Mike Geddes

CHILTON BOOK COMPANY

REPAIR MANUAL

VOLKSWAGEN FRONT WHEEL DRIVE 1974-90

All models of Cabriolet • Corrado • Dasher • Fox • GTI • Golf • Jetta • Passat • Quantum • Rabbit • Rabbit Pick-Up • Scirocco

President GARY R. INGERSOLL
Senior Vice President, Book Publishing and Research RONALD A. HOXTER
Vice President and General Manager JOHN P. KUSHNERICK
Editor-in-Chief KERRY A. FREEMAN, S.A.E.
Managing Editor DEAN F. MORGANTINI, S.A.E.
Senior Editor RICHARD J. RIVELE, S.A.E.
Editor MICHAEL J. RANDAZZO

CHILTON BOOK COMPANY
Radnor, Pennsylvania
19089

CONTENTS

GENERAL INFORMATION and MAINTENANCE

ENGINE PERFORMANCE and TUNE-UP

ENGINE and ENGINE OVERHAUL

EMISSION CONTROLS

FUEL SYSTEM

CHASSIS ELECTRICAL

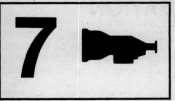

SAFETY NOTICE

Proper service and repair procedures are vital to the safe, reliable operation of all motor vehicles, as well as the personal safety of those performing repairs. This book outlines procedures for servicing and repairing vehicles using safe, effective methods. The procedures contain many NOTES, CAUTIONS and WARNINGS which should be followed along with standard safety procedures to eliminate the possibility of personal injury or improper service which could damage the vehicle or compromise its safety.

It is important to note that repair procedures and techniques, tools and parts for servicing motor vehicles, as well as the skill and experience of the individual performing the work vary widley. It is not possible to anticipate all of the conceivable ways or conditions under which vehicles may be serviced, or to provide cautions as to all of the possible hazards that may result. Standard and accepted safety precautions and equipment should be used during cutting, grinding, chiseling, prying, or any other process that can cause material removal or projectiles

Some procedures require the use of tools specially designed for a specific purpose. Before substituting another tool or procedure, you must be completly satisfied that neither your personal safety, nor the performance of the the vehicle will be endangered.

Although the information in this guide is based on industry sources and is as complete as possible at the time of publication, the possibility exists that the manufacturer made later changes which could not be included here. While striving for total accuracy, Chilton Book Company cannot assume responsibility for any errors, changes, or omissions that may occur in the compilation of this data.

PART NUMBERS

Part numbers listed in this reference are not recommendations by Chilton for any product by brand name. They are references that can be used with interchange manuals and aftermarket supplier catalogs to locate each brand supplier's discrete part number.

SPECIAL TOOLS

Special tools are recommended by the vehicle manufacturer to perform their specific job. Use has been kept to a minimum, but where absolutely necessary, they are referred to in the text by the part number of the tool manufacturer. These tools can be purchased, under the appropriate part number, from Zelenda Tool and Machine Co., 66-02 Austin St., Forrest Hills, NY 11374, or an equivalent tool can be purchased locally from a tool supplier or parts outlet. Before substituting any tool for the one recommended, read the SAFETY NOTICE at the top of this page.

ACKNOWLEDGMENTS

Chilton Book Company expresses appreciation to Volkswagen of America Inc., Detroit, MI for their generous assistance.

Manufactured in the United States of America
1234567890   9876543210

Chilton's Repair Manual: Volkswagen Front Wheel Drive 1974–90
ISBN 0–8019–8041–0 pbk.
Libary of Congress Catalog Card No. 90–055424

General Information and Maintenance

GENERAL INFORMATION AND MAINTENANCE

How To Use This Book

Chilton's Repair Manual for Volkswagen Front Wheel Drive cars covers repair and maintenance procedures for both gasoline and diesel model vehicles. Unlike many workshop manuals available to the public, this guide does not automatically assume that you have years of experience in dealing with mechanical eccentricities and the tricks of the trade that are second nature to the professional mechanic. Instead, procedures are described in easy to follow chapters, highlighted with scores of illustrations. Everything from testing your ignition coil to changing your oil filter.

The first two chapters will be the most used, since they contain maintenance and tune-up information procedures. The following chapters concern themselves with the more complex systems of your Volkswagen. This manual won't explain automatic transaxle overhaul because of the special tools and experience needed. This guide does cover just about every other practical mechanical operation possible on you car.

Before diving under your car's hood, take the time to read through the entire procedure. This will give you the overall view of what tools and supplies that will be required. Each section begins with a brief discussion of the system and what it involves, followed by adjustments, maintenance, and removal and installation procedures. When the repair is considered too complicated or special test equipment is required, we tell you how to remove the part and then how to install the new or rebuilt replacement.

Two basic mechanic's rules should be mentioned here. First, whenever the left side of the car is referred to, it is meant to specify the driver's side of the car. Conversely, the right side of the car means the passenger's side of the car. Second, most screws and bolts are removed by turning counterclockwise and tightened by turning clockwise. Safety is always the most important rule, and common sense is your best defense against injury.

TOOLS AND EQUIPMENT

It would be impossible to catalog each and every tool that you might need to perform all the operations included in this book. It would also not be wise for the amateur to rush out and buy an expensive set of tools on the theory that he may need one of them at some time. Therefore, the best approach is to proceed slowly, gathering together a quality set of those tools that are used most frequently. Don't be misled by the low cost of bargain tools, it is a better investment to spend a little more money and get a lot more quality. Always look for tools with a lifetime guarantee. As any good mechanic can tell you, there are few experiences worse than trying to work on a car or truck with bad tools. Begin accumulating those tools that are used most frequently; those associated with routine maintenance and tune-up. Your Volkswagen uses metric nuts, bolts and screws. In addition to the normal assortment of screwdrivers and pliers, you should have the following tools for routine maintenance jobs:

1. Metric wrenches, sockets and combination open-end/box wrenches to at least 19mm; note that many parts of the car also use Allen head bolts. Make sure your set includes a deep socket spark plug wrench
2. Jackstands for support
3. Band wrench for oil filters
4. Oil filler spout for pouring oil

5. Grease gun for chassis lubrication
6. Hydrometer for checking the battery
7. A container for draining oil
8. Many rags for wiping up the inevitable mess

In addition to the above items, there are several others that are not absolutely necessary, but handy to have around. These include oil dry, a transmission funnel and the usual supply of lubricants, antifreeze and fluids, although these can be purchased as needed. This is a basic list for routine maintenance, but only your personal needs and desire can accurately determine your list of tools.

The second list of tools is for tune-ups. While the tools involved here are slightly more sophisticated, they need not be outrageously expensive. There are several inexpensive tach/dwell meters on the market that are every bit as good for the average mechanic as the $100 professional model. Just be sure that it goes to at least 1200–1500 rpm on the tach scale and that it works on 4-, 6- and 8-cylinder engines. A basic list of tune up equipment could include:

1. Tach/dwell meter
2. Spark plug gap adjuster and wire feeler gauge
3. Timing light (a DC light that works from the car's battery is best, although an AC light that plugs into 110v house current will suffice at some sacrifice in brightness
4. A flat-bladed feeler gauge set
5. Valve adjusting tools (VW 10–208 and 10–209 or Tool 2078 if you are working on a 1.8 liter engine). You'll need these if you plan to adjust the valves. See Special Tools below for where to order them.

Keep your tools clean, and if they sit in your tool box for extended periods without use, make sure you spray them with silicone or oil them to prevent rust.

SPECIAL TOOLS

In addition to the above basic tool kit, there are several other tools and gauges you may find useful. These include:

1. A compression gauge. The screw-in type is slower to use, but eliminates the possibility of a faulty reading due to escaping pressure
2. A manifold vacuum gauge
3. A test light
4. An induction meter. This is used to determine whether or not there is current flowing in a wire, and thus is extremely helpful in electrical troubleshooting.
5. A torque wrench. This is necessary for all but the most basic work. The beam type models are perfectly adequate for small torque values.

However, the click (breakaway) type torque wrenches are more accurate, but are much more expensive, and must be periodically recalibrated.

NOTE: *Special tools are occasionally necessary to perform a specific job or are recommended to make a job easier. Their use has been kept to a minimum. When a special tool is indicated, it will be referred to by a manufacturer's part number, and, where possible, an illustration of the tool will be provided so that an equivalent tool may be used. These tools are available from Zelenda Tool and Machine Co., 66–02 Austin Street, Forest Hills, NY 11374.*

SERVICING YOUR CAR SAFELY

It is virtually impossible to anticipate all of the hazards involved with automotive maintenance and service, but care and common sense will prevent most accidents. The rules of safety for mechanics range from 'don't smoke around gasoline,' to 'use the proper tool for the job.' The trick to avoiding injuries is to develop safe work habits and take every possible precaution.

Do's

• Do keep a fire extinguisher and first aid kit within easy reach.
• Do wear safety glasses or goggles when cutting, drilling, grinding or prying, even if you have 20/20 vision. If you wear glasses for the sake of vision, they should be made of hardened glass that can serve also as safety glasses, or wear safety goggles over your regular glasses.
• Do shield your eyes whenever you work around the battery. Batteries contain sulphuric acid. In case of contact with the eyes or skin, flush the area with water or a mixture of water and baking soda and get medical attention immediately.
• Do use safety stands for any undercar service. Jacks are for raising vehicles; safety stands are for making sure the vehicle stays raised until you want it to come down. Whenever the car is raised, block the wheels remaining on the ground and set the parking brake.
• Do use adequate ventilation when working with any chemicals or hazardous materials. Like carbon monoxide, the asbestos dust resulting from brake lining wear can be poisonous in sufficient quantities.
• Do disconnect the negative battery cable when working on the electrical system. The secondary ignition system can contain up to 40,000 volts.
• Do follow manufacturer's directions when-

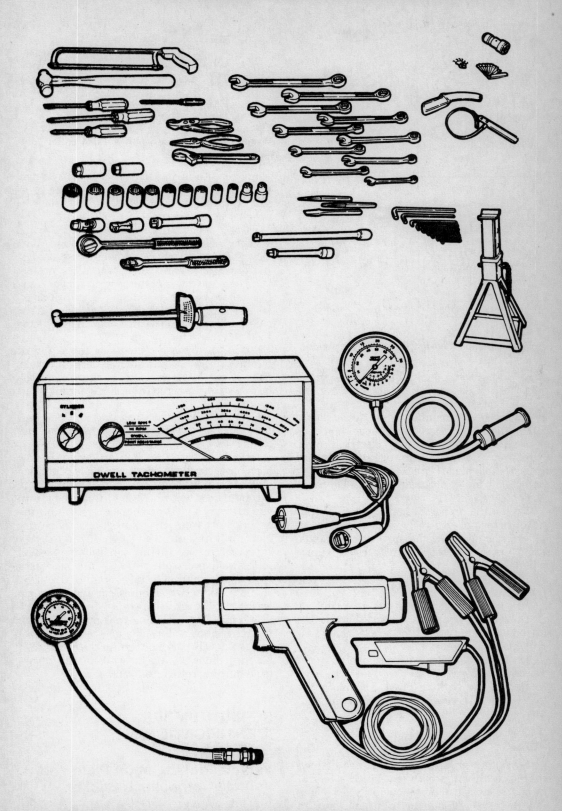

You need only a basic assortment of hand tools for most maintenance and repair jobs

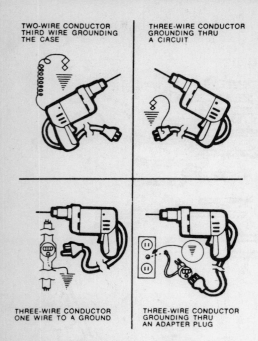

TWO-WIRE CONDUCTOR
THIRD WIRE GROUNDING
THE CASE

THREE-WIRE CONDUCTOR
GROUNDING THRU
A CIRCUIT

THREE-WIRE CONDUCTOR
ONE WIRE TO A GROUND

THREE-WIRE CONDUCTOR
GROUNDING THRU
AN ADAPTER PLUG

Power tools should always be properly grounded

Always use jackstands when working under your car

ever working with potentially hazardous materials. Both brake fluid and antifreeze are poisonous if taken internally.

• Do properly maintain your tools. Loose hammerheads, mushroomed punches and chisels, frayed or poorly grounded electrical cords, excessively worn screwdrivers, spread wrenches (open end), cracked sockets, slipping ratchets, or faulty droplight sockets can cause accidents.

• Do use the proper size and type of tool for the job being done.

• Do, when possible, pull on a wrench handle rather than push on it, and adjust your stance to prevent a fall.

• Do be sure that adjustable wrenches are tightly closed on the nut or bolt and pulled so that the face is on the side of the fixed jaw.

• Do select a wrench or socket that fits the nut or bolt. The wrench or socket should sit straight, not cocked.

• Do strike squarely with a hammer; avoid glancing blows.

• Do set the parking brake and block the drive wheels if the work requires the engine running.

Don'ts

• Don't run an engine in a garage or anywhere else without proper ventilation – EVER! Carbon monoxide is poisonous; it takes a long time to leave the human body and you can build up a deadly supply of it in your system by simply breathing in a little every day. You may not realize that you are slowly poisoning yourself. Always use power vents, windows, fans or open the garage doors.

• Don't work around moving parts while wearing a necktie or other loose clothing. Short sleeves are much safer than long, loose sleeves; hard-toed shoes with neoprene soles protect your toes and give a better grip on slippery surfaces. Jewelry such as watches, fancy belt buckles, beads or body adornment of any kind is not safe working around a car. Long hair should be hidden under a hat or cap.

• Don't use pockets for toolboxes. A fall or bump can drive a screwdriver deep into your body. Even a wiping cloth hanging from the back pocket can wrap around a spinning shaft or fan.

• Don't smoke when working around gasoline, cleaning solvents or other flammable material.

• Don't use gasoline to wash your hands; there are excellent soaps available. Gasoline may contain lead, and lead can enter the body through a cut, accumulating in the body until you are very ill. Gasoline also removes all the natural oils from the skin so that bone dry hands will suck up oil and grease.

• Don't service the air conditioning system unless you are equipped with the necessary tools and training. The refrigerant, R-12, is extremely cold when compressed, and when released into the air will instantly freeze any surface it contacts, including your eyes. Although the refrigerant is normally non-toxic, R-12 becomes a deadly poisonous gas in the presence of an open flame. One good whiff of the vapors from burning refrigerant can be fatal.

SERIAL NUMBER IDENTIFICATION

Vehicle Identification Plate and Vehicle Compliance Sticker

The Vehicle Identification Plate and Safety Compliance Sticker is located on the crossmember under the hood, just above the grille, or on the left door jamb. It is your assurance that the vehicle complies with all Federal Motor Vehicle Safety Standards (FMVSS) in effect at the time of manufacture. It also shows the month and year of manufacture and the vehicle identification number of your car.

Chassis/VIN Number

The chassis number is located on the driver's side windshield pillar on the Scirocco, Cabriolet and Dasher, and on the left front corner of the instrument panel on all Rabbit, Golf, Fox and Jetta models. The Rabbit, Golf, Fox, Jetta, Quantum and Corrado chassis number is visible through the windshield. The Dasher and Quantum chassis number is also stamped on the firewall over the windshield washer reservoir. On Corrado, you may also find the chassis number on a label plate in the luggage compartment. The Rabbit, Golf, Fox, Jetta and Scirocco chassis number is also on top of the right suspension strut mounting. It also appears on the vehicle identification plate. 1981 and later models use a seventeen digit code. On seventeen digit codes, the fifth position indicates engine and the tenth, the year. The year code will be a letter. 'B,' 1981, 'C,' 1982, etc.

Engine Number

The engine number is stamped on the engine block between the fuel pump and the distributor, on all gasoline engine models except the Fox, Corrado and Passat. The Fox's engine number is located on the left side of the engine block just below the cylinder head, and on the vehicle data plate. On Corrado, the engine number is stamped on the block near the engine oil dipstick. On Passat, the engine number is stamped on the front of the cylinder block. On diesels the engine number is stamped on the block between the fuel injection pump and the vacuum pump.

NOTE: *Beginning in May of 1987, engine codes are either composed of a combination of two letters or one number and one letter; however, the engine code continues to precede the engine number on all year models.*

Manual Transaxle

The manual transaxle type number is located on a pad above the left hand driveshaft on the Dasher, Fox and Quantum, and stamped either on or below the left hand axle yoke retainer on the Rabbit, Jetta, Scirocco and the Cabriolet. On Corrado, the type number is stamped on the drive axle casting.

The code letters and date of manufacture are stamped on the top right hand side of the bell

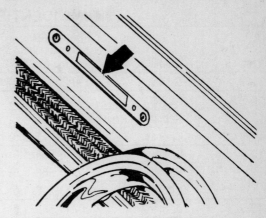

Dasher and Scirocco chassis number

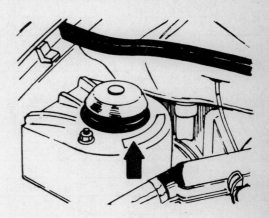

Rabbit and Jetta chassis number

housing on the 1974–75 Dasher, and on the top of the transmission above the axle yokes on the 1976 and later Dasher and Quantum. The code letters and date of manufacture for the Rabbit, Fox, Jetta and Scirocco are stamped on a pad at the lower center of the bell housing next to the starter. On Corrado the transmission code and the date of production are stamped on a pad near the starter mounting casting.

Transmission codes also appear on the vehicle data plates.

Automatic Transaxle

The automatic transmission type number for the Dasher and Quantum is stamped on the top of the rear section of the transmission. The automatic transmission type number for the Rabbit, Jetta and the Scirocco is stamped into the center of the case near the dipstick. On Corrado, the transmission type number is located on the transmission case. On Passat, the transmission type number is stamped on a pad beneath the shift lever.

ENGINE IDENTIFICATION CHART

Year	Model	Engine Displacement cu. in. (cc/liter)	Engine Series Identification	No. of Cylinders	Engine Type
1974	Dasher	90 (1,471/1.5)	XW, XV, XZ, XY	4	SOHC
1975	Dasher	97 (1,588/1.6)	YG, YH	4	SOHC
	Rabbit	90 (1,471/1.5)	FC, FG	4	SOHC
	Scirocco	90 (1,471/1.5)	FC, FG	4	SOHC
1976	Dasher	97 (1,588/1.6)	YG, YH, YK	4	SOHC
	Rabbit	97 (1,588/1.6)	EF, EE	4	SOHC
	Scirocco	97 (1,588/1.6)	EF, EE	4	SOHC
1977	Dasher	97 (1,588/1.6)	YG, YH, YK	4	SOHC
	Rabbit	97 (1,588/1.6)	EF, EE	4	SOHC
	Rabbit (Diesel)	90 (1,471/1.5)	CK	4	SOHC
	Scirocco	97 (1,588/1.6)	EF, EE	4	SOHC
1978	Dasher	97 (1,588/1.6)	YG, YH, YK	4	SOHC
	Rabbit	97 (1,588/1.6)	EF, EE	4	SOHC
	Rabbit (Diesel)	90 (1,471/1.5)	CK	4	SOHC
	Scirocco	97 (1,588/1.6)	EF, EE	4	SOHC
1979	Dasher	97 (1,588/1.6)	YG, YH, YK	4	SOHC
	Dasher (Diesel)	90 (1,471/1.5)	CK	4	SOHC
	Rabbit	90 (1,457/1.5)	EH	4	SOHC
	Rabbit (Diesel)	90 (1,471/1.5)	CK	4	SOHC
	Scirocco	97 (1,588/1.6)	FX	4	SOHC
1980	Dasher	97 (1,588/1.6)	YG, YH, YK	4	SOHC
	Dasher (Diesel)	90 (1,471/1.5)	CK	4	SOHC
	Rabbit	97 (1,588/1.6)	EH	4	SOHC
	Rabbit (Diesel)	90 (1,471/1.5)	CK	4	SOHC
	Jetta	97 (1,588/1.6)	EJ	4	SOHC
	Scirocco	97 (1,588/1.6)	FX	4	SOHC
1981	Dasher (Diesel)	97.0 (1,588/1.6)	WT, EN	4	SOHC
	Jetta	97.0 (1,588/1.6)	EJ	4	SOHC
	Jetta	105.0 (1,715/1.7)	WT, EN	4	SOHC
	Rabbit	105.0 (1,715/1.7)	WT, EN	4	SOHC
	Rabbit (Diesel)	97.0 (1,588/1.6)	CR	4	SOHC
	Scirocco	105.0 (1,715/1.7)	WT, EN	4	SOHC
1982	Jetta	105.0 (1,715/1.7)	WT, EN	4	SOHC
	Jetta (Diesel)	97.0 (1,588/1.6)	CR	4	SOHC
	Jetta (Turbo Diesel)	97.0 (1,588/1.6)	CR	4	SOHC
	Quantum	105.0 (1,715/1.7)	WT, EN	4	SOHC
	Quantum	130.8 (2,144/2.2)	WE, KX, KM	5	SOHC
	Quantum (Turbo Diesel)	97.0 (1,588/1.6)	CR	4	SOHC
	Rabbit	105.0 (1,715/1.7)	WT, EN	4	SOHC
	Scirocco	105.0 (1,715/1.7)	WT, EN	4	SOHC

ENGINE IDENTIFICATION CHART (cont.)

Year	Model	Engine Displacement cu. in. (cc/liter)	Engine Series Identification	No. of Cylinders	Engine Type
1983	Jetta	105.0 (1,715/1.7)	WT, EN	4	SOHC
	Jetta (Diesel)	97.0 (1,588/1.6)	JK, CY	4	SOHC
	Jetta (Turbo Diesel)	97.0 (1,588/1.6)	JK, CY	4	SOHC
	Quantum	130.8 (2,144/2.2)	WE, KX, KM	5	SOHC
	Quantum	105.0 (1,715,1.7)	EN, JF, WT	4	SOHC
	Quantum	109.0 (1,780/1.8)	JH	4	SOHC
	Quantum (Turbo Diesel)	97.0 (1,588/1.6)	JR, MF	4	SOHC
	Rabbit	105.0 (1,715/1.7)	WT, EN	4	SOHC
	Rabbit (Conv.)	109.0 (1,780/1.8)	JH	4	SOHC
	Rabbit (GTI)	109.0 (1,780/1.8)	JH	4	SOHC
	Rabbit (Diesel)	97.0 (1,588/1.6)	JK, CY	4	SOHC
	Scirocco	109.0 (1,780/1.8)	JH	4	SOHC
	GTI	109.0 (1,780/1.8)	JH	4	SOHC
	GLI	109.0 (1,780/1.8)	JH	4	SOHC
1984	Jetta	105.0 (1,715/1.7)	EN, JF, WT	4	SOHC
	Jetta (Diesel)	97.0 (1,588/1.6)	JP, ME	4	SOHC
	Jetta (Turbo Diesel)	97.0 (1,588/1.6)	JR, MF	4	SOHC
	Quantum	109.0 (1,780/1.8)	UM	4	SOHC
	Quantum	130.8 (2,144/2.2)	WE, KX, KM	5	SOHC
	Quantum (Turbo Diesel)	97.0 (1,588/1.62)	JR, MF	4	SOHC
	Rabbit	105.0 (1,715/1.7)	EN, JF, WT	4	SOHC
	Rabbit (Conv.)	109.0 (1,780/1.8)	GX	4	SOHC
	Rabbit (GTI)	109.0 (1,780/1.8)	HT	4	SOHC
	Rabbit (Diesel)	97.0 (1,588/1.6)	JP, ME	4	SOHC
	Scirocco	109.0 (1,780/1.8)	GX	4	SOHC
	GTI	109.0 (1,780/1.8)	HT	4	SOHC
	GLI	109.0 (1,780/1.8)	—	4	SOHC
1985	Jetta	109.0 (1,780/1.8)	GX	4	SOHC
	Jetta (Diesel)	97.0 (1,588/1.6)	ME	4	SOHC
	Jetta (Turbo Diesel)	97.0 (1,588/1.6)	MF	4	SOHC
	Quantum	109.0 (1,780/1.8)	GX	4	SOHC
	Quantum (Turbo Diesel)	97.0 (1,588/1.6)	MF	4	SOHC
	Quantum GL5	136.0 (2,226/2.2)	WE, KX, KM	5	SOHC
	Scirocco	109.0 (1,780/1.8)	JH	4	SOHC
	Cabriolet	109.0 (1,780/1.8)	JH	4	SOHC
	GTI	109.0 (1,780/1.8)	HT	4	SOHC
	GLI	109.0 (1,780/1.8)	HT	4	SOHC
	Golf	109.0 (1,780/1.8)	GX	4	SOHC
	Golf (Diesel)	97.0 (1,588/1.6)	ME	4	SOHC

ENGINE IDENTIFICATION CHART (cont.)

Year	Model	Engine Displacement cu. in. (cc/liter)	Engine Series Identification	No. of Cylinders	Engine Type
1986	Jetta	109.0 (1,780/1.8)	GX	4	SOHC
	Jetta (Diesel)	97.0 (1,588/1.6)	ME	4	SOHC
	Jetta (Turbo Diesel)	97.0 (1,588/1.6)	MF	4	SOHC
	Quantum GL5	136.0 (2,226/2.2)	WE, KX	5	SOHC
	Quantum (Turbo Diesel)	97.0 (1,588/1.6)	MF	4	SOHC
	Quantum (Syncro)	136.0 (2,226/2.2)	JT	5	SOHC
	Cabriolet	109.0 (1,780/1.8)	JH	4	SOHC
	Scirocco	109.0 (1,780/1.8)	JH	4	SOHC
	GTI	109.0 (1,780/1.8)	RD	4	SOHC
	GLI	109.0 (1,780/1.8)	RD	4	SOHC
	Golf	109.0 (1,780/1.8)	GX	4	SOHC
	Golf (Diesel)	97.0 (1,588.1/6)	ME	4	SOHC
1987	Jetta	109 (1,780/1.8)	RV	4	SOHC
	Jetta GL	109 (1,780/1.8)	PF	4	SOHC
	Jetta GLI 16V	109 (1,780/1.8)	PL	4	DOHC
	Quantum GL5	136 (2,226/2.2)	KX	5	SOHC
	Quantum Syncro	136 (2,226/2.2)	JT	5	SOHC
	Scirocco-16V	109 (1,780/1.8)	PL	4	DOHC
	Cabriolet	109 (1,780/1.8)	JH	4	SOHC
	Golf/GL	109 (1,780/1.8)	RV	4	SOHC
	Golf/GT	109 (1,780/1.8)	PF	4	SOHC
	Golf GTI 16V	109 (1,780/1.8)	PL	4	DOHC
	Fox/GL	109 (1,780/1.8)	UM	4	SOHC
1988	Jetta	109 (1,780/1.8)	RV	4	SOHC
	Jetta GL	109 (1,780/1.8)	PF	4	SOHC
	Jetta GLI 16V	109 (1,780/1.8)	PL	4	DOHC
	Jetta Carat	109 (1,780/1.8)	PF	4	SOHC
	Quantum GL5	136 (2,226/2.2)	KX	5	SOHC
	Quantum Syncro	136 (2,226/2.2)	JT	5	SOHC
	Scirocco-16V	109 (1,780/1.8)	PL	4	DOHC
	Cabriolet	109 (1,780/1.8)	JH	4	SOHC
	Golf/GL	109 (1,780/1.8)	RV	4	SOHC
	Golf/GT	109 (1,780/1.8)	PF	4	SOHC
	Golf GTI 16V	109 (1,780/1.8)	PL	4	DOHC
	Fox/GL	109 (1,780/1.8)	UM	4	SOHC

ENGINE IDENTIFICATION CHART (cont.)

Year	Model	Engine Displacement cu. in. (cc/liter)	Engine Series Identification	No. of Cylinders	Engine Type
1989	Jetta	109 (1,780/1.8)	RV	4	SOHC
	Jetta (Diesel)	97.0 (1,588/1.6)	ME	4	SOHC
	Jetta GL	109 (1,780/1.8)	PF	4	SOHC
	Jetta GLI 16V	109 (1,780/1.8)	PL	4	DOHC
	Jetta Carat	109 (1,780/1.8)	PF	4	SOHC
	Scirocco-16V	109 (1,780/1.8)	PL	4	DOHC
	Cabriolet	109 (1,780/1.8)	JH	4	SOHC
	Golf/GL	109 (1,780/1.8)	RV	4	SOHC
	Golf/GT	109 (1,780/1.8)	PF	4	SOHC
	Golf GTI 16V	109 (1,780/1.8)	PL	4	DOHC
	Fox/GL	109 (1,780/1.8)	UM	4	SOHC
1990	Jetta GL	109 (1,780/1.8)	GX	4	SOHC
	Jetta GL (Diesel)	97 (1,588/1.6)	ME	4	SOHC
	Jetta Carat	109 (1,780/1.8)	GX	4	SOHC
	Jetta GLI 16V	121 (1,984/2.0)	9A	4	DOHC
	GTI	109 (1,780/1.8)	PL	4	SOHC
	GTI 16V	121 (1,984/2.0)	9A	4	DOHC
	Golf GL	109 (1,780/1.8)	PL	4	SOHC
	Cabriolet	109 (1,780/1.8)	JH	4	SOHC
	Corrado	109 (1,780/1.8)	PG	4	SOHC w/G-Charger
	Passat GL	121 (1,984/2.0)	9A	5	DOHC
	Fox/GL	109 (1,780/1.8)	UM/JN	4	SOHC

SOHC: Single Overhead Cam.
DOHC: Dual Overhead Cam.

TRANSMISSION CODE IDENTIFICATION CHART

Model	Year	Type	Codes
Cabriolet	1985–90	5 Spd	9A, ACD, 2Y,
		Auto	TNA
Corrado	1990	5 Spd	ATB
Dasher	1974	4 Spd	ZS
		Auto	EN
	1975	4 Spd	YZ
		Auto	EO
	1976	4 Spd	YZ, XH
		Auto	ET
	1977–78	4 Spd	XK
		Auto	ET
	1979–80	4 Spd	YZ, XH
		Auto	ET
Fox/GL	1987–90	4 Spd	PW
	1989–90	5 Spd	—

TRANSMISSION CODE IDENTIFICATION CHART (cont.)

Model	Year	Type	Codes
Golf GTI	1985–90	5 Spd Auto	9A, ACN, ACH/AGS (Diesel) TJ, TL, TNA
Jetta	1980–81	4 Spd 5 Spd Auto	GC, GP FF EQ, TB
	1982–83	4 Spd 5 Spd Auto	GL, GY FR, FN TB, TC, TF, TG, TH
	1984	4 Spd 5 Spd Auto	4A FN 2H, 7A, 4K TB, TC, TF, TG, TH, TM, TR, TN
	1985–90	5 Spd Auto	9A, ACN, ACH/AGS (Diesel) TJ, TL, TNA
Passat	1990	5 Spd Auto	ACG APE
Quantum	1982–83	5 Spd Auto	2M, 3M, 5M, 9Q RJ, RU, RAC, RAF
	1984	5 Spd Auto	2W, QF, 3Z, 2N, 2M, 3M, 5Q RU, RJ, RAC, RAF, RR, RBB
	1985–88	5 Spd Auto	9Q, 2N, ABV, 3Z, 2M, 5M, 2W, 2N RAC, RAF, RU, RJ, RR, RBB, RBE
Rabbit GTI	1975–78	4 Spd Auto	GC EQ
	1979–81	4 Spd 5 Spd Auto	GC, GP FF TB, TC, TF, TG, TH
	1982–83	4 Spd 5 Spd Auto	GL, GY FR, FN TB, TC, TF, TG, TH
	1984	4 Spd 5 Spd	GL, GY 7A, 4R, FN, FR, 2H, TCA, TR, TB, TC, TF, TG, TH, TM
Scirocco	1975–78	4 Spd Auto	GC EQ
	1979–81	4 Spd 5 Spd Auto	GC, GP FF EQ, TB
	1982–83	4 Spd 5 Spd Auto	GL, GY FR, FN TB, TC, TF, TG, TH
	1984–88	5 Spd Auto	4R, 9A, 2Y, AGB (16V) TN, TNA

The code letter and date of manufacture are stamped on the front of the bell housing near the dipstick on the Dasher and Quantum, and on a pad on the upper center portion of the bell housing on the Rabbit, Jetta, Scirocco and Cabriolet. On Corrado, the transmission code and the date of production are stamped on a pad near the starter mounting casting.

Transaxle codes also appear on the vehicle data plates.

ROUTINE MAINTENANCE

NOTE: *15, 30, 45, 60, 75, and 90 thousand miles are the normal maintenance intervals. On all other intervals, you need only change the oil and filter, do routine emission control maintenance (tightening belts, checking air filter), and test the coolant for freezing temperature and replenish if necessary. If you drive under severe operating conditions, such as high speed, extended idling periods, dusty conditions or most driving under 10 miles -- more frequent maintenance (oil and filter changes, etc.) is required. Under such operating conditions, cut the normal maintenance intervals in half.*

General Maintenance

This includes changing the oil filter and oil; checking the transmission fluid level; cleaning or replacement of the air cleaner filler; testing the freezing level of the coolant and replenishing if necessary; topping up the battery electrolyte; and checking the brake fluid. This is also a good time to lubricate the door hinges and door check rods.

Tune-Up & Emission Control Maintenance

This includes checking the tension and condition of all drive belts; adjusting the valves and replacing the valve cover gasket. Do a cylinder compression test; replace the spark plugs, ignition points and condenser on gasoline engines; check the fuel filter and replace if necessary; inspect ignition wires, distributor cap and rotor on gasoline engines; check the crankcase ventilation hoses; check the fuel tank, lines and connections for leaks and wear; check the engine for leaks; check the EGR system on fuel injected gasoline engines; check clutch free-play and adjustment.

Vehicle Maintenance

Inspect the brake system for damage and leaks; inspect the brake linings and pads (front and rear), and replace as necessary; check wheels for distortion and cracks, check tires for wear and air pressure; inspect visible boots and dust seals on transaxle for ripping or leaks; check for play in the steering; check the operation of all lights and accessories (windshield wipers and blades, windshield washer fluid).

Air Cleaner

The air filter is a key part of the engine. A restrictive, dirty element will cause a reduction in fuel economy and performance and an increase in exhaust emissions. The air filter should be cleaned or replaced according to the maintenance interval chart in this chapter.

Depending on the model, year and type of engine (fuel injected, carburetor or diesel) the air cleaner element is contained in a round metal or oblong plastic container, usually connected by hoses to the intake system.

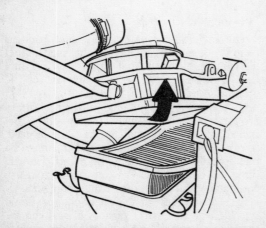

Fuel injected gasoline engine air filter is located under the fuel mixture control unit. Release the clips and raise the control unit to gain access to the air cleaner element

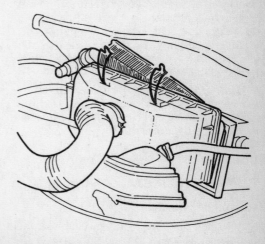

The diesel air filter is mounted directly on the intake manifold

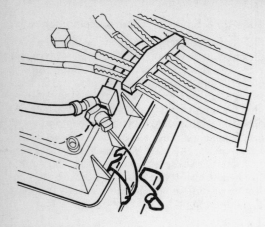

Late model Dasher air filter

REMOVAL AND INSTALLATION

1. Unsnap the cover retaining clips and lift off the cover. On models with double sets of clips, unsnap the lower clip(s) first and pull the assembly away from the bracket slightly, then unsnap the other clips and lift off the cover. On some models it may be easier to disconnect the air cleaner hose before removing the air cleaner element. To do this, loosen the hose clamp and disconnect the hose from the air inlet boot. Move the hose off to the side and out of the way.

2. Lift out the paper element. If the element is very dirty and you cannot see light through the filter, discard it.

3. If the element is only slightly dirty, tap on table top to loosen up dirt and blow compressed air through to clean it.

4. Wipe out the housing and reinstall the element.

5. Replace the cover and secure with clips. If you have a two part cover, secure the lower clip(s) first, check that the two locating pins are fully engaged in their respective mounts, then snap the remaining clips. If the air cleaner inlet hose was removed, re-connect it and tighten the hose clamp.

NOTE: *Do not run your engine without the air cleaner even for a little while. Dirt and grit will pass into the combustion chambers and cause premature wear.*

Fuel Filter

REMOVAL AND INSTALLATION

Carbureted Engines

Carbureted engines with mechanical fuel pumps have a strainer in the top cover of the fuel pump. Remove the center screw and remove the cover and strainer. Clean the

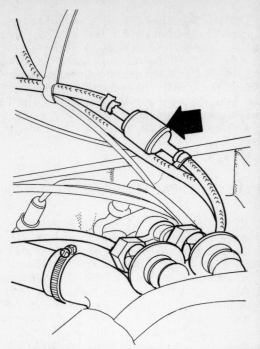

Smaller inline fuel filter usually used on carbureted models

strainer with compressed air and replace, using new gaskets. Be sure to align the notch in the cover with the groove in the body. Various models are equipped with a fuel strainer in the fuel tank attached to the sending unit. This strainer should be trouble-free.

All later models are equipped with inline fuel filters. The filters are small, usually made of plastic and are attached to the fuel line by clamps.

Fuel Injected Engines

The fuel filter removes particulate matter from the fuel system which might clog the fuel distributor block or fuel injectors. The fuel filter is installed on the pressure side of the pump.

On some fuel injected models, the fuel filters are large, metal containers. On the other fuel inejected models, a small inline filter is used. Arrows point in the direction the filter must be installed. The arrow should be pointing in the direction of fuel travel. Some fuel filters are equipped with banjo type fittings, some use O-ring seals and some just use hose clamps. Banjo type fittings use metal gaskets to seal the fitting against the filter housing. Always replace these gaskets when replacing the fuel filter. If the fuel filter has O-ring type seals, replace them.

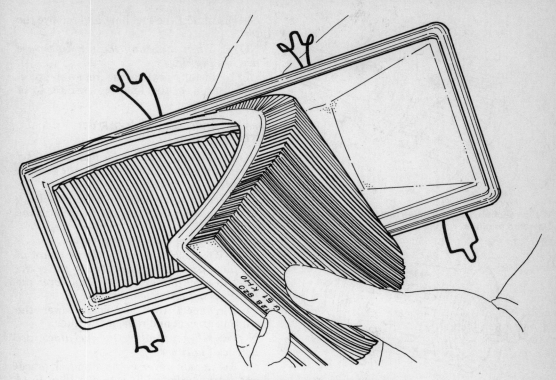

Removing the filter element from the housing

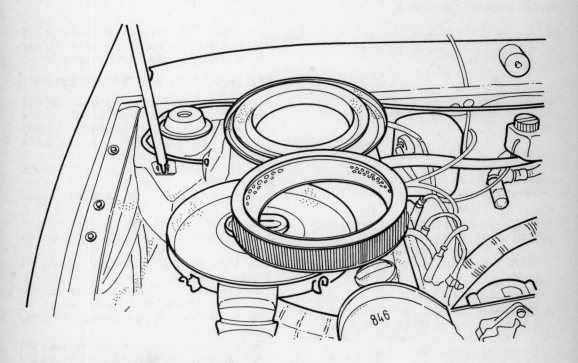

Carbureted Dasher air cleaner location

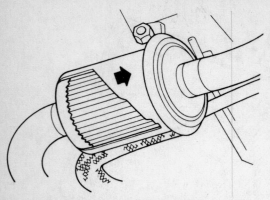

Cross section of typical inline fuel filter used on fuel injected engines

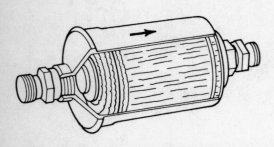

Cross section of typical canister type fuel filter used on fuel injected engines

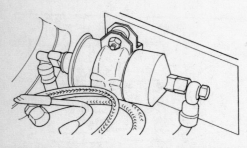

Engine compartment mounted fuel filter used on fuel injected gasoline engines

ALL EXCEPT 1985–90 CABRIOLET, CORRADO, FOX, GOLF, GTI, JETTA AND PASSAT

NOTE: *The filter is located in the engine compartment.*

1. Disconnect the negative battery cable.
2. Remove the fuel filter mounting nuts and lift the filter from the mounting bracket.
3. Loosen the filter cap and the fuel lines to relieve the pressure in the system.

CAUTION: *When relieving the pressure in the fuel system, place a container under the filter to catch the excess fuel and cover the fuel line connections with a rag.*

4. Disconnect the fuel lines and remove the filter.

NOTE: *When installing the fuel lines, use new sealing rings.*

5. To install, reverse the removal procedures. Torque the fuel lines to new filter to 14 ft. lbs. (20 Nm).

1985–90 CABRIOLET, FOX, GOLF, GTI, JETTA AND PASSAT

NOTE: *The fuel filter is located in the fuel pump assembly, mounted under the vehicle, in front of the fuel tank.*

1. Disconnect the negative battery cable.
2. Raise and safely support the rear of the vehicle.
3. Relieve the fuel system pressure.

CAUTION: *When relieving the pressure in the fuel system, place a container under the filter to catch the excess fuel and cover the fuel line connection with a rag.*

4. Disconnect the fuel lines, lower the mounting bracket and remove the filter.

NOTE: *When installing the fuel lines, use new sealing rings.*

5. To install, reverse the removal procedures. Torque the fuel lines to new filter to 14 ft. lbs. (20 Nm).

CORRADO

The Corrado is equipped with a lifetime fuel filter that does not normally require replacement unless it becomes badly contaminated.

RELIEVING FUEL SYSTEM PRESSURE

Engines equipped with electric fuel pumps maintain fuel pressure even when the engine has not been run. This residual pressure may remain in the fuel system for several hours after the engine is shut down.

To relieve the fuel system pressure, perform the following:

1. Start the engine and allow it to run at idle speed.
2. Locate the fuel pump electrical connector and disconnect it while the engine is running.
3. Allow the engine to run until it runs out of fuel and stops.
4. Connect the fuel pump connector and disconnect the negative battery cable.
5. Proceed will the necessary fuel system component repairs.

NOTE: *Have a container ready to catch the fuel that will squirt out when you loosen the clamps or couplings on the fuel system components you are working on. Wrap the connection with a rag and slowly crack the connection to vent any residual pressure from*

Remove the diesel fuel filter from the mounting studs (arrows)

the system. Once all the pressure is relieved, loosen the connection.

Diesel Engines

Three styles of fuel filters are used with diesel engines, all are canister types. Depending on year and model, the filter canister can be above or below the mounting base or clamp mounted. Clamp mounted filters are found on 1985–86 and 1989–90 Golf and Jetta.

On earlier models, the filter is mounted on the passenger's side of the car, next to the air cleaner on the Rabbit, Golf and Jetta, and next to the brake master cylinder on the Dasher and Quantum. On all later Golf and Jetta, the fuel filter is located in the engine compartment next to the fuel filter.

FILTER MOUNTED ABOVE BASE

1. If the canister is mounted above the base, remove the two filter support mounting nuts and remove the filter from the studs.

2. Turn the filter upside down and replace mounting over the studs. Install the nuts temporarily to hold the filter.

3. Use a wrench on the ends of the canister or use a band wrench to loosen the canister from the base. Have a container ready to catch the fuel as it spills out or pinch the fuel lines.

4. Turn the filter canister and base over. Unscrew the canister and discard.

5. Apply a thin film of diesel fuel to the new canister gasket and screw onto mounting base, tighten by hand. Reinstall the filter on the mounting studs and secure nuts. Start the engine, accelerate several times until engine is running smoothly (this will clear the air bubbles in the fuel system). Allow engine to idle and check for fuel leaks.

FILTER MOUNTED BELOW BASE

1. If the filter canister is mounted below the base, loosen the drain plug at the bottom of

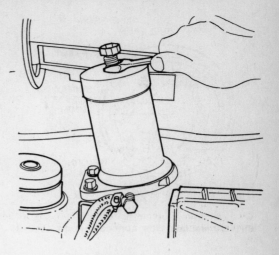

Invert the filter and loosen it

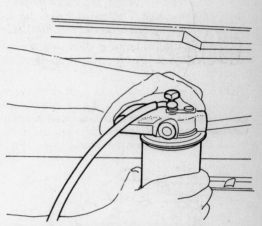

Turn the filter right side up and remove the cartridge

the canister and drain the fuel into a container. Reinstall the drain plug.

2. Use a band wrench and loosen the canister from the base. Remove by hand. Discard the old filter canister.

3. Apply a thin film of diesel fuel to the mounting gasket. Install canister and tighten by hand. Start the engine, accelerate several times until the engine is running smoothly (this will clear the air bubbles in the fuel system). Allow the engine to idle and check for fuel leaks.

CLAMP MOUNTED

1. Using clamps, pinch off the fuel lines at the fuel filter.

2. Remove the fuel lines from the filter.

NOTE: *On 1989–90 Jetta, once the two filter lines are disconnected, remove the clip from the control valve (located at the top of the can-*

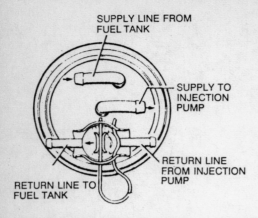

SUPPLY LINE FROM
FUEL TANK

SUPPLY TO
INJECTION
PUMP

RETURN LINE
FROM INJECTION
PUMP

RETURN LINE TO
FUEL TANK

Diesel engine fuel filter connections on 1989–90 Jetta

ister) and remove the valve leaving the two lines connected. Position the valve and the lines off to the side. This valve is delicate, so be careful during removal and installation.

3. Loosen the mounting clamp or screws and lift the filter assembly straight up. Remove the old filter.

NOTE: *When installing a new filter, coat the outside and partly fill it with diesel fuel. On 1989–90 Jetta, install new control valve O-ring seals and lubricate the seals with clean diesel fuel prior to installation.*

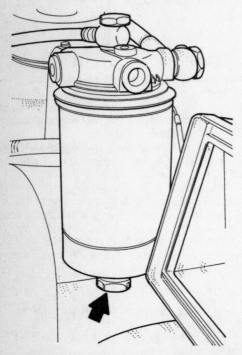

Fuel filter without vent screw. On all types of filters, water is drained by loosening the drain plug (arrow)

4. To install, reverse the removal procedures. Torque the filter assembly to mount nuts to 18 ft. lbs. Start the engine, accelerate it a few times (this will clear the air bubbles in the fuel system) and check for fuel leaks.

DRAINING WATER FROM THE DIESEL FUEL FILTER

Due to it's chemical properties, diesel fuel tends to collect water, which will settle in the bottom of the filter housing. It is very important to drain the water out periodically to ensure maximum engine performance and efficiency.

On models up to and including 1984, water is drained from the filter directly by means of a vent screw or a drain plug. On 1985–86 and 1989–90 models, water is removed from the fuel system by means of a water separator that has a drain valve on the bottom of the unit.

Fuel Filter with Primer Pump and Vent Screw

Loosen the vent screw (A) and the drain plug and drain water out into a container until clean fuel emerges. Close the vent screw, and the drain screw. Start the engine and accelerate until the engine runs smoothly.

Fuel Filter Without Primer Pump and With Vent Screw

Loosen the vent screw and drain plug and drain water out into a container until clean fuel appears. Close the drain plug and vent screw. Start the engine and accelerate a few times until the engine runs smoothly.

Fuel Filter Without Vent Screw

Disconnect the fuel return line at the injection pump. Loosen the filter drain plug and drain water out into a container until clean fuel appears. Reconnect the fuel return line at the injection pump. Start the engine and accelerate a few times until the engine runs smoothly.

1985–86 and 1989–90 With Water Separator

The water separator is located in front of the fuel tank under the right side of the vehicle. It's purpose is to remove the water from the fuel. When the water level in the separator reaches a certain point, a sensor turns on the glow plug indicator light, causing it to blink continuously alerting the driver to drain the separator.

1. Raise and support the vehicle on jackstands.

2. At the separator, connect a hose from the separator drain to a catch pan.

CAUTION: *Place a fluid catch pan under the separator to collect the excess fuel the excess fuel.*

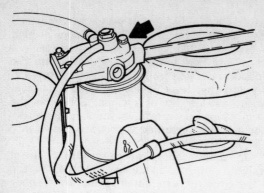

Fuel filter without primer pump and with vent screw

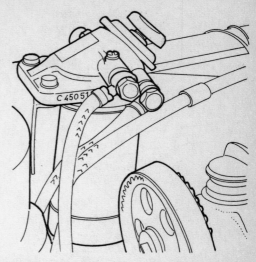

Fuel filter with primer pump and vent screw

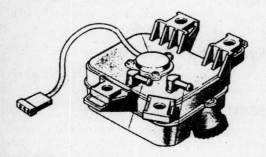

Water separator used on 1985–86 and 1989–90 Golf and Jetta

3. Open the drain valve three turns and drain the water until a steady, clear stream of fuel flows from the separator. Close the valve.

Crankcase Ventilation

CARBURETED ENGINES

Blow-by gas, caused by some of the air compressed in the cylinders leaking past the piston rings and valve guides, is routed from the camshaft cover to the air cleaner or carburetor, where it is reburned. Various models and 1975–77 Rabbits and Sciroccos incorporate a PCV valve in the hose between the valve cover and the air cleaner. To check the PCV valve, disconnect the hose from the valve cover end of the valve. Place your finger over the end of the valve. Idle speed should drop when the valve is blocked, if not, the valve is not operating and should be replaced.

Check the hoses at every tune-up for clogging or deterioration and clean or replace them as necessary. A clogged ventilation hose or PCV valve will cause excessive crankcase pressure and result in oil leaks. Keep the lines clean.

1975–76 carbureted Rabbits and Sciroccos without PCV valves often have a restrictor in the ventilation hose between the valve cover and the air cleaner elbow above the carburetor.

This restrictor has been known to cause carburetor top icing. To prevent icing, Volkswagen suggests installing a PCV valve in the those.

To replace the PCV valve, proceed as follows:

1. Disconnect the air intake hose from the air cleaner at the elbow and remove the elbow. The elbow is the round metal cap right on top of the carburetor.

2. Remove the flat, spot welded baffle plate inside the elbow.

3. Insert the replacement tube (D) so that one end sticks out of connection (A). Insert the tube as far as it will go. The tube, part number ZVP 202 851, is available from your VW dealer.

4. Push the tube clear of hole (B) and drill a 1.5mm ($^1/_{16}$ in.) hole (C) through the elbow and the tube. Fasten the tube in the elbow by fitting a sheet metal screw through the hole you just drilled. Make sure all metal shavings from the drilling are removed.

5. Install the elbow on the carburetor with tube end (D) pointing into the carburetor secondary barrel.

6. Remove the crankcase ventilation hose

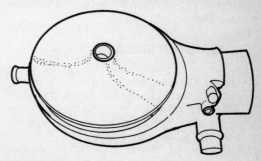

Restrictor valve modification (see PCV valve text)

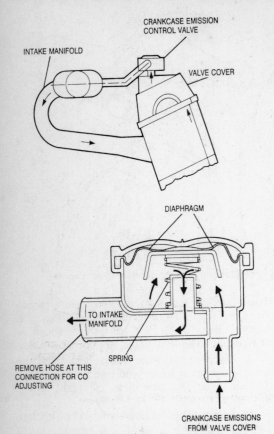

Crankcase emission control valve used on 1987–90 1.8L Jetta and Golf with Digifant II engine management systems

and remove the restrictor which is located inside the bend of the hose where it connects to the valve cover.

7. Cut about 9.5mm ($^3/_8$ in.) off the valve cover end of the hose, then measure 83mm ($3^9/_{32}$ in.) along the outside curve of the same end of the hose and cut that piece off too.

8. Install a PCV valve (part number 211 129 101) at the place where you cut the 83mm piece off the hose and attach the other end of the hose to the elbow. Use the 83mm piece to attach the PCV valve to the valve cover. Secure the hose ends with clamps.

FUEL INJECTED ENGINES

To control crankcase blow-by gasses, some fuel injected engines are equipped with crankcase breathers attached to the side of the cylinder block and some are equipped with crankcase pressure control valves or breathers located on top of the valve cover.

Block attached crankcase breathers, such as the ones found on Scirocco 16V engine, operate according to changing intake manifold vacuum. The breather contains a baffle plate that sepa-

rates oil from the blow-by gasses and returns it back to the oil pan. During conditions of high intake manifold vacuum, a large portion of crankcase blow-by gasses are drawn into the intake manifold through a restrictor located in the breather hose. When the intake manifold vacuum is low, the only a small portion of the crankcase vapors are drawn through the restrictor and the remaining vapors are routed into the air filter housing.

On engines equipped with crankcase control valves, blow-by vapors are drawn from the valve cover and are routed to the throttle body where they are re-burned with the air/fuel mixture. The crankcase emission control valve, which mounted on top of the valve cover, regulates the amount of crankcase vapors allowed to enter the throttle body.

Evaporative Canister

NOTE: *Evaporative canisters are only used on gasoline engines.*

SERVICING

The evaporative emission control system prevents the escape of raw fuel vapors (unburned hydrocarbons, or HC) into the atmosphere. Along with the activated charcoal filter canister and connector hoses, the system consists of an unvented fuel filler cap, fuel tank expansion chamber and a sealed carburetor on non-fuel injected gasoline engines. A filter cut-off valve was added to various models from 1977 and is located between the charcoal filter and the air cleaner or the throttle body. When the engine is idling or not running, the valve is closed, preventing vapors from entering the air cleaner. 1990 vehicles equipped with 2.0L engines using CIS-E Motronic engine management systems use an ON/OFF and frequency solenoid valve to control the fuel vapors from the carbon canister.

Check the components visually for cracks, broken hoses and disconnections. Also check the seal on the gas tank filler cap. Replace the cap if the seal looks worn. If any hoses are in need of replacement, use only hoses marked EVAP, available from your local automotive supply store. VW recommends that the canister be discarded and replaced every 50,000 miles.

NOTE: *The Volkswagen Rabbit Pick-up truck's canister is located under the left front fender.*

Battery

Routinely check the battery electrolyte level and specific gravity. A few minutes occasionally spent monitoring battery condition is worth saving hours of frustration when your car

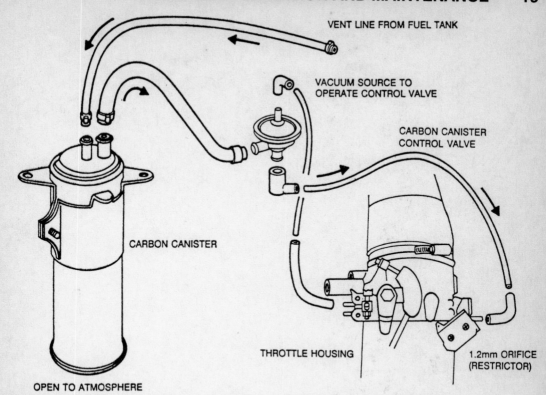

VENT LINE FROM FUEL TANK

VACUUM SOURCE TO
OPERATE CONTROL VALVE

CARBON CANISTER
CONTROL VALVE

CARBON CANISTER

THROTTLE HOUSING

1.2mm ORIFICE
(RESTRICTOR)

OPEN TO ATMOSPHERE

Evaporative emission control system used on 1987–90 1.8L Jetta and Golf with Digifant II engine management systems

won't start due to a dead battery. Only distilled water should be used to top up the battery, as tap water, in many areas, contains harmful minerals. Two tools which will facilitate battery maintenance are a hydrometer and a squeeze bulb filler. These are cheap and widely available at automotive parts stores, hardware stores and even at your local supermarket. The specific gravity of the electrolyte should be between 1.27 and 1.20. Keep the top of the battery clean, as a film of dirt can sometimes completely discharge a battery. A solution of baking soda and water may be used to clean the top surface, but be careful to flush this off with clear water and that none of the solution enters the filler holes. Clean the battery posts and clamps with a wire brush to eliminate corrosion deposits.

Special clamp and terminal cleaning brushes are available for just this purpose. Lightly coat the posts and clamps with petroleum jelly or chassis grease after cleaning them.

FLUID LEVEL (EXCEPT MAINTENANCE FREE BATTERIES)

Check the battery electrolyte level at least once a month, or more often in hot weather or during periods of extended car operation. The level can be checked through the case on trans-

lucent polypropylene batteries. The cell caps must be removed on other models. The electrolyte level in each cell should be kept filled to the split ring inside, or the line marked on the outside of the case.

If the level is low, add only distilled water (colorless, odorless drinking water) through the opening until the level is correct. Each cell is completely separate from the others, so each must be checked and filled individually.

If water is added in freezing weather, the car should be driven several miles to allow the water to mix with the electrolyte. Otherwise, the battery could freeze.

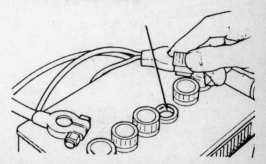

Remove the vent caps to check the electrolyte level. Electrolyte should cover the cell plates by about 1/2 in.

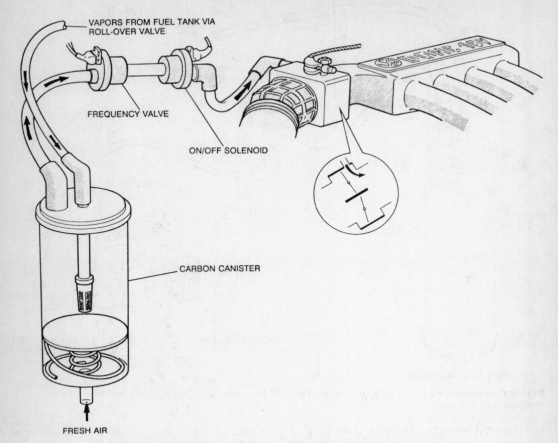

VAPORS FROM FUEL TANK VIA
ROLL-OVER VALVE

FREQUENCY VALVE

ON/OFF SOLENOID

CARBON CANISTER

FRESH AIR

Evaporative emission control system used on 2.0L 16V engines

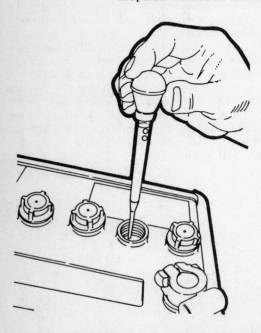

Check the specific gravity of the battery's electrolyte with a hydrometer

SPECIFIC GRAVITY (EXCEPT MAINTENANCE FREE BATTERIES)

At least once a year, check the specific gravity of the battery. It should be between 1.20 and 1.26 at room temperature.

The specific gravity can be checked with the use of an hydrometer, an inexpensive instrument available from many sources, including auto parts stores. The hydrometer has a squeeze bulb at one end and a nozzle at the other. Battery electrolyte is sucked into the hydrometer until the float is lifted from its seat. The specific gravity is then read by noting the position of the float. Generally, if after charging, the specific gravity between any two cells varies more than 50 points (0.050), the battery is bad and should be replaced.

It is not possible to check the specific gravity in this manner on sealed (maintenance free) batteries. Instead, the indicator built into the top of the case must be relied on to display any signs of battery deterioration. If the indicator is dark, the battery can be assumed to be OK. If the indicator is light, the specific gravity is low, and the battery should be charged or replaced.

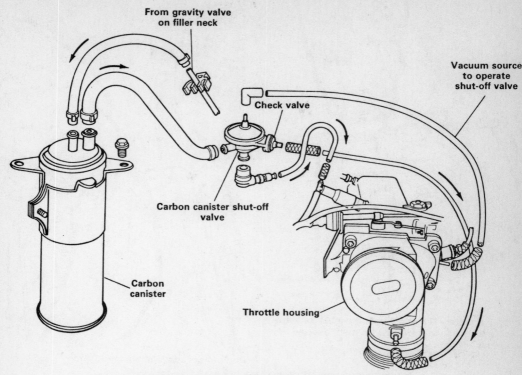

From gravity valve
on filler neck

Vacuum source
to operate
shut-off valve

Check valve

Carbon canister shut-off
valve

Carbon
canister

Throttle housing

Evaporative emission control system used on Corrado

CABLES AND CLAMPS

Once a year, the battery terminals and the cable clamps should be cleaned. Loosen the clamps and remove the cables, negative cable first. On batteries with posts on top, the use of a puller specially made for the purpose is recommended. These are inexpensive, and available in auto parts stores. Side terminal battery cables are secured with a bolt.

Clean the cable clamps and the battery terminal with a wire brush, until all corrosion, grease, etc. is removed and the metal is shiny. It is especially important to clean the inside of the clamp thoroughly, since a small deposit of foreign material or oxidation there will prevent a sound electrical connection and inhibit either starting or charging. Special tools are available for cleaning these parts, one type for conventional batteries and another type for side terminal batteries.

Before installing the cables, loosen the battery holddown clamp or strap, remove the battery and check the battery tray. Clear it of any debris, and check it for soundness. Rust should be wire brushed away, and the metal given a coat of anti-rust paint. Replace the battery and tighten the holddown clamp or strap securely, but be careful not to over-tighten, which will crack the battery case.

After the clamps and terminals are clean, reinstall the cables, negative cable last. Do not hammer on the clamps to install. Tighten the clamps securely, but do not distort them. Give the clamps and terminals a thin external coat of grease after installation, to retard corrosion.

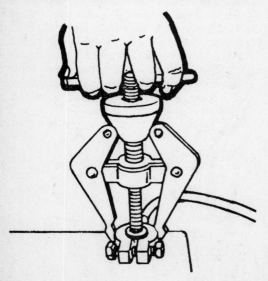

Battery cable removal tool

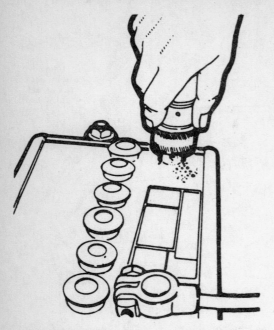

Clean the battery terminals until the metal is shiny. The cleaning tool shown can be purchased at any automotive store

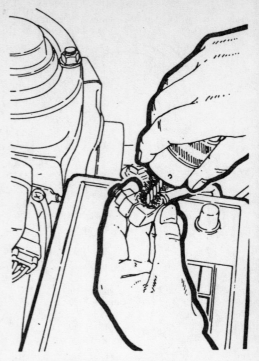

Don't forget to clean the cable ends

Check the cables at the same time that the terminals are cleaned. If the cable insulation is cracked or broken, or if the ends are frayed, the cable should be replaced with a new cable of the same length and gauge.

NOTE: *Keep flame or sparks away from the battery. It gives off explosive hydrogen gas. Battery electrolyte contains sulphuric acid. If you should splash any on your skin or in your eyes, flush the affected area with plenty of clear water. If it lands in your eyes, get medical help immediately.*

REPLACEMENT

When it becomes necessary to replace the battery, select a battery with a rating equal to or greater than the battery originally installed. Deterioration, embrittlement and just plain aging of the battery cables, starter motor, and associated wires makes the battery's job harder in successive years. The slow increase in electrical resistance over time makes it prudent to install a new battery with a greater capacity than the old.

Drive Belts

CHECKING TENSION AND ADJUSTMENT

NOTE: *Belt tension adjustment on the Corrado is done automatically by a belt tension damper and tension lever. If the belt tensioner damper fails to maintain proper drive*

belt tension, it must be adjusted using VW tool 3191 or replaced. Volkswagen recommends that this repair be referred to an authorized VW dealer.

The belt tension on most driven components is adjusted by moving the component (alternator, power steering pump etc.) within the range of a slotted or *toothed* bracket(s). Slotted brackets are used on earlier VW's and the toothed brackets are used on later Cabriolet, Fox, Golf, GTI, Jetta and Scirocco models. The newer brackets use a sliding toothed rack mechanism turned by a gear bolt which moves the alterna-

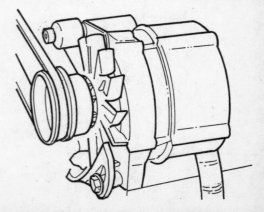

Alternator mounting on engines with slotted mounting brackets

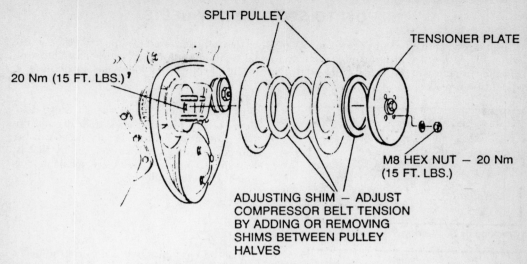

SPLIT PULLEY

TENSIONER PLATE

20 Nm (15 FT. LBS.)

M8 HEX NUT — 20 Nm
(15 FT. LBS.)

ADJUSTING SHIM — ADJUST
COMPRESSOR BELT TENSION
BY ADDING OR REMOVING
SHIMS BETWEEN PULLEY
HALVES

A/C compressor belt adjusting shims on Fox

tor side-to-side to adjust the belt tension. With this configuration, no prying tools are required. Before adjusting the belt tension on any engine, look at the alternator mounting and determine what kind of bracket is used. Adjust the belt tension using the proper procedure outlined below.

Check the belt tension every 3 months or 3,000 miles. Push in on the drive belt about midway between the crankshaft pulley and the driven component. If the belt deflects more than 14mm ($9/16$ in.) or less than 10mm ($3/8$ in.), adjustment is required.

Some late model air conditioner compressor drive belts are adjusted by varying the number of discs (shims) between the halves of the crankshaft pulley. On these models, once you tensioned the belt and if there are shims left over, don't discard them. Take the left over shims and bolt them back to the outside of the crankshaft pulley.

Engines With Slotted Brackets

1. Loosen the adjustment nut and bolt in the slotted bracket. Slightly loosen the pivot bolt.

2. Pull (don't pry) the component outward to increase tension. Push inward to reduce ten-

1. Ribbed belt pulley (alternator)
2. Ribbed belt
3. Ribbed belt pulley (G-Charger)
4. Ribbed belt idler pulley
5. Ribbed belt tensioning pulley
6. Ribbed belt pulley (water pump)
7. V-belt
8. Combination V-belt and ribbed belt pulley (crankshaft)

You need only a basic assortment of hand tools for most maintenance and repair jobs

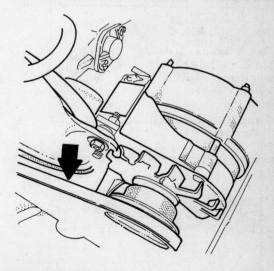

Checking belt deflection (arrow)

HOW TO SPOT WORN V-BELTS

V-Belts are vital to efficient engine operation—they drive the fan, water pump and other accessories. They require little maintenance (occasional tightening) but they will not last forever. Slipping or failure of the V-belt will lead to overheating. If your V-belt looks like any of these, it should be replaced.

Cracking or weathering

This belt has deep cracks, which cause it to flex. Too much flexing leads to heat build-up and premature failure. These cracks can be caused by using the belt on a pulley that is too small. Notched belts are available for small diameter pulleys.

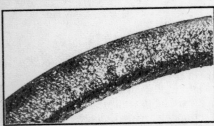

Softening (grease and oil)

Oil and grease on a belt can cause the belt's rubber compounds to soften and separate from the reinforcing cords that hold the belt together. The belt will first slip, then finally fail altogether.

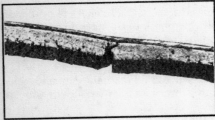

Glazing

Glazing is caused by a belt that is slipping. A slipping belt can cause a run-down battery, erratic power steering, overheating or poor accessory performance. The more the belt slips, the more glazing will be built up on the surface of the belt. The more the belt is glazed, the more it will slip. If the glazing is light, tighten the belt.

Worn cover

The cover of this belt is worn off and is peeling away. The reinforcing cords will begin to wear and the belt will shortly break. When the belt cover wears in spots or has a rough jagged appearance, check the pulley grooves for roughness.

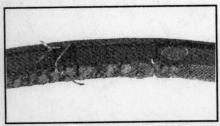

Separation

This belt is on the verge of breaking and leaving you stranded. The layers of the belt are separating and the reinforcing cords are exposed. It's just a matter of time before it breaks completely.

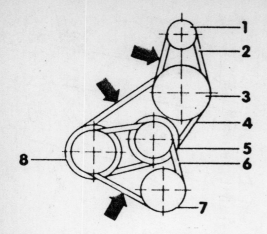

1. Alternator pulley
2. V-belt
3. A/C Compressor pulley
4. Water pump pulley
5. Power steering pump
6. Crankshaft pulley
7. V-belt
8. V-belt

Belt and pulley arrangement on Passat

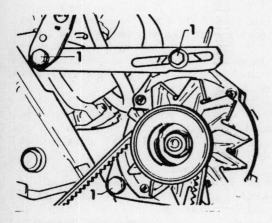

Belt tension adjustment on Passat

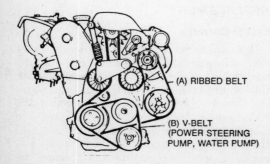

Belt routing on Corrado with air conditioning

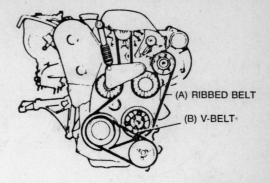

(A) RIBBED BELT

(B) V-BELT

Belt routing on Corrado without air conditioning

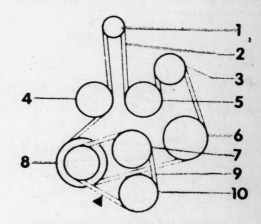

1. Ribbed belt pulley (alternator)
2. Ribbed belt
3. Ribbed belt pulley (G-Charger)
4. Tensioning pulley
5. Idler pulley
6. Ribbed belt pulley (A/C compressor)
7. V-belt pulley (water pump)
8. Combination V-belt and ribbed belt pulley
9. V-belt
10. V-belt pulley

Belt and pulley arrangement on Corrado with air conditioning

sion. Tighten the adjusting nut and bolt and the pivot bolt.

3. Components, such as the power steering pump and some air conditioner compressors, may be mounted with a double slotted adjusting bracket using a threaded bolt or bolts and locknuts to adjust and maintain tension. Loosen the locknut(s) and slightly loosen the bolt(s) in the slotted groove(s), turn the threaded adjustment bolt(s) in or out to gain correct tension. Tighten locknuts and slotted bracket bolts.

4. Recheck the drive belt tension, readjust if necessary.

5. On air conditioner compressors without a slotted bracket adjustment; remove the nuts (bolts) securing the crankshaft pulley halves.

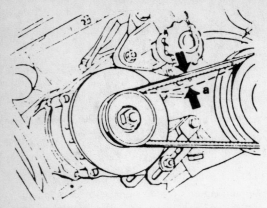

Checking belt tension on engines with toothed mounting brackets

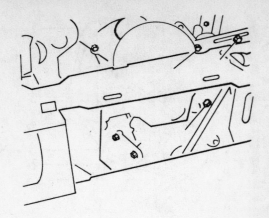

Belt tension adjustment on Fox

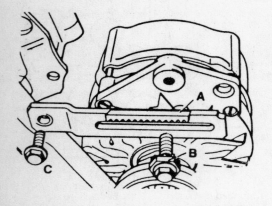

Belt tension adjustment Cabriolet, Golf, GTI, Jetta and Scirocco with toothed mounting brackets

Add or subtract spacer discs until the belt tension is correct. Secure the pulley halves. If there are any shims left over, bolt them to the front of the pulley.

Engines With Toothed Brackets

EXCEPT FOX

1. Loosen bolts **B**, **C** and the alternator pivot bolt. These bolts should be loosened until the alternator swings freely under it's own weight.
2. Tension the V-belt by turning tensioner gear **B** while checking the belt deflection with your thumb. Belt deflection for new V-belts is 8mm (0.3 in.) and 4mm (0.16 in.) for used belts.
3. Once the proper tension is achieved, tighten the tension gear to 26 ft. lbs. Torque bolt **C** to 15 ft. lbs. and the pivot bolt to 26 ft. lbs.
4. On air conditioner compressors without a bracket adjustment; remove the nuts (bolts)

securing the crankshaft pulley halves. Add or subtract spacer discs until the belt tension is correct. Secure the pulley halves. If there are any shims left over, bolt them to the front of the pulley.

FOX

1. Loosen bolts **A**, **B**, **C** and the tensioner bolt. These bolts should be loosed until the alternator swings freely under it's own weight.
2. Tension the V-belt by turning tensioner gear **C** while checking the belt deflection with your thumb. Belt deflection for new V-belts is 8mm (0.3 in.) and 4mm (0.16 in.) for used belts.
3. Once the proper tension is achieved, tighten the tension gear to 6–7 ft. lbs. Torque bolt **A** to 16 ft. lbs. and bolts **B** and **C** to 26 ft. lbs.
4. On air conditioner compressors without a bracket adjustment; remove the nuts (bolts) securing the crankshaft pulley halves. Add or subtract spacer discs until the belt tension is correct. Secure the pulley halves. If there are any shims left over, bolt them to the front of the pulley.

REPLACEMENT

Except Corrado

Belt replacement requires the loosening of the mounting and adjustment bolts as described in belt adjustment. Relax tension on the belt until removal from the pulleys is possible. Remove old belt and install new one in the reverse order. Adjust belt tension. Some late models have a front engine mount installed through the air conditioner compressor belt circle. Support the engine and remove the mount prior to belt removal and installation, reinstall mount.

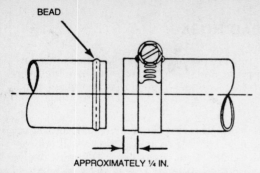

BEAD

APPROXIMATELY ¼ IN.

The hose clamp should be positioned so that the end of the clamp is ¹/₄ in. from the end of the hose

Corrado

The Corrado is equipped with a single serpentine drive belt that operates all the engine accessories. Removal, installation and tensioning of this belt is described in Chapter 3 under "Timing Belt, Removal and Installation".

CAUTION: *DO NOT attempt to service the belt that operates the G-Charger. If this is installed improperly, it may result in misalignment of the unit's drive and driven pulleys. If misalignment occurs, it will destroy the unit within seconds after the engine is started. Replacement and adjustment of this belt should be performed by an authorized VW dealer.*

Hoses

CAUTION: *Disconnect the negative battery cable when changing hoses. If the engine is warm, the cooling fan could operate even if the ignition switch is off.*

HOSE REPLACEMENT

To replace the hoses on your car, loosen the radiator cap AFTER the engine is cool and drain the coolant into a clean container. To drain the cooling system, remove the lower radiator hose at the radiator end connection.

NOTE: *Some early model Rabbits, Dashers and Sciroccos have a petcock at the bottom of the radiator for draining purposes. Check to see if yours is equipped with one.*

Loosen the clamps on the hose and remove the hose by cutting it or twisting it to break its grip on the flange. Clean all hose connections. When installing the new hose, don't overtighten the clamps or you may cut the hose. Position the hose clamps so that the end of the clamp is about 6mm (¹/₄ in.) from the end of the hose.

After the new hose in installed and the cooling system is refilled (See Cooling System, below), run the engine up to operating temperature and check for coolant leaks.

Air Conditioning

NOTE: *Operate the air conditioner for a few minutes, every two weeks or so, during the cold months. This avoids the possibility of the compressor seals drying out from lack of lubrication.*

SAFETY PRECAUTIONS

Because of the importance of the necessary safety precautions that must be exercised when working with air conditioning systems and R-12 refrigerant, a recap of the safety precautions are outlined.

1. Avoid contact with a charged refrigeration system, even when working on another part of the air conditioning system or vehicle. If a heavy tool comes into contact with a section of copper tubing or a heat exchanger, it can easily cause the relatively soft material to rupture.

2. When it is necessary to apply force to a fitting which contains refrigerant, as when checking that all system couplings are securely tightened, use a wrench on both parts of the fitting involved, if possible. This will avoid putting torque on refrigerant tubing. (It is advisable, when possible, to use tube or line wrenches when tightening these flare nut fittings.)

3. Do not attempt to discharge the system by merely loosening a fitting, or removing the service valve caps and cracking these valves. Precise control is possibly only when using the service gauges. Place a rag under the open end of the center charging hose while discharging the system to catch any drops of liquid that might escape. Wear protective gloves and goggles when connecting or disconnecting service gauge hoses.

4. Discharge the system only in a well ventilated area, as high concentrations of the gas can exclude oxygen and act as an anesthesia. When leak testing or soldering, this is particularly important, as toxic phosgene gas is formed when R-12 contacts any flame.

5. Never start a system without first verifying that both service valves are backseated, if equipped, and that all fittings are throughout the system are snugly connected.

6. Avoid applying heat to any refrigerant line or storage vessel. Charging may be aided by using water heated to less than $+125°F$ ($+51°C$) to warm the refrigerant container. Never allow a refrigerant storage container to sit out in the sun, or near any other source of heat, such as a radiator.

7. Always wear goggles when working on a system to protect the eyes. If refrigerant contacts the eye, it is advisable in all cases to see a physician as soon as possible.

HOW TO SPOT BAD HOSES

Both the upper and lower radiator hoses are called upon to perform difficult jobs in an inhospitable environment. They are subject to nearly 18 psi at under hood temperatures often over 280°F., and must circulate nearly 7500 gallons of coolant an hour—3 good reasons to have good hoses.

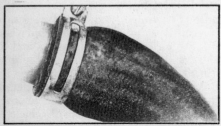

Swollen hose

A good test for any hose is to feel it for soft or spongy spots. Frequently these will appear as swollen areas of the hose. The most likely cause is oil soaking. This hose could burst at any time, when hot or under pressure.

Cracked hose

Cracked hoses can usually be seen but feel the hoses to be sure they have not hardened; a prime cause of cracking. This hose has cracked down to the reinforcing cords and could split at any of the cracks.

Frayed hose end (due to weak clamp)

Weakened clamps frequently are the cause of hose and cooling system failure. The connection between the pipe and hose has deteriorated enough to allow coolant to escape when the engine is hot.

Debris in cooling system

Debris, rust and scale in the cooling system can cause the inside of a hose to weaken. This can usually be felt on the outside of the hose as soft or thinner areas.

8. Frostbite from liquid refrigerant should be treated by first gradually warming the area with cool water, and then gently applying petroleum jelly. A physician should be consulted.

9. Always keep refrigerant can fittings capped when not in use. Avoid sudden shock to the can which might occur from dropping it, or from banging a heavy tool against it. Never carry a can in the passenger compartment of a car.

10. Always completely discharge the system before painting the vehicle (if the paint is to be baked on), or before welding anywhere near the refrigerant lines.

GENERAL SERVICING PROCEDURES

The most important aspect of air conditioning service is the maintenance of pure and adequate charge of refrigerant in the system. A refrigeration system cannot function properly if a significant percentage of the charge is lost. Leaks are common because the severe vibration encountered in an automobile can easily cause a sufficient cracking or loosening of the air conditioning fittings. As a result, the extreme operating pressures of the system force refrigerant out.

The problem can be understood by considering what happens to the system as it is operated with a continuous leak. Because the expansion valve regulates the flow of refrigerant to the evaporator, the level of refrigerant there is fairly constant. The receiver-drier stores any excess of refrigerant, and so a loss will first appear there as a reduction in the level of liquid. As this level nears the bottom of the vessel, some refrigerant vapor bubbles will begin to appear in the stream of liquid supplied to the expansion valve. This vapor decreases the capacity of the expansion valve very little as the valve opens to compensate for its presence. As the quantity of liquid in the condenser decreases, the operating pressure will drop there and throughout the high side of the system. As the R-12 continues to be expelled, the pressure available to force the liquid through the expansion valve will continue to decrease, and, eventually, the valve's orifice will prove to be too much of a restriction for adequate flow even with the needle fully withdrawn.

At this point, low side pressure will start to drop, and severe reduction in cooling capacity, marked by freeze-up of the evaporator coil, will result. Eventually, the operating pressure of the evaporator will be lower than the pressure of the atmosphere surrounding it, and air will be drawn into the system wherever there are leaks in the low side.

Because all atmospheric air contains at least some moisture, water will enter the system and mix with the R-12 and the oil. Trace amounts of moisture will cause sludging of the oil, and corrosion of the system. Saturation and clogging of the filter-drier, and freezing of the expansion valve orifice will eventually result. As air fills the system, it will interfere more and more with the normal flows of refrigerant and heat.

A list of general precautions that should be observed while servicing the air conditioning system follows:

1. Keep all tools as clean and dry as possible.

2. Thoroughly purge the service gauges and hoses of air and moisture before connecting them to the system. Keep them capped when not in use.

3. Thoroughly clean any refrigerant fitting before disconnecting it, in order to minimize the entrance of dirt into the system.

4. Plan any operation that requires opening the system beforehand in order to minimize the length of time it will be exposed to open air. Cap or seal the open ends to minimize the entrance of foreign material.

5. When adding oil, pour it through an extremely clean and dry tube or funnel. Keep the oil capped whenever possible. Do not use oil that has not been kept tightly sealed.

6. Use only refrigerant 12. Purchase refrigerant intended for use in only automotive air conditioning system. Avoid the use of refrigerant 12 that may be packaged for another use, such as cleaning, or powering a horn, as it is impure.

7. Completely evacuate any system that has been opened to replace a component, other than when isolating the compressor, or that has leaked sufficiently to draw in moisture and air. This requires evacuating air and moisture with a good vacuum pump for at least one hour.

If a system has been open for a considerable length of time it may be advisable to evacuate the system for up to 12 hours (overnight).

8. Use a wrench on both halves of a fitting that is to be disconnected, so as to avoid placing torque on any of the refrigerant lines.

ADDITIONAL PREVENTIVE MAINTENANCE CHECKS

Antifreeze

In order to prevent heater core freeze-up during air conditioner operation, it is necessary to maintain permanent type antifreeze protection of +15°F (−9°C) or lower. A reading of −15°F (−26°C) is ideal since this protection also supplies sufficient corrosion inhibitors for the protection of the engine cooling system.

NOTE: *The same antifreeze should not be used longer than the manufacturer specified.*

Radiator Cap

For efficient operation of an air conditioned car's cooling system, the radiator cap should have a holding pressure which meets manufacturer's specifications. A cap which fails to hold this pressure should be replaced.

Condenser

Any obstruction of or damage to the condenser configuration will restrict the air flow which is essential to its efficient operation. It is therefore, a good rule to keep this unit clean and in proper physical shape.

NOTE: *Bug screens are regarded as obstructions.*

Condensation Drain Tube

This single molded drain tube expels the condensation, which accumulates on the bottom of the evaporator housing, into the engine compartment.

If this tube is obstructed, the air conditioning performance can be restricted and condensation buildup can spill over onto the vehicle's floor.

GAUGE SETS

Most of the service work performed in air conditioning requires the use of a set of two gauges, one for the high (head) pressure side of the system, the other for the low (suction) side.

The low side gauge records both pressure and vacuum. Vacuum readings are calibrated from 0 to 30 in.Hg and the pressure graduations read from 0 to no less than 60 psi.

The high side gauge measures pressure from 0 to at least 600 psi.

Both gauges are threaded into a manifold that contains two hand shut-off valves. Proper manipulation of these valves and the use of the attached test hoses allow the user to perform the following services:

1. Test high and low side pressures.
2. Remove air, moisture, and contaminated refrigerant.
3. Purge the system (of refrigerant).
4. Charge the system (with refrigerant).

The manifold valves are designed so that they have no direct effect on gauge readings, but serve only to provide for, or cut off, flow of refrigerant through the manifold. During all testing and hook-up operations, the valves are kept in a closed position to avoid disturbing the refrigeration system. The valves are opened only to purge the system or refrigerant or to charge it.

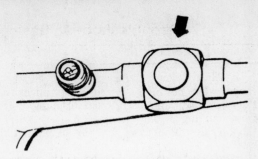

Refrigerant sight glass location (arrow) on Corrado, Golf, GTI, Jetta and Passat. The high pressure service valve is to the left of the sight glass

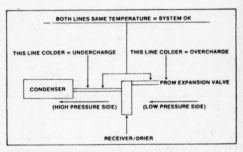

Checking refrigerant charge by line

CAUTION: *The compressed refrigerant used in the air conditioning system expands into the atmosphere at a temperature of −21.7°F (−29.8°C) or lower. This will freeze any surface, including your eyes, that it contacts. In addition, the refrigerant decomposes into a poisonous gas in the presence of a flame. Do not open or disconnect any part of the air conditioning system.*

SIGHT GLASS CHECK (REFRIGERANT LEVEL)

You can safely make a few simple checks to determine if your air conditioning system needs service. The tests work best if the temperature is warm, about 70°F (21°C).

NOTE: *This test is for the factory installed air conditioning system only. Aftermarket air conditioner testing procedures may be different. If in doubt, contact the manufacturer of your particular unit.*

1. Place the automatic transmission in Park or the manual transmission in Neutral. Set the parking brake.
2. Run the engine at a fast idle (about 2500 rpm) either with the help of a friend.
3. Set the controls for maximum cold and the highest fan speed.
4. Locate the sight glass and wipe it clean. The sight glass is located either in the high pres-

Troubleshooting Basic Air Conditioning Problems

Problem	Cause	Solution
There's little or no air coming from the vents (and you're sure it's on)	• The A/C fuse is blown • Broken or loose wires or connections • The on/off switch is defective	• Check and/or replace fuse • Check and/or repair connections • Replace switch
The air coming from the vents is not cool enough	• Windows and air vent wings open • The compressor belt is slipping • Heater is on • Condenser is clogged with debris • Refrigerant has escaped through a leak in the system • Receiver/drier is plugged	• Close windows and vent wings • Tighten or replace compressor belt • Shut heater off • Clean the condenser • Check system • Service system
The air has an odor	• Vacuum system is disrupted • Odor producing substances on the evaporator case • Condensation has collected in the bottom of the evaporator housing	• Have the system checked/repaired • Clean the evaporator case • Clean the evaporator housing drains
System is noisy or vibrating	• Compressor belt or mountings loose • Air in the system	• Tighten or replace belt; tighten mounting bolts • Have the system serviced

Sight glass condition
  Constant bubbles, foam or oil streaks
  Clear sight glass, but no cold air
  Clear sight glass, but air is cold
  Clouded with milky fluid
	
	• Undercharged system
	
	• No refrigerant at all
	• System is OK
	• Receiver drier is leaking dessicant
		
		• Charge the system
		
		• Check and charge the system
		
		• Have system checked

Large difference in temperature of lines	• System undercharged	• Charge and leak test the system
Compressor noise	• Broken valves • Overcharged • Incorrect oil level • Piston slap • Broken rings • Drive belt pulley bolts are loose	• Replace the valve plate • Discharge, evacuate and install the correct charge • Isolate the compressor and check the oil level. Correct as necessary. • Replace the compressor • Replace the compressor • Tighten with the correct torque specification
Excessive vibration	• Incorrect belt tension • Clutch loose • Overcharged • Pulley is misaligned	• Adjust the belt tension • Tighten the clutch • Discharge, evacuate and install the correct charge • Align the pulley
Condensation dripping in the passenger compartment	• Drain hose plugged or improperly positioned • Insulation removed or improperly installed	• Clean the drain hose and check for proper installation • Replace the insulation on the expansion valve and hoses
Frozen evaporator coil	• Faulty thermostat • Thermostat capillary tube improperly installed • Thermostat not adjusted properly	• Replace the thermostat • Install the capillary tube correctly • Adjust the thermostat
Low side low—high side low	• System refrigerant is low • Expansion valve is restricted	• Evacuate, leak test and charge the system • Replace the expansion valve
Low side high—high side low	• Internal leak in the compressor— worn	• Remove the compressor cylinder head and inspect the compressor. Replace the valve plate assembly if necessary. If the compressor pistons, rings or

Troubleshooting Basic Air Conditioning Problems (cont.)

Problem	Cause	Solution
Low side high—high side low (cont.)		cylinders are excessively worn or scored replace the compressor
	• Cylinder head gasket is leaking	• Install a replacement cylinder head gasket
	• Expansion valve is defective	• Replace the expansion valve
	• Drive belt slipping	• Adjust the belt tension
Low side high—high side high	• Condenser fins obstructed	• Clean the condenser fins
	• Air in the system	• Evacuate, leak test and charge the system
	• Expansion valve is defective	• Replace the expansion valve
	• Loose or worn fan belts	• Adjust or replace the belts as necessary
Low side low—high side high	• Expansion valve is defective	• Replace the expansion valve
	• Restriction in the refrigerant hose	• Check the hose for kinks—replace if necessary
	• Restriction in the receiver/drier	• Replace the receiver/drier
	• Restriction in the condenser	• Replace the condenser
Low side and high side normal (inadequate cooling)	• Air in the system	• Evacuate, leak test and charge the system
	• Moisture in the system	• Evacuate, leak test and charge the system

sure tube between the high pressure service valve and the receiver drier or on top of the receiver drier itself.

5. If you see bubbles, the system must be recharged. Very likely there is a leak at some point.

6. If there are no bubbles and air coming from the vents is warm, the system needs complete charge. If there air no bubbles and the vent air is cold, the system is ok.

7. You are probably making these tests because you think there is something wrong. As a further check, check the temperature of the two lines going to the belt driven compressor. If they are both the same temperature, the system is empty.

8. Have an assistant in the car turn the fan control on and off to operate the compressor clutch. Watch the sight glass.

9. If bubbles appear when the clutch is disengaged and disappear when it is engaged, the system is properly charged.

10. If the refrigerant takes more than 45 seconds to bubble when the clutch is disengaged, the system is overcharged. This usually causes poor cooling at low speeds.

If it is determined that the system has a leak, it should be corrected as soon as possible. Leaks may allow moisture to enter and cause a very expensive rust problem.

TESTING THE SYSTEM

1. Connect a gauge set.
2. Close both gauge set valves.

3. Mid-position both service valves.

4. Park the vehicle in the shade. Start the engine, set the parking brake, place the transmission in NEUTRAL and establish an idle of 1500 rpm.

5. Run the air conditioning system for full cooling, but NOT in the MAX or COLD mode.

6. Insert a thermometer into the center air outlet.

7. Use the accompanying performance chart for a specifications reference. If pressures are abnormal, refer to the accompanying Pressure Diagnosis Chart.

DISCHARGING THE SYSTEM

1. Connect the manifold gauge set.
2. Turn both manifold gauge set hand valves to the full open (counterclockwise) position.
3. Open both service valve slightly, from the backseated position, and allow the refrigerant to discharge *slowly*.

NOTE: *If you allow the refrigerant to rush out, it will take some refrigerant oil with it!*

EVACUATING THE SYSTEM

NOTE: *This procedure requires the use of a vacuum pump.*

1. Connect the manifold gauge set.
2. Discharge the system.
3. Connect the center service hose to the inlet fitting of the vacuum pump.
4. Turn both gauge set valves to the wide open position.

5. Start the pump and note the low side gauge reading.

6. Operate the pump for a minimum of 30 minutes after the lowest observed gauge reading.

7. Leak test the system. Close both gauge set valves. Turn off the pump and note the low side gauge reading. The needle should remain stationary at the point at which the pump was turned off. If the needle drops to zero rapidly, there is a leak in the system which must be repaired.

8. If the needle remains stationary for 3 to 5 minutes, open the gauge set valves and run the pump for at least 30 minutes more.

9. Close both gauge set valves, stop the pump and disconnect the gauge set. The system is now ready for charging.

LEAK TESTING

Some leak tests can be performed with a soapy water solution. There must be at least a $1/2$ lb. charge in the system for a leak to be detected. The most extensive leak tests are performed with either a Halide flame type leak tester or the more preferable electronic leak tester.

In either case, the equipment is expensive, and, the use of a Halide detector can be **extremely** hazardous!

CHARGING THE SYSTEM

1. Connect the gauge set.
2. Close (clockwise) both gauge set valves.
3. Mid-position the service valves.
4. Connect the center hose to the refrigerant can opener valve.
5. Make sure the can opener valve is closed, that is, the needle is raised, and connect the valve to the can. Open the valve, puncturing the can with the needle.
6. Loosen the center hose fitting at the pressure gauge, allowing refrigerant to purge the hose of air.
7. Open the low side gauge set valve and the can valve.
8. Start the engine and turn the air conditioner to the maximum cooling mode. The compressor will operate and pull refrigerant gas into the system.

NOTE: *To help speed the process, the can may be placed, upright, in a pan of warm water, not exceeding 125°F (51°C).*

9. If more than one can of refrigerant is needed, close the can valve and gauge set low side valve when the can is empty and connect a new can to the opener. Repeat the charging process until the sight glass indicates a full charge. The frost line on the outside of the can will indicate what portion of the can has been used.

10. When the charging process has been completed, close the gauge set valve and can valve. Run the system for at least five minutes to allow it to normalize.

11. Back-seat (turn fully counterclockwise) both service valves.

12. Loosen both service hoses at the gauges to allow any refrigerant to escape. Remove the gauge set and install the dust caps on the service valves.

NOTE: *Multi-can dispensers are available which allow a simultaneous hook-up of up to four 1 lb. cans of R-12.*

CAUTION: *Never exceed the recommended maximum charge for the system!*

Windshield Wipers

For maximum effectiveness and longest element life, the windshield and wiper blades should be kept clean. Dirt, tree sap, road tar and so on will cause streaking, smearing and blade deterioration if left on the glass. It is advisable to wash the windshield carefully with a commercial glass cleaner at least once a month. Wipe off the rubber blades with the wet rag afterwards. Do not attempt to move the wipers by hand, because damage to the motor and drive mechanism will result.

If the blades are found to be cracked, broken or torn, they should be replaced immediately. Replacement intervals will vary with usage, although ozone deterioration usually limits blade life to about one year or less. If the wiper pattern is smeared or streaked, or if the blade chatters across the glass, the elements should be replaced. It is easiest and most sensible to replace the elements in pairs.

There are basically three different types of refills, which differ in their method of replacement. One type has two release buttons, approximately $1/3$ of the way up from the ends of the blade frame. Pushing the buttons down releases a lock and allows the rubber filler to be removed from the frame. The new filler slides back into the frame and locks in place.

The second type of refill has two metal tabs which are unlocked by squeezing them together. The rubber filler can then be withdrawn from the frame jaws. A new refill is installed by inserting the refill into the front frame jaws and sliding it rearward to engage the remaining frame jaws. There are usually four jaws. Be certain when installing that the refill is engaged in all of them. At the end of its travel, the tabs will lock into place on the front jaws of the wiper blade frame.

The third type is a refill made from polycarbonate. The refill has a simple locking device at one end which flexes downward out of the

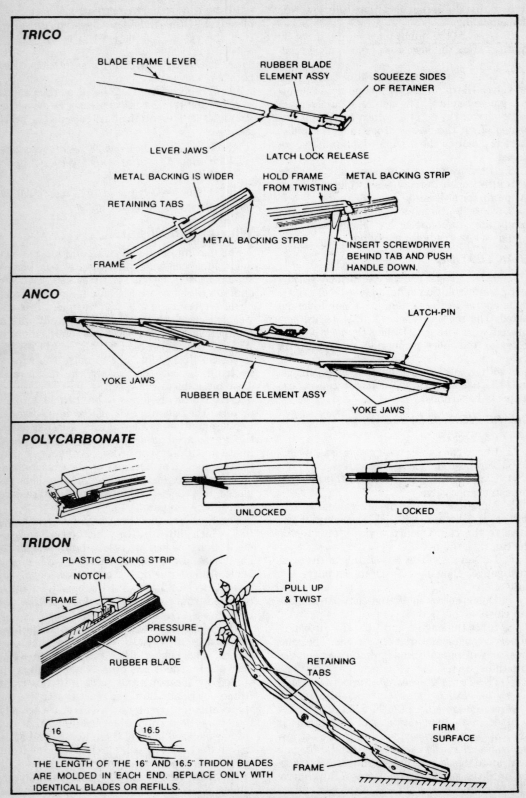

TRICO

BLADE FRAME LEVER

RUBBER BLADE ELEMENT ASSY

SQUEEZE SIDES OF RETAINER

LEVER JAWS

LATCH LOCK RELEASE

METAL BACKING IS WIDER

HOLD FRAME FROM TWISTING

METAL BACKING STRIP

RETAINING TABS

METAL BACKING STRIP

INSERT SCREWDRIVER BEHIND TAB AND PUSH HANDLE DOWN.

FRAME

ANCO

LATCH-PIN

YOKE JAWS

RUBBER BLADE ELEMENT ASSY

YOKE JAWS

POLYCARBONATE

UNLOCKED

LOCKED

TRIDON

PLASTIC BACKING STRIP

NOTCH

FRAME

PULL UP & TWIST

PRESSURE DOWN

RUBBER BLADE

RETAINING TABS

16

16.5

THE LENGTH OF THE 16" AND 16.5" TRIDON BLADES ARE MOLDED IN EACH END. REPLACE ONLY WITH IDENTICAL BLADES OR REFILLS.

FRAME

FIRM SURFACE

Wiper insert replacement

Troubleshooting Basic Windshield Wiper Problems

Problem	Cause	Solution
Electric Wipers		
Wipers do not operate— Wiper motor heats up or hums	• Internal motor defect • Bent or damaged linkage • Arms improperly installed on link- ing pivots	• Replace motor • Repair or replace linkage • Position linkage in park and rein- stall wiper arms
Wipers do not operate— No current to motor	• Fuse or circuit breaker blown • Loose, open or broken wiring • Defective switch • Defective or corroded terminals • No ground circuit for motor or switch	• Replace fuse or circuit breaker • Repair wiring and connections • Replace switch • Replace or clean terminals • Repair ground circuits
Wipers do not operate— Motor runs	• Linkage disconnected or broken	• Connect wiper linkage or replace broken linkage
Vacuum Wipers		
Wipers do not operate	• Control switch or cable inoperative • Loss of engine vacuum to wiper motor (broken hoses, low engine vacuum, defective vacuum/fuel pump) • Linkage broken or disconnected • Defective wiper motor	• Repair or replace switch or cable • Check vacuum lines, engine vacuum and fuel pump • Repair linkage • Replace wiper motor
Wipers stop on engine acceleration	• Leaking vacuum hoses • Dry windshield • Oversize wiper blades • Defective vacuum/fuel pump	• Repair or replace hoses • Wet windshield with washers • Replace with proper size wiper blades • Replace pump

groove into which the jaws of the holder fit, allowing easy release. By sliding the new refill through all the jaws and pushing through the slight resistance when it reaches the end of its travel, the refill will lock into position.

Regardless of the type of refill used, make sure that all of the frame jaws are engaged as the refill is pushed into place and locked. The metal blade holder and frame will scratch the glass if allowed to touch it.

WIPER ARM AND BLADE REPLACEMENT

To replace the complete wiper blade, lift up on the locking lever and slide the blade off of the wiper arm.

NOTE: *There are two different styles of wiper arms. On the first, the arm pivot attaching nut is covered with a plastic cap that pulls off. On the second, the arm pivot is covered by a spring-loaded metal cap that slips back off the nut.*

Lift the blade and arm up off the windshield. Simultaneously push the arm down and lift the smaller end cap up, or pull the plastic cap off to expose the retaining nut. Remove the retaining nut and apply upward pressure to remove the wiper arm. Install the arm in the reverse order of removal.

Tires and Wheels

Buy a tire pressure gauge and keep it in the glovebox of your car. Service station air gauges are generally either not working or inaccurate and should not be relied upon. The decal on the left door post gives the recommended air pressure for the standard tires. If you are driving on replacement tires of a different type, follow the inflation recommendations of the manufacturer and never exceed the maximum pressure stated on the sidewall. Always check tire pressure when the tires are cool because air pressure increases with heat and readings will be 4–6 psi higher after the tire has been run. For continued expressway driving, increase the tire pressure by a few pounds in each tire. Never mix tires of different construction on your Volkswagen. When replacing tires, ensure that the new tire(s) are the same size and type as those which will be remaining on the car. Intermixing bias ply tires with radial or bias belted can result in unpredictable and treacherous handling.

TIRE ROTATION

To equalize tire wear and thereby lengthen the mileage you obtain from your tires, rotate them every 5 or 6,000 miles. Follow the illus-

Troubleshooting Basic Wheel Problems

Problem	Cause	Solution
The car's front end vibrates at high speed	• The wheels are out of balance • Wheels are out of alignment	• Have wheels balanced • Have wheel alignment checked/adjusted
Car pulls to either side	• Wheels are out of alignment • Unequal tire pressure • Different size tires or wheels	• Have wheel alignment checked/adjusted • Check/adjust tire pressure • Change tires or wheels to same size
The car's wheel(s) wobbles	• Loose wheel lug nuts • Wheels out of balance • Damaged wheel • Wheels are out of alignment • Worn or damaged ball joint • Excessive play in the steering linkage (usually due to worn parts) • Defective shock absorber	• Tighten wheel lug nuts • Have tires balanced • Raise car and spin the wheel. If the wheel is bent, it should be replaced • Have wheel alignment checked/adjusted • Check ball joints • Check steering linkage • Check shock absorbers
Tires wear unevenly or prematurely	• Incorrect wheel size • Wheels are out of balance • Wheels are out of alignment	• Check if wheel and tire size are compatible • Have wheels balanced • Have wheel alignment checked/adjusted

Troubleshooting Basic Tire Problems

Problem	Cause	Solution
The car's front end vibrates at high speeds and the steering wheel shakes	• Wheels out of balance • Front end needs aligning	• Have wheels balanced • Have front end alignment checked
The car pulls to one side while cruising	• Unequal tire pressure (car will usually pull to the low side) • Mismatched tires • Front end needs aligning	• Check/adjust tire pressure • Be sure tires are of the same type and size • Have front end alignment checked
Abnormal, excessive or uneven tire wear See "How to Read Tire Wear"	• Infrequent tire rotation • Improper tire pressure • Sudden stops/starts or high speed on curves	• Rotate tires more frequently to equalize wear • Check/adjust pressure • Correct driving habits
Tire squeals	• Improper tire pressure • Front end needs aligning	• Check/adjust tire pressure • Have front end alignment checked

trations that are appropriate for the type of tires on your car.

TIRE DESIGN

For maximum satisfaction, tires should be used in sets of five. Mixing of different types (radial, bias-belted, fiberglass belted) should be avoided. Conventional bias tires are constructed so that the cords run bead to bead at an angle. Alternate plies run at an opposite angle. This type of construction gives rigidity to both tread and side wall. Bias belted tires are similar in construction to conventional bias ply tires. Belts run at an angle and also at a 90° angle to the bead, as in radial tires. Tread life is improved considerably over the conventional bias tire. The radial tire differs in construction, but instead of the carcass running at an angle of 90° to each other they run at an angle of 90° to the bead. This gives the tread a great deal of rigidity and the side wall a great deal of flexibility (which accounts for the characteristic bulge associated with radial tires).

INFLATION PRESSURE

Tire inflation is the most ignored item of auto maintenance. Gasoline mileage can drop as much as 0.8% for every 1 pound per square inch (psi) of under inflation.

Two items should be a permanent fixture in every glove compartment: a tire pressure gauge and a tread depth gauge. Check the tire air pressure (including the spare) regularly with a pocket type gauge. Kicking the tires won't tell you a thing, and the gauge on the service station air hose is notoriously inaccurate.

The tire pressures recommended for your car are usually found on the left door or in the owner's manual. Ideally, inflation pressure should be checked when the tires are cool. When the air becomes heated it expands and the pressure increases. Every 10° rise (or drop) in temperature means a difference of 1 psi, which also explains why the tire appears to lose air on a very cold night. When it is impossible to check the tires cold, allow for pressure build-up due to heat. If the hot pressure exceeds the cold pressure by more than 15 psi, reduce your speed, load or both. Otherwise internal heat is created in the tire. When the heat approaches the temperature at which the tire was cured, during manufacture, the tread can separate from the body.

Tread wear bands show up as horizontal bands across the tire when the tire is worn to less than $1/16$ in.

CAUTION: *Never counteract excessive pressure build-up by bleeding off air pressure (letting some air out). This will only further raise the tire operating temperature.*

Before starting a long trip with lots of luggage, you can add about 2–4 psi to the tires to make them run cooler, but never exceed the maximum inflation pressure on the side of the tire.

TREAD DEPTH

All tires have 7 built-in tread wear indicator bars that show up as 13mm ($1/2$ in.) wide smooth bands across the tire when 1.5mm ($1/16$ in.) of tread remains. The appearance of tread

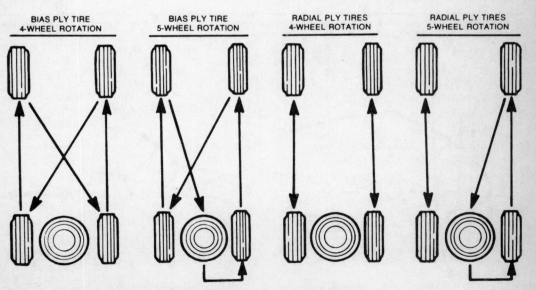

| BIAS PLY TIRE 4-WHEEL ROTATION | BIAS PLY TIRE 5-WHEEL ROTATION | RADIAL PLY TIRES 4-WHEEL ROTATION | RADIAL PLY TIRES 5-WHEEL ROTATION |

Gasoline engine oil recommendations

Tire Size Comparison Chart

"Letter" sizes			Inch Sizes	Metric-inch Sizes		
"60 Series"	"70 Series"	"78 Series"	1965–77	"60 Series"	"70 Series"	"80 Series"
		Y78-12	5.50-12, 5.60-12 6.00-12	165/60-12	165/70-12	155-12
		W78-13	5.20-13	165/60-13	145/70-13	135-13
		Y78-13	5.60-13	175/60-13	155/70-13	145-13
			6.15-13	185/60-13	165/70-13	155-13, P155/80-13
A60-13	A70-13	A78-13	6.40-13	195/60-13	175/70-13	165-13
B60-13	B70-13	B78-13	6.70-13	205/60-13	185/70-13	175-13
			6.90-13			
C60-13	C70-13	C78-13	7.00-13	215/60-13	195/70-13	185-13
D60-13	D70-13	D78-13	7.25-13			
E60-13	E70-13	E78-13	7.75-13			195-13
			5.20-14	165/60-14	145/70-14	135-14
			5.60-14	175/60-14	155/70-14	145-14
			5.90-14			
A60-14	A70-14	A78-14	6.15-14	185/60-14	165/70-14	155-14
	B70-14	B78-14	6.45-14	195/60-14	175/70-14	165-14
	C70-14	C78-14	6.95-14	205/60-14	185/70-14	175-14
D60-14	D70-14	D78-14				
E60-14	E70-14	E78-14	7.35-14	215/60-14	195/70-14	185-14
F60-14	F70-14	F78-14, F83-14	7.75-14	225/60-14	200/70-14	195-14
G60-14	G70-14	G77-14, G78-14	8.25-14	235/60-14	205/70-14	205-14
H60-14	H70-14	H78-14	8.55-14	245/60-14	215/70-14	215-14
J60-14	J70-14	J78-14	8.85-14	255/60-14	225/70-14	225-14
L60-14	L70-14		9.15-14	265/60-14	235/70-14	
	A70-15	A78-15	5.60-15	185/60-15	165/70-15	155-15
B60-15	B70-15	B78-15	6.35-15	195/60-15	175/70-15	165-15
C60-15	C70-15	C78-15	6.85-15	205/60-15	185/70-15	175-15
	D70-15	D78-15				
E60-15	E70-15	E78-15	7.35-15	215/60-15	195/70-15	185-15
F60-15	F70-15	F78-15	7.75-15	225/60-15	205/70-15	195-15
G60-15	G70-15	G78-15	8.15-15/8.25-15	235/60-15	215/70-15	205-15
H60-15	H70-15	H78-15	8.45-15/8.55-15	245/60-15	225/70-15	215-15
J60-15	J70-15	J78-15	8.85-15/8.90-15	255/60-15	235/70-15	225-15
	K70-15		9.00-15	265/60-15	245/70-15	230-15
L60-15	L70-15	L78-15, L84-15	9.15-15			235-15
	M70-15	M78-15				255-15
		N78-15				

Note: Every size tire is not listed and many size comparisons are approximate, based on load ratings. Wider tires than those supplied new with the vehicle, should always be checked for clearance.

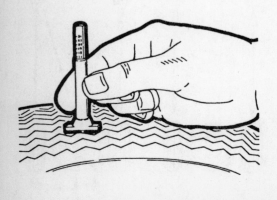

Checking tread depth using a gauge

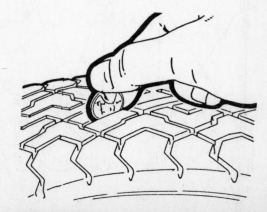

Checking tread depth using a Lincoln head penny

wear indicators means that the tires should be replaced. In fact, many states have laws prohibiting the use of tires with less than 1.5mm ($^1/_{16}$ in.) tread.

You can check your own tread depth with an inexpensive gauge or by using a Lincoln head penny. Slip the Lincoln penny into several tread grooves. If you can see the top of Lincoln's head in 2 adjacent grooves, the tires have less than 1.5mm ($^1/_{16}$ in.) tread left and should be replaced. You can measure snow tires in the same manner by using the tails side of the Lincoln penny. If you can see the top of the Lincoln memorial, it's time to replace the snow tires.

STORAGE

Store the tires at the proper inflation pressure if they are mounted on wheels. Keep them in a cool dry place, laid on their sides. If the tires are stored in the garage or basement, do not let them stand on a concrete floor. Set them on strips of wood.

BUYING NEW TIRES

When buying new tires, give some though to the following points, especially if you are considering a switch to larger tires or a different profile series:

1. All 4 tires must be of the same construction type. This rule cannot be violated. Radial, bias, and bias-belted tires must not be mixed.

2. The wheels should be the correct width for the tire. Tire dealers have charts of tire and rim compatibility. A mismatch will cause sloppy handling and rapid tire wear. The tread width should match the rim width (inside bead to inside bead) within 25mm (1 inch). For radial tires, the rim width should be 80% or less of the tire (not tread) width.

3. The height (mounted diameter) of the new tires can change speedometer accuracy, engine speed at a given road speed, fuel mileage, acceleration, and ground clearance. Tire manufacturers furnish full measurement specifications.

4. The spare tire should be usable, at least for short distance and low speed operation, with the new tires.

5. There shouldn't be any body interference when loaded, on bumps, or in turns.

NOTE: *For a more detailed description of the cooling system and servicing procedures see fluid level checks in this section.*

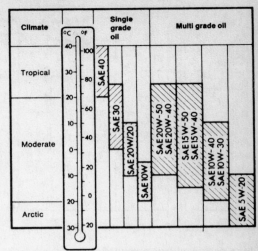

Gasoline engine oil recommendations

FLUIDS AND LUBRICANTS

Oil and Fuel Recommendations

GASOLINE ENGINES

The SAE (Society of Automotive Engineers) grade number indicates the viscosity of the engine oil, and thus its ability to lubricate at a given temperature. The lower the SAE grade number, the lighter the oil. The lower the viscosity, the easier it is to crank the engine in cold weather.

Oil viscosities should be chosen from those oils recommended for the lowest anticipated temperatures during the oil change interval.

Multi-viscosity oils (10W–30, 20W–50, etc.) offer the important advantage of being adaptable to temperature extremes. They allow easy starting at low temperatures, yet give good protection at high speeds and engine temperatures. This is a decided advantage in changeable climates or in long distance touring.

The API (American Petroleum Institute) designation indicates the classification of engine oil for use under given operating conditions. Only oils designated for use Service SF or SG should be used. Oils of the SF or SG type perform a variety of functions inside the engine in addition to the basic function as a lubricant. Through a balanced system of metallic detergents and polymeric dispersants, the oil prevents the formation of high and low temperature deposits, and also keeps sludge and dirt particles in suspension. Acids, particularly sulfuric acid, as well as other by-products of combustion, are neutralized. Both the SAE grade number and the API designation can be found on the top of the oil can.

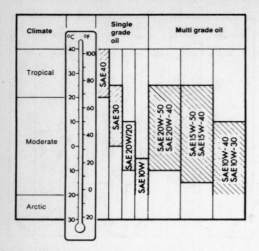

Diesel engine oil recommendations

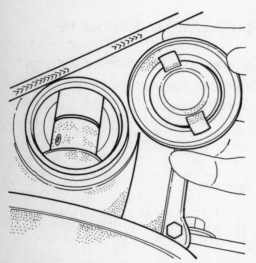

Add oil through the capped opening in the valve cover

NOTE: *Non-detergent or straight mineral oils must never be used.*

Your VW is designed to operate on lead-free fuel. The octane ratings are listed on the inside of the fuel filler door or on the door jamb. Use of leaded gasoline will render the emission control catalyst ineffective.

Oil must be selected with regard to the anticipated temperatures during the period before the next oil change. Using the chart, select the oil viscosity prior to the next oil change for the lowest expected temperature and you will be assured of easy cold starting and sufficient engine protection. The oil you pour into your engine should have the designation 'SF' or 'SG' marked on the top of its container.

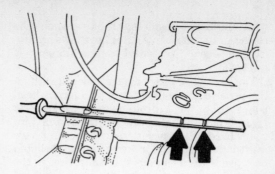

There is approximately one quart between the minimum and maximum marks on the oil dipstick

DIESEL ENGINES

The Volkswagen diesel engine is designed to run on Diesel Fuel No. 2. Since diesel fuel is generally available, supply is not usually a problem, though it is wise to check in advance. Several diesel station guides are available from fuel companies and are normally sold at diesel fuel stations.

Some U. S. States and Canadian provinces require purchasers of diesel fuel to obtain a special permit to buy diesel fuel. Check with your local VW dealer or fuel supplier for regulations in your area.

There is a difference between the refinement levels of Diesel fuel and home heating oil. While you may get away with running your diesel on home heating oil for a while, inevitably you will fill your tank with a filter and injector clogging batch of oil that will leave you stranded. Also, never allow diesel fuel to come in contact with any rubber hoses, as it will damage them.

Engine oils should be selected from the accompanying chart. The SAE viscosity number should be chosen for the lowest anticipated temperature at which the engine will be required to start not for the temperature at the time the oil is changed.

Use only oils designated by the API (American Petroleum Institute) for service 'CC' or 'CD'. The letters should appear somewhere on the oil can for example 'SF/CC' or 'SG/CD'. This indicates that the oil provides protection from rust, corrosion and high temperature deposits in diesel engines in moderate to severe service.

LEVEL CHECK

Engine oil level should be checked weekly. Always check the oil with the car on level ground and after the engine has been shut off for about five minutes. The oil dipstick is either located on the front side of engine or on the driver's side near the fuel pump.

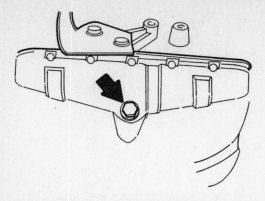

The oil drain pan is in the end of the oil drain pan

1. Remove the dipstick and wipe it clean.
2. Reinsert the dipstick.
3. Remove the dipstick again. The oil level should be between the two marks. On vehicles produced up to mid-1989, which use the round rod type dipstick, the difference between the marks is approximately one quart. On late 1989 and all 1990 VW's, the old style round rod dipstick was replaced with a flat rod type. On the flat rod type dipstick, the level between the **MIN** and **MAX** marks is approximately 0.75L (0.79 quart).
4. Add oil through the capped opening on the top of the valve cover. Select oil of the proper viscosity from the chart later in this chapter.

OIL CHANGE

Change the oil according to the maintenance interval chart in this chapter. This interval is only for average driving. If your car is being used under dusty conditions, change the oil and filter sooner. The same thing goes for cars being driven in stop and go city traffic, where acid and sludge buildup is a problem.

Always drain the oil after the engine has been run long enough to bring it to the normal operating temperature. Hot oil will flow easier and more contaminants will be removed with the oil than if it were drained cold. A large capacity drain pan, which can be purchased at any automotive supply store, will be more than paid back by savings from do-it-yourself containers for the used oil. Store the used oil in EPA approved containers and dispose of it in accordance with state or local regulations.

To change the oil and filter:
NOTE: *Always change the oil and filter at the same time on both diesel and gasoline engines.*

1. Run the engine until it reaches the normal operating temperature.
2. Slide a drain pan under the oil pan drain plug.

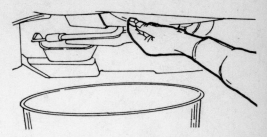

Draining engine oil — note the position of drain pan

3. Loosen the drain plug with a socket or box wrench, and then remove it by hand. Push in on the plug as you turn it out, so that no oil escapes until the plug is completely removed.
4. Allow the oil to drain into the pan.
5. Install the drain plug, making sure that the brass gasket is still on the plug. You should change the gasket at least every other oil change. Tighten the plug to 22 ft. lbs.
6. The filter is located on the front of the engine block. Reach in and turn the filter off counterclockwise. If it's tight use a filter strap wrench.
7. Carefully lower the filter from it's mounting, direct the filter into the oil pan and drain it. Throw the filter away.
8. Clean the oil filter seating area with a clean rag.
9. On gasoline engines, lightly oil the rubber seal on the new filter and spin it on to the engine following the instructions printed on the side of the filter. Tighten it until the seal is flush and then give it an additional $1/2$ to $3/4$ turn. On diesel engines, through mid-1982; if the oil filter mounting surface is ridged, tighten the filter $3/4$ turn beyond hand tight; run engine for 3–5 minutes; stop engine and torque filter to at least 18 ft. lbs. Models mid-1982 and later, having a flat filter mounting flange require the filter to be tightened following the filter manufacturers instructions.

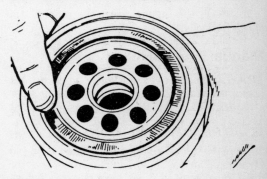

Lubricate the gasket on the new filter with clean engine oil. A dry gasket may not make a good seal and will allow the filter to leak

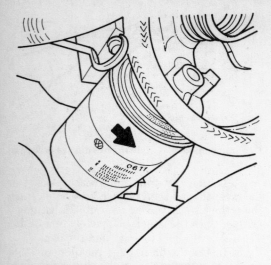

The oil filter (diesel shown) is on the side of the engine block that faces the front of the car on Rabbit, Jetta and Scirocco. On Dasher and Quantum, the filter is located on the driver's side

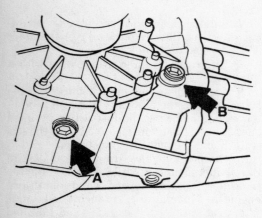

Dasher transaxle drain plug (lower left arrow) and filler plug (upper right arrow) locations

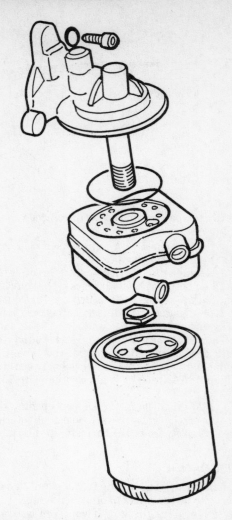

An oil cooler is used on all turbo diesel and on most gasoline engines. Always check the oil cooler for tightness when replacing the oil filter. If necessary, torque the oil cooler retaining nut to 18 ft. lbs.

10. Refill the engine, start the engine and check for leaks.

Manual Transaxle

NOTE: *Volkswagen strongly suggests that manual transmission maintenance on later model VW's be left to qualified dealers.*

FLUID RECOMMENDATIONS

From 1976 on, Volkswagen claims that the Hypoid oil in the manual transaxle does not have to be changed. They have inserted a large magnet in the bottom of the assembly to attract any gear shavings and thus keep them from causing friction among the gears. The fol-

lowing procedures are mainly for pre-1976 models.

The only equipment required is a drain pan, a wrench to fit the filler and drain plugs, and an oil suction gun. Gear oil can be purchased in gallon cans at the larger automotive supply stores. VW recommends that Hypoid gear oil fluids meeting SAE 80W, 80W/90, Mil–L–2105, API GL4 specifications be used in the manual transaxle. On Corrado and Passat, G50 synthetic and SAE 75W–90 gear oil may also be used as an acceptable substitute.

LEVEL CHECK

NOTE: *Volkswagen advises that the manual transmission lubricant need never be checked or changed. VW also recommends*

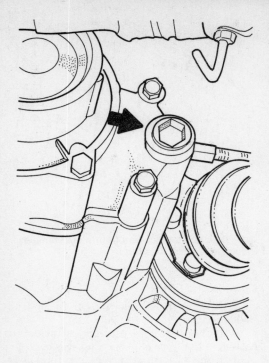

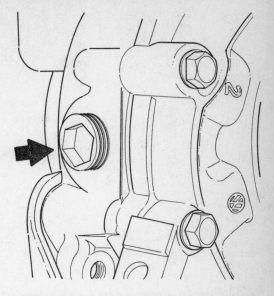

Rabbit, Jetta, Cabriolet and Scirocco manual transaxle drain plug

Oil control plug (arrow) for all manual transaxle Rabbit, Jetta and Scirocco models. For transaxles up to number 06054, the filler plug is located on the front of the transaxle case next to the back-up light switch. On later models, fill through the control plug hole

you entrust all transmission service to the dealer.

Dasher, Fox and Quantum

The oil filler plug is located on the driver's side of the transaxle at the rear of the final drive cover. Using the proper size metric Allen wrench, remove the plug, if the fluid is level with the bottom of the hole, it is correct. Add 80W–90 weight GL4 lubricant if necessary. Torque the oil filler plug to 18 ft. lbs.

Rabbit, Scirocco and Cabriolet

NOTE: *Both the transmission and the final drive gears share the same lubricant.*

For Rabbit and Scirocco transmissions up to No. 06 054, check the oil at the oil control plug.

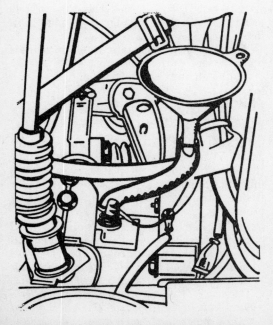

Adding transmission fluid on Golf, GTI and Jetta

Checking manual transaxle fluid level on Golf, GTI and Jetta

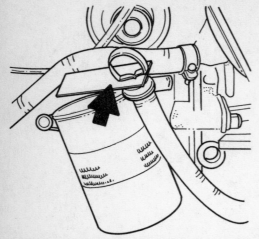

Dasher automatic transmission dipstick location (arrow)

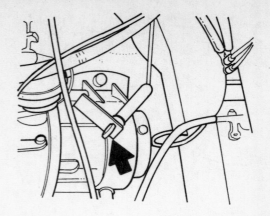

Rabbit, Jetta, Scirocco and Cabriolet automatic transaxle dipstick location

Remove the plug with a 5mm allen wrench. With the car level (the front and rear wheels on level ground or raised the same height off the ground), the oil should just begin to run out of the hole. If not, add SAE 80W or 80/90W GL-4 gear oil through the separate filler plug located on the front of the transmission near the backup light switch. A bulb syringe or an oil squirt can should do the trick.

For Rabbit and Scirocco transmissions from No. 07 954 transmissions, you check and fill the transmission through the oil control plug, using the same weight gear oil as the earlier transmissions.

Golf, GTI and Jetta

On Golf, GTI and Jetta transmissions, the oil level is checked by removing the oil filler plug located in the transmission case. On transmissions starting with 08 09 7, the filler plug is located 7mm higher.

To check the oil level:

1. Position a drain container under the oil filler plug.
2. Remove the oil filler plug and allow the oil to drain from the filler plug opening until the fluid level is even with the edge of the hole.
3. Install and tighten the plug.
4. On transmissions before 08 09 7, disconnect the speedometer cable and remove the speedometer drive gear from the transmission. Using a funnel, add approximately 0.5 qt. of gear oil through the speedometer drive gear opening. On transmissions starting with 08 07 9, the speedometer drive gear does not have to be removed to add oil to the transmission. On these models, add the required amount gear oil through the filler plug opening using a suction gun or equivalent.

Corrado and Passat

1. Remove the oil filler plug from the transaxle case.
2. If the fluid level is at or just below the bottom of the filler plug opening, it is correct.
3. If the level is not correct, add fluid as required.
4. Install and tighten the drain plug.

DRAIN AND REFILL

1. Jack up the front of the car and support it safely on stands.
2. Slide drain pan under the transaxle.
3. Remove the filler plug and then the drain plug.
4. When the oil has been completely drained, install the drain plug. Tighten to 18 ft. lbs.
5. Using the suction gun, refill the gearbox up to the level of the filler plug.
6. Install and tighten the filler plug.

Automatic Transaxle

FLUID RECOMMENDATIONS

DEXRON®II ATF is used in automatic transaxles. VW recommends that the automatic transmission fluid be replaced every 30,000 miles, or 20,000 miles if you use your car for frequent trailer towing, mountain driving, or other severe service.

NOTE: *The automatic transmission fluid used in later VW's is different in both chemical composition and color from previous models. The old fluid which was red in color has been replaced with a red/brown fluid. The new ATF changes to black/brown after a short time in the transaxle. Don't be alarmed by this color change, as it has no effect on the quality and lubricating characteristics of the*

*fluid. The new DEXRON®II can be inter-
mixed without any adverse affects.*

The final drive section of the automatic transaxle requires no attention other than an occasional level check. Top up with SAE 90 GL-5
hypoid gear oil or synthetic gear oil G50 SAE
75W90.

NOTE: *Automatic transmission is not available on the Fox or the Corrado.*

LEVEL CHECK

On late VW's, the automatic transaxle dipstick was modified. Old style dipsticks have a
fluid level instruction plate attached to the
handle. If this type of dipstick is used, the difference between the **MIN** and **MAX** marks is
0.35 qts. When checking the level cold, fill the
transmission to the **MIN** mark. Warm up the
engine to normal operating temperature and
check the level again. It should be between the
MIN and **MAX** marks. If not, add fluid as required.

The new style dipstick does not have the instruction plate attached to the handle. In addition to the **MIN** and **MAX** marks, there is a **20°**
mark at the very bottom of the dipstck. The difference between the **MIN** and **MAX** marks is
0.24 qts. When cold, fill the transmission to the
20° mark. Warm up the engine to normal operating temperature and check the level again. It
should be between the MIN and MAX marks. If
not, add fluid as required.

1. Idle the engine for a few minutes with
the selector in **N**. Apply the parking brake and
move the selector lever to **P**.

2. Remove the dipstick, wipe it clean, reinsert it, and withdraw it again.

3. The fluid level should be within the two
marks. Top up with Dexron®II automatic transmission fluid. Bear in mind that the difference
between the two marks is less than one pint.
Use a long-necked funnel to add the fluid. Fluid
should be drained and replaced at the specified
interval in the maintenance interval chart in
this chapter.

CAUTION: *DO NOT overfill the transaxle.
Too much fluid will cause damage.*

PAN AND FILTER SERVICE

Except Passat

1. Purchase the required amount of auto-

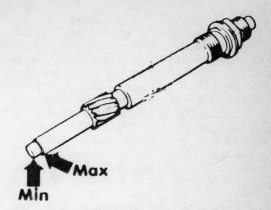

**Checking final drive fluid level on Passat with
automatic transaxle**

matic transmission fluid Dexron®II and a pan
gasket.

2. Slide a drain pan under the transmission. Jack up the front of the car and support it
safely on stands.

3. Many early models are equipped with
drain plugs in the pan. On later models, you
must loosen the pan retaining bolts to drain
the fluid.

4. On all models, loosen the front pan retaining bolts and remove the rear pan bolts.
Lower the pan and drain the oil in the drain
container. Once the oil is drained from the pan,
remove the front retaining bolts and lower the
pan.

5. Discard the old gasket and clean the pan
with solvent.

6. On models with circular oil strainers, unscrew the strainer and clean it. On models with
rectangular or not perfectly circular oil strainers, the strainer cannot be cleaned and must be
replaced. On these models, only replace the oil
strainer if the transmission fluid is contaminated.

7. Install the oil strained, but don't tighten
the bolt too much. Specified torque is only 4–14
ft. lbs.

8. Using a long-necked funnel, refill the
transmission with fluid. Check the level with
the dipstick. Run the car for a few minutes and
check again.

Passat

The transmission fluid filter used on the Passat is a replaceable element type filter similar to the one used on the engine. The filter is located on top of the transaxle and is mounted onto the ATF oil cooler. Some filters have turning lugs on top of the element that allows you to turn them by hand with the help of a rag wrapped around the filter. On filters without turning lugs, use a strap or filter wrench to loosen and tighten the filter. Once the filter is loose, allow the oil inside the filter to drain back into the transmission. Remove the filter and wipe up any fluid that may have spilled on the transmission housing. Lubricate the seal of the new filter with clean ATF and screw the filter onto the transmission. Start the engine and check the filter seating area for leaks. Check the fluid level and replenish as necessary.

Differential (Final Drive)

NOTE: *This pertains to vehicles with automatic transmission only.*

The lubricant should be changed according to the schedule in the Maintenance Intervals chart.

FLUID RECOMMENDATIONS

Use gear oil with API classification GL-5. Viscosity should be
- SAE 90 — above 30°F (–1°C)
- SAE 85W — above 0°F (–18°C)
- SAE 80W — below –30°F° (–34°C)

LEVEL CHECK

Except Passat

The lubricant level in the drive axle is checked in the same manner as the engine oil, with the engine off and the vehicle parked on a level surface. The dipstick is located to the rear of the engine oil dipstick and near the starter motor.

If the lubricant level is not at the upper mark on the dipstick additional gear oil is necessary and should be added through the dipstick filler tube. Use the proper weight oil with API classification of GL-5. Do not overfill.

Passat

The final drive uses 0.80 quart of G50 SAE 75W90 synthetic gear oil. The final drive is filled for life and does not require oil changes. The oil level is checked by removing the speedometer gear.

To check the final drive oil level:

1. Disconnect the speedometer cable from the transaxle.

2. Remove the speedometer drive gear from

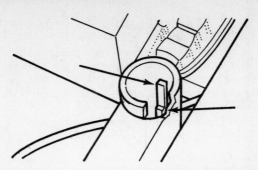

Some models have a gauge inside the radiator neck to check the coolant

the transmission and wipe it off with a clean lint-free rag.

3. Insert the speedometer drive gear back into the transaxle, remove it, then check the oil level. The level must be between the **MIN** and **MAX** marks on the lower gear shaft. The amount of oil between these two marks is 0.1 qt.

4. If the level is not as specified, add fluid as required.

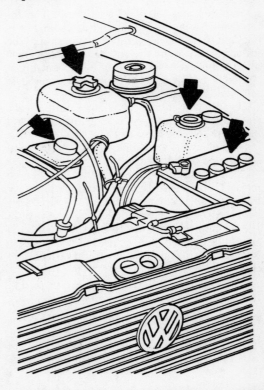

Four routine level checks—brake fluid (lower left), coolant level (upper right), windshield washer reservoir (upper right) and battery (lower right) — Rabbit, Scirocco engine compartment shown. Most cars with rear windshield wipers have an additional reservoir in the back

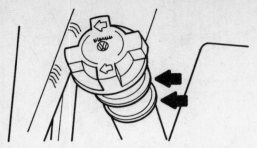

On some models, the coolant level lines are on the outside of the radiator neck

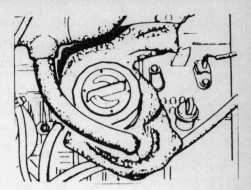

ATF filter used on Passat

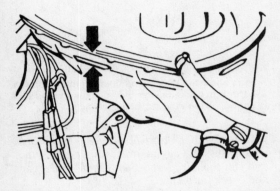

Some models are equipped with a coolant expansion tank only. When the engine is cold, the coolant level should be between the MIN and MAX marks. When the engine is warm, the coolant level should be at the MAX mark

5. Install the drive gear into the transmission and connect the speedometer cable.

DRAIN AND REFILL

NOTE: *On Passat, the oil in the final drive need not be changed.*

1. Park the car on a level surface, turn off engine and apply the parking brake.

2. Place a container of adequate capacity beneath the drain plug, located on the lower left side of the differential case, near the left axle shaft.

3. Remove the drain plug and allow the fluid to drain.

4. After draining, replace the drain plug and gasket. Do not overtighten.

5. Remove the differential dipstick and fill the differential to the upper mark on the dipstick.

Cooling System

FLUID RECOMMENDATIONS

All VW's are filled with a mixture of water and special phosphate-free antifreeze at the factory. The antifreeze has corrosion inhibitors

that prevent frost, the formation of chalk and also raise the boiling point of the water. Volkswagen recommends using VW phosphate-free antifreeze/coolant part number ZVW237 when replacing or adding coolant. Follow the instructions on the container for the proper coolant-to-water mixture.

LEVEL CHECK

Make it a habit to periodically check the coolant level in the radiator. Ideally, this should be performed when the engine is cold. When checking the coolant level on a warm or hot engine, turn the cap to the first catch to permit pressure to be released from the system. Turn the cap off counterclockwise. On some models, a gauge plate inside the radiator aids in level checking. The coolant should be maintained at the bottom of the plate.

Some models are equipped with a coolant reservoir. The reservoir is translucent and can be checked without removing the cap. Some later models have a coolant expansion tank and no radiator cap. The reservoir has low and high level marks. The coolant must be between the two marks when the engine is cold and slightly above the high mark at normal operating temperature. On models with an expansion tank and no radiator, observe the same cautions when removing the pressure cap from the expansion tank as with a radiator cap. Wrap the cap with a heavy rag and open the cap slowly to release the pressure from the cooling system.

Models equipped with an electric coolant warning device cause a light on the dash to flash until the coolant level is filled to the normal level.

DRAINING AND REFILLING

CAUTION: *Never attempt to drain the coolant from a warm engine. If you do, there's a good chance you'll be scalded. Always handle a warm radiator cap with a heavy rag.*

1. Turn the heater control to the hottest position.

2. Remove the radiator cap by turning it until it hisses. Wait for the hissing to stop, then turn it the rest of the way and remove it.

3. On early models, there is a petcock at the bottom of the radiator. Loosen it after placing a container underneath to catch the coolant. To drain the cooling system, remove the lower radiator hose at the radiator end connection. Use one of the many commercially available cleaners, that is safe to use in aluminum components, to flush out the system. These remove rust and scale which cut down on cooling efficiency.

4. After all of the coolant is drained, replace or tighten the petcock, thermostat flange or hose.

5. Remove the top water hose from the radiator and fill the system with coolant. When coolant just begins to flow out of the hose, refit the hose and continue to add coolant until the system is full. Follow the instructions on the coolant container for the proper coolant-to-water mixture.

NOTE: *Because of the use of aluminum in engines and cooling systems, be sure to use an antifreeze formulated to provide anti-corrosion protection for all metals including aluminum. The reason for removing the water hose when filling the empty system is that air pockets often form in the block which create hot spots, causing damage. Removing the hose bleeds the air from the system.*

6. Replace the radiator cap and run the engine until it's warm, then, after it cools sufficiently, recheck the coolant level and add coolant as necessary.

FLUSHING AND CLEANING THE SYSTEM

The cooling system should be drained, thoroughly flushed and refilled at least every 30,000 miles or 24 months. This operation should be done with the engine cold.

1. Remove the radiator and recovery tank caps. Run the engine till the upper radiator hose gets hot. This means that the thermostat is open and the coolant is flowing through the system.

2. Turn the engine off and place a large container under the radiator. Open the drain valve at the bottom of the radiator. Open the block drain plugs (If equipped) to speed up the draining process.

3. Close the drain valves and the block drain plugs and add water until the system is full. Repeat the draining and filling process several times, until the liquid is nearly colorless.

4. After the last draining, fill the system

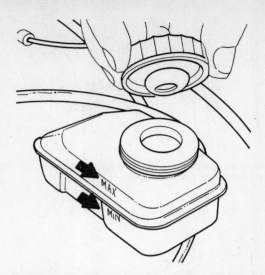

Arrows show the maximum/minimum marks on the see through brake master cylinder reservoir. Fluid is added through the capped opening

with a 50/50 mixture of ethylene glycol and water. Run the engine until the system is hot and add coolant, if necessary. Replace the caps and check for leaks.

Brake Master Cylinder

FLUID RECOMMENDATIONS

Use a good quality brake fluid that meets or exceeds DOT 3 or DOT 4 specifications.

LEVEL CHECK

The brake fluid reservoir is located on the left side of the engine compartment at the firewall. Brake fluid level should be maintained at the MAX line on the reservoir. Level can be checked visually without removing the cap on this translucent unit. If necessary, top up with a brand name hydraulic fluid which bears the DOT 3 or 4 marking. This information will be stamped on the can.

Clutch Master Cylinder

FLUID RECOMMENDATIONS

The clutch fluid system is connected to the brake fluid reservoir. Use only new brake fluid that meets or exceeds DOT 3 or DOT 4 specifications.

LEVEL CHECK

The brake fluid reservoir is located on the left side of the engine compartment at the firewall. Brake fluid level should be maintained at the MAX line on the reservoir. Level can be checked visually without removing the cap on this translucent unit. If necessary, top up with

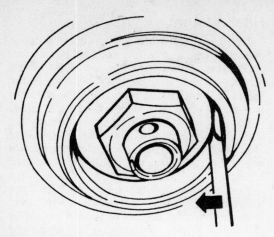

Rear wheel bearing adjustment

a brand name hydraulic fluid which bears the DOT 3 or 4 marking. This information will be stamped on the can.

Power Steering Reservoir

FLUID RECOMMENDATIONS

Use Dexron®II ATF when adding fluid to the power steering reservoir.

LEVEL CHECK

The reservoir for the power assisted steering is usually located at the rear of the engine compartment on the firewall. The fluid level should be checked at regular intervals. With the engine running (transmission in Park and parking brake applied), the fluid level should be between the 'MAX' and 'Min' marks on the outside of the reservoir. Add only Dexron®II fluid if required. If fluid is added, make sure the filler cap is secured.

CAUTION: *Stand to the side of the car when checking the fluid. Do not stand in front when the engine is running.*

Steering Gear

The rack and pinion steering gear is filled with lubricant and sealed at the factory. If you notice any leaking, have it checked at the dealer or authorized repair facility.

Chassis Greasing

These vehicles require no chassis greasing and are not equipped with grease nipples. Check the axle and driveshaft and tie rod rubber boots occasionally for leaking or cracking. At the same time, squirt a few drops of oil on the parking brake equalizer (point where cables V-off to the rear brakes). The front

wheel bearings do not require greasing unless they are disassembled.

Body Lubrication

Periodic lubrication will prevent squeaky, hard-to-open doors and lids. About every three months, pry the plastic caps off the door hinges and squirt in enough oil to fill the chambers. Press the plug back into the hinge after filling. Lightly oil the door check pivots. Finally, spray graphite lock lubricant onto your key and insert it into the door a few times.

Front Wheel Bearings

For front wheel bearing adjustment, removal, packing and installation procedures, refer to Chapter 8.

Rear Wheel Bearings

REMOVAL, PACKING AND INSTALLATION

1. Apply parking brake and loosen (but do not remove) rear wheel nuts.
2. Jack up vehicle, support it with jack stands, block the front wheels, release the parking brake and remove the wheel and tire.
3. Loosen the grease cap by striking it lightly with a rubber mallet, then remove the grease cap by prying it from drum or disc using the proper tool. DO NOT dent the cap, because it will allow water to enter.
4. Flatten lock washer and loosen axle nut, then remove lock washer, washer and brake drum or disc so as not to drop inner race of outer bearing.

NOTE: *Outer races of outer bearing and inner bearing, and oil seal can be removed together with drum or disc.*

5. Pry up spacer with a screwdriver and remove spacer and inner bearing inner race with a suitable puller.
6. Remove outer race of inner bearing from drum. Remove the oil seal at this time.
7. Remove outer race of outer bearing from drum or disc.
8. Clean the removed parts and check them for wear, damage and corrosion. If faulty, repair or replace. Check the grease cap O-ring for damage and replace it if necessary.
To install:
9. Press inner race of inner bearing into drum using a taper roller bearing installer and a press.
10. Apply sufficient grease to oil seal lip. Apply approximately 4 g (0.14 oz) of grease to inner bearing. Install the bearing and oil seal into drum or disc. Make sure that the outer end of the oil seal is flush with drum surface.

11. Press outer race of outer bearing into drum or disc using a taper rolller bearing installer and a press.

12. Apply approximately 3 g (0.11 oz) of grease to the outer bearing. Fill the boss of drum with approximately 30 g (1.06 oz) of grease.

13. Install spacer and inner race of inner bearing onto the spindle of trailing arm.

NOTE: *Stepped surface of the spacer must be faced toward the bearing.*

14. Install drum or disc, inner race of outer bearing, washer, lock washer and axle nut in this order onto the spindle. Adjust the rear wheel bearing play as described below.

15. Pack the grease cap and install it. Use a new O-ring if needed. To avoid denting the cap during installation, tap the edges lightly with a rubber mallet or use a grease cap installing tool.

NOTE: *Make sure the old lock washer is replaced with a new one.*

ADJUSTMENT

Before attempting to adjust the wheel bearings, tighten the adjustment nut while turning the wheel to seat the bearings. Wheel bearing clearance is correctly adjusted when the thrust washer under the adjusting nut can be moved slightly with a screwdriver. Do not twist or pry with the screwdriver. Install a new cotter pin.

TRAILER TOWING

Factory trailer towing packages are available for most vehicles. However, if you are installing a trailer hitch and wiring on your car, there are a few thing that you ought to know.

Trailer Weight

Trailer weight is the first, and most important, factor in determining whether or not your vehicle is suitable for towing the trailer you have in mind. The horsepower-to-weight ratio should be calculated. The basic standard is a ratio of 35:1. That is, 35 pounds of GVW for every horsepower.

To calculate this ratio, multiply you engine's rated horsepower by 35, then subtract the weight of the vehicle, including passengers and luggage. The resulting figure is the ideal maximum trailer weight that you can tow. One point to consider: a numerically higher axle ratio can offset what appears to be a low trailer weight. If the weight of the trailer that you have in mind is somewhat higher than the weight you just calculated, you might consider changing your rear axle ratio to compensate.

Hitch Weight

There are three kinds of hitches: bumper mounted, frame mounted, and load equalizing.

Bumper mounted hitches are those which attach solely to the vehicle's bumper. Many states prohibit towing with this type of hitch, when it attaches to the vehicle's stock bumper, since it subjects the bumper to stresses for which it was not designed. Aftermarket rear step bumpers, designed for trailer towing, are acceptable for use with bumper mounted hitches.

Frame mounted hitches can be of the type which bolts to two or more points on the frame, plus the bumper, or just to several points on the frame. Frame mounted hitches can also be of the tongue type, for Class I towing, or, of the receiver type, for classes II and III. Volkswagens should not be used for towing anything with a Class II or class III rating, as maximum towing capacity for these cars is limited to 1000 lbs. gross weight.

Load equalizing hitches are usually used for large trailers. Most equalizing hitches are welded in place and use equalizing bars and chains to level the vehicle after the trailer is hooked up.

The bolt-on hitches are the most common, since they are relatively easy to install.

Check the gross weight rating of your trailer. Tongue weight is usually figured as 10% of gross trailer weight. Therefore, a trailer with a maximum gross weight of 2,000 lb. will have a maximum tongue weight of 200 lb. Class I trailers fall into this category. Class II trailers are those with a gross weight rating of 2,000–3,500 lb., while Class III trailers fall into the 3,500–6,000 lb. category. Class IV trailers are those over 6,000 lb. and are for use with fifth wheel trucks, only.

When you've determined the hitch that you'll need, follow the manufacturer's installation instructions, exactly, especially when it comes to fastener torques. The hitch will be subjected to a lot of stress and good hitches come with hardened bolts. Never substitute an inferior bolt for a hardened bolt.

Wiring

Wiring the car for towing is fairly easy. There are a number of good wiring kits available and these should be used, rather than trying to design your own. All trailers will need brake lights and turn signals as well as tail lights and side marker lights. Most states require extra marker lights for overwide trailers. Also, most states have recently required backup lights for trailers, and most trailer manufacturers have been building trailers with back-up lights for several years.

Additionally, some Class I, most Class II and just about all Class III trailers will have electric brakes.

Add to this number an accessories wire, to operate trailer internal equipment or to charge the trailer's battery, and you can have as many as seven wires in the harness.

Determine the equipment on your trailer and buy the wiring kit necessary. The kit will contain all the wires needed, plus a plug adapter set which included the female plug, mounted on the bumper or hitch, and the male plug, wired into, or plugged into the trailer harness.

When installing the kit, follow the manufacturer's instructions. The color coding of the wires is standard throughout the industry.

One point to note: some domestic vehicles, and most imported vehicles, have separate turn signals. On most domestic vehicles, the brake lights and rear turn signals operate with the same bulb. For those vehicles with separate turn signals, you can purchase an isolation unit so that the brake lights won't blink whenever the turn signals are operated, or, you can go to your local electronics supply house and buy four diodes to wire in series with the brake and turn signal bulbs. Diodes will isolate the brake and turn signals. The choice is yours. The isolation units are simple and quick to install, but far more expensive than the diodes. The diodes, however, require more work to install properly, since they require the cutting of each bulb's wire and soldering in place of the diode.

One, final point, the best kits are those with a spring loaded cover on the vehicle mounted socket. This cover prevents dirt and moisture from corroding the terminals. Never let the vehicle socket hang loosely; always mount it securely to the bumper or hitch.

Cooling

ENGINE

One of the most common, if not THE most common, problems associated with trailer towing is engine overheating.

With factory installed trailer towing packages, a heavy duty cooling system is usually included. Heavy duty cooling systems are available as optional equipment on most vehicles, with or without a trailer package. If you have one of these extra capacity systems, you shouldn't have any overheating problems.

If you have a standard cooling system, without an expansion tank, you'll definitely need to get an aftermarket expansion tank kit, preferably one with at least a 2 quart capacity. These kits are easily installed on the radiator's over-

flow hose, and come with a pressure cap designed for expansion tanks.

Another helpful accessory is a Flex Fan. These fan are large diameter units are designed to provide more airflow at low speeds, with blades that have deeply cupped surfaces. The blades then flex, or flatten out, at high speed, when less cooling air is needed. These fans are far lighter in weight than stock fans, requiring less horsepower to drive them. Also, they are far quieter than stock fans.

If you do decide to replace your stock fan with a flex fan, note that if your car has a fan clutch, a spacer between the flex fan and water pump hub will be needed.

Aftermarket engine oil coolers are helpful for prolonging engine oil life and reducing overall engine temperatures. Both of these factors increase engine life.

While not absolutely necessary in towing Class I and some Class II trailers, they are recommended for heavier Class II and all Class III towing.

Engine oil cooler systems consist of an adapter, screwed on in place of the oil filter, a remote filter mounting and a multi-tube, finned heat exchanger, which is mounted in front of the radiator or air conditioning condenser.

TRANSMISSION

An automatic transmission is usually recommended for trailer towing. Modern automatics have proven reliable and, of course, easy to operate, in trailer towing.

The increased load of a trailer, however, causes an increase in the temperature of the automatic transmission fluid. Heat is the worst enemy of an automatic transmission. As the temperature of the fluid increases, the life of the fluid decreases.

It is essential, therefore, that you install an automatic transmission cooler.

The cooler, which consists of a multi-tube, finned heat exchanger, is usually installed in front of the radiator or air conditioning compressor, and hooked inline with the transmission cooler tank inlet line. Follow the cooler manufacturer's installation instructions.

Select a cooler of at least adequate capacity, based upon the combined gross weights of the car and trailer.

Cooler manufacturers recommend that you use an aftermarket cooler in addition to, and not instead of, the present cooling tank in your car radiator. If you do want to use it in place of the radiator cooling tank, get a cooler at least two sizes larger than normally necessary.

One note, a transmission cooler can, sometimes, cause slow or harsh shifting in the trans-

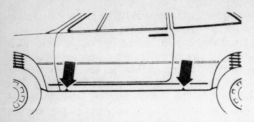

There are two jacking points on each side of the vehicle

mission during cold weather, until the fluid has a chance to come up to normal operating temperature. Some coolers can be purchased with or retrofitted with a temperature bypass valve which will allow fluid flow through the cooler only when the fluid has reached operating temperature, or above.

PUSH-STARTING AND TOWING

CAUTION: *Pushing or towing in an attempt to start a catalytic converter equipped car can cause raw gasoline to enter the converter and cause major damage.*

If your car is equipped with a manual transaxle, it may be push-started in an extreme emergency. It should be recognized that there is the possibility of damaging bumpers and/or fenders of both cars. Make sure that the bumpers of both cars are evenly matched. Depress the clutch pedal, select Second or Third gear, and switch the ignition On. When the car reaches a speed of approximately 10 or 15 mph, release the clutch to start the engine. DO NOT ATTEMPT TO PUSH-START AN AUTOMATIC TRANSMISSION EQUIPPED MODEL.

Both manual and automatic models may be towed short distances. Attach tow lines to the towing eye on the front suspension or the left or right bumper bracket at the rear. Automatic

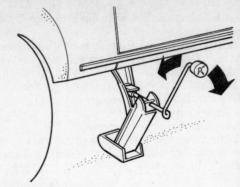

Typical tire repair jack

equipped cars must be towed in Neutral no farther than 30 miles and no faster than 30 mph, unless the front wheels are off the ground.

If you plan on towing a trailer, don't exceed the manufacturer's recommended towing weight for your VW. Towing a trailer with an automatic equipped car places an extra load on the transmission and a few items should be made note of here. Make doubly sure that the transmission fluid is at the correct level. Change the fluid more frequently if you're doing much trailer hauling. Start out in 1 or 2 and use the lower ranges when climbing hills. Aftermarket transmission coolers are available which greatly ease the load on your automatic and one should be considered if you often pull a trailer.

JACKING

Your car is equipped with a single post, crank handle jack which fits the jacking points behind the front wheel and in front of the rear wheel. These are marked with triangular sections of the body stamping. Never use the tire changing jack for anything other than that. If you intend to use this book to perform your own mainte-

Maintenance Interval Chart
(See text for a description of required maintenance)

Thousands of Miles or every 6 months	5	7.5	10	15	20	22.5	25	30	35	37.5	40	45	50
Oil Change & General Maintenance	*	*	*	*	*	*	*	*	*	*	*	*	*
Tune Up & Emission Control	—	—	—	*	—	—	—	*	—	—	—	*	—
Vehicle Maintenance	—	—	—	*	—	—	—	*	—	—	—	*	—
Fuel Injected Engine (FI)	—	FI	—	FI	—	FI	—	FI	—	FI	—	FI	—
Carburetor Engine (C)	—	C	—	C	—	C	—	C	—	C	—	C	—
Diesel Engine (D)	—	D	—	D	—	D	—	D	—	D	—	D	—
Turbo Diesel Engine (TD)	TD	—	TD	TD	TD	—	TD	TD	TD	—	TD	TD	TD

CAPACITIES

Year	Model	Engine Displacement cu. in. (cc)	Engine Crankcase (qts.) with Filter	without Filter	Transmission (pts.) 4-Spd	5-Spd	Auto.	Drive Axle (pts.)	Fuel Tank (gal.)	Cooling System (qts.)
1974	Dasher	90 (1,471)	3.2	2.6	3.2	—	6.4	1.6	12.1	12.6
1975	Dasher	97 (1,588)	3.2	2.6	3.2	—	6.4	1.6	11.9	12.6
	Rabbit	97 (1,588)	3.7	3.2	2.6	—	6.4	1.6	12.1	9.8
	Scirocco	97 (1,588)	3.7	3.2	2.6	—	6.4	1.6	12.1	9.8
1976	Dasher	97 (1,588)	3.2	2.6	3.2	—	6.4	1.6	11.9	12.6
	Rabbit	97 (1,588)	3.7	3.2	2.6	—	6.4	1.6	12.1	9.8
	Scirocco	97 (1,588)	3.7	3.2	2.6	—	6.4	1.6	12.1	9.8
1977	Dasher	97 (1,588)	3.2	2.6	3.4	—	6.4	1.6	11.9	12.6
	Rabbit	97 (1,588)	3.7	3.2	2.6	—	6.4	1.6	12.1	9.8
	Rabbit (Diesel)	90 (1,471)	3.7	3.2	2.6	—	6.4	1.6	10.6	9.8
	Scirocco	97 (1,588)	3.7	3.2	2.6	—	6.4	1.6	12.1	9.8
1978	Dasher	97 (1,588)	3.2	2.6	3.4	—	6.4	1.6	11.9	12.6
	Rabbit	89 (1,457)	3.7	3.2	2.6	4.2	6.4	1.6	10.5	9.8
	Rabbit (Diesel)	90 (1,471)	3.7	3.2	2.6	—	6.4	1.6	10.6	9.8
	Scirocco	89 (1,457)	3.2	3.2	2.6	—	6.4	1.6	10.5	9.8
1979	Dasher	97 (1,588)	3.2	2.6	3.4	—	6.4	1.6	11.9	12.6
	Dasher (Diesel)	90 (1,471)	3.7	3.2	3.2	—	6.4	1.6	11.9	11.8
	Rabbit	89 (1,457)	3.7	3.2	2.6	4.2	6.4	1.6	10.5	9.8
	Rabbit (Diesel)	90 (1,471)	3.7	3.2	3.2	4.2	6.4	1.6	10.6 ①	14.6
	Scirocco	97 (1,588)	3.7	3.2	3.2	—	6.4	1.6	10.6	9.8
1980	Dasher	97 (1,588)	3.2	2.6	3.4	—	6.4	1.6	11.9	12.6
	Dasher (Diesel)	90 (1,471)	3.7	3.2	3.2	—	6.4	1.6	11.9	11.8
	Rabbit ②	97 (1,588)	3.7	3.2	3.2	4.2	6.4	1.6	10.0	9.8 ③
	Rabbit (Diesel)	90 (1,471)	3.7	3.2	3.2	—	6.4	1.6	10.6 ①	14.6
	Rabbit (Pick-up)	97 (1,588)	3.7	3.2	3.2	4.2	6.4	1.6	15.0	14.6
	Jetta ②	97 (1,588)	3.7	3.2	3.2	4.2	6.4	1.6	10.5	10.2
	Scirocco	97 (1,588)	3.7	3.2	3.2	—	6.4	1.6	10.6	10.2
1981	Dasher (Diesel)	97 (1,588)	3.7	3.2	3.2	4.2	—	1.6	12.0	12.2
	Jetta	105 (1,715)	4.5	4.0	3.2	4.2	6.4	1.6	10.0	9.8
	Jetta (Diesel)	97 (1,588)	4.5	4.0	3.2	4.2	6.4	1.6	10.0	9.8
	Rabbit	105 (1,715)	4.5	4.0	3.2	4.2	6.4	1.6	10.0	9.8
	Rabbit (Diesel)	97 (1,588)	3.7	3.2	3.2	4.2	—	1.6	10.0	14.3
	Scirocco	105 (1,715)	4.5	4.0	3.2	4.2	6.4	1.6	10.0	9.8

CAPACITIES (cont.)

Year	Model	Engine Displacement cu. in. (cc)	Engine Crankcase (qts.) with Filter	Engine Crankcase (qts.) without Filter	Transmission (pts.) 4-Spd	Transmission (pts.) 5-Spd	Transmission (pts.) Auto.	Drive Axle (pts.)	Fuel Tank (gal.)	Cooling System (qts.)
1982	Jetta	105 (1,715)	4.8	4.3	—	4.2	6.4	1.6	10.5	10.2
	Jetta (Diesel)	97 (1,588)	4.8	4.3	—	4.2	6.4	1.6	10.5	13.8
	Jetta (Turbo Diesel)	97 (1,588)	4.8	4.3	—	4.2	6.4	1.6	10.5	13.8
	Quantum	105 (1,715)	3.6	3.2	—	4.2	6.4	1.6	16.0	11.0
	Quantum	131 (2,144)	3.6	3.2	—	4.2	6.4	1.6	16.0	11.0
	Quantum (Turbo Diesel)	97 (1,588)	4.0	3.5	—	4.2	6.4	1.6	16.0	13.0
	Rabbit	105 (1,715)	4.7	4.2	3.2	4.2	6.4	1.6	10.0	9.8
	Scirocco	105 (1,715)	4.8	4.3	—	4.2	6.4	1.6	10.5	10.2
1983	Jetta	105 (1,715)	4.3	3.7	—	4.2	6.4	1.6	10.5	5.1
	Jetta (Diesel)	97 (1,588)	4.8	4.3	—	4.2	6.4	1.6	10.5	6.9
	Jetta (Turbo Diesel)	97 (1,588)	4.8	4.3	—	4.2	6.4	1.6	10.5	6.9
	Quantum (4 cyl.)	105 (1,715)	3.6	3.2	—	4.2	6.4	1.6	16.0	5.5
	Quantum (5 cyl.)	109 (1,780)	4.0	3.5	—	4.2	6.4	1.6	16.0	5.5
	Quantum (Diesel)	130 (2,144)	4.0	3.5	—	4.2	6.4	1.6	16.0	6.5
	Quantum (Turbo-Diesel)	97 (1,588)	4.8	4.3		4.2	6.4	1.6	16.0	6.5
	Rabbit	105 (1,715)	4.3	3.7	3.2	4.2	6.4	1.6	10.0	6.9
	Rabbit	109 (1,780)	4.3	3.7	3.2	4.2	6.4	1.6	10.0	7.3
	Rabbit (Conv.)	109 (1,780)	4.3	3.7	—	4.2	6.2	1.6	10.5	7.3
	Rabbit (Diesel)	97 (1,588)	4.8	4.3	3.2	4.2	6.4	1.6	10.0	6.9
	Scirocco	105 (1,715)	4.3	3.7	—	4.2	6.4	1.6	10.5	5.1
	Scirocco	109 (1,780)	4.3	3.7	—	4.2	6.4	1.6	10.5	6.5
	GTI	109 (1,780)	4.3	3.7	3.2	4.2	6.4	1.6	10.0	7.3
	GTI (Diesel)	97 (1,588)	4.8	4.3	3.2	4.2	6.4	1.6	11.0	6.5
	GLI	109 (1,780)	4.3	3.7	3.2	4.2	—	1.6	14.5	6.5
1984	Jetta	105 (1,715)	4.3	3.7	—	4.2	6.4	1.6	10.5	5.1
	Jetta (Diesel)	97 (1,588)	4.8	4.3	—	4.2	6.4	1.6	10.5	6.9
	Quantum (4 cyl.)	109 (1,780)	3.6	3.2	—	4.2	6.4	1.6	16.0	5.5
	Quantum (5 cyl.)	130 (2,144)	4.0	3.5	—	4.2	6.4	1.6	16.0	5.5
	Quantum (Diesel)	97 (1,588)	4.0	3.5	—	4.2	6.4	1.6	16.0	6.5
	Rabbit	105 (1,715)	4.3	3.7	3.2	4.2	6.4	1.6	10.0	6.9
	Rabbit (Conv.)	109 (1,780)	4.3	3.7	—	4.2	6.2	1.6	10.5	7.3
	Rabbit (Diesel)	97 (1,588)	4.8	4.3	3.2	4.2	6.4	1.6	10.0	6.9
	Scirocco	109 (1,780)	4.3	3.7	—	4.2	6.4	1.6	10.5	6.5
	GTI	109 (1,780)	4.3	3.7	3.2	4.2	6.4	1.6	10.0	7.3
	GTI (Diesel)	97 (1,588)	4.8	4.3	3.2	4.2	6.4	1.6	11.0	6.5
	GLI	109 (1,780)	4.3	3.7	3.2	4.2	—	1.6	14.5	6.5

CAPACITIES (cont.)

Year	Model	Engine Displacement cu. in. (cc)	Engine Crankcase (qts.) with Filter	Engine Crankcase (qts.) without Filter	Transmission (pts.) 4-Spd	Transmission (pts.) 5-Spd	Transmission (pts.) Auto.	Drive Axle (pts.)	Fuel Tank (gal.)	Cooling System (qts.)
1985	Jetta	105 (1,715)	4.3	3.7	—	4.2	6.4	1.6	13.7	7.3
	Jetta (Diesel)	97 (1,588)	4.8	4.3	—	4.2	6.4	1.6	13.7	7.3
	Jetta (Turbo Diesel)	97 (1,588)	4.8	4.3	—	4.2	6.4	1.6	13.7	7.3
	Quantum (4 cyl.)	109 (1,780)	3.6	3.2	—	4.2	6.4	1.6	16.0	5.5
	Quantum (5 cyl.)	136 (2,226)	4.0	3.5	—	4.2	6.4	1.6	16.0	6.5
	Quantum (Diesel)	97 (1,588)	4.0	3.5	—	4.2	6.4	1.6	16.0	6.9
	Cabriolet	109 (1,780)	4.3	3.7	—	4.2	6.4	1.6	13.7	7.3
	Scirocco	109 (1,780)	4.3	3.7	—	4.2	6.4	1.6	13.7	6.5
	GTI	109 (1,780)	4.3	3.7	—	4.2	—	1.6	14.5	7.3
	GLI	109 (1,780)	4.3	3.7	—	4.2	—	1.6	14.5	7.3
	Golf	109 (1,780)	4.3	3.7	—	4.2	6.4	1.6	14.5	7.3
	Golf (Diesel)	97 (1,588)	4.8	4.3	—	4.2	6.4	1.6	14.5	7.3
1986	Jetta	109 (1,780)	4.3	3.7	—	4.2	6.4	1.6	13.7	7.3
	Jetta (Diesel)	97 (1,588)	4.8	4.3	—	4.2	6.4	1.6	13.7	7.3
	Jetta (Turbo Diesel)	97 (1,588)	4.8	4.3	—	4.2	6.4	1.6	13.7	7.3
	Quantum (4 cyl.)	109 (1,780)	3.6	3.2	—	4.2	6.4	1.6	16.0	5.5
	Quantum (5 cyl.)	136 (2,226)	4.0	3.5	—	4.2	6.4	1.6	16.0	6.5
	Quantum (Diesel)	97 (1,588)	4.0	3.5	—	4.2	6.4	1.6	16.0	6.9
	Cabriolet	109 (1,780)	4.3	3.7	—	4.2	6.4	1.6	13.7	7.3
	Scirocco	109 (1,780)	4.3	3.7	—	4.2	6.4	1.6	13.7	6.5
	GTI	109 (1,780)	4.3	3.7	—	4.2	—	1.6	14.5	7.3
	GLI	109 (1,780)	4.3	3.7	—	4.2	—	1.6	14.5	7.3
	Golf	109 (1,780)	4.3	3.7	—	4.2	6.4	1.6	14.5	7.3
	Golf (Diesel)	97 (1,588)	4.8	4.3	—	4.2	6.4	1.6	14.5	7.3
1987	Jetta	109 (1,780)	4.3	3.8	—	4.2	6.4	—	14.5	7.3
	Jetta GL	109 (1,780)	4.3	3.8	—	4.2	6.4	—	14.5	7.3
	Jetta GLI 16V	109 (1,780)	4.3	3.8	—	4.2	6.4	—	14.5	7.3
	Quantum GL5	136 (2,226)	4.0	3.8	—	4.2	6.4	—	15.8	8.5
	Quantum Syncro	136 (2,226)	4.0	3.5	—	5.0	6.4	1.2	18.5	8.5
	Scirocco 16V	109 (1,780)	4.3	3.8	—	4.2	6.4	—	13.8	5.1
	Cabriolet	109 (1,780)	4.3	3.8	—	4.2	6.4	—	13.8	5.1
	Golf GL	109 (1,780)	4.3	3.8	—	4.2	6.4	—	14.5	7.3
	Golf GT	109 (1,780)	4.3	3.8	—	4.2	6.4	—	14.5	7.3
	Golf GTI 16V	109 (1,780)	4.3	3.8	—	4.2	6.4	—	14.5	7.3
	Fox/GL	109 (1,780)	3.7	3.2	3.6	—	—	—	12.4	6.9 ④

CAPACITIES (cont.)

Year	Model	Engine Displacement cu. in. (cc)	Engine Crankcase (qts.) with Filter	without Filter	Transmission (pts.) 4-Spd	5-Spd	Auto.	Drive Axle (pts.)	Fuel Tank (gal.)	Cooling System (qts.)
1988	Jetta	109 (1,780)	4.3	3.8	—	4.2	6.4	—	14.5	7.3
	Jetta GL	109 (1,780)	4.3	3.8	—	4.2	6.4	—	14.5	7.3
	Jetta GLI 16V	109 (1,780)	4.3	3.8	—	4.2	6.4	—	14.5	7.3
	Jetta Carat	109 (1,780)	4.3	3.8	—	4.2	6.4	—	14.5	7.3
	Quantum GL5	136 (2,226)	4.0	3.8	—	4.2	6.4	—	15.8	8.5
	Quantum Syncro	136 (2,226)	4.0	3.5	—	5.0	6.4	1.2	18.5	8.5
	Scirocco 16V	109 (1,780)	4.3	3.8	—	4.2	6.4	—	13.8	5.1
	Cabriolet	109 (1,780)	4.3	3.8	—	4.2	6.4	—	13.8	5.1
	Golf GL	109 (1,780)	4.3	3.8	—	4.2	6.4	—	14.5	7.3
	Golf GT	109 (1,780)	4.3	3.8	—	4.2	6.4	—	14.5	7.3
	Golf GTI 16V	109 (1,780)	4.3	3.8	—	4.2	6.4	—	14.5	7.3
	Fox/GL	109 (1,780)	3.7	3.2	3.6	—	—	—	12.4	6.9 ④
1989	Jetta	109 (1,780)	4.3	3.8	—	4.2	6.4	—	14.5	7.3
	Jetta (Diesel)	97 (1,588)	4.8	4.3	—	4.2	6.4	—	13.7	7.3
	Jetta GL	109 (1,780)	4.3	3.8	—	4.2	6.4	—	14.5	7.3
	Jetta GLI 16V	109 (1,780)	4.3	3.8	—	4.2	6.4	—	14.5	7.3
	Jetta Carat	109 (1,780)	4.3	3.8	—	4.2	6.4	—	14.5	7.3
	Quantum GL5	136 (2,226)	4.0	3.8	—	4.2	6.4	—	15.8	8.5
	Quantum Syncro	136 (2,226)	4.0	3.5	—	5.0	6.4	1.2	18.5	8.5
	Scirocco 16V	109 (1,780)	4.3	3.8	—	4.2	6.4	—	13.8	5.1
	Cabriolet	109 (1,780)	4.3	3.8	—	4.2	6.4	—	13.8	5.1
	Golf GL	109 (1,780)	4.3	3.8	—	4.2	6.4	—	14.5	7.3
	Golf GT	109 (1,780)	4.3	3.8	—	4.2	6.4	—	14.5	7.3
	Golf GTI 16V	109 (1,780)	4.3	3.8	—	4.2	6.4	—	14.5	7.3
	Fox/GL	109 (1,780)	3.7	3.2	3.6	—	—	—	12.4	6.9 ④
1990	Jetta GL	109 (1,780)	4.3	3.7	—	4.2	6.2	—	14.5	7.3
	Jetta GL (Diesel)	97 (1,588)	4.7	4.2	—	4.2	6.2	—	14.5	7.3
	Jetta Carat	109 (1,780)	4.3	3.7	—	4.2	6.2	—	14.5	7.3
	Jetta GLI 16V	121 (1,984)	4.3	3.7	—	4.2	6.2	—	14.5	7.3
	GTI 16V	121 (1,984)	4.3	3.7	—	4.2	6.2	—	14.5	7.3
	GTI	109 (1,780)	4.3	3.7	—	4.2	6.2	—	14.5	7.3
	Golf GL	109 (1,780)	4.3	3.7	—	4.2	6.4	—	14.5	7.3
	Cabriolet	109 (1,780)	4.3	3.7	—	4.2	6.2	—	13.8	5.1
	Corrado	109 (1,780)	4.3	3.7	—	—	—	—	14.5	7.3
	Passat GL	121 (1,984)	4.3	3.7	—	4.2	3.2	0.8	18.5	7.3
	Fox/GL	109 (1,780)	3.7	3.2	3.6	—	—	—	12.4	6.4 ④

① Pick-up: 15.0 gals.
② Applies to fuel injected engines. Engines with carburetor, 89 cu. in. (1,457cc)
③ Rabbit Convertible: 10.2 pts.
④ Without A/C; with A/C: 6.9 qts.

Engine Performance and Tune-Up

2

TUNE-UP PROCEDURES

Your gasoline VW should be tuned including points and plugs, at least at 12,000 mile intervals. The tune-up is a good time to take a look around the engine compartment for beginning problems and head them off before they get expensive. Look for oil, fuel and coolant leaks, deteriorating radiator or heater hoses, loose and/or frayed fan belts, etc. These little items have the tendency to develop into major headaches, so don't overlook anything.

Diesel engines do not require "tune-ups" in the strict sense of the word; however, the maintenance items described above should receive the same attention. Usually, injection pump timing and idle speed are one time adjustments that are done at the time of an injection pump or injector(s) replacement or overhaul. Once curb and fast idle speeds are set, the adjustment screws should be sealed to prevent tampering and further adjustment.

Spark Plugs
(Gasoline Engines Only)

In addition to igniting the air/fuel mixture, the spark plugs in your engine can also serve as very useful diagnostic tools. Once removed, compare your spark plugs with the samples illustrated in the "Fuel Economy and tune-Up Tips" section. Typical plug conditions are shown along with their causes and remedies. Plugs which exhibit only normal wear and deposits can be cleaned, regapped, and installed. However, it is a good practice to replace them at every major tune-up.

Tool kits for spark plug changing are available at most tool outlets. The tool kit includes a spark plug socket and handle, but you will find it much more convenient to purchase a $1/2$ in. drive, $13/16$ in. spark plug socket which can be turned with a ratchet handle. Using a small extension, all four or five plugs can be removed very quickly. Before removing the spark plug leads, number the tower on the distributor cap with tape. The firing order is 1–3–4–2 or 1–2–4–5–3 (five cylinder engine). This prevents confusion in the case of distributor cap or spark plug wire replacement.

SPARK PLUG HEAT RANGE

The amount of heat the plug absorbs is determined by the length of the lower insulator. The longer the insulator (or the farther it extends into the engine), the hotter the plug will operate; the shorter the insulator the cooler it will operate. A plug that absorbs little heat and remains too cool will quickly accumulate deposits of oil and carbon since it is not hot enough to burn them off. This leads to plug fouling and consequently to misfiring. A plug that absorbs too much heat will have no deposits, but, due to

Remove the spark plug wire by grasping the boot; don't pull on the cable

GASOLINE ENGINE TUNE-UP SPECIFICATIONS

Year	Model	Engine Displacement Cu. in. (cc)	Spark Plugs Type	Gap (in.)	Distributor Point Dwell (deg.)	Point Gap (in.)	Ignition Timing (deg.)	Compression Pressure (psi)	Idle Speed (rpm)	Valve Clearance (in.) In [6]	Ex [6]
1974	Dasher	90 (1,471)	W175 T30 N8Y	0.024–0.028	44–50 ①	0.016	3 ATDC @ Idle	142–184	850–1000	0.008–0.012	0.016–0.020
1975	Dasher	97 (1,588) 90(1,471)(Canada)	W200 T30 N8Y	0.024–0.028	44–50	0.016	3 ATDC @ Idle	142–184	850–1000	0.008–0.012	0.016–0.020
	Rabbit, Scirocco	90 (1,471)	W200 T30 N8Y	0.024–0.028	44–50	0.016	3 ATDC @ Idle	142–184	850–1000	0.008–0.012	0.016–0.020
1976–79	Dasher	97 (1,588)	W215 T30 N7Y	0.024–0.028	44–50	0.016	3 ATDC @ Idle	142–184	850–1000	0.008–0.012	0.016–0.020
1976	Rabbit, Scirocco	97 (1,588)	W200 T30 N8Y	0.024–0.028	44–50	0.016	3 ATDC @ Idle	142–184	850–1000	0.008–0.012	0.016–0.020
1977	Rabbit, Scirocco	97 (1,588)	W215 T30 N7Y	0.024–0.028	44–50	0.016	3 ATDC @ Idle	142–184	850–1000	0.008–0.012	0.016–0.020
1978	Rabbit, Scirocco	89 (1,457)	W175 T30 N8Y	0.024–0.028	44–50	0.016	②	142–184	850–1000	0.008–0.012	0.016–0.020
1979	Rabbit	89 (1,457)	W175 T30 N8Y	0.024–0.032	44–50	0.016	3 ATDC @ Idle	142–184	850–1000	0.008–0.012	0.016–0.020
	Scirocco	97 (1,588)	W175 T30 N8Y	0.024–0.032	44–50	0.016	3 ATDC @ Idle	142–184	850–1000	0.008–0.012	0.016–0.020
1980–81	Dasher (49 states)	97 (1,588)	W175 T30 N8Y	0.024–0.032	44–50 ⑦	0.016 ⑦	3 ATDC @ Idle	142–184	850–1000 ⑧	0.008–0.012	0.016–0.020
	Dasher (California)	97 (1,588)	WR7DS N8GY	0.024–0.028	Electronic		3 ATDC @ Idle	142–184	880–1000	0.008–0.012	0.016–0.020
1980–83	Rabbit, Jetta, Scirocco, Quantum (49 states)	97 (1,588) ③	W175 T30 N8Y	0.024–0.032	44–50 ⑦	0.016 ⑦	3 ATDC @ Idle ⑨	142–184 ⑩	850–1000 ⑧	0.008–0.012	0.016–0.020
	Rabbit, Jetta, Scirocco, Quantum (California)	97 (1,558) ③	WR7DS N8GY	0.024–0.028	Electronic		3 ATDC @ Idle	142–184 ⑩	880–1000	0.008–0.012	0.016–0.020
1983	GTI, Scirocco	109 (1,790)	WR7DS N8GY	0.024–0.032	Electronic		6 BTDC @ Idle	131–174	875–1000	0.008–0.012	0.016–0.020
	Quantum	131 (2,144)	N8Y	0.035	Electronic		3 ATDC @ Idle	120–170	800–1000	0.008–0.012	0.016–0.020
1984	Rabbit, Jetta, GTI, Scirocco, Quantum (49 states)	105.0 (1,715)	W175 T30 N8Y	0.024–0.032	Electronic		6 BTDC @ Idle	131–174	850–1000 ⑧	0.008–0.012	0.016–0.020
	Rabbit, Jetta, GTI, Scirocco, Quantum (California)	105.0 (1,715)	WR7DS N8GY	0.024–0.028	Electronic		6 BTDC @ Idle	131–174	880–1000	0.008–0.012	0.016–0.020
1985	Scirocco, Golf, Jetta, GTI, (49 states)	109 (1,780)	WR7DS N8GY	0.024–0.032	Electronic		6 BTDC @ Idle	123–174	850–1000	0.008–0.012	0.016–0.020
	Quantum	136 (2,226)	W7DC N9YC	0.024–0.032	Electronic		6 BTDC @ Idle	123–174	850–1000	0.008–0.012	0.016–0.020

GASOLINE ENGINE TUNE-UP SPECIFICATIONS (cont.)

Year	Model	Engine Displacement Cu. in. (cc)	Spark Plugs Type	Spark Plugs Gap (in.)	Distributor Point Dwell (deg.)	Distributor Point Gap (in.)	Ignition Timing (deg.)	Compression Pressure (psi)	Idle Speed (rpm)	Valve Clearance (in.) In [6]	Valve Clearance (in.) Ex [6]
1986	Jetta	109 (1,780)	W7DTC N8GY	0.028–0.032	Electronic		6 BTDC @ Idle	123–174	800–900	Hyd.	Hyd.
	Quantum	109 (1,780)	W7DTC	0.028–0.035	Electronic		6 BTDC @ Idle	123–174	800–900	Hyd.	Hyd.
	Quantum	136 (2,226)	W7DTC	0.024–0.031	Electronic		6 BTDC @ Idle [11]	123–174	800–900	Hyd.	Hyd.
	Cabriolet	109 (1,780)	WR7DS N8GY	0.024–0.032	Electronic		6 BTDC @ Idle	123–174	850–1000	Hyd.	Hyd.
	Scirocco	110 (1,799)	F6 DTC	0.027–0.035	Electronic		6 BTDC @ Idle	123–174	800–900	Hyd.	Hyd.
	GTI	109 (1,780)	W7DTC N8GY	0.028–0.032	Electronic		6 BTDC @ Idle	123–174	800–900	Hyd.	Hyd.
	GLI	109 (1,780)	W7DTC N8GY	0.028–0.032	Electronic		6 BTDC @ Idle	123–174	800–900	Hyd.	Hyd.
	Golf	109 (1,780)	W7DTC N8GY	0.028–0.032	Electronic		6 BTDC @ Idle	123–174	800–900	Hyd.	Hyd.
1987	Jetta	109 (1,780)	WR7DS	0.024–0.032	Electronic		6 BTDC @ Idle	131–174	800–900	Hyd.	Hyd.
	Jetta GL	109 (1,780)	W7DTC	0.027–0.035	Electronic		6 BTDC @ Idle	131–174	800–900	Hyd.	Hyd.
	Jetta GLI 16V	109 (1,780)	F6DTC	0.027–0.035	Electronic		6 BTDC @ Idle	145–189	800–900	Hyd.	Hyd.
	Quantum GLS/Synchro	136 (2,226)	WR7DS	0.027–0.035	Electronic		6 BTDC @ Idle	131–174	750–850	Hyd.	Hyd.
	Scirocco 16V	109 (1,780)	F6DTC	0.027–0.035	Electronic		6 BTDC @ Idle	145–189	800–900	Hyd.	Hyd.
	Cabriolet	109 (1,780)	W7DTC	0.027–0.035	Electronic		6 BTDC @ Idle	131–174	850–1000	Hyd.	Hyd.
	Golf GL	109 (1,780)	WR7DS	0.024–0.032	Electronic		6 BTDC @ Idle	131–174	800–900	Hyd.	Hyd.
	Golf GT	109 (1,780)	W7DTC	0.027–0.035	Electronic		6 BTDC @ Idle	131–174	800–900	Hyd.	Hyd.
	Golf GTI 16V	109 (1,780)	F6DTC	0.027–0.035	Electronic		6 BTDC @ Idle	148–189	800–900	Hyd.	Hyd.
	Fox/GL	109 (1,780)	W7DTC	0.027–0.035	Electronic		6 BTDC @ Idle	131–174	800–1000	Hyd.	Hyd.

GASOLINE ENGINE TUNE-UP SPECIFICATIONS (cont.)

Year	Model	Engine Displacement Cu. in. (cc)	Spark Plugs Type	Gap (in.)	Distributor Point Dwell (deg.)	Point Gap (in.)	Ignition Timing (deg.)	Compression Pressure (psi)	Idle Speed (rpm)	Valve Clearance (in.) In ⑤	Ex ⑤
1988	Jetta	109 (1,780)	WR7DS	0.024–0.032	Electronic		6 BTDC @ Idle	131–174	800–900	Hyd.	Hyd.
	Jetta GL	109 (1,780)	W7DTC	0.027–0.035	Electronic		6 BTDC @ Idle	131–174	800–900	Hyd.	Hyd.
	Jetta GLI 16V	109 (1,780)	F6DTC	0.027–0.035	Electronic		6 BTDC @ Idle	145–189	800–900	Hyd.	Hyd.
	Jetta Carat	109 (1,780)	W7DTC	0.027–0.035	Electronic		6 BTDC @ Idle	131–174	800–900	Hyd.	Hyd.
	Quantum GLS/Synchro	136 (2,226)	WR7DS	0.027–0.035	Electronic		6 BTDC @ Idle	131–174	750–850	Hyd.	Hyd.
	Scirocco	109 (1,780)	F6DTC	0.027–0.035	Electronic		6 BTDC @ Idle	145–189	800–900	Hyd.	Hyd.
	Cabriolet	109 (1,780)	W7DTC	0.027–0.035	Electronic		6 BTDC @ Idle	131–174	850–1000	Hyd.	Hyd.
	Golf GL	109 (1,780)	WR7DS	0.024–0.032	Electronic		6 BTDC @ Idle	131–174	800–900	Hyd.	Hyd.
	Golf GT	109 (1,780)	W7DTC	0.027–0.035	Electronic		6 BTDC @ Idle	131–174	800–900	Hyd.	Hyd.
	Golf GTI 16V	109 (1,780)	F6DTC	0.027–0.035	Electronic		6 BTDC @ Idle	145–189	800–900	Hyd.	Hyd.
	Fox/GL	109 (1,780)	W7DTC	0.027–0.035	Electronic		6 BTDC @ Idle	131–174	800–1000	Hyd.	Hyd.
1989	Jetta	109 (1,780)	WR7DS	0.024–0.032	Electronic		6 BTDC @ Idle	131–174	800–900	Hyd.	Hyd.
	Jetta GL	109 (1,780)	W7DTC	0.027–0.035	Electronic		6 BTDC @ Idle	131–174	800–900	Hyd.	Hyd.
	Jetta GLI 16V	109 (1,780)	F6DTC	0.027–0.035	Electronic		6 BTDC @ Idle	145–189	800–900	Hyd.	Hyd.
	Jetta Carat	109 (1,780)	W7DTC	0.027–0.035	Electronic		6 BTDC @ Idle	131–174	800–900	Hyd.	Hyd.
	Quantum GLS/Synchro	136 (2,226)	WR7DS	0.027–0.035	Electronic		6 BTDC @ Idle	131–174	750–850	Hyd.	Hyd.
	Scirocco 16V	109 (1,780)	F6DTC	0.027–0.035	Electronic		6 BTDC @ Idle	175–189	800–900	Hyd.	Hyd.
	Cabriolet	109 (1,780)	W7DTC	0.027–0.035	Electronic		6 BTDC @ Idle	131–174	850–1000	Hyd.	Hyd.
	Golf GL	109 (1,780)	WR7DS	0.024–0.032	Electronic		6 BTDC @ Idle	131–174	800–900	Hyd.	Hyd.
	Golf GT	109 (1,780)	W7DTC	0.027–0.035	Electronic		6 BTDC @ Idle	131–174	800–900	Hyd.	Hyd.
	Golf GTI 16V	109 (1,780)	F6DTC	0.027–0.035	Electronic		6 BTDC @ Idle	145–189	800–900	Hyd.	Hyd.
	Fox/GL	109 (1,780)	W7DTC	0.027–0.035	Electronic		6 BTDC @ Idle	131–174	800–1000	Hyd.	Hyd.

GASOLINE ENGINE TUNE-UP SPECIFICATIONS (cont.)

Year	Model	Engine Displacement Cu. in. (cc)	Spark Plugs Type	Gap (in.)	Distributor Point Dwell (deg.)	Point Gap (in.)	Ignition Timing (deg.)	Com- pression Pressure (psi)	Idle Speed (rpm)	Valve Clearance (in.) In [6]	Ex [6]
1990	Jetta GL	109 (1,780)	W7DTC WR7DS	0.024– 0.031	Electronic		6 BTDC @ Idle	131–174	800–1000	Hyd.	Hyd.
	Jetta Carat	109 (1,780)	W7DTC WR7DS	0.024– 0.031	Electronic		6 BTDC @ Idle	131–174	800–1000	Hyd.	Hyd.
	Jetta GLI 16V	121 (1,984)	F6DTC	0.027– 0.035	Electronic		6 BTDC @ Idle	145–189	800–900	Hyd.	Hyd.
	GTI	109 (1,780)	WR7DS	0.028– 0.034	Electronic		6 BTDC @ Idle	131–174	800–900	Hyd.	Hyd.
	GTI 16V	121 (1,984)	F6DTC	0.027– 0.035	Electronic		6 BTDC @ Idle	145–189	800–900	Hyd.	Hyd.
	Golf GL	109 (1,780)	W7DTC WR7DS	0.024– 0.031	Electronic		6 BTDC @ Idle	131–174	800–1000	Hyd.	Hyd.
	Cabriolet	109 (1,780)	W7DTC WR7DS	0.027– 0.035	Electronic		6 BTDC @ Idle	131–174	800–1000	Hyd.	Hyd.
	Corrado	109 (1,780)	W6DPO	0.028– 0.031	Electronic		6 BTDC @ Idle	116–174	750–850	Hyd.	Hyd.
	Passat GL	121 (1,984)	F6DTC F6DSR	0.027– 0.035	Electronic		6 BTDC @ Idle	145–189	700–900 [12]	Hyd.	Hyd.
	Fox/GL	109 (1,780)	W7DTC	0.027– 0.035	Electronic		6 BTDC @ Idle	131–174	800–1000	Hyd.	Hyd.

NOTE: The underhood sticker often reflects tune-up specification changes made in production. Sticker figures must be used if they disagree with those in this chart.

HYD: equipped with hydraulic lash adjusters.

[1] 47°–53° California
[2] 3 ATDC @ Idle with CIS fuel injection; 7½ BTDC @ Idle with 34 PICT-5 Carburetor
[3] Non-California Rabbit with 1 barrel carburetor—1980; 1,457 cc (89 cu. in.)
[4] California Rabbit
[5] Non-California Rabbit with fuel injection
[6] Valve clearance need not be adjusted unless it varies more than 0.002 in. from specifications.
[7] 1981 and later have Electronic ignition
[8] w/o Idle stabilizer
[9] Non-Cal. Rabbit w/1 bbl. timing 7½° BTDC; 1983 w/Manual Trans; timing 6° BTDC
[10] 1982 and later; 131–174 psi
[11] Applies to Manual trans; Auto trans: 3 BTDC @ Idle
[12] Idle speed is computer controlled and cannot be adjusted

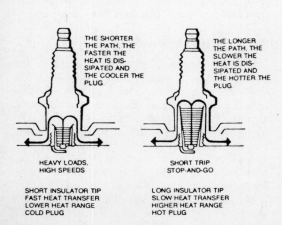

THE SHORTER THE PATH, THE FASTER THE HEAT IS DISSIPATED AND THE COOLER THE PLUG.

THE LONGER THE PATH, THE SLOWER THE HEAT IS DISSIPATED AND THE HOTTER THE PLUG.

HEAVY LOADS. HIGH SPEEDS.

SHORT TRIP STOP-AND-GO

SHORT INSULATOR TIP
FAST HEAT TRANSFER
LOWER HEAT RANGE
COLD PLUG

LONG INSULATOR TIP
SLOW HEAT TRANSFER
HIGHER HEAT RANGE
HOT PLUG

Spark plug heat range

the excessive heat, the electrodes will burn away quickly and in some instances, pre-ignition may result. Pre-ignition takes place when plug tips get so hot that they glow sufficiently to ignite the fuel/air mixture before the actual spark occurs. This early ignition will usually cause a pinging during low speeds and heavy loads. In severe cases, the heat may become high enough to start the fuel/air mixture burning throughout the combustion chamber rather than just to the front of the plug as in normal operation. At this time, the piston is rising in the cylinder making its compression stroke. The burning mass is compressed and an explosion results, forcing the piston back down in the cylinder while it is still trying to go up. Obviously, something must go, and it does—pistons are often damaged.

DIESEL ENGINE TUNE-UP SPECIFICATIONS

Year	Model	Valve Clearance Intake (in.)	Exhaust (in.)	Injection Pump Setting	Injection Nozzle Pressure (psi) New	Used	Idle Speed (rpm)	Cranking Compression Pressure (psi)
1977–78	Rabbit	0.008– ① 0.012	0.016– ① 0.020	Align Marks	1849	1706	800– ④ 850	406–493
1979–81	Dasher	0.008– ① 0.012	0.016– ① 0.020	Align Marks	1849	1706	770– 870	406–493
1979–84	Rabbit Jetta	0.008– ① 0.012	0.016– ① 0.020	Align Marks	1885 ②	1740	800– ③ 850	406–493
1985–90	Jetta	Hyd.	Hyd.	Align Marks	1885– ② 2001	1740	920– 980	406–493
1982–86	Quantum	0.008– ① 0.012	0.016– ① 0.020	Align Marks	2204– 2318	1991	900– 980	406–493

HYD: Equipped with hydraulic lash adjusters
① Warm clearance given—Cold clearance: Intake 0.006–0.010
                                   Exhaust 0.014–0.018
② Turbo diesel: New—2248–2364
               Used—2030–2200
③ 1983–84 Diesel/turbo diesel engines: 810–950
④ On later Rabbits in this year span, VW changed the idle speed to 770–870 rpm

The general rule of thumb for choosing the correct heat range when picking a spark plug is: if most of your driving is long distance, high speed travel, use a colder plug; if most of your driving is stop and go, use a hotter plug. Factory installed plugs are, of course, compromise plugs, since the factory has no way of knowing what sort of driving you do. It should be noted that most people never have occasion to change their plugs from the factory recommended heat range.

REMOVAL AND INSTALLATION

1. Grasp the spark plug boot, twist and pull straight out. Don't pull on the wire. If the boot(s) are cracked, replace them.
2. Place the spark plug socket firmly on the plug. Turn the spark plug out of the cylinder head in a counterclockwise direction.

NOTE: *The cylinder head is aluminum, which is easily stripped. Remove plugs only when the engine is cold.*

If removal is difficult, loosen the plug only slightly and drip a small amount penetrating oil onto the threads. Allow the oil time enough to work and then unscrew the plug. This will prevent damaging the threads in the cylinder head. Be sure to keep the socket straight to avoid breaking the ceramic insulator.
3. Continue on and remove the remaining spark plugs.
4. Inspect the plugs using the "Tune-Up Tips" section illustrations and then clean or dis-

card them according to condition. New spark plugs come pre-gapped, but double check the setting or reset them if you desire a different gap. The recommended spark plug gas is listed in the Tune-Up Specifications chart. Use a spark plug wire gauge for checking the gap. The wire should pass through the electrode with just a slight drag. Using the electrode bending tool on the end of the gauge, bend the side electrode to adjust the gap. Never attempt to adjust the center electrode. Lightly oil the threads of the replacement plug and install it handtight. It is a good practice to use a torque wrench to tighten the spark plugs on any car and especially since the head is aluminum. Install the ignition wire boots firmly on the spark plugs.

Spark Plug Wires

Visually inspect the spark plug cables for burns, cuts, or breaks in the insulation. Check the spark plug boots and the nipples on the distributor cap and coil. Replace any damaged wiring. If no physical damage is obvious, the wires can be checked with an ohmmeter for excessive resistance. Remove the distributor cap and leave the wires connected to the cap. Connect one lead of the ohmmeter to the corresponding electrode inside the cap and the other lead to the spark plug terminal (remove it from the spark plug for the test). Replace any wire which shows over 50,000. Generally speaking, however, resistance should not run over 35,000 and 50,000 should be considered the outer

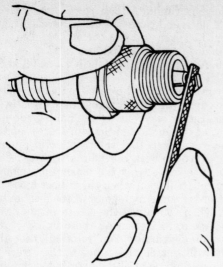

Plugs in good condition can be filed and re-used

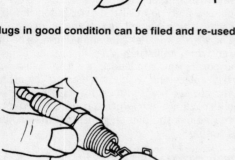

Check the plug gap with a wire gauge only

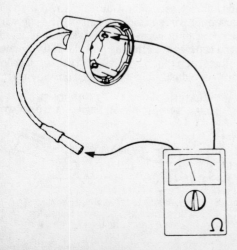

Checking plug wire resistance

limits of acceptability. It should be remembered that wire resistance is a function of length, and that the longer the cable, the greater the resistance. Thus, if the cables on your car are longer than the factory originals, resistance will be higher and quite possibly outside of these limits.

When installing a new set of spark plug cables, replace the cables one at a time so there will be no mixup. Start by replacing the longest cable first. Install the boot firmly over the spark plug. If there is any type of conduit or cover over the wires (like on Corrado), remove it. Route the new wire exactly the same as the original. Insert the nipple firmly into the tower on the distributor cap. Repeat the process for each cable. Take your time.

Firing Orders

NOTE: *To avoid confusion, remove and tag the wires one at a time, for replacement.*

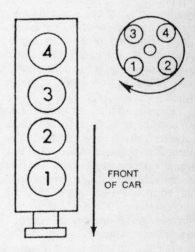

Fox Firing Order:1, 3, 4, 2
Distributor Rotation: clockwise

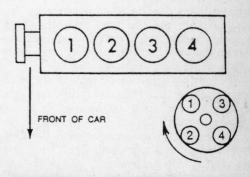

1,715cc and 1,780cc engines Firing Order: 1, 3, 4, 2
Distributor Rotation: clockwise

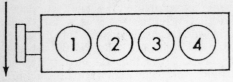

FRONT OF CAR

Diesel engine cylinder arrangement

FRONT OF ENGINE

16 Valve engines

Breaker Points and Condenser

The points function as a circuit breaker for the primary circuit of the ignition system. The ignition coil must boost the 12 volts of electrical pressure supplied by the battery to as much as 25,000 volts in order to fire the plugs. To do this, the coil depends on the points and the condenser to make a clean break in the primary circuit.

The coil has both primary and secondary circuits. When the ignition is turned on, the battery supplies voltage through the coil and onto the points. The points are connected to ground, completing the primary circuit. As the current passes through the coil, a magnetic field is created in the iron center core of the coil. When the cam in the distributor turns, the points open, breaking the primary circuit of the coil then collapses and cuts through the secondary circuit windings around the iron core. Due to electromagnetic induction, the battery voltage is increased to a level sufficient to fire the spark plugs.

When the points open, the electrical charge in the primary circuit tries to jump the gap created between the two open contacts of the points. If this electrical charge were not transferred elsewhere, the metal contacts of the points would start to change rapidly.

The function of the condenser is to absorb excessive voltage from the points when they open and thus prevent the points from becoming pitted or burned.

The ignition system must complete the above cycle each time a spark plug fires. On a four cylinder, four cylinder engine, two of the four plugs must fire once for every engine revolution. If the idle speed of an engine were 800 rev-

olutions per minute (800 rpm), the breaker points open and close two times for each revolution. For every minute the engine idles, the points open and close 1600 times (2 × 800 = 1600). And that is just at idle, what about at 55 mph?

There are two ways to check to check breaker point gap: with a feeler gauge or with a dwell meter. Either way you set the points, you are adjusting the amount of time (in degrees of distributor rotation) that the points will remain open. If you adjust the points with a feeler gauge, you are setting the maximum amount the points will open when the rubber block on the points is on a high point of the distributor cam. When you adjust the points with a dwell meter, you are measuring the number of degrees (of distributor cam rotation) that the points will remain closed before they start to open as a high point of the distributor cam approaches the rubbing block of the points.

There are two rules that should always be followed when adjusting or replacing the points. The points and condenser are a matched set; never replace one without replacing the other. If you change point gap or dwell of the engine, you also change the ignition timing. Therefore, if you adjust the points, you must also adjust the timing.

INSPECTION OF THE POINTS

1. Disconnect the high tension wire which runs between the distributor and the ignition coil.

2. Remove the metal static shield which is fitted around the distributor cap, if equipped. Remove the shield by twisting it and pulling it upward and over the cap.

3. The distributor cap is held down by two spring clips. Insert a screwdriver under their ends and release them. Lift off the cap with the spark plug wires attached. Lift off the cap with the spark plug wires attached. Wipe the inside of the cap clean with a rag and check for burned contacts, cracks or carbon tracks. Carbon tracks are dark lines running from one termi-

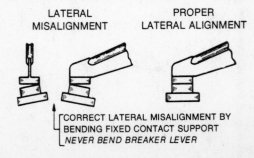

LATERAL MISALIGNMENT   PROPER LATERAL ALIGNMENT

CORRECT LATERAL MISALIGNMENT BY BENDING FIXED CONTACT SUPPORT
NEVER BEND BREAKER LEVER

Points must be correctly aligned

nal to another. They cannot be removed, so replace the cap if it has any tracks.

4. Remove the rotor from the distributor shaft by pulling it straight up. Examine the condition of the rotor, if it is cracked or if the metal tip is excessively worn or burned, it should be replaced. If not, clean the tip with a clean cloth.

CAUTION: *Do not file the contact tip on the rotor.*

5. Pry open the points with a screwdriver and check the condition of the contacts. If they are excessively worn, burned or pitted, they should be replaced.

6. If the points are in good condition, adjust them and replace the rotor and the distributor cap. If they need to be replaced, follow the replacement procedure that follows.

REPLACEMENT OF THE BREAKER POINTS AND CONDENSER

1. Remove the cap and rotor as outlined in the previous section.

2. Remove the dust shield and loosen the screws securing the points (if possible, use a magnetic screwdriver for removal to avoid losing a screw down into the distributor). Slide the point wire connector off of its terminal and remove the point set.

3. The condenser is located on the outside of the distributor body. Pull the wire connector coming from the suppressor off of the condenser terminal. Remove the screw that secures the condenser assembly to the distributor body and remove the assembly.

4. Before installing the new points and condenser, place a small dab of grease on the distributor shaft a smear it evenly around the cam. Install the new points and condenser. Tighten the condenser mounting screw but leave the points screws loose.

5. Make sure that the faces of the points meet squarely. If not, the fixed mount can be bent slightly with a little force and a pair of needle nose pliers. Do not bend the movable contact.

6. The point gap must be adjusted next. The gap is adjusted with the rubbing block of the points resting on one of the high spots of the distributor cam. To get it there, the engine can be rotated by bumping the starter with the ignition key, or the crankshaft can be turned with a wrench on the crankshaft pulley bolt; this is easier to do with the spark plugs removed.

7. Insert a 0.43mm (0.017 in.) flat feeler gauge between the points. A slight drag should be felt. If no drag can be felt, or if the gauge can't be inserted at all, insert a screwdriver into the notch provided for adjustment and use

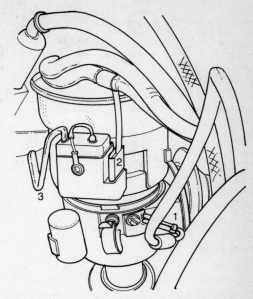

On 1979 and later distributors, unfasten ground strap (1), suppressor lead at suppressor 92), and suppressor lead at distributor body (3) to remove distributor cap

it to open or close the gap between the points until it is correct.

8. When you feel the gap is set, tighten the points screws and recheck the gap. Sometimes it takes three or four times to get it corrected, so don't feel frustrated if they seem to move around on you a little. It's not easy to feel the correct gap either. To check yourself, use gauges 0.05mm (0.002 in.) larger and smaller than 0.40mm (0.016 in.) as a test. If the points are spread slightly by a 0.45mm (0.018 in.) gauge, but not touched at all by a 0.35mm (0.014 in.) gauge, the testing should be right.

9. After all the adjustments are complete, pull a clean piece of tissue or a piece of white paper between the contacts to clear away any bits of grit.

10. Replace the dust cover, the rotor and the distributor cap. Snap on the spring clips and replace the static shield. If you have a dwell meter (recommended) you should next set the dwell. Otherwise, go on to the ignition timing section.

Dwell Angle

The dwell angle is the number of degrees of distributor cam rotation through which the points remain closed (conducting electricity). Increasing the point gap decreases dwell, while decreasing the gap increases dwell.

The dwell angle may be checked with the distributor cap and rotor installed and the engine running, or with the cap and rotor removed

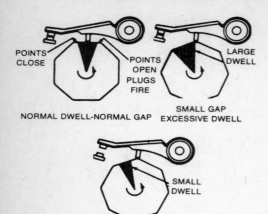

POINTS CLOSE

POINTS OPEN PLUGS FIRE

LARGE DWELL

NORMAL DWELL-NORMAL GAP

SMALL GAP EXCESSIVE DWELL

SMALL DWELL

WIDE GAP INSUFFICIENT DWELL

Dwell angle

and the engine cranking at starter speed. The meter gives a constant reading with the engine running. With the engine cranking, the meter will fluctuate between **0** dwell and the maximum figure for that setting. Never attempt to adjust the points when the ignition is on, or you may receive a shock.

ADJUSTMENT WITH A DWELL METER

NOTE: *The dwell angle on all cars with electronic ignition is set at the factory and is not adjustable.*

1. Connect a meter as per the manufacturer's instructions (usually one lead to the distributor's terminal of the coil and the other lead to a ground). Zero the meter, if necessary.

2. Check the dwell by either the cranking method, or with the engine running. If the setting is correct, the points must be adjusted.

CAUTION: *Keep your hands, hair and clothing clear of the engine fan and pulleys. Be sure the wires from the dwell meter are routed out of the way. If the engine is running, block the front wheels, put the transmission in Neutral, or Park, and set the parking brake.*

3. To change the dwell angle, turn the ignition off, loosen the points hold down screw and adjust the point gap; increase the gap to decrease dwell, and vice-versa. Tighten the hold down screw and check the dwell angle with the engine cranking. If it seems to be correct, replace the cap and rotor and check dwell with the engine running. Readjust as necessary.

4. Run the engine speed up to about 2,500 rpm, and then let off on the gas pedal; the dwell reading should not change. If it does, a worn distributor shaft, bushing or cam, or a worn breaker plate is indicted. The parts must be inspected and replaced if necessary.

5. After adjusting the dwell angle, go on to the "Ignition Timing" section following.

Electronic Ignition System

Electronic ignition systems offer many advantages over the conventional breaker point ignition system. By eliminating the points, maintenance requirements are greatly reduced. An electronic ignition system is capable of producing much higher voltage which in turn aids starting, reduces spark plug fouling and provides better emission control.

The Hall generator produces a voltage pulse which is sent to the control unit, which in turn switches the primary ignition circuit on and off.

The Hall generator, which is located in the distributor, consists of a trigger wheel that revolves with the distributor shaft and a stationary unit called the Hall sender. The Hall sender consists of a semiconductor layer positioned on a magnetically conducting element and a permanent magnet, both of which are separated by an air gap. When the trigger wheel shutter enters the air gap, it blocks the magnetic field and the Hall sender is shut off. When this occurs, the control unit will complete the primary circuit and you have the dwell period. When the shutter leaves the air gap, the magnetic field flows again. The Hall sender generates a voltage pulse to the control unit which will then interrupt the primary ignition circuit and ignition will occur.

Because temperature changes and engine load variations caused by different electrical accessories can effect idle speed, many cars equipped with the Hall generator also use an electronic idle stabilization system. This system consists of a small control unit in between the Hall generator and the main control unit. The frequency of the voltage signal sent from the Hall generator gives the idle stabilizer information on engine speed. When the idle stabilizer senses that the engine speed has dropped below a certain rpm, it will trigger the main control unit (faster than the Hall generator) which will advance the timing, causing the idle speed to increase.

ELECTRONIC IGNITION PRECAUTIONS

When working on electronic ignition systems, observe the following precautions to prevent damage to the ignition system and personal injury.

1. Connect and disconnect test equipment only when the ignition switch is OFF.

2. On the carbureted Rabbit, if you use a conventional tachometer, you will have to fabricate an adapter. See below for instructions.

3. Do not crank the engine with the starter

for compression tests, etc., until the high tension coil wire (terminal 4) is grounded.

4. Do not replace the original equipment coil with a conventional coil.

5. Do not install any kind of condenser to coil terminal 1.

6. Do not use a battery booster for longer than 1 (one) minute.

7. On the fuel injected models, do not tow cars with defective ignitions systems without disconnecting the plugs at the ignition control unit.

TACHOMETER ADAPTER FABRICATION INSTRUCTIONS (CARBURETED RABBITS)

An adapter must be used when connecting a conventional tachometer to the Hall Effect ignition system to prevent damage to the ignition components. Use the illustration as a guide. All components will be available to you locally. Connect the positive wire of the tachometer to the adapter and the negative wire to the ground.

Ignition Timing

GASOLINE ENGINE ONLY

CAUTION: *When performing this or any other operation with the engine running, be very careful of the alternator belt and pulleys. Make sure that your timing light wires don't interfere with the belt.*

Ignition timing is an important part of the tune-up. It is always adjusted after the points are gapped (dwell angle changed), on breaker point ignitions, since altering the dwell affects the timing. Three basic types of timing lights are available, the neon, the DC, and the AC powered. Of the three, the DC light is the most frequently used by professional mechanics. The bright flash put out by the DC light makes the timing marks stand out on even the brightest of days. Another advantage of the DC light is

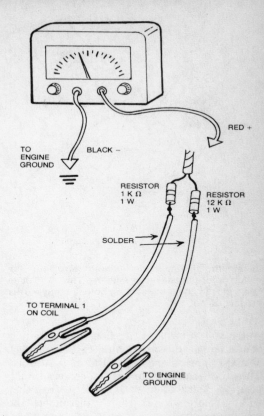

Fabricate this adapter for your tachometer on carbureted models with electronic ignition

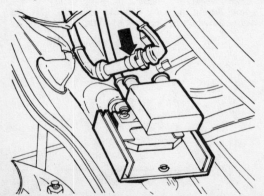

Disconnect plugs at the control unit and plug them together (electronic ignition)

that you don't need to be near an electrical outlet. Neon timing lights are available for a few dollars, but their weak flash makes it necessary to use them in a fairly dark work area. One neon light lead is attached to the spark plug and the other to the plug wire. The DC light attaches to the spark plug and the wire with an adapter and two clips attach to the battery posts for power. The AC unit is similar, except that the power cable is plugged into a house outlet. If your particular car has electronic ignition, you should use a timing light with an inductive pickup. The pickup simply clamps onto the No. 1 plug wire, eliminating an adapter. This type light is not susceptible to crossfiring or false triggering which may occur with a conventional light, due to the greater voltages produced by electronic ignitions.

BREAKER POINT IGNITION SYSTEMS

All Models

1. Attach the timing light as outlined above or according to the manufacturer's instructions. Hook-up a dwell/tachometer since you'll need an rpm indication for correct timing.

2. Locate the timing mark opening in the

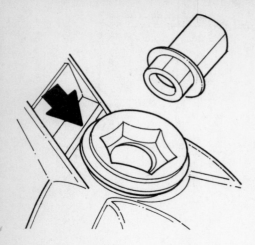

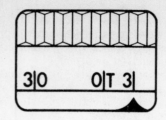

Dasher timing marks seen through opening on transmission bell housing

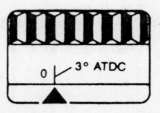

1983 4-cylinder Quantum ignition timing marks (automatic transmission)

Locate the timing mark opening (arrow) in the clutch or torque converter housing. This 1980 Jetta has a plastic cover over timing hole — many earlier models do not

clutch or torque converter housing at the rear of the engine directly behind the distributor. The **OT** mark stands for **TDC** or **0** advance. The other mark designates the correct timing position. Mark them with chalk so that they will be more visible. DON'T disconnect the vacuum line.

3. Start the engine and allow it to reach the normal operating temperature. The engine should be running at normal idle speed.

4. Shine the timing light at the marks.

5. The light should now be flashing when the timing mark and the V-shaped pointer are aligned.

6. If not, loosen the distributor hold-down bolt and rotate the distributor very slowly to align the marks.

7. Tighten the mounting nut when the ignition timing is correct.

8. Recheck the timing when the distributor is tight.

ELECTRONIC IGNITION SYSTEMS

Rabbit, Dasher and Quantum

1. Run the engine to operating temperature. Connect a tachometer.

2. Stop the engine. Disconnect the idle stabilizer plugs at the control unit and plug them together. On the carbureted Rabbit, disconnect the vacuum retard hose and plug. Models with TYF carburetor, disconnect and plug both lines.

3. Switch all electrical accessories to the **OFF** position.

4. Start the engine and check the idle speed.

5. With your timing light attached according to manufacturers instructions, shine the light on the timing hold it there. The pointer in the hole must line up with the notch in the flywheel. To adjust the timing, loosen the distributor at its base and turn it.

6. On the carbureted Rabbit, reinstall the vacuum hose(s). Idle speed should drop to 600–750 rpm.

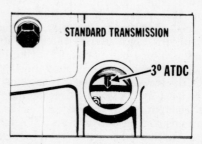

Typical timing mark for models with CIS, GTI and Scirocco (with 1.8) timed at 6° BTDC

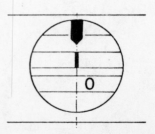

Timing mark for 1978 and 1980 34 PICT–5 carburetor (7½° BTDC)

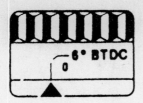

1984–85 4-cylinder Quantum ignition timing marks

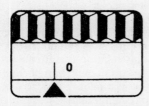

5-cylinder Quantum and Synchro ignition timing marks

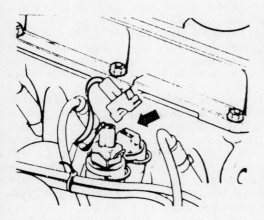

Coolant temperature sensor location (arrow) on Corrado

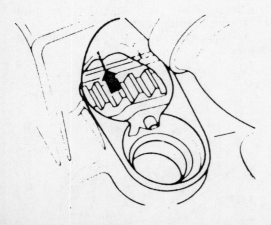

Corrado, Passat, GTI/Jetta 16 valve 2.0L engine ignition timing marks

7. Stop the engine and reconnect the plugs at the control unit. On the carbureted Rabbit, start the engine and rev it a few times to activate the idle stabilizer. On the carbureted Rabbit, the idle speed should now be 850–950 rpm.

Corrado

1. Run the engine for a few minutes to allow it reach normal operating temperature. Wait for the cooling to cycle once.

2. Stop the engine and turn the ignition

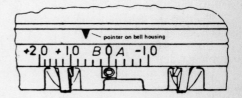

Westmoreland Rabbits with a 200mm clutch may have a "universal" flywheel. Each timing mark is equal to 2°. Marks to the left of the 0 are BTDC, to the right ATDC

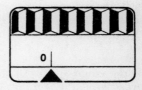

1980 electronic ignition Dashers have only one mark for correct timing (3° ATDC)

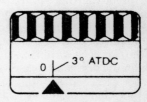

1982 4-cylinder Quantum ignition timing marks

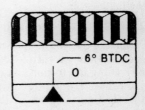

1983 4-cylinder Quantum ignition timing marks (manual transmission)

switch to the **OFF** position. Connect a timing light and tachometer to the engine.

3. Unplug the coolant temperature sensor connector. The connector is blue and is attached to the coolant sensor.

4. Start the engine and illuminate the timing marks with the timing light. The pointer in the hole must line up with the notch in the flywheel.

5. If the timing is not as specified, remove the tamper proof cap that covers the head of the distributor base clamp bolt (if installed).

6. Loosen the distributor base clamp and rotate the distributor clockwise or counterclockwise until the timing is within specs.

7. Tighten the distributor clamp and clamp base bolt.

8. Once the clamp base bolt is tight, check the timing again.

9. Check the idle speed and adjust if necessary.

10. Stop the engine, disconnect the timing light and tachometer. On Corrado, plug in the coolant temperature sensor connector.

Passat, GTI 16V and Jetta 16V 2.0L Engines

1. Run the engine for a few minutes to allow it reach normal operating temperature. Wait for the cooling fan to come on once.

2. Stop the engine and turn the ignition switch to the **OFF** position. Connect a timing light and tachometer.

3. Start the engine and illuminate the timing marks with the timing light. The pointer in the hole must line up with the notch in the flywheel.

4. If the timing is not as specified, remove the tamper proof cap that covers the head of the distributor base clamp bolt (if installed).

5. Loosen the distributor base clamp and rotate the distributor clockwise or counterclockwise until the timing is within specs.

6. Tighten the distributor clamp and clamp base bolt.

7. Once the clamp base bolt is tight, check the timing again.

8. Check the idle speed and adjust if necessary.

9. Stop the engine, disconnect the timing light and tachometer.

Cabriolet, Fox, Golf, GTI, Jetta and Scirocco

1. Run the engine for a few minutes to allow it reach normal operating temperature. Wait for the cooling fan to come on once. Make sure all electrical accessories are in the **OFF** position. On 1990 Cabriolet and 1987–90 Golf and Jetta, raise the idle speed to a minimum of 2,100 rpm four times to cancel the (computer controlled) hot start idle speed increase func-

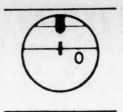

Golf, GTI, Jetta, Fox, Scirocco and Cabriolet ignition timing marks

tion, then allow the engine to idle normally. If you don't do this step, the hot re-start program stored in the computer will cause the engine idle speed to run higher than normal and affect the timing adjustment.

2. Stop the engine.

3. On Scirocco without 16V engine, Fox and 1985–89 Cabriolet, remove the vacuum hose from the distributor and plug it. On 1990 Cabriolet and 1987–90 Golf and Jetta, unplug the coolant temperature sensor connector. On early models, the connector is blue and is attached directly to the coolant temperature sensor. On later models, the connector is black and it attaches to the coolant temperature gauge.

4. Before adjusting ignition timing on 1990 Cabriolet and 1987–90 Golf and Jetta, disconnect the coolant temperature sensor connector.

5. Connect a timing light and tachometer.

6. Start the engine and illuminate the timing marks with the timing light. The pointer in the hole must line up with the notch in the flywheel. On 1990 Cabriolet and 1987–90 Golf and Jetta, have an assistant increase the engine idle speed to 2200–2300 rpm, then check the timing.

7. If the timing is not as specified, loosen the distributor base clamp and rotate the distributor clockwise or counterclockwise until the timing is within specs.

8. Tighten the distributor clamp and clamp base bolt.

Coolant temperature sensor location on 1990 Cabriolet and 1987–90 Golf and Jetta

9. Once the clamp base bolt is tight, check the timing again.

10. Check the idle speed and adjust if necessary.

11. Stop the engine and disconnect the timing light and tachometer. Plug in the coolant temperature sensor or connect the distributor vacuum line (if required).

VALVE LASH

NOTE: *1985–90 models with gas engines are equipped with hydraulic lifters. No adjustment is necessary. 1985–86 and 1989–90 models with diesel engines (Jetta and Golf), except for early production Golfs, are equipped with hydraulic valve lifters; as with the gasoline engines. No adjustment is required. A label on the valve cover will help you identify the type lifter (mechanical or hydraulic) the engine is equipped with.*

Valve adjustment is one factor which determines how far the intake and exhaust valves open into the cylinder. If the valve clearance is too large, part of the lift of the camshaft will be used in removing the excessive clearance, therefore the valves will not open far enough. This has two ill effects; one, the valve gear will become noisy as the excess clearance is taken up and, two, the engine will perform poorly. This is because intake valves which don't open the full distance will admit a smaller air/fuel mixture into the cylinders. Exhaust valves which aren't opening the full amount create a greater back pressure in the cylinder which prevents the proper air/fuel mixture from entering the cylinder.

If the valve clearance is too small, the intake and exhaust valves will not fully seat on the cylinder head when they close. When a valve seats on the cylinder head it does two things; it seals the combustion chamber so that none of the gases in the cylinder can escape and it cools itself by transferring some of the heat absorbed from the combustion process through the cylinder head and into the cooling system. Therefore, if the valve clearance is too small, the engine will run poorly (due to gases escaping from the combustion chamber), and the valves will overheat and eventually warp (since they cannot properly transfer heat unless they fully seat on the cylinder head).

While all valve adjustments must be as accurate as possible, it is better to have the valve adjustment slightly loose than tight, as burned valves can result from too tight an adjustment. Also, it is recommended that only one person perform the valve adjustment. What might be a slight drag with a feeler gauge to one person might be too tight to another.

ADJUSTMENT

The overhead cam acts directly on the valves through cam followers which fit over the springs and valves. Adjustment is made with an adjusting disc which fits into the cam follower. Different thickness disc result in changes in valve clearance.

NOTE: *VW recommends that two special tools be used to remove and install the adjustment discs. One is a pry bar to compress the valve springs and the other a pair of special pliers to remove the disc. Ask your local VW dealer for current tool part numbers. If the purchase of these tools is not possible, a flat metal plate can be used to compress the valve springs if you are careful not to gouge*

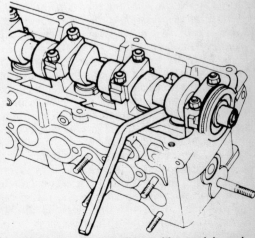

Remove the adjusting discs with special pry bar and pliers — don't press on the disc itself, but on the lip of the disc holder. Note the position of cam lobes on no. 1 cylinder. This is the correct position for measuring valve clearances.

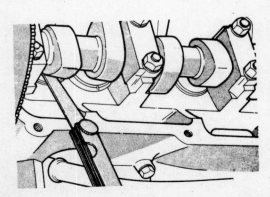

Check the valve clearance with a feeler gauge. The camshaft lobe should not be putting pressure on the valve disc

the camshaft lobes. The cam follower has two slots which permit the disc to be lifted out. Again, you may improvise by using a thin bladed screwdriver. An assistant to pry the spring down while you remove the disc would be the ideal way to perform the operation if you must improvise your own tools.

Valve clearance is checked with the engine moderately warm (coolant temperature should be about 95°F (35°C).

1. Remove the accelerator linkage (if equipped with automatic transmission), the upper drive belt cover (if necessary), the air cleaner and any hoses or lines which may be in the way.

NOTE: *When disconnecting the accelerator cable, do not allow the cable to become kinked or twisted. Route the cable neatly off to side and out of the way.*

2. Remove the cylinder head cover and cover gasket. Valve clearance is checked in the firing order; 1–3–4–2 for the 4 cylinder and 1–2–4–5–3 for the 5 cylinder engines, with the piston of the cylinder being checked at TDC of the compression stroke. Both valves will be closed at this position and the cam lobes will be pointing straight up.

NOTE: *When adjusting the clearances on the diesel engine, the pistons must not be at TDC. Turn the crankshaft 1/4 turn past TDC so that the valves do not contact the pistons when the tappets are depressed.*

3. Turn the crankshaft pulley bolt with a socket wrench to position the camshaft for checking.

NOTE: *There is a hole behind the front license plate, on Dasher models, through which a wrench can be used.*

CAUTION: *Do not turn the camshaft by the camshaft mounting bolt, this will stretch the drive belt. When turning the crankshaft pulley bolt, turn CLOCKWISE ONLY.*

4. With the No. 1 piston at TDC (1/4 turn past for the diesel) of the compression stroke, determine the clearance with a feeler gauge. Intake clearance should be 0.20–0.30mm (0.008–0.012 in.); exhaust clearance should be 0.40–0.50mm (0.016–0.020 in.) for gasoline engines, or, 0.15–0.25mm (0.006–0.010 in.) and 0.35–0.45mm (0.014–0.018 in.) for the Diesel.

5. Continue on to check the other cylinders in the firing order, turning the crankshaft to bring each particular piston to the top of the compression stroke (1/4 turn for the diesel). Record the individual clearances as you go along.

6. If measured clearance is within tolerance levels — 0.05mm (0.002 in.) — it is not necessary to replace the adjusting discs.

7. If adjustment is necessary, the discs will have to be removed and replaced with thicker or thinner ones which will yield the correct clearance. Discs are available in 0.05mm (0.002 in.) increments from 3mm (0.12 in.) to 4mm (0.16 in.).

NOTE: *The thickness of the adjusting discs are etched on one side. When installing, the marks must face the cam followers. Discs can be can be reused if they are not worn or damaged.*

8. To remove the discs; turn the cam followers so that the grooves are accessible when the pry bar is depressed.

9. Press the cam follower down with the pry bar and remove the adjusting discs with the special pliers or the screwdriver.

10. Replace the adjustment discs as necessary to bring the clearance within the 0.05mm (0.002 in.) tolerance level. If the measured clearance is larger than the given tolerance, remove the existing disc and insert a thicker one to bring the clearance up to specification. If it is smaller, insert a thinner one.

11. Recheck all valve clearances after adjustment.

12. Install the cylinder head cover with a new gasket.

13. Install the accelerator linkage, the upper drive belt cover and any wires or lines which were removed.

FUEL SYSTEM

Idle Speed Adjustment

NOTE: *The following information is being published from the latest information available at the time of publication. If the information differs from the values given on the underhood emission control label, use the data on the label.*

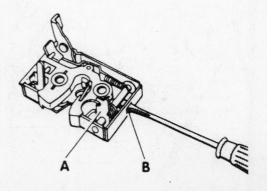

Idle speed adjusting screw — except 34 PICT (1978 and 1980) and Carter TYF

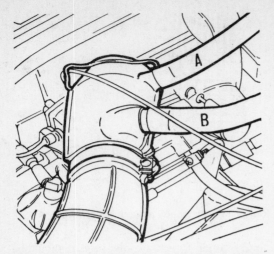

Disconnect both hoses (A) and (B) before setting idle on 1980 34 PICT–5 Rabbit. On 1978 model, disconnect only the braided charcoal filter hose

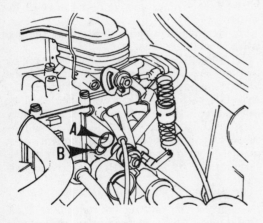

1978 34 PICT–5 idle speed screw (a) and CO screw (b) — 1980 similar

CARBURETED ENGINES

The Dasher carburetor is a Solex 32/35 DIDTA 2-barrel unit in 1974, and a Zenith 2B3 in 1975. Both have vacuum operated secondary barrels. The 1975–76 Rabbit and Scirocco use a Zenith 2B2 carburetor with a vacuum operated secondary barrel and dual floats. Some 1978 and 1980 Rabbits are equipped with the 35 PICT-5 single barrel carburetor. The 1982 and later models use a Carter TYF feedback carburetor.

Solex 32/35 DIDTA Carburetor, Zenith 2B2 and 2B3 Carburetors

1. Start the engine and run it until the normal operating temperature is reached.
2. Hook-up a tachometer to the engine and observe the idle speed.

3. If the idle speed is not specified, turn the curb idle screw to correct it. Make sure that you are turning the correct screw as shown in the illustration. Do not mistake the idle mixture screw for the curb idle screw.

Solex 34 PICT-5 Carburetor

1978 RABBIT ONLY

NOTE: *See below for 1980 Rabbit with Solex 34 PICT-5 carburetor.*

The choke must be fully open and the engine at normal operating temperature.

1. Remove the hose from the charcoal filter at the air intake elbow. Plug the hose.
2. Remove the air injection hose at the air cleaner. Plug the hose.
3. Make sure all electrical accessories are in the **OFF** position. Unplug the electric cooling fan. It must not come on when adjusting the idle speed.
4. Connect a tachometer. Adjust the idle speed to specification at the idle speed adjusting screw **A**. The CO content can be adjusted at screw **B** if a CO meter is available.
5. Disconnect the tachometer, reconnect all hoses and plug in the cooling fan.

1980 RABBIT ONLY

NOTE: *See above 1978 Rabbit with Solex 34 PICT-5 carburetor for illustrations showing locations of idle speed and mixture screws.*

1. The engine must be at operating temperature and the choke must be fully open.
2. Remove the two hoses from the carburetor air intake elbow and plug the two hose inlets in the elbow. The air intake elbow sits right on top of the carburetor.
3. Remove both of the air injection hoses at

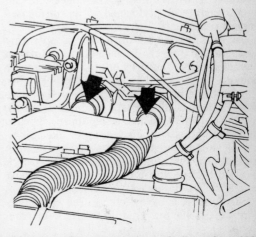

Remove air injection hoses and plug valves 1980 34 PICT–5. For 1978 34 PICT–5, remove the air injection hose at the air cleaner and plug the hose

the air injection valves, located side by side in the front middle of the engine. Plug the air injection valves.

4. Shut off all electrical equipment, including the air conditioner (if installed).

5. Connect a tachometer, timing light and CO meter (if available) to the engine.

CAUTION: *See Tachometer Adaptation (Carbureted Rabbits), under the electronic ignition section above for method of connecting tachometer. If you do not follow these instructions, you will damage your ignition system!*

6. Start the engine. Rev the engine a few times to start the idle stabilizer.

7. Check the idle; it should be 850–950 rpm. If the idle is not correct, disconnect the plugs at the control unit and plug them together (see electronic ignition system above).

8. Remove the vacuum advance and retard hoses, then plug the hoses.

9. Adjust the idle speed to 800–1000 rpm at the idle adjustment screw. Check the timing.

10. If the timing was off, recheck the idle speed.

11. Reconnect the advance and retard hoses. Adjust the CO lever at the CO adjusting screw.

12. Reconnect the control unit.

13. Rev the engine to reactivate idle stabilizer and check the idle speed and CO. Idle speed should be 850–950 rpm.

14. If the idle speed is still not correct, replace the control unit or the idle stabilizer.

CARTER TYF

The Carter TYF in an electrically controlled carburetor requiring special equipment for adjustment. The adjustment procedure calls for a special duty cycle meter which is not commonly available to the backyard mechanic. Unless you have access to this meter it is suggested that the procedure be performed by an authorized service technician.

1. Run the engine until normal operating temperature is reached. The electric cooling fan should come on at least once. Make sure the choke is fully opened and not sticking. Remove the breather hose from the side of the valve cover. Shut off all electrical equipment including the air conditioner (if so equipped). The radiator fan must not be running for idle adjustment, so unplug it. Disconnect the vacuum hoses to the distributor and plug them. Check ignition timing with a timing light and adjust to $7\frac{1}{2}°$ BTDC if necessary. Connect hoses.

2. Connect a tachometer to the engine according to the tach manufacturer's instructions.

3. Connect the duty cycle meter to the test connector on the left strut tower.

4. Start the engine, and run at 2000 rpm

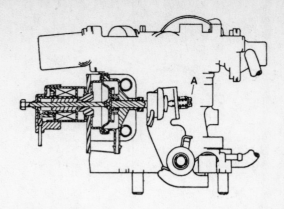

Carter TYF idle speed adjustment at screw "A"

for 5 seconds. Check the idle speed, it should be 850–1000 rpm. Duty cycle should be fluctuating between 20% and 50%.

5. To adjust the idle speed, disconnect both idle stabilizer plugs and connect the plugs together

6. Remove the vacuum hoses from the distributor and plug them.

7. Adjust the idle speed to 820–900 rpm by turning the idle screw at the front of the bracket mounted idle kickback switch on the side of the carburetor. Duty cycle should still be fluctuating between 20% and 50%. If the duty cycle reading is incorrect the car should be taken to a professional for adjustment, as a tamper-proof plug must be removed from the carburetor body to make the required adjustment.

NOTE: *On air conditioned cars, turn the compressor on and set the controls to MAX cold and FAST fan speed before setting idle speed to 820–900 rpm.*

8. Stop engine, reconnect the idle stabilizer plugs and vacuum hoses at the distributor.

FUEL INJECTED ENGINES

CIS Fuel Injection

1976–80 MODELS

1. To adjust the idle speed; run the engine until normal operating temperature is reached. The cooling fan must cycle at least once.

2. Adjust the ignition timing to specifications with the vacuum hoses connected and the engine at idle.

3. With a tachometer connected following the tach manufacturer's instructions, adjust the idle speed to specifications shown in the chart or on the underhood sticker. The idle adjustment screw is located on the throttle chamber near the accelerator linkage.

4. If a CO meter and CO adjusting tool (VW-P377) are available the CO idle mixture can be

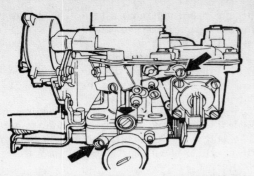

Idle mixture adjusting screw 1974 Dasher California (upper), 49 states (lower). Idle speed cover is at center

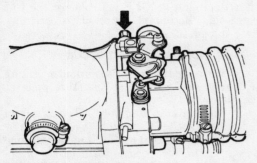

Idle speed adjusting screw (arrow) — CIS fuel injection (Rabbit shown)

adjusted. If these special tools are not available, take your car to a qualified mechanic for adjustment.

5. To adjust CO, remove the charcoal filter hose from the air cleaner. Turn on the headlights to high beam. Unplug the cooling fan (it must not come on during the idle speed adjustment). On 1980 California vehicles, disconnect the oxygen sensor connector.

6. Remove the plug from the CO adjusting hole and insert CO adjusting tool (VW-P377). Turn the adjusting tool clockwise (in) to raise the percentage of CO and counterclockwise (out) to lower the percentage of CO. Always con-

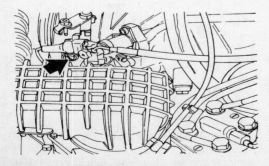

Dasher idle speed adjustment screw — CIS fuel injection

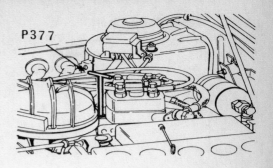

CO adjustment tool (PC77) — CIS fuel injection; note plug resting on battery

sult the emissions label or state or local requirements for proper CO concentrations.

CAUTION: *Do not push down on the adjusting tool or accelerate the engine with the tool in place.*

7. Remove the tool after each adjustment and accelerate the engine briefly before reading the CO value.

NOTE: *The plug covering the CO adjustment is attached to a long thin wire with a loop at the end. The plug is located next to the fuel distributor, which is identified by the four injector hoses attached at the top. Remove the plug by pulling on the wire loop.*

1981–84 MODELS EXCEPT 5-CYLINDER ENGINES

1. The engine must be at normal operating temperature.

2. Disconnect the crankcase breather hose at the cam cover and plug, on models through 1982. On 1983 models, except the 5 cylinder, allow hose opened to air. On 1982 Rabbit, Pick-Up, Scirocco and Jetta without an oxygen sensor, disconnect the charcoal filter hose from the air inlet boot. The canister is located on the left front apron.

3. Disconnect the two idle stabilizer plugs from the control unit and connect them together. Make sure all electrical accessories are turned to the **OFF** position. Unplug the electric cooling fan. The fan must not come on when adjusting the idle speed.

4. Connect a tachometer and timing light. Check the timing, adjust if necessary.

5. Check the idle speed against the specifications chart or the underhood sticker. Adjust the idle using the idle adjustment screw on the throttle chamber.

NOTE: *Only adjust the idle when the fan is not on.*

6. The CO adjustment on these engines is sealed to prevent unauthorized adjustment. The only way CO levels can be adjusted on these models is with special dealer tools which are very expensive.

Tach. Conv. Chart.

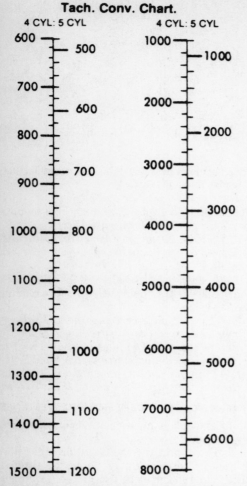

4 CYL: 5 CYL	4 CYL: 5 CYL
600 — 500	1000 — 1000
700 — 600	2000 — 2000
800 — 700	3000 — 3000
900 —	4000 —
1000 — 800	5000 — 4000
1100 — 900	6000 — 5000
1200 — 1000	7000 — 6000
1300 — 1100	8000 —
1400 — 1200	
1500 —	

Use this chart to convert the 4-cylinder tachometer reading to true idle speed on 5-cylinder models

1981–84 5-CYLINDER ENGINES

1. Check that there are no leaks in the exhaust system and connect Siemens 451 tester or equivalent according to the manufacturer's instructions. Make sure the TDC sending unit is installed snugly into the transmission housing.

2. Remove the cap from the T-connector.

3. Disconnect both crankcase breather hoses from the cylinder head cover and plug both T-connections at the cylinder head cover.

4. Disconnect both plugs at the idle stabilizer and plug the connectors together to bypass the unit. Make sure the connectors are tight.

5. Turn OFF all accessories. If any fuel lines were disconnected or replaced, start the engine and run it to 3000 rpm several times, then let idle for at least 2 minutes.

6. Start the engine and allow it to reach normal operating temperature. The radiator fan must come on at least once.

NOTE: *The radiator fan must not be running during all tests and adjustments.*

7. Check and adjust the idle speed if necessary using the idle speed adjusting screw located on the throttle housing.

8. The CO adjustment on these engines is sealed to prevent unauthorized adjustment. The only way CO levels can be adjusted on these models is with special dealer tools which are very expensive.

9. Check and adjust the ignition timing if necessary. Turn ignition OFF.

10. Readjust the idle speed, if necessary, then turn ignition OFF and remove the test equipment. Reconnect the crankcase breather hose and idle stabilizer.

1985–86 CABRIOLET AND SCIROCCO

1. Warm up the engine to normal operating temperature. The cooling fan must cycle at least once.

2. Stop the engine and turn all electrical accessories to the OFF position.

3. Unplug the cooling fan. It must not come on during the idle speed adjustment.

4. Connect a tachometer and timing light to the engine.

5. Start the engine and check the timing. Remember to remove and plug the line from the distributor advance. Adjust as necessary and connect the line to the distributor advance once the timing is within specs.

6. Pinch the hose going to the idle boost valve with a clamp.

7. Disconnect the cylinder head cover and crankcase breather hoses. Bend both hoses upward so they vent to the atmosphere.

8. Disconnect the hose that runs from the carbon canister to the air intake elbow at the

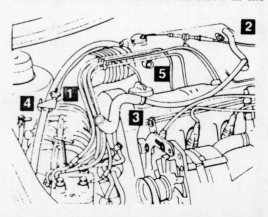

Hose locations for idle speed adjustment on Golf, GTI and Jetta with CIS fuel injection

T-connector. There are two hose connection on the canister. This hose is the one on the outside of the canister closest to the left wheel housing.

9. Check the idle speed with the tach and adjust to specification using the idle speed adjusting screw located in the throttle housing.

10. The CO adjustment on these engines is sealed to prevent unauthorized adjustment. The only way CO levels can be adjusted on these models is with special dealer tools which are very expensive.

11. Re-check the timing and adjust as necessary.

12. Stop the engine and connect all hoses. Disconnect the timing light and the tachometer. Plug in the cooling fan.

1985–86 GOLF, GTI AND JETTA

1. Warm up the engine to normal operating temperature. The cooling fan must cycle at least once.

2. Stop the engine and turn all electrical accessories to the **OFF** position.

3. Unplug the cooling fan. It must not come on during the idle speed adjustment.

4. Connect a tachometer and timing light to the engine.

5. Start the engine and check the timing. Adjust as necessary.

NOTE: *If any fuel lines were disconnected or replaced, start the engine and run it to 3000 rpm several times, then let idle for at least 2 minutes.*

6. Pinch and clamp hose (1) of the idle speed boost valve.

7. Remove hose (2) from the intake manifold and hose (3) from the air intake boot. Bend both hoses upward so they vent to the atmosphere.

8. Remove T- connector (4) from the carbon canister at the air intake boot. Rotate the T-connector 90° and insert the blank side with the 1.5mm (0.059 in.) restrictor into the air intake boot opening. Some engines are not equipped with this type of restrictor T- connector. If so, purchase plug 026 133 382D or equivalent plug that has the 1.5mm (0.059 in.) orifice built in.

9. Check the idle speed with the tach. If not as specified, use idle speed adjusting screw (5) to adjust it.

10. The CO adjustment on these engines is sealed to prevent unauthorized adjustment. The only way CO levels can be adjusted on these models is with special tools which are very expensive.

11. Re-check the timing and adjust as necessary.

12. Stop the engine and connect all hoses. Dis-

connect the timing light and the tachometer. Plug in the cooling fan.

CIS-E Fuel Injection

NOTE: *Certain 1.8L engines are equipped with a manual pre-heat valve located on the air cleaner housing. The valve is marked "S" (summer) and "W" (winter). When adjusting the idle speed, position the valve to S (unless work area is below freezing). After servicing, return the valve to the position that matches climate conditions.*

GOLF, GTI AND JETTA (EXCEPT 16V)

1. Warm up the engine to normal operating temperature. The cooling fan must cycle at least once.

2. Stop the engine and turn all electrical accessories to the **OFF** position.

3. Unplug the cooling fan. It must not come on during the idle speed adjustment.

4. Connect a tachometer and timing light to the engine.

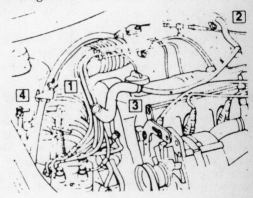

Hose locations for idle speed adjustment on Golf, GTI and Jetta with CIS-E fuel injection (except 16 valve)

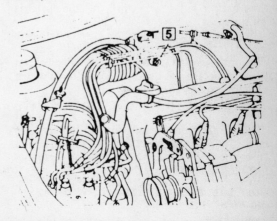

Idle speed adjusting screw on Golf, GTI and Jetta with CIS-E fuel injection (except 16 valve)

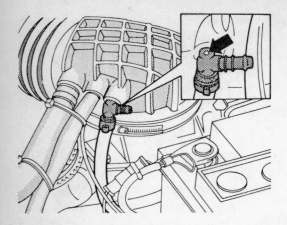

T-connector positioning for idle speed check on Scirocco 16V (Golf, GTI and Jetta 1.8L 16V similar)

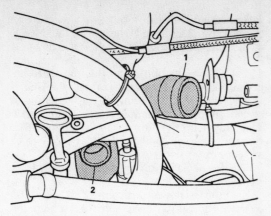

Crankcase hose positioning for idle speed check on Scirocco 16V (Golf, GTI and Jetta 1.8L 16V similar)

5. Start the engine and check the timing. Adjust as necessary.

NOTE: *If any fuel lines were disconnected or replaced, start the engine and run it to 3000 rpm several times, then let idle for at least 2 minutes.*

6. Remove hose (2) from the intake manifold and hose (3) from the air intake boot. Bend both hoses upward so they vent to the atmosphere.

7. Remove T- connector (4) from the carbon canister at the air intake boot. Rotate the T-connector 90° and insert the blank side with the 1.5mm (0.059 in.) restrictor into the air intake boot opening. Some engines are not equipped with this type of restrictor T- connector. If so, purchase plug 026 133 382D or equivalent plug that has the 1.5mm (0.059 in.) orifice built in.

8. Check the idle speed with the tach. If not as specified, use idle speed adjusting screw (5) to adjust it. First turn the screw all the way in, then back it out slowly until the idle speed is within specs.

9. The CO adjustment on these engines is sealed to prevent unauthorized adjustment. The only way CO levels can be adjusted on these models is with special dealer tools which are very expensive.

10. Re-check the timing and adjust as necessary.

11. Stop the engine and connect all hoses. Install the T-connector in it's original position. Disconnect the timing light and the tachometer. Plug in the cooling fan.

GOLF, GTI, JETTA AND SCIROCCO WITH 16V ENGINES

Engine idle speed is controlled by the idle stabilizer valve and is not adjustable. To check the idle speed, perform the following:

1. Warm up the engine to normal operating temperature. The cooling fan must cycle at least once. Make sure the there are no exhaust leaks.

2. Stop the engine and turn all electrical accessories to the **OFF** position.

3. Unplug the cooling fan. It must not come on during the idle speed check.

4. Connect a tachometer and timing light to the engine.

5. Start the engine and check the timing. Adjust as necessary.

NOTE: *If any fuel lines were disconnected or replaced, start the engine and run it to 3000 rpm several times, then let idle for at least 2 minutes.*

6. Remove the large crankcase breather hose (1) from crankcase vent (2) opening and bend the hose upward so that it vents to the atmosphere.

7. Remove the angled T-connector from the the intake air boot. Turn the T-connector 90° and insert blank side with 1.5mm (0.059 in.) restrictor into the hole in the intake boot as shown in the accompanying illustration.

8. Turn the ignition switch to the **ON** position and listen to the idle stabilizer valve. It should hum or vibrate when the key is turned on. If not, refer to Chapter 4 for test procedures to see if the valve is working properly.

9. Start the engine and check the idle speed.

10. The CO adjustment on these engines is sealed to prevent unauthorized adjustment. The only way CO levels can be adjusted on these models is with special dealer tools which are very expensive.

11. Connect the T-connector to the air intake boot in it's original position and connect the large hose to the crankcase vent.

12. Disconnect the test equipment and plug in the cooling fan.

QUANTUM WITH 4-CYLINDER ENGINES

1. The following must be checked prior to adjustment: engine oil temperature at normal operating 176°F (80°C), radiator fan and air conditioning off, no exhaust system leaks and oxygen sensor operating properly. When warming up the engine, make sure the cooling fan cycles once.

2. Connect a tachometer and timing light to the engine.

3. Start the engine and check the timing. Adjust as necessary.

NOTE: *If any fuel lines were disconnected or replaced, start the engine and run it to 3000 rpm several times, then let idle for at least 2 minutes.*

4. Clamp the idle speed boost hose tightly to prevent flow.

5. Pull the breather hoses from the cylinder head to allow fresh air to circulation (hose at intake manifold and hose from air cleaner).

6. Remove the protective cap from the carbon canister T-connector and leave it open.

7. Start the engine and check the idle speed. If the idle speed is not within specs, adjust it using the idle speed screw located in the throttle housing.

8. The CO adjustment on these engines is sealed to prevent unauthorized adjustment. The only way CO levels can be adjusted on these models is with special dealer tools which are very expensive.

9. Install the T-connector cap and connect the hoses.

10. Disconnect the test equipment and plug in the cooling fan.

QUANTUM WITH 5-CYLINDER ENGINES

Engine idle speed is controlled by the idle stabilizer and cannot be adjusted. To check the idle speed, perform the following:

1. The following must be checked prior to adjustment: engine oil temperature at normal operating 176°F (80°C), radiator fan and air conditioning off, no exhaust system leaks and oxygen sensor operating properly. When warming up the engine, make sure the cooling fan cycles once.

2. Connect a tachometer and timing light to the engine.

3. Start the engine and check the timing. Adjust as necessary. Unplug the cooling fan. It must not come on during the idle speed check.

NOTE: *If any fuel lines were disconnected or replaced, start the engine and run it to 3000 rpm several times, then let idle for at least 2 minutes.*

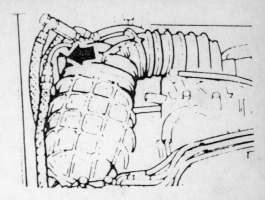

Charcoal canister T-connection location on 5-cylinder engine

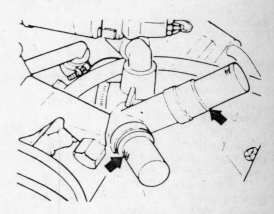

Sealing off the crankcase ventilation hoses on 5-cylinder engine for idle speed adjustment

4. Disconnect both crankcase ventilation hoses and seal them with masking tape or plug them.

5. Remove the cap from the carbon canister T-connector and leave it open.

6. Turn the ignition switch to the **ON** position and listen to the idle stabilizer valve. It should hum or vibrate when the key is turned on. If not, refer to Chapter 4 for test procedures to see if the valve is working properly.

7. Start the engine and check the idle speed.

8. The CO adjustment on these engines is sealed to prevent unauthorized adjustment. The only way CO levels can be adjusted on these models is with special dealer tools which are very expensive.

9. Install the carbon canister cap and connect the crankcase hoses.

10. Disconnect the test equipment and plug in the cooling fan.

FOX

1. Warm up the engine to normal operating

temperature. The cooling fan must cycle at least once. Make sure the there are no exhaust leaks.

2. Stop the engine and turn all electrical accessories to the **OFF** position.

3. Unplug the cooling fan. It must not come on during the idle speed check.

4. Connect a tachometer and timing light to the engine.

5. Start the engine and check the timing. Adjust as necessary.

NOTE: *If any fuel lines were disconnected or replaced, start the engine and run it to 3000 rpm several times, then let idle for at least 2 minutes.*

6. Unplug the connectors from the idle speed boost valves.

7. Pull the crankcase breather hose (2) from the valve cover and vent it to the atmosphere.

8. Remove the suction hose from the charcoal canister.

9. Pinch the idle boost solenoid hose and clamp it.

10. Start the engine and check the idle speed. If the idle speed is not within specs, adjust it by turning the idle speed screw (4) located in the throttle housing.

11. The CO adjustment on these engines is sealed to prevent unauthorized adjustment. The only way CO levels can be adjusted on these models is with special dealer tools which are very expensive.

12. Stop the engine and disconnect the test equipment. Connect all hoses. Plug in the idle boost valve and cooling fan connectors.

PASSAT

Idle speed is controlled by the idle stabilization system and is not adjustable.

Digifant II

1987–90 GOLF, JETTA AND 1990 CABRIOLET

1. Start engine and run until it reaches normal operating temperature. The cooling fan must cycle at least once.

2. Turn all electrical accessories to the **OFF** position.

3. Connect a timing light and tachometer to the engine.

4. Start the engine and let it idle. Disconnect the coolant temperature sensor.

5. Rev the engine over 2100 rpm at least four times and then let it idle normally. This cancels the hot start idle function.

6. Check the timing. Adjust as necessary.

7. Check the idle speed. To adjust the idle speed to specification, turn the idle adjusting

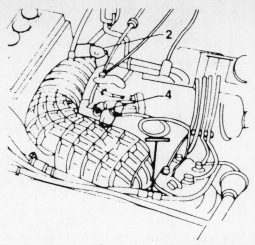

Crankcase breather hose and idle speed adjustment location on Fox

screw (1). Turn clockwise to decrease rpm and counterclockwise to increase.

8. When all adjustments are complete, reconnect the coolant temperature sensor.

9. Check the timing again, then remove all test equipment.

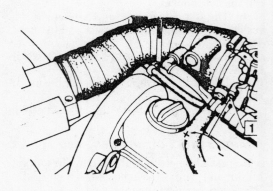

Idle speed adjusting screw location on 1987–90 Golf, Jetta and 1990 Cabriolet (Digifant II)

Diesel Injection System

IDLE SPEED/MAXIMUM SPEED ADJUSTMENTS

Volkswagen diesel engines have both an idle speed and a maximum speed adjustment. The maximum engine speed adjustment prevents the engine from over-revving and destroying itself. The adjusters are located side by side on top of the injection pump. The screw closest to the engine is the idle speed adjuster, while the outer screw is the maximum speed adjuster.

Because the diesel engine has no conven-

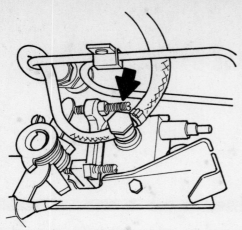

Adjust diesel engine idle speed at the inner screw (arrow). Adjust the maximum speed at the outer screw (no arrow). Lock screws in place with sealer

A special adaptor (VW 1324) is necessary to hook up an external tachometer on diesel engines

tional ignition, you will need a special adapter (VW 1324) to connect your tachometer. VW makes a ignition tester for diesel engines (part number 1367), if you wish to purchase one. DO NOT use the tachometer on the instrument panel (if so equipped), as they are notorious for being inaccurate. You should check with the manufacturer of your tachometer to see if it will work with diesel engines.

NOTE: *The sticker on your pre-1978 Rabbit may indicate an idle range of 850–950 rpm. This has been altered by Volkswagen to 770–870 rpm.*

1. The idle and maximum speed must be adjusted with the engine warm (normal operating temperature) and all the electrical accessories switched to the **OFF** position.

2. Adjust all engines to the specified idle speed.

3. When adjustment is correct, lock the locknut on the screw and apply non-hardening thread sealer (Loctite® or similar) to prevent the screw from vibrating loose.

4. The maximum speed for all engines is between 5500 and 5600 rpm (through 1980). From 1981 on, the maximum speed for all engines is 5300–5400 rpm or 5050–5150 (turbo). If it is not in this range, loosen the screw and correct the speed (turning the screw clockwise decreases rpm).

5. Lock the nut on the adjusting screw and apply a dab of thread sealer.

CAUTION: *Do not attempt to squeeze more power out of your engine by raising the maximum speed. If you do, you'll probably be in for a major overhaul in the not too distant future.*

Engine and Engine Overhaul

3

ENGINE ELECTRICAL

Point Type Ignition System Ignition Coil

COIL RESISTANCE CHECK

1. Label, then disconnect all wires from the coil terminals.
2. Measure the **primary** resistance between terminal 15 (+) and terminal 1 (–). Resistance should be 1.7–2.1Ω.
3. Measure the **secondary** resistance between terminal 1 (–) and the coil wire terminal (terminal 4). Resistance should be 7000–12,000Ω.
4. If the resistance is not as specified, replace the ignition coil.

REMOVAL AND INSTALLATION

1. Tag and disconnect the negative and positive terminal wires from the top of the coil.
2. Remove the coil wire from the coil.
3. Using a flat screwdriver, loosen the adjusting screw which secures the coil inside the clamp.
4. Remove the coil from the vehicle.
5. Install in the reverse order.

Electronic Ignition System Ignition Coil

A defective Hall ignition coil cannot be checked with standard coil testing equipment. If there is no high tension current and all other components of the ignition system check out, see if you're getting a spark from the coil wire to the distributor cap by unplugging the coil wire at the distributor, holding the end of it with insulated pliers about 13mm ($^1/_2$ in.) from ground (engine block, etc.) and turning over the engine. If a weak or no spark is obtained, try replacing the coil.

PRELIMINARY SYSTEM CHECKS

1. Make sure that ignition is in **OFF** position before test equipment or system connectors are either connected or disconnected.
2. When cranking engine without starting, as for a compression test, disconnect wire from distributor, and connect to ground. Do not hand hold wire.
3. DO NOT install a standard ignition coil in the system.
4. DO NOT connect a condenser/suppressor or powered test light to negative terminal of ignition coil.
5. DO NOT connect any 12-volt test instruments to positive terminal of ignition coil, as this could damage electronic components.
6. When boost-starting, DO NOT connect a quick-charger for more than 1 minute, nor exceed 16.5 volts with booster.

COIL RESISTANCE CHECK

Quantum, Golf, GTI, Jetta (except 16V), Scirocco (except 16V) and Cabriolet

1. Label, then disconnect the wires from the ignition coil terminals
2. With an ohmmeter, measure the *primary* resistance between positive terminal **15** and negative terminal **1** as shown in the accompanying illustration. The resistance should be 0.52–0.76Ω for CIS/CIS-E equipped cars and 0.65–0.79Ω for cars equipped with Digifant II.
3. Measure the *secondary* resistance between negative terminal **1** and the coil tower as shown in the accompanying illustration. The resistance should be 2400–3500 for CIS/CIS-E

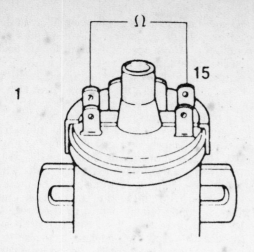

Measuring ignition coil primary resistance — Golf, GTI, Jetta Scirocco (except 16-valve) and Cabriolet

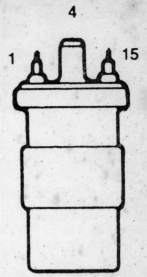

Ignition coil terminal identification on Passat, Corrado, Scirocco 16-valve, GTI 16-valve, Jetta 16-valve engines

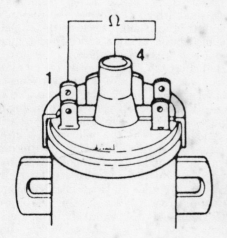

Measuring ignition coil secondary resistance — Golf, GTI, Jetta Scirocco (except 16-valve) and Cabriolet

equipped cars and 6900–8500 for cars equipped with Digifant II.

4. If the resistance is not as specified, replace the ignition coil.

Passat, Corrado, Scirocco 16V, GTI 16V and Jetta 16V

1. Label, then disconnect the wires from the ignition coil terminals.

2. With an ohmmeter, measure the *primary* resistance between terminals **1** and **15**. The resistance should be 0.6–0.8Ω.

3. With an ohmmeter, measure the *secondary* resistance between terminals **15** and **4**. The resistance should be 6900–8500Ω.

4. If the resistance is not as specified, replace the ignition coil.

Fox

1. Label, then disconnect the wires from the ignition coil terminals

2. With an ohmmeter, measure the *primary* resistance between positive terminal **4** and negative terminal **1** as shown in the accompanying illustration. The resistance should be 0.52–0.76Ω.

3. Measure the *secondary* resistance between negative terminal **1** and terminal **15** as shown in the accompanying illustration. The resistance should be 2400–3500Ω.

4. If the resistance is not as specified, replace the ignition coil.

REMOVAL AND INSTALLATION

1. Tag and disconnect the negative and positive terminal wires from the top of the coil.

2. Remove the coil wire from the coil.

3. Disconnect the engine ground strap from the coil, if installed. On CIS-E Motronic coils, unplug the harness connector from the power stage module on the side of the coil.

4. Using a flatblade screwdriver, loosen the adjusting screw which secures the coil inside the clamp.

5. Remove the coil from the vehicle.

6. Installation is the reverse of the removal procedure.

Ballast Resistor

CHECKING

All 1976 and later Dashers and other later models, have replaced the ballast resistor with a resistor wire which runs from terminal 15 (+) of the ignition coil to terminal C15 at the back of the fuse block/relay panel. The color of the resistor wire is usually clear with violet stripes.

To test the resistor wire, disconnect it from the ignition coil and unplug multipin connector C from the back of the fuse/relay panel. Connect an ohmmeter to each end of the resistor wire (resistor wire is terminal C15 at the fuse/relay panel). The resistance should be between 0.85–0.95Ω for the Rabbit, Golf, Jetta and Scirocco, 0.52–0.76Ω for the Fox and approximately 1 for Dasher and Quantum. The old type ballast resistor can also be checked using this method. Before checking, disconnect all wires from the ballast resistor.

Distributor

Some distributors incorporate both centrifugal advance and vacuum advance and retard ignition timing mechanisms. Centrifugal advance is controlled by two weights located beneath the breaker plate. As engine speed increases, centrifugal force moves the weights out from the distributor shaft and advances the ignition by changing the position of the cam in relation to the shaft. This advanced positioning of the cam will then open the breaker points sooner and ignite the air fuel mixture quickly enough in relation to piston speed. Centrifugal advance is necessary because as engine speed increases, the time period available to ignite the mixture decreases. At idle speed, the ignition setting is, say, 3° ATDC. This is adequate for the spark plug to ignite the mixture at 925 rpm, but not at 2,500 rpm. The weights, governed by spring, move out at a predetermined rate to advance the timing to match engine speed.

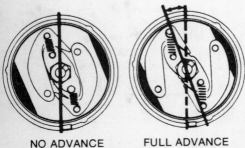

NO ADVANCE   FULL ADVANCE

Centrifugal advance weight operation

Centrifugal advance is not completely sufficient to provide the proper advance under all conditions. To compensate for different load and speed conditions, there is vacuum advance/retard. Under light load conditions, such as very gradual acceleration and low speed cruising, the throttle opening is not sufficient to draw enough air/fuel mixture into the cylinder. Vacuum advance is used to provide the extra spark advance needed to ignite the smaller mixture. The round can on the side of the distributor is the vacuum advance/retard unit. The rubber hose supplies vacuum from the intake manifold to draw on the diaphragm in the unit which is connected by a link to the breaker plate in the distributor. Under part throttle operation, the vacuum advance moves the breaker plate as necessary to provide the correct advance for efficient operation. At idle, the vacuum retard unit retards the timing to reduce exhaust emission.

The distributor is gear driven by an intermediate shaft which also drives the fuel pump. The distributor shaft also turns the oil pump. The distributor location varies from engine to engine and is easily accessible.

Hall effect type distributors have no centrifugal or vacuum advance. These type of distributors use a Hall sensor which is actuated by a trigger wheel. The trigger wheel contains four windows, one for each cylinder. Before the piston reaches TDC, the hall sensor transmits a signal to the ECU. The ECU determines engine speed and crankshaft position from this signal. Ignition timing is calculated by the ECU according to engine load and speed based on information from a network of engine sensors. The computer will advance the timing as the engine speed increases and retard the timing with increases in engine load.

REMOVAL AND INSTALLATION

NOTE: *Aside from replacing the cap, rotor, breaker points (if equipped), and the condenser, refer all distributor repair to a VW dealer or ignition specialty shop. They are equipped with a distributor test machine which permits diagnosis of any problems.*

1. Disconnect the coil high tension wire from the distributor. This is the large wire which goes into the center of the cap.
2. Detach the smaller primary wire which also connects from the coil to the distributor or unfasten the spring clip and disconnect the connector plug at the distributor housing. Unplug any wire connectors from base of the distributor.
3. Unsnap the clips and remove the distributor cap. Position it out of the way.
4. Use the crankshaft pulley nut or bump

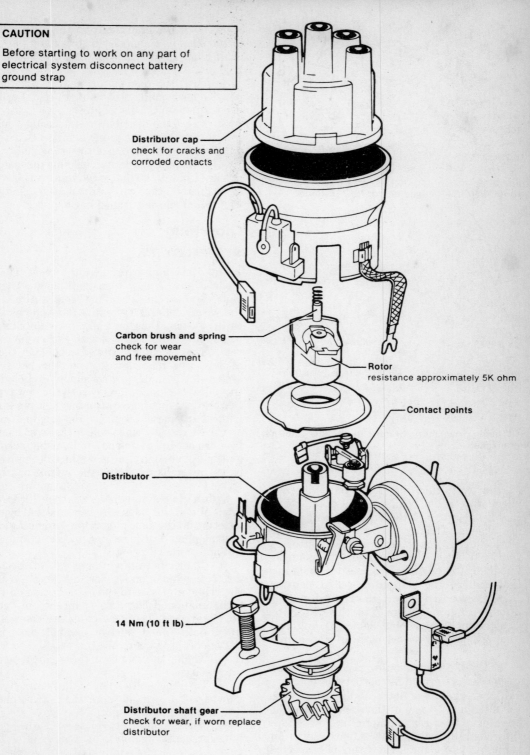

CAUTION

Before starting to work on any part of
electrical system disconnect battery
ground strap

Distributor cap
check for cracks and
corroded contacts

Carbon brush and spring
check for wear
and free movement

Rotor
resistance approximately 5K ohm

Contact points

Distributor

14 Nm (10 ft lb)

Distributor shaft gear
check for wear, if worn replace
distributor

Typical breaker point type distributor

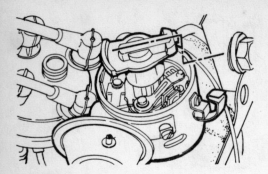

Rotor/distributor alignment for No. 1 cylinder

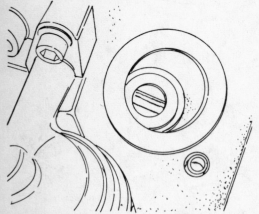

Oil pump driveshaft slot must be parallel with the crankshaft

the starter to turn the engine until the rotor aligns with the index mark on the outer edge of the distributor and the engine timing marks are aligned. Chapter 2 shows all the timing mark illustrations. Matchmark the bottom of the distributor housing and its mounting flange on the engine. This is extra insurance that you'll get the distributor back in correctly.

5. Loosen and remove the hex bolt and lift off the retaining flange. Lift the distributor straight out of the engine. Some distributor retaining bolts are sealed with an anti-tamper cap.

6. Check the distributor gasket for wear. If the gasket is worn or damaged, replace it.

If the engine has not been disturbed while the distributor was out, then reinstall the distributor in the reverse order of removal. Carefully align the matchmarks. After the distributor is in place and all the wiring is connected, adjust the ignition timing and check the idle speed as described in Chapter 2.

If the engine has been rotated while the distributor was out, i.e., accidently started, then proceed as follows:

1. Turn the crankshaft so that the No. 1 piston is on its compression stroke and the OT timing marks are aligned with the V-shaped pointer.

2. Turn the distributor so that the rotor points approximately 15° before the No. 1 cylinder position on the distributor.

3. Insert the distributor and, using a long screwdriver, turn the pump shaft so that it is parallel to the centerline of the crankshaft.

4. Install the distributor, aligning the matchmarks. Tighten the flange retaining nut.

5. Install the cap. Adjust the ignition timing and idle as outlined in Chapter 2.

Glow Plug

SYSTEM CHECK

The 1982 and later diesels (except Turbo models) have a new type quick-glow system. Nominal glow time is seven seconds. Although the wiring for this system is the same as the earlier system, the glow plugs and relay cannot be paired or interchanged with earlier parts or vice versa, except for 1978 Dasher. On these models, you can convert from the old type system to the new type by simply exchanging the old style plugs and relay with the new type. Because of the higher combustion pressure with Turbodiesel engines the engine may smoke excessively when cold if the swirl chambers are not fully warmed up. By using normal glow plugs enough heat is produced to prevent excessive smoking when the engine is first started.

Quick glow system plugs are identified by a brass nut on the plugs wire terminal and by red lettering on the glow plug relay. **Normal glow** system plugs are identified by an aluminum nut and white lettering.

1. Connect a test light between No. 4 cylinder (rear cylinder on Dasher and Quantum and the cylinder closest to the driver's side on the Golf, Rabbit and Jetta) glow plug and a suitable engine ground. The glow plugs are connected by a flat, coated busbar (located near the bottom of the cylinder head).

2. Unplug the wire from the engine temperature sensor.

3. Turn the ignition key to the heating (preglow) position for no more than 15 seconds. The test light should light.

4. There should be voltage the the glow plug for approximately five seconds after the glow plug indicator lamp goes out. Voltage is applied as a normal part of the controlled preheat period. If not, possible problems include the glow plug relay, the ignition switch and the fuse box relay plater and the glow plug fuse or a break in the wire to the relay terminal.

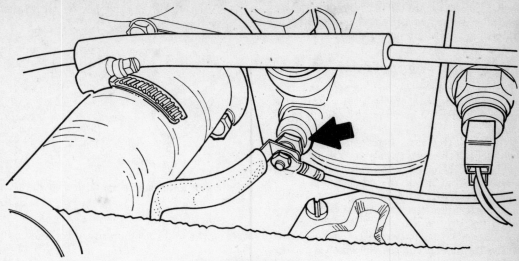

No. 4 cylinder glow plug

5. If the test lamp lights, perform the individual glow plug checks as described below.

INDIVIDUAL GLOW PLUG TEST

1. Remove the wire and busbar from the glow plugs.
2. Connect a test light to the battery positive terminal.
3. Touch the test light probe to each glow plug in turn.
4. If the test light lights, the plug is good and the cause of the problem may lie in the fuel system.
5. If the test light does not light, replace the plug.

A common cause of glow plug failure is worn glow plug tips. This is due to faulty injector operation in the related cylinder. This type of condition has nothing to do with the operation of the glow plugs. If you find that you are constantly replacing glow plugs, and have eliminated all possible electrical faults, check the fuel injector(s) for damage or have the injectors

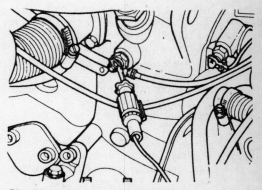

Checking glow plug supply voltage

pressure and leak tested by a diesel injector repair shop.

REMOVAL AND INSTALLATION

1. Loosen the nut and disconnect the wire from the glow plug terminal.
2. Using the proper size socket, remove the plug from engine.
3. Install the new plug and torque it to 29 ft. lbs. on Quantum, Rabbit and Dasher and 22 ft. lbs. on Golf and Jetta.

NOTE: *Do not exceed the specified torque when installing the glow plug. Doing so will close the plug ring gap and cause premature failure.*

4. Connect the wire to the glow plug terminal and tighten the nut.

Alternator

Your car is equipped with either a Bosch or Motorola alternator, which produce alternating current (AC), as opposed to generators, which

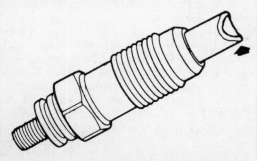

Worn tips are a common cause of glow plug failure

produce direct current (DC). The regulators on these alternators are contained on the alternator housing, therefore no adjustments are possible.

ALTERNATOR PRECAUTIONS

To prevent damage to the alternator and regulator, the following precautionary measures must be taken when working with the electrical system.

1. Never reverse battery connections. Always check the battery polarity visually. This is to be done before any connections are made to be sure that all of the connections correspond to the battery ground polarity of the car.

2. Booster batteries for starting must be connected properly. Make sure that the positive cable of the booster battery is connected to the positive terminal of the battery which is getting the boost.

3. Disconnect the battery cables before using a fast charger; the charger has a tendency to force current through the diodes in the opposite direction for which they were designed. This burns out the diodes.

4. Never use a fast charger as a booster for starting the vehicle.

5. Never disconnect the battery cables while the engine is running.

6. Do not ground the alternator output terminal.

7. Do not operate the alternator on an open circuit with the field energized.

8. Do not attempt to polarize an alternator.

9. Disconnect the battery cables before using an electric arc welder on the car.

REMOVAL AND INSTALLATION

The alternator and voltage regulator are combined in one housing. No voltage adjustment can be made with this unit. As with the distributor, repairs to the alternator should be made by an authorized VW dealer. The regulator can be replaced without removing the alternator, just unbolt it from the rear.

1. Disconnect the battery cables and remove any interference needed to gain access to the alternator and it's mounting bolts.

2. Remove the multiconnector retaining bracket and unplug the connector from the rear of the alternator. Label each wire and terminal with masking tape to ensure proper assembly.

3. Loosen and remove the top mounting nut and bolt.

4. Using a hex socket inserted through the timing belt cover (it is not necessary to remove the cover), loosen the lower mounting bolt. Some alternators have a toothed bracket and tensioning gear for belt tension adjustment.

Remove the lower alternator bolt through the timing cover

Loosen the bracket mounting, pivot and cradle bolts.

5. Slide the alternator over and remove the alternator belt.

6. Remove the lower nut and bolt. Don't lose the spacers or rubber isolators.

7. Remove the alternator.

NOTE: *Remember when installing the alternator that it is not necessary to polarize the system.*

8. Install the alternator with the lower bolt. Don't tighten at this point.

9. Install the alternator belt over the pulleys.

10. Loosely install the top mounting bolt and pivot the alternator over until the belt is correctly tensioned as explained in Chapter 1.

11. Finally tighten the top and bottom bolts.

12. Connect the alternator and battery wires. Install any interfering component at this time.

Voltage Regulator

The voltage regulator is attached to the rear of the alternator. Since no adjustment can be performed on the regulator, it is serviced by replacement ONLY.

1. Remove the regulator mounting screws.

2. Disconnect the electrical connectors and remove the regulator.

3. To install, reverse the removal procedures. Care must be taken to install the electrical connectors in their proper location. Label the wires and connection points with masking tape to ensure proper assembly.

Battery

REMOVAL AND INSTALLATION

CAUTION: *Battery electrolyte (acid) is highly corrosive and can damage both you and the paintwork. Be careful when lifting*

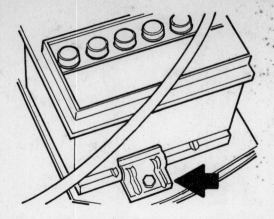

The battery is retained by a clamp

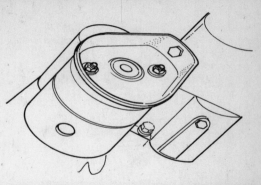

Rabbit and Scirocco old type manual transmission starter installation — be sure bolts (2) have enough clearance in the elongated holes of the bracket (1) so there is no strain

the battery in and out of the engine compartment.

1. Disconnect the battery cables, negative cable first.
2. Put on heavy work gloves.
3. Loosen the retaining clamp bolt and remove the clamp.
4. Disconnect the small electrical lead for the computer sensor.
5. Lift the battery carefully out of the tray.
6. Clean all corrosion deposits from the battery tray and the retaining plate. Spray them with rust preventive paint.

7. Install the battery in reverse order of removal. Polish the inside of the cables and give them a coat of grease or silicone compound before installation.

Starter

REMOVAL AND INSTALLATION

All Models Except Dasher Diesel, Corrado, Passat and Fox with Air Conditioning

1. Disconnect the battery ground cable.
2. Jack up the right front of the car and support on jackstands.

Troubleshooting Basic Charging System Problems

Problem	Cause	Solution
Noisy alternator	• Loose mountings • Loose drive pulley • Worn bearings • Brush noise • Internal circuits shorted (High pitched whine)	• Tighten mounting bolts • Tighten pulley • Replace alternator • Replace alternator • Replace alternator
Squeal when starting engine or accelerating	• Glazed or loose belt	• Replace or adjust belt
Indicator light remains on or ammeter indicates discharge (engine running)	• Broken fan belt • Broken or disconnected wires • Internal alternator problems • Defective voltage regulator	• Install belt • Repair or connect wiring • Replace alternator • Replace voltage regulator
Car light bulbs continually burn out—battery needs water continually	• Alternator/regulator overcharging	• Replace voltage regulator/alternator
Car lights flare on acceleration	• Battery low • Internal alternator/regulator problems	• Charge or replace battery • Replace alternator/regulator
Low voltage output (alternator light flickers continually or ammeter needle wanders)	• Loose or worn belt • Dirty or corroded connections • Internal alternator/regulator problems	• Replace or adjust belt • Clean or replace connections • Replace alternator or regulator

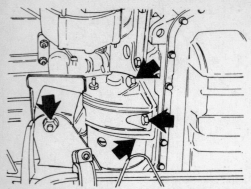

Dasher diesel starter removal — remove the engine mount and carrier on the starter side (arrows)

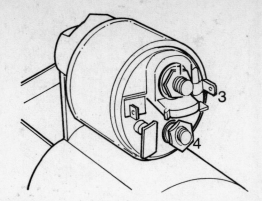

Rabbit, Jetta, Scirocco starter installation — (1) from battery (+) terminal, (2) from terminal 15a to ignition coil terminal 15, (3) from starter switch and (94) field winding connection

3. Mark with tape and then disconnect the two small wires from the starter solenoid. One wire connects to the ignition coil and the second to the ignition switch through the wiring harness.

4. Disconnect the large cable, which is the positive battery cable, from the solenoid.

5. Remove the starter retaining nuts and/or bolts.

6. Pull the starter straight out.

7. To install, lift the starter into place on the engine, support it by hand and install the mounting fasteners. On 1.6L and 1.8L Golf, GTI and Jetta engines with manual transmissions, torque the starter mounting bolts to 43 ft. lbs. On all other models, torque the starter mounting bolts to 14 ft. lbs.

8. Connect starter solenoid wires. Make sure that the wires are connected to the proper terminals and make sure the wire nuts are tight.

9. Lower the vehicle.

10. Connect the negative battery cable.

Dasher Diesel and Fox with Air Conditioning

1. Disconnect the battery ground cable.

2. Support the weight of the engine with either Volkswagen special tool 10-222 or use a jack with a block of wood under the oil pan. Don't jack the engine too high, just take the weight off the motor mounts. Be careful not to bend the oil pan.

3. On Dasher diesel, remove the engine/transmission cover plate.

4. On Dasher diesel, unbolt and remove the starter side motor mount and carrier. On Fox, remove the mounting bolts from the engine mount support, rubber engine mount lower nut and clamp screw. Then, remove the engine mount support and mount.

5. Disconnect and mark the starter wiring.

6. Remove the bolts holding the starter and remove the starter.

7. Install the starter and tighten the nuts and bolt to 14 ft. lbs.

8. Connect the starter solenoid wires. Make sure that the wires are connected to the proper terminals and the wire nuts are tight.

9. Install the engine mounts and related components.

10. Lower the engine or remove the engine support.

11. Connect the battery cable.

Corrado and Passat

1. Disconnect the battery ground cable.

2. Support the weight of the engine with either Volkswagen special tool 10-222 (and lug set 10-222A) or use a jack with a block of wood under the oil pan. Don't jack the engine too high, just take the weight off the motor mounts. Be careful not to bend the oil pan.

3. Label and disconnect the wiring from the starter solenoid. On Corrado, some of the wires are secured by a clip. Pry the ends of the clip a

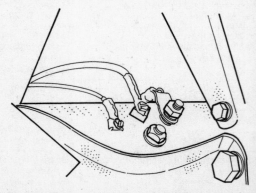

Dasher starter installation — (A) from starter switch, (B) from terminal 15 on coil, (C) from battery (+) terminal

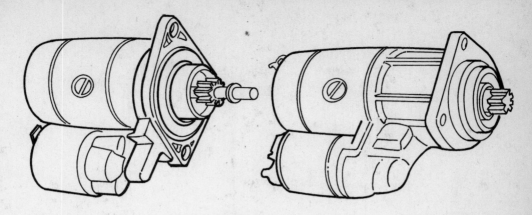

New and old type starter motors

part and remove the wiring. On Passat the starter/alternator wiring harness is secured by two wire ties. Cut these ties to release the starter wiring harness.

4. Unplug the harness connector(s) from the starter solenoid. On Corrado, there is a single connector. On Passat, there is one black and one white connector.

5. Support the starter by hand.

6. Remove the upper starter mounting bolt.

7. Pull the starter out and lower it to the ground.

8. To install, lift the starter into place and install the upper mounting bolt. Torque the bolt to 44 ft. lbs on both Corrado and Passat.

9. Connect the starter solenoid wires. Make sure that the wires are connected to their respective terminals and make sure the wire nuts are tight. On Corrado, neatly tuck the wiring back into the clip and bend the clip ends to hold the wires in place. On Passat, install two new wire ties and pull them tight.

10. Lower the engine or remove the engine support.

11. Connect the negative battery cable.

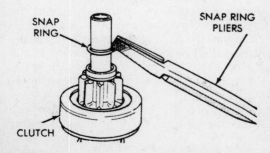

Remove the circlip to remove the starter drive

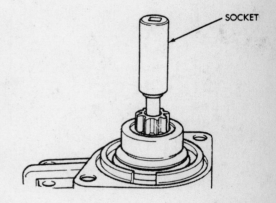

Remove the stop ring over the circlip with a socket

OVERHAUL

1. Remove the solenoid.

2. Remove the end bearing cap.

3. Loosen both of the long housing screws.

4. Remove the lockwasher and spacer washers.

5. Remove the long housing screws and remove the end cover.

6. Pull the brushes out of the brush housing.

7. Remove the brush housing assembly.

8. Loosen the nut on the solenoid housing, remove the sealing disc, and remove the solenoid operating lever.

9. Loosen the large screws on the side of the starter housing and remove the field coil along with the brushes from the starter housing. Measure the length of the brushes. Brushes should be 7–13mm ($^{9}/_{32}$–$^{1}/_{2}$ in.) long.

NOTE: *If the brushes require replacement, the field coil and brushes and/or the brush housing and its brushes must be replaced as a unit. Have the armature commutator*

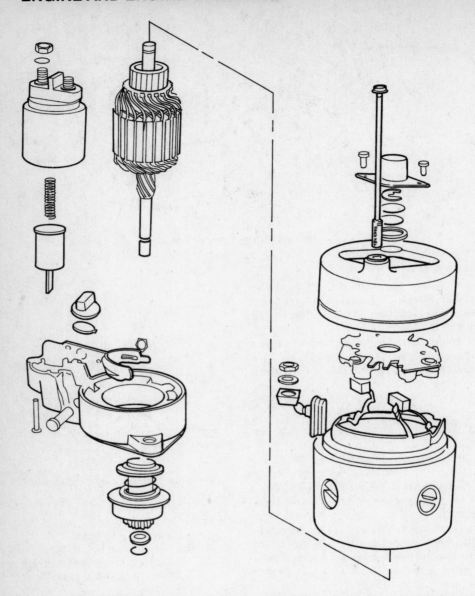

Exploded view of typical starter (Dasher and old type Rabbit, Jetta and Scirocco)

turned at a machine shop if it is out-of-round, scored, or grooved.

10. If the starter drive is being replaced, push the stop ring down using a socket and remove the circlip at the end of the shaft. Remove the snapring and starter drive.

11. Press the starter bushing from the cover.

To assemble the starter:

12. To install the cover bushing, immerse the cover in hot water for five minutes, then press in a new bushing.

13. Install the starter drive with a new snapring. Install a new stop ring onto the armature shaft and press down with a socket until the circlip can be installed easily. Use a new circlip. Make sure the stop ring turns easily on the armature shaft once the circlip is seated in the grooves of the armature shaft. Slide the armature and drive assembly into the starter housing.

14. Replace the brushes if they are not within the specified length. This is described below.

15. Place the field coil and brush assembly into the starter housing and install the the two side retaining screws.

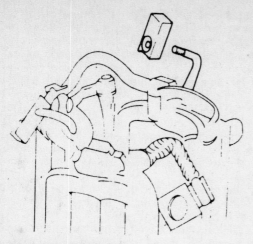

Starter brush removal

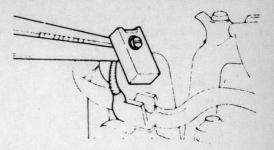

Starter brush installation

BRUSH REPLACEMENT

1. Remove the brush from the brush holder by smashing the end to free it from the lead.

2. Clean the old solder and corrosion from the lead with sandpaper.

3. Insert the end of the lead into the new brush.

4. Solder the lead into the brush by filling the brush opening with rosin core solder. A small soldering iron rated at about 150 watts is recommended to do the job.

5. Smooth the outer surface of the soldered connection with a jewelers file or sandpaper until the surface of the brush is flat.

16. Install the solenoid operating lever, sealing disc and housing nut.

17. Install the brush housing.

18. Install the brushes into the brush housing.

19. Install the end cover and long cover screws.

20. Install the spacer washers and lockwashers.

21. Install the two long housing screws.

22. Install the bearing end cap.

23. Connect the actuating lever to the starter solenoid and install the solenoid.

SOLENOID REPLACEMENT

1. Remove the starter.

2. Remove the nut which secures the connector strip on the end of the solenoid.

3. Take out the two retaining screws on the mounting bracket and withdraw the solenoid after it has been unhooked from the operating lever.

4. Installation is the reverse of removal. In order to facilitate engagement of the lever the pinion should be pulled out as far as possible when inserting the solenoid.

ENGINE MECHANICAL

Design

GASOLINE ENGINE

Rabbit, Golf, Scirocco, Cabriolet and Jetta

The engine is an inline 4-cylinder with single overhead camshaft. The engine is inclined 30° to the rear. The center of gravity is in front of the axle, thereby providing lighter steering and better handling. The crankshaft runs in five bearings with thrust being taken on the center bearing. The cylinder block is cast iron. A steel reinforced belt drives the intermediate shaft and camshaft. The intermediate shaft drives the oil pump, distributor, and fuel pump.

BATTERY AND STARTER SPECIFICATIONS

(All models use 12 volt, negative ground system)

Year/Model	Battery Amp Hour Capacity	Lock Test			No Load Test			Brush Spring Tension (oz)	Minimum Brush Length (in)
		Amps	Volts	Torque (ft. lbs.)	Amps	Volts	RPM		
All	45/54*	280–370	7.5	2.42	33–55	11.5	6000–8000	35.5	0.5

*w/AC

The cylinder head is lightweight aluminum alloy. The intake and exhaust manifolds are mounted on the same side of the cylinder head. The valves are opened and closed by the camshaft lobes operating on cupped cam followers which fit over the valves and springs. This design results in lighter valve train weight and fewer moving parts.

1990 Cabriolets receive the Digifant II engine management system similar to the one used on later Golfs and Jettas. The 1990 Cabriolet is capable of producing 94 horsepower.

1986–89 Scirocco and GTI (16V DOHC)

In the latter part 1986 Volkswagen introduced its 1.8L, DOHC, 16 valve, fuel injected 4cyl. engine in the Scirocco, as an option to the standard 1.8L, single overhead cam engine. This engine will also be offered in the GTI as of the 1987 model year.

The cylinder head has a cross flow design and is made of light weight aluminum allow. The block is a standard Volkswagen inline 4 cyl., modified with greater oil pump capacity, and special piston cooling oil jets. In addition to these modifications the DOHC engine gets new pistons to create a 10.0:1 compression ratio, a bhp of 123 at 5800 rpm, and a torque of 120 ft. lbs. at 4250 rpm.

The combustion chamber is contained completely within the cylinder head. The exhaust valves are vertical with the intake valves angled 25° to the engines centerline. This helps to provide a narrow combustion chamber. The spark plug is located in the center of the combustion chamber which allows a shorter ignition flame path.

When combined with the narrow combustion chamber, this results in rapid burning of the fuel air mixture and less potential for ignition knock.

The cylinder head is lightweight aluminum silicone alloy. The 25° angle of the intake valves also allows for a relatively narrow cylinder head design.

The intake valve diameter is 31.75mm (1.25 in.) and the exhaust valves are 28mm (1.10 in.). The valves are surface hardened with stelite. The valve seats in the cylinder head are made from sintered steel.

The exhaust valve stems are partially filled with sodium to improve heat dissipation. At normal operating temperatures, the sodium is in liquid form. The motion of the valves causes the sodium to travel back and forth from the valve head area to the stem. The liquid sodium acts as a medium to remove heat from the valve head area and transfer it to the valve stem where it is removed through the valve guide to the cylinder head coolant jacket. Under no cir-

cumstances should either the intake or the exhaust valves be resurfaced. If these valves show signs of wear or damage they must be replaced and the old valves disposed of properly to prevent personal injury. Refer disposal of the valves to a qualified machine shop technician.

The camshafts are driven by a single toothed belt. The belt drives the exhaust camshaft in an arrangement similar to the normal 1.8L engine. The exhaust camshaft then drives the intake camshaft through a single roller chain and sprockets attached to the backs of the camshafts.

The camshafts and pulleys must be installed together in the cylinder head so the timing marks line up as pictured

The camshaft drive belt and all pulleys have been widened from 19mm (0.748 in.) to 25mm (0.984 in.). The tooth pitch of the belt and pulleys are also deeper.

1990 GTI, Jetta GLI 16V and Passat (16V DOHC)

In 1990, VW introduced the 16V dual overhead cam 2.0L engine. The engine retains many of the design characteristics of it's 1.8L 16V cousin. The 2.0L engine features the following design modifications:

• A CIS-E Motronic fuel management system
• Cylinder bore increased by 1.5mm to 82.5mm
• Stoke increased 6.4mm to 92.8mm
• Compression ratio increased from 10.0:1 to 10.8:1
• Two knock sensors

The net effect of the changes is an engine that is capable of producing 134 horsepower at 5,800 rpm and 134 ft. lbs. of torque at 4,440 rpm.

Corrado

The 158 horsepower G60 engine is built on the same platform as the 1.8L engine used in the GTI. This engine features a heat treated cylinder head with a stronger head gasket, longer and stronger wrist pins, stronger connecting rod bolts and a forged (instead of cast) crankshaft. Engine fuel and emissions management is provided by a modified Digifant engine management system. The most distinguishing characteristic of the G60 engine is the addition of a belt driven G-Charger (supercharger). The G-Charger provides a wider torque range and improved engine response.

Dasher, Fox and Quantum

The 4-cylinder engine is identical to the Rabbit or Scirocco engine except for the way it is mounted. While the Rabbit and Scirocco engine is transverse, or mounted sideways in the engine compartment, the Dasher and Fox engine is mounted straight ahead in the traditional fashion. Engines are inclined 30° to the right.

The Quantum 5-cylinder engine is an inline engine with a single overhead camshaft and fuel injection. The engine is installed in the straight ahead manner and tilted to the right. The crankshaft runs in six main bearings, the cylinder block is made of cast iron and the cylinder head is light weight aluminum alloy. The oil pump is driven by the crankshaft, while the distributor is camshaft driven.

DIESEL ENGINE

VW introduced the diesel engine option on 1977 Rabbit models and 1979 Dashers. Diesel engines were used through 1986 and disappeared during 1897–88. The diesel re-appeared in 1989 as an option in the Jetta and is thus far available in 1990.

The key difference between the gasoline and diesel engine is that the diesel does not use a carburetor or electrical ignition system. There are no plugs, points or coil to replace. Combustion occurs when a fine mist of diesel fuel is sprayed into hot compressed air ($1650°F$) [$899°C$] under high pressure (850 psi). The air is heated by the compression as the piston moves up on the compression stroke. The diesel engine has a compression ratio of 23.5:1 compared to the gasoline engine's compression ration of 8.2:1.

VW's diesel block, flywheel, bearings and crankshaft are identical to those in the Rabbit gasoline engine. The connecting rod wrist pins were strengthened and new pistons and cylinder head, made of aluminum for lightness, were designed.

The cylinder head has an overhead camshaft to actuate the valves and the cam is driven by a flexible toothed belt which also operates the fuel injection pump.

The Volkswagen diesel has a spherical pre-combustion chamber in which combustion begins. The burning fuel/air mixture is given a swirl pattern by the chamber's shape. The swirl promotes more complete combustion as the combustion process continues in the main combustion chamber. Using the swirl chamber has other advantages: it reduces the peak load which the force of combustion would normally exert on pistons, rods, bearings and crankshaft, enabling VW to use many standard components.

Warm weather starts and warm engine starts are immediate, as with a gasoline version. Starting a cold engine on a chilly day is different and takes slightly longer. Each of the cylinders has an electric glow plug to preheat them for cold starts. Depending on how cold it is, the driver must wait from 15 to 60 seconds before starting. A light on the dashboard indicates when preheating is completed. Once the engine is warmed up, there is no need to preheat for subsequent restarting.

The VW diesel is also equipped with a manual cold start device that looks like a choke knob. It advances the timing for the fuel injection so that the fuel is injected into the hot compressed air earlier to make the engine start more easily. The engine accelerates better and the puff of blue smoke typical of a cold starting diesel is reduced. Once the car is driven away, the knob is pushed in.

TURBODIESEL ENGINE

The turbo diesel engine shares the basic design and principals of the normally aspirated diesel, however various modifications have been made to suit the special requirements of turbocharging.

Modifications include: a new cylinder head alloy, new materials used in the valves, valve seats and swirl chambers-all of which improve heat resistance. A new cylinder head gasket is used to provide better heat resistance and sealing. The engine block has been reinforced to accept 12mm stretch type cylinder head bolts. Piston cooling jets have been installed in the block to provide a spray of oil to help cool the pistons and internal temperatures. The pistons have been modified and strengthened, while the piston rings have been redesigned to provide better sealing and wear characteristics. The surface of the crankshaft connecting rod journals have been hardened to increase torsional rigidity and the front crank pulley size has been increased to help reduce vibration.

Engine Overhaul Tips

Most engine overhaul procedures are fairly standard. In addition to specific parts replacement procedures and complete specifications for your individual engine, this chapter also is a guide to accepted rebuilding procedures. Examples of standard rebuilding practice are shown and should be used along with specific details concerning your particular engine.

Competent and accurate machine shop services will ensure maximum performance, reliability and engine life. Procedures marked with the micrometer symbol shown above should be performed by a competent machine shop, and are provided so that you will be familiar with the procedures necessary to perform a successful overhaul.

In most instances it is more profitable for the

do-it-yourself mechanic to remove, clean and inspect the component, buy the necessary parts and deliver these to a shop for actual machine work.

On the other hand, much of the rebuilding work that does not require machine shop services (crankshaft, block, bearings, piston rods, and other component replacement) is well within the scope of the do-it-yourself mechanic.

Tools

The tools required for an engine overhaul or parts replacement will depend on the depth of your involvement. With a few exceptions, they will be the tools found in a mechanic's tool kit (see Chapter 1). More in-depth work will require any or all of the following:
• A dial indicator (reading in thousandths) mounted on a universal base
• Micrometers and telescope gauges
• Jaw and screw-type pullers
• Scraper
• Valve spring compressor
• Ring groove cleaner
• Piston ring expander and compressor
• Ridge reamer
• Cylinder hone or glaze breaker
• Plastigage®
• Engine stand
Use of most of these tools is illustrated in this chapter. Many can be rented for a one-time use from a local parts jobber or tool supply house specializing in automotive work.

Occasionally, the use of special tools is called for. See the information on Special Tools and Safety Notice in the front of this book before substituting another tool.

Inspection Techniques

Procedures and specifications are given in this chapter for inspecting, cleaning and assessing the wear limits of most major components. Other procedures such as Magnaflux® and Zyglo® can be used to locate material flaws and stress cracks. Magnaflux® is a magnetic process applicable only to ferrous materials. The Zyglo® process coats the material with a flourescent dye penetrant and can be used on any material. Checks for suspected surface cracks can be more readily made using spot check dye. The dye is sprayed onto the suspected area, wiped off and the area sprayed with a developer. Cracks will show up brightly.

Overhaul Tips

Aluminum has become extremely popular for use in engines, due to its low weight. Observe the following precautions when handling aluminum parts:

• Never hot tank aluminum parts (the caustic hot-tank solution will eat the aluminum.
• Remove all aluminum parts (identification tag, etc.) from engine parts prior to the tanking.
• Always coat threads lightly with engine oil or anti-seize compounds before installation, to prevent seizure.
• Never over-torque bolts or spark plugs especially in aluminum threads. Stripped threads in any component can be repaired using any of several commercial repair kits (Heli-Coil®, Microdot®, Keenserts®, etc.).

When assembling the engine, pre-lube all power-pack components (pistons, bearings, bearing caps, thrust washers, ect.) to provide lubrication at initial start-up. Any product specifically formulated for this purpose can be used, but clean engine oil is recommended.

When semi-permanent (locked, but removable) installation of bolts or nuts is desired, threads should be cleaned and coated with Loctite® or other similar, commercial non-hardening sealant.

Repairing Damaged Threads

Several methods of repairing damaged threads are available. Heli-Coil® (shown here), Keenserts® and Microdot® are among the most widely used. All involve basically the same principle—drilling out stripped threads, tapping the hole and installing a prewound insert—making welding, plugging and oversize fasteners unnecessary.

Two types of thread repair inserts are usually supplied—a standard type for most Inch Coarse, Inch Fine, Metric Course and Metric Fine thread sizes and a spark lug type to fit most spark plug port sizes. Consult the individ-

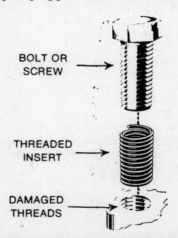

BOLT OR
SCREW

THREADED
INSERT

DAMAGED
THREADS

Damaged bolt holes can be repaired with thread repair inserts

Standard thread repair insert (left) and spark plug thread insert (right)

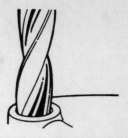

Drill out the damaged threads with specified drill. Drill completely through the hole or to the bottom of a blind hole

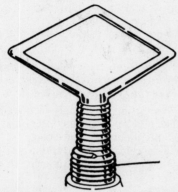

Screw the threaded insert onto the installation tool until the tang engages the slot. Screw the insert into the tapped hole until it is $1/4$–$1/2$ turn below the top surface. After installation break off the tang with a hammer and punch

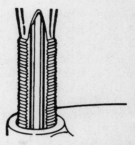

With the tap supplied, tap the hole to receive the thread insert. Keep the tap well oiled and back it out frequently to avoid clogging the threads

ual manufacturer's catalog to determine exact applications. Typical thread repair kits will contain a selection of prewound threaded inserts, a tap (corresponding to the outside diameter threads of the insert) and an installation tool. Spark plug inserts usually differ because they require a tap equipped with pilot threads and a combined reamer/tap section. Most manufacturers also supply blister-packed thread repair inserts separately in addition to a master kit containing a variety of taps and inserts plus installation tools.

Before effecting a repair to a threaded hole, remove any snapped, broken or damaged bolts or studs. Penetrating oil can be used to free frozen threads; the offending item can be removed with locking pliers or with a screw or stud extractor. After the hole is clear, the thread can be repaired, as follows:

CHECKING ENGINE COMPRESSION

A noticeable lack of engine power, excessive oil consumption and/or poor fuel mileage measured over an extended period are all indicators of internal engine wear. Worn piston rings,

scored or worn cylinder bores, blown head gaskets, sticking or burnt valves and worn valve seats are all possible culprits here. A check of each cylinder's compression will help you locate the problems.

As mentioned in the "Tools and Equipment" section of Chapter 1, a screw-in type compression gauge is more accurate that the type you simply hold against the spark plug hole, although it takes slightly longer to use. It's worth it to obtain a more accurate reading. Follow the procedures below for gasoline and diesel engined cars.

Gasoline Engines

1. Warm up the engine to normal operating temperature.

2. Remove all spark plugs.

3. Disconnect the high tension lead from the ignition coil.

4. On carbureted cars, fully open the throttle either by operating the carburetor throttle linkage by hand or by having an assistant "floor" the accelerator pedal. On fuel injected cars, disconnect the cold start valve and all injector connections.

5. Screw the compression gauge into the No. 1 spark plug hole until the fitting is snug.

NOTE: *Be careful not to crossthread the plug hole. On aluminum cylinder heads use extra car, as the threads in these heads are easily ruined.*

The screw-in type compression gauge is more accurate

6. Ask an assistant to depress the accelerator pedal fully on both carbureted and fuel injected cars. Then, while you read the compression gauge, ask the assistant to crank the engine two or three times in short bursts using the ignition switch.

7. Read the compression gauge at the end of each series of cranks, and record the highest of these readings. Repeat this procedure for each of the engine's cylinders. Compare the highest reading of each cylinder to the compression pressure specification in the "Tune-Up Specifications" chart in Chapter 2. A cylinder compression pressure is usually acceptable if it is not less than 80% of maximum. The difference between each cylinder should be no more than 12–14 psi.

8. If a cylinder is unusually low, pour a tablespoon of clean engine oil into the cylinder through the spark plug hole and repeat the compression test. If the compression comes up after adding the oil, it appears that the cylinder's piston rings or bore are damaged or worn. If the pressure remains low, the valves may not be seating properly (a valve job is needed), or the head gasket may be blown near that cylin-der. If compression in any two adjacent cylinders is low, and if the addition of oil doesn't help the compression, there is leakage past the head gasket. Oil and coolant water in the combustion chamber can result from this problem. There may be evidence of water droplets on the engine dipstick when a had gasket has blown.

Diesel Engines

Checking cylinder compression on diesel engines is basically the same procedure as on gasoline engines except for the following:

1. A special compression gauge adaptor suitable for diesel engines (because these engines have much greater compression pressures) must be used.

2. Remove the injector tubes and remove the injectors from each cylinder.

NOTE: *Don't forget to remove the washer underneath each injector, otherwise, it may get lost when the engine is cranked.*

3. When fitting the compression gauge adaptor to the cylinder head, make sure the bleeder of the gauge (if equipped) is closed.

4. When reinstalling the injector assemblies, install new washers underneath each injector.

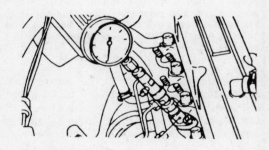

Diesel engines require a special compression gauge adaptor

Standard Torque Specifications and Fastener Markings

In the absence of specific torques, the following chart can be used as a guide to the maximum safe torque of a particular size/grade of fastener.

- There is no torque difference for fine or coarse threads.
- Torque values are based on clean, dry threads. Reduce the value by 10% if threads are oiled prior to assembly.
- The torque required for aluminum components or fasteners is considerably less.

U.S. Bolts

SAE Grade Number	1 or 2			5			6 or 7		
Number of lines always 2 less than the grade number.									
Bolt Size (Inches)—(Thread)	Ft./Lbs.	Kgm	Nm	Ft./Lbs.	Kgm	Nm	Ft./Lbs.	Kgm	Nm
¼—20	5	0.7	6.8	8	1.1	10.8	10	1.4	13.5
—28	6	0.8	8.1	10	1.4	13.6			
⁵/₁₆—18	11	1.5	14.9	17	2.3	23.0	19	2.6	25.8
—24	13	1.8	17.6	19	2.6	25.7			
⅜—16	18	2.5	24.4	31	4.3	42.0	34	4.7	46.0
—24	20	2.75	27.1	35	4.8	47.5			
⁷/₁₆—14	28	3.8	37.0	49	6.8	66.4	55	7.6	74.5
—20	30	4.2	40.7	55	7.6	74.5			
½—13	39	5.4	52.8	75	10.4	101.7	85	11.75	115.2
—20	41	5.7	55.6	85	11.7	115.2			
⁹/₁₆—12	51	7.0	69.2	110	15.2	149.1	120	16.6	162.7
—18	55	7.6	74.5	120	16.6	162.7			
⅝—11	83	11.5	112.5	150	20.7	203.3	167	23.0	226.5
—18	95	13.1	128.8	170	23.5	230.5			
¾—10	105	14.5	142.3	270	37.3	366.0	280	38.7	379.6
—16	115	15.9	155.9	295	40.8	400.0			
⅞— 9	160	22.1	216.9	395	54.6	535.5	440	60.9	596.5
—14	175	24.2	237.2	435	60.1	589.7			
1— 8	236	32.5	318.6	590	81.6	799.9	660	91.3	894.8
—14	250	34.6	338.9	660	91.3	849.8			

Metric Bolts

Relative Strength Marking	4.6, 4.8			8.8		
Bolt Markings						
Bolt Size Thread Size x Pitch (mm)	Ft./Lbs.	Kgm	Nm	Ft./Lbs.	Kgm	Nm
6 x 1.0	2–3	.2–.4	3–4	3–6	.4–.8	5–8
8 x 1.25	6–8	.8–1	8–12	9–14	1.2–1.9	13–19
10 x 1.25	12–17	1.5–2.3	16–23	20–29	2.7–4.0	27–39
12 x 1.25	21–32	2.9–4.4	29–43	35–53	4.8–7.3	47–72
14 x 1.5	35–52	4.8–7.1	48–70	57–85	7.8–11.7	77–110
16 x 1.5	51–77	7.0–10.6	67–100	90–120	12.4–16.5	130–160
18 x 1.5	74–110	10.2–15.1	100–150	130–170	17.9–23.4	180–230
20 x 1.5	110–140	15.1–19.3	150–190	190–240	26.2–46.9	160–320
22 x 1.5	150–190	22.0–26.2	200–260	250–320	34.5–44.1	340–430
24 x 1.5	190–240	26.2–46.9	260–320	310–410	42.7–56.5	420–550

GENERAL ENGINE SPECIFICATIONS

Year	Model	Engine Displacement cu. in. (cc)	Fuel System Type	Net Horsepower @ rpm	Net Torque @ rpm (ft. lbs.)	Bore × Stroke (in.)	Compression Ratio	Oil Pressure @ rpm
1974	Dasher	89.7 (1471)	2 bbl Solex	75 @ 5800 ①	81 @ 4000	3.01 × 3.15	8.5:1	40 @ 2500
1975	Dasher	96.8 (1588)	2 bbl Zenith	81 @ 5500	90 @ 3300	3.13 × 3.15	8.0:1	40 @ 2500
	Rabbit, Scirocco	89.7 (1471)	2 bbl Zenith	70 @ 6000	81 @ 3500	3.01 × 3.15	8.2:1	40 @ 2500
1976	Rabbit, Scirocco	96.8 (1588)	2 bbl Zenith	71 @ 5600	82 @ 3300	3.13 × 3.15	8.2:1	40 @ 2500
1976–77	Dasher	96.8 (1588)	CIS Fuel Inj.	79 @ 5500 ②	90 @ 3300	3.13 × 3.15	8.0:1	40 @ 2500
1977	Rabbit, Scirocco	96.8 (1588)	CIS Fuel Inj.	78 @ 5500 ③	90 @ 3300	3.13 × 3.15	8.0:1	40 @ 2500
1977–80	Rabbit (Diesel)	89.7 (1471)	Fuel Inj.	48 @ 5000	56.5 @ 3000	3.01 × 3.15	23.5:1	27 @ 2000
1978	Scirocco	88.9 (1457)	CIS Fuel Inj.	73 @ 5800	73 @ 3500 ④	3.13 × 2.89	8.0:1	28 @ 2000
1978–79	Dasher	97.0 (1588)	CIS Fuel Inj.	78 @ 5500 ③	84 @ 3200 ②	3.13 × 3.15	8.0:1	28 @ 2000
	Rabbit	88.9 (1457)	CIS Fuel Inj.	71 @ 5800 ⑤	73 @ 3500 ④	3.13 × 2.89	8.0:1	28 @ 2000
1979	Scirocco	97.0 (1588)	CIS Fuel Inj.	78 @ 5500 ①	84 @ 3200 ⑥	3.13 × 3.15	8.0:1	28 @ 2000
1979–80	Dasher (Diesel)	89.7 (1471)	Fuel Inj.	48 @ 5000	56.5 @ 3000	3.01 × 3.15	23.5:1	28 @ 2000
1980	Dasher	97.0 (1588)	CIS Fuel Inj.	76 @ 5500	83 @ 3200	3.13 × 3.15	8.2:1	40 @ 2500
	Rabbit	89.0 (1457)	1 bbl Solex	62 @ 5400	76.6 @ 3000	3.13 × 2.89	8.0:1	28 @ 2000
	Rabbit, Jetta, Scirocco	97.0 (1588)	CIS Fuel Inj.	71 @ 5500	83 @ 3200	3.13 × 3.15	8.2:1	28 @ 2000
1981	Dasher (Diesel)	97.0 (1588)	Fuel Inj.	52 @ 4800	72 @ 3000	3.01 × 3.40	23.0:1	28 @ 2000
	Jetta	97.0 (1588)	Fuel Inj.	78 @ 5500	84 @ 3200	3.13 × 3.15	8.0:1	28 @ 2000
	Jetta	105.0 (1715)	Fuel Inj.	74 @ 5000	90 @ 3000	3.13 × 3.40	8.2:1	28 @ 2000
	Rabbit	105.0 (1715)	Fuel Inj.	74 @ 5000	90 @ 3000	3.13 × 3.40	8.2:1	28 @ 2000
	Rabbit	105.0 (1715)	1 bbl.	65 @ 5000	88 @ 2800	3.13 × 3.40	8.2:1	28 @ 2000
	Rabbit (Diesel)	97.0 (1588)	Fuel Inj.	52 @ 4800	72 @ 3000	3.01 × 3.40	23.0:1	28 @ 2000
	Scirocco	105.0 (1715)	Fuel Inj.	74 @ 5000	90 @ 3000	3.13 × 3.40	8.2:1	28 @ 2000
1982	Jetta	105.0 (1715)	CIS Fuel Inj.	74 @ 5000	90 @ 3000	3.13 × 3.40	8.2:1	28 @ 2000
	Jetta (Diesel)	97.0 (1588)	Fuel Inj.	52 @ 4800	72 @ 2000	3.01 × 3.40	23.0:1	28 @ 2000
	Jetta (Turbo Diesel)	97.0 (1588)	Fuel Inj.	68 @ 4500	98 @ 2800	3.01 × 3.40	23.0:1	74 @ 5000
	Quantum	105.0 (1715)	CIS Fuel Inj.	74 @ 5000	90 @ 3000	3.13 × 3.40	8.2:1	28 @ 2000
	Quantum (Turbo Diesel)	97.0 (1588)	Fuel Inj.	68 @ 4500	98 @ 2800	3.01 × 3.40	23.0:1	74 @ 5000
	Quantum	130.8 (2144)	CIS Fuel Inj.	100 @ 5100	112 @ 3000	3.12 × 3.40	8.2:1	28 @ 2000
	Rabbit	105.0 (1715)	CIS Fuel Inj.	74 @ 5000	90 @ 3000	3.13 × 3.40	8.2:1	28 @ 2000
	Rabbit	105.0 (1715)	1 bbl.	65 @ 5000	88 @ 2800	3.13 × 3.40	8.2:1	28 @ 2000
	Rabbit (Diesel)	97.0 (1588)	Fuel Inj.	52 @ 4800	72 @ 3000	3.01 × 3.40	21.0:1	74 @ 5000
	Scirocco	105.0 (1715)	CIS Fuel Inj.	74 @ 5000	90 @ 3000	3.13 × 3.40	8.2:1	28 @ 2000

GENERAL ENGINE SPECIFICATIONS (cont.)

Year	Model	Engine Displacement cu. in. (cc)	Fuel System Type	Net Horsepower @ rpm	Net Torque @ rpm (ft. lbs.)	Bore × Stroke (in.)	Compression Ratio	Oil Pressure @ rpm
1983	Jetta	105.0 (1715)	CIS Fuel Inj.	74 @ 5000	90 @ 3000	3.13×3.40	8.2:1	28 @ 2000
	Jetta (Diesel)	97.0 (1588)	Fuel Inj.	52 @ 4800	72 @ 2000	3.01×3.40	23.0:1	28 @ 2000
	Jetta (Turbo Diesel)	97.0 (1588)	Fuel Inj.	68 @ 4500	98 @ 2800	3.01×3.40	23.0:1	74 @ 5000
	Quantum	105.0 (1715)	CIS Fuel Inj.	74 @ 5000	90 @ 3000	3.13×3.40	8.2:1	28 @ 2000
	Quantum	109.0 (1780)	CIS Fuel Inj.	88 @ 5500	96 @ 3250	3.19×3.40	9.0:1	28 @ 2000
	Quantum	130.8 (2144)	CIS Fuel Inj.	100 @ 5100	112 @ 3000	3.12×3.40	8.2:1	28 @ 2000
	Quantum (Turbo Diesel)	97.0 (1588)	Fuel Inj.	68 @ 4500	98 @ 2800	3.01×3.40	23.0:1	74 @ 5000
	Rabbit	105.0 (1715)	CIS Fuel Inj.	74 @ 5000	90 @ 3000	3.13×3.40	8.2:1	28 @ 2000
	Rabbit	105.0 (1715)	1 bbl.	65 @ 5000	88 @ 2800	3.13×3.40	8.2:1	28 @ 2000
	Rabbit (Conv.)	109.0 (1780)	CIS Fuel Inj.	74 @ 5000	90 @ 3000	3.13×3.40	8.2:1	28 @ 2000
	Rabbit GTI	109.0 (1780)	CIS Fuel Inj.	90 @ 5500	100 @ 3000	3.19×3.40	8.5:1	28 @ 2000
	Rabbit (Diesel)	97.0 (1588)	Fuel Inj.	52 @ 4800	97 @ 2800	3.01×3.40	23.0:1	74 @ 5000
	Scirocco	105.0 (1715)	CIS Fuel Inj.	74 @ 5000	90 @ 3000	3.13×3.40	8.2:1	28 @ 2000
	Scirocco	109.0 (1780)	CIS Fuel Inj.	90 @ 5500	100 @ 3000	3.19×3.40	8.5:1	28 @ 2000
	GTI	109.0 (1780)	CIS Fuel Inj.	90 @ 5500	100 @ 3000	3.19×3.40	8.5:1	28 @ 2000
	GLI	109.0 (1780)	CIS Fuel Inj.	90 @ 5500	100 @ 3000	3.19×3.40	8.5:1	28 @ 2000
	GTI (Diesel)	97.0 (1588)	Fuel Inj.	52 @ 4800	72 @ 3000	3.01×3.40	23.0:1	74 @ 5000
1984	Jetta	105.0 (1715)	CIS Fuel Inj.	74 @ 5000	90 @ 3000	3.13×3.40	8.2:1	28 @ 2000
	Jetta (Diesel)	97.0 (1588)	Fuel Inj.	52 @ 4800	72 @ 2000	3.01×3.40	23.0:1	28 @ 2000
	Jetta (Turbo Diesel)	97.0 (1588)	Fuel Inj.	68 @ 4500	98 @ 2800	3.01×3.40	23.0:1	74 @ 5000
	Quantum	109.0 (1780)	CIS Fuel Inj.	88 @ 5500	96 @ 3250	3.19×3.40	9.0:1	28 @ 2000
	Quantum	130.0 (2144)	CIS Fuel Inj.	100 @ 3000	112 @ 3000	3.12×3.40	8.2:1	28 @ 2000
	Quantum (Turbo Diesel)	97.0 (1588)	Fuel Inj.	68 @ 4500	98 @ 2800	3.01×3.40	23.0:1	74 @ 5000
	Rabbit	105.0 (1715)	1 bbl.	65 @ 5000	88 @ 2800	3.13×3.40	8.2:1	28 @ 2000
	Rabbit (Conv.)	109.0 (1780)	CIS Fuel Inj.	90 @ 5500	100 @ 3000	3.19×3.40	8.5:1	28 @ 2000
	Rabbit (GTI)	109.0 (1780)	CIS Fuel Inj.	90 @ 5500	100 @ 3000	3.19×3.40	8.5:1	28 @ 2000
	Rabbit (Diesel)	97.0 (1588)	Fuel Inj.	52 @ 4800	97 @ 2800	3.01×3.40	23.0:1	74 @ 5000
	Rabbit	105.0 (1715)	CIS Fuel Inj.	74 @ 5000	90 @ 3000	3.13×3.40	8.2:1	28 @ 2000
	Scirocco	109.0 (1780)	CIS Fuel Inj.	90 @ 5500	100 @ 3000	3.19×3.40	8.5:1	28 @ 2000
	GTI (Diesel)	97.0 (1588)	Fuel Inj.	52 @ 4800	72 @ 3000	3.01×3.40	23.0:1	74 @ 5000
	GTI	109.0 (1780)	CIS Fuel Inj.	90 @ 5500	100 @ 3000	3.19×3.40	8.5:1	28 @ 2000
	GLI	109.0 (1780)	CIS Fuel Inj.	90 @ 5500	100 @ 3000	3.19×3.40	8.5:1	28 @ 2000
1985	Jetta	109.0 (1780)	CIS Fuel Inj.	85 @ 5250	98 @ 3000	3.19×3.40	8.5:1	28 @ 2000
	Jetta (Diesel)	97.0 (1588)	Fuel Inj.	52 @ 4800	72 @ 2000	3.01×3.40	23.0:1	28 @ 2000
	Jetta (Turbo Diesel)	97.0 (1588)	Fuel Inj.	68 @ 4500	48 @ 2800	3.01×3.40	23.0:1	74 @ 5000
	Quantum	109.0 (1780)	CIS Fuel Inj.	88 @ 5500	96 @ 3250	3.19×3.40	9.0:1	28 @ 2000
	Quantum (Turbo Diesel)	97.0 (1588)	Fuel Inj.	68 @ 4500	98 @ 2800	3.01×3.40	23.0:1	74 @ 5000
	Quantum	136.0 (2226)	Fuel Inj.	110 @ 5500	122 @ 2500	3.19×3.40	8.5:1	28 @ 2000
	Cabriolet	109.0 (1780)	CIS Fuel Inj.	90 @ 5500	100 @ 3000	3.19×3.40	8.5:1	28 @ 2000
	Scirocco	109.0 (1780)	CIS Fuel Inj.	90 @ 5500	100 @ 3000	3.19×3.40	8.5:1	28 @ 2000
	GTI	109.0 (1780)	CIS Fuel Inj.	100 @ 5500	107 @ 3000	3.20×3.40	10.0:1	28 @ 2000
	GLI	109.0 (1780)	CIS Fuel Inj.	100 @ 5500	107 @ 3000	3.20×3.40	10.0:1	28 @ 2000
	Golf	109.0 (1780)	CIS Fuel Inj.	85 @ 5250	98 @ 3000	3.19×3.40	8.5:1	28 @ 2000
	Golf (Diesel)	97.0 (1588)	Fuel Inj.	52 @ 4800	70 @ 2000	3.01×3.40	23.0:1	74 @ 5000

GENERAL ENGINE SPECIFICATIONS (cont.)

Year	Model	Engine Displacement cu. in. (cc)	Fuel System Type	Net Horsepower @ rpm	Net Torque @ rpm (ft. lbs.)	Bore × Stroke (in.)	Com- pression Ratio	Oil Pressure @ rpm
1986	Jetta	109.0 (1780)	CIS Fuel Inj.	88 @ 5500	110 @ 3250	3.19 × 3.40	9.0:1	28 @ 2000
	Jetta (Diesel)	97.0 (1588)	Fuel Inj.	52 @ 4800	72 @ 2000	3.01 × 3.40	23.0:1	28 @ 2000
	Jetta (Turbo Diesel)	97.0 (1588)	Fuel Inj.	68 @ 4500	98 @ 2800	3.01 × 3.40	23.0:1	74 @ 5000
	Quantum	109.0 (1780)	CIS Fuel Inj.	88 @ 5500	96 @ 3250	3.19 × 3.40	9.0:1	28 @ 2000
	Quantum (Turbo Diesel)	97.0 (1588)	Fuel Inj.	68 @ 4500	98 @ 2800	3.01 × 3.40	23.0:1	74 @ 5000
	Quantum	136.0 (2226)	Fuel Inj.	110 @ 5500	122 @ 2500	3.19 × 3.40	8.5:1	28 @ 2000
	Cabriolet	109.0 (1780)	CIS Fuel Inj.	90 @ 5500	100 @ 3000	3.19 × 3.40	8.5:1	28 @ 2000
	Scirocco	109.0 (1780)	CIS Fuel Inj.	90 @ 5500	100 @ 3000	3.19 × 3.40	8.5:1	28 @ 2000
	GTI	109.0 (1780)	CIS Fuel Inj.	100 @ 5500	110 @ 3250	3.20 × 3.40	10.0:1	28 @ 2000
	GLI	109.0 (1780)	CIS Fuel Inj.	100 @ 5500	110 @ 3250	3.20 × 3.40	10.0:1	28 @ 2000
	Golf	109.0 (1780)	CIS Fuel Inj.	85 @ 5250	98 @ 3000	3.19 × 3.40	9.0:1	28 @ 2000
	Golf (Diesel)	97.0 (1588)	Fuel Inj.	52 @ 4800	70 @ 2000	3.01 × 3.40	23.0:1	74 @ 5000
1987	Jetta	109.0 (1780)	Digifant II	100 @ 5400	107 @ 3400	3.19 × 3.40	10.0:1	28 @ 2000
	Jetta GL	109.0 (1780)	Digifant II	105 @ 5400	110 @ 3400	3.19 × 3.40	10.0:1	28 @ 2000
	Jetta GLI 16V	109.0 (1780)	CIS-E Fuel Inj.	123 @ 5800	120 @ 4250	3.19 × 3.40	10.0:1	28 @ 2000
→	Quantum GL5	136.0 (2226)	CIS-E Fuel Inj.	110 @ 5500	122 @ 2400	3.19 × 3.40	8.5:1	28 @ 2000
	Quantum Syncro	136.0 (2226)	CIS-E Fuel Inj.	115 @ 5500	126 @ 3000	3.19 × 3.40	8.5:1	28 @ 2000
	Scirocco 16V	109.0 (1780)	CIS-E Fuel Inj.	123 @ 5800	120 @ 4250	3.19 × 3.40	10.0:1	28 @ 2000
	Cabriolet	109.0 (1780)	CIS-E Fuel Inj.	90 @ 5500	100 @ 3000	3.19 × 3.40	9.0:1	28 @ 2000
	Golf GL	109.0 (1780)	Digifant II	100 @ 5400	107 @ 3400	3.19 × 3.40	10.0:1	28 @ 2000
	Golf GT	109.0 (1780)	Digifant II	105 @ 5400	110 @ 3400	3.19 × 3.40	10.0:1	28 @ 2000
	Golf GTI 16V	109.0 (1780)	CIS-E Fuel Inj.	123 @ 5800	120 @ 4250	3.19 × 3.40	10.0:1	28 @ 2000
	Fox/GL	109.0 (1780)	CIS-E Fuel Inj.	81 @ 5500	93 @ 3250	3.19 × 3.40	9.0:1	28 @ 2000
1988	Jetta	109.0 (1780)	Digifant II	100 @ 5400	107 @ 3400	3.19 × 3.40	10.0:1	28 @ 2000
	Jetta GL	109.0 (1780)	Digifant II	105 @ 5400	110 @ 3400	3.19 × 3.40	10.0:1	28 @ 2000
	Jetta GLI 16V	109.0 (1780)	CIS-E Fuel Inj.	123 @ 5800	120 @ 4250	3.19 × 3.40	10.0:1	28 @ 2000
	Jetta Carat	109.0 (1780)	Digifant II	105 @ 5400	110 @ 3400	3.19 × 3.40	10.0:1	28 @ 2000
	Quantum GL5	136.0 (2226)	CIS-E Fuel Inj.	110 @ 5500	122 @ 2400	3.19 × 3.40	8.5:1	28 @ 2000
	Quantum Syncro	136.0 (2226)	CIS-E Fuel Inj.	115 @ 5500	126 @ 3000	3.19 × 3.40	8.5:1	28 @ 2000
	Scirocco 16V	109.0 (1780)	CIS-E Fuel Inj.	123 @ 5800	120 @ 4250	3.19 × 3.40	10.0:1	28 @ 2000
	Cabriolet	109.0 (1780)	CIS-E Fuel Inj.	90 @ 5500	100 @ 3000	3.19 × 3.40	9.0:1	28 @ 2000
	Golf GL	109.0 (1780)	Digifant II	100 @ 5400	107 @ 3400	3.19 × 3.40	10.0:1	28 @ 2000
	Golf GT	109.0 (1780)	Digifant II	105 @ 5400	110 @ 3400	3.19 × 3.40	10.0:1	28 @ 2000
	Golf GTI 16V	109.0 (1780)	CIS-E Fuel Inj.	123 @ 5800	120 @ 4250	3.19 × 3.40	10.0:1	28 @ 2000
	Fox/GL	109.0 (1780)	CIS-E Fuel Inj.	81 @ 5500	93 @ 3250	3.19 × 3.40	9.0:1	28 @ 2000
1989	Jetta	109.0 (1780)	Digifant II	100 @ 5400	107 @ 3400	3.19 × 3.40	10.0:1	28 @ 2000
	Jetta.0 (Diesel)	97.0 (1588)	Fuel Inj.	52 @ 4800	72 @ 2000	3.01 × 3.40	23.0:1	28 @ 2000
	Jetta GL	109.0 (1780)	Digifant II	105 @ 5400	110 @ 3400	3.19 × 3.40	10.0:1	28 @ 2000
	Jetta GLI 16V	109.0 (1780)	CIS-E Fuel Inj.	123 @ 5800	120 @ 4250	3.19 × 3.40	10.0:1	28 @ 2000
	Jetta Carat	109.0 (1780)	Digifant II	105 @ 5400	110 @ 3400	3.19 × 3.40	10.0:1	28 @ 2000
	Scirocco 16V	109.0 (1780)	CIS-E Fuel Inj.	123 @ 5800	120 @ 4250	3.19 × 3.40	10.0:1	28 @ 2000
	Cabriolet	109.0 (1780)	CIS-E Fuel Inj.	90 @ 5500	100 @ 3000	3.19 × 3.40	9.0:1	28 @ 2000
	Golf GL	109.0 (1780)	Digifant II	100 @ 5400	107 @ 3400	3.19 × 3.40	10.0:1	28 @ 2000
	Golf GT	109.0 (1780)	Digifant II	105 @ 5400	110 @ 3400	3.19 × 3.40	10.0:1	28 @ 2000
	Golf GTI 16V	109.0 (1780)	CIS-E Fuel Inj.	123 @ 5800	120 @ 4250	3.19 × 3.40	10.0:1	28 @ 2000
	Fox/GL	109.0 (1780)	CIS-E Fuel Inj.	81 @ 5500	93 @ 3250	3.19 × 3.40	9.0:1	28 @ 2000

GENERAL ENGINE SPECIFICATIONS (cont.)

Year	Model	Engine Displacement cu. in. (cc)	Fuel System Type	Net Horsepower @ rpm	Net Torque @ rpm (ft. lbs.)	Bore × Stroke (in.)	Compression Ratio	Oil Pressure @ rpm
1990	Jetta GL	109.0 (1780)	Digifant II	100 @ 5400	107 @ 3400	3.19×3.40	10.0:1	29 @ 2000
	Jetta GL.0 (Diesel)	97.0 (1588)	Fuel Inj.	52 @ 4800	71 @ 2000	3.01×3.40	23.0:1	29 @ 2000
	Jetta Carat	109.0 (1780)	Digifant II	105 @ 5400 ⑦	110 @ 3400 ⑧	3.19×3.40	10.0:1	29 @ 2000
	Jetta GLI 16V	121.0 (1984)	CIS-E Motronic Fuel Inj.	134 @ 5800	133 @ 4400	3.25×3.65	10.8:1	29 @ 2000
	GTI	109.0 (1780)	Digifant II	105 @ 5400 ⑦	110 @ 3400 ⑧	3.19×3.40	10.0:1	29 @ 2000
	GTI 16V	121.0 (1984)	CIS-E Motronic Fuel Inj.	134 @ 5800	133 @ 4400	3.25×3.65	10.8:1	29 @ 2000
	Golf GL	109.0 (1780)	Digifant II	100 @ 5400	107 @ 3400	3.19×3.40	10.0:1	29 @ 2000
	Cabriolet	109.0 (1780)	Digifant II	94 @ 5400	100 @ 3000	3.19×3.40	10.0:1	29 @ 2000
	Corrado	109.0 (1780)	Digifant II	158 @ 5600	166 @ 4000	3.19×3.40	8.0:1	29 @ 2000
	Passat GL	121.0 (1984)	CIS-E Motronic Fuel Inj.	134 @ 5800	133 @ 4400	3.25×3.65	10.8:1	29 @ 2000
	Fox/GL	109.0 (1780)	CIS-E Fuel Inj.	81 @ 5500	93 @ 3250	3.19×3.40	9.0:1	29 @ 2000

① 71 @ 5800—California
② 77 @ 5500—California
③ 76 @ 5500—California
④ 72 @ 3500—California
⑤ 70 @ 5800—California
⑥ 83 @ 3200—California
⑦ 100 @ 5400—California
⑧ 107 @ 3400—California

TORQUE SPECIFICATIONS

All readings in ft. lbs.

Years	Engine Displacement cu. in. (cc)	Cylinder Head Bolts	Main Bearing Bolts	Rod Bearing Bolts	Crankshaft Pulley Bolts	Flywheel Bolts	Manifold Intake	Manifold Exhaust	Spark Plugs
1974–80	⑥	54 ①	47	33	58	54	18	18	22
1975–81	⑦	②	47	33 ③	58	54	18	18	22
1977–81	⑧	61 ④	47	33	58	54	—	18	—
1982	97.0 Diesel (1,588)	⑤	47	33 ③	56	54	—	18	—
	105.0 (1,715)	②	47	33 ③	58	54	18	18	22
	130.8 (2,144)	②	47	33 ③	58	54	18	18	22
1983	97.0 Diesel (1,588)	⑤	47	33 ③	56	54	18	18	22
	105.0 (1,715)	②	47	33 ③	58	54	18	18	22
	109.0 (1,780)	②	47	33 ③	58	54	18	18	22
	130.8 (2,144)	②	47	36 ③	58	54	18	18	22

TORQUE SPECIFICATIONS (cont.)

Years	Engine Displacement cu. in. (cc)	Cylinder Head Bolts	Main Bearing Bolts	Rod Bearing Bolts	Crankshaft Pulley Bolts	Flywheel Bolts	Manifold Intake	Manifold Exhaust	Spark Plugs
1984	97.0 Diesel (1,588)	⑤	47	33 ③	56	54	—	18	—
	105.9 (1,715)	②	47	33 ③	58	54	18	18	14
	109.0 (1,780)	②	47	33 ③	58	54	18	18	14
	120.0 (1,970)	②	47	33 ③	58	54	18	18	14
1985	97.0 Diesel (1,588)	⑤	48	33 ③	130	72	18	18	—
	109.0 (1,780)	②	47	33 ③	145	54	18	18	14
	120.0 (1,970)	②	47	33 ③	145	54	18	18	14
	130.8 (2,144)	②	47	33 ③	145	54	18	18	14
1986	97.0 Diesel (1,588)	⑤	48	③	—	72	18	18	—
	109.0 (1,780)	②	47	33 ③	145	54	18	18	14
	136.0 (2,226)	②	47	33 ③	331	54	18	18	14
1987	109.0 (1,780)	②	47	33 ③	145 ④	54	18	18	14
	136.0 (2,226)	②	47	33 ③	253	54	18	18	14
1988	109.0 (1,780)	②	47	33 ③	145 ④	54	18	18	14
	136.0 (2,226)	②	47	33 ③	331	54	18	18	14
1989	97.0 Diesel (1,588)	②	48	③	—	72	18	18	—
	109.0 (1,780)	②	47	33 ③	145 ④	54	18	18	14
	97.0 Diesel (1,588)	⑤	48	③	—	72	—	18	—
	109.0 (1,780)	②	48	③	—	74	18	18	14
	121.0 (1,984)	⑥	48	③	—	74	15	18	15

① Cold; 61 ft. lbs. warm 1978–79 54 ft. lbs. plus 1/4 turn (polygon bolts).
After 1,000 miles, loosen each cylinder head bolt 1/3 turn (120°) in reverse of numbered sequence. Then, re-tighten to specification.
② With 12 points (polygon) head bolds
Torque in 4 steps:
1st step—29 ft/lbs.
2nd step—43 ft/lbs.
3rd step—additional 1/2 turn (180 degrees) further in one movement (two 90 degree turns are permissible)
Note tightening sequence
Do not retorque at 1000 miles
With 6 point (hex) head bolts
Torque in steps to 54 ft. lbs. with engine cold, when engine is warmed up, torque to 61 ft. lbs.
Head bolts must be retorqued after 1000 miles.
③ Stretch bolts: 22 ft. lbs. plus 1/4 (90°) turn.
④ Cold; 69 ft. lbs. warm. After 1,000 miles, loosen each cylinder head bolt 1/3 turn (120°) in reverse of the numbered sequence. Then, re-tighten to specification.
⑤ See text for proper bolt torque procedure.
⑥ Dasher gasoline engine only.
⑦ Gasoline engine, except Dasher.
⑧ All diesel engines.

CRANKSHAFT AND CONNECTING ROD SPECIFICATIONS

All measurements are given in inches.

Year	Engine Displacement cu. in. (cc)	Crankshaft				Connecting Rod		
		Main Brg. Journal Dia.	Main Brg. Oil Clearance	Shaft End-play	Thrust on No.	Journal Diameter	Oil Clearance ①	Side Clearance ①
1974–81	90.0 (1,471)	2.1260	0.001–0.003	0.003–0.007	3	1.811	0.001–0.003	0.015
	97.0 (1,588) Gasoline and Diesel	2.1260	0.001–0.003	0.003–0.007	3	1.811	0.001–0.003	0.015
	105.0 (1,715)	2.1260	0.001–0.003	0.003–0.007	3	1.811	0.001–0.003	0.015
1982	97.0 (1,588) Diesel	2.1260	0.001–0.003	0.003–0.007	3	1.811	0.001–0.003	0.015
	105.0 (1,715)	2.1260	0.001–0.003	0.003–0.007	3	1.811	0.001–0.003	0.015
	120.0 (1,970)	2.3609–② 2.3617	0.002–0.004	0.0027–0.0050	1 at flywheel	2.1644 2.1653	0.0008–0.0027	0.004–0.016
	130.8 (2,144)	2.2822	0.0006–0.0030	0.003–0.007	4	1.811	0.0006–0.0020	0.016
1983	97.0 (1,588) Diesel	2.1260	0.001–0.003	0.003–0.007	3	1.811	0.0049 ①	0.015
	105.0 (1,715)	2.1260	0.001–0.003	0.003–0.007	3	1.811	0.049 ①	0.015
	109.0 (1,780)	2.1260	0.001–0.003	0.003–0.007	3	1.881	0.001–0.003	0.015
	120.0 (1,970)	2.3609– 2.3617	0.002–0.004	0.0027–0.0050	1 at flywheel	2.1644 2.1653	0.0008–0.0027	0.004–0.016
	130.8 (2,144)	2.28220	0.0006–0.0030	0.003–0.007	4	1.811	0.0006–0.0020	0.016
1984	97.0 (1,588) Diesel	2.1260	0.001–0.003	0.003–0.007	3	1.811	0.0049 ①	0.015
	105.0 (1,715)	2.1260	0.001–0.003	0.003–0.007	3	1.811	0.0049 ①	0.015
	109.0 (1,780)	2.1260	0.001–0.003	0.003–0.007	3	1.881	0.001–0.003	0.015
1985	97.0 (1,588) Diesel	2.1260	0.001–0.003	0.003–0.007	3	1.811	0.0049	0.015
	109.0 (1,780)	2.1260	0.001–0.003	0.003–0.007	3	1.881	0.0049	0.015
	136.0 (2,226)	2.1260	0.001–0.003	0.003–0.007	3	1.811	0.001–0.003	0.015
1986	97.0 (1,588) Diesel	2.1260	0.001–0.003	0.003–0.007	3	1.811	0.0049	0.015
	109.0 (1,780)	2.1260	0.001–0.003	0.003–0.007	3	1.881	0.0049	0.015
	136.0 (2,226)	2.2820	0.001–0.003	0.003–0.007	3	1.881	0.0006–0.0020	0.015
1987	109.0 (1,780)	2.1260	0.001–0.003	0.003–0.007	3	1.881	0.0049	0.015
	136.0 (2,226)	2.2820	0.001–0.003	0.003–0.007	3	1.881	0.0006–0.0020	0.015

CRANKSHAFT AND CONNECTING ROD SPECIFICATIONS (cont.)

Year	Engine Displacement cu. in. (cc)	Crankshaft				Connecting Rod		
		Main Brg. Journal Dia.	Main Brg. Oil Clearance	Shaft End-play	Thrust on No.	Journal Diameter	Oil Clearance ①	Side Clearance ①
1988	109.0 (1,780)	2.1260	0.001–0.003	0.003–0.007	3	1.881	0.0049	0.015
	136.0 (2,226)	2.2820	0.001–0.003	0.003–0.007	3	1.881	0.0006–0.0020	0.015
1989	97.0 (1,588) Diesel	2.1260	0.001–0.003	0.003–0.007	3	1.881	0.0049	0.015
	109.0 (1,780)	2.1260	0.001–0.003	0.003–0.007	3	1.881	0.0049	0.015
1990	97.0 (1,588)	2.1260	0.001–0.003	0.003–0.007	3	1.880–1.881	0.005	0.015
	109.0 (1,780)	2.1260	0.001–0.003	0.003–0.007	3	1.880–1.881	0.0005	0.015
	121.0 (1,984)	2.1251–2.1276	0.0007–0.0020	0.0027–0.0060	3	1.880–1.881	0.0004–0.0040	0.0019–0.0120

① Wear limit.
② Applies to Journal No. 1, 2, 3.
    Journal No. 4—1.5739–1.5748

Engine

REMOVAL AND INSTALLATION

NOTE: *A good rule of thumb to follow when removing engines from all models is to label all hoses, electrical wires, and linkages and their connections with tape. Number each tape tag and the place it connects; this should help eliminate the hassles of "Where does this go?" during installation. Also, if you have a camera handy, snap a few pictures of the engine compartment before you start removing anything.*

Dasher with Gasoline Engine

1. Disconnect the battery cables. On fuel injected engines, release the fuel system pressure.
2. Remove the exhaust manifold heater hose and breather hose from the air cleaner.
3. Remove the air cleaner assembly.
4. On carbureted models, pull the clip off the accelerator cable and detach the cable. On fuel injected models, disconnect the electrical connectors and wiring harnesses for the fuel injectors, cold start valve, oxygen sensor and frequency valve (if equipped), and detach the control pressure regulator lines.
5. Loosen the upper adjustment nut on the clutch cable and detach it. Move the cable of to the side and out of the way.
6. On carbureted models only, disconnect the fuel line from the fuel pump, drain it, plug it, and place it out of the way. On fuel injected

models, disconnect the air duct. Remove the cold start valve. Remove the fuel injectors from the cylinder head (protect the ends with caps) and the accelerator cable. Remove the air flow sensor with the fuel distributor and place out of the way.
7. Detach emission control hoses. Remove power steering pump and V-belts, if equipped.
8. Disconnect the wiring from the alternator.
9. Detach the clip and remove the heater cable.

CAUTION: *Do not disconnect refrigerant lines on cars equipped with air conditioning.*

10. On cars with air conditioning:

a. Remove the horn, compressor and condenser assemblies.

b. Move the compressor and condensers out of the way, without disconnecting the refrigerant lines.

c. Disconnect the vacuum hoses and brake booster hose, if equipped.

11. Disconnect the front engine mounts and remove the mount bracket.

CAUTION: *When draining the coolant, keep in mind that cats and dogs are attracted by the ethylene glycol antifreeze, and are quite likely to drink any that is left in an uncovered container or in puddles on the ground. This will prove fatal in sufficient quantity. Always drain the coolant into a sealable container. Coolant should be reused unless it is contaminated or several years old.*

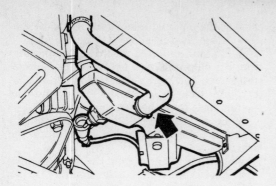

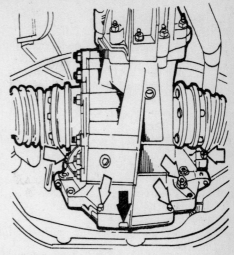

Remove the bottom hose on models without drain plugs to drain the radiator

12. Drain the coolant from the radiator. The plug is located near the lower hose, or remove the hose on models without the drain plug. Drain the cylinder block at the plug near the starter.

13. Disconnect the electrical wire from the coil and distributor, oil pressure and temperature sending units, fan and the thermal switch on the radiator.

14. Disconnect the radiator and heater hoses from the engine. Detach the heater valve cable.

15. Loosen the radiator shroud retainers. Remove the mounting bolts and nuts and lift out the radiator and fan from the engine compartment.

16. Raise the front of the car and safely support it.

17. Remove the starter.

18. Disconnect the exhaust pipe from the manifold.

19. Detach the engine side mounts.

20. Loosen the upper engine-to-transmission bolts. Remove the lower bolts. If the car is equipped with an automatic transmission, remove the three torque converter-to-flywheel bolts by working through the starter hole. Use a bar or locking device to hold the flywheel. Also disconnect the automatic transmission vacuum hose.

21. Support the transmission with a floor jack.

22. Lower the car until the wheels are on the ground.

23. Attach the hoist to the engine lift points. Make sure the lifting bracket fasteners are tight before connecting the hoist.

24. Raise the engine/transmission until the transmission touches the steering rack.

25. Adjust your jack or support so that the transmission is held firmly.

26. Remove the upper engine-to-transmission bolts.

27. Pry the engine and transmission apart and remove the intermediate plate. Install a

Remove the lower engine/transmission bolts and flywheel cover (arrows)

On automatic transmissions, remove the converter-to-flywheel bolts through the starter mounting hole (Dasher and Quantum)

bar or cable to the torque converter housing on automatic transmission equipped cars to prevent the converter from falling out.

28. Remove the engine by slowly lifting and turning simultaneously.

CAUTION: *Do this very carefully to avoid damaging the halfshafts or transmission.*

To install:

29. Lower the engine into the vehicle. Be careful not to damage the input shaft of the transmission during installation.

30. Install the upper engine-to-transaxle bolts. Torque the bolts to 40 ft. lbs.

31. Install the engine-to-transaxle (manual) or torque converter (automatic) bolts. Use new bolts. Torque the torque converter bolts to 25 ft. lbs., engine to transaxle bolts to 40 ft.lbs.

32. Install the engine side mount bolts and torque them to 32 ft. lbs.

33. Connect the exhaust pipe to the manifold. Use new gaskets as required.

34. Install the starter and connect the wiring.

35. Lower the car.

36. Install the radiator and fan.

37. Connect the heater cable, heater hoses and radiator hoses.

38. Connect the thermal switch, cooling fan, temperature sending unit and distributor wires.

39. Install the coolant drain plugs and fill the cooling system.

40. Install the front engine mounts and bracket.

41. On cars equipped with air conditioning, connect the brake booster and vacuum hoses. Mount the compressor and condenser units.

42. Connect the heater cable and install the cable clip.

43. Connect the alternator wiring. Make sure the wire nuts are tight.

44. Connect the emission control hoses. If equipped, install the power steering pump and V-belt. Tension the belt.

45. On fuel injected engines: install the air flow sensor and fuel distributor, fuel injectors and accelerator cable and air duct. On carbureted engines, connect the fuel line to the fuel pump.

46. Connect and adjust the clutch cable.

47. On fuel injected engines: connect the control pressure regulator lines, and frequency valve, cold start valve and fuel injector wiring. On carbureted engine connect and adjust the accelerator cable. Secure the cable with the cable clip.

48. Install the air cleaner assembly and the exhaust manifold heater and breather hoses.

49. Connect the battery cables.

Dasher with Diesel Engine

1. Disconnect the battery cables.

2. Set the heat control to **HOT**. Remove the lower radiator hose and remove the thermostat to drain the coolant. Remove the thermoswitch electrical connector and the radiator brace at the bottom of the radiator, remove the top radiator shroud, upper hose, radiator mounting bolts, and remove the radiator and fan.

CAUTION: *When draining the coolant, keep in mind that cats and dogs are attracted by the ethylene glycol antifreeze, and are quite likely to drink any that is left in an uncovered container or in puddles on the ground. This will prove fatal in sufficient quantity. Always drain the coolant into a sealable container. Coolant should be reused unless it is contaminated or several years old.*

3. Remove the supply and return lines from the injection pump. Disconnect the throttle cable from the pump and remove the cable mounting bracket. Disconnect the cold start cable at the pin, and remove the electrical connector from the fuel shut-off solenoid.

4. Disconnect the electrical connectors from the oil pressure switch, coolant temperature sensor and glow plugs. Remove the radiator hose from the cylinder head and the vacuum hose from the vacuum pump.

5. Loosen the clutch cable adjusting nuts.

6. Disconnect the clutch cable from the lever.

7. Remove the hose from the water pump.

8. Loosen the right engine mount.

9. Remove the alternator.

10. Remove the front engine mounts.

11. Disconnect the exhaust pipe from the manifold, and the pipe bracket from the transmission.

12. Loosen the left engine mount.

13. Remove the starter.

14. Remove the engine-to-transmission bolts, and the flywheel cover bolts.

15. Attach a lifting chain to the engine and raise the engine until the transmission touches the steering rack. Make sure the lifting bracket fasteners are tight before connecting the hoist. Remove the left engine mount.

16. Support the transmission with a floor jack and raise and turn the engine at the same time to remove.

To install:

17. Lower the engine into the vehicle and install the flywheel cover bolts and the engine-to-transmission bolts. Install the left engine mount. Tighten the engine-to-transmission bolts to 40 ft. lbs. and the engine mount bolts to 29 ft. lbs.

18. Install the starter.

19. Mount the exhaust pipe bracket to the transmission and connect the exhaust pipe to the manifold. Use new gaskets as required. Torque the exhaust manifold nuts to 18 ft. lbs.

20. Install the front engine mounts and torque the bolts to 29 ft. lbs.

21. Install the alternator.

22. Connect the water pump hose.

23. Install the right engine mount and torque the bolts to 29 ft. lbs.

24. Connect the clutch cable to the adjusting lever and adjust it.

25. Connect the vacuum pump hose and the radiator hose to the cylinder head.

26. Connect the glow plug, coolant temperature sensor and oil pressure switch electrical connectors.

27. Connect the fuel shut-off solenoid wiring. Connect the throttle cable to the mounting bracket and the fuel injection pump. Attach the injection pump supply and return lines. Adjust the throttle and cold start cables.

28. Install the radiator and fan and connect

the wiring and hoses. Install the thermostat with a new gasket.

29. Connect the battery cables. Refill the cooling system and adjust the belt tension.

4-Cylinder Quantum Gasoline Engine

1. Relieve the fuel system pressure. Disconnect the battery cables.

2. Set the heater control to full **OPEN**, remove the radiator cap and drain the cooling system. Remove the radiator hoses from the engine.

CAUTION: *When draining the coolant, keep in mind that cats and dogs are attracted by the ethylene glycol antifreeze, and are quite likely to drink any that is left in an uncovered container or in puddles on the ground. This will prove fatal in sufficient quantity. Always drain the coolant into a sealable container. Coolant should be reused unless it is contaminated or several years old.*

3. If equipped, remove the power steering mounting bolts, the drive belt and move the pump aside, leaving the hoses attached.

4. Disconnect the electrical connectors from the thermo-time switch, the alternator and the control pressure regulator.

5. Disconnect the distributor vacuum hoses from the distributor.

6. Remove the control pressure regulator bolts and move the regulator aside, with the fuel lines attached.

7. Disconnect the radiator fan wires. Remove the radiator bolts and the radiator assembly with the air duct.

8. Remove the clip on the clutch cable and disconnect the cable. Position the cable off to the side and out of the way.

9. Remove the left engine mount nut.

10. Disconnect the coolant temperature sender wire from the engine, oxygen sensor, thermo-switch, the Hall sending unit wire and the coil wire from the distributor.

11. Disconnect the electrical connectors from the auxiliary air regulator, the cold start and the frequency valves.

12. Remove the emissions canister hose from the air duct.

13. Remove the preheater hose and the cold start valve (leave the fuel line attached).

14. Disconnect the distributor vacuum hose from the intake manifold. Remove the accelerator cable, the crankcase breather hose and the brake booster hose.

15. Remove the fuel injectors (protect them with caps), the fuel distributor (leave the lines attached) and move them aside.

NOTE: *If equipped with air conditioning, remove the following components: the throttle body housing, the auxiliary air regulator, the horn bracket, the crankcase pulley nuts, the drive belt, the compressor bracket bolts, the compressor and the condenser. Position and tie the compressor and the condenser off to the side and out of the way.*

16. Remove the right engine mount nuts.

17. Remove the exhaust pipe at the manifold.

18. Remove the starter wiring and the starter. Remove the lower engine-to-transmission bolts and the flywheel cover plate.

19. If equipped with an automatic transaxle, remove the torque converter-to-driveplate bolts. Attach the engine support tool VW 785/1B or equivalent to the transmission and support it.

20. Loosen the nuts on the outer half of the damper pulley and remove the drive belt.

21. Remove the air conditioning compressor bracket mounting bolts and move the compressor off to the side and out of the way (with the lines attached).

22. Attach the engine sling US-1105 or equivalent to the engine, support it with a vertical hoist and lift the engine slightly, then remove the right engine mount.

23. Remove the upper engine-to-transmission bolts, separate the engine from the transmission. Lift and turn the engine to remove it from the vehicle.

NOTE: *If equipped with an automatic transmission, secure the torque converter to the transmission to keep it from falling out.*

To install:

24. Lower the engine into the vehicle and install the engine-to-transmission bolts. Torque the bolts to 40 ft. lbs.

25. Install the right engine mount and torque the bolts to 25 ft. lbs.

26. Mount the air conditioning compressor. Torque the upper mounting bolts to 22 ft. lbs. and the lower bolts to 18 ft. lbs.

27. Slip the drive belt onto the damper pulley and tighten the outer pulley half nuts.

28. If equipped with automatic transmission, install the torque converter-to-flywheel bolts and torque them to 22 ft. lbs.

29. Install the lower engine-to-transmission bolts and torque them to 40 ft. lbs.

30. Install the starter and connect the wiring.

31. Connect the exhaust pipe to the exhaust manifold and torque the nuts to 26 ft. lbs. Use a new gasket as required.

32. Install the right engine mount nuts and torque them to 26 ft. lbs.

33. Mount the air conditioning compressor and install all related components. Torque the upper air conditioning compressor mounting

bolts to 22 ft. lbs. and the lower bolts to 18 ft. lbs.

34. Install the fuel distributor and fuel injectors.

35. Connect the crankcase and brake booster hoses. Connect and adjust the accelerator cable. Connect the distributor vacuum hose to the intake manifold.

36. Install the cold start valve and connect the pre-heater hose.

37. Connect the emissions canister hose to the air duct.

38. Plug in the frequency valve, cold start and auxiliary air regulator connectors.

39. Connect the Hall sending unit and coil wire to the distributor. Connect the oxygen sensor, thermoswitch and temperature sending unit wires.

40. Install the left engine mount. Torque the nuts to 26 ft. lbs.

41. Connect and adjust the clutch cable. Install the cable clip.

42. Install the radiator and fan assembly with the air duct. Plug in the radiator fan wires.

43. Install the control pressure regulator.

44. Connect the distributor vacuum advance hose.

45. Connect the wires to the control pressure regulator, alternator and the thermo-time switch.

46. Mount the power steering pump and torque the bolts to 15 ft. lbs.

47. Connect the radiator hoses.

48. Connect the battery cables. Refill the cooling system and adjust the belt tension.

5-Cylinder Quantum

1. Disconnect the negative battery cable.

2. Move the heater control valve to fully **OPEN** and remove the radiator cap from the expansion tank.

3. At the power steering pump, remove the drive belt cover, the drive belt, the mounting bolts and the pump. Move the pump aside with the hoses connected.

4. Remove the grille and the radiator cover.

5. Remove the lower radiator hose and drain the coolant.

CAUTION: *When draining the coolant, keep in mind that cats and dogs are attracted by the ethylene glycol antifreeze, and are quite likely to drink any that is left in an uncovered container or in puddles on the ground. This will prove fatal in sufficient quantity. Always drain the coolant into a sealable container. Coolant should be reused unless it is contaminated or several years old.*

6. Remove the front bumper with the energy absorber.

5-cylinder engine front bumper and energy absorber removal

7. Remove the vacuum hoses from the intake manifold, the upper radiator hose, the radiator hose from the thermostat housing and the heater hose (drain the remaining coolant).

8. Disconnect the electrical connectors from the oil pressure switch, the control pressure regulator and the thermo-time switches.

9. Remove the cylinder head cover ground wire.

10. Remove the control pressure regulator (leave the lines attached) and the ball joint circlip (disconnect it at the pushrod).

11. Remove the alternator drive belt, the bracket bolts and the alternator assembly.

12. Remove the air duct and the front engine stop.

13. Disconnect the electrical connectors from the cold start valve, the frequency valve and the throttle switch. Disconnect the electrical leads at the idle stabilizer valve, the Hall sender at the distributor and the oxygen sensor.

14. Remove the accelerator cable circlip and disconnect the cable rod from the throttle body.

15. Remove the distributor cap, the cold start valve and the vacuum hose from the thermo valve.

16. Remove the fuel injection cooling hose.

17. Remove the fuel injectors from the intake manifold (leave the fuel lines connected).

NOTE: *When removing the fuel injectors and the cold start valve, place caps on the ends to protect them from damage.*

18. Remove the air filter housing bolts and the filter.

NOTE: *If equipped with an automatic transmission, disconnect (and plug) the oil cooler hoses.*

19. Remove the heater hoses. Remove the exhaust pipe bracket from the engine and transmission assembly.

NOTE: *If equipped with air conditioning, remove the drive belt, the electrical connector at the compressor, the compressor bracket to engine bolts and the compressor assembly. Move it off to the side and out of the way. Tie the compressor to some convenient point in the engine compartment. DO NOT allow the compressor to hang by the pressure hoses.*

20. Attach the supporting tool 2084 to the crankshaft pulley and remove the crankshaft bolt.

21. Of the four crankshaft pulley bolts, remove 2 and loosen 2. To loosen the pulley, tap lightly on the remaining bolts. Remove the bolts and the pulley

NOTE: *When removing the pulley from the crankshaft, leave the drive belt sprocket attached to the crankshaft.*

22. Remove the front engine mount and the subframe-to-body bolts. Remove the exhaust pipe from the exhaust manifold and the support bracket.

23. Disconnect the starter cables and remove the starter.

24. Remove the torque converter-to-flywheel bolts, the bolts can be removed through the starter hole. Remove the lower engine-to-transmission bolts. Unhook the shift rod clip and disconnect the rod.

25. Remove the rubber plugs from the left side frame member. Using the support tool VW 785/1 or equivalent, connect it to the transmission and to the frame member, then adjust to make contact with the transmission.

26. Remove both engine mount nuts and the upper engine to transmission bolts (leave one bolt in place).

27. Attach the engine support tool US 1105 or equivalent and the lift tool 9019 or equivalent to the engine.

NOTE: *If equipped with an automatic transmission, secure the torque converter before removing the engine from the transmission.*

28. Remove the last engine-to-transmission bolt and lift the engine, while prying the engine apart from the transmission. Remove the engine from the vehicle.

To install:

29. Lower the engine into the vehicle and install a engine-to-transmission bolt to hold the engine in place. Install the remaining bolts and also the engine mount nuts. Torque the transmission-to-engine bolts to 22 ft. lbs. for 8mm bolts, 32 ft. lbs. for 10mm bolts and 43 ft. lbs. for 12mm bolts. Torque the engine mount nuts to 32 ft. lbs.

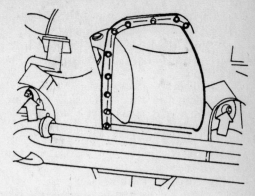

5-cylinder engine side mounts

30. Install the left frame side member rubber plugs and remove the support fixtures from the engine.

31. Connect the shift rod and install a new circlip.

32. Install the lower engine-to-transmission bolts. Torque to 22 ft. lbs. for 8mm bolts, 32 ft. lbs. for 10mm bolts and 43 ft. lbs. for 12mm bolts. Install the converter-to-flywheel bolts (working through the starter hole) and torque them to 22 ft. lbs.

33. Install the starter and connect the starter wiring.

34. Connect the exhaust pipe using a new gasket. Torque the manifold nuts to 18 ft. lbs.

35. Install the front engine mounts and subframe-to-body bolts. Torque the sub-frame-to-body bolts to 28 ft. lbs., then tighten them an additional 1/4 turn (90°). Torque the mount nuts to 33 ft. lbs.

36. When installing the crankshaft pulley, align the match mark on the sprocket with the mark on the pulley. When installing the crankshaft bolt, lubricate the threads with Loctite® 573 or equivalent. Torque the damper pulley center bolt to 331 ft. lbs. and the crankshaft pulley bolts to 14 ft. lbs.

37. Install the air conditioning compressor,

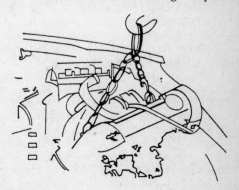

5-cylinder engine removal

drive belt and connect the electrical wiring. Torque the mounting bolts to 29 ft. lbs.

38. Mount the exhaust pipe bracket to the engine and transmission. Torque the mounting bolts to 22 ft. lbs.

39. Connect the heater hoses.

40. If equipped with automatic transmission, unplug and connect the transmission cooler lines.

41. Install the air filter housing and filter.

42. Install the fuel injectors and connect the fuel injector cooling hose.

43. Connect the vacuum hose to the thermo valve. Install the distributor cap and cold start valve.

44. Plug in the oxygen sensor, Hall sender unit (at the distributor), idle stabilizer valve, frequency valve (at the throttle switch) and cold start valve electrical connectors.

45. Install the front engine stop and torque the bolts to 33 ft. lbs. Connect the air inlet duct.

46. Install the alternator.

47. Install the ball joint circlip and the control pressure regulator.

48. Attach the cylinder head cover ground wire.

49. Plug in the thermo-time, control regulator and oil pressure switch electrical connectors.

50. Connect the heater, thermostat and upper radiator, and install the manifold (vacuum) hoses.

51. Install the energy absorber and front bumper assemblies.

52. Connect the lower radiator hose.

53. Install the radiator cover and grille.

54. Install the power steering pump, drive belt and and drive belt cover. Torque the power steering pump mounting bolts to 15 ft. lbs.

55. Connect the battery cables, fill the cooling system and adjust the drive belt tension.

Quantum TurboDiesel

1. Disconnect the battery cables.

2. Remove the horn and the cover plates of the engine and the transmission.

3. Move the heater control valve to fully **OPEN** and remove the radiator cap.

4. Remove the two lower hoses of the thermostat housing and drain the coolant.

CAUTION: *When draining the coolant, keep in mind that cats and dogs are attracted by the ethylene glycol antifreeze, and are quite likely to drink any that is left in an uncovered container or in puddles on the ground. This will prove fatal in sufficient quantity. Always drain the coolant into a sealable container. Coolant should be reused unless it is contaminated or several years old.*

5. Unplug the electrical connections from the fan, the thermoswitch and the series resistor near the alternator.

6. Remove the radiator to engine coolant hose, the radiator bolts, the right fan connector and the radiator.

7. Remove the fuel supply and the return lines from the fuel injector. Cap the lines to prevent the entry of dirt into the fuel system.

8. Disconnect the accelerator cable from the fuel injection pump and from the support bracket.

9. Disconnect the cold start cable.

10. Unplug the electrical connector at the fuel shut-off solenoid and remove the gear shift indicator switch with the wiring from the bracket.

11. Remove the air filter-to-turbocharger (air filter) hose.

12. Unplug the electrical connector from the oil pressure switch, the coolant temperature sensors and the glow plugs.

13. Remove the power steering bracket bolts (leave the lines attached) and move the pump off to the side and out of the way.

14. Disconnect the hose from the vacuum pump.

15. Remove the clutch cable lock plate and unhook the cable.

16. Remove the two nuts from both engine mounts and the engine torque support bolts at the front of the engine.

17. Remove the alternator and the front engine stop.

NOTE: *If equipped with air conditioning, remove the pulley nuts from the compressor, the drive belt, the compressor bracket bolts and the compressor. Position and tie the compressor off to the side and out of the way so that the hoses are not under strain. DO NOT allow the compressor to hang freely by the hoses.*

18. Disconnect the exhaust pipe and oil lines (supply and return) from the turbocharger. Remove the turbocharger from it's mounting bracket. Cap the ends of the oil lines to prevent leakage and dirt from entering.

19. Disconnect the electrical connectors and remove the starter. Place the starter on the engine subframe.

20. Remove the two bottom engine-to-transmission bolts and the flywheel cover plate bolts.

NOTE: *If equipped with an automatic transmission, remove the cover plate and the torque converter mounting bolts.*

21. Install the engine support bar VW 785/1B or equivalent under the front of the transmission and support it.

22. Attach the engine lifting tool US 1105 or equivalent and a vertical lift to the engine and

lift the engine and transmission assembly free of the engine mounts.

23. Adjust the support bar under the transmission.

24. Remove the three upper transmission-to-engine bolts and pry the engine from the transmission.

NOTE: *If equipped with an automatic transmission, secure the torque converter-to-the transmission to keep it from falling out.*

25. Lift the engine from the engine compartment.

To install:

NOTE: *Before installing the engine, place the starter on the sub-frame.*

26. Lower the engine into the engine compartment and shake the engine until it seats on the transmission housing.

27. Install the three upper engine-to-transmission bolts and torque them to 41 ft. lbs.

28. If equipped with automatic transmission, install the torque converter and cover plate bolts. Torque the converter bolts to 22 ft. lbs. and the cover plate bolts to 7 ft. lbs.

29. Install the flywheel cover plate bolts (manual transmissions) and torque them to 7 ft. lbs. Install the two bottom engine-to-transmission bolts and torque them to 41 ft. lbs.

30. Remove the engine support bars.

31. Mount the starter and connect the starter wiring. Torque the starter mounting bolts to 15 ft. lbs.

32. Install the turbocharger with an new gasket. Connect the oil lines and exhaust pipe (with a new gasket) to the turbo. Torque the exhaust pipe nuts and turbo-to-manifold nuts to 18 ft. lbs.

33. Mount the air conditioning compressor, install the drive belt and pulley nuts. Torque the 8mm bracket bolts to 18 ft. lbs. and the 12mm bolts to 59 ft. lbs.

34. Install the engine mount nuts and the torque support bolts. Torque the mount nuts to 25 ft. lbs.

35. Connect the clutch cable and install the lock plate.

36. Connect the vacuum pump hose.

37. Install the power steering pump and torque the mounting bolts to 15 ft. lbs.

38. Plug in the glow plug, coolant temperature sensor and oil pressure switch electrical connectors.

39. Connect and adjust the cold start and accelerator cables.

40. Connect the fuel lines to the injection pump.

41. Install the radiator and plug in the fan wire. Connect the coolant hose.

42. Plug in the alternator series resistor, thermoswitch and fan electrical connectors.

43. Install the cover plates and the horn.

44. Connect the battery cables. Fill the cooling system and adjust the drive belt tension.

Scirocco, Cabriolet, 1979–84 Rabbit, Pick-Up and Jetta with Gasoline Engines

The engine and transmission assembly is removed from the vehicle with the transmission attached. If the vehicle is carbureted, ignore any procedures that pertain to fuel injection.

1. On 1979 fuel injected vehicles equipped with equipped with air conditioning: Turn ON the ignition and the air conditioning control (engine not running), remove the compressor clutch bolt, press the clutch from the air conditioning compressor shaft (using a $5/8$ in. $\times$ 18 UNF bolt), turn OFF the ignition and the air conditioning. Disconnect the compressor clutch wire.

2. Disconnect the negative battery cable. On Scirocco 16V, remove the battery from the engine compartment.

3. Remove the fuel tank cap to relieve the pressure on the fuel system.

NOTE: *If equipped with an automatic transmission, place the selector lever in the PARK position and disconnect the positive battery cable.*

4. Remove the air intake duct between the fuel distributor and the throttle housing.

5. Remove the radiator cap. Turn the heater temperature control valve to fully **OPEN**. Place a container under the thermostat housing, remove the thermostat flange and drain the coolant.

CAUTION: *When draining the coolant, keep in mind that cats and dogs are attracted by the ethylene glycol antifreeze, and are quite likely to drink any that is left in an uncovered container or in puddles on the ground. This will prove fatal in sufficient quantity. Always drain the coolant into a sealable container. Coolant should be reused unless it is contaminated or several years old.*

6. Remove the upper radiator and heater hoses from the engine. Unplug the electrical connector from the radiator fan motor and the thermoswitch.

7. Remove the radiator mounting nuts, the upper radiator clamp clip, the clamp and the radiator.

8. Disconnect the alternator, thermoswitch, oil pressure switch, warm-up regulator and distributor wiring.

9. On 1979 fuel injected vehicles equipped with equipped with air conditioning: Turn the drive belt tensioner with an open end wrench until a 10mm Allen wrench can be inserted into the socket head bolts. Remove the tensioner bolts and the tensioner. Remove the alternator,

the timing belt cover and the compressor mounting bracket bolts (under the timing cover). Disconnect the pre-heat hose. Remove the diagonal braces, the support brace and the compressor bracket. Move and tie the compressor off to the side and out of the way; DO NOT disconnect the refrigerant hoses and do not allow the compressor to hang freely by the hoses.

10. Remove the pre-heat tube from the rear of the engine.

11. Remove the distributor vacuum hoses and the EGR temperature valve.

12. Remove the coil and the coolant temperature sensor wires.

CAUTION: *Use care when disconnecting the fuel lines. Fuel under pressure may still be in the lines and if sprayed, may cause fire or personal injury.*

13. Place a suitable container (to catch the fuel) under the cold start valve, then remove the fuel line and the warm-up regulator.

14. Remove the electrical connectors from the cold start valve and the auxiliary air regulator.

15. At the throttle body (fuel injected engines), remove the vacuum lines of the brake booster and the vacuum amplifier (if equipped).

16. Remove the PCV hose from the cylinder head cover.

17. At the throttle body (fuel injected engines), pull back the accelerator cable clip and disconnect the cable from the ball. Loosen the accelerator cable locknut and remove the cable from the cylinder head cover. Position the cable off the side and out of the way.

18. On fuel injected engines, remove the fuel injector rail, then position the entire assembly aside. Cover the fuel injector openings with masking tape to prevent the entry of dirt. Move the fuel and vacuum lines off to the side and out of the way. On Scirocco, remove the intake manifold.

19. Unplug the electrical connectors from the starter, the back-up light switch and the ground cable from the transmission.

20. If equipped with a manual transmission, at the clutch cable, loosen the locknut, remove the clip from under the clutch lever and the cable. If equipped with an automatic transmission, disconnect the selector cable from the transmission and the bracket. On Scirocco and Cabriolet with automatic transmission, loosen the accelerator pedal cable and disconnect it from the operating rod and the bracket.

21. Remove the speedometer cable clamp and the cable.

22. Remove the upper starter bolts and the starter.

23. Remove the nuts from the exhaust flex-

pipe and the relay shaft. Disconnect the lever from the relay shaft.

24. Remove the driveshafts from the mounting flanges.

25. Remove the horn (move aside), the front mount cup bolts, the cup and the front mount.

26. At both front wheels, remove the axle nuts.

27. At both steering knuckles, remove the ball joint lock bolts. Using a large pry bar, pry the ball joints from the bearing housings.

28. Swing the wheel and strut assembly away from the vehicle. Remove the drive axles from the wheel hubs.

NOTE: *With the driveshafts removed, reconnect the ball joints and lock bolts so that the vehicle may be lowered on its wheels.*

29. Remove the entire rear mount and the right front wheel and tire assembly.

30. Attach an engine sling tool US–1105, 2024A or equivalent to the engine and using an overhead crane, lift the engine slightly.

31. On manual transmissions: Remove the clip from the gearshift lever rod. Remove the rod from the selector shaft lever and the relay shaft with the gearshift lever rod attached. Open the clip on the front of the selector rod and remove the rod from the relay lever.

32. Remove the right and left side engine mount-to-body bolts.

33. Carefully Lower the engine and transmission assembly onto a dolly.

34. Raise the vehicle and slide the engine and transmission assembly clear of the vehicle.

To install:

35. With the engine/transmission positioned on the dolly, slide the engine under the vehicle and re-connect the crane to the lifting brackets.

36. Carefully, raise the engine and transmission into the vehicle and align as follows: Move the engine from side to side until the rear mount is straight. Then, move the engine assembly in the front to rear direction until the left and right mounts are centered in their brackets. Tighten the right, left and rear mount bolts to 25–30 ft. lbs. Position the front mount cup until the rubber core is centered in the cup. Now, torque the cup bolts to 38 ft. lbs. On all models, make sure that the exhaust system is aligned properly before completing the rest of the installation procedure. Re-align the exhaust system if necessary.

37. On manual transmissions: Insert the selector rod into the relay lever. Spread the ends of the circlip and install it in the groove at the front of the selector rod. Insert the gearshift lever rod (with selector lever and relay shaft attached) into the selector shaft and install the circlip.

38. Mount the right front wheel and tire as-

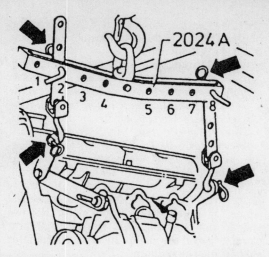

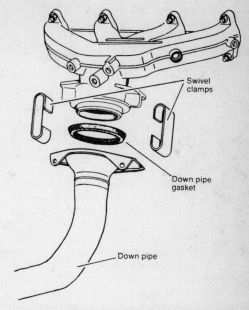

Using VW engine support tool 2024A to lift engine from vehicle

Swivel type exhaust pipe mounting on 1983 models

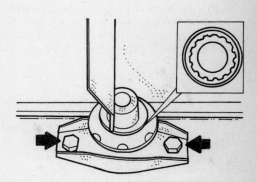

sembly. Install the transmission mounting nuts.

39. Bolt the drive axles to the wheel hubs. Center the wheel and strut assembly.

40. Connect the ball joints to the steering knuckles and install the ball joint lock bolts. Torque the bolts to 36 ft. lbs.

41. Install the axle nuts and torque to 174 ft. lbs.

42. Install the horn.

43. Connect the driveshafts to the mounting flanges on the transmission. Torque the mounting bolts to 30–33 ft. lbs.

44. Connect the relay shaft lever and install the relay shaft and exhaust flex pipe nuts.

45. Install the starter. Torque the starter mounting bolts to 33 ft. lbs. for 10mm and 54 ft. lbs. for 12mm.

46. Connect the speedometer cable to the transmission and install the cable clamp.

47. If equipped with an automatic transmission, connect and adjust the selector cable. If equipped with a manual transmission, connect the clutch cable to the selector lever, install the cable clip and adjust the locknut.

48. Connect the ground wire to the transmission. Connect the back-up light switch and starter wiring.

49. On fuel injected engines, install the fuel injectors.

50. On fuel injected engines, position the accelerator cable onto the cylinder head cover and install the cable locknut. Pull the cable tight and connect the cable end to the locking ball by depressing the ball spring, then secure the cable with the cable clip.

51. Connect the PCV hose to the cylinder head cover.

Rabbit, Jetta, Scirocco — align the front mount so the rubber core is centered in the housing

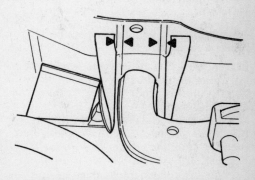

Move the engine/transmission front to rear to center the left and right transmission mounts in the brackets — Rabbit, Jetta, Scirocco

52. On fuel injected engines, connect the vacuum amplifier and brake booster vacuum lines to the throttle body.

53. Plug in the cold start valve and auxiliary air regulator electrical connectors.

54. Install the warm up regulator and connect the fuel line to the cold start valve.

55. Connect the coolant temperature and coil wires.

56. Install the EGR valve and connect the distributor vacuum hoses.

57. Connect the pre-heat tube to the rear of the engine.

58. On 1979 fuel injected vehicles equipped with equipped with air conditioning: Install the compressor bracket, support brace and diagonal braces and mount the compressor. Slip the drive belt onto the pulley. Install the alternator adjusting bracket and snug the bolts to tension the belt. Using a small prybar, pry on the adjusting bracket and tension the belt until there is approximately 10mm ($^3/_8$ in.) deflection between the compressor and the crankshaft pulleys (check with thumb pressure). Once the belt is tensioned properly, torque the alternator bracket bolts to 17 ft. lbs. Install the alternator and timing belt covers.

59. Connect the distributor, warm-up regulator, oil pressure switch, thermo-switch and alternator wiring.

60. Install the radiator and connect the fan motor wiring.

61. Connect the upper radiator and heater hoses to the engine

62. Install the thermostat flange with a new gasket.

63. Connect the air intake duct to the fuel distributor and throttle housing.

64. Connect the battery cables.

65. On 1979 fuel injected vehicles equipped with air conditioning: Connect the clutch wire. Position the compressor clutch on the compressor shaft and install the clutch bolt.

66. Fill the cooling system and connect the battery cables.

1985–90 Golf, GTI and Jetta Gasoline Engines Except 2.0L 16V

The engine and transmission assembly are removed from the vehicle together.

1. Disconnect the battery cables and remove the battery.

2. Relieve the fuel system pressure.

NOTE: *If equipped with an automatic transmission, place the selector lever in the PARK position.*

3. Remove the air intake duct between the fuel distributor and the throttle housing.

4. Remove the radiator cap. Turn the heater temperature control valve to fully

OPEN. Place a container under the thermostat housing, remove the thermostat flange and drain the coolant.

CAUTION: *When draining the coolant, keep in mind that cats and dogs are attracted by the ethylene glycol antifreeze, and are quite likely to drink any that is left in an uncovered container or in puddles on the ground. This will prove fatal in sufficient quantity. Always drain the coolant into a sealable container. Coolant should be reused unless it is contaminated or several years old.*

5. Remove the upper radiator and heater hoses from the engine. Remove the electrical connector from the radiator fan motor. Remove the radiator mounting nuts, the upper radiator clamp clip and the clamp. Remove the radiator shroud and the radiator.

6. At the front of the vehicle, remove the apron, the trim and the grille. Disconnect the headlight electrical connectors and the hood release cable from the hood latch assembly.

NOTE: *If equipped with power steering, remove the drive belt and the pump mounting bolts. Remove the power steering pump and move it aside. DO NOT disconnect the power steering pressure lines and DO NOT allow the pump to hang freely by the hoses..*

7. Remove the electrical connectors from the following components: the alternator, the thermoswitch, the oil pressure switch, the warm-up regulator and the distributor.

NOTE: *If equipped with air conditioning, remove the trim panel and the lower apron. Remove the condenser and duct work from the crossmember and radiator. Remove the idle boost valve vacuum hose and the air filter assembly. Disconnect the air flow assembly and the compressor, then move it aside. Tie the compressor off to the side and out of the way. DO NOT disconnect the refrigerant hoses and DO NOT allow the compressor to hang freely by the hoses.*

8. Remove the pre-heat tube from the rear of the engine.

9. Remove the distributor vacuum hoses and the EGR temperature valve.

10. Remove the coil and the coolant temperature sensor, the Lambda (oxygen) sensor and the knock sensor wires.

CAUTION: *Use care when disconnecting the fuel lines. Fuel under pressure may still be in the lines and if sprayed, may cause fire or personal injury.*

11. Place a container under the cold start valve, then remove the fuel line and the warm-up regulator.

12. Remove the electrical connectors from the cold start valve and the auxiliary air regulator.

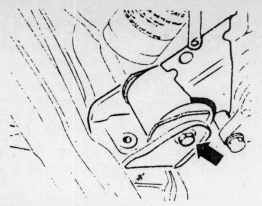

Early version front rubber mount

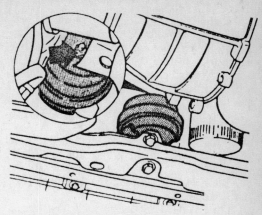

Later version front rubber mount

13. At the throttle body, remove the vacuum lines of the brake booster, the vacuum amplifier and the vacuum amplifier (if equipped).

14. Remove the PCV hose from the cylinder head cover.

15. At the throttle body, pull back the accelerator cable clip and disconnect the cable from the ball. Loosen the accelerator cable locknut and remove the cable from the cylinder head cover.

16. Remove the fuel injectors, then position the entire assembly aside. Cover the fuel injector openings with masking tape to prevent the entry of dirt.

17. Disconnect the electrical connectors from the starter, the back-up light switch and the ground cable from the transmission.

18. If equipped with a manual transmission, at the clutch cable, loosen the locknut, remove the clip from under the clutch lever and remove the cable. If equipped with an automatic transmission, disconnect the selector cable from the transmission and the bracket.

19. Remove the speedometer cable clamp and the cable. Remove the upper starter bolts and the starter.

20. If equipped with a manual transmission, remove the transmission and upshift indicator vacuum switches. If equipped with an automatic transmission, remove the CIS-E wiring harness.

NOTE: *On the GTI/GLI models, remove the idle stabilizer control valve, the throttle plate switch and the knock sensor.*

21. Remove the nuts from the exhaust flexpipe and the relay shaft. Disconnect the lever from the relay shaft.

22. Remove the driveshafts from the mounting flanges.

23. Remove the horn (move aside) and the front mount cup bolts. Remove the cup and the front mount. There are two kinds of front mounts. Earlier mounts are the rubber bushing type which were replaced with a hydraulic mount in January of 1985. To remove the rubber bushing type front mount, remove the mounting bolt and disengage the transmission from the mount by turning it slightly side to side. Hydraulic mounts are removed in the same manner except that they are held in place by an acorn nut instead of a bolt.

24. Remove the three rear engine mounting nuts.

NOTE: *On vehicles equipped with the 16 valve engine, the intake manifold will have to be removed in order to remove the engine.*

25. Attach an engine sling tool VW–2024A or equivalent to the engine. Using an overhead crane, lift the engine slightly.

26. On manual transmissions: Remove the clip from the gearshift lever rod, the rod from the selector shaft lever and the relay shaft with the gearshift lever rod. Open the clip on the front of the selector rod and remove the rod from the relay lever.

27. Remove the right and left side engine mount to body bolts.

28. Slightly lower and tilt the engine and transmission. Lift the engine/transmission assembly, turning it slightly, out of the car.

To install:

29. Lower the engine/transmission assembly into the car and install the right and left engine mount-to-body bolts. Torque to 33 ft. lbs. for 10mm bolts or 54 ft. lbs. for 12mm bolts.

30. On manual transmissions: Insert the selector rod into the relay lever. Spread the ends of the circlip and install it in the groove at the front of the selector rod. Insert the gearshift lever rod (with selector lever and relay shaft attached) into the selector shaft and install the circlip.

31. Install the rear engine mounting nuts. On 16V engines, install the intake manifold with a new gasket.

32. Install the front engine mounts. Lubricate the bolt threads with engine oil prior to installation. For the old style rubber bushing type mounts, torque the bolt to 37 ft. lbs. On the new hydraulic mounts, torque the acorn nut to 22 ft. lbs.

33. Install the horn.

34. Connect the driveshafts to the mounting flanges. Torque the bolts to 30–33 ft. lbs. Torque the ball joint-to-steering knuckle bolt to 36 ft. lbs. and the drive axle nut to 174 ft. lbs.

35. Connect the relay shaft lever and the exhaust flex pipe.

36. On GLI/GTI models, install the knock sensor, throttle plate switch and idle stabilizer control valve.

37. On automatic transmissions, install the CIS-E wiring harness and make sure that it is routed neatly. On manual transmissions, install the upshift indicator and transmission switches.

38. Install the starter, connect the speedometer cable and install the cable clamp.

39. Connect the selector (automatic transmission) or clutch (manual transmission) cables.

40. Connect the transmission ground, back-up light switch and starter wiring.

41. Install the fuel injectors.

42. Position the accelerator cable onto the cylinder head cover and install the cable locknut. Pull the cable tight and connect the cable end to the locking ball by depressing the ball spring, then secure the cable with the cable clip.

43. Connect the PCV hose to the cylinder head cover.

44. Connect the vacuum amplifier (if equipped) and brake booster vacuum lines to the throttle body.

45. Plug in the cold start valve and auxiliary air regulator electrical connectors.

46. Install the warm up regulator and connect the fuel line to the cold start valve.

47. Connect the coolant temperature, coil, oxygen sensor, knock sensor wires.

48. Install the EGR valve and connect the distributor vacuum hoses.

49. Connect the pre-heat tube to the rear of the engine.

50. If equipped with air conditioning: Install the compressor the mounting bracket and tighten the mounting bolts. Connect the air flow assembly and the idle boost vacuum hose. Install the air duct work, lower apron and trim panel.

51. Connect the distributor wiring and plug in the warm-up regulator, oil pressure switch, thermoswitch and alternator connectors.

52. Install the power steering pump and drive belt. Torque the mounting bolts to 14 ft. lbs.

53. Connect the hood release cable to the hood latch.

54. Plug in the headlight connectors.

55. Install the front grille, trim and apron.

56. Install the radiator and connect the fan wiring and upper radiator and heater hoses.

57. Install the thermostat flange with a new gasket.

58. Connect the air intake duct.

59. Install the battery and connect the battery cables.

60. Fill the cooling system and adjust the drive belt tension.

GTI and Jetta GLI 16V 2.0L Engines

After removing the battery and front apron, the engine/transmission assembly is removed the same way as described above for 1.8L engines.

During installation, perform the following:

• Place a light coating of MoS_2 grease on the splines of the transmission shaft.

• Make sure the guide sleeves for centering the engine and transmission are in place on the engine block. If not, install them.

• When lowering the engine into the engine compartment, make sure there is enough clearance for the driveshafts.

• Once the engine is in place and the mounts installed, first tighten engine mount **A** to 18 ft. lbs. then transmission mount **B** to 22 ft. lbs. Lubricate the the mount and mounting bracket bolts with clean engine oil prior to installation.

• Loosen the front bonded rubber bushing on the engine mounts and align the bushing until all tension is removed from it. Once aligned, torque mounting bracket bolt **E** to 44 ft. lbs. and **F** to 52 ft. lbs.

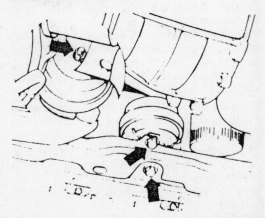

Loosen the front bonded rubber bushing (arrows) on the engine mount and align without tension

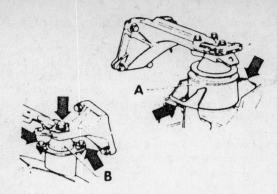

Rear engine (A) and transmission (B) mounts

• Torque the drive shaft flange bolts to 33 ft. lbs.

• Torque the exhaust pipe-to-manifold nuts to 30 ft. lbs.

• Torque the power steering pump bracket bolts to 18 ft. lbs.

Rabbit and Jetta Diesel and Turbodiesel Engines

The engine and transmission assembly is removed from the vehicle with the transmission attached.

1. Disconnect the negative battery cable.

2. Turn the heater control to fully **OPEN**. Remove the radiator cap and the radiator hose at the thermostat housing and drain the cooling system. Remove the thermostat flange.

CAUTION: *When draining the coolant, keep in mind that cats and dogs are attracted by the ethylene glycol antifreeze, and are quite likely to drink any that is left in an uncovered container or in puddles on the ground. This will prove fatal in sufficient quantity. Always drain the coolant into a sealable container. Coolant should be reused unless it is contaminated or several years old.*

3. Remove the fuel filter. Cap the fuel line connections to prevent leakage.

4. Remove the radiator hoses.

5. Disconnect the wiring from the radiator fan motor and the thermoswitch. Remove the radiator mounting nuts and upper clamp. Lift the radiator out of the vehicle.

6. Disconnect the brake booster hose from the vacuum pump.

7. Remove the alternator.

8. Disconnect the electrical connectors at the fuel shut-off solenoid, the glow plugs, the oil pressure switch and the coolant temperature sensor.

9. Remove the heater and the expansion tank hoses.

10. At the injection pump, disconnect the accelerator cable with the bracket and remove the fuel supply and the return lines from the injection pump. Cap the ends of the lines to prevent leakage and the entry of dirt into the system.

11. Disconnect the cold start cable.

12. If equipped with air conditioning: Remove the timing belt cover, loosen the timing belt tensioner, and remove the timing belt from the injection pump sprocket. Using a suitable puller (US 4484 or equivalent), remove the injection pump sprocket from the shaft of the pump. Remove the injection pump mounting plate bolts, support and remove the pump (the fuel lines should already have been disconnected). Remove the air conditioning belt tensioner, water pump pulley and drive belt. Remove the alternator and drive belt (if not already removed). Remove the windshield washer reservoir and set it off to the side and out of the way. Remove the air conditioning drive belt, the electrical connector at the compressor, the compressor bracket-to-engine bolts and the compressor assembly, then move it off to the side and support with wire leaving the hoses connected. DO NOT support the compressor with the hoses under tension or allow the compressor to hang freely by the hoses.

13. If equipped with power steering: Remove the drive belt, the bracket bolts (leave the lines attached) and tie the assembly off to the side and out of the way. DO NOT allow the pump to hang freely by the hoses.

14. Disconnect the electrical connectors from the starter, back-up switch and the transmission mount ground wire.

15. If equipped with a manual transmission, disconnect the clutch cable and route it off to the side and out of the way.

16. Remove the speedometer cable clamp

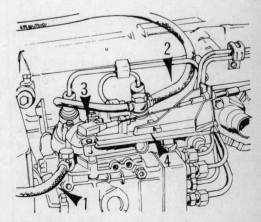

Detach and mark the fuel lines at the injection pump. (1) fuel supply line, (2) return line, (3) accelerator cable and (4) remove bracket — diesel

and disconnect the speedometer cable from the transmission.

17. Remove the upper starter bolt.

18. On non-turbocharged engines, remove the exhaust pipe nuts or spring clips and disconnect the exhaust pipe from the manifold.

19. If equipped with a turbocharger: Remove the turbocharger-to-exhaust manifold bolts, the turbocharger-to-transmission bracket, the air intake ducts and the oil lines. Remove the turbocharger from the engine. Cap the oil lines to prevent leakage.

20. Disconnect the relay shaft lever.

21. Unbolt and disconnect the halfshafts from the drive flanges.

22. Remove the lower starter bolt and remove the starter.

23. Remove the horn and set it off to the side.

24. Remove the front mount cup bolts and remove the cup and the front mount.

25. Drain the oil and unscrew the oil filter.

CAUTION: *The EPA warns that prolonged contact with used engine oil may cause a number of skin disorders, including cancer! You should make every effort to minimize your exposure to used engine oil. Protective gloves should be worn when changing the oil. Wash your hands and any other exposed skin areas as soon as possible after exposure to used engine oil. Soap and water, or waterless hand cleaner should be used.*

26. Remove the axle hub nuts and disconnect the lower ball joints from the steering knuckles.

27. Raise the vehicle, swing the strut assemblies away from the vehicle and pull out the drive shafts.

28. Reconnect the ball joints so that the vehicle may be lowered to the ground.

29. Remove the rear engine mount and the right front wheel.

30. Attach the engine support tool US 1105 or equivalent and a vertical lift to the engine, then lift it slightly.

NOTE: *If equipped with a manual transmission, remove the relay shaft and the gearshift lever rods.*

31. Remove both side engine mount to body bolts.

32. Lower the engine and transmission assembly onto a dolly. Raise the vehicle and slide the dolly from under the vehicle.

To install:

33. With the engine/transmission positioned on the dolly, slide the engine under the vehicle and re-connect the crane to the lifting brackets.

34. Carefully, raise the engine and transmission into the vehicle and align as follows: Move the engine from side to side until the rear mount is straight. Then, move the engine assembly in the front to rear direction until the left and right mounts are centered in their brackets. Tighten the right, left and rear mount bolts to 25–30 ft. lbs. Position the front mount cup until the rubber core is centered in the cup. Now, torque the cup bolts to 38 ft. lbs. On all models, make sure that the exhaust system is aligned properly before completing the rest of the installation procedure. Re-align the exhaust system if necessary.

35. Mount the right front wheel.

36. Disconnect the ball joints and raise the front end.

37. Swing the strut assemblies away from the vehicle and insert the drive shafts.

38. Attach the ball joint to the wheel bearing housing and torque the locknut to 36 ft. lbs. Install the axle nuts and torque them to 174 ft. lbs.

39. Install a new oil filter.

40. Mount the horn.

41. Mount the starter and install the lower starter bolt. Do not tighten at this time.

42. Connect the halfshafts to the drive flanges and torque the mounting bolts to 30 ft. lbs.

43. Connect the relay shaft lever.

44. If equipped, install the turbocharger onto the engine, connect the oil lines and attach the exhaust pipe. Use new gaskets.

45. On non-turbocharged engines, connect the exhaust flex pipe to the manifold and torque the nuts to 18 ft. lbs.

46. Install the upper starter bolts and torque all the bolts to 33 ft. lbs.

47. Connect the speedometer to the transmission and install the cable clamp.

48. On manual transmission, connect and adjust the clutch cable.

49. Connect the transmission ground, back-up switch and starter wiring.

50. If equipped with power steering, install the power steering pump and the drive belt.

51. If equipped with air conditioning: Attach the compressor bracket to the engine block and torque the mounting bolts to 18 ft. lbs. Mount the compressor and tensioner on the bracket. Install the windshield washer bottle. Place the alternator drive belt onto the compressor clutch pulley, and do the same for the air conditioning drive belt. Install the water pump pulley and torque the pulley bolts to 14 ft. lbs. Adjust the belt tension to 10mm ($^3/8$ in.) deflection, and tighten the compressor mounting and tensioning bolts to 22 ft. lbs. Install the injection pump, sprocket and timing belt as described later in this chapter. Install the timing belt cover cover with a new gasket.

52. Connect the cold start cable.

53. Connect the fuel lines to the injection pump. Do not mix up the supply and return lines. VW has marked the return lines with **OUT** to prevent this from happening.

54. Connect the expansion tank and heater hoses.

55. Connect the temperature sensor, oil pressure switch, glow plug and fuel shut-off solenoid wires.

56. Install the radiator and connect the thermoswitch and fan motor wiring.

57. Install the radiator hoses.

58. Install a new fuel filter.

59. Install the thermostat flange with a new gasket.

60. Connect the negative battery cable, fill the cooling system and crankcase. Adjust the belt tension and injection pump timing.

Fox

The engine is lifted out of the vehicle after separation from the transmission.

1. Disconnect the battery ground cable and remove the battery.

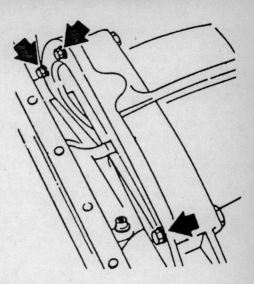

Converter cover plate removal — Fox

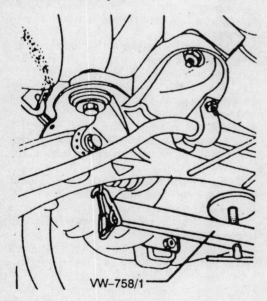

VW-758/1

Transmission support tool installation — Fox

CAUTION: *The battery tube located on the right side of the engine may contain a small amount of battery electrolyte which contains sulfuric acid. When removing the battery, wear protective gloves and goggles to prevent personal injury.*

2. Open the heating valve and the cap on the coolant expansion tank. Drain the coolant by removing the hoses. Then separate the electrical connector from the radiator fan.

CAUTION: *When draining the coolant, keep in mind that cats and dogs are attracted by the ethylene glycol antifreeze, and are quite likely to drink any that is left in an uncovered container or in puddles on the ground. This will prove fatal in sufficient quantity. Always drain the coolant into a sealable container. Coolant should be reused unless it is contaminated or several years old.*

NOTE: *Do not disconnect or loosen any refrigerant hose connections during engine removal on cars equipped with air conditioning.*

3. On cars equipped with air conditioning: Remove the condenser from the radiator. Loosen the compressor support bolts and remove the compressor and the condenser. Tie the air conditioning compressor and condenser off to the side and out of the way without disconnecting any refrigerant lines. DO NOT allow the compressor to hang freely by the hoses.

4. Disconnect the radiator thermo switch and remove the radiator cover. Disconnect the motor mount and remove the rubber bushing. Remove the radiator with the air ducts and fan.

5. Disconnect the clutch cable.

6. Disconnect the alternator, oil pressure switches and oxygen sensor wiring.

7. Disconnect the wiring harnesses at the thermostat flange, auxiliary air regulator and cold start valve.

8. Disconnect the throttle cable from the throttle body. Route the cable off to the side and out of the way.

8. Disconnect the vacuum hoses from the intake manifold and the throttle body.

9. From the distributor, disconnect the ig-

nition coil wire, vacuum advance hoses and Hall effect sender wire.

10. Remove the fuel injectors. Cover the injector openings with masking tape to prevent the entry of dirt.

11. Unbolt and remove the cold start valve (leave the fuel line connected).

12. Loosen the charcoal canister clamp and move the canister to the rear of the engine so that it out of your way.

13. Remove the engine stop.

14. Disconnect the air intake duct from the intake manifold and move it off to the side and out of the way.

15. Remove the right and left engine mounting nuts.

16. Disconnect the starter wiring and remove the starter from the engine.

17. Remove the two lower engine to transmission bolts. Then remove the cover plate bolts and the cover plate.

18. Disconnect the exhaust pipe from the manifold at the flange. Then remove the bolt from the exhaust pipe support and remove the exhaust pipe from the manifold.

19. Install transmission support bar VW-758/1 or equivalent with slight preload.

20. Install chain US-1105 or equivalent on the engine lifting eyes, located on the left side of the cylinder head.

21. Lift the engine until its weight is taken off the engine mounts.

22. Adjust the support bar to contact the transmission.

23. Separate the engine and transmission.

24. Carefully lift the engine out of the engine compartment so as not to damage the transmission main shaft, clutch and body.

To install:

NOTE: *When installing a replacement block on Fox, the oil pump drive bushing does not come with the new block. You must purchase one. Before installing the new block, make sure to install the oil pump drive bushing between the oil pump shaft and the distributor drive gear. If this bushing is not installed, the engine will have little oil pressure or none at all. This would be very bad for you and your engine.*

25. Lubricate the clutch release bearing and transmission main shaft splines with MOS_2 grease or an equivalent. Do Not lubricate the guide sleeve or the clutch release bearing.

26. Carefully guide the engine into the vehicle and attach to the transmission while keeping weight off of the motor mounts.

27. Install and tighten the upper engine-to-transmission bolts.

28. Remove the transmission support bar and lower the engine onto the engine mounts.

Install the upper engine-to-transmission bolts and torque them to 42 ft. lbs. Install the cover plate and torque the mounting bolts to 7 ft. lbs. Install the engine mount nuts and snug them.

NOTE: *The engine mounts and subframe bracket bolts will will be torqued later with the engine running at idle speed.*

29. Connect the exhaust pipe to the manifold with a new gasket and torque the pipe nuts to 22 ft. lbs. Attach the pipe to the support bracket and torque the support bolt to 18 ft. lbs.

30. Install the starter and connect the starter wiring. Torque the starter mounting bolts to 18 ft. lbs.

31. Connect the air intake duct to the intake manifold.

32. Install the engine stop.

33. Move the charcoal canister back to the front of the engine and tighten the mounting clamp.

34. Install the cold start valve and torque the mounting bolts to 7 ft. lbs.

35. Install the fuel injectors.

36. Connect the Hall effect sender wire, vacuum unit hose and the ignition coil wire to the distributor.

37. Connect the intake manifold and throttle body vacuum hoses.

38. Connect and adjust the throttle cable.

39. Connect the cold start valve, auxiliary regulator, thermostat flange, oxygen sensor, oil pressure and alternator wiring.

40. Connect and adjust the clutch cable.

41. Install the radiator, fan and duct assemblies. Install the radiator cover and connect the thermoswitch.

42. If equipped with air conditioning: Mount the compressor and install the drive belt. Mount the condenser onto the radiator.

43. Connect the radiator fan wire and install the radiator hoses.

44. Refill the cooling system, adjust the belt tension, install the battery and connect the battery cables.

45. Run the engine at idle speed and torque the engine mount nuts to 30 ft. lbs., the body engine front mounting carrier fasteners to 47 ft. lbs. and the block front mounting bracket to 22 ft. lbs.

Corrado and Passat

The engine and transmission are removed through top of the vehicle.

1. Disconnect the battery cables and drain the cooling system.

CAUTION: *When draining the coolant, keep in mind that cats and dogs are attracted by the ethylene glycol antifreeze, and are quite likely to drink any that is left in an uncov-*

ered container or in puddles on the ground. *This will prove fatal in sufficient quantity. Always drain the coolant into a sealable container. Coolant should be reused unless it is contaminated or several years old.*

2. Disconnect and label all electrical connectors, wiring harnesses and vacuum hoses.

3. Disconnect the accelerator cable from the throttle body.

4. Unbolt the condenser from the radiator and move it off to the side and out of the way.

5. Remove the upper radiator cover and unplug the fan wire and thermoswitch connectors. Disconnect the coolant hose from the upper radiator hose flange. Disconnect the lower radiator, expansion tank and coolant pipe hoses. Remove the air ducts and the radiator and fan assembly.

6. Unbolt and remove the power steering pump and tie it off to the side and out of the way. DO NOT disconnect the hydraulic hoses from the pump or allow the pump to hang freely by the hoses.

7. If equipped with air conditioning, remove the compressor mounting bolts and tie the compressor (with mount) off to the side and out of the way. DO NOT disconnect the refrigerant hoses or allow the compressor to hang freely by the hoses.

CAUTION: *DO NOT discharge the air conditioning system.*

8. On Corrado, disconnect the intercooler tubes and plug them.

9. If equipped with automatic transmission, place the gearshift selector lever in **PARK** and disconnect the cable from the gearshift lever on the transmission. If equipped with manual transmission, disconnect the gearshift cable from the transmission gearshift lever. Disconnect the selector cable (with linkage lever) from the transmission. Do not allow the cables to become twisted or kinked.

10. Disconnect the speedometer cable from the transmission.

11. Remove the upper engine/transmission bolts.

12. On Corrado, disconnect the air intake hose from the air flow sensor. Remove the fuel injectors. Cover the injector opening with masking tape to prevent the entry of dirt.

13. Disconnect the exhaust pipe from the exhaust manifold.

14. Remove the three right engine mount bolts.

15. Remove the hex head bolt from the left transmission mount.

NOTE: *On Corrado equipped with ABS, the left transmission bolt is hard to get at. On these vehicles, remove the cooling system overflow reservoir to gain access to this bolt.*

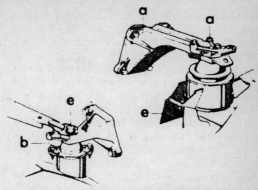

Engine/transmission mount fastener locations — Passat

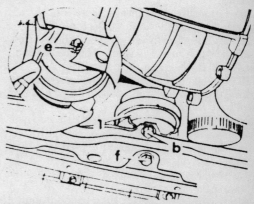

Engine/transmission mount fastener locations (continued) — Passat

16. Remove the front transmission mount nut. Discard the nut and purchase a new one.

17. Connect engine lifting support 2024A or equivalent to the engine lifting eyes and attach a vertical engine hoist to the lifting support.

18. Remove the inner right CV-joint heat shield.

19. Unbolt the driveshafts from the transmission flanges, swing them upward and tie them off.

20. Disconnect the rear engine mounts. Discard the nuts and purchase new ones.

21. Carefully raise the engine from the engine compartment and maneuver out of the vehicle.

To install:

22. Check the clutch release bearing for wear. Lubricate the splines of the release bearing driveshaft with a light coat of MoS_2 grease.

23. Make sure the locating dowels for centering the engine and transmission are in place on the cylinder block.

NOTE: *When lowering the engine, make sure that there is enough clearance for the engine to clear the driveshafts.*

24. Lower the engine onto the rear engine mount first, then install the transmission mounts. Loosen the front engine mount bracket. Align all the engine mount supports with their bushings before installing the mounting fasteners keeping as much tension off the mounts as possible. Once the mounts are aligned properly, install the mounting fasteners. Using the accompanying illustrations (for fastener identification), torque fastener **A** to 18 ft. lbs., fastener **B** to 22 ft. lbs., fastener **E** to 44 ft. lbs. and fastener **F** to 53 ft. lbs.

25. Connect the driveshafts and torque the flange bolts to 33 ft. lbs.

26. Install the inner right CV-joint heat shield.

27. Connect the air intake hose from the air flow sensor. Install the fuel injectors.

28. Connect the exhaust pipe to the exhaust manifold with a new gasket. Torque the pipe nuts to 30 ft. lbs.

29. Install the upper engine/transmission bolts. Torque the 10mm bolts to 33 ft. lbs. and the 12mm bolts to 41 ft. lbs.

30. Connect the speedometer cable to the transmission.

31. Connect the gearshift and selector cables.

32. On Corrado, connect the intercooler tubes.

33. If equipped, install the air conditioning compressor (and mount).

34. Install the power steering pump and torque the mounting bolts to 15–18 ft. lbs.

35. Install the radiator and air duct ducts. Connect the radiator fan and thermoswitch wires and all coolant hoses. Install the radiator upper cover.

36. Mount the condenser to the radiator.

37. Connect all vacuum hoses, wiring harnesses and electrical connectors.

38. Fill the cooling system and connect the battery cables.

Camshaft (Valve) Cover

REMOVAL AND INSTALLATION

Remove air cleaner assembly or loosen and relocate the air cleaner snorkel or box (depending on year and model). Disconnect the fuel line and accelerator cable (if necessary) and any other vacuum lines, hoses, support brackets, spark plug wires that will interfere with the cover removal. Disconnect the crankcase breather hose from the cover connection. Remove the cover retaining bolts and the cover. Clean all mounting surfaces. Install a new cover gasket and seal. Lubricate the seal with grease or a suitable sealant before installing it. Install the cover in the reverse order of re-

moval. Torque the cover fasteners to 7 ft. lbs. DO NOT overtighen them or you may warp the cover and overcompress the gasket.

Thermostat

REMOVAL AND INSTALLATION

All 4-Cylinder Engines

The thermostat is located in the bottom radiator hose neck on the water pump.

1. Drain the cooling system.

CAUTION: *When draining the coolant, keep in mind that cats and dogs are attracted by the ethylene glycol antifreeze, and are quite likely to drink any that is left in an uncovered container or in puddles on the ground. This will prove fatal in sufficient quantity. Always drain the coolant into a sealable container. Coolant should be reused unless it is contaminated or several years old.*

2. Remove the two retaining bolts from the lower water pump neck.

NOTE: *It's not necessary to disconnect the hose.*

3. Move neck, with hoses attached, out of the way.

4. Remove the thermostat.

5. Install a new O-ring seal on the water pump neck. Lubricate the seal with silicone compound prior to installation.

6. Install the thermostat with the spring end up.

7. Replace the water pump neck and tighten the two retaining bolts to 7 ft. lbs.

5-Cylinder

The thermostat is located in the lower radia-

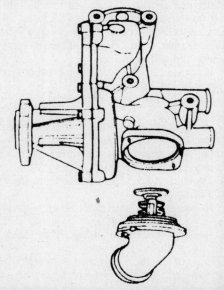

Typical thermostat assembly (Fox shown here)

tor hose neck, on the left side of the engine block, behind the water pump housing.

1. Drain the cooling system.

CAUTION: *When draining the coolant, keep in mind that cats and dogs are attracted by the ethylene glycol antifreeze, and are quite likely to drink any that is left in an uncovered container or in puddles on the ground. This will prove fatal in sufficient quantity. Always drain the coolant into a sealable container. Coolant should be reused unless it is contaminated or several years old.*

2. Remove the two retaining bolts from the lower water pump neck.

NOTE: *It's not necessary to disconnect the hose.*

3. Move neck, with hoses attached, out of the way.

4. Carefully pry the thermostat out of the engine block.

5. Install a new O-ring seal on the water pump neck. Lubricate the seal with silicone compound prior to installation.

6. Install the thermostat.

NOTE: *When installing the thermostat, the spring end should be pointing toward the engine block.*

7. Reposition the water pump neck and tighten the retaining bolts to 7 ft. lbs.

Intake Manifold
REMOVAL AND INSTALLATION
Carbureted Engines

1. Remove the air cleaner. Drain the cooling system.

CAUTION: *When draining the coolant, keep in mind that cats and dogs are attracted by the ethylene glycol antifreeze, and are quite likely to drink any that is left in an uncovered container or in puddles on the ground. This will prove fatal in sufficient quantity. Always drain the coolant into a sealable container. Coolant should be reused unless it is contaminated or several years old.*

2. Disconnect the accelerator cable.

3. Disconnect the EGR valve connections.

4. Detach all electrical leads.

5. Disconnect the coolant hoses.

6. Disconnect the fuel line from the carburetor.

7. Remove the vacuum hoses from the carburetor.

8. Loosen and remove the six retaining bolts and lift off the manifold.

To install:

9. Install a new gasket. Fit the manifold and tighten the bolts from the inside out. Tightening torque is 18 ft. lbs.

10. Connect the vacuum hoses to the carburetor.

11. Connect the fuel line to the carburetor.

12. Connect the coolant hoses.

13. Connect all electrical leads.

14. Connect the EGR valve.

15. Connect the accelerator cable.

16. Install the air cleaner and refill the cooling system.

NOTE: *See Throttle Linkage Adjustment in Chapter 5 for correct adjustment of the throttle cable.*

Fuel Injected Engines

1. Disconnect the air duct from the throttle valve body. On Corrado, also disconnect the flexible hose that connects the throttle body to the G-Charger, the hose that connects the idle stabilizer valve to the G-Charger inlet pipe and the intercooler hose. Drain the cooling system.

CAUTION: *When draining the coolant, keep in mind that cats and dogs are attracted by the ethylene glycol antifreeze, and are quite likely to drink any that is left in an uncovered container or in puddles on the ground. This will prove fatal in sufficient quantity. Always drain the coolant into a sealable container. Coolant should be reused unless it is contaminated or several years old.*

2. Disconnect the accelerator cable.

3. Remove the injectors or injector/fuel rail assembly and disconnect the line from the cold start valve. Have a small plastic container handy to catch the excess fuel.

4. Disconnect all coolant hoses.

5. Disconnect all vacuum and emission control hoses. Label all hoses for installation.

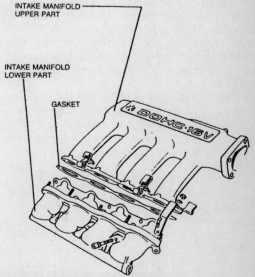

16-valve engine intake manifold

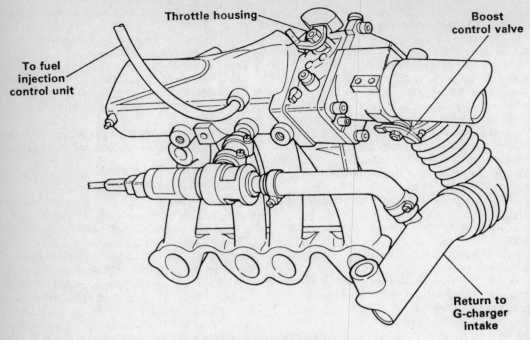

Throttle housing

Boost control valve

To fuel injection control unit

Return to G-charger intake

Corrado intake manifold assembly

6. Remove the auxiliary air regulator.

7. Disconnect all electrical connectors. Label all wires for installation.

8. Disconnect the EGR line from the exhaust manifold.

9. Loosen and remove the retaining bolts and lift off the manifold with the throttle body attached. It is easier to remove the throttle body with the intake manifold off the engine. On Corrado, do not disturb the boost control linkage. This linkage is adjusted at the factory and should not be tampered with. Clean the intake manifold gasket mating surfaces throughly. Make sure that all traces of the old gasket material are removed. Inspect the intake manifold for cracks and the gasket surfaces for warpage. If the manifold is damaged, replace it.

NOTE: *The intake manifold on the 16 valve engine is removed in two halves (upper and lower). The upper half is removed first. The gasket between the halves should be replaced if the manifold is separated.*

To install:

10. Install a new gasket. Install the manifold and tighten the bolts to 18 ft. lbs. (eight valve engines). On 16 valve engines, torque the upper-to-lower bolts to 15 ft. lbs.

11. Connect the EGR valve to the exhaust manifold.

12. Plug in all electrical connectors.

13. Install the auxiliary air regulator with a new gasket.

14. Connect all vacuum and emission control hoses.

15. Connect the coolant hoses.

16. Install the cold start valve with a new gasket. Install the fuel injectors using new injector seals.

17. Connect and adjust the accelerator cable.

18. Fill the cooling system and connect the air intake duct to the throttle body. On Corrado, connect the G-Charger, the idle stabilizer and intercooler hoses.

Diesel Engines

1. Disconnect the negative battery cable.

2. Drain the cooling system.

CAUTION: *When draining the coolant, keep in mind that cats and dogs are attracted by the ethylene glycol antifreeze, and are quite likely to drink any that is left in an uncovered container or in puddles on the ground. This will prove fatal in sufficient quantity. Always drain the coolant into a sealable container. Coolant should be reused unless it is contaminated or several years old.*

3. Disconnect the hose that runs between the air duct and the turbocharger (turbo-diesel only).

4. Remove the air cleaner.

5. Disconnect and plug all lines coming from the brake booster vacuum pump and remove the pump.

6. Disconnect the PCV line.

7. Disconnect and remove the blow-off

valve and then disconnect the hose which runs from the intake manifold to the turbocharger (turbodiesel only).

8. Remove the intake manifold from the engine. Clean the intake manifold gasket mating surfaces throughly. Make sure that all traces of the old gasket material are removed. Inspect the intake manifold for cracks and the gasket surfaces for warpage. If the manifold is damaged, replace it.

To install:

9. Install the manifold onto the engine with a new gasket. Tighten the bolts from the center towards the ends, alternating from center.

10. Connect the intake manifold-to-turbo-charger hose (turbo-diesels only). Install the blow-off valve.

11. Connect the PCV line.

12. Install the brake booster vacuum pump and connect the vacuum lines.

13. Install the air cleaner.

14. On turbodiesel engines, connect the air duct-to-turbocharger hose.

15. Fill the cooling system.

16. Connect the negative battery cable.

Exhaust Manifold

REMOVAL AND INSTALLATION

NOTE: *Some diesel and gasoline engines use two spring clamps to connect the exhaust pipe to the manifold. If spring clips are used, they require the use of a special wedge tool kit 3140 for removal and installation. Removal and installation of the spring clamps is described at the end of this chapter.*

1. Disconnect the EGR tube from the exhaust manifold (if equipped).

2. Remove the air pump components or any other type of interference which would prevent access to the exhaust manifold.

3. Remove the air cleaner hose from the exhaust manifold.

4. Disconnect the intake manifold support and the heat deflector shield, if equipped. Raise and support the front end.

5. Separate the front exhaust pipe from the manifold or turbocharger and remove any heat shields. If the front exhaust pipe is in the way, unbolt it from the converter and remove it completely. On Scirocco with automatic transmission, remove the starter motor heat shied, starter wiring and remove the starter.

NOTE: *Some exhaust systems use nuts to connect the exhaust pipe to the manifold, while others use spring clamps. If spring clamps are used, the gasket (which looks like a donut) is re-useable unless it was leaking or damaged. If the gasket is good, use it again.*

6. Unplug the connector from the oxygen sensor and unscrew the sensor from the exhaust manifold.

7. Remove the CO probe tube and tube clamp from the manifold, if equipped.

8. Remove turbocharger (turbodiesels only).

9. Remove the and remove the manifold from the engine. Clean the cylinder head and manifold mating surfaces. Make sure that all traces of the old gasket material are removed. Inspect the intake manifold for cracks and the gasket surfaces for warpage. If the manifold is damaged, replace it.

To install:

10. Using a new gasket, install the exhaust manifold. Tighten the nuts to 18 ft. lbs. Work from the inside out.

11. Connect the CO probe tube to the manifold and install the tube clamp (if equipped).

12. If equipped, screw the oxygen sensor into the exhaust manifold with a new gasket and plug in the connector. Lubricate the threads of the sensor with high temperature sealant and torque the sensor nut to 37 ft. lbs. Make sure that the sealant is applied only to the threads of the nut and not the slots of the sensor.

13. Connect the front exhaust pipe to the turbocharger or manifold using a new gasket as required. On Scirocco with automatic transmission, install the starter, wiring and starter heat shield.

14. Install the heat deflector shield and intake manifold support. Torque the heat deflector shield fasteners to 7 ft. lbs.

15. Connect the air cleaner hose to the manifold.

16. Install any interfering component that was removed to gain access to the exhaust manifold.

17. Connect the EGR tube (if equipped).

Turbocharger

REMOVAL AND INSTALLATION

TurboDiesel Engines

1. Disconnect the negative battery cable and ground strap. Drain the engine oil and remove the oil filter. Whenever the turbocharger is replaced, especially in cases of a turbo failure, it is good maintenance practice to change the oil and filter. If the turbo failed, metal particles from the compressor shaft bearings will have contaminated the old engine oil. Not changing the oil and filter may allow these particles to wipe the compressor shaft bearings of the new turbocharger and destroy it. The amount of money spent on oil and a filter is rel-

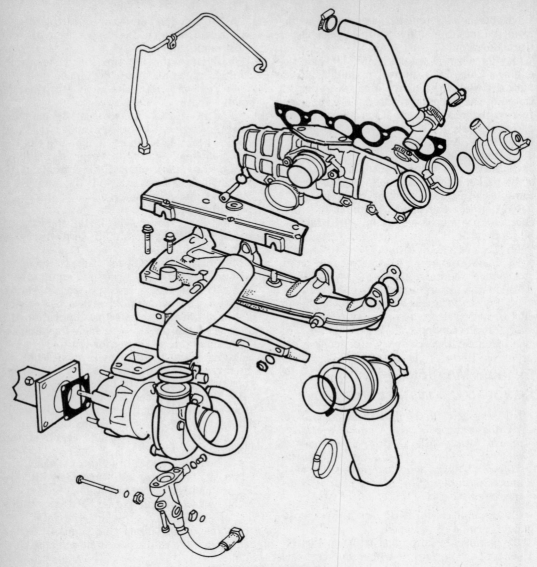

Turbocharger mounting

atively cheap insurance to ensure successful and sustained operation of the turbo.

CAUTION: *The EPA warns that prolonged contact with used engine oil may cause a number of skin disorders, including cancer! You should make every effort to minimize your exposure to used engine oil. Protective gloves should be worn when changing the oil. Wash your hands and any other exposed skin areas as soon as possible after exposure to used engine oil. Soap and water, or waterless hand cleaner should be used.*

2. Remove the engine and transmission cover shield to gain access to the turbocharger.
3. Loosen the stabilizer bar clamps on both sides of the stabilizer and push the bar down out of the way.
4. Remove the turbocharger heat shield mounting nuts. Disconnect the oil return line from the adapter flange at the bottom of the turbo. Plug the end of the line to prevent leakage.
5. Loosen the oil return connector bolt at the bottom of the adapter. Remove the side support bolt and remove the adapter from the bottom of the turbo. Have a container ready to catch the oil.
6. Remove the turbocharger-to-intake manifold and air cleaner hoses.
7. Loosen and remove the oil supply line to the turbocharger.

8. Remove the exhaust pipe-to-turbocharger mounting bolts.

9. Remove the turbocharger exhaust manifold mounting bolts. Remove the turbocharger.

To install:

10. Position the turbocharger on the exhaust manifold and hand tighten the two mounting bolts. Torque the manifold-to-turbocharger bolts to 50 ft. lbs.

11. Fill the upper oil supply connection on the turbocharger with oil. This ensures proper bearing pre-lube during start up.

12. Connect the turbocharger-to-air intake manifold and air cleaner hoses.

13. Attach the adapter to the bottom of the turbo with a new O-ring seal. Install the side and bottom bolts and torque them to 18 ft. lbs.

14. Connect the oil return line to the adapter and install the heat shields.

15. Raise the stabilizer bar to it's original position and install the stabilizer bar clamps.

16. Install the engine and transmission covers.

17. Connect the ground strap and negative battery cable. Install a new oil filter and fill the crankcase to the proper level.

18. When installation is complete, start the engine and allow to idle for several minutes. Do not increase engine speed above idle until the turbocharger oil supply system has had a chance to fill.

Air Conditioning Compressor

REMOVAL AND INSTALLATION

1. Discharge the air conditioning system as described in Chapter 1.

2. Disconnect the clutch wire from the compressor.

3. Remove the camshaft drive belt cover or any other interfering component needed to gain access to the compressor (pulley shields, ect.)

3. Loosen the compressor mounting bracket or tensioner bolts and slip the drive belt from the pulley. On Corrado, once the serpentine belt is off the air conditioning compressor pulley allow it to hang from the remaining pulleys.

4. Remove the diagonal and support braces, if installed.

5. Disconnect the refrigerant lines from the compressor. Cap the lines immediately to prevent the entry of dirt and moisture into the system.

6. Remove the compressor mounting bracket bolts and lift the unit out of the vehicle.

To install:

7. Mount the compressor and install the mounting bracket bolts.

8. Connect the refrigerant lines to the compressor.

9. Install the drive belt and adjust the tension as described in Chapter 1.

10. Install any interfering component that was removed to gain access to the compressor.

11. Connect the clutch wire.

12. Evacuate, charge and leak test the system.

Radiator and Fan

REMOVAL AND INSTALLATION

4-Cylinder Gasoline Engines

1. Disconnect the negative battery cable and drain the cooling system.

CAUTION: *When draining the coolant, keep in mind that cats and dogs are attracted by the ethylene glycol antifreeze, and are quite likely to drink any that is left in an uncovered container or in puddles on the ground. This will prove fatal in sufficient quantity. Always drain the coolant into a sealable container. Coolant should be reused unless it is contaminated or several years old.*

NOTE: *Various late models have the radiator retained by locating tabs at the bottom and two mounting brackets at the top. Disconnect hoses and wiring connectors, disconnect top brackets and remove radiator and fan assembly.*

2. Remove the inner shroud mounting bolts.

3. Disconnect the lower radiator hose.

4. Disconnect the thermo-switch lead and fan motor wiring. At this point (and depending on what vehicle you are working on), unbolt and remove the fan(s) from the radiator. This will make removing the radiator easier. On vehicle equipped with air conditioning, remove the condenser from the radiator (leaving lines connected) and position it off to the side and out of the way.

5. Remove the lower radiator shroud.

6. Remove the lower radiator mounting bolts.

7. Disconnect the upper radiator hose.

8. Detach the upper radiator shroud, air duct work and support braces.

9. Disconnect the heater and intake manifold hoses.

10. Remove the side mounting bolts and top clip and lift the radiator and fan(s) out as an assembly from the mounts.

To install:

11. Set the radiator and fan(s) assembly onto the mounts and install the mounting bolts and toe clips.

12. Connect the heater and intake manifold hoses.

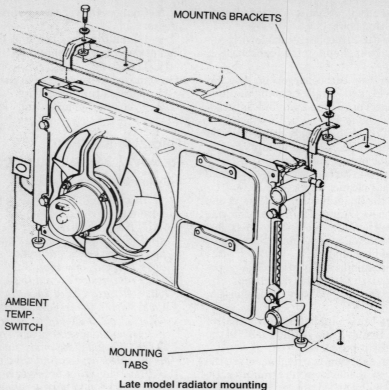

MOUNTING BRACKETS

AMBIENT
TEMP.
SWITCH

MOUNTING
TABS

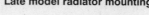

Late model radiator mounting

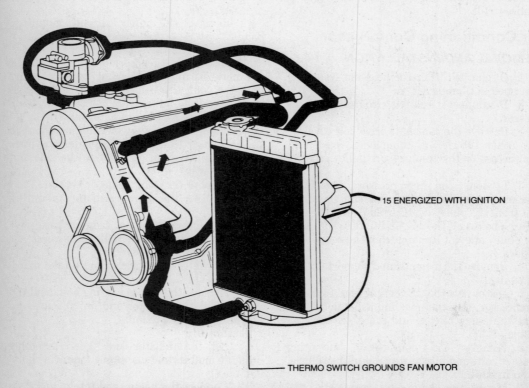

15 ENERGIZED WITH IGNITION

THERMO SWITCH GROUNDS FAN MOTOR

Carbureted Dasher cooling system. The thermo switch controls fan operation

13. Attach the support braces, air duct work and the upper radiator shroud.

14. Connect the upper radiator hose.

15. Install the lower radiator mounting bolts.

16. Install the lower radiator mounting shroud.

17. Connect the thermoswitch lead and fan motor wiring. If the fan(s) were removed, install them at this time. Mount the condenser if equipped with air conditioning.

18. Connect the lower radiator hose.

19. Install the inner shroud mounting bolts.

20. Fill the cooling system and connect the negative battery cable. Start the engine, allow it to warm up check for coolant leaks.

5-Cylinder Engines

1. Drain the cooling system and disconnect the negative battery cable.

CAUTION: *When draining the coolant, keep in mind that cats and dogs are attracted by the ethylene glycol antifreeze, and are quite likely to drink any that is left in an uncovered container or in puddles on the ground. This will prove fatal in sufficient quantity. Always drain the coolant into a sealable container. Coolant should be reused unless it is contaminated or several years old.*

2. Remove the three pieces of the radiator cowl.

3. Disconnect the fan motor wiring and remove the fan motor assembly. Take care in removing the fan motor connectors to avoid bending them.

4. Remove the upper and lower radiator hoses and the coolant tank supply hose.

5. Disconnect the coolant temperature switch located on the lower right side of the radiator.

6. Remove the radiator mounting bolts and lift out the radiator.

To install:

7. Lower the radiator into the engine compartment and install the mounting bolts.

8. Connect the coolant temperature switch.

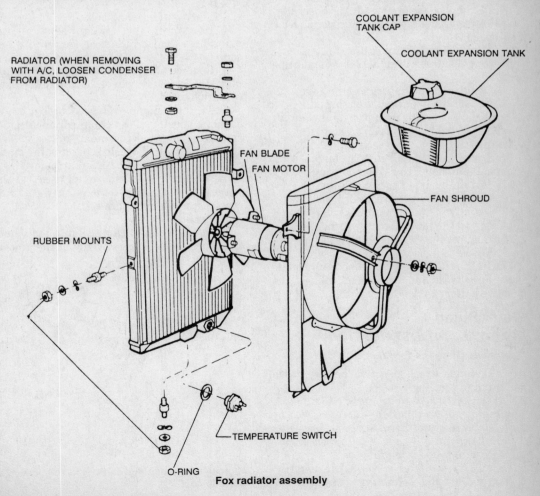

Fox radiator assembly

9. Connect the coolant supply, lower and upper radiator hoses.

10. Install the fans and connect the fan motor wiring.

11. Install the three radiator cowl pieces.

12. Fill the cooling system and connect the negative battery cable.

Diesel Engines

NOTE: *The 1984–86 Quantum turbodiesel has two cooling fans on the radiator.*

1. Drain the cooling system and disconnect the negative battery cable.

CAUTION: *When draining the coolant, keep in mind that cats and dogs are attracted by the ethylene glycol antifreeze, and are quite likely to drink any that is left in an uncovered container or in puddles on the ground. This will prove fatal in sufficient quantity. Always drain the coolant into a sealable container. Coolant should be reused unless it is contaminated or several years old.*

2. Remove the inner shroud mounting bolts.

3. Disconnect the lower radiator hose.

4. Disconnect the thermostatic switch lead, if equipped.

5. Remove the lower radiator shroud.

6. Remove the lower radiator mounting bolts.

7. Disconnect the upper radiator hose.

8. Detach the upper radiator shroud.

9. Remove the side mounting bolts and lift the radiator and fan out as an assembly.

To install:

10. Lower the radiator into the engine compartment and install the side mounting bolts.

11. Install the upper radiator shroud.

12. Connect the upper radiator hose.

13. Install the lower mounting bolts.

14. Install the lower radiator shroud.

15. Connect the thermoswitch lead.

16. Connect the lower radiator hose.

17. Install the inner shroud mounting bolts.

18. Fill the cooling system and connect the negative battery cable.

Water Pump

REMOVAL AND INSTALLATION

4-Cylinder Gasoline Engines

1. Disconnect the negative battery cable and drain the cooling system.

CAUTION: *When draining the coolant, keep in mind that cats and dogs are attracted by the ethylene glycol antifreeze, and are quite likely to drink any that is left in an uncovered container or in puddles on the ground. This will prove fatal in sufficient quantity. Always drain the coolant into a sealable con-*

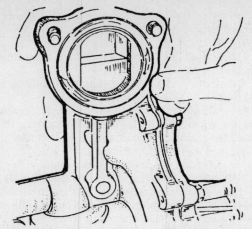

Check the condition of the O-ring seal before installing the water pump

tainer. Coolant should be reused unless it is contaminated or several years old.

2. If required, remove the alternator and drive belt.

3. Remove the timing belt cover.

4. Disconnect the lower radiator hose, engine hose, and heater hose from the water pump.

5. Remove the pump-to-housing retaining bolts. Make a note of where the different length bolts are located.

6. Turn the pump slightly and lift it out of the pump housing. If the pump is stubborn, tap around the edges of the pump with a rubber mallet to loosen it, then separate the pump from the pump housing. Clean the pump housing gasket surface to remove all traces of the gasket material. Remove the pump pulley and transfer it to the new pump.

To install:

7. Install a new O-ring seal into the pump. Make sure the seal seats evenly in the groove.

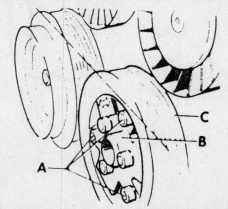

Aligning the water pump and crankshaft pulleys on Corrado

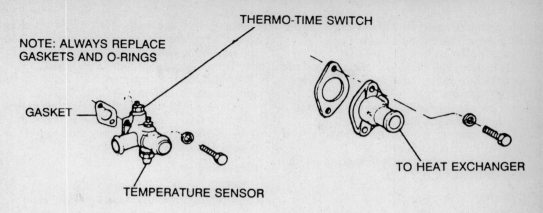

NOTE: ALWAYS REPLACE
GASKETS AND O-RINGS

THERMO-TIME SWITCH

GASKET

TEMPERATURE SENSOR

TO HEAT EXCHANGER

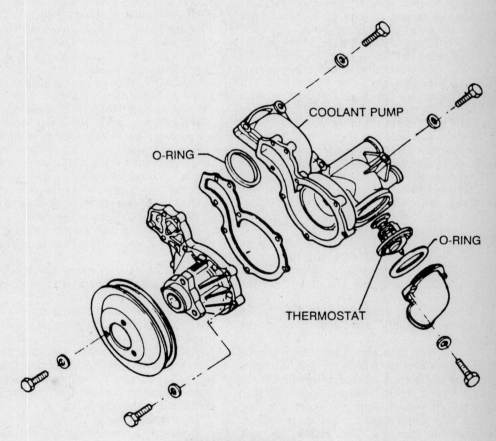

COOLANT PUMP

O-RING

O-RING

THERMOSTAT

Fox water pump assembly

Lubricate the seal with a liberal coat of silicone compound prior to installation.

8. Place the new pump gasket onto the pump housing and install the pump onto the gasket. Install one of the mounting bolts to hold the pump and gasket in place. Make sure all the gasket bolt holes are aligned properly with the holes in the housing before installing the remaining bolts. Torque the bolts to 7 ft. lbs. Torque the pulley bolts (on all models except Corrado) to 15 ft. lbs. and adjust the belt tension. On Corrado, once the water pump is in place, the water pump pulley must be aligned with the crankshaft pulley. To do this, loosen inner pulley bolts (**A**) and rotate the inner adjusting portion of the pulley (**B**) until the water

pump pulley (**C**) is even with with the crankshaft pulley. Once the pulleys are even, tighten the inner pulley bolts.

NOTE: *On 1985–90 Golf models install the water pump pulley with the word "Klima" facing outward.*

9. Connect the radiator and heater hoses.

10. Install the timing belt cover.

11. If removed, install the alternator and adjust the drive belt tension.

12. Fill the cooling system and adjust the drive belt tension.

5-Cylinder

NOTE: *Some replacement water pumps for five cylinder engines have a larger O-ring seal groove that does not accept the standard 4mm O-ring seal. Instead, an oversized 5mm seal must be used. Pumps that require a 5mm seal are stamped with a "5" on the water pump bolt flange area. Make sure that you use the proper O-ring seal when installing the water pump.*

1. Disconnect the negative battery cable and drain the cooling system.

CAUTION: *When draining the coolant, keep in mind that cats and dogs are attracted by the ethylene glycol antifreeze, and are quite likely to drink any that is left in an uncovered container or in puddles on the ground. This will prove fatal in sufficient quantity. Always drain the coolant into a sealable container. Coolant should be reused unless it is contaminated or several years old.*

2. Remove the V-belts, timing belt covers and timing belts as outlined in this chapter.

3. Unscrew the three water pump pulley retaining bolts and remove the pulley. Set the pulley aside.

4. Unscrew the intermediate shaft drive sprocket retaining bolt and remove the sprocket.

5. Unscrew the water pump retaining bolts and remove the pump from its housing. If the pump is stubborn, tap around the edges of the pump with a rubber mallet to loosen it, then separate the pump from the pump housing. Clean the pump housing gasket surface to remove all traces of the gasket material. Remove the pump pulley and transfer it to the new pump.

To install:

6. Install a new O-ring seal into the pump. Make sure the seal seats evenly in the groove. Lubricate the seal with a liberal coat of silicone compound prior to installation.

7. Place the new pump gasket onto the pump housing and install the pump onto the gasket. Install one of the mounting bolts to hold the pump and gasket in place. Make sure

all the gasket bolt holes are aligned properly with the holes in the housing before installing the remaining bolts. Torque the bolts to 15 ft. lbs. Torque the pulley bolts to 15 ft. lbs.

8. Mount the intermediate drive shaft sprocket and install the retaining bolt.

9. Install the timing belt, timing belt covers and drive belts. Adjust the drive belt tension.

10. Refill the cooling system and connect the negative battery cable.

Diesel Engine

NOTE: *Some replacement water pumps on Quantum turbo-diesel engines have a larger O-ring seal groove that does not accept the standard 4mm O-ring seal. Instead, an oversized 5mm seal must be used. Pumps that require a 5mm seal are stamped with a "5" on the water pump bolt flange area. Make sure that you use the proper O-ring seal when installing the water pump.*

1. Drain the cooling system.

CAUTION: *When draining the coolant, keep in mind that cats and dogs are attracted by the ethylene glycol antifreeze, and are quite likely to drink any that is left in an uncovered container or in puddles on the ground. This will prove fatal in sufficient quantity. Always drain the coolant into a sealable container. Coolant should be reused unless it is contaminated or several years old.*

2. Remove the alternator and drive belt.

3. Remove the timing belt cover.

4. Disconnect the lower radiator hoses, engine hose and heater hose from the water pump.

5. Remove the pump retaining bolts. Note where the different length bolts are located, for installation.

6. Turn the pump slightly and lift it out of the engine block. If the pump is stubborn, tap around the edges of the pump with a rubber mallet to loosen it, then separate the pump from the pump housing. Clean the pump housing gasket surface to remove all traces of the gasket material. Remove the pump pulley and transfer it to the new pump.

To install:

7. Install a new O-ring seal into the pump. Make sure the seal seats evenly in the groove. Lubricate the seal with a liberal coat of silicone compound prior to installation.

8. Place the new pump gasket onto the pump housing and install the pump onto the gasket. Install one of the mounting bolts to hold the pump and gasket in place. Make sure all the gasket bolt holes are aligned properly with the holes in the housing before installing the remaining bolts. Torque the bolts to 7 ft. lbs. Torque the pulley bolts to 14–15 ft. lbs.

9. Connect the heater, radiator and engine hoses.

10. Install the timing belt cover.

11. Install the alternator and adjust the drive belt tension.

12. Fill the cooling system and connect the negative battery cable.

Cylinder Head

REMOVAL AND INSTALLATION

Carbureted Engines

The engine should be cold before the cylinder head can be removed. The head is retained by ten socket head bolts. It can be removed without removing the intake and exhaust manifolds.

NOTE: *Beginning approximately July 1977, 12 point socket head bolts were used in place of 6 point older version. These should be used in complete sets only and need not be retorqued after the mileage interval.*

1. Rotate the crankshaft to set No. 1 cylinder at TDC with timing marks aligned. Disconnect the battery ground cable.

2. Drain the cooling system.

CAUTION: *When draining the coolant, keep in mind that cats and dogs are attracted by the ethylene glycol antifreeze, and are quite likely to drink any that is left in an uncovered container or in puddles on the ground. This will prove fatal in sufficient quantity. Always drain the coolant into a sealable container. Coolant should be reused unless it is contaminated or several years old.*

3. Remove the air cleaner. Disconnect the fuel line from the carburetor.

4. Disconnect the radiator, heater, and choke hoses.

5. Disconnect all electrical wires and emission control vacuum hoses. Remove the spark plug wires. The spark plugs can be left in the head if you choose to do so.

CAUTION: *Remove air conditioner compressor with lines attached and place out of the way. DO NOT disconnect any hoses or allow the unit to hang freely by the hoses.*

6. Separate the exhaust manifold from the exhaust pipe.

7. Disconnect the EGR line from the exhaust manifold. Remove the EGR valve and filter from the intake manifold.

8. Remove the carburetor from the intake manifold.

9. Disconnect the air pump fittings.

10. Remove the timing belt cover and belt. Remove the valve cover and valve cover gasket.

11. Loosen the cylinder head bolts in the sequence of 10 to 1 as shown in the illustration.

12. Remove the bolts and lift the cylinder

head straight off. Clean the head and block gasket surfaces throughly.

To install:

13. Install the new cylinder head gasket with the words **TOP** or **OBEN** up (Oben is German meaning top or above). Lower the head onto the gasket.

14. Install bolts Nos. 10 and 8 first, these holes are smaller and will properly locate the gasket and cylinder head.

15. Install the remaining bolts. Tighten them in three stages in the 1 through 10 sequence shown. Cylinder head tightening torque is 54 ft. lbs. 12 point bolts should be tightened to 54 ft. lbs., then tightened 1/4 turn more.

NOTE: *After approximately 1000 miles, retighten the cylinder head bolts. Torque them, with the engine hot (operating temperature) to 61 ft. lbs. This is for six point bolts only, 12 point bolts do not have to be retorqued.*

16. Install and tension the timing belt. Install the timing belt and valve covers. Use a new valve cover gasket.

17. Connect the air pump fittings.

18. Install the carburetor with a new gasket.

19. Install the EGR valve and filter on the intake manifold. Connect the EGR valve line.

20. Connect the exhaust pipe to the exhaust manifold with a new gasket.

21. Mount the air conditioning compressor.

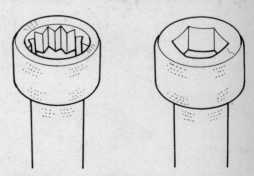

New and old style head bolts

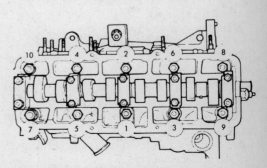

Cylinder head torque sequence — installing. Reverse the sequence when removing

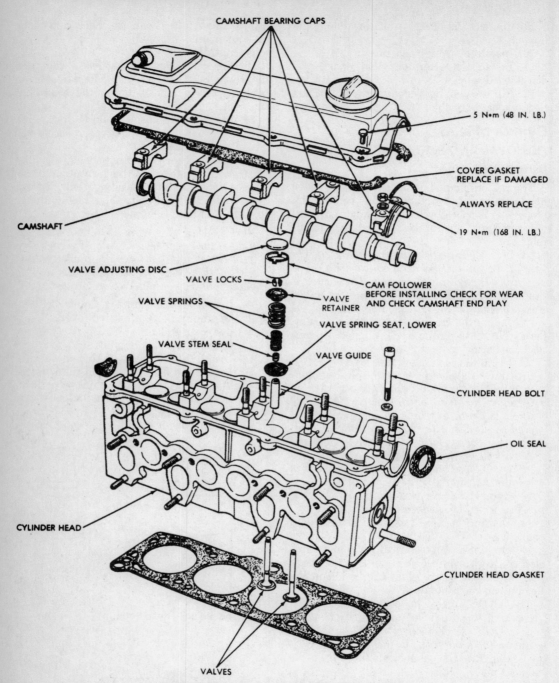

CAMSHAFT BEARING CAPS

5 N•m (48 IN. LB.)

COVER GASKET
REPLACE IF DAMAGED

ALWAYS REPLACE

CAMSHAFT

19 N•m (168 IN. LB.)

VALVE ADJUSTING DISC

VALVE LOCKS

CAM FOLLOWER
BEFORE INSTALLING CHECK FOR WEAR
AND CHECK CAMSHAFT END PLAY

VALVE SPRINGS

VALVE
RETAINER

VALVE SPRING SEAT, LOWER

VALVE STEM SEAL

VALVE GUIDE

CYLINDER HEAD BOLT

OIL SEAL

CYLINDER HEAD

CYLINDER HEAD GASKET

VALVES

Exploded view of engine camshaft and cylinder head

22. Connect the spark plug wires. Connect all the vacuum hoses and electrical wires.

23. Connect the choke, radiator and heater hoses.

24. Connect the fuel line to the carburetor. Install the air cleaner.

25. Fill the cooling system.

26. Connect the negative battery cable.

Adjust the ignition timing and the idle speed.

Fuel Injected Engines

NOTE: *12 point socket stretch type head bolts are now used in place of the older six point bolts. These should be used in complete sets only and need not be retorqued after any mileage interval. These bolts may only be*

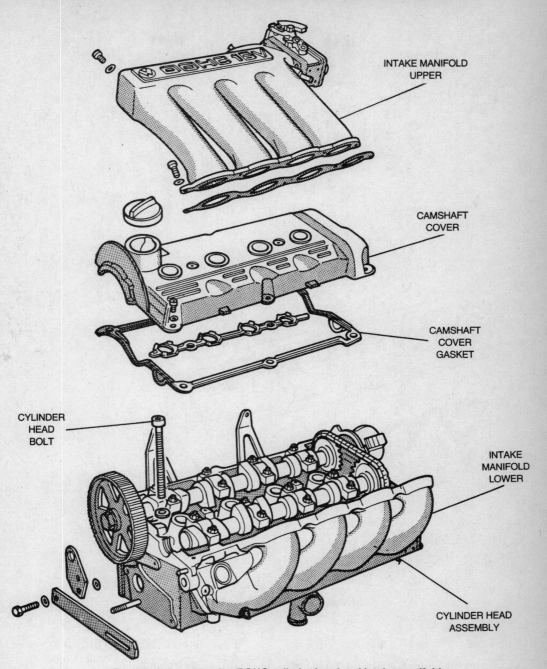

INTAKE MANIFOLD
UPPER

CAMSHAFT
COVER

CAMSHAFT
COVER
GASKET

CYLINDER
HEAD
BOLT

INTAKE
MANIFOLD
LOWER

CYLINDER HEAD
ASSEMBLY

Exploded view, 16-valve DOHC cylinder head and intake manifold

used once and should be replaced at every overhaul. *THROW THE OLD BOLTS AWAY!!! These bolts do not require retorquing after any mileage interval.*

1. Rotate the crankshaft to set No. 1 cylinder at TDC with timing marks aligned. Disconnect the battery ground cable.
2. Drain the cooling system.

CAUTION: *When draining the coolant, keep in mind that cats and dogs are attracted by the ethylene glycol antifreeze, and are quite likely to drink any that is left in an uncovered container or in puddles on the ground. This will prove fatal in sufficient quantity. Always drain the coolant into a sealable container. Coolant should be reused unless it is contaminated or several years old.*

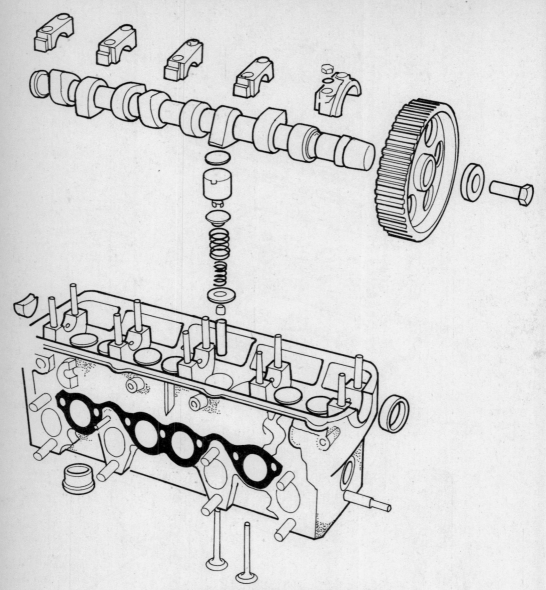

Diesel engine camshaft and cylinder head

3. Loosen and remove all the accessory drive belts.

4. Remove the alternator and alternator mounting bracket as required.

5. Disconnect the air inlet ductwork from the throttle body assembly.

4. Disconnect the throttle cable from the throttle body assembly.

6. Remove the injectors and disconnect the line from the cold start valve, if equipped.

7. Disconnect the radiator and heater hoses. On Corrado, disconnect the hoses from the G-Charger inlet pipe and the intercooler.

8. Disconnect all the emission control vacuum lines. Label lines for installation.

9. Remove the valve cover and valve cover gasket. If equipped, remove the camshaft cover plate.

10. Remove the auxiliary air regulator from the intake manifold, if equipped.

11. Disconnect all electrical lines. Remove the spark plugs. Label all lines and wires for installation.

CAUTION: *Remove air conditioner compressor with lines attached and tie it off to the side and out of the way. DO NOT disconnect*

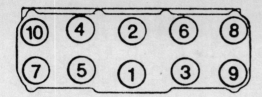

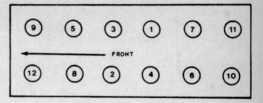

Cylinder head bolt tightening sequence — 4 cylinder 8-valve engines. Loosen the head bolts in reverse of the tightening sequence

5-cylinder head bolt tightening sequence

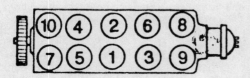

Cylinder head bolt tightening sequence — 4 cylinder 16-valve engines. Loosen the head bolts in reverse of the tightening sequence

each bolt, in sequence, an additional 180° turn. Two 90° turns are permissible. Further tightening is not necessary.

NOTE: *With 6-point bolts, retorque the bolts to 61 ft. lbs., hot, after 1000 miles of driving.*

any lines or allow the compressor to hang freely.

12. Separate the exhaust manifold from the exhaust pipe.

13. Remove the EGR line from the exhaust manifold, if equipped.

14. Remove the intake manifold.

15. Remove the timing belt covers and belt. After removing the rear cover on Corrado, disconnect the belt tensioning damper from the alternator mounting bracket an unbolt the bracket from the head. The tesnioner damper is held to the bracket by a collar nut and a hex head set screw.

16. Loosen the cylinder head bolts in the reverse of the tightening sequence.

17. Remove the bolts and lift the head straight off. Remove the old cylinder head gasket.

18. Clean the head and block surfaces throughly and check the flatness of the cylinder block with a feeler gauge and a metal straight edge. Maximum allowable distortion is 0.1mm (0.004 in.).

To install:

19. Install the new cylinder head gasket with the TOP or OBEN (German for top or above) facing upward.

CAUTION: *Do not reuse the cylinder head bolts.*

20. Install bolts No. 10 and 8 on 4 cylinder engines first; these holes are smaller and will properly locate the gasket and cylinder head.

21. Install the remaining bolts. Tighten them in three stages using the sequence shown in the illustration. Cylinder head bolts must be torqued cold. 12 point bolts should be tightened to first 29 ft. lbs., then 43 ft. lbs., then tighten

22. On Corrado, install the alternator mounting bracket before attaching the rear drive belt cover. Do not tension the bracket. The belt tensioning damper bushing must be be able to rotate freely. Connect the belt tensioner damper to the bracket and attach the bracket to the head. Torque the bracket mounting bolts to 26 ft. lbs. and the tensioner collar nut to 18 ft. lbs.

23. Install the timing belt and timing belt covers. Adjust the timing belt tension.

24. Install the intake manifold with new gaskets.

25. Connect the EGR to the exhaust manifold, if equipped.

26. Connect the exhaust manifold to the exhaust pipe with a new gasket.

27. Install the air conditioning compressor.

29. Connect all electrical wires. Install the spark plugs.

30. Install the auxiliary air regulator onto the intake manifold, if equipped.

31. Install the valve cover with a new gasket.

32. Connect all emission control vacuum lines.

33. Connect the radiator and heater hoses. On Corrado, connect the G-Charger and intercooler hoses.

34. Connect the line to the cold start valve and install the fuel injectors.

35. Connect and adjust the throttle cable.

36. Connect the air inlet ductwork to the throttle body.

37. Install the alternator mounting bracket and alternator as required.

38. Install the accessory drive belts and adjust the drive belt tension.

39. Fill the cooling system and connect the negative battery cable.

Rabbit, Dasher and Jetta Diesel and Turbo Engines

The engine should be cold when the head is removed to avoid chances of warpage.

CAUTION: *Diesel cylinder heads cannot be resurfaced.*

1. Disconnect the negative battery cable.
2. Drain the cooling system.

CAUTION: *When draining the coolant, keep in mind that cats and dogs are attracted by the ethylene glycol antifreeze, and are quite likely to drink any that is left in an uncovered container or in puddles on the ground. This will prove fatal in sufficient quantity. Always drain the coolant into a sealable container. Coolant should be reused unless it is contaminated or several years old.*

3. Remove the air cleaner and duct.
4. Clean and disconnect the fuel (injector) lines. Cap the ends of the lines to prevent the entry of dirt into the fuel system.
5. Tag and disconnect all electrical wires and leads.
6. If equipped, disconnect and plug all lines coming from the brake booster vacuum pump and remove the pump.
7. Disconnect the air supply tubes (turbo diesels only) and then unbolt and remove the intake manifold.
8. Disconnect and plug all lines coming from the power steering pump and remove the pump and V-belt (if equipped).
9. Disconnect and remove the oil supply and return lines from the turbocharger (if equipped).
10. Remove the exhaust manifold heat shields (if equipped). Remove the glow plugs and the fuel injectors.
11. Separate the exhaust pipe from the exhaust manifold or turbocharger and then remove the manifold.

NOTE: *On turbodiesels, the exhaust manifold is removed with the turbocharger and wastegate still attached.*

12. Disconnect all radiator and heater hoses where they are attached to the cylinder head and position them out of the way.
13. Remove the drive belt cover and the drive belt.
14. Remove the PCV hose.
15. Remove the cylinder head cover.
16. Loosen the cylinder head bolts in the reverse order of the tightening sequence.
17. Remove the bolts and lift the cylinder head straight off.

NOTE: *If the head sticks, loosen it by compression or rap it upward with a soft rubber mallet. Do not force anything between the head and the engine block to pry it upward; this may result in serious damage to the gasket seating surfaces.*

18. Clean the cylinder head and engine block mating surfaces thoroughly and then install the new gasket without any sealing compound.

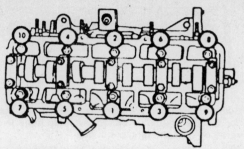

Cylinder head bolt tightening sequence — diesel and turbodiesel engines. Loosen the head bolts in reverse of the tightening sequence

Make sure the words **TOP** or **OBEN** are facing up when the gasket is installed. Depending upon the piston height above the top surface of the engine block, there are 3 gaskets of different thicknesses which can be used. The gasket thickness is determined by the number of identification notches in the gasket. Be sure that the new gasket has the same number of notches as the gasket being replaced. If the engine is be overhauled with a short block or new pistons, the piston height must be measured and a gasket selected from the measurement. If the piston height for mechanical lifter equipped engines is: 0.60–0.8mm (0.025–0.032 in.) use a 1.4mm (0.055 in.) gasket; 0.85–0.90mm (0.033–0.036 in.) use a 1.5mm (0.059 in.) gasket; 0.95–1.00mm (0.037–0.040 in.) use a 1.5mm (0.063 in.) gasket. For engines with hydraulic lifters, gasket thickness is determined by the number of notches on the gasket. The following gives the piston height with it's corresponding gasket notch number: 0.66–0.86mm (0.026–0.034 in.) use a 1 notch gasket; 0.69–0.89mm (0.027–0.035 in.) use a 2 notch gasket; 0.90–1.00mm (0.036–0.040 in.) use a 3 notch gasket. Piton height measurement for diesel engines is described later in this chapter.

19. Turn the crankshaft to TDC, then turn the crankshaft back until all the pistons are nearly equal height in the cylinders.
20. Place the cylinder head on the engine block and turn the camshaft gear so that the cam lobes for the No.1 cylinder point upwards. Install bolts No. 8 and 10 first. These holes are smaller and will properly locate the head on the engine block.
21. Install the remaining bolts and tighten as follows:

6 point bolts:

• Step 1—Tighten the head bolts in numbered sequence to 35 ft. lbs.
• Step 2—Re-tighten the head bolts in numerical sequence to 50 ft. lbs.
• Step 3—Re-tighten the head bolts in numbered sequence to 65 ft. lbs.

• Run the engine until the cooling fan comes on at least once. Stop the engine and re-tighten the head bolts in the same order to 65 ft. lbs. **12 point bolts:**
• Step 1 – Tighten the head bolts in numbered sequence to 29 ft. lbs.
• Step 2 – Re-tighten the head bolts in numbered sequence to 43 ft. lbs.
• Step 3 – Finally, make each head bolt a 180° turn tighter. Two 90° turns are permissible.
• Run the engine until the cooling fan comes on at least once. Stop the engine and re-tighten the head bolts in the same order an additional 1/4 turn (90°). Tighten the bolt in one continuous motion. Two 45° turns are NOT premissable.
22. Installation of all other components is in the reverse order of removal.
23. With 6 point bolts, after about 1000 miles of operation, remove the cylinder head cover and loosen each cylinder head bolt 1/3 of turn (30°) in reverse of the tightening sequence. Then, re-torque each bolt to 65 ft. lbs. in the numbered sequence. This is done 1 bolt at a time, in the proper sequence, without interruption. This can be done with the engine warm or cold. With 12 point bolts, after about 1000 miles, remove the cylinder head cover and retighten the cylinder head bolts, turning the bolts in sequence 1/4 turn (90°) WITHOUT loosening them first. This is done 1 bolt at a time, in the proper sequence, without interruption. This can be done with the engine warm or cold.

Quantum Turbodiesel Engine

The engine should be cold when the head is removed to avoid chances of warpage.
NOTE: *Cylinder head installation requires the use of VW special tools 3070/1 and 2065 A. Before attempting to remove the cylinder head, check on the availability of these special tools.*
CAUTION: *Diesel cylinder heads cannot be resurfaced.*
1. Rotate the crankshaft to set No. 1 cylinder at TDC with timing marks aligned. Disconnect the negative battery cable.
2. Drain the cooling system.
CAUTION: *When draining the coolant, keep in mind that cats and dogs are attracted by the ethylene glycol antifreeze, and are quite likely to drink any that is left in an uncovered container or in puddles on the ground. This will prove fatal in sufficient quantity. Always drain the coolant into a sealable container. Coolant should be reused unless it is contaminated or several years old.*
3. Remove the air cleaner and duct.
4. Clean and disconnect the fuel (injector) lines. Cap the ends of the lines to prevent the entry of dirt into the fuel system.
5. Tag and disconnect all electrical wires and leads.
6. If equipped, disconnect and plug all lines coming from the brake booster vacuum pump and remove the pump.
7. Disconnect the air supply tubes and then unbolt and remove the intake manifold.
8. Disconnect and plug all lines coming from the power steering pump and remove the pump and V-belt (if equipped).
9. Disconnect and remove the oil supply and return lines from the turbocharger.
10. Remove the exhaust manifold heat shields. Remove the glow plugs and the fuel injectors.
11. Separate the exhaust pipe from the turbocharger and then remove the manifold. The exhaust manifold is removed with the turbocharger and wastegate still attached.
12. Disconnect all radiator and heater hoses where they are attached to the cylinder head and position them out of the way.
13. Remove the drive belt cover and the drive belt.
14. Remove the PCV hose.
15. Remove the cylinder head cover.
16. Loosen the cylinder head bolts in the reverse order of the tightening sequence.
17. Remove the bolts and lift the cylinder head straight off.
NOTE: *If the head sticks, loosen it by compression or rap it upward with a soft rubber mallet. Do not force anything between the head and the engine block to pry it upward; this may result in serious damage.*
18. Clean the cylinder head and engine block mating surfaces thoroughly check for warpage and damage.
To install:
19. Turn the crankshaft until the No. 1 piston is at TDC.
20. Turn the crankshaft back 1/4 turn until all the pistons are at nearly the same height in the cylinders.
21. Lock the camshaft with setting bar 2065 A or equivalent.
22. Install the drive belt as described in this chapter.
23. Install two guide pins 3070/1 into the intake manifold side of the block. These help locate the head to the block.
24. Install the new gasket without any sealing compound. Make sure the words **TOP** or **OBEN** are facing up when the gasket is installed.
NOTE: *Depending upon the piston height above the top surface of the engine block, there are 3 gaskets of different thicknesses*

which can be used. The gasket thickness is determined by the number of identification notches in the gasket. Be sure that the new gasket has the same number of notches as the gasket being replaced. If the engine was overhauled with a short block or new pistons, the piston height must be measured and a gasket selected from the measurement. If the piston height is: 0.66–0.79mm (0.026–0.031 in.) use a 1 notch gasket; 0.80–0.89mm (0.032–0.035 in.) use a 2 notch gasket; 0.90–1.00mm (0.036–0.040 in.) use a 3 notch gasket. Piston height measurement is described later in this chapter.

25. Place the cylinder head on the engine block and install bolts No. 8 and 10 first. These holes are smaller and will properly locate the head on the engine block.

26. Install the remaining bolts and remove the guide pins. Torque the bolts in sequence using 3 steps: 29 ft. lbs., 43 ft. lbs., an additional $1/2$ turn (180°) and retorque an additional $1/4$ (90°) turn, after warming the engine.

27. Installation of all other components is in the reverse order of removal.

28. After about 1000 miles, remove the cylinder head cover and retighten the cylinder head bolts, turning the bolts in sequence $1/4$ turn (90°) WITHOUT loosening them first. This is done 1 bolt at a time, in the proper sequence.

CLEANING AND INSPECTION

CAUTION: *Do not place a diesel cylinder head down in the normal position until the injectors and inserts are removed or damage to the injectors an result. Inserts are removed by placing a drift through the injector hole and tapping the insert out. DO NOT resurface diesel engine cylinder heads.*

1. Remove the intake and exhaust manifolds if still mounted. Remove all water hose connections, and the injectors combustion chamber inserts and glow plugs if diesel engine.

2. Place the head on wooden blocks and remove the camshaft, cam followers and end seals.

NOTE: *Keep the valve adjusting shims and cam followers in order from the valves they were removed from for reinstallation ("tag and bag").*

3. Working in a clean area, use spray solvent or brush cleaning solvent on the cylinder head top, sides and combustion chamber surfaces to remove any grease, dirt or oil, and help soften carbon deposits. After cleaning with solvent, wash the head with hot water and wipe dry.

4. Turn the head so the combustion chambers are facing up. Support the head on wooden blocks so damage to the cam bearing cap mounting studs will not occur.

5. Mount a rotary wire carbon cleaning brush in an electric drill and clean the combustion chambers and valve heads.

6. Use a dull scraper to remove any old cylinder head gasket material remaining on the gasket surface. Use safe solvent on a rag to wipe the combustion chambers and gasket surface, wipe dry with a clean rag.

7. A complete inspection of the cylinder head (combustion chambers, valves, guides etc.) can be done after the valves and springs are removed.

RESURFACING

After the head gasket mounting surface has been cleaned, check the head for flatness. Place a straightedge across the gasket surface. Using feeler gauges, determine the clearance between the straightedge and head surface. Measure along the length at the center and across both diagonals. Check clearance at several points along the straightedge. The allowable distortion of the cylinder head is 0.1mm (0.004 in.). If clearance is greater the head will have to be resurfaced. VW cautions that the diesel cylinder head cannot be resurfaced, and if over specs., must be replaced. The gasoline engine cylinder head should not be resurfaced to a point where measurement from the valve cover to head gasket mounting surfaces is less than 132.5mm (5.2185 inches). Cylinder head replacement is indicated if measurement is less than specified.

Cylinder head resurfacing can be handled by most local automotive machine shops.

Valves and Springs
REMOVAL AND INSTALLATION

1. Number the valve heads (in order) with a permanent marker for reinstallation identification.

2. Block the head on wooden supports in a position that permits use of the type of valve spring removing tool you are going to use. VW

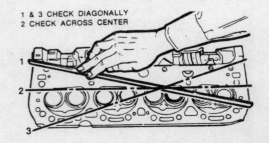

Check the cylinder head for warpage

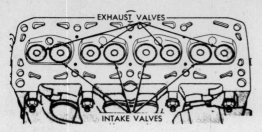

Valve identification

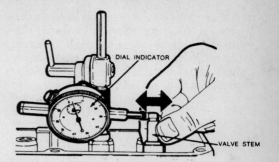

Check the valve guide-to-stem clearance

uses tool VW 541, although you should be able to perform the job with several other available removers, the locking C-clamp type is popular.

3. Compress the valve springs and remove the stem locks and retainers. Remove the valve springs. Keep the parts from each valve separate and in order for reinstallation ("tag and bag"). Remove the lower valve spring seats and valve stem oil seals. Remove the valves, keep them in order in case the identification marking wears off.

4. Clean valve faces, tips and combustion chambers with a rotary wire brush or bench grinder wire wheel. Do not wire brush the valve stems, take care not to damage the valve seats. Remove the carbon, do not just burnish. If a stubborn carbon deposit is encountered, use a blunt drift to break the carbon loose. Again use caution around the valve seat.

5. Use a valve guide cleaning brush and safe solvent to clean the valve guides.

6. If a water leak is suspected, or the valve seats, guides or valves need machine work, take the head and parts to the machine shop. Now is also a good time to have the head super cleaned in a cold parts cleaner, the machine shop can handle the job. However, never allow the aluminum head to be hot tanked, this will damage the head and make replacement necessary.

7. After all machine work has been done, any required new parts on hand, reassemble the head in the reverse order. Always install new valve guide oil seals using the protectors provided to prevent damage to the seal.

8. Refer to the following sections for details on machine work and cylinder head component checking.

9. Valve adjustment can be done after the head is reassembled and the cam followers, shims and camshaft installed. Refer to Chapter 2 for necessary tools and procedure. Be sure the heel of the camshaft lobe (greatest clearance) is over the valve (cam follower) you are checking.

INSPECTION

After all cylinder head parts have been removed and cleaned, examine them for any visual signs of wear. Badly worn parts should

be replaced, slightly grooved or burnt valves or seats can be machined. Check the valve-stem-to guide clearance. Having a new intake or exhaust valve around would make the job easier, however if they are not on hand proceed with the following. Insert the valve into the guide it came from. Lift the head of the valve away from the valve seat slightly. Wiggle the valve from side to side. A small amount of play is usual, a large amount of play indicates wear in either the valve stem, guide or both. Measure the valve stem with a micrometer and compare the reading to original "specs" to determine whether the stem or guide is responsible for the excessive clearance. Compare the valve springs, obvious length difference indicates wear. Cracked, broken or damaged spring should be replaced. Examine the valve spring seats, retainers and locks for grooves or wear, replace as necessary.

REFACING VALVES AND SEATS

CAUTION: *Under no circumstances should either the exhaust or the intake valves in the 16 valve 1.8L engine and Corrado be resurfaced. These valves are sodium filled and may explode if the sodium filling is exposed*

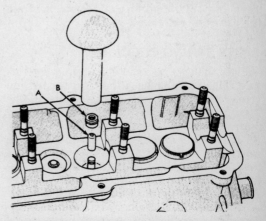

Use protector (A) when installing valve stem seal (B). Installation tool is above seal

to extreme heat or water. These valves must be replaced with new ones, and properly disposed of, if there are any signs of wear. Proper disposal of the sodium filled valves should be referred to a qualified machine shop technician.

Valve and valve seat refacing requires special equipment, the automotive machine shop can handle the job for you.

VW recommends that the exhaust valves not be refaced on a machine and should be hand lapped only.

Intake valves are refaced to the angle shown on the specifications chart in this chapter. Both intake and exhaust valves are available having shorter stems which provide the use of maximum thickness valve adjusting discs if too much material has been removed from the valve seats when they are refaced. Valve seats can be refaced with either grinding stones or reamers. A true valve seat can not be machined unless the valve guide is within specifications, and not worn. Valve guides are replaceable, but if the valve seat is damaged and cannot be repaired a new cylinder head is required. Consult your machine shop for their advice.

HAND LAPPING VALVES

Invert the cylinder head, lightly lubricate the valve stem and install the valves in the head as numbered. Slightly raise the valve from the valve seat and apply a small amount of valve grinding compound to the valve seat.

Moisten the suction cup on the lapping tool and attach to the valve head. Rotate the lapping tool and valve between the palms of your hands, change position and lift the tool often to prevent grooving. Lap the valve, until a smooth polished surface is evident on the valve and valve seat. Remove the valve from the head and clean away all traces of lapping compound from the valve and valve seat.

VALVE SPRING CHECKING

Place the cleaned valve spring on a flat surface. Measure the height of the spring and rotate it against a carpenter's square. If the spring height varies 1.5mm ($\frac{1}{16}$ in.), by comparison, or if distortion of more than 1.5mm ($\frac{1}{16}$ in.) is present when the spring is rotated, replace the spring. After the valve and spring is installed, measure the distance between the lower spring pad and lower edge of the upper retainer. Check the measurement with the specifications chart. If the installed height is incorrect, add special shim washers between the spring pad and the spring. Use only washers designed for this purpose.

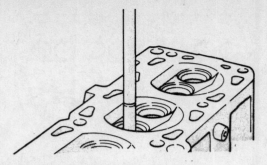

Use a press to install new valve guides

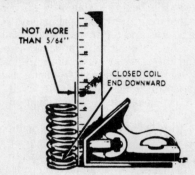

Check the valve spring free length and squareness

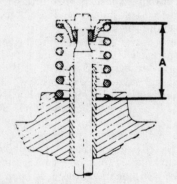

Valve spring installed height (A)

VALVE SEATS

REMOVAL AND INSTALLATION

Valve seats which are worn or burnt can usually be machined to the correct angle and width. VW recommends that if the seat can not be saved by machine work the head should be replaced. In some cases a new seat can be installed, consult an automotive machine shop for their advice.

Valve Guides

REMOVAL AND INSTALLATION

Worn valve guides can be replaced by the automotive machine shop. The job requires special equipment which they have. In some cases a worn valve guide can be knurled which is a process where metal is displaced and raised, thereby reducing clearance. Consult the machine shop for their advice.

Oil Pan

REMOVAL AND INSTALLATION

Dasher, Fox and Quantum Gasoline Engines

1. Drain the oil pan. Loosen the motor mounts.

CAUTION: *The EPA warns that prolonged contact with used engine oil may cause a number of skin disorders, including cancer! Protective gloves should be worn when changing the oil. Wash your hands and any other exposed skin areas as soon as possible after exposure to used engine oil.*

2. Support and slightly raise the engine with an overhead hoist.
3. Gradually loosen the engine crossmember mounting bolts. Remove the left and right side engine mounts.
4. Lower the crossmember very carefully.
5. Loosen and remove the oil pan retaining bolts.
6. Lower the pan from the car.
7. Install the pan using a new gasket and sealer.
8. Tighten the retaining bolts in a criss-cross pattern. Tighten the hex head bolts to 14 ft. lbs., or the Allen head bolts to 7 ft. lbs.
9. Raise the crossmember. Tighten the cross-member bolts to 42 ft. lbs. and the engine mounting bolts to 32 ft. lbs.
10. Refill the engine with oil. Start the engine and check for leaks.

All Gasoline Engines Except Dasher and Quantum

1. Drain the oil pan.
CAUTION: *The EPA warns that prolonged contact with used engine oil may cause a number of skin disorders, including cancer! You should make every effort to minimize your exposure to used engine oil. Protective gloves should be worn when changing the oil. Wash your hands and any other exposed skin areas as soon as possible after exposure to used engine oil. Soap and water, or waterless hand cleaner should be used.*

2. Loosen and remove the socket or Allen head oil pan retaining bolts. On Corrado and Passat, use VW special tool or equivalent to remove the oil pan bolts on the flywheel side.
3. Lower the pan from the car.
4. Clean all the gasket surfaces throughly and coat the block surface with VW D 000 300

or equivalent sealant before positioning the gasket.

5. Install the pan using a new gasket.
6. Tighten the hex headed bolts to 14–15 ft. lbs., or Allen bolts to 7 ft. lbs. in a criss-cross pattern.
7. Refill the engine with oil. Start the engine and check for leaks.

Diesel Engines

1. Drain the oil pan.
CAUTION: *The EPA warns that prolonged contact with used engine oil may cause a number of skin disorders, including cancer! You should make every effort to minimize your exposure to used engine oil. Protective gloves should be worn when changing the oil. Wash your hands and any other exposed skin areas as soon as possible after exposure to used engine oil. Soap and water, or waterless hand cleaner should be used.*

2. Support and slightly raise the engine with an overhead hoist.
3. Gradually loosen the engine crossmember mounting bolts. Remove the front and rear side engine mounts.
4. Lower the crossmember very carefully.
5. Loosen and remove the oil pan retaining bolts.
6. Lower the pan from the car.
7. Install the pan using a new gasket and sealer on the block surface.
8. Tighten the retaining bolts in a criss-cross pattern. Tighten hex head bolts to 14–15 ft. lbs., or Allen head bolts to 7 ft. lbs.
9. Raise the crossmember. Tighten the cross-member bolts to 42 ft. lbs. and the engine mounting bolts to 32 ft. lbs.

Oil Pump

REMOVAL AND INSTALLATION

4-Cylinder Gasoline Engines

1. Remove the oil pan.
2. Remove the two mounting bolts that hold the pump to the block. One bolt is longer than the other.
3. Pull oil pump down and out of the engine.
4. Unscrew the bolts and separate the pump halves.
5. Remove the driveshaft and gears from the upper body.
6. Clean the bottom half in solvent. Pry up the metal edges to remove the filter screen for cleaning.
7. Examine the gears and driveshaft for wear or damage. Replace them if necessary.
8. Reassemble the pump halves. Check the pump gear backlash with a feeler gauge in-

serted between the gear teeth. It should be 0.05–0.20mm (0.002–0.008 in.). Check the gear axial play with a straight edge and feeler gauge. Insert the feeler gauge between the top of the pump housing and straight edge. Maximum permissible axial play is 0.15mm (0.006 in.).

9. Prime the pump with oil and position onto the block. Install the mounting bolts. Torque the long bolt to 15 ft. lbs. and the short one to 7 ft. lbs.

10. Install the oil pan with a new gasket. Fill the crankcase to the proper level.

5-Cylinder Engines

1. Remove the timing belt cover and remove the timing belt.

2. Remove the drive belt sprocket from the crankshaft.

3. Remove the oil dip stick and drain the crankcase.

CAUTION: *The EPA warns that prolonged contact with used engine oil may cause a number of skin disorders, including cancer! You should make every effort to minimize your exposure to used engine oil. Protective gloves should be worn when changing the oil. Wash your hands and any other exposed skin areas as soon as possible after exposure to used engine oil. Soap and water, or waterless hand cleaner should be used.*

4. Remove the engine-to-subframe bolts, raise the engine slightly and remove the oil pan.

5. Remove the oil pickup tube bolts and the tube.

6. Remove the oil pump to engine bolts and the oil pump.

7. Remove the gasket and clean the gasket mounting surfaces.

8. At the rear of the oil pump, remove the end cover bolts and the cover.

9. Check the pump for wear and/or damage, replace the parts if necessary. Remove the pressure relief valve, clean it in solvent and check the relief spring for wear. Torque the relief valve to 26 ft. lbs.

10. Pack the pump with petroleum jelly and reassemble the pump.

To install:

11. Mount the oil pump with a new gasket to the block and install the mounting bolts. Torque the pump-to-engine bolts to 14 ft. lbs.

12. Attach the oil pump pick-up tube to the pump using new gaskets. Torque the mounting bolts to 7 ft. lbs.

13. Install the oil pan with a new gasket. Lower the engine and install the engine-to-subframe bolts.

14. Fill the crankcase and insert the dipstick.

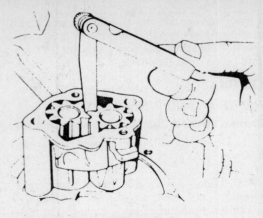

Checking oil pump gear backlash

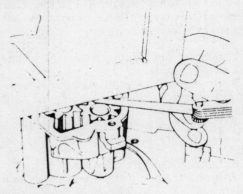

Checking oil gear axial play

15. Install the drive belt sprocket onto the crankshaft.

16. Install the drive belt and drive belt covers.

17. Start the engine and check for leaks.

Diesel Engines

1. Remove the oil pan as described above.

2. Remove the two mounting bolts that hold the pump to the block. One bolt is longer than the other.

3. Pull oil pump down and out of the engine.

4. Unscrew the bolts and separate the pump halves.

5. Remove the driveshaft and gears from the upper body.

6. Clean the bottom half in solvent. Pry up the metal edges to remove the filter screen for cleaning.

7. Examine the gears and driveshaft for wear or damage. Replace them if necessary.

8. Reassemble the pump halves. Check the pump gear backlash with a feeler gauge inserted between the gear teeth. It should be 0.05–0.20mm (0.002–0.008 in.). Check the gear axial play with a straight edge and feeler gauge.

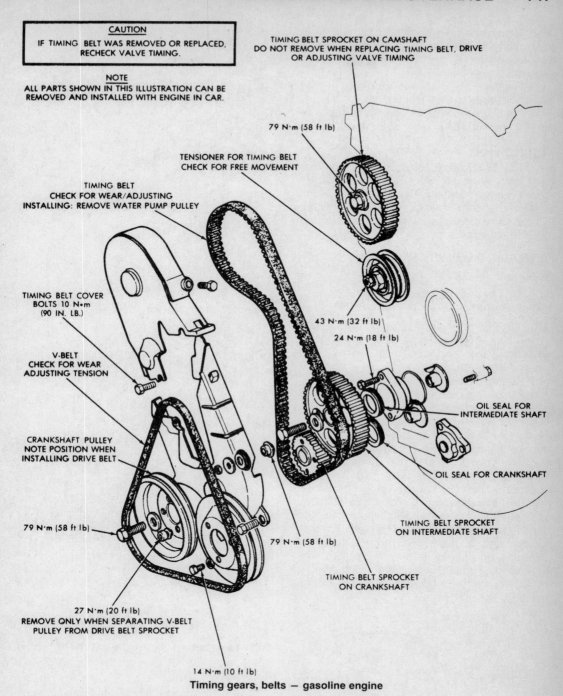

CAUTION

IF TIMING BELT WAS REMOVED OR REPLACED, RECHECK VALVE TIMING.

NOTE

ALL PARTS SHOWN IN THIS ILLUSTRATION CAN BE REMOVED AND INSTALLED WITH ENGINE IN CAR.

TIMING BELT SPROCKET ON CAMSHAFT DO NOT REMOVE WHEN REPLACING TIMING BELT, DRIVE OR ADJUSTING VALVE TIMING

79 N·m (58 ft lb)

TENSIONER FOR TIMING BELT CHECK FOR FREE MOVEMENT

TIMING BELT CHECK FOR WEAR/ADJUSTING INSTALLING: REMOVE WATER PUMP PULLEY

TIMING BELT COVER BOLTS 10 N•m (90 IN. LB.)

43 N·m (32 ft lb)

24 N·m (18 ft lb)

V-BELT CHECK FOR WEAR ADJUSTING TENSION

OIL SEAL FOR INTERMEDIATE SHAFT

CRANKSHAFT PULLEY NOTE POSITION WHEN INSTALLING DRIVE BELT

OIL SEAL FOR CRANKSHAFT

79 N·m (58 ft lb)

79 N·m (58 ft lb)

TIMING BELT SPROCKET ON INTERMEDIATE SHAFT

TIMING BELT SPROCKET ON CRANKSHAFT

27 N·m (20 ft lb) REMOVE ONLY WHEN SEPARATING V-BELT PULLEY FROM DRIVE BELT SPROCKET

14 N·m (10 ft lb)

Timing gears, belts — gasoline engine

Insert the feeler gauge between the top of the pump housing and straight edge. Maximum permissible axial play is 0.15mm (0.006 in.).

9. Prime the pump with oil and position onto the block. Install the mounting bolts. Torque the long bolt to 15 ft. lbs. and the short one to 7 ft. lbs.

10. Install the oil pan with a new gasket. Fill the crankcase to the proper level.

Timing Belt Cover

REMOVAL AND INSTALLATION

1. Loosen the alternator mounting bolts and if equipped, the power steering pump and air conditioner compressor bolts if their drive belts will interfere with cover removal.

2. Pivot the alternator or driven component and slip the drive belt from the pulleys.

3. Unscrew the belt cover retaining nuts and remove the cover. On some models with two piece covers, it may be necessary to remove the crankshaft pulley.

4. Reposition the spacers and nuts on the mounting studs so they will not get lost.

5. Service vehicle as necessary and reinstall the belt cover in the reverse order of removal.

Timing Belt

NOTE: *The timing belt is designed to last for more than 60,000 miles and normally does not require tension adjustment. If the belt is removed, breaks or is replaced, the basic valve timing must be checked and the belt re-tensioned.*

REMOVAL AND INSTALLATION

Gasoline Engines

DASHER, FOX AND QUANTUM
1979–84 RABBIT, SCIROCCO, PICK-UP AND JETTA

NOTE: *Timing belt installation will be less confusing if the engine is set for No. l cylinder at TDC (top dead center) prior to belt removal or replacement.*

1. Remove front belt cover(s).

2. Turn the engine until the 0° mark on the flywheel is aligned with the stationary pointer on the bell housing. On 4 cylinder engines, turn the camshaft until the mark on the rear of the sprocket is aligned with the upper edge of the rear drive belt cover, at the left side of the engine. On 5 cylinder engines, turn the camshaft until the mark on the sprocket lines up with the left side edge of the camshaft housing. The notch on the crankshaft pulley should align with the dot on the intermediate shaft sprocket and the distributor rotor (remove distributor cap) should be pointing toward the mark on the rim of the distributor housing.

3. Remove the crankshaft accessories drive pulley(s).

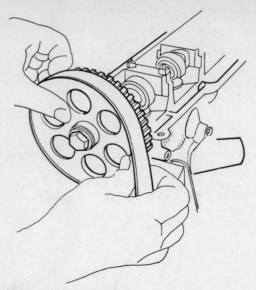

Work the belt off the gear

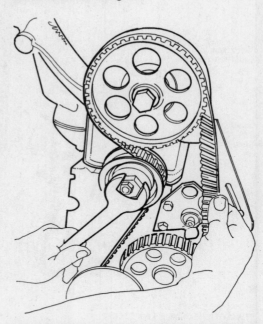

Belt tension is correct when the belt can be twisted 90°

4. On 4-cylinder engines, hold the large nut on the tensioner pulley and loosen the smaller pulley lock nut. Turn the tensioner counterclockwise to relieve the tension on the timing belt.

5. On 5-cylinder engines, loosen the water pump bolts and turn the pump clockwise to relieve timing belt tension.

6. Slide the timing belt from the pulleys.

7. Install timing belt and retension with

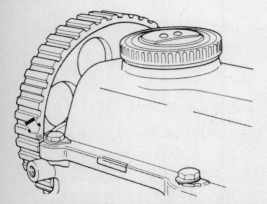

Align the camshaft timing mark with the edge of the cylinder head

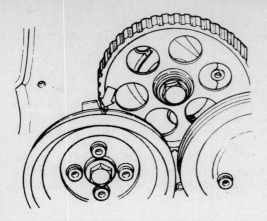

Align the timing marks on crankshaft and intermediate shaft

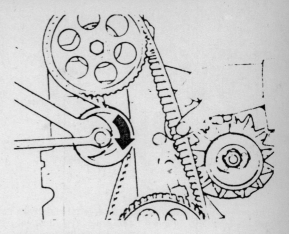

Tensioning the drive belt

pulley or water pump. Reinstall the crankshaft pulley(s). Recheck alignment of timing marks.

CAUTION: *If the timing marks are not correctly aligned with the No. 1 piston at TDC of the compression stroke and the belt is installed, valve timing will be incorrect. Poor performance and possible engine damage can result from improper valve timing.*

8. Check the timing belt tension. The tension is correct when the belt can be twisted 90° with the thumb and index finger along the straight run between the camshaft sprocket and the water pump.

9. Turn the engine two complete revolutions (clockwise rotation) and align the flywheel mark at TDC. Recheck belt tension and timing marks. Readjust as required.

10. Reinstall the cam belt cover and drive belts in the reverse order of removal.

PASSAT, GOLF, GTI, JETTA, CABRIOLET AND SCIROCCO (8-VALVE ENGINES)

1. Remove the drive belts, vibration dampener, pulleys and timing belt cover.

2. Loosen the tensioner and work the old belt off the timing gears.

3. Install the new drive belt onto the crankshaft and intermediate shaft sprockets.

4. Mount the pulley and vibration damper onto the crankshaft with the fasteners. The installation of these pulleys is required for proper belt timing.

5. Align the mark on the camshaft sprocket with the mark on the cylinder head cover and the crankshaft pulley dampener mark is aligned with the mark on the intermediate shaft.

6. Install the drive belt on the camshaft sprocket.

7. To tension the drive belt: Engage the

flats of the large pulley nut with an open end wrench and loosen the smaller pulley locknut. Tension the belt by turning the tensioner in a CLOCKWISE direction. Proper tension is achieved when you can twist the belt 90° with your thumb and index finger along the straight run between the camshaft and intermediate sprockets. When you can do this, tighten the tensioner locknut and tighten (holding the large nut stationary). The distributor rotor (remove distributor cap) should be pointing toward the mark on the rim of the distributor housing. If not, turn the distributor until the mark and the rotor align. If necessary, remove and reinstall the distributor.

8. Turn the crankshaft twice in the normal direction of engine rotation and recheck the belt tension.

9. Remove the crankshaft pulley and vibration dampener and install the lower timing belt cover.

10. Install the upper drive belt cover, V-belt pulley, vibration damper and V-belt.

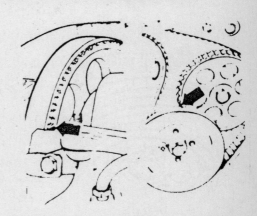

Camshaft and intermediate shaft sprocket alignment

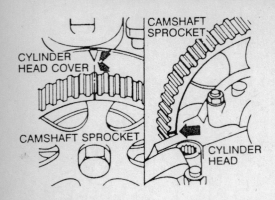

The mark on the camshaft sprocket must align with the mark on the cylinder head cover (valve cover installed)

16-VALVE ENGINES

NOTE: *Timing belt replacement can be accomplished with the valve cover on or off the engine.*

1. Remove the V-belts, vibration dampener, pulleys and timing belt covers.
2. Loosen the tensioner and work the old belt off the timing gears.
3. Install the drive belt onto the crankshaft and intermediate shaft sprockets.
4. Install the lower drive belt cover.
5. Install the vibration dampener. The offset holes must be in the right position.
6. If the valve cover is installed, align the marks on the camshaft sprocket with the pointer mark on the cylinder head cover. If the valve cover was removed, the mark on the camshaft sprocket must be aligned with mark on the edge of the cylinder head.
7. Align the mark on the vibration dampener with the mark on the drive belt cover.
8. Install the drive belt on the camshaft sprocket.

9. Engage the flats of the large pulley nut with an open end wrench and tension the belt by turning the tensioner in a CLOCKWISE direction. Proper tension is achieved when you can twist the belt 90° with your thumb and index finger along the straight run between the camshaft and intermediate sprockets. When you can do this, install the tensioner locknut and tighten to 33 ft. lbs. (holding the large nut stationary).
10. Turn the crankshaft twice in the normal direction of engine rotation and recheck the belt tension. Make sure all the timing marks are aligned properly.
11. Install the upper drive belt cover, V-belt pulley and V-belts.

CORRADO

NOTE: *It is not necessary to bring the the No.1 piston is NOT when replacing the timing belt. Timing belt replacement may be accomplished with the valve cover on or off the engine.*

1. Remove the V-belts, vibration dampener, pulleys and timing belt covers.
2. Loosen the tensioner and work the old belt off the timing gears.
3. Install the drive belt onto the crankshaft and intermediate shaft sprockets.
4. Mount the pulley and vibration damper onto the crankshaft with the fasteners. The installation of these pulleys is required for proper belt timing.
5. If the valve cover is installed, align the two dots on the camshaft sprocket with the mark on the cylinder head cover. If the valve cover was removed, the two dots on the camshaft sprocket must be aligned with mark on the edge of the cylinder head.

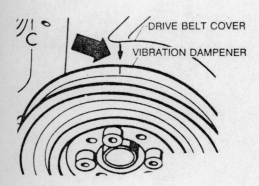

The mark on the camshaft sprocket must align with the edge of the cylinder head (valve cover removed)

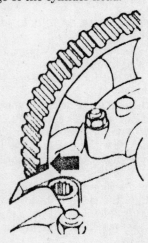

On Corrado, align the mark on the camshaft sprocket with the edge of the cylinder head (valve cover removed)

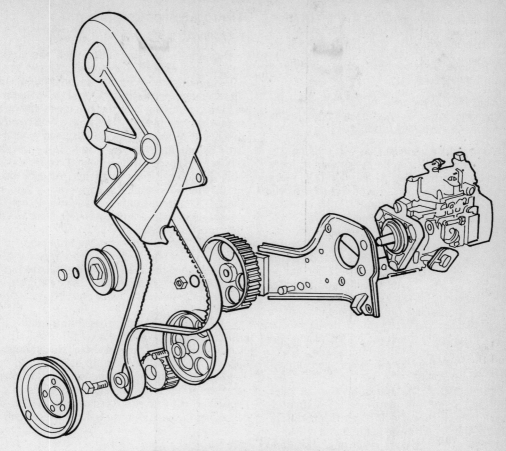

Timing belt installation — diesel engine

6. Align the mark on the crankshaft pulley/vibration damper with the mark on the intermediate sprocket. The No.1 piston should be at TDC (**0** mark on the flywheel aligned with the

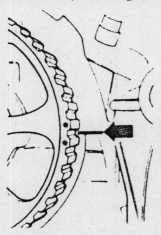

On Corrado, align the mark on the valve cover with two dots on the camshaft sprocket (valve cover installed)

pointer on the bellhousing. Mount the drive belt on the camshaft sprocket.

7. Engage the flats of the large pulley nut with an open end wrench and tension the belt by turning the tensioner in a CLOCKWISE direction. Proper tension is achieved when you can twist the belt 90° with your thumb and index finger along the straight run between the camshaft and intermediate sprockets. When you can do this, install the tensioner locknut and torque to 33 ft. lbs. (holding the large nut stationary).

8. Turn the crankshaft twice in the normal direction of engine rotation and recheck the belt tension. Make sure all the timing marks are aligned properly.

9. Remove the crankshaft pulley and vibration dampener and install the lower timing belt cover.

10. Install the upper drive belt cover, V-belt pulley, vibration damper and drive belt.

Diesel Engines

NOTE: *This procedure will require a number of special tools and a certain working knowledge of diesel engines. You may wish to have the work performed by an authorized service technician.*

1. Remove the camshaft (valve) cover and the timing belt cover(s).

NOTE: *The drive belt must be checked for proper tension and must be centered in the sprockets before checking timing.*

2. Turn the engine so that No. 1 cylinder is at TDC. The No. 1 cylinder camshaft lobes should be pointing upward and the TDC mark on the flywheel should be aligned with the bellhousing mark.

3. Fix the camshaft in position with tool VW 2065 or 2065A. Align the tool as follows: Turn the camshaft until one end of the tool touches the cylinder head. Measure the gap at the other end of the tool with a feeler gauge. Take half of the measurement and insert a feeler gauge of that thickness between the tool and the cylinder head. Turn the camshaft so the tool rests on the feeler gauge. Insert a feeler gauge of the same thickness on the other side, between the tool and the cylinder head.

4. Lock the injector pump sprocket in position with pin 2064.

5. Check that the marks on the sprocket, pump and mounting plate are approximately aligned. Check that the TDC mark on the flywheel is aligned with the bellhousing mark.

6. After the camshaft is set in position and the timing at TDC (flywheel and bellhousing marks aligned) loosen the camshaft sprocket mounting bolt 1 turn.

7. Tap the back of sprocket with a rubber hammer to loosen. Hand tight the bolt to remove endplay.

8. Loosen the belt adjuster and remove the belt from the injector pump sprocket.

9. Turn the injector pump sprocket until the marks on the sprocket, pump and mounting bracket align. Insert pin 2064 through the hole in the sprocket and mounting bracket to lock in position.

10. Reinstall the camshaft drive belt. Tighten the camshaft mounting bolt to 33 ft. lbs. Remove the camshaft setting bar and the lock pin from the injector pump sprocket. Install VW tool VW210 (Belt tension gauge).

11. Adjust tension by turning the tensioner clockwise, reading on the tension gauge should be 12–13. Lock tensioner in position.

12. Turn the crankshaft 2 complete turns (clockwise rotation) and recheck belt tension. Strike the drive belt once with a rubber hammer between the camshaft and injector pump sprockets to eliminate play.

13. Recheck timing, readjust if necessary.

Timing Sprockets
REMOVAL AND INSTALLATION

Depending on year and model, the timing sprockets are located on the shaft by a key, a self-contained drive lug, or in the case of early diesel engine camshaft, a tapered fit. All sprockets are retained by a bolt. To remove any or all sprockets, removal of the timing belt cover(s) and belt is required. The old hex head washered style bolt on many engine crankshaft sprockets has been replaced with a new 12 point stretch bolt that do not have a washer. At each overhaul, this bolt sould be throw away and replaced. The crankshaft threads can accept the new style bolts; however, washers from the old bolt must not be used.

NOTE: *When removing the crankshaft pulley, it is not necessary to remove the four bolts which hold the outer component drive pulley to the timing belt sprocket. Remove the component drive belt, center retaining bolt and crankshaft pulley.*

1. Remove the center retaining bolt.
2. Gently pry the sprocket off the shaft.
3. If the sprocket is stubborn in coming off, use a gear puller. Don't hammer on the sprocket. On diesel engine camshafts, loosen the center bolt one turn and tap the rear of the sprocket with a rubber hammer. When the sprocket loosens, remove bolt and sprocket.

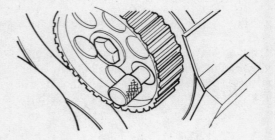

Holding the sprocket

4. Remove the sprocket and key. Inspect the key and keyway for scoring. Polish scored keys and keyways with fine emery cloth. If the key is excessively damaged, replace it.

5. Install the sprocket in the reverse order of removal.

6. On all engines, except those listed below, tighten all sprocket bolts to 58 ft. lbs. Models having a crankshaft sprocket with a self contained index lug require 145 ft. lbs. on center bolt.

• 16 valve Scirocco: torque the camshaft sprocket bolt to 48 ft. lbs.

• 4-cylinder Quantum (gasoline engines): torque 12mm crankshaft sprocket bolts to 59 ft. lbs. (lubricate threads with locking compound).

• Quantum turbo-diesel: torque the camshaft bolt to 33 ft. lbs.

• Corrado: Torque the camshaft and intermediate sprocket bolts to 58 ft. lbs. Always replace the crankshaft bolt with a new one. This is a 12 point stretch type bolt. Torque this bolt in two steps: First torque the bolt to 66 ft. lbs, then tighten an additional $1/2$ turn (180°). Two $1/4$ (90°) turns are permissible. Use special tool 3099 or its equivalent to loosen and tighten the bolt.

• Passat: Torque the camshaft and intermediate sprocket bolts to 48 ft. lbs. Always replace the crankshaft bolt with a new one. This is a 12 point stretch type bolt. Torque this bolt in two steps: First torque the bolt to 66 ft. lbs, then tighten an additional $1/2$ turn (180°). Two $1/4$ (90°) turns is permissible. Two $1/4$ (90°) turns are permissible. Use special tool 3099 or its equivalent to loosen and tighten the bolt.

• 16 valve Golf/Jetta/GTI: Torque the intermediate shaft, intake and exhaust sprockets to 48 ft. lbs. Lubricate the crankshaft bolt threads with oil and torque to 133 ft. lbs. On Jetta's produced starting in March of 1989, the old style hex head, washered crankshaft bolt was replaced with a 12 point stretch bolt that has a collar. This bolt is to be discarded at each overhaul. It cannot be reused. The bolt may be used on pre-March 1989 engines; however the washer from the old bolt must be discarded. Torque the 12 point bolt in two steps: First torque the bolt to 66 ft. lbs, then tighten an additional $1/2$ turn (180°). Two $1/4$ (90°) turns are permissible. Use special tool 3099 or its equivalent to loosen and tighten the bolt.

• Jetta diesel/Turbodiesel: On these engines the old style 14mm hex head crankshaft sprocket bolt was replaced with a 12 point stretch type bolt. The 12 point bolt is to be discarded at each overhaul. It cannot be reused. Torque the 12 point bolt in two steps: First torque the bolt to 66 ft. lbs, then tighten an additional $1/2$ turn (180°). Two $1/4$ turns are permissible. Use special tool 3099 or its equivalent to loosen and tighten the bolt.

• Fox: Torque the camshaft and intermediate shaft sprocket bolts to 59 ft. lbs. On engines up to and including serial number JN 707 652, lubricate the threads of the crankshaft bolt and torque to 133 ft. lbs. This bolt is a hex head washered type bolt. On engines starting with serial number JN 707 65, the hex head bolt was replaced with a 12 point stretch bolt with a collar. This bolt is to be discarded at each overhaul. It cannot be reused. The bolt may be used on all engines; however the washer from the old bolt must be discarded. Torque the 12 point

bolt in two steps: First torque the bolt to 66 ft. lbs, then tighten an additional $1/2$ turn (180°). Two $1/4$ turns are permissible. Use special tool 3099 or its equivalent to loosen and tighten the bolt.

CAUTION: *On 16 valve engines, make sure the camshaft sprockets are installed so that the curved portion of the sprocket key faces the surface of the engine block. If the sprocket is installed incorrectly, the timing will be advanced and cause the valves to hit the pistons.*

7. Install the timing belt, check valve timing, tension belt, and install the cover.

Camshaft(s) and Bearings
REMOVAL AND INSTALLATION
All Engines Except 16 Valve

NOTE: *The No.4 camshaft bearing has been eliminated on 1988–90 Cabriolets.*

1. Remove the timing belt cover(s), the timing belt, camshaft drive sprocket and camshaft (valve) cover.

NOTE: *Number the bearing caps from front to back. Scribe an arrow facing front. The caps are off-set and must be installed correctly. Factory number on the caps are not always on the same side.*

2. Remove the camshaft sprocket and the Woodruff key.

3. Remove the front and rear bearing caps. Loosen the remaining bearing cap nuts diagonally in several steps, starting from the outside caps near the ends of the head and work toward the center. Remember, the camshaft is under pressure from the valve spring.

4. Remove the bearing caps.

5. Install new oil seal and end plug in cylinder head. Lightly coat the camshaft(s) bearing journals and lobes with a film of assembly lube or heavy engine oil.

6. Install the camshaft so that the lobes for the No.1 cylinder are pointing upward. Torque the camshaft bearing nuts in reverse of the removal sequence to 15 ft. lbs.

7. Install the drive sprocket and timing belt. Check valve clearance and adjust if necessary. Install remaining parts in reverse order of removal.

16 Valve Engines

On the 16 valve 1.8L and 2.0L DOHC engines, the camshafts are driven by a single toothed belt. The belt drives the exhaust camshaft in an arrangement similar to the eight valve 1.8L engine. The exhaust camshaft then drives the intake camshaft through a single roller chain and sprockets attached to the backs of the camshafts.

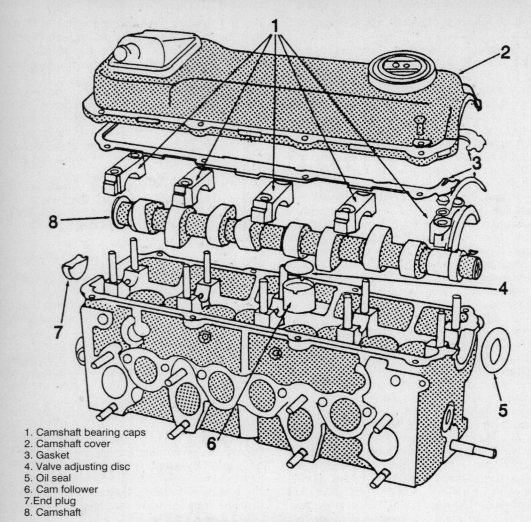

1. Camshaft bearing caps
2. Camshaft cover
3. Gasket
4. Valve adjusting disc
5. Oil seal
6. Cam follower
7. End plug
8. Camshaft

Typical 8-valve gasoline engine camshaft assembly

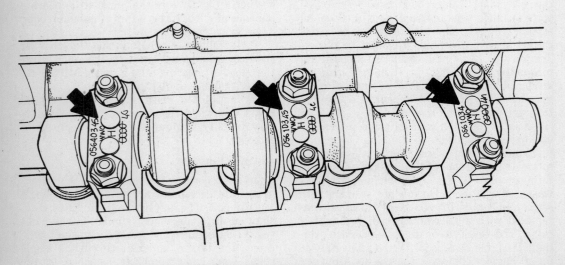

The camshaft bearings are numbered for identification (arrows)

The camshafts and pulleys must be installed together in the cylinder head so all the timing marks line up.

The camshaft drive belt and all pulleys have been widened and the tooth pitch of the belt and pulleys are also deeper.

1. Remove the timing belt cover.

2. Remove the bolts from the upper intake manifold and remove the manifold and gasket.

3. Remove the bolts from the cylinder head cover and remove the cover and gaskets.

4. Turn the engine to TDC on cylinder No. 1, then loosen and remove the timing belt.

5. Remove the camshaft sprockets and the drive train. Matchmark the intake sprocket to the drive chain with an indelible marker or equivalent before removal. DO NOT scratch, inscribe, punch, number or mark the drive chain in any way.

6. On the intake camshaft, remove bearing caps 5 and 7 as well as the last bearing caps. Then loosen bearing caps 6 and 8 alternately and diagonally.

7. On the exhaust camshaft, remove bearing caps 1 and 3 as well as the first and last bearing caps. Then loosen bearing caps 2 and 4 alternately and diagonally.

NOTE: *First and last bearing caps are located either at the front and/or rear of the camshafts and are not numbered.*

8. Remove the remaining bearing cap bolts and remove the cam shafts.

9. Install the camshaft drive chain so that the marks on the chain sprockets are matched at the base of the cylinder head, directly across from each other.

10. On the intake camshaft, install and

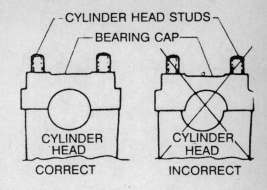

Proper camshaft bearing positioning for 8-valve engines

tighten bearing caps 6 and 8 alternately and diagonally to 11 ft. lbs.

11. Install and tighten the remaining bearing caps to 11 ft. lbs.

12. On the exhaust camshaft, tighten bearing caps 2 and 4 alternately and diagonally to 11 ft. lbs. 13. Install and tighten the remaining bearing caps to 11 ft. lbs.

14. Position and install the camshaft sprocket. Torque the camshaft sprockets to 48 ft. lbs.

CAUTION: *Make sure the camshaft sprockets are installed so that the curved portion of the sprocket key faces the surface of the engine block. If the sprocket is installed incorrectly, the timing will be advanced and cause the valves to hit the pistons.*

15. Install the drive belt and adjust the timing.

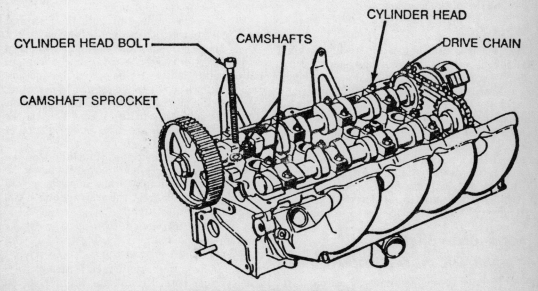

16-valve engine cylinder head assembly

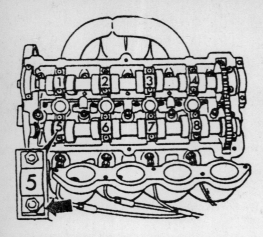

Camshaft bearing torque sequence for 16-valve engines

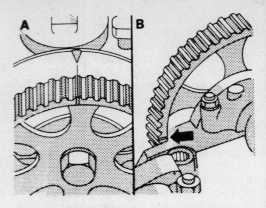

Exhaust camshaft pulley timing mark at TDC

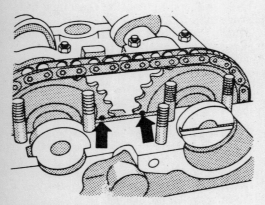

Camshaft sprocket timing marks at TDC

16. Install the remaining components in the reverse order of their removal.

INSPECTION

Degrease the camshaft using a safe solvent. Visually inspect the cam lobes and bearing journals for excessive wear. If a lobe is questionable or a bearing journal scored, the camshaft should be replaced. Check the lobes and journals with a micrometer. Measure the lobes from nose to heel. If all intake or all exhaust lobes do not measure the same, replace the camshaft. If the lobes and journals appear intact, place the front and rear journals in V-blocks. Position a dial indicator on the center journal and rotate the camshaft. If deviation exceeds 0.01mm (0.0004 in.) replace the camshaft.

Intermediate Shaft

REMOVAL AND INSTALLATION

1. Remove timing belt cover(s), timing belt and intermediate shaft drive sprocket.

2. Remove fuel pump and distributor (gasoline engines). Remove drive key from the intermediate shaft.

3. Remove the mounting flange retaining bolts. Reinstall sprocket bolt and remove the flange and shaft by pulling on the sprocket bolt.

4. Remove flange from the intermediate shaft and install new oil seal.

5. Install in reverse order of removal. Lubricate the oil seal lips. When installing the mounting flange be sure the oil return hole is at the bottom. Tighten the flange mounting bolts to 18 ft. lbs.

Pistons and Connecting Rods
Gasoline Engines

REMOVAL AND INSTALLATION

1. Follow the instructions under Timing Belt and Cylinder Head removal.

2. Remove the oil pan.

3. Turn the crankshaft until the piston to be removed is at the bottom of travel.

4. Make sure the connecting rod and cap are marked for reference as to cylinder location and position match (scribe across rod end and cap so cap will be installed in mating position). Mark piston heads from front to back, in order, for reinstallation identification. The marks should face towards the drive pulley section of the engine.

5. Place a rag down the cylinder bore on the head of the piston to be removed. Remove the cylinder top ridge and carbon deposits with a ridge reamer, following the instructions of the reamer's manufacturer.

CAUTION: *Do not cut too deeply or remove more than 0.8mm ($^1/_{32}$ in.) from the ring travel area when removing the ridge.*

6. Remove the rag and metal cuttings from the cylinder bore. Remove the connecting rod cap and bearing insert.

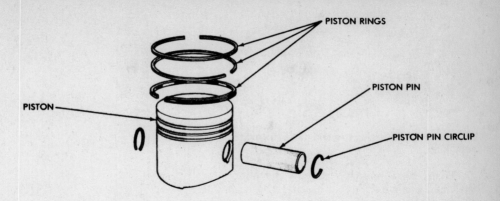

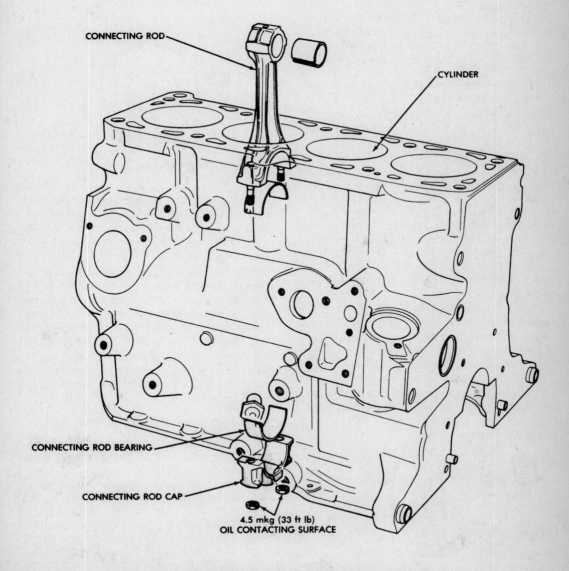

Cylinder block, piston, connecting rods and bearings

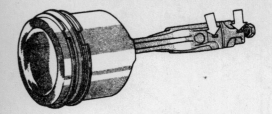

Matchmark the connecting rod and cap before disassembly

7. Push the connecting rod up the bore slightly and remove the upper bearing insert.

8. Push the connecting rod and piston assembly up and out of the cylinder with a hammer handle.

9. Wipe any dirt or oil from the connecting rod bearing saddle and rod cap. Install the bearing inserts (if to be reused) in the connecting rod and cap. Install cap and secure with rod bolts.

10. Remove the rest of the rod and piston assemblies in a like manner.

CAUTION: *When removing the pistons, take care not to score the crankshaft journals or cylinder walls.*

11. Lubricate the piston, rings and cylinder wall. Install and lubricate the upper bearing insert. Install a piston ring compressor over the rings and top of the piston. Be sure the piston ring ends are staggered (See following section). Lower the piston and rod assembly into the cylinder bore with the arrow on the piston head facing the front of the engine. When the ring compressor contacts the top of the engine block, use a wooden hammer handle to tap the piston into the bore.

NOTE: *If unusual resistance is encountered when starting the piston into the cylinder bore, it is possible that a ring slipped out of the compressor and is caught at the top of the cylinder. Remove the piston and reinstall compressor or else you will break some rings.*

12. Guide the connecting rod down the cylinder bore and over the crankshaft journal taking

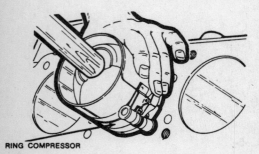

RING COMPRESSOR

Installing the piston

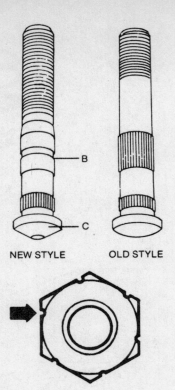

NEW STYLE   OLD STYLE

Stretch-type rod bolt identification

care not to score the wall or shaft. Install the lower bearing insert into the connecting rod cap. Lubricate the insert and mount the cap on the rod with matchmarks aligned. Install rod bolts and tighten to specifications.

NOTE: *Engines using rod bolts with a smooth surface between threads and short knurled shank and having a round head containing six notches are stretch type bolts and cannot be reused. Always use new bolts when servicing.*

13. Install remaining piston and rod assemblies in a like manner, turn the crankshaft each time so the crank journal of the piston being installed is at the bottom of travel.

CLEANING AND INSPECTION

After removing the piston and rod assemblies from the engine, take and assembly and clamp the connecting rod into a vise with the lower edge of the piston just resting on the vise jaws. Use a ring expanding tool and remove the piston rings from the piston. Save the top compression ring and tag with cylinder location number. The old ring can be used later to check the cylinder bore for wear. Clean the top of the piston with a dull scraper, use care not to gouge the piston when removing the carbon deposits. Clean the ring grooves using an appropriate

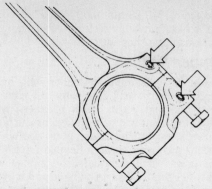

When assembling the connecting rod and cap, align the forged marks

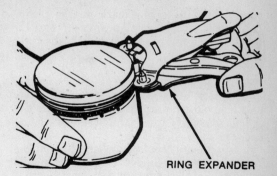

RING EXPANDER

Remove the piston rings

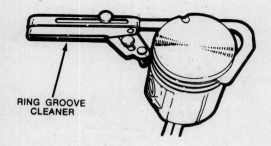

RING GROOVE CLEANER

Ring groove cleaner

groove cleaning tool. A broken piston ring can be used if a groove cleaner is not available. Once again, use care not to cut too deeply or gouge the ring seat. After all the pistons have had the rings removed and grooves cleaned, soak them in safe solvent. Do not use a wire brush or caustic solvent on the pistons.

After the pistons have been cleaned and wiped dry inspect them for scuffing, scoring, cracks, pitting or excessive ring groove wear. If wear is evident, the piston must be replaced. Hold the connecting rod in one hand and grasp the piston in the other hand, twist the piston and rod in opposite directions. If excessive clearance (looseness) is detected, the piston pin, connecting rod bushing or piston and rod may require replacement. The automotive machine shop can handle the job for you. If you are not sure of the extent of wear present or what component needs replacing, take the assemblies to the machine shop and have them checked.

Make sure the piston, connecting rod and rod cap are marked with the number of the cylinder the assembly came from. Remove the piston from the connecting rod by inserting a small blunt drift in the small cutout provided on each side of the piston at the piston pin ends. Pry upward on the circlip to compress, and remove both circlips. Use a blunt drift slightly smaller than the diameter of the piston

pin to gently drive the pin out. If resistance is encountered when removing the piston pin, submerge the pistons in hot water of 140°F to expand the metal and then carefully drive the pin out. Inspect the piston pin, connecting rod bushing and piston pin bore for galling, scoring or excessive wear. If wear is evident, consult the machine shop for advice as to what repair is necessary.

Measure, or have the machine shop measure the piston with a micrometer. Turn the piston upside down and take a measurement at a point 16mm (⁵⁄₈ in.) below the lower edge of the piston, 90° away from the piston pin holes. Compare the reading to specifications, replace piston as needed.

Check the cylinder bore (see following section) to determine if wear indicates excessive clearance requiring cylinder boring and oversize piston installation. If the original pistons are to be reused, lubricate the piston pin and rod bushing and reinstall the connecting rod. Make sure the matchmarks you made on the connecting rod are on the same side of the piston (arrow facing front) as they were before removal. Factory forge marks at the bottom of the connecting rod and cap face must be mounted on the intermediate shaft side of the

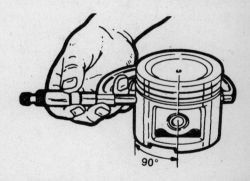

Measure the piston at a point 90° from the wrist pin boss

engine when the arrow mark on the piston head is facing front. Install pistons on connecting rods in the reverse order of removal.

CYLINDER BORE

Measurements can be made with a special dial indicator, telescope gauge and micrometer, or with an old compression ring taken from the piston removed from the cylinder being checked.

Measurements should be taken at a number of places in each cylinder: at the top, middle and bottom at two points at each location: that is, at a point 90° from the crankshaft, as well as a point parallel to the crankshaft. The difference between the greatest measurement of the cylinder wall and the diameter measurement of the piston (see Cleaning and Inspection) is the piston clearance. If slightly excessive clearance is indicated and the cylinder is not tapered too much, finish honing of the cylinder and a slightly larger (oversize) piston may be all that is required. A great amount of wear will require cylinder boring and standard oversize pistons.

If the necessary precision tools to check the bore are not on hand and the engine is out of the car and disassembled, have the machine shop check it out for you. One way to get an idea of cylinder wear, when no instruments are available, is to use an old compression ring taken from the cylinder being checked. Place the piston ring into the bore just below the removed ridge. Make sure the ring is square in the bore (push into place with the piston head). Take a set of feeler gauges and measure the gap between the ends of the ring. Push the ring down the bore to the end of the piston travel and take a measurement. The taper of the cylinder is roughly 0.3 times the difference of the ring gap readings. The amount of taper should

not exceed 0.18–0.23mm (0.007–0.009 in.). If it does, the block probably requires reboring. Consult the machine shop for their advice.

CYLINDER HONING

Honing or deglazing the cylinder walls helps new piston rings seat faster for oil control. Refer to the instruction sheet packaged with the new rings that will be installed for the manufacturer's recommendation. If no special instructions are given, chuck a flexible drive hone into a power drill, lubricate the stones and insert into cylinder. Start the hone and move it up and down in the cylinder at a rate that will produce a 60° crosshatch pattern. Take care not to extend the hone below cylinder bore, or to withdraw it from the bore when operating. After developing the pattern wash the cylinder with a detergent and water solution to remove abrasive dust. Dry cylinder wall and wipe several times with a clan rag soaked in engine oil.

PISTON RINGS

After the cylinder bore has been finish honed, or determined to be in satisfactory condition, ring end gap clearance can be checked. Compress the piston rings to be used in each cylinder, one at a time, into that cylinder. Press the ring down the bore to a point about 25mm (1 inch) below the top with an inverted piston. Measure the distance between the two ends (ring gap) of the ring with feeler gauges and compare to specifications. Pull the ring from the cylinder and file the ends with a fine file to gain required clearance, if necessary. Roll the outside of the ring around the piston groove it will be installed in to check for burrs or unremoved carbon deposits. Dress the groove with a fine file if necessary. Hold the ring in the groove and measure between top of ring and groove with a set of feeler gauges to check side clearance. If clearance is excessive, a new piston may be required or, in some cases, a spacer can be installed. Consult the machine shop for their advice.

Install the piston rings on the piston starting with the lower oil control ring. Always refer to the ring manufacturer's instruction sheet for guidance. Be sure, when installing a three piece expander type oil ring, that the ends of the expander are butted together and do not overlap. Hold the butter edges together and install the lower rail first. Install with the ring gap about 19mm (³/₄ in.) away from the butter point of the expander. Install the upper rail on the opposite side, ³/₄ away from the butted point of the expander. Use a ring expander and install the compression rings, second ring first. Most compression rings will have a top mark of some kind, be sure the mark is facing up.

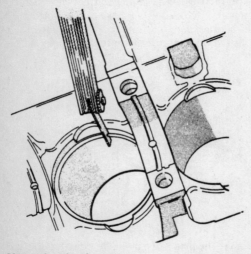

Measuring the ring gap

NOTE: *Before installing the piston ring compressor, while assembling the engine, be sure the piston ring locations are staggered. The end gaps should be at three equal spacings, never in a straight line. Avoid installing the rings with their ends in line with the piston pin bosses and the thrust direction. Always refer to the ring manufacturer's instruction sheet for guidance.*

PISTON AND CONNECTING RODS DIESEL ENGINE

The same basic procedures apply to the diesel engine as the gasoline engine. The one important difference is that whenever new pistons or short block are installed, the piston projection must be checked.

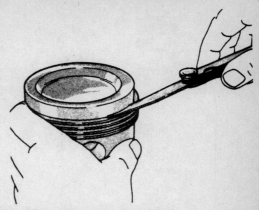

Measuring the ring side clearance

Piston projection measurement on diesel engines — note spacer (arrow)

A spacer (VW385/17) and bar with dial indicator (VW 382/7) are necessary, and should be set up as shown to measure the maximum amount of piston projection above the deck height. To measure the piston height of particular cylinder, bring the piston up so that the top of the piston is dead flush with the surface of the block. Mount the indicator and spacer onto the cylinder deck. Slide the indicator over and zero the indicator stylus on the top of the piston. Now, slowly (very slowly) rotate the crankshaft until a deflection is read on the indicator. This is a very tricky reading, because you have to catch the indicator deflection before the piston starts on the downward travel. Take several readings per cylinder to get an average.

After piston height has been determined, a head gasket of suitable thickness must be used. Head gasket thickness is coded by the number of notches located on the edge and by a part number on the gasket near the notches. Always install a gasket with the same number of notches as the one removed. Consult your VW dealer if new pistons are installed.

Depending upon the piston height above the top surface of the engine block, there are 3 gaskets of different thicknesses which can be used. The gasket thicknesses vary depending on whether the engine is equipped with hydraulic or mechanical lifters. You can tell what kind of lifters the engine has from the sticker on the valve cover.

If the piston height for mechanical lifter equipped engines is:
• 0.60–0.80mm (0.025–0.032 in.) use a 1.4mm (0.055 in.) gasket
• 0.85–0.90mm (0.033–0.036 in.) use a 1.5mm (0.059 in.) gasket
• 0.95–1.00mm (0.037–0.040 in.) use a 1.6mm (0.063 in.) gasket

For engines with hydraulic lifters, gasket thickness is determined by the number of notches on the gasket. The following gives the piston height with it's corresponding notch number:
• 0.65–0.85mm (0.026–0.034 in.) use a 1 notch gasket
• 0.70–0.90mm (0.027–0.035 in.) use a 2 notch gasket
• 0.90–1.00mm (0.036–0.040 in.) use a 3 notch gasket

Rear Main Oil Seal

NOTE: *The front crankshaft oil seal can be changed after the crank pulley and drive sprocket have been removed. A number of special tools from VW are required.*

REPLACEMENT

The rear main oil seal is located in a housing on the rear of the cylinder block. To replace the seal on the Dasher or Quantum, it is necessary to remove the transmission and perform the work from underneath the car or remove the

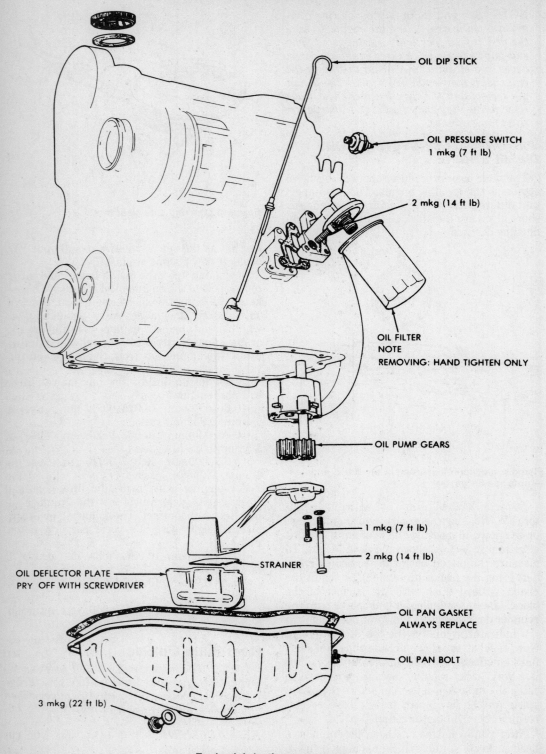

OIL DIP STICK

OIL PRESSURE SWITCH
1 mkg (7 ft lb)

2 mkg (14 ft lb)

OIL FILTER
NOTE
REMOVING: HAND TIGHTEN ONLY

OIL PUMP GEARS

1 mkg (7 ft lb)

2 mkg (14 ft lb)

STRAINER

OIL DEFLECTOR PLATE
PRY OFF WITH SCREWDRIVER

OIL PAN GASKET
ALWAYS REPLACE

OIL PAN BOLT

3 mkg (22 ft lb)

Engine lubrication components

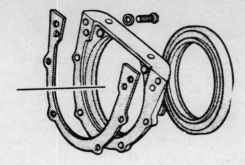

Rear main oil seal (circular)

A rear main oil seal protector is necessary when installing the new seal

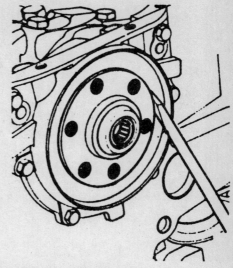

Rear main oil seal removal

engine and perform the work on an engine stand or work bench. See Transmission Removal and Installation section in Chapter 7.

On all other models, the engine should be removed from the car.

1. Remove the transmission and flywheel.

2. Using a screwdriver or VW seal remover tool, very carefully pry or pull the old seal out of the support ring.

3. Remove the seal.

4. Lightly oil the replacement seal and then press it into place using a a VW seal installation tool, canister top or other circular piece of flat metal. Be careful not to damage the seal or score the crankshaft.

5. Install the flywheel and transmission.

Crankshaft and Bearings

REMOVAL, INSPECTION, AND INSTALLATION

1. Rod bearings can be installed when the pistons have been removed for servicing (rings etc.) or, in most cases, while the engine is still in the car. Bearing replacement, however, is far easier with the engine out of the car and disassembled.

2. For in car service, remove the oil pan, spark plugs and front cover if necessary. Turn the engine until the connecting rod to be serviced is at the bottom of its travel. Remove the bearing cap and push the piston and rod assembly up the cylinder bore until enough room is gained for bearing insert removal. Take care not to push the rod assembly up too far or the top ring will engage the cylinder ridge or come out of the cylinder and require head removal for reinstallation.

3. Clean the rod journal, the connecting rod end and the bearing cap after removing the old bearing inserts. Install the new inserts in the rod and bearing cap, lubricate them with oil. Position the rod over the crankshaft journal and install the rod cap. Make sure the cap and rod numbers match, torque the rod bolts to specifications.

NOTE: *See note under Step 11 of Piston and Connecting Rod Section pertaining to the reuse of rod bolts.*

4. Main bearings may be replaced while the engine is still in the car by rolling them out and in.

5. Special roll-out pins are available from automotive parts houses or can be fabricated from a cotter pin. The roll out pin fits in the oil hole of the main bearing journal. When the crankshaft is rotated opposite the direction of the bearing lock tab, the pin engages the end of the bearing and rolls out the insert.

6. Remove main bearing cap and roll out upper bearing insert. Remove insert from main bearing cap. Clean the inside of the bearing cap and crankshaft journal.

NOTE: *Main bearing inserts with the lubrication grooves must be installed in the block.*

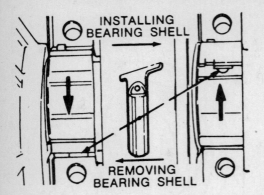

Remove or install the upper bearing insert using a roll-out pin

Inserts without grooves are installed in the baring caps.

7. Lubricate and roll upper insert into position, make sure the lock tab is anchored and the insert is not cocked. Install the lower bearing insert into the cap, lubricate and install on the engine. Make sure the main bearing cap is installed facing in the correct direction and torque to specifications.

8. With the engine out of the car. Remove the manifolds, cylinder head, front cover, timing belt and gears, oil pan, oil pump, flywheel, front and rear main seals and brackets.

9. Remove the piston and rod assemblies. Remove the main bearing caps after marking them for position and direction.

10. Remove the crankshaft and bearing inserts. Clean the engine block and cap bearing saddles. Clean the crankshaft and inspect for wear. Check the bearing journals with a micrometer for out-of-round condition and to determine what size rod and main bearing inserts to install.

11. Install the main bearing upper inserts into the engine block. (See previous Note.)

12. Lubricate the bearing inserts and the crankshaft journals. Slowly and carefully lower the crankshaft into position.

13. Install the bearing inserts into the bearing caps, install the caps working from the middle out. Torque cap bolts to specifications in stages, rotate the crankshaft after each torque stage.

14. Remove bearing caps, one at a time and check the oil clearance with Plastigage®. Reinstall if clearance is within specifications. Check the crankshaft endplay, if within specifications install connecting rod and piston assemblies with new rod bearing inserts. Check connecting rod bearing oil clearance and rod side play, if correct and assemble the rest of the engine.

BEARING OIL CLEARANCE

Remove cap from the bearing to be checked. Using a clean, dry rag, thoroughly clean all oil from crankshaft journal and bearing insert.

NOTE: *Plastigage® is soluble in oil. Therefore, oil on the journal or bearing could result in erroneous readings.*

Place a piece of Plastigage® along the full width of the insert, reinstall cap, and torque to specifications.

NOTE: *Specifications are given in the engine specifications earlier in this chapter.*

Remove bearing cap, and determine bearing clearance by comparing width of Plastigage® to the scale on Plastigage® envelope. Journal taper is determined by comparing width of the Plastigage® strip near its ends. Rotate crankshaft 90° and retest, to determine journal eccentricity.

NOTE: *Do not rotate crankshaft with Plastigage® installed. If bearing insert and journal appear intact, and are within tolerances, no further main bearing service is required. If bearing or journal appear defective, cause of failure should be determined before replacement.*

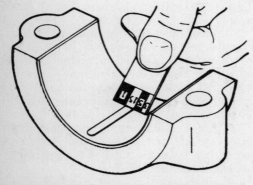

Measure the Plastigage® to determine bearing clearance

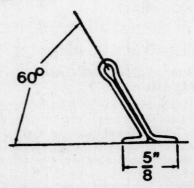

Homemade bearing rollout pin

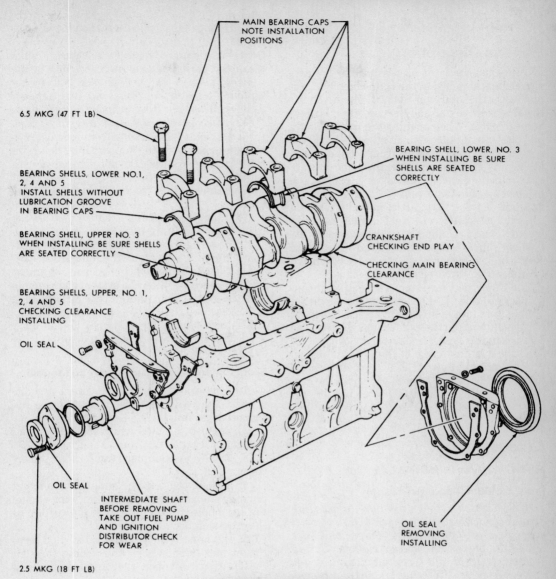

MAIN BEARING CAPS
NOTE INSTALLATION
POSITIONS

6.5 MKG (47 FT LB)

BEARING SHELLS, LOWER NO.1,
2, 4 AND 5
INSTALL SHELLS WITHOUT
LUBRICATION GROOVE
IN BEARING CAPS

BEARING SHELL, UPPER NO. 3
WHEN INSTALLING BE SURE SHELLS
ARE SEATED CORRECTLY

BEARING SHELLS, UPPER, NO. 1,
2, 4 AND 5
CHECKING CLEARANCE
INSTALLING

OIL SEAL

OIL SEAL

INTERMEDIATE SHAFT
BEFORE REMOVING
TAKE OUT FUEL PUMP
AND IGNITION
DISTRIBUTOR CHECK
FOR WEAR

2.5 MKG (18 FT LB)

BEARING SHELL, LOWER, NO. 3
WHEN INSTALLING BE SURE
SHELLS ARE SEATED
CORRECTLY

CRANKSHAFT
CHECKING END PLAY

CHECKING MAIN BEARING
CLEARANCE

OIL SEAL
REMOVING
INSTALLING

Cylinder block and crankshaft

CRANKSHAFT ENDPLAY/CONNECTING ROD SIDE PLAY

Place a pry bar between a main bearing cap and crankshaft casting taking care not to damage any journals. Pry backward and forward and measure the distance between the thrust bearing and crankshaft with a feeler gauge. Compare reading with specifications. If too great a clearance is determined, a larger thrust bearing or crank machining may be required. Consult an automotive machine shop for their advice.

Connecting rod clearance between the rod and crank throw casting can be checked with a feeler gauge. Pry the rod carefully to one side as far as possible and measure the distance on the other side of the rod.

CRANKSHAFT REPAIRS

If a journal is damaged on the crankshaft, repair is possible by having the crankshaft machined to a standard undersize.

In most cases, however, since the crankshaft must be removed from the engine, some thought should be given to replacing the damaged crankshaft with a reground shaft kit. A reground crankshaft kit contains the necessary main and rod bearings for installation. The shaft has been ground and polished to undersize specifications and will usually hold up well if installed correctly.

EXHAUST SYSTEM

General Discription

The exhaust system is suspended by hangers and clamps attached to the frame member. Annoying rattles and noise vibrations in the exhaust system are usually caused by misalignment of parts. When aligning the system, leave all bolts and nuts loose until all parts are properly aligned, then tighten from front to rear. Make sure that you are wearing some form of eye protection when removing or installing the exhaust system, to prevent eye injury from falling road dirt and rust particles. Never work on the exhaust system of a vehicle that has been recently used. Exhaust systems reach extremely high temperatures and can cause severe burns. Always allow the car to cool down before starting any repairs to the exhaust.

The Catalytic Converter is an emission control device added to a gasoline engines exhaust system to reduce hydrocarbon and carbon monoxide pollutants in the exhaust gas stream. The catalyst in the converter is not servicable.

Periodic maintenance of the exhaust system is not required. However, if the vehicle is raised for other service, it is advisable to check the general condition of the catalytic converter, exhaust pipes, muffler, hangers, flanges and fasteners.

Exhaust Pipe

REMOVAL AND INSTALLATION

Front Exhaust Pipe (Non-Turbo)

NOTE: *Some front exhaust pipes are equipped with swivel type joints that connect the pipe to the manifold. These joints are held in place with spring clamps. Spring clamp removal and installation requires the use of a special VW wedge kit that may be purchased at your local VW dealer. If the front exhaust pipe does have the spring clamp type connection, removal and installation procedures are located at the end of this chapter.*

1. Disconnect the oxygen sensor harness and remove the heat shields (if installed).
2. Remove the air duct from the upper shell cover if equipped.
3. Loosen (Do not remove) the nuts which hold the front exhaust pipe to the exhaust port of the engine.
4. Disconnect the front and rear exhaust pipes.
5. Disconnect the front exhaust pipe and bracket.
6. While holding the front exhaust pipe with one hand, remove the flange nuts which hold the front exhaust pipe to the exhaust port.

The front exhaust pipe can then be disconnected.

NOTE: *Be sure to install a new gasket at the exhaust port. Use only nuts specified by the manufacturer. Do not remove the gasket placed between the front and rear exhaust pipes. When the front exhaust pipe needs to be replaced, the gasket must be replaced also.*

7. Raise and connect the front exhaust pipe to the exhaust port and support it by hand. Install the flange nuts (Do not tighten at this time).
8. Connect the front exhaust pipe and bracket.
9. Connect the front exhaust pipe to the rear. Leave the flange nuts loose.
10. Starting from the front and working towards the rear, tighten all the nuts properly.
11. Check the system for proper alignment and clearance between the system components and the body. Align the system by loosening and tightening the brackets and hangers.
12. Install the upper shell cover and air duct.
13. Install the heat shields and connect the oxygen sensor harness.

Front Exhaust Pipe (Turbocharged Models)

1. Remove the turbocharger covers, and disconnect the center exhaust pipe. Remove the turbocharger unit.
2. Remove the nuts which hold the turbocharger bracket to the front exhaust pipe.
3. Remove underguard and right undercover.
4. Loosen the engine mount bracket and pitching stopper. Then slightly raise the engine until the bolts protrude beyond the surface of the crossmember.
5. Disconnect the front exhaust pipe from the engines exhaust port, and remove through the clearance between the crossmember and the cylinder head.

CAUTION: *Do not damage the power steering pipe which is located along the crossmember. Be sure to remove the bolts only after the engine has cooled off.*

6. Install the gasket onto the stud bolts at the engine's exhaust port with its flat surface facing the engine. If the gasket is tilted, it may catch on a thread and then will not drop down over the bolt.

NOTE: *Be sure to install a new gasket.*

7. Temporarily tighten the front exhaust pipe to engine's exhaust port with the nuts.

NOTE: *Use only nuts designed by the manufacturer.*

8. Lower the engine. Tighten the engine mount bracket and properly adjust the pitching stopper.

9. Install the underguard and right undercover.

10. Connect the front exhaust pipe to the turbocharger bracket.

NOTE: *Use only bolts designed by the manufacturer. Be sure to install a new gasket on the inlet of the turbocharger.*

11. Properly tighten the front exhaust pipe at the engine's exhaust port.

12. Connect the O_2 sensor connector.

13. Install the turbocharger unit, center the exhaust pipe and turbocharger covers.

Center Exhaust Pipe

REMOVAL AND INSTALLATION

Turbo Vehicles Only

1. Remove the two turbocharger covers.

2. Disconnect the O_2 sensor connector.

3. Remove the flange nuts which hold the center exhaust pipe to turbocharger unit.

NOTE: *Before removing the flange nuts, allow the turbocharger unit and exhaust pipe to cool.*

4. Remove the flange nuts from the transmission side.

5. Disconnect the center and rear exhaust pipes.

6. Disconnect the center exhaust pipe from the bracket located on the lower side of the transmission.

7. Remove the center exhaust pipe from the body.

CAUTION: *Do not allow the turbocharger cover mounting bracket to interfere with the brake pipe cover located in the front toeboard. Be sure not to damage the steering universal joint. Do not damage the gasket used on the lower side of the turbocharger unit or turbocharger cover.*

8. Install the gasket onto the stud bolts on the turbocharger unit. Connect the center exhaust pipe flange and temporarily tighten it with nuts.

CAUTION: *Be sure not to damage the gasket used on the lower side of the turbocharger unit and turbocharger cover.*

NOTE: *Use only nuts and bolts designed by the manufacturer and be sure to install a new gasket.*

9. Temporarily connect the center exhaust pipe and bracket located on the transmission side.

10. Temporarily connect the center and rear exhaust pipes, and center exhaust pipe to the bracket located on the lower side of the transmission with new nuts.

11. Tighten the nuts and bolts at the turbocharger unit bracket, (on the transmission side) and the bracket (on the lower side of the transmission), in that order.

NOTE: *Gasket used between the center and rear exhaust pipes may be reused but not removed. When a new center exhaust pipe is installed, replace the old gasket with a new one.*

12. Install turbocharger covers.

Rear Exhaust Pipe

REMOVAL AND INSTALLATION

1. Disconnect the ASV hose from the ASV (49 state 2WD carburetor model only).

2. Disconnect the rear exhaust pipe from the front exhaust pipe (Non-Turbo), center exhaust pipe (turbocharged models).

3. Disconnect the rear exhaust pipe from the muffler assembly. To prevent damage to the bumper or rear skirt by the muffler, wrap a cloth around the tail pipe.

4. Remove rear exhaust pipe from the rubber cushion.

5. Temporarily connect the rear exhaust pipe and the muffler assembly.

6. Temporarily connect the rear exhaust pipe and the front exhaust pipe (Non-Turbo), center exhaust pipe (turbocharged models).

7. Insert exhaust pipe bracket into the rubber cushion.

8. Adjust the clearance between the temporarily installed parts and tighten to specified torque.

NOTE: *Be sure to install bolts, springs, and self locking nuts in the order indicated in the figure. Always install new self locking nuts.*

Muffler Assembly

REMOVAL AND INSTALLATION

1. Remove the bolts, self locking nuts or sleeve clamps which hold the rear exhaust pipe to the muffler assembly.

2. Remove the left and right rubber cushions from the muffler assembly and detach the muffler assembly.

3. Installation is in the reverse order of the removal procedure.

NOTE: *Be sure to install new self locking nuts and gaskets.*

Aligning the Exhaust System

1. After installing exhaust system parts, check to make sure clearances between parts and car body are larger than specified values.

2. If any clearance is not, loosen all connections.

3. Adjust when necessary to obtain proper clearances.

4. Tighten all connections properly.

Mid Muffler Shield

REPAIR

To due corrosion and vibration, the center and corner welds that attach the mid-muffler shield often break. If this happens, the shield can be re-welded without having to replace the whole muffler assembly. To do this: loosen the exhaust hangers and lower the muffler assembly. Clamp the heat shield to the muffler using vise grips. Arc weld the heat shied to the muffler at the four points shown in the illustration. Re-hang the exhaust system.

Spring Clamps

REMOVAL AND INSTALLATION

Some front exhaust pipes are equipped with swivel type joints that connect the pipe to the exhaust manifold. These joints are held in place with two spring clamps. Spring clip removal and installation requires the use of a special VW wedge kit 3140 or suitable equivalent. Check on the availability of the this kit before attempting to disconnect the front exhaust pipe from the rest of the exhaust system.

To remove:

1. Allow the exhaust system to cool down.
2. Using a large set of pliers, move the exhaust pipe to the left side of the vehicle until short wedge 3140/2 can be inserted into the right clamp and to the right to insert the wedge into the left clamp.

NOTE: *The wedge must be completely inserted into the clamp. The shoulders of the wedge should butt up against the edges of the clamp.*

3. Move the exhaust pipe over to the right (with both wedges installed), remove the left wedge and clamp as a unit from the left side of the vehicle. Do the same for the right wedge and clamp. Insert art here

To release clamp:

4. Mount the clamp and wedge in a vise as shown. Position the clamp across the vise so that the blade of the wedge is between the jaws of the vise.
5. Insert starting wedge 3140/1 next to the other (short) wedge. Drive the starting wedge into the other wedge with a rubber mallet to release the clamp.

CAUTION: *Exercise extreme care when removing the wedge from the spring clamp. The combination of the blow from the hammer and the spring tension of the clamp will release the wedges with considerable force. Have a rag filled box or other device ready to catch the tool. Wear protective eye and face gear when performing this operation.*

To install:

6. Place the clamp on its side across the jaws of the vise.
7. Using the rubber mallet, drive the starting wedge into the clamp.

CAUTION: *DO NOT try to spread a bare clamp (new or untensioned) with the short wedge 3140/2 without using starting wedge 3140/1 first. Due to the tension exerted by the clamp, this could hurt you severely.*

8. Drive the short wedge into the clamp unto the shoulder of the tool butts against the edge of the clamp.
9. Remove and invert the clamp and knock the starting wedge out of the clamp. Leave the short wedge in place.
10. Install the clamps and remove the short wedges. The clamps must seat properly in the notches in the exhaust pipe flange and manifold.

Troubleshooting Engine Mechanical Problems

Problem	Cause	Solution
External oil leaks	• Fuel pump gasket broken or improperly seated	• Replace gasket
	• Cylinder head cover RTV sealant broken or improperly seated	• Replace sealant; inspect cylinder head cover sealant flange and cylinder head sealant surface for distortion and cracks
	• Oil filler cap leaking or missing	• Replace cap
	• Oil filter gasket broken or improperly seated	• Replace oil filter
	• Oil pan side gasket broken, improperly seated or opening in RTV sealant	• Replace gasket or repair opening in sealant; inspect oil pan gasket flange for distortion
	• Oil pan front oil seal broken or improperly seated	• Replace seal; inspect timing case cover and oil pan seal flange for distortion
	• Oil pan rear oil seal broken or improperly seated	• Replace seal; inspect oil pan rear oil seal flange; inspect rear main bearing cap for cracks, plugged oil return channels, or distortion in seal groove
	• Timing case cover oil seal broken or improperly seated	• Replace seal
	• Excess oil pressure because of restricted PCV valve	• Replace PCV valve
	• Oil pan drain plug loose or has stripped threads	• Repair as necessary and tighten
	• Rear oil gallery plug loose	• Use appropriate sealant on gallery plug and tighten
	• Rear camshaft plug loose or improperly seated	• Seat camshaft plug or replace and seal, as necessary
	• Distributor base gasket damaged	• Replace gasket
Excessive oil consumption	• Oil level too high	• Drain oil to specified level
	• Oil with wrong viscosity being used	• Replace with specified oil
	• PCV valve stuck closed	• Replace PCV valve
	• Valve stem oil deflectors (or seals) are damaged, missing, or incorrect type	• Replace valve stem oil deflectors
	• Valve stems or valve guides worn	• Measure stem-to-guide clearance and repair as necessary
	• Poorly fitted or missing valve cover baffles	• Replace valve cover
	• Piston rings broken or missing	• Replace broken or missing rings
	• Scuffed piston	• Replace piston
	• Incorrect piston ring gap	• Measure ring gap, repair as necessary
	• Piston rings sticking or excessively loose in grooves	• Measure ring side clearance, repair as necessary
	• Compression rings installed upside down	• Repair as necessary
	• Cylinder walls worn, scored, or glazed	• Repair as necessary
	• Piston ring gaps not properly staggered	• Repair as necessary
	• Excessive main or connecting rod bearing clearance	• Measure bearing clearance, repair as necessary
No oil pressure	• Low oil level	• Add oil to correct level
	• Oil pressure gauge, warning lamp or sending unit inaccurate	• Replace oil pressure gauge or warning lamp
	• Oil pump malfunction	• Replace oil pump
	• Oil pressure relief valve sticking	• Remove and inspect oil pressure relief valve assembly
	• Oil passages on pressure side of pump obstructed	• Inspect oil passages for obstruction

Troubleshooting Engine Mechanical Problems (cont.)

Problem	Cause	Solution
No oil pressure (cont.)	• Oil pickup screen or tube obstructed	• Inspect oil pickup for obstruction
	• Loose oil inlet tube	• Tighten or seal inlet tube
Low oil pressure	• Low oil level	• Add oil to correct level
	• Inaccurate gauge, warning lamp or sending unit	• Replace oil pressure gauge or warning lamp
	• Oil excessively thin because of dilution, poor quality, or improper grade	• Drain and refill crankcase with recommended oil
	• Excessive oil temperature	• Correct cause of overheating engine
	• Oil pressure relief spring weak or sticking	• Remove and inspect oil pressure relief valve assembly
	• Oil inlet tube and screen assembly has restriction or air leak	• Remove and inspect oil inlet tube and screen assembly. (Fill inlet tube with lacquer thinner to locate leaks.)
	• Excessive oil pump clearance	• Measure clearances
	• Excessive main, rod, or camshaft bearing clearance	• Measure bearing clearances, repair as necessary
High oil pressure	• Improper oil viscosity	• Drain and refill crankcase with correct viscosity oil
	• Oil pressure gauge or sending unit inaccurate	• Replace oil pressure gauge
	• Oil pressure relief valve sticking closed	• Remove and inspect oil pressure relief valve assembly
Main bearing noise	• Insufficient oil supply	• Inspect for low oil level and low oil pressure
	• Main bearing clearance excessive	• Measure main bearing clearance, repair as necessary
	• Bearing insert missing	• Replace missing insert
	• Crankshaft end play excessive	• Measure end play, repair as necessary
	• Improperly tightened main bearing cap bolts	• Tighten bolts with specified torque
	• Loose flywheel or drive plate	• Tighten flywheel or drive plate attaching bolts
	• Loose or damaged vibration damper	• Repair as necessary
Connecting rod bearing noise	• Insufficient oil supply	• Inspect for low oil level and low oil pressure
	• Carbon build-up on piston	• Remove carbon from piston crown
	• Bearing clearance excessive or bearing missing	• Measure clearance, repair as necessary
	• Crankshaft connecting rod journal out-of-round	• Measure journal dimensions, repair or replace as necessary
	• Misaligned connecting rod or cap	• Repair as necessary
	• Connecting rod bolts tightened improperly	• Tighten bolts with specified torque
Piston noise	• Piston-to-cylinder wall clearance excessive (scuffed piston)	• Measure clearance and examine piston
	• Cylinder walls excessively tapered or out-of-round	• Measure cylinder wall dimensions, rebore cylinder
	• Piston ring broken	• Replace all rings on piston
	• Loose or seized piston pin	• Measure piston-to-pin clearance, repair as necessary
	• Connecting rods misaligned	• Measure rod alignment, straighten or replace
	• Piston ring side clearance excessively loose or tight	• Measure ring side clearance, repair as necessary
	• Carbon build-up on piston is excessive	• Remove carbon from piston

Troubleshooting the Serpentine Drive Belt

Problem	Cause	Solution
Tension sheeting fabric failure (woven fabric on outside circumference of belt has cracked or separated from body of belt)	• Grooved or backside idler pulley diameters are less than minimum recommended • Tension sheeting contacting (rubbing) stationary object • Excessive heat causing woven fabric to age • Tension sheeting splice has fractured	• Replace pulley(s) not conforming to specification • Correct rubbing condition • Replace belt • Replace belt
Noise (objectional squeal, squeak, or rumble is heard or felt while drive belt is in operation)	• Belt slippage • Bearing noise • Belt misalignment • Belt-to-pulley mismatch • Driven component inducing vibration • System resonant frequency inducing vibration	• Adjust belt • Locate and repair • Align belt/pulley(s) • Install correct belt • Locate defective driven component and repair • Vary belt tension within specifications. Replace belt.
Rib chunking (one or more ribs has separated from belt body)	• Foreign objects imbedded in pulley grooves • Installation damage • Drive loads in excess of design specifications • Insufficient internal belt adhesion	• Remove foreign objects from pulley grooves • Replace belt • Adjust belt tension • Replace belt
Rib or belt wear (belt ribs contact bottom of pulley grooves)	• Pulley(s) misaligned • Mismatch of belt and pulley groove widths • Abrasive environment • Rusted pulley(s) • Sharp or jagged pulley groove tips • Rubber deteriorated	• Align pulley(s) • Replace belt • Replace belt • Clean rust from pulley(s) • Replace pulley • Replace belt
Longitudinal belt cracking (cracks between two ribs)	• Belt has mistracked from pulley groove • Pulley groove tip has worn away rubber-to-tensile member	• Replace belt • Replace belt
Belt slips	• Belt slipping because of insufficient tension • Belt or pulley subjected to substance (belt dressing, oil, ethylene glycol) that has reduced friction • Driven component bearing failure • Belt glazed and hardened from heat and excessive slippage	• Adjust tension • Replace belt and clean pulleys • Replace faulty component bearing • Replace belt
"Groove jumping" (belt does not maintain correct position on pulley, or turns over and/or runs off pulleys)	• Insufficient belt tension • Pulley(s) not within design tolerance • Foreign object(s) in grooves • Excessive belt speed • Pulley misalignment • Belt-to-pulley profile mismatched • Belt cordline is distorted	• Adjust belt tension • Replace pulley(s) • Remove foreign objects from grooves • Avoid excessive engine acceleration • Align pulley(s) • Install correct belt • Replace belt
Belt broken (Note: identify and correct problem before replacement belt is installed)	• Excessive tension • Tensile members damaged during belt installation • Belt turnover • Severe pulley misalignment • Bracket, pulley, or bearing failure	• Replace belt and adjust tension to specification • Replace belt • Replace belt • Align pulley(s) • Replace defective component and belt

Troubleshooting the Serpentine Drive Belt (cont.)

Problem	Cause	Solution
Cord edge failure (tensile member exposed at edges of belt or separated from belt body)	• Excessive tension • Drive pulley misalignment • Belt contacting stationary object • Pulley irregularities • Improper pulley construction • Insufficient adhesion between tensile member and rubber matrix	• Adjust belt tension • Align pulley • Correct as necessary • Replace pulley • Replace pulley • Replace belt and adjust tension to specifications
Sporadic rib cracking (multiple cracks in belt ribs at random intervals)	• Ribbed pulley(s) diameter less than minimum specification • Backside bend flat pulley(s) diameter less than minimum • Excessive heat condition causing rubber to harden • Excessive belt thickness • Belt overcured • Excessive tension	• Replace pulley(s) • Replace pulley(s) • Correct heat condition as necessary • Replace belt • Replace belt • Adjust belt tension

Troubleshooting Basic Starting System Problems

Problem	Cause	Solution
Starter motor rotates engine slowly	• Battery charge low or battery defective • Defective circuit between battery and starter motor • Low load current • High load current	• Charge or replace battery • Clean and tighten, or replace cables • Bench-test starter motor. Inspect for worn brushes and weak brush springs. • Bench-test starter motor. Check engine for friction, drag or coolant in cylinders. Check ring gear-to-pinion gear clearance.
Starter motor will not rotate engine	• Battery charge low or battery defective • Faulty solenoid • Damage drive pinion gear or ring gear • Starter motor engagement weak • Starter motor rotates slowly with high load current • Engine seized	• Charge or replace battery • Check solenoid ground. Repair or replace as necessary. • Replace damaged gear(s) • Bench-test starter motor • Inspect drive yoke pull-down and point gap, check for worn end bushings, check ring gear clearance • Repair engine
Starter motor drive will not engage (solenoid known to be good)	• Defective contact point assembly • Inadequate contact point assembly ground • Defective hold-in coil	• Repair or replace contact point assembly • Repair connection at ground screw • Replace field winding assembly
Starter motor drive will not disengage	• Starter motor loose on flywheel housing • Worn drive end busing • Damaged ring gear teeth • Drive yoke return spring broken or missing	• Tighten mounting bolts • Replace bushing • Replace ring gear or driveplate • Replace spring
Starter motor drive disengages prematurely	• Weak drive assembly thrust spring • Hold-in coil defective	• Replace drive mechanism • Replace field winding assembly
Low load current	• Worn brushes • Weak brush springs	• Replace brushes • Replace springs

Troubleshooting the Cooling System

Problem	Cause	Solution
High temperature gauge indication—overheating	• Coolant level low	• Replenish coolant
	• Fan belt loose	• Adjust fan belt tension
	• Radiator hose(s) collapsed	• Replace hose(s)
	• Radiator airflow blocked	• Remove restriction (bug screen, fog lamps, etc.)
	• Faulty radiator cap	• Replace radiator cap
	• Ignition timing incorrect	• Adjust ignition timing
	• Idle speed low	• Adjust idle speed
	• Air trapped in cooling system	• Purge air
	• Heavy traffic driving	• Operate at fast idle in neutral intermittently to cool engine
	• Incorrect cooling system component(s) installed	• Install proper component(s)
	• Faulty thermostat	• Replace thermostat
	• Water pump shaft broken or impeller loose	• Replace water pump
	• Radiator tubes clogged	• Flush radiator
	• Cooling system clogged	• Flush system
	• Casting flash in cooling passages	• Repair or replace as necessary. Flash may be visible by removing cooling system components or removing core plugs.
	• Brakes dragging	• Repair brakes
	• Excessive engine friction	• Repair engine
	• Antifreeze concentration over 68%	• Lower antifreeze concentration percentage
	• Missing air seals	• Replace air seals
	• Faulty gauge or sending unit	• Repair or replace faulty component
	• Loss of coolant flow caused by leakage or foaming	• Repair or replace leaking component, replace coolant
	• Viscous fan drive failed	• Replace unit
Low temperature indication—undercooling	• Thermostat stuck open	• Replace thermostat
	• Faulty gauge or sending unit	• Repair or replace faulty component
Coolant loss—boilover	• Overfilled cooling system	• Reduce coolant level to proper specification
	• Quick shutdown after hard (hot) run	• Allow engine to run at fast idle prior to shutdown
	• Air in system resulting in occasional "burping" of coolant	• Purge system
	• Insufficient antifreeze allowing coolant boiling point to be too low	• Add antifreeze to raise boiling point
	• Antifreeze deteriorated because of age or contamination	• Replace coolant
	• Leaks due to loose hose clamps, loose nuts, bolts, drain plugs, faulty hoses, or defective radiator	• Pressure test system to locate source of leak(s) then repair as necessary
	• Faulty head gasket	• Replace head gasket
	• Cracked head, manifold, or block	• Replace as necessary
	• Faulty radiator cap	• Replace cap
Coolant entry into crankcase or cylinder(s)	• Faulty head gasket	• Replace head gasket
	• Crack in head, manifold or block	• Replace as necessary
Coolant recovery system inoperative	• Coolant level low	• Replenish coolant to FULL mark
	• Leak in system	• Pressure test to isolate leak and repair as necessary
	• Pressure cap not tight or seal missing, or leaking	• Repair as necessary
	• Pressure cap defective	• Replace cap
	• Overflow tube clogged or leaking	• Repair as necessary
	• Recovery bottle vent restricted	• Remove restriction

Troubleshooting the Cooling System (cont.)

Problem	Cause	Solution
Noise	• Fan contacting shroud	• Reposition shroud and inspect engine mounts
	• Loose water pump impeller	• Replace pump
	• Glazed fan belt	• Apply silicone or replace belt
	• Loose fan belt	• Adjust fan belt tension
	• Rough surface on drive pulley	• Replace pulley
	• Water pump bearing worn	• Remove belt to isolate. Replace pump.
	• Belt alignment	• Check pulley alignment. Repair as necessary.
No coolant flow through heater core	• Restricted return inlet in water pump	• Remove restriction
	• Heater hose collapsed or restricted	• Remove restriction or replace hose
	• Restricted heater core	• Remove restriction or replace core
	• Restricted outlet in thermostat housing	• Remove flash or restriction
	• Intake manifold bypass hole in cylinder head restricted	• Remove restriction
	• Faulty heater control valve	• Replace valve
	• Intake manifold coolant passage restricted	• Remove restriction or replace intake manifold

NOTE: *Immediately after shutdown, the engine enters a condition known as heat soak. This is caused by the cooling system being inoperative while engine temperature is still high. If coolant temperature rises above boiling point, expansion and pressure may push some coolant out of the radiator overflow tube. If this does not occur frequently it is considered normal.*

Emission Controls

EMISSION CONTROLS

NOTE: *The following information is being published from the latest information available at the time of publication. If the information contained herein differs from that which is listed on the vehicles emission label, use the specifications given on the label.*

General Emissions Service

Most of the following emission control procedures and, in fact, assemblies, are for gasoline engines. Diesel engine emissions are controlled by the virtually complete burning of the diesel fuel in the cylinders. For the most part, emission control maintenance on the diesel is restricted to checking the crankcase ventilation hoses, the air cleaner, and the fuel tank lines and connections for leaks and wear. Replace the fuel filter at regular intervals and perform an occasional engine compression test.

PCV VALVE

Every 15,000 miles, check the PCV valve. Every 30,000 miles replace the PCV valve. Inspect and clean all hoses and connections. Replace any that show signs of deterioration.

EVAPORATIVE EMISSION CONTROL SYSTEM

Make a visual check of all system hoses and filters every 10,000 miles. Replace the charcoal filter every 50,000 miles.

DUAL DIAPHRAGM DISTRIBUTOR

Check the condition of the vacuum lines every 10,000 miles.

EXHAUST GAS RECIRCULATION SYSTEM

Inspect and check the hoses regularly. Reset the mileage switch if equipped, as necessary. Replace the EGR filter every 30,000 miles.

AIR INJECTION

Visually inspect the pump, control valve and hoses every 10,000 miles. Clean the pump filter every 10,000 miles. Replace the pump filter every 20,000 miles or two years.

CATALYTIC CONVERTER

Check for damage and tight connections every 30,000 miles. Reset the indicator light as necessary (if so equipped).

AIR CLEANER

Replace the air cleaner element every 15,000 miles.

Crankcase Ventilation System

OPERATION

The purpose of the crankcase ventilation system is twofold. It keeps harmful vapor by-products of combustion from escaping into the atmosphere and prevents the building of crankcase pressure which in turn causes gasket failure and oil leaks. Crankcase vapors are recirculated from the camshaft cover through a hose to the air cleaner. Here they are mixed with the air/fuel mixture and burned in the combustion chamber.

NOTE: *1975–76 Rabbits and Sciroccos are equipped with either a PCV valve on the hose between the valve cover and the air cleaner, or a restrictor inserted inside this hose. Volkswagen suggests that the models with the restrictors would be less prone to carburetor icing if the restrictor were removed and replaced with a PCV valve. See Chapter 1 under PCV valve for replacement procedures.*

SERVICE

Service the crankcase ventilation valve at the

interval suggested in Chapter 1. Remove the crankcase ventilation valve (if so equipped) which is connected to the camshaft cover, and clean it with a safe spray solvent. At every tune-up, examine the hoses for clogging or deterioration. Replace the hoses as necessary.

Evaporative Emission Controls

This system prevents the escape of raw fuel vapors (unburned hydrocarbons or HC) into the atmosphere. The system consists of a sealed carburetor, unvented fuel tank filler cap, fuel tank expansion chamber, an activated charcoal filter canister and connector hoses. Fuel vapors which reach the filter deposit hydrocarbons on the surface of the charcoal filter element. Fresh air enters the filter when the engine is running and forces the hydrocarbons to the air cleaner where they join the air/fuel mixture and are burned. Many 1979 and later models are equipped with a charcoal filter valve which prevents vapors from escaping from the canister when the engine is not running.

SERVICE

Maintenance of the system consists of checking the condition of the various connector hoses and the charcoal filter at 10,000 mile intervals. The charcoal filter should be replaced at 50,000 mile intervals.

Dual Diaphragm Distributor

The purpose of the dual diaphragm distributor (if so equipped) is to improve exhaust emissions during one of the engine's dirtier operating modes, idling. The distributor has a vacuum retard diaphragm, in addition to a vacuum advance diaphragm. A temperature

Checking distributor advance temperature valve

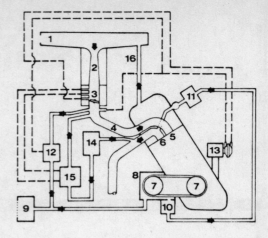

1. Air cleaner
2. Carburetor
3. Throttle plate
4. Intake manifold
5. Intake valve
6. Exhaust valve
7. Air pump belt
8. Air pump
9. Air pump air cleaner
10. High pressure valve
11. Check valve
12. Control valve
13. Distributor
14. EGR filter
15. EGR valve
16. Crankcase ventilation

Dasher emission control system — 1974–75

valve shuts off vacuum from the carburetor when coolant temperature is below 130°F (55°C).

TESTING

Advance Diaphragm

1. Connect a timing light to the engine. Check the ignition timing as described in Chapter 2.
2. Remove the retard (inner) hose from the distributor and plug it. Increase the engine speed. The ignition timing should advance. If it doesn't, then the vacuum unit is faulty and must be replaced.

Temperature Valve

1. Remove the temperature valve and place the threaded portion in hot water.
2. Create a vacuum by sucking on the angled connection.
3. The valve must be open above approximately 130°F (55°C).

Exhaust Gas Recirculation (EGR)

To reduce NOx (oxides of nitrogen) emissions, metered amounts of cooled exhaust gases are added to the air/fuel mixture. The recirculated exhaust gas lowers the peak flame temperature during combustion to cut the output of oxides of nitrogen. Exhaust gas from the manifold passes through a filter where it is cleaned. The EGR valve controls the amount of this exhaust gas which is allowed into the intake man-

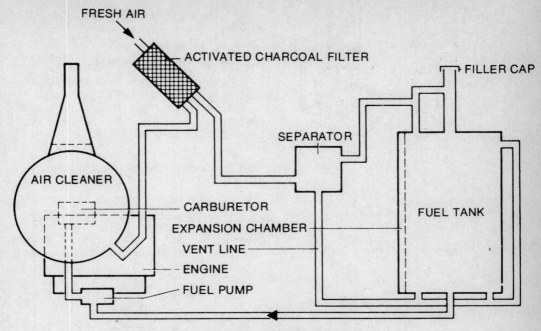

Typical evaporative emission control system

ifold. There is no EGR at idle, partial at slight throttle and full EGR at mid-throttle.

1974–75 MODELS

1974–75 models have an EGR filter and a 2-stage EGR valve. The first stage is controlled by the temperature valve. The second stage is controlled by the microswitch on the carburetor throttle valve. The switch opens the valve when the throttle valve is open between 30–67°F (–1 to +19°C) for manual transmission, or 23–63°F (–5 to +17°C) for automatic transmission.

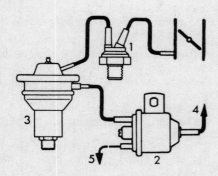

1. Temperature valve
2. Two-way valve
3. EGR valve
4. To brake booster
5. To micro switch

EGR operation — 1974-75

1976 MODELS

The EGR filter was discontinued on 1976 models but the 2-stage EGR valve was retained. On Federal vehicles, only the first stage is connected; California vehicles use both stages.

First stage EGR is controlled by engine vacuum and coolant temperature. The EGR valve is open above approximately 120°F (49°C) coolant temperature and below approximately 80°F (27°C). (At idle and during full throttle acceleration (engine hot), there is no EGR since the engine vacuum is too low to open the valve.

The second stage is controlled by temperature, engine vacuum and microswitch on the carburetor throttle valve. Vacuum is always present at the second stage and the valve is opened at about 120°F (49°C) coolant temperature. When the throttle valve opens between 25°F (–4°C) and 67°F (19°C), the microswitch activates the 2-way valve and allows engine vacuum to reach the second stage.

1976 AND LATER MODELS

The EGR valve on fuel injected models is controlled by a temperature valve and a vacuum amplifier. The valve is located on the intake manifold.

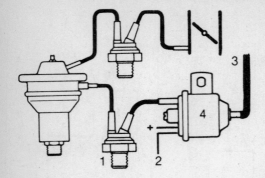

1. Temperature valve for EGR 2nd stage
2. To micro switch on throttle valve
3. Vacuum hose to brake booster
4. Two way valve

Two stage EGR operation — 1976 and later

TESTING

EGR Valve, Checking the First Stage 1974–76 Carbureted Engines

1. Disconnect the vacuum line from the end of the EGR valve.
2. Disconnect the vacuum hose from the distributor vacuum unit and extend hose.
3. Start the engine and allow it to idle.
4. Connect the line from the anti-backfire valve to the EGR valve. The engine should stumble or stall.
5. If the idle stays even, the EGR line is clogged or the EGR valve is defective, or the filter is clogged.

EGR Valve, Checking the Second Stage 1974–76 Carbureted Engines

The EGR valve second stage is on all 1974–75 USA and California models and on 1976 California Rabbits and Sciroccos only. The system includes a microswitch located on the side of the carburetor near the throttle valve. To check the system, manually operate the switch with the engine at idle. If the engine speed drops or the engine stalls, the switch is operating correctly. If not, check the microswitch, the EGR filter and the EGR return lines for blockage.

EGR Valve—Fuel Injected Models

Be sure the vacuum lines are not leaking. Replace any that are leaking or cracked.
1. Warm the engine to normal operating temperature.
2. Run the engine at idle.
3. Remove the vacuum hose from the EGR valve.
4. Remove the vacuum hose from the vacuum retard on the distributor (if so equipped) and connect it to the EGR valve.

5. If the engine speed does not change, the EGR valve is clogged or damaged.

EGR Temperature Valve (1974–76)

1. Remove the temperature valve and place the threaded portion in hot water.
2. Create a vacuum by sucking on the angled connection. The valve should be closed below approximately 120°F (49°C).

EGR Temperature Valve—Fuel Injected Models

Warm the engine to normal operating temperature. With the engine at idle, attach a vacuum gauge between the EGR temperature control valve and the EGR valve. The valve should be replaced if the gauge shows less than 2 in.Hg.

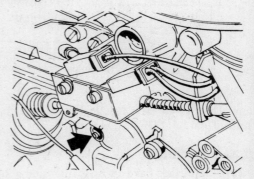

Manually operate micro-switch (arrow) to check 2nd stage EGR valve

EGR Deceleration Valve (1976 and Later)

NOTE: *1976 USA models, except California manual transmission Dashers are equipped with deceleration valves. No automatic transmission Volkswagens have deceleration valves. Rabbits and Sciroccos first received deceleration valves in 1977.*

1. Remove the hose from the deceleration valve. Plug the hose.
2. Run the engine for a few seconds at 3,000 rpm.
3. Snap the throttle valve closed.
4. With your finger, check for suction at the hose connection.
5. Remove the hose from the connector.
6. Run the engine at about 3,000 rpm. No suction should be felt.

EGR Vacuum Amplifier (1976 and Later)

NOTE: *1976 Dashers are equipped with EGR Vacuum Amplifiers, while Rabbits and Sciroccos first received them in 1977.*

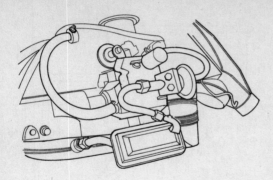

EGR system components — carbureted engine

1. Run the engine at idle.
2. Connect a vacuum gauge between the vacuum amplifier and the throttle valve port.
3. The gauge should read 0.2–0.3 in.Hg. If not, check the throttle plate for correct position or check the port for obstruction.
4. Connect a vacuum gauge between the vacuum amplifier and the temperature valve.
5. Replace the vacuum amplifier if the gauge reads less than 2 in.Hg.

MAINTENANCE

The only maintenance is to replace the EGR filter (1974–75 models only) and to reset the EGR elapsed mileage switch as described below.

Resetting the Elapsed Mileage Switch

Resetting of the elapsed mileage switch is described later in this chapter.

FILTER REPLACEMENT

1. Disconnect the filter EGR line fittings.
2. Remove the filter and discard.
3. Install the new filter into the EGR lines and securely tighten fittings.

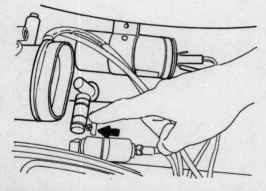

Checking EGR deceleration valve (fuel injected engines)

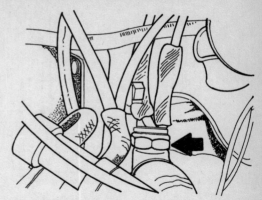

Checking EGR temperature valve (fuel injected engines)

REMOVAL AND INSTALLATION

EGR Valve

1. Disconnect the vacuum hose from the EGR valve.
2. Unbolt the EGR line fitting on the opposite side of the valve.
3. Remove the two retaining bolts and lift the EGR valve from the intake manifold.
4. Install the EGR valve in the reverse order of removal. Use a new gasket at the intake manifold.

Dashpot

Adjustments

See appropriate section under Carburetor, in Chapter 5 for dashpot adjustments.

Air Injection

The air injection system used on most carbureted engines, except the 1978 and 1980 Rabbit with 34 PICT-5 carburetor and later models equipped with a TYF carburetor, includes a belt driven air pump, filter, check valve, anti-backfire valve or gulp valve, and connecting hoses and air lines. The system reduces exhaust emissions by pumping fresh air to the exhaust manifold or directly behind the exhaust valves where it combines with the hot exhaust gas to burn away excess hydrocarbons and reduce carbon monoxide.

The air injection systems on the 1978, 1980, 1982 and later Rabbits do not have air pumps. Instead, air is drawn from the air cleaner through a silencer to two check valves. The valves turn blue when overheated. If the valves are blue, replace them.

MAINTENANCE

Required maintenance on the air pump consists of visually checking the pump, control valves, hoses and lines every 10,000 miles.

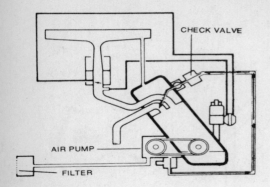

Typical air injection system schematic

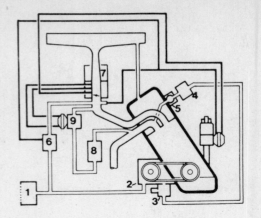

1. Air pump filter
2. Air pump
3. Relief valve
4. Check valve
5. Air manifold
6. Anti-backfire valve
7. Carburetor
8. EGR filter
9. EGR valve

Typical air injection and EGR systems schematic

Clean the air pump filter element at this interval. The filter element should be replaced every 20,000 miles or two years.

TESTING AND SERVICE

Air Pump and Hoses

1. Disconnect the hose from the check valve and plug the valve opening.
2. With the engine idling, check for air flow from the hose. If no air flows from the hose, the hoses are kinked or damaged, the diverter valve is defective or the air pump is defective (it cannot be repaired, only replaced).

Diverter Valve

1. Disconnect the vacuum hose from the F or 1 connection.
2. Disconnect the hose from the S or 2 connection and connect it to F or 1.
3. With the engine idling, if no air comes from the muffler on the diverter valve the hoses are kinked or damaged or the air pump is defective. If air flows, the diverter valve is OK.

2-Way Valve

1. Idle the engine and pull the electrical lead from the 2-way valve.

2. Ground the valve and connect a test wire directly from the battery to the valve.

3. Increase the engine rpm and check for air output at the diverter valve.

4. If no air flows from the diverter valve, the vacuum line is kinked or disconnected or

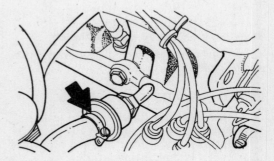

Checking air pump and hoses

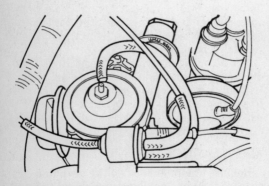

Checking Rabbit, Scirocco diverter valve

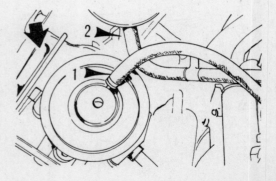

Checking Dasher diverter valve

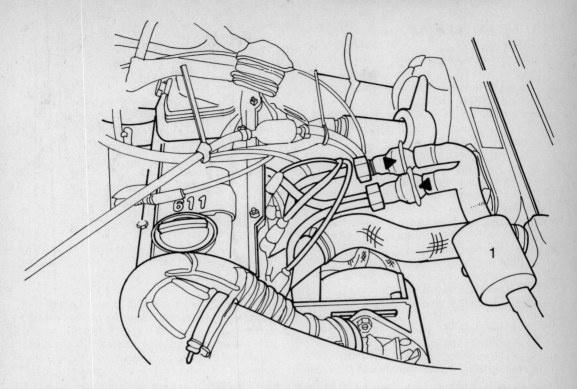

1978–1980 Rabbit with 34 PICT–4 carburetor check valves (arrows) and silencer (1) in air injection system. If valves turn blue, replace them

the diverter valve is bad. If air flows, the 2-way valve is OK.

Anti-Backfire Valve

A defective anti-backfire valve could be indicated by the engine backfiring while coasting.

1. Disconnect the hose from the valve.

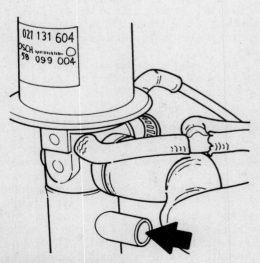

Checking the anti-backfire valve

2. Start the engine and run it briefly at higher than normal fast idle.

3. Snap the throttle valve closed. As the throttle snaps shut, suction should be felt at the valve for about 1-3 seconds. If not, the vacuum hose is kinked or blocked, the hose between manifold and valve is kinked or blocked or the valve is defective.

Catalytic Converter

Many models are equipped with catalytic converters located in the exhaust system. This device contains noble metals acting as catalysts to convert hydrocarbons and carbon monoxide into harmless water and carbon dioxide. Required maintenance on the catalytic converter involves checking the condition of the ceramic insert every 30,000 miles. On earlier models, as this interval is reached, an indicator light on the dash will glow. Once service to the converter is performed, the "CAT" warning light must be reset. Resetting of the "CAT" waring light is described later in this chapter. Not all models are equipped with warning lights.

CAUTION: *Never attempt to remove the converter from a just-run or warm engine. Catalytic temperatures can reach 1,900°F (1,038°C), so be careful!*

TESTING AND SERVICE

CAUTION: *Do not drop or strike the converter assembly or damage to the ceramic insert will result.*

Damage and overheating of the catalytic converter, indicated by the flickering of the "CAT" warning light, can be caused by the following:

1. Engine misfire caused by faulty spark plug, ignition wires and so on.
2. Improper ignition timing.
3. CO valve set too high.
4. Faulty air pump diverter valve.
5. Faulty temperature sensor.
6. Engine under strain caused by trailer hauling, high speed driving in hot weather, etc.

A faulty converter is indicated by one of the following symptoms:

1. Poor engine performance.
2. The engine stalls.
3. Rattling in the exhaust system.
4. A CO reading greater than 0.4% at the tail pipe.

• Check or replace the converter as follows:

1. Disconnect the temperature sensor.
2. Loosen and remove the bolts holding the converter to the exhaust system and the chassis.
3. Remove the converter.
4. Hold the converter up to a strong light and look through both ends, checking for blockages. If the converter is blocked, replace it.
5. Install the converter in the reverse order of removal.

Maintenance Reminder Lights

Not all VW's are equipped with maintenance reminder lights.

RESETTING

EGR and Oxygen Sensor Warning Light

On all models so equipped, there is an EGR warning light that is located in the instrument cluster. This system also uses a mileage counter. When the mileage reaches 15,000 miles, it will trip the EGR warning light. This light tells the driver that the EGR and emission systems should be inspected and checked for proper operation.

On all models so equipped, there is an oxygen sensor (**OXS**) light located in the instrument cluster. This system also uses a mileage counter. When the mileage counter reaches 30,000 miles, it will trip the **OXS** warning light. This indicates that the oxygen sensor should be replaced.

Once the system has been serviced, reset the light(s) as follows:

On some Rabbits and Pick-Ups, remove the

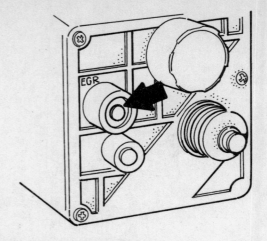

Reset the EGR light switch

instrument panel cover trim plate. Locate the mileage counter rest arms at the top left corner of the speedometer housing. Pull the release arms to reset the mileage counter. The left are is used to reset the EGR warning light and the right arm is used to reset the oxygen sensor warning light.

On all other models, locate the mileage counter which is usually found under the hood near the firewall, inline with the speedometer cable. To locate the counter, follow the speedometer cable up from the transmission towards the firewall. Once the counter is located, push in the black reset button marked **EGR** or the white reset button marked **OXS**. Both of these buttons are located right on the face of the mileage counter.

"CAT" Warning Light

The CAT warning light in the speedometer should come on at 30,000 mile intervals to remind you to have the catalytic converter serviced.

The light can be reset by pushing the button marked CAT on the switch. The light on the speedometer should go out.

Oxygen Sensor

The oxygen sensor is located in the front exhaust pipe or is screwed into the exhaust manifold. Its primary function is to sense the content of the exhaust gases and relay information to the ECU. When the level of oxygen in the exhaust system is high, the oxygen sensor will send a low voltage signal of 100–500 mV to the Electronic Control Unit (ECU). The control unit will increase the current to the differential pressure regulator.

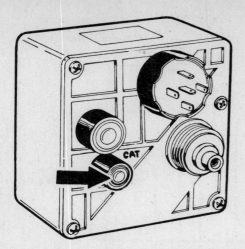

Reset the catalytic converter elapsed mileage odometer

When the current to the differential pressure regulator is increased, the plate valve will deflect to the left to restrict the flow of fuel to the lower chamber. This reduces the pressure to the lower chamber causing the pressure regulating valves to deflect downward. The result is increased fuel flow to the injectors and an enriched fuel mixture.

If the amount of oxygen in the exhaust system is low, indicating a rich mixture, the

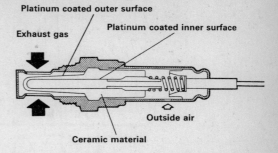

Platinum coated outer surface

Exhaust gas

Platinum coated inner surface

Outside air

Ceramic material

Cross section of typical oxygen sensor

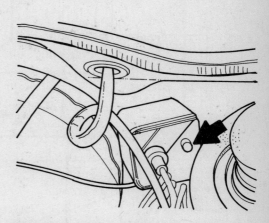

Oxygen sensor reset button

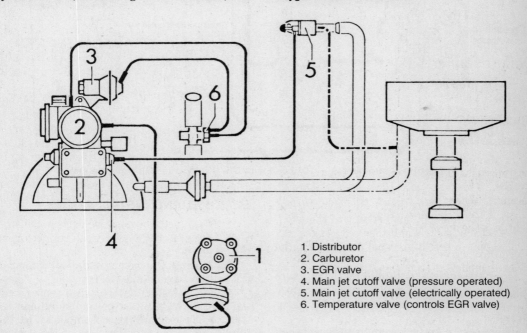

1. Distributor
2. Carburetor
3. EGR valve
4. Main jet cutoff valve (pressure operated)
5. Main jet cutoff valve (electrically operated)
6. Temperature valve (controls EGR valve)

Emission control hoses — 1978 carbureted Rabbit

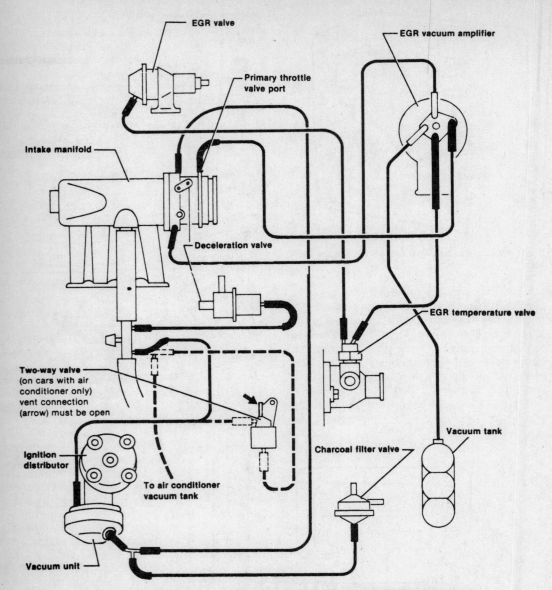

Emission control hoses — 1979 and later CIS USA except California manual

sensor voltage will be high. This signal is approximately 500–900 mV, is sent to the ECU. The electronic control unit then reduces the current signal to the differential pressure regulator.

When the current to the differential pressure regulator is reduced, the plate valve will move to the right and allow more fuel into the lower chamber.

The pressure in the lower chamber will then increase and defect the pressure regulating valve upward. The quantity of the fuel delivered to the injectors is then reduced and the fuel mixture is leaned.

REMOVAL AND INSTALLATION

1. Disconnect the negative battery cable.
2. Disconnect the electrical connector at the oxygen sensor.
3. Unscrew the oxygen sensor and remove it from the exhaust manifold.
4. Before installing the oxygen sensor, coat the threads with anti-seize compound and install. Apply the anti-sieze compound to the threads only and not the slots of the sensor. Torque the sensor to 37 ft. lbs.
5. Connect the electrical sensor to the oxygen sensor. Connect the negative battery cable.

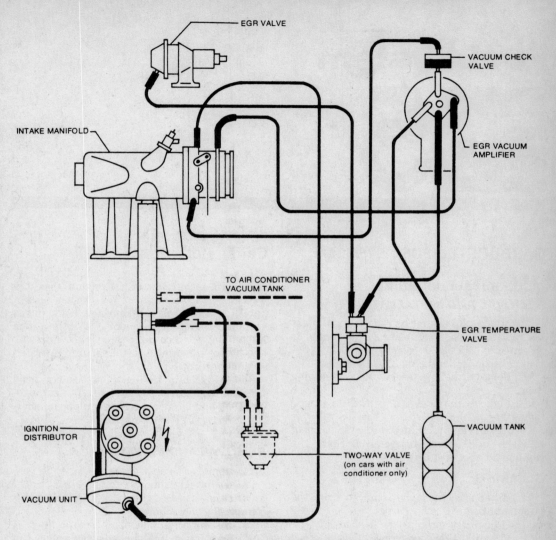

Emission control hoses — 1976-77 with CIS California automatic transmission

Fuel System

CARBURETED FUEL SYSTEM

Mechanical Fuel Pump

REMOVAL AND INSTALLATION

The fuel pump cannot be repaired and must be replaced when defective. The pump is mounted on the side of the engine block.

1. Disconnect and plug both fuel lines.
2. Remove the two socket head retaining bolts.
3. Remove the fuel pump and its plastic flange.
4. Install the pump in the reverse order of removal. Use a new flange seal. Start the engine and check for leaks.

CLEANING

The filter screen can be removed from the pump and cleaned.

1. Disconnect and plug the fuel lines.
2. Remove the center screw.
3. Remove the screen and gasket. Clean the screen in a safe solvent.
4. Replace the screen.
5. Install a new gasket and replace the cover.

NOTE: *Make sure that the depression in the pump cover engages the projection on the body of the pump or the cover will not seal properly.*

Carburetor

The 1974 Dasher uses a Solex 32/35 DIDTA two barrel carburetor with a vacuum operated secondary throttle. The 1975 Dasher uses a Zenith 2B3 two barrel carburetor. It too, has a vacuum operated secondary throttle. The Rabbit and Scirocco carburetor is a Zenith 2B2 two barrel which also has a vacuum operated secondary throttle.

Some 1978 and 1980 Rabbits are equipped with a single barrel Solex 34 PICT–5 carburetor. 1982 and later carburetor equipped models use a Carter TYF feedback model.

REMOVAL AND INSTALLATION

1. Remove the air cleaner.
2. Disconnect and plug the fuel lines.
3. Drain some of the coolant and then disconnect the choke hoses.
4. Disconnect and label all vacuum lines.
5. Disconnect and label all electrical leads.
6. Remove the clip which secures the throt-

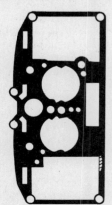

New and old style carburetor gaskets are not interchangeable. 1975 Dashers, Rabbits and Sciroccos use old type: 1976 Rabbits and Sciroccos use new types

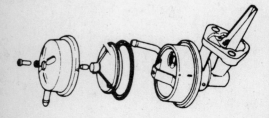

Exploded view of fuel pump showing filter screen

Troubleshooting Basic Fuel System Problems

Problem	Cause	Solution
Engine cranks, but won't start (or is hard to start) when cold	• Empty fuel tank • Incorrect starting procedure • Defective fuel pump • No fuel in carburetor • Clogged fuel filter • Engine flooded • Defective choke	• Check for fuel in tank • Follow correct procedure • Check pump output • Check for fuel in the carburetor • Replace fuel filter • Wait 15 minutes; try again • Check choke plate
Engine cranks, but is hard to start (or does not start) when hot—(presence of fuel is assumed)	• Defective choke	• Check choke plate
Rough idle or engine runs rough	• Dirt or moisture in fuel • Clogged air filter • Faulty fuel pump	• Replace fuel filter • Replace air filter • Check fuel pump output
Engine stalls or hesitates on acceleration	• Dirt or moisture in the fuel • Dirty carburetor • Defective fuel pump • Incorrect float level, defective accelerator pump	• Replace fuel filter • Clean the carburetor • Check fuel pump output • Check carburetor
Poor gas mileage	• Clogged air filter • Dirty carburetor • Defective choke, faulty carburetor adjustment	• Replace air filter • Clean carburetor • Check carburetor
Engine is flooded (won't start accompanied by smell of raw fuel)	• Improperly adjusted choke or carburetor	• Wait 15 minutes and try again, without pumping gas pedal • If it won't start, check carburetor

tle linkage to the carburetor. Detach the linkage, being careful not to lose any washers or bushings.

7. Unbolt the carburetor from the manifold and remove it. If the carboretor is to be left off the engine for any length of time, cover the intake manifold opening with masking tape to prevent anything from falling into the engine.

To install:

8. Clean the carburetor and intake manifold surfaces and lay the new gasket onto the intake manifold. ALWAYS use a new gasket.

9. Set the carburetor on top of the gasket and tighten the nuts in a criss-cross pattern. Don't overtighten.

10. Connect and adjust the throttle linkage.

11. Connect the electrical leads and vacuum lines.

12. Connect the choke hoses.

13. Connect the fuel lines.

14. Install the air cleaner and fill the cooling system to the proper level.

ADJUSTMENTS

Solex 32/35DIDTA Carburetor — 1974 Dasher

THROTTLE GAP ADJUSTMENT (BASIC SETTING)

This adjustment is made at the adjuster screw located in the linkage on the carburetor, below and to the right of the automatic choke unit.

1. Open the choke and close the throttle.

2. Turn the first stage adjusting screw out until there is a gap between it and its stop. The first stage throttle valve should be fully closed now.

3. Turn the adjusting screw in until it just touches its stop.

4. Turn the screw in 1/4 turn more and lock it.

5. The second stage throttle (secondary) should only be adjusted when it is definitely maladjusted.

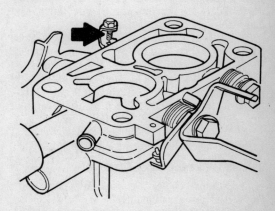

Second stage adjusting screw (arrow) — 1974 Dasher

a. Loosen the adjusting screw until the secondary throttle closes.

b. Turn the screw in 12 turn and lock it.

c. Adjust the idle mixture after this adjustment.

FUEL LEVEL ADJUSTMENT

This adjustment is made with the carburetor installed on the engine. Incorrect fuel level can cause stalling or high speed miss.

1. Remove the air cleaner.

2. Remove the five carburetor cover mounting screws.

3. Plug the fuel inlet with a finger and lift off the carburetor cover and gasket. Set them to the side, leaving the linkages attached.

4. On models with the original equipment float, which is shaped like a child's top, with the float in the up, or closed, position, the distance from the edge of the float rim to the carburetor surface (minus the gasket) should be 16–17mm.

5. Adjust the float by varying the thickness of the fiber sealing ring under the float needle valve.

6. On models with the modified float, which is more rectangular in shape, with the float in the up, or closed, position, measure from the top edge of the float closest to the throttle chambers down to the carburetor surface (minus the gasket). The distance should be 37–39mm.

7. Adjust the float by bending the tab that contacts the needle valve.

NOTE: *For added accuracy, when measuring the float level, make all measurements with the carburetor top at a 45° angle so that the stop ball in he needle valve is not unnaturally pushed down by the weight of the float.*

FAST IDLE ADJUSTMENT

It will be necessary to remove the carburetor from the engine to perform this operation.

1. Turn the carburetor upside down and drain the fuel from it.

2. With the carburetor upside down, close the choke tightly and measure the gap between the lower edge of the throttle valve and the housing wall with a drill. The measurement should be: All Except Calif. Manual Trans. 0.80–0.85mm (0.030–0.034 in.); Calif. Manual Trans. 0.60–0.70mm (0.024–0.028 in.).

3. Adjust the fast idle speed at the eyebolt fitted in the choke lever attachment.

CHOKE VALVE GAP ADJUSTMENT

1. Remove the automatic choke cover with the water hoses still attached.

2. Push the plunger rod down into its seat, then move the choke valve toward the fully closed position.

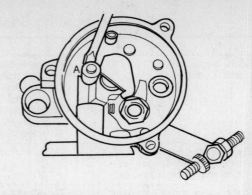

Adjust the choke gap by bending the lever (a)

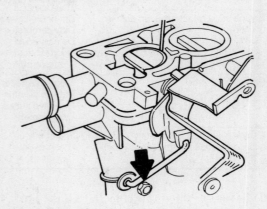

Fast idle adjuster (arrow) — 1974 Dasher

3. With an appropriate size drill measure the gap between the choke valve and the carburetor housing. It should be: all Except Calif. 3.5–4.0mm (0.142–0.154 in.); Calif. 3.5–3.7mm (0.134–0.146 in.).

4. Adjust the choke gap by bending the lever arm attached to the plunger rod.

NOTE: *When installing the choke spring inside the choke cover, the loop in the spring must go over the protruding choke lever. Insert the spring so that it uncoils in a clockwise direction (facing you).*

AUTOMATIC CHOKE ADJUSTMENT

Align the mark on the automatic choke cover with the mark on the carburetor by loosing the three retaining screws and turning the choke cover with the hoses still attached.

DASHPOT ADJUSTMENT

The purpose of the dashpot is to keep the throttle from snapping shut and stalling the engine. The dashpot has a plunger that extends when the throttle is closed suddenly. The plunger contacts a tab on the throttle lever and holds the throttle open slightly for a second,

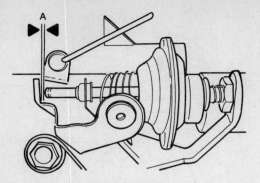

1974 Dasher dashpot adjustment

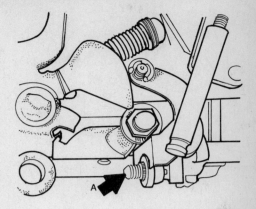

then closes the throttle slowly over the period of another second or so.

NOTE: *Not all models have dashpots.*

1. Close the throttle valve and make sure the choke is fully open. You may have to run the car up to operating temperature.

2. Press the dashpot plunger in as far as it will go.

3. Measure the gap between the plunger and its striking surface. It should be 1mm (0.04 in.).

4. Adjust by loosening the lock nut and moving the dashpot on its threads.

NOTE: *There is a dashpot kit available. The kit includes special washers which fit between the dashpot spring and the plunger mount.*

Zenith 2B3 Carburetor—1975 Dasher

THROTTLE GAP ADJUSTMENT

To adjust first stage throttle gap:

1. The choke must be open and the first stage (primary) throttle closed.

2. Turn the first stage throttle valve stop screw until there is a gap between it and the lever moves.

3. Turn the screw in until it just touches the lever.

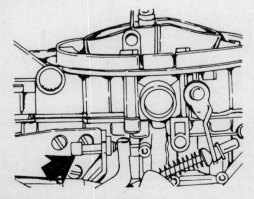

First stage throttle gap adjustment — 1975 Dasher, 1975-76 Rabbit and Scirocco

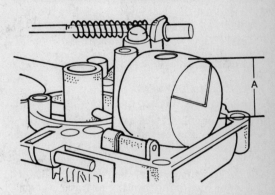

Second stage throttle gap adjustment (a) — 1975 Dasher, 1975-76 Rabbit and Scirocco

Checking the float level — 1975 Dasher, 1975-76 Rabbit and Scirocco

4. Turn screw in 1/4 turn more.

5. Adjust the idle speed and CO level.

To adjust the second stage (secondary) throttle gap, proceed as follows.

6. The choke must be open and the first stage throttle must be closed.

7. Turn the second stage (secondary) adjusting screw until there is no clearance in the lever it is mounted on.

8. From this position, turn the screw out 1/4 turn. There should be noticeable clearance at the lever.

FUEL LEVEL ADJUSTMENT

Remove the top of the carburetor. You may not have to remove the entire carburetor from the engine to perform this operation.

1. With the carburetor top upside down and canted at a 45° angle to prevent the damping ball in the needle valve from settling too deeply due to the weight of the float, measure from the highest tip of the first stage float to the carburetor surface (minus the gasket). The distance for the first stage float should be 28mm ± 0.5mm (1.10 in. ± 0.02 in.).

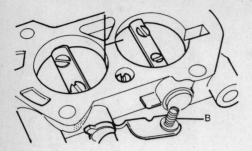

Fast idle adjustment (A) gap, (B) adjuster screw — 1975 Dasher, Rabbit and Scirocco

2. Adjust the second stage float in the same manner. The distance for the second stage float should be 30mm ± 0.5mm (1.20 ± 0.02 in.).

3. Adjust the float level by bending the float bracket.

CAUTION: *If the float height must be adjusted, remove the float from the carburetor to prevent damage to the needle valve.*

FAST IDLE ADJUSTMENT

It will be necessary to remove the carburetor from the engine to perform this procedure.

1. Turn the carburetor upside down and drain the fuel from it.

2. With the carburetor upside down, close the choke tightly and measure the gap between the lower edge of the throttle valve and the housing wall with a drill. The measurement should be: 0.45–0.50mm (0.018–0.020 in.).

3. Adjust the gap at the adjusting screw (beside the first stage valve) which is facing up when the carburetor is upside down.

CHOKE VALVE GAP ADJUSTMENT

1. Remove the automatic choke cover. You should be able to remove the cover without unfastening the water hoses.

2. Open and close the choke to make sure its internal spring is working. If not, remove

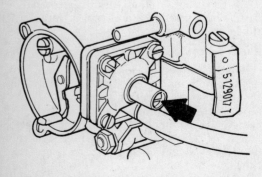

Choke gap adjustment — 1975 Dasher, Rabbit and Scirocco

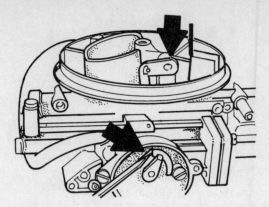

Checking the choke gap — 1975 Dasher, Rabbit and Scirocco

the vacuum cover at the side of the choke assembly and check the spring.

3. Push the choke lever to its stop (arrow) and hold the rod there with a rubber band.

4. Equalize the bushing and lever clearances by pushing the choke valve slightly open (see arrow B).

5. Check the choke gap with an appropriate size drill. The gap should be between 3.8–4.2mm (0.152–0.168 in.).

6. Adjust the choke valve gap by turning the screw in the end of the vacuum unit at the side of the choke assembly. Lock the adjusting screw by dabbing a little paint or thread sealant over its end.

NOTE: *When installing the automatic choke cover, the choke lever (protruding part) must fit in the loop on the coiled spring.*

AUTOMATIC CHOKE ADJUSTMENT

Align the mark on the automatic choke cover with the mark on the carburetor by loosening the three retaining across and turning the choke with the hoses still attached.

DASHPOT ADJUSTMENT

For explanation of dashpot function, see 1974 Dasher dashpot procedure.

NOTE: *Not all models are equipped with dashpots.*

1. Close the throttle valve and make sure the choke is fully open. You may have to run the car up to the operating temperature.

2. Push the plunger in as far as it will go and measure the gap between the end of the plunger and its striking surface. The gap should be 3mm (0.122 in.).

3. Adjust by loosening the lock nut and moving the dashpot on its threads.

Fast idle adjustment — 1976 Rabbit and Scirocco

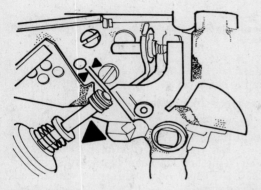

Dashpot adjustment — 1975 Dasher, 1975-76 Rabbit and Scirocco

Zenith 2B2 Carburetor, 1975–76 Rabbit and Scirocco

THROTTLE GAP ADJUSTMENT

See 1975 Dasher Zenith 2B3 section, above, for throttle gap adjustment procedures.

FUEL LEVEL ADJUSTMENT

This fuel level adjustment is the same as the procedures followed for the Zenith 2B3 Carburetor used in the 1975 Dasher. See above for procedures.

1975 FAST IDLE ADJUSTMENT

See 1975 Dasher 2B3 Carburetor section, above, for fast idle gap adjustment.

1976 FAST IDLE ADJUSTMENT

On these models it is not necessary to remove the carburetor. The engine must be at normal operating temperature.

1. Set the ignition timing.
2. Disconnect and plug the hose from the choke pull-down unit.
3. Open the throttle valve slightly and close the choke valve.
4. Close the throttle valve. The choke valve should be fully open again.
5. Set the stop screw of the fast idle cam on the highest step. Start the engine.

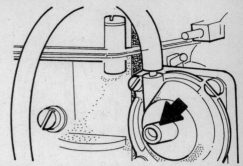

Choke gap adjustment — 1976 Rabbit and Scirocco

6. Adjust the speed with the screw (arrow) to: 3150–3250 rpm manual transmission or 3350–3450 rpm automatic transmission.

CHOKE GAP ADJUSTMENT

NOTE: *See 1975 Dasher 2B3 Carburetor section for 1975 Rabbit Scirocco choke gap adjustment illustration.*

1. Remove the automatic choke cover.
2. Close the choke valve and push the choke rod to the stop (arrow).
3. Hold the choke in position with a rubber band (a).
4. Push the choke lever (b) down slightly to equalize the clearances.
5. Check the choke gap between the edge of the carburetor wall and the edge of the valve with a drill. It should be:
• 1975: 4.8mm (0.19 in.) with vacuum delay valve.
• 1976: 3.5mm (0.14 in.) primary activated.
• 5.0mm (0.20 in.) secondary activated.
6. Adjust the gap by turning the screw on the choke vacuum unit in to decrease the gap or out to increase the gap.

AUTOMATIC CHOKE

Align the mark on the automatic choke cover with the mark on the carburetor.

AUTOMATIC CHOKE TEMPERATURE SWITCH

The temperature switch must be removed from the carburetor and checked with an ohmmeter. Connect an ohmmeter across the 2 blades. It should read 0Ω below 107°F (42°C), and infinity above 136°F (58°C).

DASHPOT ADJUSTMENT

Dashpot adjustments are the same as those for Zenith 2B3 Carburetor (1975 Dasher), above.

Solex 34 PICT–5 — 1978 Rabbit Only

THROTTLE VALVE BASIC ADJUSTMENT

You need a vacuum gauge to set the throttle valve. The stop screw (1) is set at the factory,

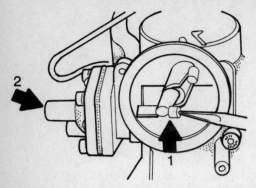

Adjusting the choke valve — 1978 carbureted Rabbit. Adjusting screw (2) is the same on the 1980 carbureted Rabbit

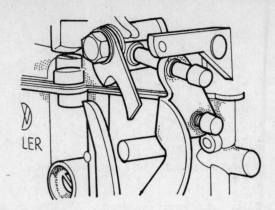

Basic throttle adjustment — 1978 carbureted Rabbit

and should not be moved. If the screw is accidentally turned, proceed as follows. Make no adjustment at screw (2).

1. Run the engine at idle.
2. Remove the vacuum advance hose at the carburetor and connect a vacuum gauge.
3. Remove the plastic screw cap and turn the stop screw in until the gauge indicates vacuum.
4. Turn the stop screw out until the gauges indicates no vacuum. Turn the screw an additional 1/4 turn and install the plastic cap.
5. Adjust the idle and CO.

CHOKE VALVE ADJUSTMENT

1. Remove the cover from the automatic choke and fully close the choke.
2. Push the choke rod in the direction of the arrow and check the gap between the choke valves and the air horn wall. It should be 2.8–3.3mm (0.11–0.13 in.).
3. Adjust the gap with the adjusting screw (2).
4. Reassemble the choke cover. There is an

index mark on the choke housing and another on the choke cover.

FAST IDLE ADJUSTMENT

The engine should be at normal operating temperature.

1. Run the engine with the screw on the 3rd step of the fast idle cam. The speed should be 2350–2450 rpm. Adjust this speed with the adjusting screw.
2. Stop the engine. Open the choke valve fully and check the gap between the adjusting screw and fast idle cam. It should be 0.20mm (0.008 in.).

ALTITUDE CORRECTION

Cars that are generally operated above 3600 feet may require altitude correction, which is made by backing out the two screws (arrows) until they are flush with the carburetor body. Adjust the idle and CO content.

Solex 34 PICT–5 — 1980 RABBIT

PART THROTTLE HEATER

This carburetor is equipped with a heating element which partly pre-heats the throttle channel while the engine temperature is below 167°F (75°C). This allows the engine to run smoother during warm-up time and prevents excessive use of the choke valve.

To test the part throttle heater, disconnect its wire and connect a test light between the throttle heater lead and the positive battery terminal. The heating element is working if the test light lights up. If the light fails to light, the element is bad and must be replaced.

MAIN JET SHUT-OFF SYSTEM

The shut-off valve is vacuum activated by the vacuum control unit, located on the fender inside the engine compartment next to the brake master cylinder. A relay is activated via

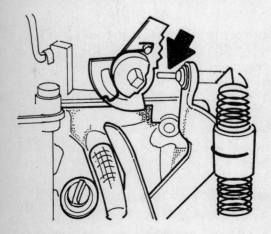

Adjust fast idle gap — 1978 Rabbit

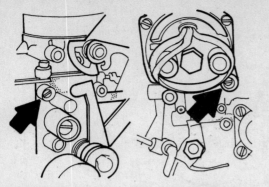

Altitude adjustment — 1978 carbureted Rabbit

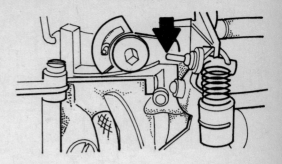

Fast idle adjustment — 1978 carbureted Rabbit. 1980 carbureted Rabbit similar

terminal 15 of the fuse panel and shuts off the fuel flow to the main jet if voltage is less than 5 volts at terminal 15 or when the ignition is cut-off.

To test the system, proceed as follows:

1. Run the engine at idle and disconnect the electrical connector from the front of the vacuum control unit.

2. The engine should stall. If not, check the vacuum tubes for blockage and check the vacuum control unit (see below for procedures). If these are not the problem, replace the main jet cut-off valve.

IDLE SHUT-OFF VALVE

1. Run the engine at idle.

2. Pull the electrical connector from the idle shut-off valve.

3. The engine should stall. If not, replace the idle shutoff valve.

AUTOMATIC CHOKE

The automatic choke is operated by the electrical heating element inside the choke and coolant temperature. When coolant temperature is below 61°F (16°C), the electrical heating element in the choke receives current from thermoswitch 1 and the resistor wire. Approxi-

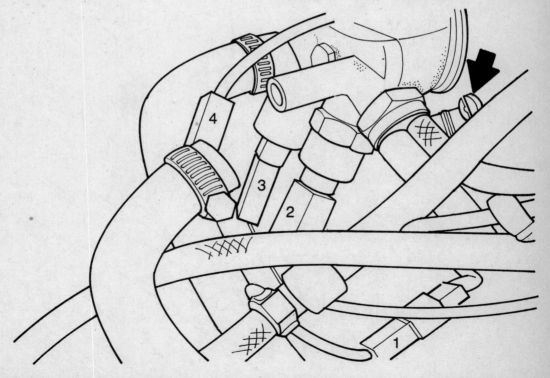

1980 Rabbit carburetor (1) part throttle heater connection (2) thermoswitch 1, (3) thermoswitch 2, (4) choke heater connection. Large black arrow indicates idle jet

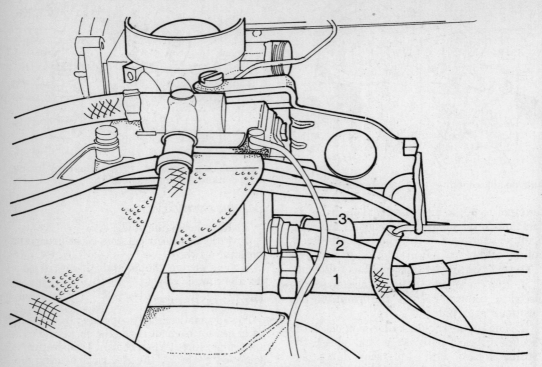

Second view of 1980 Rabbit carburetor (1) cold start valve, (2) main jet cutoff valve, (3) idle shutoff valve

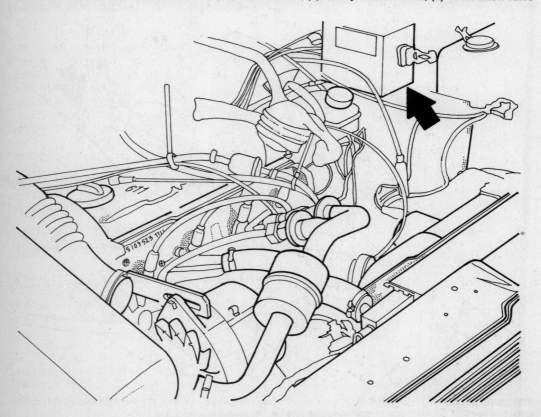

1980 Rabbit 34 PICT-5 vacuum control unit (arrow)

mately 9 volts of current is applied at this point.

When the engine temperature (coolant) is between 61°F (16°C) and 167°F (75°C), the resistor wire is bypassed by thermoswitch 2 and the heating element in the choke receives full battery voltage (12 volts).

When the coolant temperature exceeds 167°F (75°C), all electrical activation of the choke valve is switched off, thermoswitch 1 opens interrupting the current to the heating element while the choke fully opens.

To test the choke system, proceed as follows:

1. Unplug the choke heating element connector and connect the positive lead of a voltmeter to the female part of the connector (part leading into the wiring harness). Connect the negative lead of the voltmeter to the carburetor ground wire. Turn on the ignition.

2. With the coolant temperature below 59°F (15°C), record the voltage.

3. Run the engine up above 131°F (55°C) and check the voltage again. Compare the two readings. The first reading should be one or two volts below the second reading.

4. With the engine at operating temperature (the cooling fan must have come on at least once), the voltmeter should have no reading. If it does, check the thermoswitches.

To test the thermoswitches, remove the switches and connect an ohmmeter between the terminals on each thermoswitch. Thermoswitch 1 opens when the temperature reaches 167°F (75°C) and closes when the temperature drops to 149°F (65°C). Thermoswitch 2 closes when the temperature reaches 131°F (55°C) and opens when the temperature drops to 61°F (16°C).

SETTING THE CHOKE VALVE GAP

1. Set the cold idle speed adjuster screw in its upper notch.

2. Connect a manually operated vacuum pump to the connection on the pulldown unit and build up vacuum.

3. Close the choke valve by hand with the lever and check the choke valve gap with a drill. The gap should be 3.0–3.7mm (0.123–0.146 in.).

4. Adjust the gap using the adjusting screw on the pulldown unit. After adjusting, lock the screw with sealant or a dab of paint.

SETTING THE FAST IDLE SPEED

1. Run the engine up to operating temperature and make sure the ignition setting and the idle adjustment are correct.

2. Run the engine at idle and set the adjust-

ing screw on its third notch on the choke valve lever.

3. Open the choke valve fully by hand using the choke valve lever.

4. Connect a tachometer and check the rpm.

CAUTION: *See Electronic Ignition Precaution in chapter two for warning about connecting tachometers to electronic ignition systems.*

5. The fast idle speed should be between 2350–2450 rpm. If not, adjust with fast idle adjustment screw. Lock screw with safety cap after adjustment.

Cold Start Valve

The cold start valve enriches the air/fuel mixture when engine temperature is below 60°F (15°C) by injecting fuel into the throttle chamber through a passage parallel to the main jet. Test the valve for continuity with a test light or ohmmeter. The test light should light and the ohmmeter should reach 80Ω. If test light fails to light and ohmmeter reads infinity, replace the valve.

THROTTLE KICKER (AIR CONDITIONED VEHICLES ONLY)

The throttle kicker increases the idle speed to prevent stalling when the air conditioner is engaged. To test, proceed as follows:

1. Run the engine up to operating temperature and check the ignition timing (see Chapter 2). Unplug the idle stabilizer (control unit) and plug the two plugs together (see electronic ignition section in chapter two). Remove the retard and advance vacuum hoses and plug them. Make sure the basic idle speed and CO adjustments areas correct (See Chapter 2).

2. Reconnect the advance and retard hoses and reconnect the plugs for the idle stabilizer (control unit).

3. Rev the engine to start the idle stabilizer (control unit) and note the ignition timing at idle.

4. Switch on the air conditioner (coldest temperature setting, highest fan speed), the ignition timing should not change.

5. If the timing changes, adjust the throttle kicker screw where it contacts the throttle valve lever until the correct setting (no timing change) is reached. Seal the screw with Loctite® or equivalent sealant.

VACUUM CONTROL VALVE

The vacuum control unit has two functions. It houses both the relay for the main jet cutoff valve and the relay for the throttle kicker on air conditioner equipped vehicles.

To test the main jet cutoff valve relay, per-

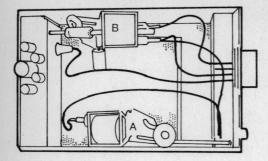

1980 carbureted Rabbit vacuum control unit: (a) main jet cutoff valve relay, (b) throttle kicker relay (air conditioned cars only)

form the steps under the heading Main Jet Cutoff Valve, above. If the engine continues to run and you are sure the vacuum lines are not clogged and the valve is working replace the relay inside the vacuum control unit.

To test the throttle kicker relay, run the engine and turn the air conditioner on and then turn it off. The kicker should move in and out. If it doesn't connect the vacuum retard hose from the distributor to the throttle kicker vacuum connector. If the kicker moves, replace the relay. If the kicker does not move, replace the throttle kicker.

Carter TYF—1982 and Later

THROTTLE GAP ADJUSTMENT

Throttle gap is set at the factory and should not be tampered with.

FAST IDLE ADJUSTMENT

1. Run the engine until it reaches normal operating temperature. Make sure that the timing and idle speed are set to specifications.
2. Run the engine at idle and set the fast idle adjustment screw to the second step of the fast idle cam.
3. Disconnect the purge valve. Disconnect and plug the vacuum hose at the EGR valve.
4. Connect a tachometer as per the manufacturer's instructions and check that the engine speed is 2800–3200 rpm. If not, turn the fast idle screw until it is.
5. Reconnect the purge valve and the vacuum hose at the EGR valve.

CHOKE GAP ADJUSTMENT

1. Set the cold idle speed adjuster screw in its upper notch.
2. Connect a manually operated vacuum pump to the connection on the pulldown unit and build up vacuum.
3. Close the choke valve by hand with the lever and check the choke valve gap with a drill.

The gap should be 3.0–3.7mm (0.123–0.146 in.); 4.0mm (0.154 in.) for 1982; 4.2mm (0.165 in.) for 1983.

4. Adjust the gap using the adjusting screw in the end of the vacuum unit at the side of the choke unit. After adjusting, lock the screw with sealant.

THROTTLE LINKAGE ADJUSTMENT

All Models

Throttle linkage adjustments are not normally required. However, it is a good idea to make sure that the throttle valve(s) in the carburetor open all the way when the accelerator pedal is held in the wide-open position. Only the primary (first stage) throttle valve will open when the pedal is pushed with the engine off: the secondary throttle on Volkswagen 2-barrel carburetors is vacuum operated.

Make note of the following:

• Always be careful not to kink or twist the cables during installation or adjustment. This can cause rapid wear and binding.

• On the Rabbits and Sciroccos, the accelerator cable will only bend one way, make sure you install it with the bends in the right positions.

• On 1974–75 Dashers, when installing new accelerator cable, the hole in the fire wall must be enlarged to 16mm ($^5/_8$ in.). Adjust these cables at the pedal clamp.

NOTE: *When installing new cables, all bends should be as wide as possible, and fittings between which the inner cable is exposed must be aligned.*

OVERHAUL

NOTE: *Specific directions and specifications for carburetor overhaul are usually contained in the rebuilding kit.*

Efficient carburetion depends greatly on careful cleaning and inspection during overhaul since dirt, gum, water, or varnish in or on the carburetor parts are often responsible for poor performance.

Overhaul your carburetor in a clean, dustfree area. Carefully disassemble the carburetor, referring often to the exploded views. Keep all similar and look-alike parts segregated during disassembly and cleaning to avoid accidentally interchange during assembly. Make a note of all jet sizes.

When the carburetor is disassembled, wash all parts (except diaphragms, electric choke units, pump plunger, and any other plastic, leather, fiber, or rubber parts) in clean carburetor solvent. Do not leave parts in the solvent any longer than is necessary to sufficiently loosen the deposits. Excessive cleaning may remove the special finish from the float bowl

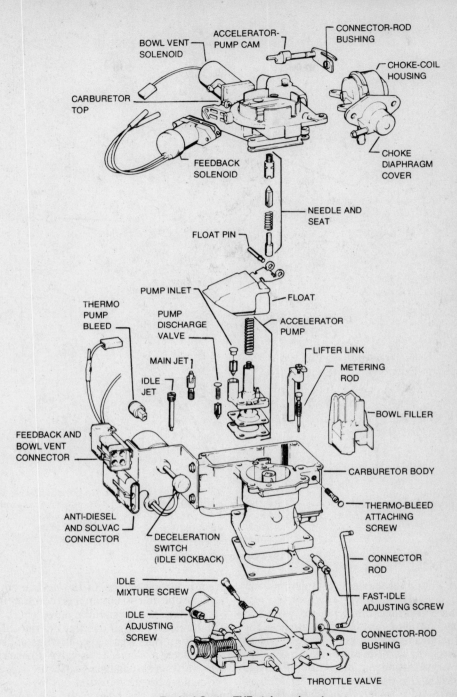

Typical Carter TYF style carburetor

and choke valve bodies, leaving these parts unfit for service. Rinse all parts in clean solvent and blow them dry with compressed air or allow them to air dry. Wipe clean all cork, plastic, leather, and fiber parts with a clean, lint-free cloth.

Blow out all passages and jets with compressed air and be sure that there are no re-strictions or blockages. Never use wire or similar tools to clean jets, fuel passages, or air bleeds. Clean all jets and valves separately to avoid accidental interchange.

Check all parts for wear or damage. If wear or damage is found, replace the defective parts. Especially check the following:

1. Check the float needle and seat for wear.

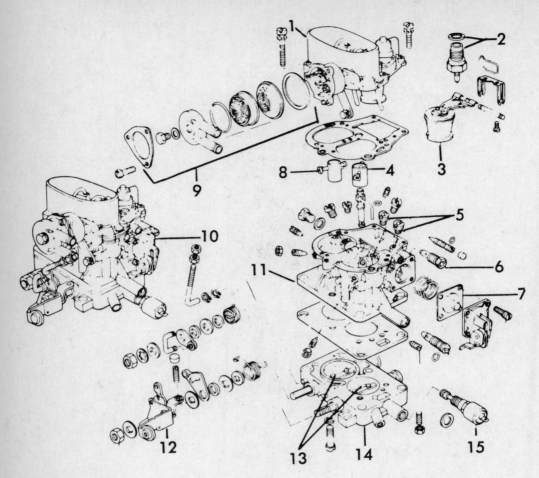

1. Top housing
2. Float needle valve assembly
3. Float
4. Venturi
5. Main jets
6. Idle jet
7. Accelerator pump assembly
8. Venturi
9. Automatic choke assembly
10. Assembled view of carburetor
11. Carburetor bowl assembly
12. Throttle lever assembly
13. Throttle valves
14. Throttle plate
15. By-pass cutoff valve

1974 Dasher carburetor

If wear is found, replace the complete assembly.

2. Check the float hinge pin for wear and the float(s) for dents or distortion. Replace the float if fuel has leaked into it.

3. Check the throttle and choke shaft bores for wear or an out-of-round condition. Damage or wear to the throttle arm, shaft, or shaft bore will often require replacement of the throttle body. These parts require a close tolerance of fit. Wear may allow air leakage, which could adversely affect starting and idling.

NOTE: *Throttle shafts and bushings are not included in overhaul kits. They can be purchased separately.*

4. Inspect the idle mixture adjusting needles for burrs or grooves. Any such condition requires replacement of the needle, since you will not be able to obtain a satisfactory idle.

5. Test the accelerator pump check valves. They should pass air one way but not the other. Test for proper seating by blowing and sucking on the valve. Replace the valve if necessary. If the valve is satisfactory, wash the valve again to remove breath moisture.

6. Check the bowl cover for warped surfaces with a straightedge.

7. Closely inspect the valves and seats for wear and damage, replacing as necessary.

8. After the carburetor is assembled, check the choke valve for freedom of operation.

Carburetor overhaul kits are recommended for each overhaul. These kits contain all gaskets and new parts to replace those that deteriorate most rapidly. Failure to replace all parts

Carburetor Specifications

Year	Model	Carburetor Type	Main Jet		Air Correction Jet		Idle Fuel Jet		Idle Air Jet		Accelerator Pump Discharge (cm³/stroke)	
			Primary	Secondary	Primary	Secondary	Primary	Secondary	Primary	Secondary	Fast	Slow
1974	Dasher (Calif. M/T)	Solex 32/35	x122.5	x142.5	130	140	g45	g45	180	180	0.3−0.5	0.75−1.05
	Dasher (Calif. A/T)	Solex 32/35	x120	x145	140	140	g45	g45	180	180	0.3−0.5	0.75−1.05
	Dasher (Fed. M/T)	Solex 32/35	x135	x140	150	150	g52.5	g52.5	180	180	0.3−0.5	0.75−1.05
	Dasher (Fed. A/T)	Solex 32/35	x130	x140	140	140	g52.5	g52.5	180	180	0.3−0.5	0.75−1.05
1975	Dasher (US all)	Zenith 2B3	x117.5	x137.5	140	92.5	52.5	65	130	110	−	0.75−1.05
	Rabbit, Scirocco (US all)	Zenith 2B2	x115	x115	140	92.5	52.5	70	135	100	−	0.75−1.05
1976	Rabbit, Scirocco (US all)	Zenith 2B2	x117.5	x110	130	92.5	52.5	65	135	140	1.3−1.7①	0.6−0.9②
1978	Rabbit	34 PICT-5	x127.5	−	120Z	−	52.5	−	120	−	③	③
1980	Rabbit	34 PICT-5	x127.5	−	120Z	−	④	−	120	−	⑤	⑤

① Cold
② Warm
③ Rate given as 0.85−1.15 cm³/stroke
④ Come in sizes 50.0/55.0/57.5 The jet size is stamped on the float housing next to plug on front of carburetor
⑤ Rate given as 0.8−1.2 cm³/stroke
M/T Manual trans.
A/T Automatic trans.
Fed. Non-California USA car.
NOTE: Refer to instruction sheet with carburetor rebuilding kit for "specs" — 1981 and later models

supplied with the kit (especially gaskets) can result in poor performance later.

Some carburetor manufacturers supply overhaul kits of three basic types: minor repair; major repair; and gasket kits. Basically, they contain the following: **Minor Repair Kits**
- All gaskets
- Float needle valve
- Volume control screw
- All diaphragms
- Spring for the pump diaphragm **Major Repair Kits**
- All jets and gaskets
- All diaphragms
- Float needle valve
- Volume control screw
- Pump ball valve
- Float
- Complete intermediate rod
- Intermediate pump lever
- Some cover holddown screws and washers

Gasket Kits
- All gaskets

After cleaning and checking all components, reassemble the carburetor, using new parts and referring to the exploded view. When reassembling, make sure that all screws and jets are tight in their seats, but do not overtighten, as the tips will be distorted. Tighten all screws gradually, in rotation. Do not tighten needle valves into their seats; uneven jetting will result. Always use new gaskets. Be sure to adjust the float level when reassembling.

GASOLINE FUEL INJECTION SYSTEMS

General Descriptions

CONTINUOUS INJECTION SYSTEM (CIS)

The Continuous Injection Systems (CIS) is an independent mechanical system. That is, no pump or other component is driven by the engine. The basic operating principle is to continuously inject fuel into the intake side of the engine by means of an electric pump. The amount of fuel delivered is metered by an air flow measuring device. CIS is a mechanical system, there is no electronic brain deciding when or how much fuel to inject.

The primary fuel circuit consists of an electric pump, which pulls fuel from the tank. Fuel then passes through an accumulator. The accumulator is basically a container in the fuel line. It houses a spring-loaded diaphragm that provides fuel damping and delays pressure build-up when the engine is first started. When the engine is shut down, the expanded chamber in the accumulator keeps the system under enough pressure for good hot restarts with no vapor locking. Fuel flows through a large, paper element filter to the mixture control assembly.

The mixture control assembly is the heart of the CIS system. It houses the air flow sensor and the fuel distributor. The air sensor is a round plate attached to a counterbalanced

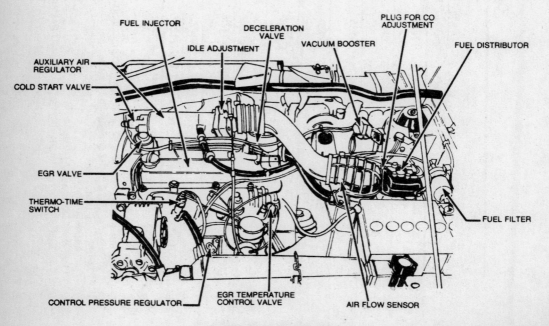

Typical CIS fuel injection

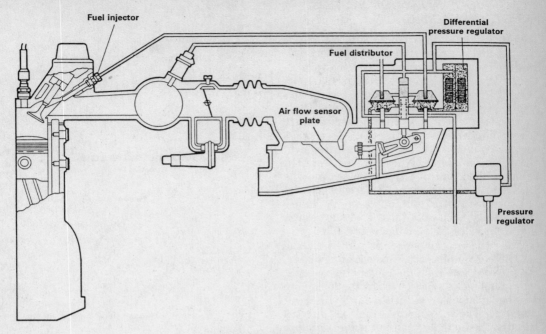

CIS fuel injection system

lever. The plate and lever are free to move up-and-down on a fulcrum. Accelerator pedal linkage connects to a throttle butterfly, which is upstream (closer to the manifold and intake valves) of the air sensor. Stepping on the gas opens the throttle valve. Increased air, demanded by the engine, is sucked through the air cleaner and around the air sensor plate.

In the air funnel, where the air sensor plate is located, the quantity of intake air lifts the plate until an equilibrium is reached between air flow and hydraulic counterpressure acting on the lever through a plunger. This is the control plunger. In this balanced position, the plunger stays at a level in the fuel distributor to open small metering slits, one for each cylinder in the engine. Fuel under controlled pressure from the pump goes through the slits to the injectors supply opening. The slit meters the right amount of fuel.

In order to maintain a precise fuel pressure, a pressure regulator, or pressure relief valve, is located in the primary fuel circuit of the fuel distributor. Excess fuel is diverted back to the tank through a return line. To make sure the amount of fuel going through the control plunger slits depends only on their area, an exact pressure differential must always be maintained at the openings. This pressure is controlled by a differential-pressure valve. There's one valve for each cylinder. The valve consists of a spring loaded steel diaphragm and an outlet to the injectors. The diaphragm separates the upper and lower chambers.

The valve keeps an exact pressure differential of 1.42 psi between upper chamber pressure and lower chamber pressure. Both pressures act on the spring loaded steel diaphragm which opens the outlet to the injectors. The size of the outlet opening is always just enough to maintain that 1.42 psi pressure differential at the metering slit. The diaphragm opens more if a larger amount of fuel flows. If less fuel enters the upper chamber, the diaphragm opens less and less fuel goes to the injectors. An exact pressure differential between upper and lower chamber is kept constant. Diaphragm movement is actually only a few hundreths of a millimeter (thousandths of an inch).

A warm-up regulator can alter the pressure on the control plunger according to engine and outside air temperature. For warm-up running, it lowers the pressure so that the air sensor plate can go higher for the same air flow. This exposes more metering slit area, and more fuel flows for a richer mixture. An auxiliary air valve passes extra air to create a richer (than throttle valve position calls for) mixture. For cold starts, a separate injector is used to squirt fuel into the intake manifold. This injector is electronically controlled. A thermo-time switch, screwed into the engine, limits the amount of time the valve is open and at higher temperatures, cuts it off.

CONTINUOUS INJECTION SYSTEM ELECTRONIC (CIS-E)

The CIS-E is an electronically controlled continuous fuel injection system. This system utilizes the basic CIS mechanical system for injection, with electrically controlled correction functions. The electronic portion of the system consists of an air flow sensor position indicator, thermo-time switch, coolant temperature sensor, electronic control unit (ECU), transistorized ignition switching unit, micro-switch, throttle valve switch, altitude correction indicator, lambda control and oxygen sensor. The mechanical portion of the CIS-E system consist of a mixture control unit, differential pressure regulator, auxiliary air valve, cold start valve, injector nozzles, fuel pump and fuel filter.

When the ignition switch is turned on, the electric fuel pump is activated causing pressurized fuel to move from the tank to the accumulator. Fuel pulsations exerted by the fuel pump are then damped or smoothed out by the accumulator. The pressurized fuel is directed through the fuel filter and to the fuel distributor or mixture control unit. A differential pressure regulator (DPR) located on the side of fuel distributor is used to control fuel pressure. A potentiometer has been added to the CIS system to sense the position of the sensor plate. The frequency solenoid and warm-up pressure regulator are not used in the CIS-E fuel injection system. The system pressure regulator valve has been removed from the fuel distributor and replaced by an external, diaphragm type, pressure regulator. This regulator contains an additional port which is used to return fuel from the differential pressure regulator.

The differential pressure regulator (DPR) is an electro-magnetic operated pressure regulator. It receives an electronic signal in milliamps from the electronic control unit (ECU). The higher the milliamp signal the higher the differential between the upper and lower chamber pressures, resulting in a richer mixture. The lower the milliamp signal the lower the differential pressure resulting in a leaner mixture.

In the CIS-E fuel injection system, system pressure is always present in the upper chamber of the fuel distributor. The metering slit in the control barrel regulates the amount of fuel delivered to the upper chamber depending on the air flow sensor position and control plunger position. The amount of fuel delivered to the injectors and consequently fuel mixture, is adjusted by the differential pressure regulator.

The following is a list of the CIS-E system components with a description of how they work.

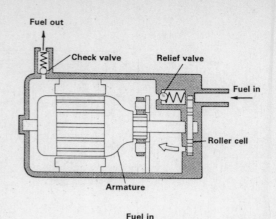

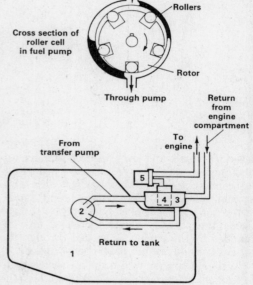

1. Fuel tank
2. Sending unit with transfer pump
3. Fuel supply reservoir
4. Fuel pump
5. Accumulator

CIS-E fuel injection fuel pump

Mixture Control Valve

The air-flow sensor contains a plate, mounted on a hinged lever, which moves in a cone shaped venturi. The air sensor measures the amount of air entering the engine and controls the amount of fuel injected by moving the control plunger in the fuel distributor.

The flow of intake air through the air cone lifts the sensor plate causing the sensor lever to lift the control plunger in the fuel distributor. As the control plunger rises, it allows more fuel to flow from the metering slits and to the injectors.

Since the air sensor is constantly measuring the intake air and controlling the amount of

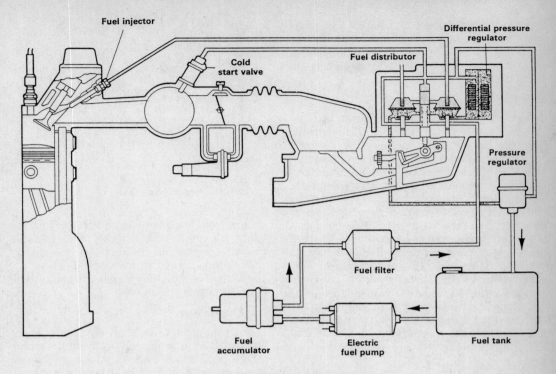

CIS-E fuel injection supply system

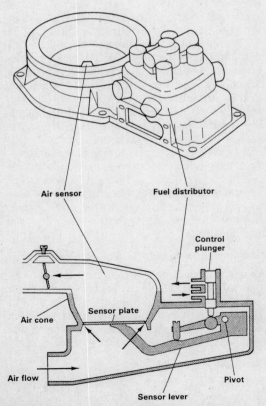

Mixture control unit used on CIS-E fuel injection systems

fuel by raising or lowering the control plunger, the basic air/fuel mixture is always correct.

Differential Pressure Regulator

The differential pressure regulator (DPR) is located on the side of the fuel distributor. It consists of a plate valve joined between two electromagnets. The plate valve regulates the fuel flow into the lower chamber of the fuel distributor. This determines the differential pressure, which is the difference in pressure between the upper and lower chambers in the fuel distributor.

By varying the electric current to the differential pressure regulator and changing the strength of the magnets, the plate valve can be moved. By changing the opening, the quantity of the fuel allowed into the lower the chamber of the fuel distributor can be regulated. This in turn changes differential pressure.

The differential pressure regulator is activated by an electrical signal from the electronic control unit (ECU) in measurements of miliamps. The operating range is from minus (–) 50–150 mA. Differential pressure will be from 0–24 psi. (0 bar to 1.6 bar) less than system pressure.

The differential pressure regulator is designed that should the Electronic Control Unit (ECU) malfunction or an electrical failure occur, the plate valve will defect enough under system pressure of about 0.4 bar. This combined with the 0.2 bar difference caused by the pressure regulation springs in the fuel distributor will enable the vehicle to be drivable in the event of such an electrical failure.

Fuel Pump

An electric fuel pump is used to provide a fuel pressure of 60–80 psi. There is a check valve located in the pump that will aid in the hot starting process. This check valve works in conjunction with the accumulator to maintain a constant pressure in the system when the engine is not running.

The fuel pump is controlled by a relay to prevent it from operating should the engine stall or cut off. Some vehicles are equipped with a transfer pump located in the fuel tank and attached to the fuel tank sending unit. This pump delivers fuel to a separate reservoir which supplies the fuel for the main pump.

The fuel pump is solely depended upon the fuel flowing through it for cooling and lubrication. The fuel pump is subject to damage if it is ever allowed to run dry.

Accumulator

The accumulator is located between the fuel pump and the fuel filter. When the fuel pump is running, a diaphragm inside of the accumulator moves to the stop against spring pressure. When the fuel pump is off, the fuel is stored under pressure in the accumulator thereby maintaining residual fuel pressure. The residual pressure is maintained by the spring slowly pushing the diaphragm to the right, forcing a small amount of fuel through an orifice in the reed valve. This in turn helps to maintain residual fuel pressure and also avoiding vapor lock.

The accumulator reduces fuel pump noise as well as protects the metal diaphragm in the fuel distributor from rapid pressure build up during pump operation.

Pressure Regulator

The control pressure regulator and pressure relief valve are not use in the CIS-E system. A diaphragm type pressure regulator is used to maintain system pressure at approximately 78.3 psi. (5.4 bar).

When the engine is started, fuel enters from the main return port of the fuel distributor and works against the regulating spring. The diaphragm assembly moves up along with the valve body which is moved by the closing pressure spring to open the sealing plate. The valve body then contacts its stop and the regulation of system pressure will begin by way of the regulating valve. Excess fuel along with the spill

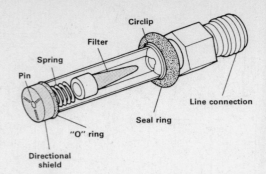

CIS-E fuel injector cross section

volume from the lower chamber in the fuel distributor is now returned back to the fuel tank by way of the opened sealing plate.

The pressure regulator also acts as a one way check valve to maintain pressure in the system once the engine is shut off.

Cold Start Valve

The cold start valve is an electrically operated solenoid valve located in the intake manifold. It provides the necessary fuel enrichment to all cylinders during cold start conditions. The electro-magnetic coil in the cold start valve receives current from the starter. It is grounded by the thermo-time switch so that the injector sprays only during cranking.

The Quantum 5 cylinder is equipped with and additional starting enrichment to supplement the cold start valve. When the starter is activated the control unit increases the current to the differential pressure regulator thus, the fuel mixture is enriched. The amount of starting enrichment is dependent upon the engine coolant temperature. Maximum starting enrichment time is 1.5 seconds, during which time current to the differential pressure regulator can briefly go as high as 150 mA provided the engine is cold. Starting enrichment is possible an will also occur during warm engine starting, however it is at its highest level when the engine is cold.

Thermo-Time Switch

The thermo-time switch senses engine temperature and controls the cold start valve at a specified temperature and on/off time limit measured in seconds. The thermo-time switch controls the cold start valve so that the engine will not flood if it fails to start immediately.

Auxiliary Air Regulator

During cold engine operation, the auxiliary air regulator acts like a fast idle cam to slightly increase idle speed while the engine is warming up. The auxiliary air regulator provides addi-

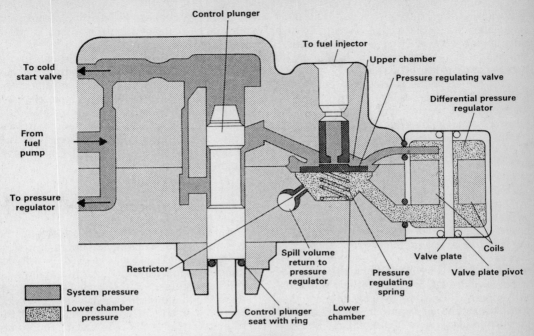

Control plunger

To fuel injector

Upper chamber

Pressure regulating valve

Differential pressure regulator

To cold start valve

From fuel pump

To pressure regulator

Restrictor

Spill volume return to pressure regulator

Pressure regulating spring

Valve plate

Coils

Valve plate pivot

Control plunger seat with ring

Lower chamber

System pressure

Lower chamber pressure

CIS-E fuel distributor

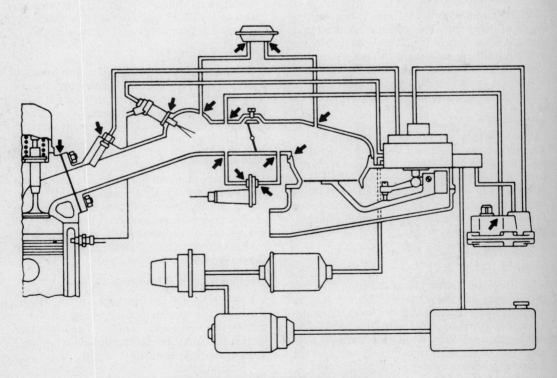

Check the CIS for vacuum leaks at arrows

tional air for idling during warm up. This is accomplished when the engine is cold. At such time, a gate way valve in side of the auxiliary air regulator is open and air is allowed to bypass the closed throttle valve.

After the engine is started, current is supplied by the fuel pump relay to the electric heating element of the auxiliary air regulator, this in turn warms the bi-metal strip gradually causing the gate valve to close.

Idle Air Stabilizer Valve

The Quantum 5 cylinder, GTI, GLI and the 16 valve engine use a air idle stabilization system to control idle speed. This system insures that the idle speed remains constant at predetermined levels during all engine operating conditions. For example: When the engine is cold — below 122°F (50°C) — the idle will be approximately 1000 rpm. When the engine is warm — above 122°F (50°C) the idle will be approximately 850 rpm. When the engine is warm, with the air condition compressor engaged, the idle will be approximately 900–950 rpm.

The idle air stabilization valve, which eliminates the auxiliary air regulator, consist of an electric motor with 2 windings and a turning angle of about 90°. The valve is operated by a cycled voltage signal which is generated by the control unit. By regulating the duty cycle, the valve position can be controlled, resulting in the idle speed being maintained at a predetermined level.

Fuel Injector

The injectors in the CIS-E system open at a predetermined pressure. The fuel is always present in the lines between the fuel distributor and the injectors to ensure good starting. As the pressure in the fuel distributor increases (when the engine is started), the valves open and spray continuously. The amount of fuel injected will be determined by control pressure and the position of the control plunger.

Fuel Distributor

The fuel distributor has under gone a few improvements making it more efficient than previous versions. It is smaller and made of aluminum. The pressure relief valve has been eliminated, the pressure regulating springs have been re-located to the lower chambers and the differential pressure regulator is mounted directly to the fuel distributor.

The volume of the upper chamber has been made smaller, resulting in quicker response time and better starting efficiency. The control plunger is position on an O-ring when the engine is not operating. There is now a few mil-

limeters play between the sensor plate arm and the control plunger when the engine is not in operation.

System pressure is always present in the upper chamber of the fuel distributor. The metering slit in the control barrel regulates the amount of fuel delivered to the upper chamber depending on the air flow sensor position and control plunger position. The amount of fuel delivered to the injectors and consequently fuel mixture, is adjusted by the differential pressure regulator.

Fuel Filter

There are basically 3 fuel filters used in the CIS-E system:
• Inline filter—This filter is located on the pressure side of the pump so that in any event the filter should become clogged it will not damage the pump by causing it to run dry.
• Filter/strainer—This filer is located on the end of the fuel pick-up tube inside of the tank. Vehicles with a transfer pump in the tank, the strainer is attached to the end of the pump. This filter does not require service except when replacing the fuel pump.
• Mini fuel filter—Some vehicles incorporate a small filter located in the hollow bolt that connects the pressure line to fuel distributor.

OXYGEN SENSOR

The oxygen sensor is located in the front exhaust pipe or in the exhaust manifold. Its primary function is to sense the content of the exhaust gases and relay information to the ECU. For more information about the oxygen sensor, refer to Chapter 4.

Potentiometer

The potentiometer is a variable resistor that sends a voltage signal to the control unit based on the sensor plate position. It consists of a wiper brush moving against a carbon film. The voltage signal supplied by it is primarily for cold acceleration enrichment. It is located on the side of the air sensor housing.

Electronic Control Unit (ECU)

The electronic control unit (ECU) is the brains of the electronic fuel system. It determines the operation for the fuel injection system base on the following inputs received:
• Engine temperature
• Engine speed
• Sensor plate position
• Starter signal
• Atmospheric pressure
The control unit generates output signals to the differential pressure regulator based on the input signals received, thus providing the

proper air/fuel mixture for all engine operating conditions.

Coolant Temperature Sensor

The coolant temperature sensor is located in the bottom of the cylinder coolant outlet. It senses the temperature of the engine coolant. The coolant temperature sensor is considered to be a negative temperature coefficient (NTC) resistor, which means that as the engine coolant temperature increases its resistance decreases, vice versa.

When a signal from the temperature sensor is received by the control unit, the control unit provides additional fuel to the injectors during starting and engine warm-up. The lower the temperature of the coolant, the more fuel will be provided to the engine.

Altitude Sensor

An altitude sensor is used on the Quantums with the 5 cylinder engine. It is located next the control unit. This sensor is used to send a voltage signal to the control unit that is based on altitude. The signal is used to adjust the fuel mixture for changes in air pressure.

In high altitude areas the air is thinner, therefore the engine has less oxygen available to burn. Under these conditions, the altitude sensor sends a resistance signal to the control unit. This resistance signal results in a lower current being sent to the differential pressure regulator. As a result, less fuel is delivered to the engine to maintain the correct air/fuel ratio. At sea level the sensor remains open and has no affect on the fuel mixture.

Full Throttle Enrichment

Some engines are equipped with a full throttle enrichment. The full throttle enrichment will only take place after the engine has reached operating temperature and provides additional fuel for increased performance requirements of the engine.

When the engine speed is above 4000 rpm and the throttle is fully open, the full throttle switch closes, sending a voltage signal to the electronic control unit. The control unit increases current at the differential pressure regulator to a fixed rate that is approximately 3 mA above the basic adjustment value to enrich the fuel mixture.

CONTINUOUS INJECTION SYSTEM ELECTRONIC MOTRONIC (CIS-E MOTRONIC)

The CIS-E Motronic fuel injection system is used on the 1990 2.0L 16 valve engine.

The CIS-E Motronic fuel injection system and its components are similar to the CIS-E

fuel injection system. The following a list of CIS-E Motronic refinements:

- Fuel Injection Control
- Oxygen sensor regulation with adaptive learning capability
- Dual map ignition control system with individual cylinder knock control
- Idle speed control
- Fuel tank ventilation control
- Permanent memory for self-diagnosis

DIGIFANT II FUEL INJECTION SYSTEM

Digifant II is further development of the Digifant system. The Digifant II system uses a knock sensor. The control unit circuitry for the idle stabilization system is incorporated in the electronic control unit.

Through the use of sophisticated electronic controls, all functions of the fuel and ignition systems are carefully controlled to provide a fuel efficient engine with good performance. The Cabriolet and received the Digifant II engine management system in 1990.

The following is a list of the Digifant II system components with descriptions.

Crankcase Control Valve

The crankcase emission control system is a closed system. Therefore, no crankcase emissions are discharged into the atmosphere. During operation the blow-by gases from the crankcase will be drawn from the valve cover to the throttle body. A crankcase emission control valve which is mounted to the valve cover regulates the amount of crankcase emissions entering the throttle body.

Electronic Control Unit (ECU)

The heart of the Digifant II system is the electronic control unit (ECU). The control unit incorporates all the functions of the fuel system and provides both the actuation signal for the fuel injectors and optimum ignition timing point for all engine operating conditions.

The control unit (ECU) receives the following inputs:

- Engine speed
- Intake air volume
- Coolant temperature
- Oxygen content in the exhaust gas
- Battery voltage
- Throttle position
- Intake air temperature

Digifant II therefore provides complete fuel injection and ignition control throughout the entire range of entire speed, load and temperature conditions. The injector opening time and ignition timing points are programmed in the control unit.

Fail safe functions are programmed into the

control units memory so the system will continue to operate in the event of a fault in the coolant temperature sensor, oxygen sensor or knock sensor. The ECU provides the ground for the fuel injectors. If the engine speed reaches 6500 rpm the ECU interrupts the ground to the injectors, shutting off the fuel supply.

Power Supply Relay

The power supply relay provides battery voltage to the ECU and fuel injectors.

Fuel Pump Relay

The fuel pump relay provides battery voltage to the fuel pump and the oxygen sensor heating element.

Fuel Delivery System

The Digifant II fuel delivery system is similar to the system used with the CIS-E and CIS-E Motronic fuel injection systems. However, the fuel pump pressure is reduced and the fuel accumulator has been eliminated. The fuel pump is a roller cell design and is cooled and lubricated by the fuel flowing through it. The fuel pump has a check valve on the output side to help maintain residual pressure when the pump has been shut off. The fuel pressure regulator has a check valve as well which also aids in maintaining residual pressure. Maintaining residual pressure on the fuel system prevent vapor lock during start-up.

The transfer pump in the fuel take which supplies fuel to the reservoir is the same as used n the CIS-E fuel systems. The fuel filter is a lifetime fuel filter and does not need replacing unless contaminated.

Fuel Injectors

The Digifant II fuel injector assembly includes, the injectors, the fuel pressure regulator, the service port for fuel pressure testing and injector wiring harness.

Digifant II fuel injectors are electronically on/off valves. A solenoid actuates a needle valve allowing fuel to be forced through the injector nozzle. All 4 injectors open at the same time and inject fuel directly into the intake manifold near the intake valve. Injector opening time is regulated by the ECU, based on inputs from the various engine sensors.

The injectors are supplied 12 volts by the power supply relay. The ECU grounds the injector to control opening time. Internal resistance of each injector is 14–18Ω. When checking all 4 injectors at the same time, the resistance should be 3.7–5.0Ω.

The complete assembly can be removed by removing the allen head mounting bolts. The in-

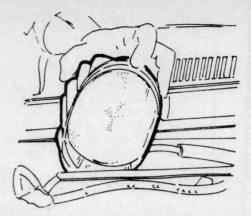

Rubber boot must be tight. Always give air ducts the once-over for leaks or cracks. Vacuum leaks will upset system and the engine will never run correctly

jectors can be separated from the fuel rail by removing the U-clip.

The plastic injector inserts in the cylinder head have been changed to accept the new style injector. A 10mm wrench is needed to remove and install the inserts. When installing the inserts into the cylinder head, use D6 sealing compound or equivalent.

Fuel Pressure Regulator

The fuel pressure regulator maintains approximately 2.5 bar of pressure at idle and up to 3.0 bar when the engine is under load. This is done by regulating the amount of fuel that is returned to the reservoir. The regulator mounts to the fuel injector assembly. A small filter screen installed in the inlet of the regulator helps control the amount of fuel that is returned to the fuel reservoir by moving the diaphragm inside the regulator. When the engine is shut off, the check valve closes and seals to maintain residual fuel pressure to prevent vapor lock during restarting.

Air Filter Housing

The Digifant II system is equipped with a vacuum operated preheat valve for the air intake system. The preheat valve is located on the air filter housing. A vacuum thermoswitch senses intake air temperature. The sensor controls the amount of vacuum to the preheat valve. The preheat valve regulates the amount of preheated air that is delivered to the intake manifold. Intake air is drawn into the filter housing behind the right headlight. The air flow sensor is bolted to the air filter housing.

Air Flow Sensor

The air flow sensor measures the amount of air entering the intake manifold and sends a

Corrado fuel delivery system

voltage signal to the ECU. Intake air opens the air flow sensor flap which actuates the potentiometer to determine the voltage signal. The signal and the engine speed information supplied by the Hall sender are used as the principal inputs for the determination of fuel injector opening duration and ignition timing points. A compensation flap is connected to the air sensor and dampens sudden movements of the air sensor flap due to oscillations of the intake air.

Intake Air Temperature Sensor

An intake temperature sensor is mounted in the air flow sensor housing. It is a negative temperature coefficient (NTC) resistor, which means its resistance value drops as its temperature increases. The signal it supplies to the control unit is used to modify fuel injection rate depending on intake air temperature.

Coolant Temperature Sensor

The coolant temperature sensor is also a negative temperature coefficient resistor (NTC). The resistance signal it produces is used by the control unit to determine cold start enrichment. It also provides a signal to continue to enrich the mixture during engine warm-up. The signals from this sensor also provide correction to ignition timing based on engine speed.

Oxygen Sensor

With Digifant II, a separate control unit and frequency value are not needed. The sensor is connected directly to the Digifant II ECU. The control unit uses the voltage signal from the oxygen sensor and adjusts the opening time of the injector to maintain proper air/fuel mixture. A heated oxygen sensor is used and is located at the front of the catalytic converter. Replacement interval for the oxygen sensor is every 60,000 miles.

Throttle Switches

The idle and full throttle switches are wired in parallel. The switches are mounted on the throttle housing. A voltage signal is sent to the ECU when the throttle switch and throttle plates are closed. The switch opens when the throttle has been opened approximately 1°. The idle switch signal is used for operation of idle stabilizer valve, operation of deceleration fuel shut off and activation of the special ignition timing map of deceleration. The full throttle switch closes about 10° before full throttle. This signal is used for full throttle enrichment.

Ignition System

The map controlled ignition system operates on the principle of a timing map which is programmed into the ECU. Information on engine load, speed and coolant temperature are provided to the ECU in the form of voltage signals. In the ECU, these signals are processed so that the ignition coil, is controlled via terminal No. 1 in accordance with the programmed ignition map.

An engine speed signal comes from the Hall sender in the distributor and measurement of engine load is accomplished through a signal from the air sensor potentiometer. These 2 signals establish the ignition timing point. They

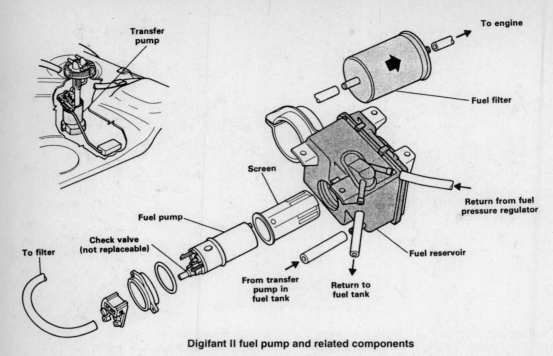

Digifant II fuel pump and related components

are stored in the ignition map in the control units memory as 256 single operational points, 16 fixed points for each engine load point and 16 for each rpm point.

The engine coolant temperature sensor signals the control unit to correct the ignition timing based on engine temperature. Throughout the engine warm-up phase, ignition timing is constantly being corrected. Once the engine reaches operating temperature, the timing is determined by the map. Ignition timing is also corrected through the used of a knock sensor.

Exhaust System

Two exhaust systems are used. A single take down pipe on the 100 hp engine and a double take down pipe on the 105 hp engine. The 100 hp engine take down pipe is made from hot aluminized steel and stainless steel for long life and freedom from corrosion. The swivel joint is similar to that which was used on vehicles with the CIS-E fuel injection.

The 105 hp engine has a double take down pipe and a larger exhaust manifold for better flow. This helps to improve the engine's torque and horsepower characteristics. The swivel joints on the 105 hp engine are made of corrugated stainless steel which connects the take down pipe to the exhaust manifold flange. This is the same part as used on the 16 valve engines.

Knock Sensor

The knock sensor is attached to the left side

of the cylinder block, next to cylinder No. 2. It is a piezoelectric crystal encased in a metal and plastic housing.

Vibrations in the engine will cause the quartz crystal in the knock sensor to generate a small voltage. By monitoring this voltage, the ignition control unit can determine when ignition knock or detonation occurs. The ignition control unit will retard the ignition timing to prevent the ignition knock.

The construction of the knock sensor is slightly different than previous versions. A steel bushing is located inside the sensor housing. This is to prevent the quartz crystal inside the sensor from being crushed or damaged by overtightening the installation bolt. The installation torque for this new sensor is 11–18 ft. lbs. no washers should be used on the installation bolt.

Knock Sensor Regulation

If a cylinder develops ignition knock, the Digifant II control unit will sense this through the knock sensor mounted on the engine block. The control unit will then retard the ignition timing 3° for that cylinder. If the knocking stops, the ignition timing will be advanced in steps of 0.33° back to the preprogrammed value.

If the knocking continues or recurs, the ignition timing can be retarded up to 15° for each cylinder. The difference between the 2 cylinders is limited to 9°.

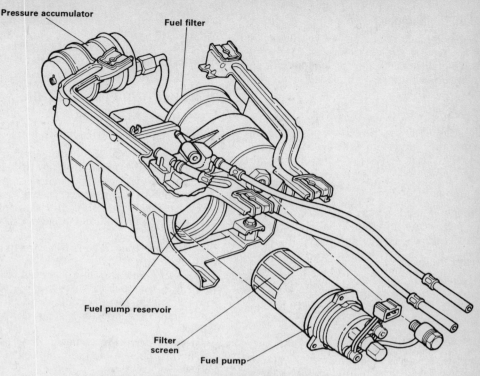

Pressure accumulator

Fuel filter

Fuel pump reservoir

Filter screen

Fuel pump

CIS-E Motronic fuel pump and related components

Ignition Distributor

The ignition distributor has no centrifugal or vacuum advance. It contains a Hall sender which is operated by a trigger wheel. The trigger wheel has four apertures, one for each cylinder. The hall sender sends a voltage signal to the ECU for each cylinder. From this signal, the control unit determines engine speed and crankshaft position.

Idle Stabilization

The idle stabilization system used on the Digifant II system insures that the idle speed remains constant at predetermined levels. The system controls the amount of air bypassing the throttle plate. If the engine idle speed varies from the value stored in the control unit, the idle stabilizer valve will adjust the volume of air entering the engine at idle. This maintains idle speed within certain limits. The idle stabilizer is operated by the ECU. The ECU receives inputs from the following components, the throttle switch, the coolant temperature switch, the A/C compressor clutch is engaged, the current to the idle stabilizer is increased. The increase in current opens the valve further to allow additional air to bypass the throttle plate. This additional air maintains the correct idle speed during engine loads at idle.

Electrical current is passed through a set of electrical windings inside the valve. This creates a magnetic field which regulates the position of the valve plunger.

Evaporative Emission System

The carbon canister stores fuel vapors from the fuel tank when the engine is shut off. During normal driving, fuel tank vapors are drawn into the throttle housing via the carbon canister control valve. The fuel vapors are drawn into the throttle housing via a 1.2mm orifice. At idle, the control valve is closed (low vacuum to control valve) and the carbon canister is not purged.

Manual Transmission

Digifant II vehicles equipped with manual transmission use a vacuum amplifier. The purpose of the amplifier is to increase vacuum at idle to the brake booster. The carbon canister vent line is not disconnected when checking or adjusting CO content. It is important that these 2 vacuum hoses are not reversed.

Automatic Transmission

Digifant II vehicles equipped with automatic transmission use a vacuum amplifier. The purpose of the amplifier is to increase vacuum at idle to the brake booster. The carbon canister vent line is not disconnected when checking or adjusting CO content.

Air Flap Potentiometer

The air flap potentiometer is a variable resistor connected to the air flow sensor that provides a signal for determining fuel system enrichment. It is a internal component of air flow sensor.

Fuel Filter

The fuel filter, which removes foreign particles from the fuel system, is attached to the fuel reservoir in front of the fuel tank on the right side of the vehicle.

Fuel Pump

The fuel pump is an electric pump which delivers fuel to the injectors. It is located inside the fuel reservoir.

Transfer Pump

The transfer pump supplies the fuel pump reservoir with fuel from the tank. It is located inside the fuel tank and is attached to the fuel tank sending unit.

Fuel Screen

The fuel screen is a strainer which removes foreign particles from the fuel system. It is located in from of the fuel pump, inside the fuel reservoir, inlet of each injector and inlet of fuel pressure regulator.

Idle Stabilization Valve

The idle stabilization valve is an electronically controlled valve used to maintain idle speed at a predetermined level by regulating intake air at idle. It is located on a rubber mount near the top of the intake manifold and valve cover.

Power Supply Relay

The power supply relay, when energized by the ignition switch, provides battery voltage to the ECU and fuel injectors. It is located in the relay panel.

Electric Fuel Pump

LOCATION

• Rabbit, Scirocco and Cabriolet: The fuel pump is mounted in front of the right rear axle
• Corrado, Fox, Passat, GTI/Jetta 16 valve w/2.0L engine: The fuel pump, fuel pump reservoir, accumulators and fuel filter are all located under the vehicle
• Dasher: The fuel pump is mounted below the fuel accumulator near the rear wheel
• Quantum: The fuel pump is located in the gas tank
• Rabbit Pick-up Truck: The fuel pump is mounted on the passenger's side near the front

of the fuel tank, which is located near the center of the vehicle
• Golf, Jetta and GTI: fuel pump is on the passenger's side in front of the rear wheel and is accessible through a cover plate

REMOVAL AND INSTALLATION

CIS Fuel Injection System

ALL MODELS EXCEPT QUANTUM

1. Raise the vehicle and support it on jack stands. Disconnect the battery ground cable.
2. Remove the right rear wheel on all cars. On the Rabbit Pick-up truck, you will probably have an easier go of it if you raise all four wheels off the ground and support the vehicle on jackstands.
3. Remove the gas tank filler cap to release the fuel pressure.
4. Clamp off the line between the fuel pump and the fuel tank with a pair of soft jawed vise grips or other suitable lock pliers. Don't clamp the line too tightly or you may damage it.
5. Disconnect the clamped line from the fuel pump. There's bound to be a little gas in the line, so be careful.
6. If your vehicle has an accumulator mounted next to the fuel pump, disconnect the fuel lines from the accumulator. Disconnect the wiring from the fuel pump and remove all other lines after marking them for assembly.
7. Loosen and remove the retaining nuts and remove the fuel pump on Dashers and pre 1979 Rabbits and Sciroccos. On 1979–86 Rabbits, Jettas, GTIs and Sciroccos, including the Rabbit Pick-up, remove the nuts on the lower bracket, loosen the nut on the upper slotted bracket where it connects to the body and slide the pump out.
8. Slide the fuel pump into the mounting bracket and install the pump/bracket fasteners.
9. Connect the fuel lines and wiring to the pump. Make sure that the new seal washers are installed on the fuel discharge line.
10. Lower the vehicle. Start the engine and check for leaks.

QUANTUM

1. Pull up carpet under rear cargo area, revealing fuel pump access.
2. Remove cover over sending unit.
3. Detach fuel return hose, fuel supply hose, and vent hose from top of fuel pump.
4. Disconnect electrical wire from sending unit and fuel pump.
5. Loosen fuel pump attaching screws and pull fuel pump out in one motion.
6. Slide the fuel pump into the mounting bracket and install the pump/bracket fasteners.

7. Connect the fuel lines and wiring to the pump. Make sure that the new seal washers are installed on the fuel discharge line.

8. Connect the negative battery cable.

9. Start the engine and check for leaks.

CIS-E, CIS-E Motronic and Digifant Fuel Injection Systems

The fuel pump is normally located under the vehicle near the fuel tank or in front of the rear axle on the right side. It is attached to a bracket which also accommodates the fuel filter and the accumulator as an assembly.

1. Disconnect the negative battery cable.

2. Relieve the fuel system pressure. Wrap a cloth around the connection to catch any escaping fuel.

NOTE: *When replacing the old fuel pump with a new pump, the new pump may have a positive lock connector that differs from the earlier pumps. The electrical connectors of the fuel pump wiring harness must be changed when installing this newer pump.*

3. Raise the vehicle and support it safely.

4. Disconnect the electrical connector from the fuel pump.

5. Remove both wire terminals from the connector housing.

6. Discard the old connector and protective boot.

7. Install the new protective boot over the wires and insert the wire terminals into the new connector.

8. Slide the protective boot over the connector.

9. Disconnect fuel line from the fuel pump.

10. Remove the lower pump cover (if equipped), pump mounting bolts and remove the pump.

To install:

11. Position the fuel pump it place and secure it with the mounting bolts. Make sure the tabs in the pump housing catch in the retaining ring recess.

12. Install new O-ring seals when connecting the fuel lines to the pump. Lubricate the O-rings with clean fuel prior to installation.

13. Connect the electrical connector to the fuel pump.

14. Lower the vehicle.

15. Connect the negative battery cable. Turn the ignition switch on and off several times to pressurize the system.

16. Raise the and support it safely, start the engine and observe for fuel leaks. When the engine is started after a fuel pump replacement, you may here knocking or clunking noises from the rear of the vehicle for about 5–20 seconds. This is normal due to fuel filling the accumulator under pressure from the pump. Do not attempt to remedy this situation if it occurs.

17. Shut the engine off and lower the vehicle.

TESTING

Operating Test

ALL MODELS

1. Have an assistant operate the starter. Listen near the fuel pump location to determine if the pump is running.

2. If the pump is not running, check the wiring and the fuse on the front of the fuel pump relay.

3. If the fuse is good, replace the fuel pump relay.

4. If the fuel pump still does not operate, and you're sure there are no loose connections in the wiring, the fuel pump is faulty and must be replaced.

Delivery Rate Test

CIS FUEL INJECTION SYSTEM

1. Check the condition of the fuel filter. Make sure it is clean and that fuel flows through the lines freely.

2. Connect a jumper wire between the No. 1 terminal on the ignition coil and ground.

3. Disconnect the return fuel line and hold it in a measuring container with a capacity of more than 1 liter.

4. Have an assistant run the starter for 30 seconds while watching the quantity of fuel delivered.

The minimum allowable flow for the 1975–78 Rabbit and Scirocco is 750cc in 30 seconds; 900cc in 30 seconds for 1979 and later Rabbits, Jettas and Sciroccos.

For Dashers with the type A fuel pump, identified by the fuel inlet and outlet ports being at opposite end of the pump, the pump must delivery 1 liter of fuel in 32 seconds. For Dashers with the type B fuel pump, identified by the inlet and outlet ports forming a 90° angle through the center of the pump, the pump must delivery 1 liter of fuel in 40 seconds. Quantum fuel pump must delivery 700cc of fuel in 30 seconds.

NOTE: *For the above test, the battery must be fully charged. Also, make sure you have plenty of fuel in the tank.*

If your pump fails its specific test, check for a dirty fuel filter, blocked lines or blocked fuel tank strainer (if so equipped). If all of these are in good condition, replace the pump.

CIS-E AND CIS-E MOTRONIC FUEL INJECTION SYSTEM

1. Disconnect the fuel return line at the fuel distributor.

2. Place the return line in a 1 quart capacity measuring container.

3. Remove the fuel pump relay and install US 4480/3 or equivalent remote control apparatus.

4. Operate the fuel pump for exactly 30 seconds.

5. Delivery quantity should be 675cc CIS-E equipped vehicles and 760cc for 2.0L 16 valve engines that use CIS-E Motronic. This is the maximum flow rate with 12.0 volts available at the fuel pump.

6. If the fuel pump delivery is incorrect, check the following:
- Fuel line leaks
- Blocked fuel lines
- Blocked fuel filter
- Blocked fuel tank screen
- Voltage at the fuel pump with the pump operating

7. If all systems are in good order, replace the fuel pump.

DIGIFANT II FUEL INJECTION SYSTEM

1. Connect pressure gauge US 1076 or VW 1318 (or equivalent) to fuel line T-piece. If using VW 1318/3A or equivalent pressure gauge, the lever must be in a closed position.

2. Remove fuel pump relay and bridge terminals 30 and 87 with tool US 4480/3.

3. Run fuel pump and observe pressure. Pressure must be a minimum of 36 psi. If not, continue with next test.

4. Be sure that the fuel tank is at least half full of fuel. Disconnect fuel return line at pressure regulator.

5. Attach about 4 ft. of fuel line to the return line of the pressure regulator. Place other end of fuel line into a 1 liter measuring container. Plug the return line with the cap from the CO measuring tube or any suitable plug.

6. Remove the fuel pump relay and bridge terminals 30 and 87 with tool US 4480/3.

7. Run the fuel pump for exactly 30 seconds. Delivery quantity should be at least 500cc.

8. If delivery quantity is not within specification, check the fuel flow from the tank before and after the fuel filters. If fuel flow from the tank is not obstructed, continue with the next test.

Injector

REMOVAL AND INSTALLATION

Except Corrado

1. Disconnect the negative battery cable.

2. Relieve the fuel system pressure. Wrap a cloth around the connection to catch any escaping fuel.

3. Clean the area around the fuel injectors. Using two wrenches, hold the injector with one wrench and loosen the fuel line fitting with the other.

4. Remove the fuel line from the injector, do not allow the injector to turn.

5. Carefully pull the injector out from the insert. A injector extractor tool may be required on injectors that are difficult to remove.

6. If required, use a 13mm hex head socket tool, remove the injector upper insert from the cylinder head.

7. Remove the lower insert and sealing ring from the cylinder head.

To install:

8. Install a new sealing washer and the lower insert into the cylinder head.

9. Coat the upper insert threads with D-6 sealing compound or equivalent. Thread the upper insert into the cylinder head.

10. Using a 13mm hex head socket tool, tighten the the upper insert to 15 ft. lbs.

11. Make sure all O-rings are in place on the injector. Lubricate the O-rings with fuel prior to installing.

12. Push the injector firmly in position into the upper insert seat.

13. Connect the fuel line to the injector (use both wrenches).

14. Turn the ignition switch on and off several times to pressurize the system. Check for fuel leaks before starting the engine and after starting.

Corrado

1. Disconnect the negative battery cable.

2. Remove the idle stabilizer valve and set it off to the side.

3. Remove the valve cover.

4. Remove the intake manifold support.

5. Disconnect the harness connector from the connector at the end of the wiring guide.

6. Gently pry the wiring guide from the fuel distributor retainers.

7. Remove the fuel distributor mounting bolts.

8. Pull the entire injector assembly with the fuel distributor and wiring guide from the cylinder head. If required, use a 13mm hex head socket tool, remove the injector upper insert from the cylinder head. Remove the

lower insert and sealing ring from the cylinder head.

To install:

9. Install a new sealing washer and the lower insert into the cylinder head. Coat the upper insert threads with D-6 sealing compound or equivalent. Thread the upper insert into the cylinder head. Using a 13mm hex head socket tool, tighten the the upper insert to 15 ft. lbs.

10. Position the injector assembly (with wiring guide and fuel distributor) onto the cylinder head. Push the injectors firmly in position into the upper insert seat. Make sure the O-rings are in place on each injector. Lubricate the O-rings with fuel prior to installing.

11. Install and tighten the fuel distributor mounting bolts.

12. Push the wiring guide into the retainer and connect the wiring harness.

13. Install the intake manifold support.

14. Install the valve cover.

15. Install the idle stabilizer valve.

16. Connect the negative battery cable.

INJECTOR SPRAY PATTERN

A bad injector can cause a number of problems:

1. Hot restart troubles
2. Rough idle
3. Hesitation
4. Poor power.

Hot starting complaints can come from an injector or injectors that are leaking fuel droplets when they're supposed to be completely shut.

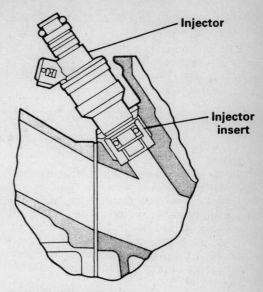

Fuel injector installation

The next three problems can be caused by a bad spray pattern from one or more of the injectors. Dribble patterns, fire hose shots, and uneven sprays will produce hesitation, stumbling and general lack of power.

On-Car Testing

With care, you can check injectors without a tester, but if you suspect injector problems, it's worth having them checked on a test stand. To watch spray patterns on the car, switch the ignition on, pull an injector out of the head, and

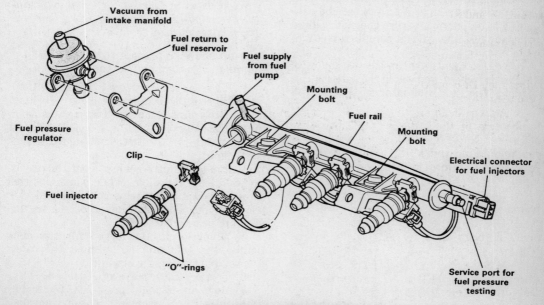

Typical fuel injector assembly

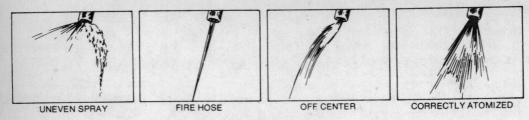

| UNEVEN SPRAY | FIRE HOSE | OFF CENTER | CORRECTLY ATOMIZED |

Fuel injector spray patterns

lift the air sensor plate with your fingers (carefully). When you let the plate down quickly, you should get a fine, cone-shaped spray of fuel. If not, the injector should come off and be cleaned or replaced. Repeat the test for each injector. Hot start complaints call for a different procedure. Crank the starter and pull each injector in turn. If an injector drips fuel, it's defective and should be replaced.

Off-Car Testing

Testing injectors out of the car is the most accurate method for determining whether or not they're causing performance problems. Individual injectors are expensive items, and immediately trashing suspect injection valves is not wise. New and old injectors can be mixed in the set for that engine, so only defective units need be replaced. Unfortunately, injector test equipment is very expensive. So carefully consider the cost of having the injectors tested by a qualified test facility before jumping into a major purchase of test equipment.

Bosch and several other companies manufacture injector test stands. A tester kit usually includes a hand pump, pressure gauge, test-fluid bottle, and test line. All you need do is bolt it to a stand.

On the test stand, you can operate the valve as much as you like and watch the pattern. Use a suitable test fluid, not gasoline! With the injector filled with fluid and bled, tighten the test line fitting. Slowly work the handle, without going over 21 psi. Pressure should build up and the injector shouldn't leak. Next, build up pressure with the test valve open until the injector squirts. Opening pressure for all CIS cars is 35–52 psi. and all other cars is 44–59 psi.

Throttle Cable

ADJUSTMENT

Most throttle cable slack adjustments are made at the two locknuts where the cable is mounted on the valve cover or by moving the cable grommet.

Except Below

1. Check that the throttle valve is closed (in the idle position).
2. If adjustment is necessary, loosen locknut and turn the adjusting nut until the throttle cable is free of slack or tension.

NOTE: *On automatic transmission models, make sure the throttle cable levers on the transmission are moved the whole way into their rest positions. Some models do not use transmission cables.*

1985–90 Scirocco (Except 16 Valve) and Cabriolet w/Automatic Transmission

1. Place the selector lever in the **P** position.
2. Loosen the accelerator cable adjusting nut and disconnect the accelerator cable from the throttle lever.
3. Loosen the throttle cable adjusting nut and locknut.
4. Pull the throttle cable out until all play is removed from the cable. While doing this the throttle valves must remain closed and the transmission operating lever must be in the closed position.
5. When the play is removed from the cable tighten the adjusting nut against the cable bracket and tighten the locknut.
6. Connect the accelerator pedal cable.
7. Have an assistant press the accelerator cable until the operating lever on the transmission lever contacts the kick-down stop. Turn

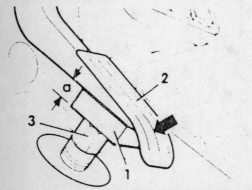

Install a 15mm spacer between the gas pedal and the pedal stop

CHILTON'S
FUEL ECONOMY
& TUNE-UP TIPS

Tune-up • Spark Plug Diagnosis • Emission Controls

Fuel System • Cooling System • Tires and Wheels

General Maintenance

55 WAYS TO IMPROVE FUEL ECONOMY

CHILTON'S FUEL ECONOMY & TUNE-UP TIPS

Fuel economy is important to everyone, no matter what kind of vehicle you drive. The maintenance-minded motorist can save both money and fuel using these tips and the periodic maintenance and tune-up procedures in this Repair and Tune-Up Guide.

There are more than 130,000,000 cars and trucks registered for private use in the United States. Each travels an average of 10-12,000 miles per year, and, and in total they consume close to 70 billion gallons of fuel each year. This represents nearly ⅔ of the oil imported by the United States each year. The Federal government's goal is to reduce consumption 10% by 1985. A variety of methods are either already in use or under serious consideration, and they all affect you driving and the cars you will drive. In addition to "down-sizing", the auto industry is using or investigating the use of electronic fuel delivery, electronic engine controls and alternative engines for use in smaller and lighter vehicles, among other alternatives to meet the federally mandated Corporate Average Fuel Economy (CAFE) of 27.5 mpg by 1985. The government, for its part, is considering rationing, mandatory driving curtailments and tax increases on motor vehicle fuel in an effort to reduce consumption. The government's goal of a 10% reduction could be realized — and further government regulation avoided — if every private vehicle could use just 1 less gallon of fuel per week.

How Much Can You Save?

Tests have proven that almost anyone can make at least a 10% reduction in fuel consumption through regular maintenance and tune-ups. When a major manufacturer of spark plugs sur-

---

TUNE-UP

1. Check the cylinder compression to be sure the engine will really benefit from a tune-up and that it is capable of producing good fuel economy. A tune-up will be wasted on an engine in poor mechanical condition.

2. Replace spark plugs regularly. New spark plugs alone can increase fuel economy 3%.

3. Be sure the spark plugs are the correct type (heat range) for your vehicle. See the Tune-Up Specifications.

Heat range refers to the spark plug's ability to conduct heat away from the firing end. It must conduct the heat away in an even pattern to avoid becoming a source of pre-ignition, yet it must also operate hot enough to burn off conductive deposits that could cause misfiring.

The heat range is usually indicated by a number on the spark plug, part of the manufacturer's designation for each individual spark plug. The numbers in bold-face indicate the heat range in each manufacturer's identification system.

Manufacturer	Typical Designation
AC	R **45** TS
Bosch (old)	WA **145** T30
Bosch (new)	HR **8** Y
Champion	RBL **15** Y
Fram/Autolite	4**15**
Mopar	P-**62** PR
Motorcraft	BRF-**42**
NGK	BP **5** ES-15
Nippondenso	W **16** EP
Prestolite	14GR **5** 2A

Periodically, check the spark plugs to be sure they are firing efficiently. They are excellent indicators of the internal condition of your engine.

On AC, Bosch (new), Champion, Fram/Autolite, Mopar, Motorcraft and Prestolite, a higher number indicates a hotter plug. On Bosch (old), NGK and Nippondenso, a higher number indicates a colder plug.

4. Make sure the spark plugs are properly gapped. See the Tune-Up Specifications in this book.

5. Be sure the spark plugs are firing efficiently. The illustrations on the next 2 pages show you how to "read" the firing end of the spark plug.

6. Check the ignition timing and set it to specifications. Tests show that almost all cars have incorrect ignition timing by more than 2°.

veyed over 6,000 cars nationwide, they found that a tune-up, on cars that needed one, increased fuel economy over 11%. Replacing worn plugs alone, accounted for a 3% increase. The same test also revealed that 8 out of every 10 vehicles will have some maintenance deficiency that will directly affect fuel economy, emissions or performance. Most of this mileage-robbing neglect could be prevented with regular maintenance.

Modern engines require that all of the functioning systems operate properly for maximum efficiency. A malfunction anywhere wastes fuel. You can keep your vehicle running as efficiently and economically as possible, by being aware of your vehicle's operating and performance characteristics. If your vehicle suddenly develops performance or fuel economy problems it could be due to one or more of the following:

PROBLEM	POSSIBLE CAUSE
Engine Idles Rough	Ignition timing, idle mixture, vacuum leak or something amiss in the emission control system.
Hesitates on Acceleration	Dirty carburetor or fuel filter, improper accelerator pump setting, ignition timing or fouled spark plugs.
Starts Hard or Fails to Start	Worn spark plugs, improperly set automatic choke, ice (or water) in fuel system.
Stalls Frequently	Automatic choke improperly adjusted and possible dirty air filter or fuel filter.
Performs Sluggishly	Worn spark plugs, dirty fuel or air filter, ignition timing or automatic choke out of adjustment.

Check spark plug wires on conventional point type ignition for cracks by bending them in a loop around your finger.

Be sure that spark plug wires leading to adjacent cylinders do not run too close together. (Photo courtesy Champion Spark Plug Co.)

7. If your vehicle does not have electronic ignition, check the points, rotor and cap as specified.

8. Check the spark plug wires (used with conventional point-type ignitions) for cracks and burned or broken insulation by bending them in a loop around your finger. Cracked wires decrease fuel efficiency by failing to deliver full voltage to the spark plugs. One misfiring spark plug can cost you as much as 2 mpg.

9. Check the routing of the plug wires. Misfiring can be the result of spark plug leads to adjacent cylinders running parallel to each other and too close together. One wire tends to pick up voltage from the other causing it to fire "out of time".

10. Check all electrical and ignition circuits for voltage drop and resistance.

11. Check the distributor mechanical and/or vacuum advance mechanisms for proper functioning. The vacuum advance can be checked by twisting the distributor plate in the opposite direction of rotation. It should spring back when released.

12. Check and adjust the valve clearance on engines with mechanical lifters. The clearance should be slightly loose rather than too tight.

SPARK PLUG DIAGNOSIS

Normal

APPEARANCE: This plug is typical of one operating normally. The insulator nose varies from a light tan to grayish color with slight electrode wear. The presence of slight deposits is normal on used plugs and will have no adverse effect on engine performance. The spark plug heat range is correct for the engine and the engine is running normally.

CAUSE: Properly running engine.

RECOMMENDATION: Before reinstalling this plug, the electrodes should be cleaned and filed square. Set the gap to specifications. If the plug has been in service for more than 10-12,000 miles, the entire set should probably be replaced with a fresh set of the same heat range.

Oil Deposits

APPEARANCE: The firing end of the plug is covered with a wet, oily coating.

CAUSE: The problem is poor oil control. On high mileage engines, oil is leaking past the rings or valve guides into the combustion chamber. A common cause is also a plugged PCV valve, and a ruptured fuel pump diaphragm can also cause this condition. Oil fouled plugs such as these are often found in new or recently overhauled engines, before normal oil control is achieved, and can be cleaned and reinstalled.

RECOMMENDATION: A hotter spark plug may temporarily relieve the problem, but the engine is probably in need of work.

Incorrect Heat Range

APPEARANCE: The effects of high temperature on a spark plug are indicated by clean white, often blistered insulator. This can also be accompanied by excessive wear of the electrode, and the absence of deposits.

CAUSE: Check for the correct spark plug heat range. A plug which is too hot for the engine can result in overheating. A car operated mostly at high speeds can require a colder plug. Also check ignition timing, cooling system level, fuel mixture and leaking intake manifold.

RECOMMENDATION: If all ignition and engine adjustments are known to be correct, and no other malfunction exists, install spark plugs one heat range colder.

Carbon Deposits

APPEARANCE: Carbon fouling is easily identified by the presence of dry, soft, black, sooty deposits.

CAUSE: Changing the heat range can often lead to carbon fouling, as can prolonged slow, stop-and-start driving. If the heat range is correct, carbon fouling can be attributed to a rich fuel mixture, sticking choke, clogged air cleaner, worn breaker points, retarded timing or low compression. If only one or two plugs are carbon fouled, check for corroded or cracked wires on the affected plugs. Also look for cracks in the distributor cap between the towers of affected cylinders.

RECOMMENDATION: After the problem is corrected, these plugs can be cleaned and reinstalled if not worn severely.

MMT Fouled

APPEARANCE: Spark plugs fouled by MMT (Methycyclopentadienyl Maganese Tricarbonyl) have reddish, rusty appearance on the insulator and side electrode.

CAUSE: MMT is an anti-knock additive in gasoline used to replace lead. During the combustion process, the MMT leaves a reddish deposit on the insulator and side electrode.

RECOMMENDATION: No engine malfunction is indicated and the deposits will not affect plug performance any more than lead deposits (see Ash Deposits). MMT fouled plugs can be cleaned, regapped and reinstalled.

High Speed Glazing

APPEARANCE: Glazing appears as shiny coating on the plug, either yellow or tan in color.

CAUSE: During hard, fast acceleration, plug temperatures rise suddenly. Deposits from normal combustion have no chance to fluff-off; instead, they melt on the insulator forming an electrically conductive coating which causes misfiring.

RECOMMENDATION: Glazed plugs are not easily cleaned. They should be replaced with a fresh set of plugs of the correct heat range. If the condition recurs, using plugs with a heat range one step colder may cure the problem.

Ash (Lead) Deposits

APPEARANCE: Ash deposits are characterized by light brown or white colored deposits crusted on the side or center electrodes. In some cases it may give the plug a rusty appearance.

CAUSE: Ash deposits are normally derived from oil or fuel additives burned during normal combustion. Normally they are harmless, though excessive amounts can cause misfiring. If deposits are excessive in short mileage, the valve guides may be worn.

RECOMMENDATION: Ash-fouled plugs can be cleaned, gapped and reinstalled.

Detonation

APPEARANCE: Detonation is usually characterized by a broken plug insulator.

CAUSE: A portion of the fuel charge will begin to burn spontaneously, from the increased heat following ignition. The explosion that results applies extreme pressure to engine components, frequently damaging spark plugs and pistons.

Detonation can result by over-advanced ignition timing, inferior gasoline (low octane) lean air/fuel mixture, poor carburetion, engine lugging or an increase in compression ratio due to combustion chamber deposits or engine modification.

RECOMMENDATION: Replace the plugs after correcting the problem.

EMISSION CONTROLS

13. Be aware of the general condition of the emission control system. It contributes to reduced pollution and should be serviced regularly to maintain efficient engine operation.

14. Check all vacuum lines for dried, cracked or brittle conditions. Something as simple as a leaking vacuum hose can cause poor performance and loss of economy.

15. Avoid tampering with the emission control system. Attempting to improve fuel econ-

FUEL SYSTEM

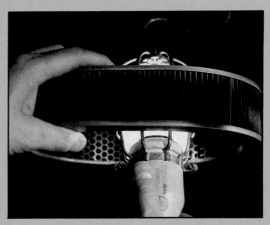

Check the air filter with a light behind it. If you can see light through the filter it can be reused.

Extremely clogged filters should be discarded and replaced with a new one.

18. Replace the air filter regularly. A dirty air filter richens the air/fuel mixture and can increase fuel consumption as much as 10%. Tests show that ⅓ of all vehicles have air filters in need of replacement.

19. Replace the fuel filter at least as often as recommended.

20. Set the idle speed and carburetor mixture to specifications.

21. Check the automatic choke. A sticking or malfunctioning choke wastes gas.

22. During the summer months, adjust the automatic choke for a leaner mixture which will produce faster engine warm-ups.

COOLING SYSTEM

29. Be sure all accessory drive belts are in good condition. Check for cracks or wear.

30. Adjust all accessory drive belts to proper tension.

31. Check all hoses for swollen areas, worn spots, or loose clamps.

32. Check coolant level in the radiator or expansion tank.

33. Be sure the thermostat is operating properly. A stuck thermostat delays engine warm-up and a cold engine uses nearly twice as much fuel as a warm engine.

34. Drain and replace the engine coolant at least as often as recommended. Rust and scale

TIRES & WHEELS

38. Check the tire pressure often with a pencil type gauge. Tests by a major tire manufacturer show that 90% of all vehicles have at least 1 tire improperly inflated. Better mileage can be achieved by over-inflating tires, but never exceed the maximum inflation pressure on the side of the tire.

39. If possible, install radial tires. Radial tires deliver as much as ½ mpg more than bias belted tires.

40. Avoid installing super-wide tires. They only create extra rolling resistance and decrease fuel mileage. Stick to the manufacturer's recommendations.

41. Have the wheels properly balanced.

omy by tampering with emission controls is more likely to worsen fuel economy than improve it. Emission control changes on modern engines are not readily reversible.

16. Clean (or replace) the EGR valve and lines as recommended.

17. Be sure that all vacuum lines and hoses are reconnected properly after working under the hood. An unconnected or misrouted vacuum line can wreak havoc with engine performance.

23. Check for fuel leaks at the carburetor, fuel pump, fuel lines and fuel tank. Be sure all lines and connections are tight.

24. Periodically check the tightness of the carburetor and intake manifold attaching nuts and bolts. These are a common place for vacuum leaks to occur.

25. Clean the carburetor periodically and lubricate the linkage.

26. The condition of the tailpipe can be an excellent indicator of proper engine combustion. After a long drive at highway speeds, the inside of the tailpipe should be a light grey in color. Black or soot on the insides indicates an overly rich mixture.

27. Check the fuel pump pressure. The fuel pump may be supplying more fuel than the engine needs.

28. Use the proper grade of gasoline for your engine. Don't try to compensate for knocking or "pinging" by advancing the ignition timing. This practice will only increase plug temperature and the chances of detonation or pre-ignition with relatively little performance gain.

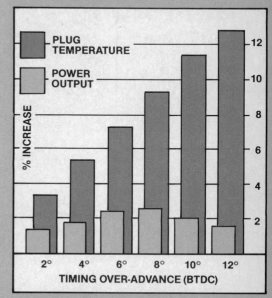

Increasing ignition timing past the specified setting results in a drastic increase in spark plug temperature with increased chance of detonation or preignition. Performance increase is considerably less. (Photo courtesy Champion Spark Plug Co.)

that form in the engine should be flushed out to allow the engine to operate at peak efficiency.

35. Clean the radiator of debris that can decrease cooling efficiency.

36. Install a flex-type or electric cooling fan, if you don't have a clutch type fan. Flex fans use curved plastic blades to push more air at low speeds when more cooling is needed; at high speeds the blades flatten out for less resistance. Electric fans only run when the engine temperature reaches a predetermined level.

37. Check the radiator cap for a worn or cracked gasket. If the cap does not seal properly, the cooling system will not function properly.

42. Be sure the front end is correctly aligned. A misaligned front end actually has wheels going in differed directions. The increased drag can reduce fuel economy by .3 mpg.

43. Correctly adjust the wheel bearings. Wheel bearings that are adjusted too tight increase rolling resistance.

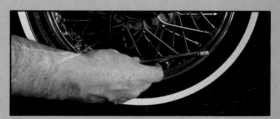

Check tire pressures regularly with a reliable pocket type gauge. Be sure to check the pressure on a cold tire.

GENERAL MAINTENANCE

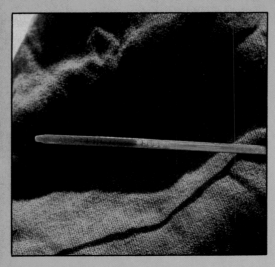

Check the fluid levels (particularly engine oil) on a regular basis. Be sure to check the oil for grit, water or other contamination.

A vacuum gauge is another excellent indicator of internal engine condition and can also be installed in the dash as a mileage indicator.

44. Periodically check the fluid levels in the engine, power steering pump, master cylinder, automatic transmission and drive axle.

45. Change the oil at the recommended interval and change the filter at every oil change. Dirty oil is thick and causes extra friction between moving parts, cutting efficiency and increasing wear. A worn engine requires more frequent tune-ups and gets progressively worse fuel economy. In general, use the lightest viscosity oil for the driving conditions you will encounter.

46. Use the recommended viscosity fluids in the transmission and axle.

47. Be sure the battery is fully charged for fast starts. A slow starting engine wastes fuel.

48. Be sure battery terminals are clean and tight.

49. Check the battery electrolyte level and add distilled water if necessary.

50. Check the exhaust system for crushed pipes, blockages and leaks.

51. Adjust the brakes. Dragging brakes or brakes that are not releasing create increased drag on the engine.

52. Install a vacuum gauge or miles-per-gallon gauge. These gauges visually indicate engine vacuum in the intake manifold. High vacuum = good mileage and low vacuum = poorer mileage. The gauge can also be an excellent indicator of internal engine conditions.

53. Be sure the clutch is properly adjusted. A slipping clutch wastes fuel.

54. Check and periodically lubricate the heat control valve in the exhaust manifold. A sticking or inoperative valve prevents engine warm-up and wastes gas.

55. Keep accurate records to check fuel economy over a period of time. A sudden drop in fuel economy may signal a need for tune-up or other maintenance.

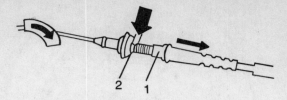

Positioning the throttle cable

the adjusting nut to hold the cable in this position and tighten the locknut.

Scirocco 16 Valve

On the 16 valve engine, the accelerator cable is adjusted by moving the retainer clip on the notched cable housing. The cable is properly adjusted when the gas pedal is fully depressed, there is about 1mm (0.039 in.) of play before contacting the stop at the wide open throttle position.

Quantum 5 Cylinder

If the linkage is out of adjustment, the transmission will shift poorly. The adjustment is correct when the throttle valve and transmission operating lever rest against the stop in the idle position. If not, adjust as follows.

1. Remove the circlips at the ball sockets.
2. Remove the pushrod at the ball pin.
3. Move the throttle linkage against the idle stop, then push the linkage against the bracket stop.
4. Adjust the length of the pushrod so that the ball socket will drop onto the ball without moving the linkage off the stop or tensioning the cable.
5. Install the ball socket circlips.

1985–90 Golf, Jetta and GTI w/Automatic Transmissions

1. Warm up the engine to normal operating temperature, then shut it off.
2. Place the shifter lever in the **P** position.
3. Loosen the accelerator pedal adjustment nut and set the cable off to the side.
4. Loosen the nuts on the cable jacket.
5. Pull the cable jacket out until all play is removed from the cable. While doing this the throttle plates must remain closed and the transmission linkage must stay in the no-throttle position.
6. When all the play is removed, tighten the jacket nuts.
7. Connect the accelerator cable and have an assistant depress the gas pedal all the way down.

8. Turn the cable adjusting nut until the transmission accelerator linkage contacts the kick-down stop. Tighten the cable locknut.

1985–90 Golf, Jetta and GTI w/Manual Transmissions and Fox

To check the throttle cable adjustment, have an assistant press the gas pedal all the way to the floor. Open the hood and make sure the throttle valve just reaches the full throttle position. There should be approximately 1mm (0.04 in.) clearance between the throttle valve and the throttle valve stop. If not, adjust the throttle cable as follows:

1. Pull the throttle cable adjusting grommet out of the adjusting bracket.
2. Remove the positioning clip until the throttle valve just reaches the full throttle position.
3. Install the positioning clip.
4. Push the grommet back into the retaining bracket. Re-check the gap and adjust as necessary.

NOTE: *Remember, if there is no play in the cable the throttle lever will bottom out and stretch the cable. If there is too much play, transmission performance will be reduced.*

Passat w/Manual Transmission

To check the throttle cable adjustment, have an assistant press the gas pedal all the way to the floor. Open the hood and make sure the throttle valve just reaches the full throttle position. There should be approximately 1mm (0.04 in.) clearance between the throttle valve and the throttle valve stop. If not, adjust the throttle cable as follows:

1. Remove the retaining clip from the cable adjuster.
2. Slide the adjuster back and forth until the gap between the throttle valve and the throttle valve stop is 1mm (0.04 in.).
3. Install the clip in the groove closest to the grommet.
4. Re-check the gap and adjust as necessary.

NOTE: *Remember, if there is no play in the cable the throttle lever will bottom out and stretch the cable. If there is too much play, transmission performance will be reduced.*

Passat w/Automatic Transmission

NOTE: *This adjustment requires a 15mm spacer, special VW adapter kit 1594, an ohmmeter and an assistant.*

1. Place the 15mm spacer between the accelerator pedal and the pedal stop.

2. Have an assistant press the gas pedal down all the way and hold it there.

3. Open the throttle by pulling on the accelerator cable sleeve and move the retaining clip to hold it in this position.

4. Connect the kick-down switch adapter (from VW kit 1594) to the kick-down switch connector and connect the ohmmeter to the adapter. The ohmmeter should read infinity.

5. Have the assistant slowly press the gas pedal until the throttle is in the fully open position. The ohmmeter should read 0Ω and the accelerator pedal should be just about to make contact with the pedal stop.

Fuel Distributor
REMOVAL AND INSTALLATION

1. Release the pressure in the system by loosening the fuel line on the control pressure regulator (large connector). Have a rag ready to catch the fuel that escapes.

2. Mark the fuel lines in the top of the distributor so that you will be able to put them back in their correct positions.

NOTE: *Using different colored paints is usually a good marking device. When you mark each line, be sure to mark the spot where it connects to the distributor.*

3. Clean the fuel lines, then remove them from the distributor. Remove the little looped wire plug (the CO adjusting screw plug). Remove the two retaining screws in the top of the distributor.

NOTE: *When removing the fuel distributor be sure the control plunger does not fall out from underneath.*

4. If the control plunger has been removed, moisten it with gasoline before installing. The small shoulder on the plunger is inserted first.

NOTE: *Always use new gaskets and O-ring when removing and installing fuel distributor. Lock all retaining screws with Loctite® or its equivalent.*

DIESEL FUEL SYSTEM

The diesel fuel system is an extremely complex and sensitive system. Very few repairs or adjustments are possible by the owner. Any service other than that listed here should be referred to an authorized VW dealer or diesel specialist. Injection pump repair requires experience, very expensive calibration/test equipment and a large number of special tools. This type of work should be referred to a shop that specializes in diesel engine injection pump overhaul.

Any work done to the diesel fuel injection should be done with absolute cleanliness. Even

Diesel engine fuel injector (do not disassemble)

the smallest specks of dirt will have a disastrous effect on the injection system.

Do not attempt to remove the fuel injectors. They are very delicate and must be removed with a special tool to prevent damage. The fuel in the system is also under tremendous pressure (1700–1850 psi), so it's not wise to loosen any lines with the engine running. Exposing your skin to the spray from the injector at working pressure can cause fuel to penetrate the skin.

REMOVAL AND INSTALLATION

1. Loosen the injector lines using line wrench 3035 or equivalent.

NOTE: *Remove the injector lines as a complete set. DO NOT attempt to bend or alter the configuration of the lines in any way. These lines are pre-formed for precise flow.*

2. Remove the injectors from the cylinder head using special VW socket SW 27 or its equivalent.

3. Next, remove the injector heat shields from the cylinder head. This should be done as part of an injector replacement.

4. Install the new heat shields into the head as shown in the illustration.

5. Install the injectors into the head and torque to 51 ft. lbs.

6. Connect the injector lines and torque the line nuts to 18 ft. lbs.

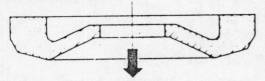

Diesel engine heat shield installation

Injection Pump

REMOVAL AND INSTALLATION

1. Remove the timing belt cover(s).

2. Remove the cylinder head cover and the plug cover on top of the bell housing.

3. Turn the crankshaft to place the No. 1 cylinder on TDC of the compression stroke (the TDC mark on the flywheel must align with the pointer).

4. Loosen the camshaft nut and tap the back of the camshaft sprocket with a rubber mallet until it is loose, then remove the sprocket.

5. Fasten the setting bar tool VW–2065A or equivalent to the end of the camshaft. Turn the camshaft until 1 end of the bar touches the cylinder head. Using a feeler gauge, measure the clearance at the other end. Using 2 feeler gauges of half of the acquired measurement, insert them between each end of the bar and the cylinder head.

6. Loosen the tensioner pulley and remove the timing belt from the engine.

7. Loosen the shaft nut from the injection pump sprocket.

8. Install the sprocket puller tool VW–3032 or equivalent and apply tension to the injection pump sprocket.

9. Using a light hammer, strike the puller spindle head with a few light blows to loosen the sprocket from the tapered shaft.

10. Remove the injection pump shaft nut and the sprocket.

11. Using a line nut wrench tool VW–3035 or equivalent, disconnect the fuel lines from the injection pump and cover the openings with a clean cloth.

CAUTION: *To avoid damaging the injection pump plunger, DO NOT loosen the bolts on the fuel distributor head.*

12. Disconnect the fuel cut-off valve, the accelerator and the cold start cables from the injection pump.

13. Remove the injection pump to mounting bracket bolts and the injection pump from the engine.

14. Set the injection timing (align the mark on top of the injection pump with the mark on the mounting plate) and reverse the removal procedures. Torque the injection pump mounting bolts to 18 ft. lbs., the injection pump sprocket nut to 33 ft. lbs. and the fuel injection line nuts to pump to 18 ft. lbs.

NOTE: *When installing the fuel supply and the return pipe union screws, DO NOT interchange them; the return pipe union screw is marked with OUT on the head.*

INJECTION PUMP TIMING

1. Remove the timing belt.

2. Turn the crankshaft to place the No. 1 cyl on TDC of the compression stroke (the TDC mark on the flywheel must align with the pointer).

NOTE: *The cold start cable MUST NOT be pulled in (the actuation lever on the injection pump must be in NEUTRAL).*

3. Turn the injection pump sprocket so that the mark on the sprocket is aligned with the mark on the mounting plate.

4. Using the pin tool 2064, insert it through the sprocket hole, locking the sprocket to the injection pump.

5. Loosen the camshaft nut and tap the back of the camshaft sprocket with a rubber mallet until it is loose, then remove the sprocket.

6. Fasten the setting bar tool VW–2065A or equivalent to the end of the camshaft. Turn the camshaft until the end of the bar touches the cylinder head. Using a feeler gauge, measure the clearance at the other end. Using 2 feeler gauges of half of the acquired measurement, insert them between each end of the bar and the cylinder head.

7. Install the camshaft sprocket, torque the sprocket nut to 33 ft. lbs. (45 Nm) and remove the setting bar tool.

8. Install the timing belt and remove the lock pin tool from the injection pump sprocket.

9. Tension the drive belt by turning the tensioner pulley clockwise until belt flex of 13mm ($^1/_2$ in.) is established between the camshaft and the pump sprockets.

10. Turn the crankshaft 2 complete revolutions and check the belt tension.

NOTE: *It may be necessary to strike the timing belt between the camshaft and the pump sprockets with a rubber mallet to eliminate the play in the drive belt.*

11. Remove the sealing plug on the injection pump head, then install the adapter tool VW–2066 or equivalent and a dial micrometer (preload the micrometer to 2.5mm).

12. Slowly turn the engine counterclockwise until the dial gauge stops moving, then zero the micrometer.

13. Turn the engine clockwise until the TDC mark on the flywheel aligns with the pointer on the bell housing.

NOTE: *The adjusting value is 0.90–0.95mm (0.036–0.038 in.) for the diesel engine or 0.95–1.00mm (0.038–0.040 in.) for the turbodiesel.*

14. If adjustment of the pump is necessary, loosen the two upper mounting bolts, the rear support bolt and the lower front bolt through the sprocket, then turn the pump until the correct value is reached.

15. To complete the installation, reverse the removal procedures. Torque the pump cover plug to 11 ft. lbs. Check the delivery rate, the idle and the maximum speeds.

Adjustments

ACCELERATOR CABLE ADJUSTMENT

The ball pin on the pump lever should be pointing up and be aligned with the mark in the slot. The accelerator cable should be attached at the upper hole in the bracket. With the pedal in the full throttle position, adjust the cable so that the pump lever contacts the stop with no binding or strain.

COLD START CABLE ADJUSTMENT

When the cold start knob on the dash is pulled out, the fuel injection pump timing is advanced 2.5°. This improves cold starting and running until the engine warms up.

1. Insert the washer on the cable.
2. Insert the cable in the bracket with the rubber bushing. Install the cable in the pin.
3. Install the lockwasher.
4. Move the lever to the zero position (direction of arrow). Pull the inner cable tight and tighten the clamp screw.

Glow Plugs

See Chapter 3, under the "Engine Electrical" section for glow plug testing, removal and installation.

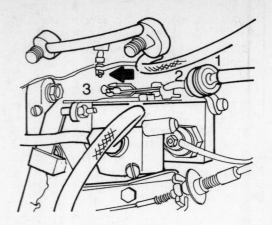

Cold start cable adjustment

FUEL TANK

REMOVAL AND INSTALLATION

Rabbit (Except Pick-up), Golf, GTI, 1975–84 Scirocco and Jetta

1. Disconnect the battery.
2. Remove the drain plug and empty the tank. Disconnect the remove fuel pump if removal of the pump is necessary to gain clearance to remove the tank.
3. Disconnect the parking brake cables at the parking brake lever.
4. If required, disconnect and plug the rear brake lines.
5. If required, remove the rear axle mounting nuts and pull the rear axle down.
6. Disconnect the sending unit ground wire, gauge wire and transfer pump wiring.
7. Loosen the clamps and pull off the fuel line(s).

NOTE: *If more than one fuel line attaches to the sending unit, mark the lines to avoid confusion when assembly.*

8. Disconnect any other breather lines. Disconnect the filler pipe.
9. Remove the rubber exhaust hangers if they hinder removal of the fuel tank.
10. Remove the fuel tank straps and allow the tank to come down far enough to see if there are any other vent hoses to be disconnected.
11. After removing all vent hoses, remove the tank.

NOTE: *Many earlier models do not have these vent lines.*

To install:

12. Raise and support the tank. If you have to connect any vent lines, do so at this time, before securing the tank straps. Make sure that all breather and vent lines are not kinked. Use new clamps on all connections

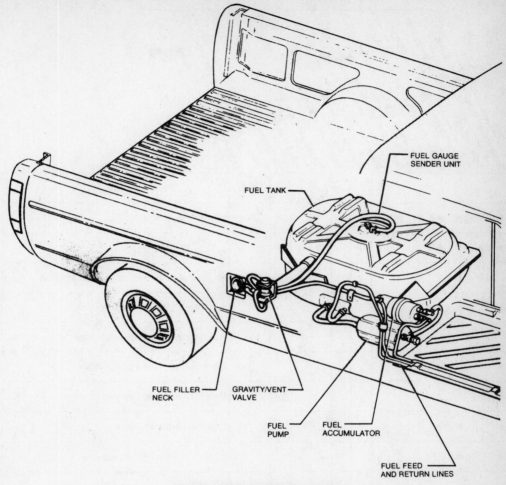

FUEL GAUGE
SENDER UNIT

FUEL TANK

FUEL FILLER
NECK

GRAVITY/VENT
VALVE

FUEL
PUMP

FUEL
ACCUMULATOR

FUEL FEED
AND RETURN LINES

Rabbit pickup fuel tank assembly

13. Install the rubber exhaust hangers, if they were removed.

14. Connect the filler pipe and any breather lines.

15. Connect the fuel lines. Use new clamps on all connections.

16. Connect the transfer pump, gauge and sending unit wires.

17. Install the rear axle and tighten the rear axle nut to specification.

18. Connect the rear brake lines and bleed the brakes.

19. Connect the parking brake cables to the lever and adjust.

20. Install the fuel pump.

21. Install the drain plug and fill the tank.

22. Connect the negative battery cable.

Rabbit Pick-up

The fuel tank is located to the rear of the cab.

1. Disconnect the battery.

2. Drain the fuel from the tank using a conventional siphon.

3. Remove and match mark all hoses from the tank, except for the breather hose in the sending unit.

4. Remove the wires from the sending unit.

5. Loosen the straps holding the tank and unhook them from their brackets.

6. Lower the tank and unhook the vent hose in the sending unit.

7. Remove the fuel tank.

8. To install, raise and support the tank. Connect the vent hose and the sending unit wire. Connect and tighten the tank straps.

9. Connect the sending unit wires.

10. Connect the hoses to the tank.

11. Fill the tank and connect the negative battery cable.

Dasher and Quantum

1. Disconnect the negative battery cable.

Engine does not start or starts poorly when cold	Engine does not start or starts poorly when warm	Irregular idle (engine shakes) when warm	Irregular idle (engine shakes) during warm-up	Engine idle (engine shakes) with engine warm	Engine does not draw fuel smoothly (backfires)	Insufficient power	Engine runs on (diesels)	Excessive fuel consumption	Flat spot during acceleration	Idle CO value too high	Idle CO value too low	Idle speed cannot be adjusted (too high)	Engine stalls immediately after starting	Cause(s)
▶	▶	▶	▶		▶			▶			▶			Vacuum system leaking
▶	▶		▶					▶	▶	▶	▶			Air flow sensor plate and/or control plunger not moving smoothly
▶							▶							Air flow sensor plate stop incorrectly set
▶			▶											Auxiliary air valve does not open
												▶		Auxiliary air valve does not close
▶	▶			▶									▶	Electric fuel pump not operating
▶														Defective cold start system
		▶	▶				▶	▶		▶				Leaking cold start valve
▶			▶											Incorrect cold control pressure
	▶		▶	▶	▶	▶			▶				▶	Warm control pressure too high
		▶	▶		▶			▶	▶	▶			▶	Warm control pressure too low
			▶	▶					▶				▶	Incorrect system pressure
	▶													Fuel system pressure leakage
▶	▶	▶			▶			▶						Injection valve(s) leaking, opening pressure too low
		▶	▶			▶			▶					Unequal fuel delivery between cylinders
▶	▶	▶	▶					▶	▶	▶	▶	▶		Basic idle and/or CO adjustment incorrect
						▶								Throttle plate does not open completely

2. Remove the trunk floor mat.

3. Drain the fuel tank.

4. Disconnect and label the fuel and over-flow lines.

5. Disconnect the electrical plugs from the fuel tank gauge sending unit.

6. Detach the vent line from the tank.

7. Remove all the retaining bolts from the trunk floor.

8. Detach the filler tube from the tank filler neck and lower the tank.

To install:

9. Raise and support the tank. Connect the filler tube to the filler neck.

10. Install the trunk floor retaining bolts.

11. Connect the vent line to the tank.

12. Connect the fuel tank gauge sending unit wiring.

13. Connect the fuel lines. Use new clamps.

14. Install the trunk floor mat.

15. Fill the tank and connect the negative battery cable.

16. Reseal the edge of the lower trunk floor to prevent leaks.

Fox

1. Disconnect the negative battery cable.

2. Remove the luggage compartment cover.

3. Remove the access cover to the fuel gauge sending unit.

4. Disconnect the supply line to the main fuel pump.

5. Disconnect the return line to the fuel tank.

6. Unplug the fuel gauge and transfer pump connectors.

7. Using VW tool US 2021A or equivalent spanner, unscrew the fuel gauge sending unit from the tank.

8. Siphon the fuel from the fuel gauge sending unit opening.

9. Raise the rear of the vehicle and support safely.

10. Place a support or stand under the fuel tank.

11. Remove the clamp that connects the filler pipe to the tank.

12. Remove the fuel tank strap nuts.

13. Work the filler pipe hose from the tank.

14. Disconnect the breather hoses and lower the tank.

To install:

15. Raise and support the tank, while connecting the breather hoses. Use new hose clamps as required.

16. Connect the filler pipe hose to the tank.

17. Lower the vehicle.

18. Screw the fuel gauge sending unit into the tank.

19. Plug in the fuel gauge and transfer pump connectors.

20. Connect the fuel tank return and fuel pump supply lines.

21. Install the fuel gauge sending unit access cover.

22. Install the luggage compartment cover.

23. Fill the tank and connect the negative battery cable.

1985–90 Scirocco and Cabriolet

1. Disconnect the negative battery cable and drain the fuel tank.

2. Remove the rear right wheel housing cover.

3. Disconnect the large breather hose from the filler neck.

4. Pull the gravity valve down leaving the hoses connected.

5. Unbolt the fuel pump bracket from the body and lower the pump.

6. Remove the fuel tank screw.

7. Disconnect the fuel pump hose and pull the blue hose from the return line.

8. Disconnect the brake hoses from both sides of the rear axle and plug them.

9. Disconnect the rear axle from both sides of the body and allow it to swing down and rest on the handbrake cable guides.

10. Unhook the rear muffler support lugs.

11. Disconnect the filler hose from the tank.

12. Support the tank, remove the tank fasteners and lower the tank enough to disconnect the fuel gauge sending unit wires and breather hoses.

13. Remove the fuel tank.

To install:

NOTE: *If installing a new or used tank, make of note of where the old foam strips were installed and install new foam strips on the replacement tank in the same locations.*

14. Raise and support tank. Connect the small breather hoses and fuel gauge sending unit wires. Install the tank fasteners.

NOTE: *When connecting the breather hoses, position the hose clips so that they do not make contact with the body.*

15. Connect the filler hose to the tank and connect the rear muffler support lugs.

16. Raise the rear axle off the handbrake cable guides and install.

17. Connect the brake hoses and bleed the brakes.

18. Connect the return line and fuel pump hose.

19. Install the fuel tank screw.

20. Raise the fuel pump and attach the fuel pump bracket to the body.

21. Put the gravity valve back into its original (raised) position.

22. Connect the large breather hose to the filler neck.

NOTE: *When connecting the breather hose, position the hose clip so that it does not make contact with the body.*

23. Install the right rear wheel housing cover.

24. Fill the tank and connect the negative battery cable.

Corrado and Passat

1. Disconnect the negative battery cable.

2. Remove the luggage compartment cover.

3. Remove the access cover to the fuel gauge sending unit.

4. Disconnect all fuel lines from the tank.

5. Unplug the fuel gauge and transfer pump connectors.

6. Using VW tool US 2021A or equivalent spanner, unscrew the threaded retainer from the fuel gauge sending unit and remove the unit from the tank.

7. Siphon the fuel from the fuel gauge sending unit opening.

8. Raise the rear of the vehicle and support safely.

9. Place a support or stand under the fuel tank.

10. Remove the clamp that connects the filler pipe to the tank.

11. Remove the fuel tank strap nuts.

12. Work the filler pipe hose from the tank.

13. Disconnect the breather hoses and lower the tank.

To install:

14. Raise and support the tank, while connecting the breather hoses. Use new hose clamps as required. If spring clamps are used, always use new clamps.

15. Connect the filler pipe hose to the tank.

16. Lower the vehicle.

17. Install the fuel gauge sending unit into the tank making sure that the arrow on the top of the tank is aligned with the matchmark on the unit. Use a new sealing ring and lubricate it with clean engine oil prior to installatiom.

18. Plug in the fuel gauge and transfer pump connectors.

19. Connect the fuel hoses.

20. Install the fuel gauge sending unit access cover.

21. Install the luggage compartment cover.

22. Fill the tank and connect the negative battery cable.

Chassis Electrical

UNDERSTANDING AND TROUBLESHOOTING ELECTRICAL SYSTEMS

With the rate at which both import and domestic manufacturers are incorporating electronic control systems into their production lines, it won't be long before every new vehicle is equipped with one or more on-board computer. These electronic components (with no moving parts) should theoretically last the life of the vehicle, provided nothing external happens to damage the circuits or memory chips.

While it is true that electronic components should never wear out, in the real world malfunctions do occur. It is also true that any computer-based system is extremely sensitive to electrical voltages and can not tolerate careless or haphazard testing or service procedures. An inexperienced individual can literally do major damage looking for a minor problem by using the wrong kind of test equipment or connecting test leads or connectors with the ignition switch ON. When selecting test equipment, make sure the manufacturers instructions state that the tester is compatible with whatever type of electronic control system is being serviced. Read all instructions carefully and double check all test points before installing probes or making any test connections.

The following section outlines basic diagnosis techniques for dealing with computerized automotive control systems. Along with a general explanation of the various types of test equipment available to aid in servicing modern electronic automotive systems, basic repair techniques for wiring harnesses and connectors is given. Read the basic information before attempting any repairs or testing on any computerized system, to provide the background of information necessary to avoid the most common and obvious mistakes that can cost both time and money. Although the replacement and testing procedures are simple in themselves, the systems are not, and unless one has a thorough understanding of all components and their function within a particular computerized control system, the logical test sequence these systems demand can not be followed. Minor malfunctions can make a big difference, so it is important to know how each component affects the operation of the overall electronic system to find the ultimate cause of a problem without replacing good components unnecessarily. It is not enough to use the correct test equipment; the test equipment must be used correctly.

Safety Precautions

CAUTION: *Whenever working on or around any computer based microprocessor control system, always observe these general precautions to prevent the possibility of personal injury or damage to electronic components.*

• Never install or remove battery cables with the key ON or the engine running. Jumper cables should be connected with the key OFF to avoid power surges that can damage electronic control units. Engines equipped with computer controlled systems should avoid both giving and getting jump starts due to the possibility of serious damage to components from arcing in the engine compartment when connections are made with the ignition ON.

• Always remove the battery cables before charging the battery. Never use a high output charger on an installed battery or attempt to use any type of "hot shot" (24 volt) starting aid.

• Exercise care when inserting test probes into connectors to insure good connections without damaging the connector or spreading the pins. Always probe connectors from the rear (wire) side, NOT the pin side, to avoid accidental shorting of terminals during test procedures.

• Never remove or attach wiring harness connectors with the ignition switch ON, especially to an electronic control module.

• Do not drop any components during service procedures and never apply 12 volts directly to any component (like a solenoid or relay) unless instructed specifically to do so. Some component electrical windings are designed to safely handle only 4 or 5 volts and can be destroyed in seconds if 12 volts are applied directly to the connector.

• Remove the electronic control module if the vehicle is to be placed in an environment where temperatures exceed approximately 176°F (80°C), such as a paint spray booth or when arc or gas welding near the control unit location in the vehicle.

ORGANIZED TROUBLESHOOTING

When diagnosing a specific problem, organized troubleshooting is a must. The complexity of a modern automobile demands that you approach any problem in a logical, organized manner. There are certain troubleshooting techniques that are standard:

1. Establish when the problem occurs. Does the problem appear only under certain conditions? Were there any noises, odors, or other unusual symptoms?

2. Isolate the problem area. To do this, make some simple tests and observations; then eliminate the systems that are working properly. Check for obvious problems such as broken wires, dirty connections or split or disconnected vacuum hoses. Always check the obvious before assuming something complicated is the cause.

3. Test for problems systematically to determine the cause once the problem area is isolated. Are all the components functioning properly? Is there power going to electrical switches and motors? Is there vacuum at vacuum switches and/or actuators? Is there a mechanical problem such as bent linkage or loose mounting screws? Doing careful, systematic checks will often turn up most causes on the first inspection without wasting time checking components that have little or no relationship to the problem.

4. Test all repairs after the work is done to make sure that the problem is fixed. Some causes can be traced to more than one component, so a careful verification of repair work is important to pick up additional malfunctions that may cause a problem to reappear or a different problem to arise. A blown fuse, for example, is a simple problem that may require more than another fuse to repair. If you don't look for a problem that caused a fuse to blow, for example, a shorted wire may go undetected.

Experience has shown that most problems tend to be the result of a fairly simple and obvious cause, such as loose or corroded connectors or air leaks in the intake system; making careful inspection of components during testing essential to quick and accurate troubleshooting. Special, hand held computerized testers designed specifically for diagnosing the HEI-EST system are available from a variety of aftermarket sources, as well as from the vehicle manufacturer, but care should be taken that any test equipment being used is designed to diagnose that particular computer controlled system accurately without damaging the control module (ECM) or components being tested.

NOTE: *Pinpointing the exact cause of trouble in an electrical system can sometimes only be accomplished by the use of special test equipment. The following describes commonly used test equipment and explains how to put it to best use in diagnosis. In addition to the information covered below, the manufacturer's instructions booklet provided with the tester should be read and clearly understood before attempting any test procedures.*

TEST EQUIPMENT

Jumper Wires

Jumper wires are simple, yet extremely valuable, pieces of test equipment. Jumper wires are merely wires that are used to bypass sections of a circuit. The simplest type of jumper wire is merely a length of multistrand wire with an alligator clip at each end. Jumper wires are usually fabricated from lengths of standard automotive wire and whatever type of connector (alligator clip, spade connector or pin connector) that is required for the particular vehicle being tested. The well equipped tool box will have several different styles of jumper wires in several different lengths. Some jumper wires are made with three or more terminals coming from a common splice for special purpose testing. In cramped, hard-to-reach areas it is advisable to have insulated boots over the jumper wire terminals in order to prevent accidental grounding, sparks, and possible fire, especially when testing fuel system components.

Jumper wires are used primarily to locate open electrical circuits, on either the ground (–) side of the circuit or on the hot (+) side. If an electrical component fails to operate, connect the jumper wire between the component and a good ground. If the component operates only with the jumper installed, the ground circuit is open. If the ground circuit is good, but the component does not operate, the circuit between the power feed and component is open. You can sometimes connect the jumper wire directly from the battery to the hot terminal of the component, but first make sure the component uses 12 volts in operation. Some electrical components, such as fuel injectors, are designed to operate on about 4 volts and running 12 volts directly to the injector terminals can burn out the wiring. By inserting an inline fuseholder between a set of test leads, a fused jumper wire can be used for bypassing open circuits. Use a 5 amp fuse to provide protection against voltage spikes. When in doubt, use a voltmeter to check the voltage input to the component and measure how much voltage is being applied normally. By moving the jumper wire successively back from the lamp toward the power source, you can isolate the area of the circuit where the open is located. When the component stops functioning, or the power is cut off, the open is in the segment of wire between the jumper and the point previously tested.

CAUTION: *Never use jumpers made from wire that is of lighter gauge than used in the circuit under test. If the jumper wire is of too small gauge, it may overheat and possibly melt. Never use jumpers to bypass high resistance loads (such as motors) in a circuit. Bypassing resistances, in effect, creates a short circuit which may, in turn, cause damage and fire. Never use a jumper for anything other than temporary bypassing of components in a circuit.*

12 Volt Test Light

The 12 volt test light is used to check circuits and components while electrical current is flowing through them. It is used for voltage and ground tests. Twelve volt test lights come in different styles but all have three main parts; a ground clip, a probe, and a light. The most commonly used 12 volt test lights have pick-type probes. To use a 12 volt test light, connect the ground clip to a good ground and probe wherever necessary with the pick. The pick should be sharp so that it can penetrate wire insulation to make contact with the wire, without making a large hole in the insulation. The wraparound light is handy in hard to reach areas or where it is difficult to support a wire to push a probe pick into it. To use the wrap around light, hook the wire to probed with the hook and pull the trigger. A small pick will be forced through the wire insulation into the wire core.

CAUTION: *Do not use a test light to probe electronic ignition spark plug or coil wires. Never use a pick-type test light to probe wiring on computer controlled systems unless specifically instructed to do so. Any wire insulation that is pierced by the test light probe should be taped and sealed with silicone after testing.*

Like the jumper wire, the 12 volt test light is used to isolate opens in circuits. But, whereas the jumper wire is used to bypass the open to operate the load, the 12 volt test light is used to locate the presence of voltage in a circuit. If the test light glows, you know that there is power up to that point; if the 12 volt test light does not glow when its probe is inserted into the wire or connector, you know that there is an open circuit (no power). Move the test light in successive steps back toward the power source until the light in the handle does glow. When it does glow, the open is between the probe and point previously probed.

NOTE: *The test light does not detect that 12 volts (or any particular amount of voltage) is present; it only detects that some voltage is present. It is advisable before using the test light to touch its terminals across the battery posts to make sure the light is operating properly.*

Self-Powered Test Light

The self-powered test light usually contains a 1.5 volt penlight battery. One type of self-powered test light is similar in design to the 12 volt test light. This type has both the battery and the light in the handle and pick-type probe tip. The second type has the light toward the open tip, so that the light illuminates the contact point. The self-powered test light is dual purpose piece of test equipment. It can be used to test for either open or short circuits when power is isolated from the circuit (continuity test). A powered test light should not be used on any computer controlled system or component unless specifically instructed to do so. Many engine sensors can be destroyed by even this small amount of voltage applied directly to the terminals.

Open Circuit Testing

To use the self-powered test light to check for open circuits, first isolate the circuit from the vehicle's 12 volt power source by disconnecting the battery or wiring harness connector. Connect the test light ground clip to a good ground and probe sections of the circuit sequentially with the test light. (start from either end of the circuit). If the light is out, the open is between the probe and the circuit ground. If the light is on, the open is between the probe and end of the circuit toward the power source.

Short Circuit Testing

By isolating the circuit both from power and from ground, and using a self-powered test light, you can check for shorts to ground in the circuit. Isolate the circuit from power and ground. Connect the test light ground clip to a good ground and probe any easy-to-reach test point in the circuit. If the light comes on, there is a short somewhere in the circuit. To isolate the short, probe a test point at either end of the isolated circuit (the light should be on). Leave the test light probe connected and open connectors, switches, remove parts, etc., sequentially, until the light goes out. When the light goes out, the short is between the last circuit component opened and the previous circuit opened.

NOTE: *The 1.5 volt battery in the test light does not provide much current. A weak battery may not provide enough power to illuminate the test light even when a complete circuit is made (especially if there are high resistances in the circuit). Always make sure that the test battery is strong. To check the battery, briefly touch the ground clip to the probe; if the light glows brightly the battery is strong enough for testing. Never use a self-powered test light to perform checks for opens or shorts when power is applied to the electrical system under test. The 12 volt vehicle power will quickly burn out the 1.5 volt light bulb in the test light.*

Voltmeter

A voltmeter is used to measure voltage at any point in a circuit, or to measure the voltage drop across any part of a circuit. It can also be used to check continuity in a wire or circuit by indicating current flow from one end to the other. Voltmeters usually have various scales on the meter dial and a selector switch to allow the selection of different voltages. The voltmeter has a positive and a negative lead. To avoid damage to the meter, always connect the negative lead to the negative (–) side of circuit (to ground or nearest the ground side of the circuit) and connect the positive lead to the positive (+) side of the circuit (to the power source or the nearest power source). Note that the negative voltmeter lead will always be black and that the positive voltmeter will always be some color other than black (usually red). Depending on how the voltmeter is connected into the circuit, it has several uses.

A voltmeter can be connected either in parallel or in series with a circuit and it has a very high resistance to current flow. When connected in parallel, only a small amount of current will flow through the voltmeter current path; the rest will flow through the normal circuit current path and the circuit will work normally. When the voltmeter is connected in series with a circuit, only a small amount of current can flow through the circuit. The circuit

will not work properly, but the voltmeter reading will show if the circuit is complete or not.

Available Voltage Measurement

Set the voltmeter selector switch to the 20V position and connect the meter negative lead to the negative post of the battery. Connect the positive meter lead to the positive post of the battery and turn the ignition switch ON to provide a load. Read the voltage on the meter or digital display. A well charged battery should register over 12 volts. If the meter reads below 11.5 volts, the battery power may be insufficient to operate the electrical system properly. This test determines voltage available from the battery and should be the first step in any electrical trouble diagnosis procedure. Many electrical problems, especially on computer controlled systems, can be caused by a low state of charge in the battery. Excessive corrosion at the battery cable terminals can cause a poor contact that will prevent proper charging and full battery current flow.

Normal battery voltage is 12 volts when fully charged. When the battery is supplying current to one or more circuits it is said to be "under load". When everything is off the electrical system is under a "no-load" condition. A fully charged battery may show about 12.5 volts at no load; will drop to 12 volts under medium load; and will drop even lower under heavy load. If the battery is partially discharged the voltage decrease under heavy load may be excessive, even though the battery shows 12 volts or more at no load. When allowed to discharge further, the battery's available voltage under load will decrease more severely. For this reason, it is important that the battery be fully charged during all testing procedures to avoid errors in diagnosis and incorrect test results.

Voltage Drop

When current flows through a resistance, the voltage beyond the resistance is reduced (the larger the current, the greater the reduction in voltage). When no current is flowing, there is no voltage drop because there is no current flow. All points in the circuit which are connected to the power source are at the same voltage as the power source. The total voltage drop always equals the total source voltage. In a long circuit with many connectors, a series of small, unwanted voltage drops due to corrosion at the connectors can add up to a total loss of voltage which impairs the operation of the normal loads in the circuit.

INDIRECT COMPUTATION OF VOLTAGE DROPS

1. Set the voltmeter selector switch to the 20 volt position.

2. Connect the meter negative lead to a good ground.

3. Probe all resistances in the circuit with the positive meter lead.

4. Operate the circuit in all modes and observe the voltage readings.

DIRECT MEASUREMENT OF VOLTAGE DROPS

1. Set the voltmeter switch to the 20 volt position.

2. Connect the voltmeter negative lead to the ground side of the resistance load to be measured.

3. Connect the positive lead to the positive side of the resistance or load to be measured.

4. Read the voltage drop directly on the 20 volt scale.

Too high a voltage indicates too high a resistance. If, for example, a blower motor runs too slowly, you can determine if there is too high a resistance in the resistor pack. By taking voltage drop readings in all parts of the circuit, you can isolate the problem. Too low a voltage drop indicates too low a resistance. If, for example, a blower motor runs too fast in the MED and/or LOW position, the problem can be isolated in the resistor pack by taking voltage drop readings in all parts of the circuit to locate a possibly shorted resistor. The maximum allowable voltage drop under load is critical, especially if there is more than one high resistance problem in a circuit because all voltage drops are cumulative. A small drop is normal due to the resistance of the conductors.

HIGH RESISTANCE TESTING

1. Set the voltmeter selector switch to the 4 volt position.

2. Connect the voltmeter positive lead to the positive post of the battery.

3. Turn on the headlights and heater blower to provide a load.

4. Probe various points in the circuit with the negative voltmeter lead.

5. Read the voltage drop on the 4 volt scale. Some average maximum allowable voltage drops are:

    FUSE PANEL — 7 volts
    IGNITION SWITCH — 5volts
    HEADLIGHT SWITCH — 7 volts
    IGNITION COIL (+) — 5 volts
    ANY OTHER LOAD — 1.3 volts

NOTE: *Voltage drops are all measured while a load is operating; without current flow, there will be no voltage drop.*

Ohmmeter

The ohmmeter is designed to read resistance (ohms) in a circuit or component. Although there are several different styles of ohmmeters, all will usually have a selector switch which permits the measurement of different ranges of resistance (usually the selector switch allows the multiplication of the meter reading by 10, 100, 1000, and 10,000). A calibration knob allows the meter to be set at zero for accurate measurement. Since all ohmmeters are powered by an internal battery (usually 9 volts), the ohmmeter can be used as a self-powered test light. When the ohmmeter is connected, current from the ohmmeter flows through the circuit or component being tested. Since the ohmmeter's internal resistance and voltage are known values, the amount of current flow through the meter depends on the resistance of the circuit or component being tested.

The ohmmeter can be used to perform continuity test for opens or shorts (either by observation of the meter needle or as a self-powered test light), and to read actual resistance in a circuit. It should be noted that the ohmmeter is used to check the resistance of a component or wire while there is no voltage applied to the circuit. Current flow from an outside voltage source (such as the vehicle battery) can damage the ohmmeter, so the circuit or component should be isolated from the vehicle electrical system before any testing is done. Since the ohmmeter uses its own voltage source, either lead can be connected to any test point.

NOTE: *When checking diodes or other solid state components, the ohmmeter leads can only be connected one way in order to measure current flow in a single direction. Make sure the positive (+) and negative (–) terminal connections are as described in the test procedures to verify the one-way diode operation.*

In using the meter for making continuity checks, do not be concerned with the actual resistance readings. Zero resistance, or any resistance readings, indicate continuity in the circuit. Infinite resistance indicates an open in the circuit. A high resistance reading where there should be none indicates a problem in the circuit. Checks for short circuits are made in the same manner as checks for open circuits except that the circuit must be isolated from both power and normal ground. Infinite resistance indicates no continuity to ground, while zero resistance indicates a dead short to ground.

RESISTANCE MEASUREMENT

The batteries in an ohmmeter will weaken with age and temperature, so the ohmmeter must be calibrated or "zeroed" before taking measurements. To zero the meter, place the selector switch in its lowest range and touch the two ohmmeter leads together. Turn the calibration knob until the meter needle is exactly on zero.

NOTE: *All analog (needle) type ohmmeters must be zeroed before use, but some digital ohmmeter models are automatically calibrated when the switch is turned on. Self-calibrating digital ohmmeters do not have an adjusting knob, but its a good idea to check for a zero readout before use by touching the leads together. All computer controlled systems require the use of a digital ohmmeter with at least 10 mega-ohms impedance for testing. Before any test procedures are attempted, make sure the ohmmeter used is compatible with the electrical system or damage to the on-board computer could result.*

To measure resistance, first isolate the circuit from the vehicle power source by disconnecting the battery cables or the harness connector. Make sure the key is OFF when disconnecting any components or the battery. Where necessary, also isolate at least one side of the circuit to be checked to avoid reading parallel resistances. Parallel circuit resistances will always give a lower reading than the actual resistance of either of the branches. When measuring the resistance of parallel circuits, the total resistance will always be lower than the smallest resistance in the circuit. Connect the meter leads to both sides of the circuit (wire or component) and read the actual measured ohms on the meter scale. Make sure the selector switch is set to the proper ohm scale for the circuit being tested to avoid misreading the ohmmeter test value.

CAUTION: *Never use an ohmmeter with power applied to the circuit. Like the self-powered test light, the ohmmeter is designed to operate on its own power supply. The normal 12 volt automotive electrical system current could damage the meter.*

Ammeters

An ammeter measures the amount of current flowing through a circuit in units called amperes or amps. Amperes are units of electron flow which indicate how fast the electrons are flowing through the circuit. Since Ohms Law dictates that current flow in a circuit is equal to the circuit voltage divided by the total circuit resistance, increasing voltage also increases the current level (amps). Likewise, any decrease in resistance will increase the amount of amps in a circuit. At normal operating voltage, most circuits have a characteristic amount of amperes, called "current draw" which can be measured using an ammeter. By referring to a specified current draw rating, measuring the amperes, and comparing the two values, one can determine what is happening within the circuit to

aid in diagnosis. An open circuit, for example, will not allow any current to flow so the ammeter reading will be zero. More current flows through a heavily loaded circuit or when the charging system is operating.

An ammeter is always connected in series with the circuit being tested. All of the current that normally flows through the circuit must also flow through the ammeter; if there is any other path for the current to follow, the ammeter reading will not be accurate. The ammeter itself has very little resistance to current flow and therefore will not affect the circuit, but it will measure current draw only when the circuit is closed and electricity is flowing. Excessive current draw can blow fuses and drain the battery, while a reduced current draw can cause motors to run slowly, lights to dim and other components to not operate properly. The ammeter can help diagnose these conditions by locating the cause of the high or low reading.

Multimeters

Different combinations of test meters can be built into a single unit designed for specific tests. Some of the more common combination test devices are known as Volt/Amp testers, Tach/Dwell meters, or Digital Multimeters. The Volt/Amp tester is used for charging system, starting system or battery tests and consists of a voltmeter, an ammeter and a variable resistance carbon pile. The voltmeter will usually have at least two ranges for use with 6, 12 and 24 volt systems. The ammeter also has more than one range for testing various levels of battery loads and starter current draw and the carbon pile can be adjusted to offer different amounts of resistance. The Volt/Amp tester has heavy leads to carry large amounts of current and many later models have an inductive ammeter pickup that clamps around the wire to simplify test connections. On some models, the ammeter also has a zero-center scale to allow testing of charging and starting systems without switching leads or polarity. A digital multimeter is a voltmeter, ammeter and ohmmeter combined in an instrument which gives a digital readout. These are often used when testing solid state circuits because of their high input impedance (usually 10 megohms or more).

The tach/dwell meter combines a tachometer and a dwell (cam angle) meter and is a specialized kind of voltmeter. The tachometer scale is marked to show engine speed in rpm and the dwell scale is marked to show degrees of distributor shaft rotation. In most electronic ignition systems, dwell is determined by the control unit, but the dwell meter can also be used to check the duty cycle (operation) of some electronic engine control systems. Some tach/dwell meters are powered by an internal battery, while others take their power from the vehicle battery in use. The battery powered testers usually require calibration much like an ohmmeter before testing.

Special Test Equipment

A variety of diagnostic tools are available to help troubleshoot and repair computerized engine control systems. The most sophisticated of these devices are the console type engine analyzers that usually occupy a garage service bay, but there are several types of aftermarket electronic testers available that will allow quick circuit tests of the engine control system by plugging directly into a special connector located in the engine compartment or under the dashboard. Several tool and equipment manufacturers offer simple, hand held testers that measure various circuit voltage levels on command to check all system components for proper operation. Although these testers usually cost about $300–$500, consider that the average computer control unit (or ECM) can cost just as much and the money saved by not replacing perfectly good sensors or components in an attempt to correct a problem could justify the purchase price of a special diagnostic tester the first time it's used.

These computerized testers can allow quick and easy test measurements while the engine is operating or while the vehicle is being driven. In addition, the on-board computer memory can be read to access any stored trouble codes; in effect allowing the computer to tell you where it hurts and aid trouble diagnosis by pinpointing exactly which circuit or component is malfunctioning. In the same manner, repairs can be tested to make sure the problem has been corrected. The biggest advantage these special testers have is their relatively easy hookups that minimize or eliminate the chances of making the wrong connections and getting false voltage readings or damaging the computer accidentally.

NOTE: *It should be remembered that these testers check voltage levels in circuits; they don't detect mechanical problems or failed components if the circuit voltage falls within the preprogrammed limits stored in the tester PROM unit. Also, most of the hand held testers are designed to work only on one or two systems made by a specific manufacturer.*

A variety of aftermarket testers are available to help diagnose different computerized control systems. Kent-Moore Tool Company 29784 Little Mack Roseville, MI 48066–2298, markets a device which plugs directly into the assembly line diagnostic link (ALDL). The tester makes diagnosis a simple matter of pressing the correct buttons and, by changing the internal PROM or inserting a different diagnosis cartridge, it will work on any model from full size to subcompact, over a wide range of years. An adapter is supplied with the tester to allow connection to all types of ALDL links, regardless of the number of pin terminals used. By inserting an updated PROM into the tester, it can be easily updated to diagnose any new modifications of computerized control systems.

Wiring Harnesses

The average automobile contains about $1/2$ mile of wiring, with hundreds of individual connections. To protect the many wires from damage and to keep them from becoming a confusing tangle, they are organized into bundles, enclosed in plastic or taped together and called wire harnesses. Different wiring harnesses serve different parts of the vehicle. Individual wires are color coded to help trace them through a harness where sections are hidden from view.

A loose or corroded connection or a replacement wire that is too small for the circuit will add extra resistance and an additional voltage drop to the circuit. A ten percent voltage drop can result in slow or erratic motor operation, for example, even though the circuit is complete. Automotive wiring or circuit conductors can be in any one of three forms:
1. Single strand wire
2. Multistrand wire
3. Printed circuitry

Single strand wire has a solid metal core and is usually used inside such components as alternators, motors, relays and other devices. Multistrand wire has a core made of many small strands of wire twisted together into a single conductor. Most of the wiring in an automotive electrical system is made up of multistrand wire, either as a single conductor or grouped together in a harness. All wiring is color coded on the insulator, either as a solid color or as a colored wire with an identification stripe. A printed circuit is a thin film of copper or other conductor that is printed on an insulator backing. Occasionally, a printed circuit is sandwiched between two sheets of plastic for more protection and flexibility. A complete printed circuit, consisting of conductors, insulating material and connectors for lamps or other components is called a printed circuit board. Printed circuitry is used in place of individual wires or harnesses in places where space is limited, such as behind instrument panels.

Wire Gauge

Since computer controlled automotive electrical systems are very sensitive to changes in resistance, the selection of properly sized wires is critical when systems are repaired. The wire gauge number is an expression of the cross section area of the conductor. The most common system for expressing wire size is the American Wire Gauge (AWG) system.

Wire cross section area is measured in circular mils. A mil is $\frac{1}{1000}$ in. (0.001 in.); a circular mil is the area of a circle one mil in diameter. For example, a conductor $\frac{1}{4}$ in. in diameter is 0.250 in. or 250 mils. The circular mil cross section area of the wire is 250 squared (250^2)or 62,500 circular mils. Imported vehicle models usually use metric wire gauge designations, which is simply the cross section area of the conductor in square millimeters (mm^2).

Gauge numbers are assigned to conductors of various cross section areas. As gauge number increases, area decreases and the conductor becomes smaller. A 5 gauge conductor is smaller than a 1 gauge conductor and a 10 gauge is smaller than a 5 gauge. As the cross section area of a conductor decreases, resistance increases and so does the gauge number. A conductor with a higher gauge number will carry less current than a conductor with a lower gauge number.

NOTE: *Gauge wire size refers to the size of the conductor, not the size of the complete wire. It is possible to have two wires of the same gauge with different diameters because one may have thicker insulation than the other.*

12 volt automotive electrical systems generally use 10, 12, 14, 16 and 18 gauge wire. Main power distribution circuits and larger accessories usually use 10 and 12 gauge wire. Battery cables are usually 4 or 6 gauge, although 1 and 2 gauge wires are occasionally used. Wire length must also be considered when making repairs to a circuit. As conductor length increases, so does resistance. An 18 gauge wire, for example, can carry a 10 amp load for 10 feet without excessive voltage drop; however if a 15 foot wire is required for the same 10 amp load, it must be a 16 gauge wire.

An electrical schematic shows the electrical current paths when a circuit is operating properly. It is essential to understand how a circuit works before trying to figure out why it does not. Schematics break the entire electrical system down into individual circuits and show only one particular circuit. In a schematic, no attempt is made to represent wiring and components as they physically appear on the vehicle; switches and other components are shown as simply as possible. Face views of harness connectors show the cavity or terminal locations in all multi-pin connectors to help locate test points.

If you need to backprobe a connector while it is on the component, the order of the terminals must be mentally reversed. The wire color code can help in this situation, as well as a keyway, lock tab or other reference mark.

NOTE: *Wiring diagrams are not included in this book. As vehicles have become more complex and available with longer option lists, wiring diagrams have grown in size and complexity. It has become almost impossible to provide a readable reproduction of a wiring diagram in a book this size. Information on ordering wiring diagrams from the vehicle manufacturer can be found in the owner's manual.*

WIRING REPAIR

Soldering is a quick, efficient method of joining metals permanently. Everyone who has the occasion to make wiring repairs should know how to solder. Electrical connections that are soldered are far less likely to come apart and will conduct electricity much better than connections that are only "pig-tailed" together. The most popular (and preferred) method of soldering is with an electrical soldering gun. Soldering irons are available in many sizes and wattage ratings. Irons with higher wattage ratings deliver higher temperatures and recover lost heat faster. A small soldering iron rated for no more than 50 watts is recommended, especially on electrical systems where excess heat can damage the components being soldered.

There are three ingredients necessary for successful soldering; proper flux, good solder and sufficient heat. A soldering flux is necessary to clean the metal of tarnish, prepare it for soldering and to enable the solder to spread into tiny crevices. When soldering, always use a resin flux or resin core solder which is non-corrosive and will not attract moisture once the job is finished. Other types of flux (acid core) will leave a residue that will attract moisture and cause the wires to corrode. Tin is a unique metal with a low melting point. In a molten state, it dissolves and alloys easily with many metals. Solder is made by mixing tin with lead. The most common proportions are 40/60, 50/50 and 60/40, with the percentage of tin listed first. Low priced solders usually contain less tin, making them very difficult for a beginner to use because more heat is required to melt the solder. A common solder is 40/60 which is well suited for all-around general use, but 60/40 melts easier, has more tin for a better joint and is preferred for electrical work.

Soldering Techniques

Successful soldering requires that the metals to be joined be heated to a temperature that will melt the solder—usually 360–460°F (182–238°C). Contrary to popular belief, the purpose of the soldering iron is not to melt the solder itself, but to heat the parts being soldered to a temperature high enough to melt the solder when it is touched to the work. Melting flux-cored solder on the soldering iron will usually destroy the effectiveness of the flux.

NOTE: *Soldering tips are made of copper for good heat conductivity, but must be "tinned" regularly for quick transference of heat to the project and to prevent the solder from sticking to the iron. To "tin" the iron, simply heat it and touch the flux-cored solder to the tip; the solder will flow over the hot tip. Wipe the excess off with a clean rag, but be careful as the iron will be hot.*

After some use, the tip may become pitted. If so, simply dress the tip smooth with a smooth file and "tin" the tip again. An old saying holds that "metals well cleaned are half soldered." Flux-cored solder will remove oxides but rust, bits of insulation and oil or grease must be removed with a wire brush or emery cloth. For maximum strength in soldered parts, the joint must start off clean and tight. Weak joints will result in gaps too wide for the solder to bridge.

If a separate soldering flux is used, it should be brushed or swabbed on only those areas that are to be soldered. Most solders contain a core of flux and separate fluxing is unnecessary. Hold the work to be soldered firmly. It is best to solder on a wooden board, because a metal vise will only rob the piece to be soldered of heat and make it difficult to melt the solder. Hold the soldering tip with the broadest face against the work to be soldered. Apply solder under the tip close to the work, using enough solder to give a heavy film between the iron and the piece being soldered, while moving slowly and making sure the solder melts properly. Keep the work level or the solder will run to the lowest part and favor the thicker parts, because these require more heat to melt the solder. If the soldering tip overheats (the solder coating on the face of the tip burns up), it should be retinned. Once the soldering is completed, let the soldered joint stand until cool. Tape and seal all soldered wire splices after the repair has cooled.

Wire Harness and Connectors

The on-board computer (ECM) wire harness electrically connects the control unit to the various solenoids, switches and sensors used by the control system. Most connectors in the engine compartment or otherwise exposed to the elements are protected against moisture and dirt which could create oxidation and deposits on the terminals. This protection is important because of the very low voltage and current levels used by the computer and sensors. All connectors have a lock which secures the male and female terminals together, with a secondary lock holding the seal and terminal into the connector. Both terminal locks must be released when disconnecting ECM connectors.

These special connectors are weather-proof and all repairs require the use of a special terminal and the tool required to service it. This tool is used to remove the pin and sleeve terminals. If removal is attempted with an ordinary pick, there is a good chance that the terminal will be bent or deformed. Unlike standard blade type terminals, these terminals cannot be straightened once they are bent. Make certain that the connectors are properly seated and all of the sealing rings in place when connecting leads. On some models, a hinge-type flap provides a backup or secondary locking feature for the terminals. Most secondary locks are used to improve the connector reliability by retaining the terminals if the small terminal lock tangs are not positioned properly.

Molded-on connectors require complete replacement of the connection. This means splicing a new connector assembly into the harness. All splices in on-board computer systems should be soldered to insure proper contact. Use care when probing the connections or replacing terminals in them as it is possible to short between opposite terminals. If this happens to the wrong terminal pair, it is possible to damage certain components. Always use jumper wires between connectors for circuit checking and never probe through weather-proof seals.

Open circuits are often difficult to locate by sight because corrosion or terminal misalignment are hidden by the connectors. Merely wiggling a connector on a sensor or in the wiring harness may correct the open circuit condition. This should always be considered when an open circuit or a failed sensor is indicated. Intermittent problems may also be caused by oxidized or loose connections. When using a circuit tester for diagnosis, always probe connections from the wire side. Be careful not to damage sealed connectors with test probes.

All wiring harnesses should be replaced with identical parts, using the same gauge wire and connectors. When signal wires are spliced into a harness, use wire with high temperature insulation only. With the low voltage and current levels found in the system, it is important that the best possible connection at all wire splices be made by soldering the splices together. It is seldom necessary to replace a complete harness. If replacement is necessary, pay close attention to insure proper harness routing. Secure the harness with suitable plastic wire clamps to prevent vibrations from causing the harness to wear in spots or contact any hot components.

NOTE: *Weatherproof connectors cannot be replaced with standard connectors. Instructions are provided with replacement connector and terminal packages. Some wire harnesses have mounting indicators (usually pieces of colored tape) to mark where the harness is to be secured.*

In making wiring repairs, it's important that you always replace damaged wires with wires that are the same gauge as the wire being replaced. The heavier the wire, the smaller the gauge number. Wires are color-coded to aid in identification and whenever possible the same color coded wire should be used for replacement. A wire stripping and crimping tool is necessary to install solderless terminal connectors. Test all crimps by pulling on the wires; it should not be possible to pull the wires out of a good crimp.

Wires which are open, exposed or otherwise damaged are repaired by simple splicing. Where possible, if the wiring harness is accessible and the damaged place in the wire can be located, it is best to open the harness and check for all possible damage. In an inaccessible harness, the wire must be bypassed with a new insert, usually taped to the outside of the old harness.

When replacing fusible links, be sure to use fusible link wire, NOT ordinary automotive wire. Make sure the fusible segment is of the same gauge and construction as the one being replaced and double the stripped end when crimping the terminal connector for a good contact. The melted (open) fusible link segment of the wiring harness should be cut off as close to the harness as possible, then a new segment spliced in as described. In the case of a damaged fusible link that feeds two harness wires, the harness connections should be replaced with two fusible link wires so that each circuit will have its own separate protection.

NOTE: *Most of the problems caused in the wiring harness are due to bad ground connections. Always check all vehicle ground connections for corrosion or looseness before performing any power feed checks to eliminate the chance of a bad ground affecting the circuit.*

Repairing Hard Shell Connectors

Unlike molded connectors, the terminal contacts in hard shell connectors can be replaced. Weatherproof hard-shell connectors with the leads molded into the shell have non-replaceable terminal ends. Replacement usually involves the use of a special terminal removal tool that depress the locking tangs (barbs) on the connector terminal and allow the connector to be removed from the rear of the shell. The connector shell should be replaced if it shows any evidence of burning, melting, cracks, or breaks. Replace individual terminals that are burnt, corroded, distorted or loose.

NOTE: *The insulation crimp must be tight to prevent the insulation from sliding back on the wire when the wire is pulled. The insulation must be visibly compressed under the crimp tabs, and the ends of the crimp should be turned in for a firm grip on the insulation.*

The wire crimp must be made with all wire strands inside the crimp. The terminal must be fully compressed on the wire strands with the ends of the crimp tabs turned in to make a firm grip on the wire. Check all connections with an ohmmeter to insure a good contact. There should be no measurable resistance between the wire and the terminal when connected.

Mechanical Test Equipment

Vacuum Gauge

Most gauges are graduated in inches of mercury (in. Hg), although a device called a manometer reads vacuum in inches of water (in. H_2O). The normal vacuum reading usually varies between 18 and 22 in. Hg at sea level. To test engine vacuum, the vacuum gauge must be connected to a source of manifold vacuum. Many engines have a plug in the intake manifold which can be removed and replaced with an adapter fitting. Connect the vacuum gauge to the fitting with a suitable rubber hose or, if no manifold plug is available, connect the vacuum gauge to any device using manifold vacuum, such as EGR valves, etc. The vacuum gauge can be used to determine if enough vacuum is reaching a component to allow its actuation.

Hand Vacuum Pump

Small, hand-held vacuum pumps come in a variety of designs. Most have a built-in vacuum gauge and allow the component to be tested without removing it from the vehicle. Operate the pump lever or plunger to apply the correct amount of vacuum required for the test specified in the diagnosis routines. The level of vacuum in inches of Mercury (in. Hg) is indicated on the pump gauge. For some testing, an additional vacuum gauge may be necessary.

Intake manifold vacuum is used to operate various systems and devices on late model vehicles. To correctly diagnose and solve problems in vacuum control systems, a vacuum source is necessary for testing. In some cases, vacuum can be taken from the intake manifold when the engine is running, but vacuum is normally provided by a hand vacuum pump. These hand vacuum pumps have a built-in vacuum gauge that allow testing while the device is still attached to the component. For some tests, an additional vacuum gauge may be used.

HEATING AND AIR CONDITIONING SYSTEM

The heater core and blower on most models are contained in the heater box (fresh air housing) located in the center of the passenger compartment under the dashboard. On most air conditioned models, the evaporator is located in the heater box. On air conditioned Dashers and most Quantums the evaporator is located under the hood separate from the heater box.

The blower fan on non-air conditioned models before 1977 is open-bladed, much like an airplane propeller. The blower fan on all air conditioned models and non-air conditioned models after 1977 is of the turbine type.

On some models, the fan and core can be removed without removing the heater box. The fan should be accessible from under the hood on these models, while the heater core is accessible from inside the passenger compartment.

CAUTION: *When working on air conditioning components, use extreme caution. The system is filled with refrigerant which is poisonous if mixed with an open flame, and can freeze your skin if allowed to contact it. Be careful!*

Heater Case

REMOVAL AND INSTALLATION

Without Center Console

1. Disconnect the battery ground cable.
2. Drain the cooling system.

CAUTION: *When draining the coolant, keep in mind that cats and dogs are attracted by the ethylene glycol antifreeze, and are quite likely to drink any that is left in an uncovered container or in puddles on the ground. This will prove fatal in sufficient quantity. Always drain the coolant into a sealable container. Coolant should be reused unless it is contaminated or several years old.*

3. Remove the windshield washer container from its mounts and remove the ignition coil only if they prevent access to the heater components under the hood.

Heater hose connections at the firewall

4. Disconnect the two hoses from the heater core connections at the firewall.

5. Unplug the blower fan electrical connectors. Some models are equipped with an external series resistor mounted on the heater box. Do not try to remove the wires from the resistor.

6. Remove the heater control knobs on the dash.

7. Remove the two retaining screws and remove the controls from the dash complete with brackets.

8. Some models have a cable attached to a lever which is operated by a round knob on the dashboard. Remove the cable from the lever.

9. Remove either the clips or the screws holding the heater box in place and remove the heater box with the heater controls.

To install:

10. When installing the new type of housing in Rabbits and Sciroccos originally equipped with the older model heater box, proceed as follows: Make a hole by cutting along the line **W**. Clip the connections after installing the new air outlet pipe and seal the joint with a suitable adhesive.

11. Mount and install the heater box (with controls) and install the retaining clips or screws.

12. On those models with cable operated lever, connect the cable to the lever.

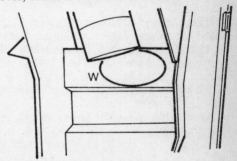

Cut along line (W) for Rabbit and Scirocco

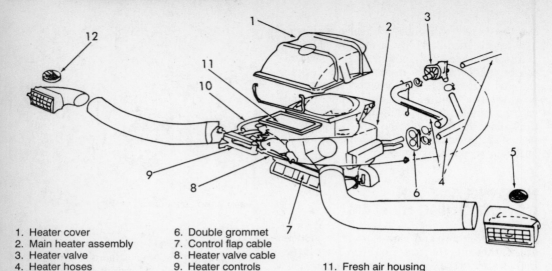

1. Heater cover
2. Main heater assembly
3. Heater valve
4. Heater hoses
5. Vent for side windows
6. Double grommet
7. Control flap cable
8. Heater valve cable
9. Heater controls
10. Cutoff flap cable
11. Fresh air housing
12. Vent for side windows

Dasher heater assembly

13. Mount the controls to the dash and secure with the two retaining screws.

14. Install the heater control knobs.

15. Plug in the blower fan connectors.

16. Connect the hoses to the heater core at the fire wall.

17. Install the ignition coil and windshield washer reservoir if they were removed.

18. Fill the cooling system to the proper level.

19. Connect the negative battery cable.

With Center Console

1. Disconnect the negative battery cable.

2. Drain the engine coolant.

CAUTION: *When draining the coolant, keep in mind that cats and dogs are attracted by the ethylene glycol antifreeze, and are quite likely to drink any that is left in an uncovered container or in puddles on the ground. This will prove fatal in sufficient quantity. Always drain the coolant into a sealable container. Coolant should be reused unless it is contaminated or several years old.*

3. Trace the heater hoses coming from the firewall and disconnect them. One leads to the back of the cylinder head and the other leads to the heater valve located above and behind the oil filter.

4. Detach the cable for the heater valve.

5. Remove the center console.

6. Remove the left and right covers below the instrument panel.

7. Pull off the fresh air/heater control knobs.

8. Pull off the trim plate.

9. Remove the screws for the controls.

10. Remove the center cover mounting screws and remove the cover.

11. Detach the right, left and center air ducts.

12. Remove the heater housing retaining spring.

13. Remove the cowl for the air plenum which is located under the hood and in front of the windshield.

14. Remove the heater housing mounting screws and remove the heater housing. The mounting screws are under the hood where the air plenum was. Remove all the old sealing material and relace with new.

To install:

15. Mount the heater housing and install the mounting screws.

16. Install the air plenum cowl.

17. Install the heater housing retaining spring.

18. Connect the right, left and center air ducts.

19. Install the center cover.

20. Install the control assembly screws.

21. Mount the trim plate.

22. Install the fresh air/heater control knobs.

23. Install the lower left and right instrument panel covers.

24. Install the center console.

25. Connect the heater cable valve.

26. Connect the heater hoses.

27. Fill the cooling system to the proper level.

28. Connect the negative battery cable.

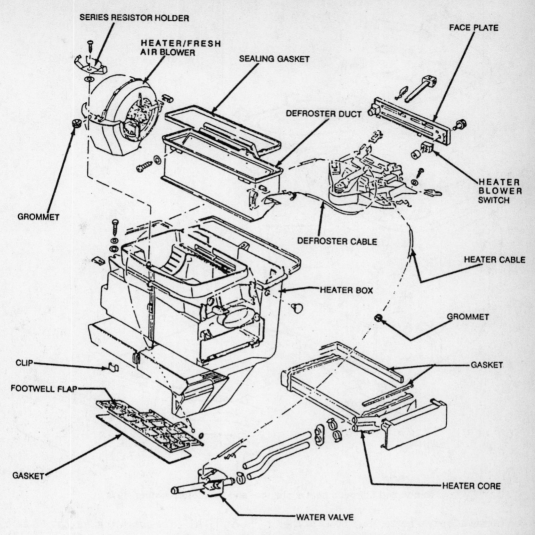

Scirocco and Cabriolet heater box assembly

Heater Core
REMOVAL AND INSTALLATION

All Except Fox

NOTE: *On some 1977 and later models, it is possible to remove the heater core without removing the heater box.*

1. Disconnect the negative battery cable.
2. Drain the cooling system.

CAUTION: *When draining the coolant, keep in mind that cats and dogs are attracted by the ethylene glycol antifreeze, and are quite likely to drink any that is left in an uncovered container or in puddles on the ground. This will prove fatal in sufficient quantity. Always drain the coolant into a sealable container. Coolant should be reused unless it is contaminated or several years old.*

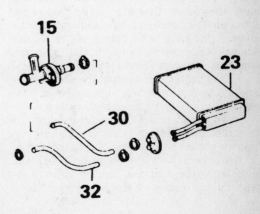

Rabbit, Scirocco and Jetta heater core (23), hoses (30 and 32) and heater control valve (15)

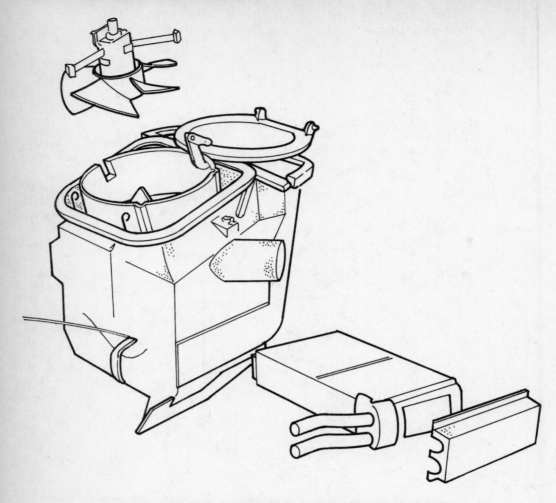

Rabbit and Scirocco heat exchanger and fan motor, through 1977

3. Remove the two heater inlet hoses at the firewall.

4. Inside the car, remove the center console side panels, if equipped. Locate the heater core cover located on the side of the case. Press down on the retaining tabs and remove the cover. If the unit has a core cover in its side, remove the screws or unclip the cover and remove it. The core should pull out.

5. The heater core can now be slid from the case. If the retaining lugs lugs break off, don't worry, they can be replaced with screws.

6. To install, insert the heater core into the case. Install the heater core cover, making sure that the gasket on the cover is properly fitted.

7. Connect the heater hoses at the fire wall. Make sure the seal fits tightly without any gaps. Fill the cooling system to the proper level.

Fox

1. Disconnect the negative battery cable.
2. Drain the engine coolant.

CAUTION: *When draining the coolant, keep in mind that cats and dogs are attracted by the ethylene glycol antifreeze, and are quite likely to drink any that is left in an uncovered container or in puddles on the ground. This will prove fatal in sufficient quantity. Always drain the coolant into a sealable container. Coolant should be reused unless it is contaminated or several years old.*

3. Disconnect the heater inlet hoses at the firewall.

4. Inside the vehicle, remove the center console side panels. Disconnect the temperature control cables at the heater case.

5. Remove the left and right air distribution ducts.

6. In the engine compartment, remove the cowl cover and remove the air distribution housing cover.

7. Inside the vehicle, remove the lower housing retaining clips and remove the housing.

NOTE: *On vehicles equipped with A/C the heater box also contains the A/C system evaporator mounted in the lower housing cover. When removing the lower cover on these models lay the cover and evaporated aside WITHOUT disconnecting the refrigerant lines.*

8. Remove the bolts retaining the heater case and remove the case.

9. Remove the clips holding the case together and split the case, the heater core can now be removed.

10. To install, insert the heater core into the case and reassemble the case.

11. Install the case into the vehicle. Attach the lower heater case cover to the heater case. Install the air distribution ducts and the control cables.

12. Install the center console side panels. Reconnect the heater inlet hoses. Install the air distribution housing cover and the cowl.

13. Fill the cooling system to the proper level.

Heater Blower

REMOVAL AND INSTALLATION

1974-76 Models

1. Remove the heater box. See procedure above.

2. On Rabbit and Scirocco, remove the screws holding the heater cover in place and remove the heater cover. Remove the circular cutoff flap by unhooking it from its hinge. On Dashers, remove the heater cover by pulling out its pins.

3. On the Rabbit and Scirocco, the heater blower should pull right out of the assembly.

4. On Dashers, remove the clips holding the heater box halves together and separate the halves. The fan should just pull out.

5. Installation is the reverse of removal.

NOTE: *On the Dasher, when installing the fan in the heater box halves, make sure the wiring connections on the fan face the wiring harness on the heater box. Also, when jointing the housing halves, make sure there is no side to side play in the blower motor.*

1977-84 Rabbit, Dasher, Jetta, Quantum and 1977-90 Scirocco

1. Remove the heater unit from the vehicle. See above for procedures.

2. Remove the screws holding the cover on the heater box and remove the cover. Remove the blower motor cover, if so equipped.

3. Remove the electrical connections from the blower motor after matchmarking them to insure that you assemble them in the correct order.

4. Remove the clamp or screws holding the motor in place and remove the motor.

5. Installation is the reverse of removal.

Fox

1. Disconnect the negative battery cable.

2. Remove the front cover sealing gasket.

3. Remove the water deflector.

4. Loosen the fresh air housing cover retaining clips and remove the *front* fresh air housing cover.

5. If equipped with air conditioning, undo the lock and disconnect the air distribution flap levers.

6. Remove the *rear* fresh air housing cover.

7. If equipped with air conditioning, disconnect (and label) the vacuum servo motor hoses

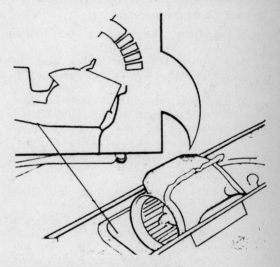

Fox blower removal and installation

and hoses from the grommets in the lower portion of the fresh air housing covers.

8. Remove the thermal resistor and thermal circuit breaker from the support.

9. Loosen the blower motor mounting screw and disconnect the blower wiring connectors.

10. Remove the lower fresh air covers.

11. Maneuver the fan and motor towards the front of the car and remove it from the fresh air (blower) housing.

To install:

12. Install the fan and motor assembly into the fresh air (blower) housing.

13. Install the lower fresh air covers.

14. Connect the blower wiring and install the blower motor mounting screw.

15. Attach the thermal circuit breaker and thermal resistor the support.

16. Connect the hoses to the lower fresh air

housing covers and connect the vacuum servo motor hoses.

17. Install the rear fresh air housing cover.

18. If equipped with air conditioning, connect the air distribution flap levers and engage the lock.

19. Install the front fresh air housing cover and lock the retaining clips.

20. Install the water deflector.

21. Connect the negative battery cable and check the blower operation at all speeds.

1985–90 Golf, GTI and Jetta

NOTE: *The blower motor is located behind the glove box and it may be necessary to remove the glove box to gain access to the motor.*

WITHOUT AIR CONDITIONING

1. Disconnect the wires at the blower motor.

2. At the blower motor flange near the cowl, disengage the retaining lug (pull down on the lug).

3. Turn the motor in the clockwise direction, to release it from it's mount, then lower it from the plenum.

4. To install, reverse the removal procedures. Use a new gasket or sealant as required.

WITH AIR CONDITIONING

1. Disconnect the wires from the blower motor.

2. Remove the three mounting screws and pull the motor from the plenum.

3. To install, reverse the removal procedures. Use a new gasket or sealant as required.

RADIO

NOTE: *Most radios are a dealer installed option.*

REMOVAL AND INSTALLATION

Except 1987–90 Models With Heidleberg V and VI — Electronically Tuned

1. Remove the knobs from the radio.

2. Remove the nuts from the radio control shafts.

3. Detach the antenna lead from the jack on the radio case.

CAUTION: *Never operate the radio without a speaker; severe damage to the output transistor will result. If the speaker must be replaced, use a speaker of the correct impedance (ohms) or else the output transistors will be damaged and require replacement.*

4. Detach the power and speaker leads.

5. Remove the radio support nuts and bolts.

6. Withdraw the radio from beneath the dashboard.

7. Insert the radio into the dashboard and install the radio support fasteners.

8. Connect the power and speaker leads.

9. Connect the antenna leads.

10. Install the control shafts and knobs.

Heidleberg V

The Heidleberg V, CR radio is equipped with an electronic locking circuit to deter radio theft. Whenever the radio is removed or the battery is disconnected, the locking circuit code must be entered in order for the radio to operate. There are 2 codes that can be entered, the first is the original factory code. The second is the programmed personal code entered by the vehicle owner. If the codes are not entered the radio will not operate. If the correct code is not entered in 6 tries the radio becomes electronically locked-up and must be replaced.

The Heidleberg V radio is retained in the instrument panel by means of lock clips at the sides of the radio body. To remove the radio from its mounting position, 2 special tools are required. Insert the tools, into the holes, in the side of the radio face plate. The tools will "click" into position. With the tools installed the radio can be pulled from the instrument panel. Disconnect the electrical leads to complete the removal. When installing the radio, be sure to connect the electrical leads in their proper position.

Heidleberg VI

The Heidleberg VI fix coded radio is equipped with an electronic locking circuit to deter radio theft. The Heidelberg radio is assigned a fixed four digit security code when it leaves the factory. Unlike the Heidelberg V system, this code cannot be changed. The Heidleberg VI radio is identified by white lettering on the faceplate and separate knobs for the fader, bass and treble controls. After two attempts at entering the security code, the radio will lock up electronically. This is indicated by a **SAFE** display. Unlike the previous generation, the radio will not lock up no matter how many incorrect coding attempts are made. The reactivation procedure can be repeated indefinitely.

The Heidleberg VI radio is retained in the instrument panel by means of lock clips at the sides of the radio body. To remove the radio from its mounting position, two special tools are required. Insert the tools, into the holes, in the side of the radio face plate. The tools will "click" into position. With the tools installed the radio can be pulled from the instrument panel. Disconnect the electrical leads to complete the removal. When installing the radio, be sure to connect the electrical leads in their proper position.

WINDSHIELD WIPERS

Wiper Refill

REPLACEMENT

1. Pull the wiper arms up off the windshield.

2. Using a pair of pliers, squeeze the two steel inserts at the open end of the blade.

3. Pull the insert of the rubber filler.

4. Remove the rubber filler.

5. Insert the new rubber filler making sure that the retainers engage the recesses in the second grooves.

6. Slide the metal inserts into the upper grooves of the rubber blade so that the notch in the insert faces the rubber. Engage the projections in grooves on both sides.

Blade and Arm

REMOVAL AND INSTALLATION

Front and Rear

NOTE: *There are two different styles of wiper arms. On the first, the arm pivot at-*

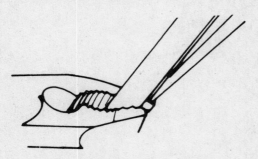

Squeezing the wiper blade insert

Notch in the blade insert

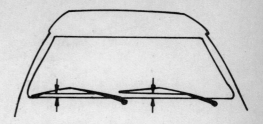

Blade-to-molding clearance

taching nut is covered with a plastic cap that pulls off. On the second, the arm pivot is covered by a spring-loaded metal cap that slips back off the nut.

1. Lift the blade and arm up off the windshield.

2. Simultaneously push the arm down and lift the smaller end cap up, or pull the plastic cap off, to expose the retaining nut.

3. Remove the retaining nut and lift the arm off the shaft.

4. Install the arm in the reverse order of removal. When properly installed, the blade-to-windshield molding clearance should be as follows (right — passenger side and left — driver side). Blade clearance is adjusted by holding the base of the wiper arm with pliers and bending the arm where at the point where it connects to the blade.

- Corrado:
  Right arm: 25mm
  Leftarm: 44.5mm
- Fox: 45.5mm for both arms
- Passat:
  Front right arm: 50mm
  Front left arm: 20mm
  Rear arm (wagon only): 20mm
- Scirocco w/Single blade: 55.5mm
- Scirocco w/Double blade and Cabriolet
  Front right: 35mm
  Left front:63.5mm
  Rear: 30mm
- 1979–84 Rabbit, Jetta and Pick-Up:
  Right arm: 30mm
  Left arm: 63.5mm
- 1985 Golf, GTI and Jetta:
  Right and left front arms: 61mm
  Rear arm: 10mm from the bottom and 20mm from the window center line
- Dasher: 30mm for both arms

Front Wiper Motor

REMOVAL AND INSTALLATION

Dasher and Quantum

NOTE: *Do not remove the wiper drive crank from the wiper motor shaft. If it must be re-*

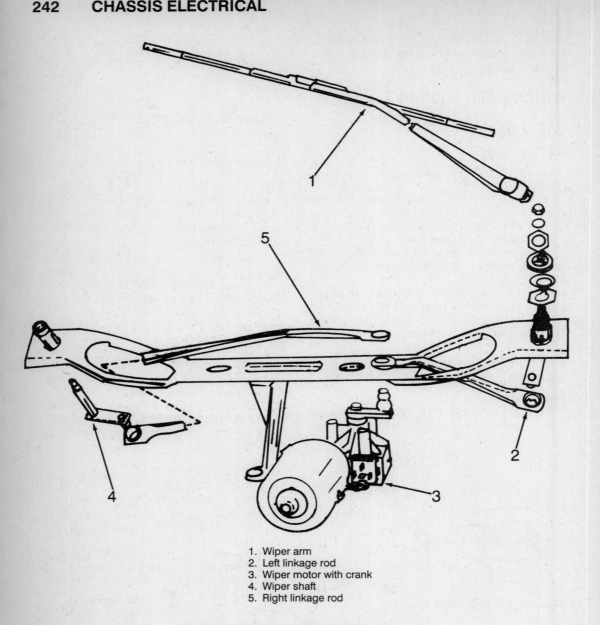

1. Wiper arm
2. Left linkage rod
3. Wiper motor with crank
4. Wiper shaft
5. Right linkage rod

Dasher windshield wiper components

moved for any reason, matchmark the shaft, motor and crank for installation.

1. Unplug the multiconnector from the wiper motor.
2. Remove the motor-to-linkage bracket retaining screws.
3. Carefully pry the motor crank out of the two linkage arms.
4. Remove the motor from the car.

5. Install the motor in the reverse order of removal. The crank arm should be at a right angle to the motor.

1974–84 Rabbit, Scirocco and Jetta

When removing the wiper motor, leave the mounting frame in place. On all models with two front wiper arms, do not remove the wiper drive crank from the motor shaft.

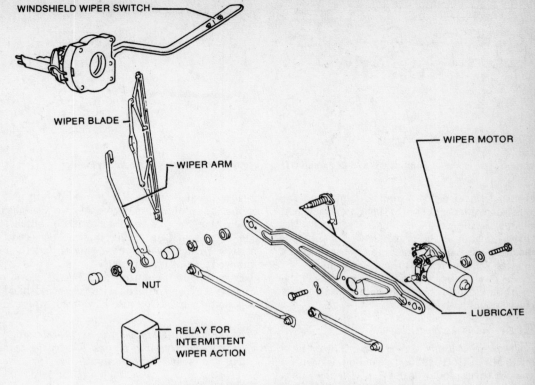

WINDSHIELD WIPER SWITCH

WIPER BLADE

WIPER ARM

NUT

WIPER MOTOR

LUBRICATE

RELAY FOR
INTERMITTENT
WIPER ACTION

Rabbit, Jetta and Scirocco front wiper motor and linkage

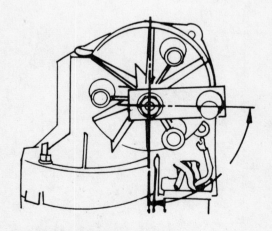

Dasher wiper motor-to-arm angle

On Sciroccos with one front wiper arm, match-mark the drive crank and motor arm and then remove the arm.

NOTE: *If, for any reason you must remove the wiper drive crank from the motor shaft on two wiper arm models, matchmark both parts for reassembly.*

1. Access is with the hood open. Disconnect the battery ground cable.

2. Detach the connecting rods or motor crank arm from the motor.

3. Pull off the wiring plug.

4. Remove the four mounting bolts. You may have to energize the motor for access to the top bolt.

5. Remove the motor. Reverse the procedure for installation.

1985–90 Golf, Fox, GTI, Jetta, Scirocco, Cabriolet, Corrado and Passat

1. Disconnect the electrical connector to the wiper motor.

2. Disconnect the crank arm from the wiper arm assembly. Make a note or drawing of the crank arm installation angle before removing.

3. Remove the retaining nut and the crank arm from the wiper motor shaft.

4. Remove the motor mounting bolts and the motor from the vehicle.

5. To install, run the motor and turn it off (it will stop in the **PARK** position).

6. Install the motor.

7. On Golf, Jetta and GTI, to install the

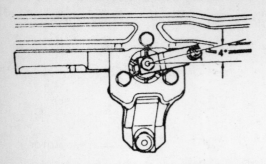

Wiper motor crank alignment on Golf, Jetta and GTI

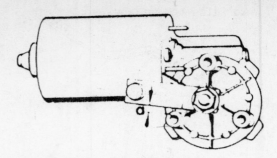

Wiper motor crank alignment on Passat

crank arm, raise it 4° from horizontal on the right side and connect it to the motor shaft. On Passat, if the crank is aligned properly, the threaded hole in the crank drive housing will just be covered by the crank. On all other models, set the crank at the original angle.

8. To complete the installation, connect the crank arm to the wiper assembly and reverse the removal procedures.

Rear Motor

There are 2 kinds of rear wiper motors used on Rabbits. Until 1976, a gear housing with a smooth cover plate was used; later models used a ribbed gear housing. Parts are different and cannot be combined between the two systems, except that the new style wiper motor bracket can be installed on earlier models. Sciroccos' motors are totally interchangeable, and their linkage remains unchanged.

Dasher, Fox, Quantum and Passat station wagons are also equipped with rear windshield wipers (optional). Golf also has a rear wiper.

NOTE: *On all models, do not interchange the wires of terminal 53 and 53a on the rear wiper switch. Damage to the motor will result.*

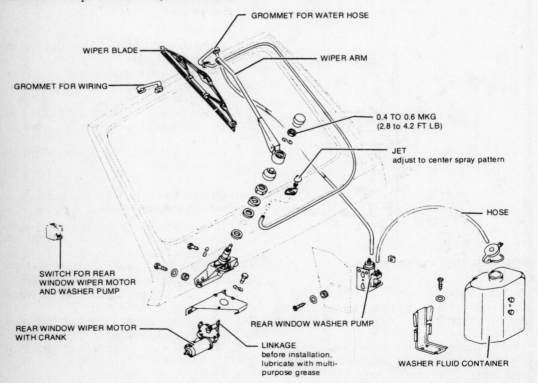

Rabbit and Scirocco rear wiper motor and linkage

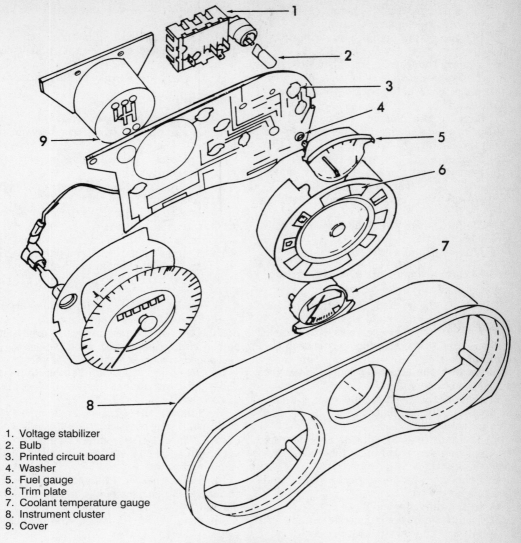

1. Voltage stabilizer
2. Bulb
3. Printed circuit board
4. Washer
5. Fuel gauge
6. Trim plate
7. Coolant temperature gauge
8. Instrument cluster
9. Cover

Dasher instrument panel

INSTRUMENTS AND SWITCHES

Instrument Cluster/Panel

REMOVAL AND INSTALLATION

Dasher

1974–77

1. Disconnect the battery ground cable.
2. Unscrew the speedometer cable from the rear of the cluster.
3. Using needle nosed pliers, detach the retaining springs on either side of the cluster.
4. Pivot the instrument cluster out of the dash.
5. Disconnect the multi-connector plug at the rear of the cluster.

6. Remove the cluster from the dash.
To install:
7. Support the cluster and connect the multi-plug connector.
8. Mount the cluster to the dash and connect the side cluster retaining springs.
9. Connect the speedometer cable to the speedometer at the rear of the cluster.
10. Connect the negative battery cable.

1978–81

1. Remove the radio or shelf.
2. Pull the knobs off the fresh air control and fan switch.
3. Remove the six instrument cluster to dashboard retaining screws.

4. Snap out the light, emergency flasher and rear window defogger switches.

5. Disconnect the air fan switch electrical connector.

6. Remove the instrument cluster and disconnect the speedometer cable and the multipoint connector from the back of the cluster.

To install:

7. Support the cluster and connect the multi-point plug and speedometer cable to the rear of the cluster.

8. Plug in the air fan switch connector.

9. Push the rear window defogger, emergency and light switches into the cluster.

10. Install the cluster-to-dash retaining screws.

11. Mount the fan switch and fresh air control knobs.

12. Mount the radio or shelf.

1975–84 Rabbit, Jetta and 1978–81 Scirocco

1. Disconnect the battery ground cable.

2. Remove the fresh air controls trim plate.

3. Remove the radio and glove box.

4. Unscrew the speedometer drive cable from the back of the speedometer. Detach the electrical plug.

5. Remove the attaching screw inside the radio/glove box opening.

6. Remove the instrument cluster. Reverse the procedure for installation.

To install:

7. Mount the instrument cluster and install the attaching screw through the radio/glove box opening.

8. Connect the electrical plug and speedometer cable.

9. Install the radio and glove box.

10. Mount the fresh air controls trim plate.

11. Connect the negative battery cable.

1982–84 Scirocco

1. Disconnect battery ground cable.

2. Remove the two Phillips head screws on the inner top surface of the instrument compartment.

3. Start to pull down on the instrument cluster and remove the screws in the top of the cluster.

4. Tip out the top of the instrument cluster.

5. Remove the speedometer cable by twisting the tabs of the plastic fixture around the end of the cable. On some vehicles, the speedometer cable is attached by a nut.

6. Disconnect the multi-point connector and remove instrument cluster.

To install:

7. Support the cluster and connect the multi-point plug connector.

8. Connect the speedometer cable.

9. Mount the cluster and install the lower retaining screws.

10. Install the two Phillips head screws on the inner top surface of the instrument compartment.

11. Connect the negative battery cable.

Quantum

1. Disconnect battery ground strap.

2. Carefully pry off switch trim below instruments.

3. Pull heater control knobs off and press out heater control trim.

4. Remove Phillips head screws holding heater control trim to panel.

5. Remove Phillips screws around perimeter of instrument cluster.

6. Disconnect all wiring to switches and warning lamps. Remove all trim panels.

7. Start to pull down on the instrument cluster and remove the screws in the top of the cluster.

8. Tip out the top of the instrument cluster.

9. Remove the speedometer cable by twisting the tabs of the plastic fixture around the end of the cable. On some vehicles, the speedometer cable is attached by a nut.

10. Disconnect the multi-point connector and remove instrument cluster.

To install:

11. Support the cluster and connect the multi-point plug connector.

12. Connect the speedometer cable.

13. Mount the cluster and install the lower retaining screws.

14. Install the two Phillips head screws on the inner top surface of the instrument compartment.

15. Install the trim panels and connect all switch wiring.

16. Install the Phillips heads screws around the cluster perimeter.

17. Install the heater control-to-trim panel screws.

18. Press in the heater control trim and mount the heater control knobs.

19. Mount the lower instrument trim.

20. Connect the negative battery cable.

1985–90 Golf, Fox, GTI, Jetta and Scirocco/Cabriolet

1. Pull off all of the temperature control knobs and levers.

2. Unclip the control lever trim plate, unplug the electrical connectors and remove the plate.

3. Remove the retaining screws and the instrument panel trim plate.

4. Remove the retaining screws and pull out the instrument panel.

5. Squeeze the clips on the speedometer cable head and remove the cable from the instrument cluster.

6. Disconnect all of the vacuum hose and the electrical connections.

To install:

7. Support the cluster and connect the electrical and vacuum hoses.

8. Connect the speedometer cable.

9. Mount the instrument panel and install the panel retaining screws.

10. Install the trim plate with retaining screws.

11. Install the control lever trim plate and plug in the electrical connectors. Secure the plate with the clip.

12. Mount the temperature control knobs and levers.

Corrado

1. Disconnect the negative battery.

2. Remove the five shelf screws.

3. Remove the two plastic nuts and pull out the storage tray.

4. Release the clips and pull out the storage box.

5. Remove the left cover. This cover is held in place by one oval head and six multi-purpose screws.

6. Remove the steering wheel.

7. Gently pry off the two upper left trim plate cover caps. Remove the four screws and remove the upper left trim plate.

8. Gently pry out the vents from the instrument panel.

9. Remove the radio or glove box.

10. Gently pry the trim plate from the cassette storage box, remove the screws and withdraw the box from the center console.

11. Pull off the temperature control knobs and sliding levers.

12. Gently pry the trim plate from the face of the heating and ventilation controls and remove the control assembly from the center console.

13. Remove the retaining screws and remove the center console trim plate.

14. Remove the instrument panel cover and steering steering column switch.

15. Remove the bolt cover caps from the left and right sides of the panel and remove the hex bolt that is under each cap.

16. Remove the hex nut from the rear of the console.

17. Remove the hex nuts located in the rear of the plenum panel. These nuts can only be seen with the aid of a small inspection mirror.

18. Pull the instrument panel slightly forward until there is sufficient clearance to disconnect the cables from the rear of the panel.

19. Remove the instrument panel.

To install:

20. Support the instrument panel and connect the cables.

21. Mount the panel and install the hex nuts in the rear of the plenum panel.

22. Install the rear console hex nut.

23. Install the left and right side hex bolts with cover caps.

24. Install the steering column switch and the instrument panel cover.

25. Install the center console trim plate.

26. Insert the ventilation controls into the center console. Install the control assembly trim plate.

27. Mount the temperature control knobs and sliding levers.

28. Install the cassette storage box and trim plate.

29. Install the radio, glove box and vents.

30. Install the upper left trim plate and cover caps.

31. Install the steering wheel.

32. Install the left cover.

33. Install the storage box, storage tray and five shelf screws. During installation of the storage box, the locating pins must be pushed firmly in the trim plate retainers.

34. Connect the negative battery cable.

Passat

1. Disconnect the negative battery cable.

2. Remove the front and center consoles.

3. Remove the screws from the passenger's side storage tray. To remove the storage tray, pull it down at an angle. Be careful not to damage the pins.

4. Reach into the driver's side storage tray and turn each fitting 90°. Remove the pins and unclip the driver's side storage tray. Remove the screws and pull the tray downward and out at an angle to remove it.

5. Remove the center trim plate.

6. Remove the instrument panel retaining screws.

7. Press the controls inward and under the instrument panel.

8. Drill out the shear bolts and lower the steering column.

9. Disconnect and label all electrical and ground wires.

10. Trace the wiring harnesses from the instrument panel to the fuse/relay box and disconnect them at the box.

11. Remove the cover caps from both sides of the instrument panel and remove the screw from under each cap.

12. Pull the air intake housing retainers upward.

13. Remove the front panel support screws,

loosen the rear support screws and fold the support back out of the way.

14. Working from inside the air plenum opening, disconnect the speedometer cable, remove the retaining pins and work the instrument panel from the mounting brackets.

To install:

15. Connect the speedometer cable and push the instrument panel onto the mounting brackets and secure with the retaining pins.

16. Raise the panel supports and snug the rear support screws. Mount the panel to the support and install the front support screws. Leave the rear screws slightly loose until the panel is aligned properly, then tighten them properly.

17. Push the air intake housing retainers down. Check for proper seating of the the air intake ducting on the heater housing.

18. Install the side panel screws and cover caps.

19. Connect the instrument panel wiring harnesses to the fuse box.

20. Connect all ground and electrical wires.

21. Raise the steering column and install new shear bolts.

22. Raise the controls and pull them back into the panel.

23. Install the panel retaining screws.

24. Install the center trim plate.

25. Install the driver's side storage tray by first inserting the clips in the instrument panel, then install the screws. Make sure the screws securing the cover and tray to the A pillar are tight.

26. Install the passenger's side storage tray.

27. Install the front and center consoles.

28. Connect the negative battery cable.

Windshield Wiper/Washer Switch

REMOVAL AND INSTALLATION

1. Using your hands, pull off the steering wheel cover.

2. Remove the steering wheel lock nut and spacer.

3. Using a wheel puller, remove the steering wheel.

4. Remove the three retaining screws and remove the combination turn signal/headlight switch.

5. Remove the windshield wiper/washer switch from the steering column.

To install:

6. Install the windshield wiper/washer switch onto the steering column.

7. Install the combination turn signal/headlight switch.

8. Install the steering wheel, lock nut and spacer.

9. Install the steering wheel cover.

Headlight Switch

REMOVAL AND INSTALLATION

NOTE: *A modified headlight switch has been installed on 1989 Cabriolets and Jettas produced from November of 1988. The new includes two additional terminals. The new switch is NOT interchangeable with the old one.*

1. Remove the steering wheel.

2. Remove the three retaining screws and remove the combination turn signal, headlight switch.

3. Installation is the reverse of the removal procedure.

Back-Up Light Switch

The back-up light switch is mounted on the transaxle. For removal and installation procedures, refer to Chapter 7.

Speedometer Cable

REMOVAL AND INSTALLATION

Dasher and Quantum

1. Unscrew the speedometer cable from the rear of the instrument cluster.

2. Unsnap the rubber grommets from the dash panel support and the firewall.

3. Pull the speedometer cable through the holes from the engine compartment.

4. Use pliers to unscrew the cable from the transaxle.

NOTE: *Some models may have the EGR mileage counter box mounted between the speedometer and the transmission. In this case the speedometer cable is unscrewed from the EGR box*

5. Installation is the reverse of removal.

Corrado and Passat

The speedometer cable is pushed into the rear of the instrument cluster and then into the speedometer. The cable engages the speedometer by means of spring in the cable housing.

1. Remove the instrument cluster and pull it out far enough so that the speedometer cable/cover assembly is accessible.

2. Disengage the speedometer cable from the rear of the instrument cluster.

3. Unsnap the rubber grommets from the dash panel support and the firewall.

4. Pull the speedometer cable through the holes from the engine compartment.

5. Use pliers to unscrew the cable from the transaxle.

6. Installation is the reverse of the removal procedure.

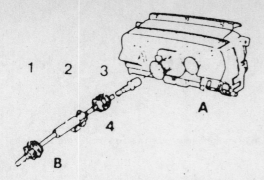

Speedometer cable assembly on Corrado and Passat

Rabbit, Golf, Scirocco, Jetta and GTI

The speedometer cable should not be kinked or greased. When installing the Scirocco speedometer cable, attach the cable to the bracket so the speedometer cable will not contact the clutch cable.

1. Unscrew the speedometer cable from the rear of the instrument cluster and from the EGR elapsed mileage counter.

2. Unsnap the rubber grommets from the dash panel support and the firewall.

3. Pull the speedometer cable through the holes.

4. The other end of the cable is attached to the EGR counter and transaxle.

5. Installation is the reverse of removal.

The speedometer cable should not be kinked or greased. When installing the Scirocco speedometer cable, attach it to the bracket to avoid the speedometer cable contacting the clutch cable.

LIGHTING

Headlights

REMOVAL AND INSTALLATION

Dasher—Single Headlight Models

1. Remove the grille. The retaining screws are located on the left of the VW insignia and one each between the VW and the headlight.

2. Remove the three headlight retaining ring screws.

NOTE: *Do not disturb the two headlight aiming screws or it will be necessary to re-aim the headlights.*

3. Remove headlight retaining ring.

4. Pull the headlight out of the housing and unplug the multiconnector.

5. Replace the new bulb in the reverse order of removal. Make sure that the three lugs on the bulb engage the slots in the housing.

Dasher—Dual Headlight Models

1. Remove the radiator grille. Pry up the two retaining clips, one located at each end of the top of the grille. Unsnap the four plastic tabs along the top of the grille and remove it.

2. Remove the three small screws and remove the retaining ring. Don't fiddle with the spring loaded adjusting screws or you will have to have the light re-aimed. Pull the light out and unhook it.

3. When installing new headlight, be aware that the outside lights have both high beam and low beam filaments while the inside lights have only high beam filaments. Be sure to mention which one you need when buying replacement.

4. When installing, make sure the glass lugs on the light engage in the support ring.

1975–81 Scirocco

1. Remove the grille. There are about fourteen screws located inside the grids of the grille. Remove these and remove the grille.

2. The headlights are removed in the same manner as the Dasher dual headlight model. See above for procedures. The Scirocco dual headlights are arranged the same as the Dasher.

1982–90 Scirocco

NOTE: *Depending on model, your car could be equipped with either Halogen sealed beam or incandescent sealed beam units. Always replace a burned out sealed beam with a new like unit.*

1. Remove the black moldings below the headlights.

2. Remove the screws retaining the headlamp mounting bracket.

3. Gently pull the headlamp from the support, unplug the connector from the back of the unit and remove the sealed beam.

4. Install in the reverse order.

1975–80 Rabbit

1. Remove the grille. On Westmoreland Rabbits (those made in the U.S., with square headlamps), the radiator grille is retained by two snap tabs and four fasteners on earlier models and by four screws along the top of the grille on later models. On the earlier models, remove the fasteners with a small punch. New fasteners will be needed to install the grille.

On the Rabbit equipped with round headlights, remove the screws and clips along the top and sides of the grille.

2. Remove the head light on all models by removing the retaining ring screws and removing the ring and the light. Unhook the electrical connector.

3. When installing new light, be sure to align the lugs in the light with their positions in the frame.

1981–84 Rabbit

NOTE: *Depending on model, your vehicle could be equipped with either Halogen sealed beam or incandescent sealed beam units. Always replace a burned out sealed beam with a new like unit.*

ROUND SEALED BEAM

1. Remove the screws and clips along the top and side of the grille and remove the grille.
2. Remove the three retaining screws that hold the headlamp mounting bracket.
3. Gently pull the headlamp from the support, unplug the connector from the back of the unit and remove the sealed beam.
4. Install in the reverse order.

RECTANGULAR SEALED BEAM

1. Remove the four screws located around the headlamp trim cover and remove the cover.
2. Remove the four screws retaining the headlamp mounting bracket.
3. Gently pull the headlamp from the support, unplug the connector from the back of the unit and remove the sealed beam.
4. Install in the reverse order.

Cabriolet

1. Remove the grille.
2. Unplug the connector from the back of the headlight.
3. Remove the retainer ring screws and remove the light.
4. Installation is the reverse of the removal procedure.

Jetta, Golf and GTI

Remove the grille by removing the two screws and the clip, swinging the side grille forward and lifting it out of the lower support holders. Remove the four screws and tensioner spring (Golf) in the face of the ring and remove the headlight after unhooking its electrical connector. When inserting new light, make sure the lugs in the light align with their supports in the ring.

Be aware when buying new headlights that the two inner lights have only high beam filaments while the outer two have both low and high beam filaments.

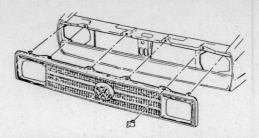

Grille and retaining pins used on Westmoreland Rabbits

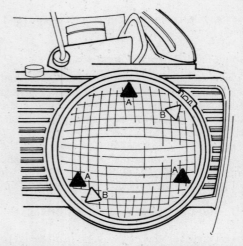

Screws at points (A) remove the headlight. Screws at points (B) are used for aiming

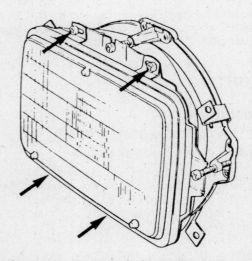

Remove the screws holding the trim ring on Jetta and Westmorlend Rabbits. Do not disturb the headlight aiming screws, top and right side

Quantum

NOTE: *Never substitute an incandescent sealed beam for one of the Halogen design.*

1. Open the hood. Loosen the lower parking/signal lamp retaining screws until the cover lens can be removed.

2. Remove the two lower and one upper screws that retain the headlamp trim housing.

3. Remove the four screws that mount the headlamp retaining bracket.

4. Gently pull the headlamp from the support, unplug the connector from the back of the sealed beam.

5. Install in the reverse order.

Fox

The headlight and side marker lights are removed as one unit.

1. Remove the two clamps from the top of the headlight frame.

2. Remove the headlight frame.

3. Unplug the connector from the back of the headlight.

4. Working from inside the engine compartment, remove the four screws and remove the headlight/side marker light as an assembly.

5. Installation is the reverse of the removal procedure.

Corrado

1. Gently pry the trim plate from the front of the light. The trim plate is fastened to the headlight supporting frame by six tabs.

2. Release the retaining clip on each side of the frame and pull the headlight and parking lamp assembly forward.

3. Unplug the connector from the back of the headlight and remove the headlight from the reflector housing.

4. Installation is the reverse of the removal procedure.

Passat

1. Remove the four retaining screws and remove the front panel.

2. Unplug the connector from the back of the headlight.

3. Remove the four headlight housing retaining screws and pull the headlight out of the housing.

4. Installation is the reverse of the removal procedure.

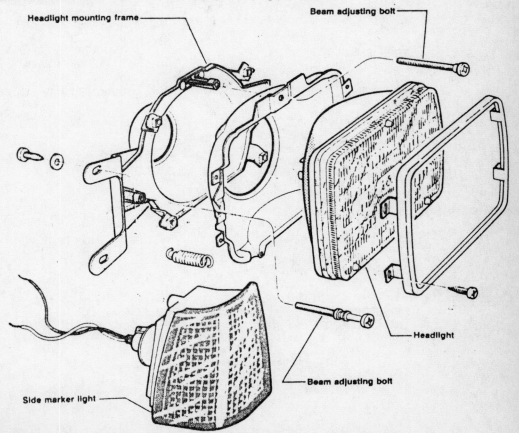

Fox headlight and side marker light assembly

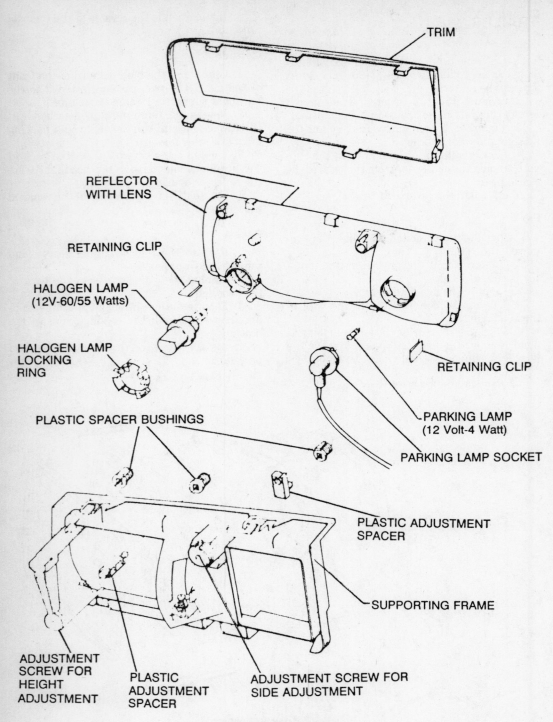

TRIM

REFLECTOR
WITH LENS

RETAINING CLIP

HALOGEN LAMP
(12V-60/55 Watts)

HALOGEN LAMP
LOCKING
RING

PLASTIC SPACER BUSHINGS

RETAINING CLIP

PARKING LAMP
(12 Volt-4 Watt)

PARKING LAMP SOCKET

PLASTIC ADJUSTMENT
SPACER

SUPPORTING FRAME

ADJUSTMENT
SCREW FOR
HEIGHT
ADJUSTMENT

PLASTIC
ADJUSTMENT
SPACER

ADJUSTMENT SCREW FOR
SIDE ADJUSTMENT

Corrado headlight assembly

TRAILER WIRING

Wiring the car for towing is fairly easy. There are a number of good wiring kits available and these should be used, rather than trying to design your own. All trailers will need brake lights and turn signals as well as tail lights and side marker lights. Most states require extra marker lights for overwide trailers. Also, most states have recently required back-up lights for trailers, and most trailer manufacturers have been building trailers with back-up lights for several years.

Additionally, some Class I, most Class II and just about all Class III trailers will have electric brakes.

Add to this number an accessories wire, to operate trailer internal equipment or to charge the trailer's battery, and you can have as many as seven wires in the harness.

Determine the equipment on your trailer and buy the wiring kit necessary. The kit will contain all the wires needed, plus a plug adapter set which included the female plug, mounted on the bumper or hitch, and the male plug, wired into, or plugged into the trailer harness.

When installing the kit, follow the manufacturer's instructions. The color coding of the wires is standard throughout the industry.

One point to note: some domestic vehicles, and most imported vehicles, have separate turn signals. On most domestic vehicles, the brake lights and rear turn signals operate with the same bulb. For those vehicles with separate turn signals, you can purchase an isolation unit so that the brake lights won't blink whenever the turn signals are operated, or, you can go to your local electronics supply house and buy four diodes to wire in series with the brake and turn signal bulbs. Diodes will isolate the brake and turn signals. The choice is yours. The isolation units are simple and quick to install, but far more expensive than the diodes. The diodes, however, require more work to install properly, since they require the cutting of each bulb's wire and soldering in place of the diode.

One, final point, the best kits are those with a spring loaded cover on the vehicle mounted socket. This cover prevent dirt and moisture from corroding the terminals. Never let the vehicle socket hang loosely; always mount it securely to the bumper or hitch.

CIRCUIT PROTECTION

The Dasher fuse/relay panel is located under the hood on the driver's side fender. The fuse/relay panel on all other models is located in the lower left side of the dashboard. Use VW ceramic fuses. VW recommends that relays be replaced by your dealer.

Fuses

Fuses are listed according to numbers on the fuse box cover.

Troubleshooting the Heater

Problem	Cause	Solution
Blower motor will not turn at any speed	• Blown fuse • Loose connection • Defective ground • Faulty switch • Faulty motor • Faulty resistor	• Replace fuse • Inspect and tighten • Clean and tighten • Replace switch • Replace motor • Replace resistor
Blower motor turns at one speed only	• Faulty switch • Faulty resistor	• Replace switch • Replace resistor
Blower motor turns but does not circulate air	• Intake blocked • Fan not secured to the motor shaft	• Clean intake • Tighten security
Heater will not heat	• Coolant does not reach proper temperature • Heater core blocked internally • Heater core air-bound • Blend-air door not in proper position	• Check and replace thermostat if necessary • Flush or replace core if necessary • Purge air from core • Adjust cable
Heater will not defrost	• Control cable adjustment incorrect • Defroster hose damaged	• Adjust control cable • Replace defroster hose

Troubleshooting Basic Dash Gauge Problems

Problem	Cause	Solution
Coolant Temperature Gauge		
Gauge reads erratically or not at all	• Loose or dirty connections • Defective sending unit	• Clean/tighten connections • Bi-metal gauge: remove the wire from the sending unit. Ground the wire for an instant. If the gauge registers, replace the sending unit.
	• Defective gauge	• Magnetic gauge: disconnect the wire at the sending unit. With ignition ON gauge should register COLD. Ground the wire; gauge should register HOT.
Ammeter Gauge—Turn Headlights ON (do not start engine). Note reaction		
Ammeter shows charge	• Connections reversed on gauge	• Reinstall connections
Ammeter shows discharge	• Ammeter is OK	• Nothing
Ammeter does not move	• Loose connections or faulty wiring	• Check/correct wiring
	• Defective gauge	• Replace gauge
Oil Pressure Gauge		
Gauge does not register or is inaccurate	• On mechanical gauge, Bourdon tube may be bent or kinked	• Check tube for kinks or bends preventing oil from reaching the gauge
	• Low oil pressure	• Remove sending unit. Idle the engine briefly. If no oil flows from sending unit hole, problem is in engine.
	• Defective gauge	• Remove the wire from the sending unit and ground it for an instant with the ignition ON. A good gauge will go to the top of the scale.
	• Defective wiring	• Check the wiring to the gauge. If it's OK and the gauge doesn't register when grounded, replace the gauge.
	• Defective sending unit	• If the wiring is OK and the gauge functions when grounded, replace the sending unit
All Gauges		
All gauges do not operate	• Blown fuse • Defective instrument regulator	• Replace fuse • Replace instrument voltage regulator
All gauges read low or erratically	• Defective or dirty instrument voltage regulator	• Clean contacts or replace
All gauges pegged	• Loss of ground between instrument voltage regulator and car	• Check ground
	• Defective instrument regulator	• Replace regulator
Warning Lights		
Light(s) do not come on when ignition is ON, but engine is not started	• Defective bulb • Defective wire	• Replace bulb • Check wire from light to sending unit
	• Defective sending unit	• Disconnect the wire from the sending unit and ground it. Replace the sending unit if the light comes on with the ignition ON.
Light comes on with engine running	• Problem in individual system • Defective sending unit	• Check system • Check sending unit (see above)

Troubleshooting Basic Turn Signal and Flasher Problems

Most problems in the turn signals or flasher system can be reduced to defective flashers or bulbs, which are easily replaced. Occasionally, problems in the turn signals are traced to the switch in the steering column, which will require professional service.

F = Front   R = Rear   ● = Lights off   o = Lights on

Problem		Solution
Turn signals light, but do not flash		• Replace the flasher
No turn signals light on either side		• Check the fuse. Replace if defective. • Check the flasher by substitution • Check for open circuit, short circuit or poor ground
Both turn signals on one side don't work		• Check for bad bulbs • Check for bad ground in both housings
One turn signal light on one side doesn't work		• Check and/or replace bulb • Check for corrosion in socket. Clean contacts. • Check for poor ground at socket
Turn signal flashes too fast or too slow		• Check any bulb on the side flashing too fast. A heavy-duty bulb is probably installed in place of a regular bulb. • Check the bulb flashing too slow. A standard bulb was probably installed in place of a heavy-duty bulb. • Check for loose connections or corrosion at the bulb socket
Indicator lights don't work in either direction		• Check if the turn signals are working • Check the dash indicator lights • Check the flasher by substitution
One indicator light doesn't light		• On systems with 1 dash indicator: See if the lights work on the same side. Often the filaments have been reversed in systems combining stoplights with taillights and turn signals. Check the flasher by substitution • On systems with 2 indicators: Check the bulbs on the same side. Check the indicator light bulb. Check the flasher by substitution

Troubleshooting Basic Lighting Problems

Problem	Cause	Solution
Lights		
One or more lights don't work, but others do	• Defective bulb(s) • Blown fuse(s) • Dirty fuse clips or light sockets • Poor ground circuit	• Replace bulb(s) • Replace fuse(s) • Clean connections • Run ground wire from light socket housing to car frame
Lights burn out quickly	• Incorrect voltage regulator setting or defective regulator • Poor battery/alternator connections	• Replace voltage regulator • Check battery/alternator connections
Lights go dim	• Low/discharged battery • Alternator not charging • Corroded sockets or connections • Low voltage output	• Check battery • Check drive belt tension; repair or replace alternator • Clean bulb and socket contacts and connections • Replace voltage regulator
Lights flicker	• Loose connection • Poor ground • Circuit breaker operating (short circuit)	• Tighten all connections • Run ground wire from light housing to car frame • Check connections and look for bare wires
Lights "flare"—Some flare is normal on acceleration—if excessive, see "Lights Burn Out Quickly"	• High voltage setting	• Replace voltage regulator
Lights glare—approaching drivers are blinded	• Lights adjusted too high • Rear springs or shocks sagging • Rear tires soft	• Have headlights aimed • Check rear springs/shocks • Check/correct rear tire pressure
Turn Signals		
Turn signals don't work in either direction	• Blown fuse • Defective flasher • Loose connection	• Replace fuse • Replace flasher • Check/tighten all connections
Right (or left) turn signal only won't work	• Bulb burned out • Right (or left) indicator bulb burned out • Short circuit	• Replace bulb • Check/replace indicator bulb • Check/repair wiring
Flasher rate too slow or too fast	• Incorrect wattage bulb • Incorrect flasher	• Flasher bulb • Replace flasher (use a variable load flasher if you pull a trailer)
Indicator lights do not flash (burn steadily)	• Burned out bulb • Defective flasher	• Replace bulb • Replace flasher
Indicator lights do not light at all	• Burned out indicator bulb • Defective flasher	• Replace indicator bulb • Replace flasher

Drive Train

7

MANUAL TRANSAXLE

Transaxle describes a unit which combines the transmission gears and the drive axle gears in one housing. Volkswagen is a past master at this type of assembly, it being the design used in the VW Beetle for over thirty years. Besides being mounted in the front of the vehicle instead of the rear as in the Beetle, the Rabbit, Jetta and Scirocco transaxle is rather unconventional in that it is mounted side by side with the engine. The Dasher and Fox transaxle is mounted behind the engine, much like a conventional automobile engine/transmission layout, except that the differential is mounted ahead of the transmission.

Transaxle Identification

The transaxle can be identified by numbers in 2 places on the transaxle housing. The transaxle code letters and the date of production are located on top of the bell housing and the transaxle type number is located on the side of the bell housing.

Adjustments

SHIFT LINKAGE

Dasher, to Chassis No. 3–5 2 044 764

1. Shift into Neutral.
2. Remove the round floor cover.
3. Loosen the nuts and move the bearing housing so that the shift lever inclines approximately 5° to the rear.
4. Tighten the nuts.
5. Shift into 2nd gear.
6. Loosen the stop plate bolts.
7. Adjust the plate so that the shift lever has 10–16mm lateral movement at the shift knob.

NOTE: *Moving the plate to the right increases play; moving the plate to the left decreases play.*

8. Tighten the bolts. Check the shift pattern and make sure that reverse engages easily.

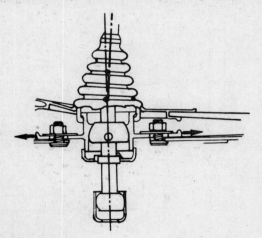

Neutral adjustment — Dasher to chassis number 3-5 2 044 764

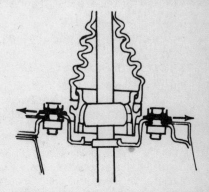

Second gear adjustment — Dasher to chassis number 3-5 2 044 764

Dasher from Chassis No. 3–5 2 044 765 and Quantum

An adjusting tool, VW 3014 or 3057, must be used on these models.

1. Place the lever in Neutral.
2. Working under the car, loosen the clamp nut.
3. Inside the car, remove the gear lever knob and the shift boot. It is not necessary to remove the console. Align the centering holes of the lever housing and the lever bearing housing.
4. Install the tool with the locating pin toward the front. Push the lever to the left side of the tool cutout. Tighten the lower knurled knob to secure the tool.
5. Move the top slide of the tool to the left stop and tighten the upper knurled knob.
6. Push the shift lever to the right side of the cutout. Align the shift rod and shift finger under the car, and tighten the clamp nut. Remove the tool.
7. Place the lever in 1st. Press the lever to the left side against the stop. Release the lever: it should spring back 6–12mm. If not, move the lever housing slightly sideways to correct. Check that all gears can be engaged easily, particularly reverse.

Fox

1. Shift into Neutral.
2. Remove the gear shift lever knob and shift boot.
3. Loosen the clamp nuts and check that shift finger slides freely on the shift rod.
4. Move the gear shift lever to the right side, between 3rd and 4th gear position. The gear shift lever should remain perpendicular to the ball housing.
5. With the inner shift lever in neutral and the gear shift lever between 2nd and 3rd gear, tighten the clamp nut.
6. Check the engagement of all gears, including reverse, and make sure that the gear shift lever moves freely.

Rabbit, Scirocco, Cabriolet and 1980–84 Jetta

1974–76 MODELS WITH ADJUSTABLE LINKAGE

1. Adjust the long rod over the left drive-shaft coupling to a length of 163–165mm.
2. Adjust the short angle rod that attaches to the final drive housing to a length of 30–32mm.
3. Make the lower part of the floorshift lever vertical (in the side to side plane) in the 1st gear position by loosening the bearing plate that supports the end of the long shift rod that connects to the bottom of the floorshift lever.

Tighten the mounting nuts when the lever is vertical.

4. Make the lower part of the floorshift lever vertical (in the fore and aft plane) in the Neutral position by pulling up the boot and loosening the two lever plate bolts. Move the plate until the lever is vertical.

1977 AND LATER MODELS WITH ADJUSTABLE LINKAGE

This category includes some late 1976 models, and is for Rabbits from chassis no. 176 3 000 001, Sciroccos from chassis no. 536 2 000 001 and all Jettas.

1. Align the holes of the lever housing plate with the holes of the lever bearing plate. With the shifter in neutral.
2. Loosen the shift rod clamp so that the selector lever moves easily on the shift rod. On 4-speed transaxles, pull the boot off the lever housing under the car and push it out of the

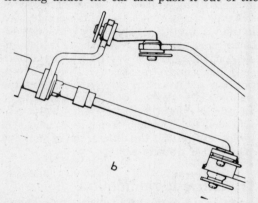

The long rod on the rabbit and Scirocco shift linkage is to be adjusted to a length (B) of 163–165mm

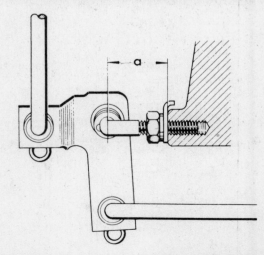

Adjust the relay lever (A) to 30–32mm on Rabbit and Scirocco with adjustable linkage

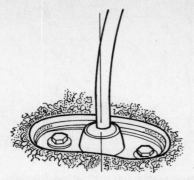

Adjusting the shift lever on Rabbit and Scirocco with adjustable linkage

way. It may be necessary to loosen the screws in the coverplate to free the boot.

3. Check that the shift finger (the rubber covered protrusion at the bottom of the shifter) is in the center of the stopping plate.

4. Adjust the shift rod end so that (A) is 19mm (7mm for 5–speed transaxles). Tighten the shift rod clamp and check the shifter operation.

MODELS WITH NON-ADJUSTABLE LINKAGE

1. Make the lower part of the floorshift lever vertical (in the side to side plane) in the 1st gear position by loosening the bearing plate that supports the end of the long shift rod that connects to the bottom of the floorshift lever. Tighten the mounting nuts when the lever is vertical.

2. Make the lower part of the floorshift lever vertical (in the fore and aft plane) in the Neutral position by pulling up the boot and loosening the two lever plate bolts. Move the plate until the lever is vertical.

1985–90 Golf and Jetta

1. Place the shifter lever into the Neutral position.

2. Under the vehicle, loosen the clamp on the shifter rod.

NOTE: *The shifter lever MUST move freely on the shifter rod.*

3. Remove the shifter knob and the boot.

4. Position the gauge alignment tool VW–3104 on the shifting mechanism (lock it in place).

5. Place the transaxle selector lever in the Neutral position.

6. Align the shift rod with the selector lever and torque the clamp to 19 ft. lbs.

NOTE: *The shifter linkage MUST NOT be under load during the adjustment.*

7. To complete the installation, reverse the removal procedures. Check the shifting of the gears.

Corrado and Passat

NOTE: *This procedure requires the use of VW shift lever adjusting gauge 3192 or its equivalent.*

1. Place the gearshift lever in Neutral.

2. Remove the gearshift lever knob and shift boot assembly.

3. Loosen the shift and select cable lever bolts until the operating levers move freely.

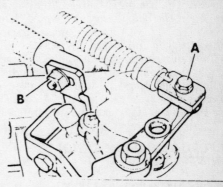

Manual transmission operating cables on Corrado and Passat

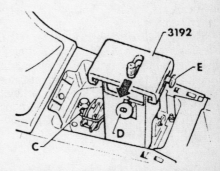

Gearshift adjuster tool installation on Corrado and Passat

4. Loosen bolt **C** which is shown in the accompanying illustration.

5. Install the shift lever adjusting gauge.

6. Pivot the locating pin (on the gauge) under the bearing plate and tighten nut **D**.

7. Press the gearshift lever into the left detent of the gauge slide.

8. Press the gearshift lever and slide to the left stop and tighten with bolt **E**.

9. Move the gearshift lever to the right detent and tighten bolt **C**.

10. Install wedge and locating pin 3192/1 or its equivalent. Push the wedge in between the gearshift lever and cover until there is no play. The wedge must not raise the gearshift lever.

11. Connect the operating cables with the gearshift lever in this position.

12. Remove the wedge, pin and adjusting gauge.

13. Start the engine, press the clutch pedal in and wait about 3–6 seconds to allow the input shaft to stop rotating.

14. Shift all the gears and check for smooth and proper engagement. If any gear binds or drags, check the transaxle rod travel as follows: Shift into 1st gear. Press the shift lever to the left, up to stop and release it. While doing this have an assistant observe the shift rod on the transaxle. The rod must travel 1.2mm up and down when the shift lever is activated. If the rod travel is not within specs, press the shift lever to the left and loosen the selector cable nut (the cable should have a minimal amount of play at this point). Push the cable toward the instrument panel and tighten the nut to increase the cable play.

15. Install the shift boot and gearshift lever knob.

SELECTOR SHAFT LOCKBOLT ADJUSTMENT

Rabbit, Scirocco and Jetta Only

These selector shaft lockbolt adjustments are for Rabbits, Sciroccos and Jettas only. The adjustments are the same for both 4- and 5-speed manual transaxles.

NOTE: *For 5-speed transaxle 5th gear lockbolt adjustment, see the following section.*

Make this adjustment if, after completing the linkage adjustment, the linkage still feels spongy or jams. There are 2 kinds of lockbolts: those with plastic caps (1975) or those with lockrings (1976 and later). The lockbolt is located on the top of the transaxle.

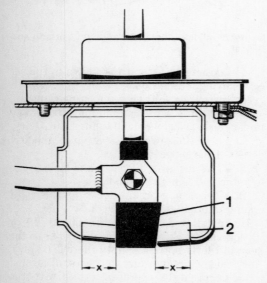

1977 and later Rabbit, Jetta and Scirocco. Shift finger (1) must be in the center of the stopping gate (2)

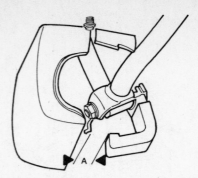

Adjusting the shift rod end (A) on 1977 and later Rabbit, Jetta and Scirocco

1975 MODELS

1. Remove the linkage from the selector shaft lever and put the transaxle in Neutral.

2. Turn the slotted plunger until the plunger hits bottom. The nut will start to move out.

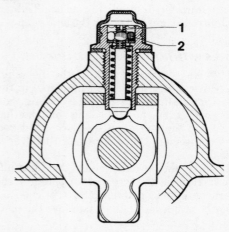

On 1975 Rabbit and Scirocco, turn the plunger (1) until the nut (2) starts to move

3. From here, turn the plunger back 1/4 turn and install the plastic cap.

4. Reconnect the linkage.

1976 AND LATER MODELS

1. Disconnect the shift linkage and put the transaxle in Neutral.

2. Loosen the locknut and turn the adjusting sleeve in until the lockring lifts off the sleeve.

3. Turn the adjusting sleeve back until the lockring just contacts the sleeve. Tighten the locknut.

4. Turn the shaft slightly. The lockring should lift as soon as the shaft is turned.

5. Reconnect the linkage.

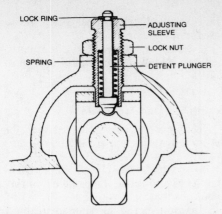

On 1976 and later Rabbit, Jetta and Scirocco, loosen the locknut and turn the adjusting sleeve

5th GEAR LOCKBOLT ADJUSTMENT

Rabbit, Scirocco and Jetta Only

This adjustment is made with the transaxle in neutral. The 5th gear lockbolt is located on top of the transaxle next to the selector shaft lockbolt. It has a large protective cap over it.

1. Remove the protective cap.
2. Loosen the locknut and tighten the adjusting sleeve until the detent plunger in the center of the sleeve just begins to move up.
3. Loosen the adjusting sleeve ⅓ of a turn and tighten the locknut. Make sure the transaxle shifts in and out of 5th gear easily. Replace the protective cap.

Back-Up light Switch

The Dasher and Quantum back-up light switch is screwed into the back of the gear shift housing above the shift lever for manual transaxles.

The Fox back-up light switch is screwed into the back of the transaxle housing.

The back-up light switch on the manual Rabbit, Scirocco and Cabriolet is mounted in one of three positions: screwed into the front face of the transaxle beside the oil filler plug; screwed into the top of the transaxle case to the left of the shift linkage; mounted as a microswitch on top of the transaxle with a lever that is activated by the external shift linkage.

The manual transaxle Jetta back-up light switch is screwed into the top of the transaxle case to the left of the shift linkage.

On Corrado and Passat, the back-up light switch is mounted in a bracket that bolts to the top of the gearshift housing.

The Rabbit, Scirocco, Corrado and Passat microswitch can be adjusted by bending the bracket. No other back-up light switch can be adjusted.

Transaxle

REMOVAL AND INSTALLATION

Dasher

1. Disconnect the negative battery cable.
2. Disconnect the exhaust pipe from the manifold and its bracket on the transaxle.
3. Remove the square-headed bolt on the shift linkage. Later models have a hex head bolt.
4. Press the shift linkage coupling off.
5. Disconnect the clutch cable.
6. Disconnect the speedometer cable.
7. Detach the axle shafts from the transaxle.
8. Remove the starter.
9. Remove the inspection plate.
10. Remove the engine-to-transaxle bolts.
11. Remove the transaxle crossmember.
12. Support the transaxle with a jack.
13. Pry the transaxle out from the engine.
14. Lift the transaxle out of the car with an assistant.
15. Observe the following when installing the transaxle.

   a. When installing the transaxle crossmember, do not fully tighten the bolts until the transaxle is aligned and fully installed in the vehicle.

   b. Tighten the engine-to-transaxle bolts to 40 ft. lbs.

   c. Tighten the axle shaft bolts to 33 ft. lbs.

   d. On models with the rubber core rear transaxle mount, the rubber core must be centered in its housing.

   e. Make sure there is a 10mm clearance between the header pipe and the floor of the vehicle.

   f. Adjust the clutch (see section in this chapter).

Quantum

1. Disconnect battery ground strap.
2. Disconnect exhaust pipe from the manifold and its bracket.
3. Unhook the clutch cable.
4. Detach speedometer cable.
5. Remove upper engine/transaxle bolts.
6. Remove engine support bolts on both sides of engine block (front).
7. Remove front muffler and exhaust pipe.
8. Unbolt both driveshafts (halfshafts) at the transaxle.

NOTE: *On Quantum Syncro, models the driveshaft to the rear axle assembly will also have to be removed in order to remove the transaxle.*

9. Disconnect back-up light wiring.

10. Remove the inspection plate on bottom of transaxle case.

11. Remove starter bolt.

12. Remove shift rod coupling bolt. Pry off shift rod coupling ball with a prybar.

13. Pull off shift rod coupling from shift rod.

14. Place a jack under the transaxle and lift slightly.

15. Remove transaxle support bolts, and transaxle rubber mounts.

16. Remove front transaxle support bolts, lower transaxle/engine support bolts.

17. Slowly pry transaxle from engine.

18. Lower transaxle out of the car.

19. During installation, make sure mainshaft splines are clean and lubricated with a molybdenum disulfide grease. Make sure inspection plate is properly seated, and that all engine/transaxle mounting bolts are aligned and free of tension (holes lined up) before tightening everything. Readjust shift mechanism if necessary. Observe the following torques:

• Transaxle-to-engine: 40 ft. lbs.
• Driveshaft-to-drive flange: 33 ft. lbs.
• Front transaxle support-to-transaxle: 18 ft. lbs.
• Transaxle-to-body: 80 ft. lbs.

Fox with 4-Speed Transaxle

1. Disconnect the battery ground cable.

2. Disconnect the exhaust pipe from the manifold and its bracket on the transaxle.

3. Remove the square-headed bolt on the shift linkage. Later models have a hex head bolt.

4. Press the shift linkage coupling off.

5. Disconnect the clutch cable.

6. Disconnect the speedometer cable.

7. Detach the halfshafts from the transaxle.

8. Remove the starter.

9. Remove the inspection plate.

10. Remove the engine-to-transaxle bolts.

11. Remove the transaxle crossmember.

12. Support the transaxle with a jack.

13. Pry the transaxle out from the engine.

14. Lift the transaxle out of the car with an assistant.

15. Observe the following when installing the transaxle.

a. When installing the transaxle crossmember, do not fully tighten the bolts until the transaxle is aligned and fully installed in the vehicle.

b. Tighten the engine-to-transaxle bolts to 40 ft. lbs.

c. Tighten the halfshaft bolts to 33 ft. lbs. (45 Nm).

d. On models with the rubber core rear transaxle mount, the rubber core must be centered in its housing.

e. Make sure there is a 10mm clearance between the header pipe and the floor of the vehicle.

f. Adjust the clutch.

Fox with 5-Speed Transaxle

1. Disconnect the negative battery cable.

2. Remove the upper engine-to-transaxle bolts.

3. Disconnect the clutch cable from the clutch lever and route the cable off to the side and out of the way.

4. Disconnect the speedometer cable from the transaxle.

5. Disconnect the exhaust pipe from the manifold and its bracket on the transaxle.

6. Remove the engine stop bolts from the block.

7. Disconnect the front exhaust pipe from the catalytic converter.

8. Unbolt the exhaust pipe support from the transaxle.

9. Unbolt the axleshafts from the transaxle flanges. Tie the shafts up and out of the way.

10. Unplug the back-up switch wire.

11. Unbolt and remove the cover plate.

12. Remove the starter.

13. Remove the bolt from the shift rod coupling and pry the linkage from the coupling.

14. Pull the shift rod coupling from the shift rod.

15. Support the transaxle with a jack or support tool 2071 and raise the transaxle slightly.

16. Remove the transaxle support bar bolts and pivot the support to the rear. Remove the support bar mount.

17. Remove the lower engine/transaxle bolts.

18. Using a large prybar, separate the transaxle from the engine and lower from the vehicle using the jack.

To install:

19. Make sure the mainshaft splines are clean, then lightly lubricate them with MoS_2 grease or spray.

20. Raise the transaxle onto the engine and install the lower engine/transaxle bolts. Torque the bolts to 40 ft. lbs.

21. Install the mounts and mounting support brackets. Torque the transaxle mounting fasteners to the following specifications:

• Sub-frame support-to-body — 40 ft. lbs.
• Mount-to-bracket — 18 ft. lbs.
• Mount-to-body — 80 ft. lbs.
• Front bracket-to-transaxle — 40 ft. lbs.

NOTE: *Make sure the engine/transaxle mounts are aligned and free of tension before tightening the fasteners. All the mount rubber cores should be centered in the mount.*

22. Connect the shift rod coupling to the shift rod.

23. Connect the shift rod linkage to the shift rod coupling. Torque the shift rod bolt to 14 ft. lbs.

24. Install the starter. Torque the starter mounting bolts to 14 ft. lbs.

25. Install the cover plate and torque the bolts to 7 ft. lbs. Make sure the cover plate is properly seated.

26. Plug in the back-up switch wire.

27. Connect the axleshaft to the transaxle. Torque the flange bolts to 30 ft. lbs.

28. Attach the exhaust pipe support to the transaxle.

29. Connect the front exhaust pipe to the catalytic converter.

30. Install the engine stop bolts and torque them to 18 ft. lbs.

31. Connect the exhaust pipe to the bracket and manifold. Torque the manifold nuts to 22 ft. lbs.

32. Connect the speedometer and clutch cables.

33. Install the upper engine/transaxle bolts. Torque the bolts to 40 ft. lbs.

1975–84 Rabbit, Scirocco, Pick-Up and Jetta

The engine and transaxle may be removed together as explained under "Engine, Removal and Installation" or the transaxle may be removed alone, as explained here.

1. Disconnect the battery ground cable.

2. Support the left end of the engine at the lifting eye with the appropriate VW support tool. For 16V Scirocco, use support bar 10–222A with base 3180.

3. Remove the left transaxle mount bolts (between the transaxle and the firewall and ground strap.)

4. Turn the engine until the lug on the flywheel (to the left to the TDC mark) aligns with the flywheel timing pointer. The transaxle/engine must be in this position to be separated.

5. Detach the speedometer drive cable, backup light wire, and clutch cable.

6. Remove the engine-to-transaxle bolts.

7. Disconnect the shift linkage.

8. Detach the transaxle ground strap.

9. Remove the starter.

10. Remove the engine mounting support near the starter.

11. Remove the rear transaxle mount.

12. Unbolt and wire up the driveshafts.

13. From underneath, remove the bolts for the large cover plate, but don't remove it. Unbolt the small cover plate on the firewall side of the engine. Remove the engine to transaxle nut immediately below the small plate.

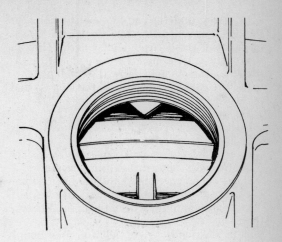

Align the lug on the flywheel with the timing pointer to remove the Rabbit, Jetta or Scirocco transaxle

14. Press the transaxle off the dowels and remove it from below the car.

15. During installation, the recess in the flywheel edge must be at 3:00 o'clock (facing the left end of the engine). Tighten the engine to transaxle bolts to 47 ft. lbs. Tighten the engine mounting support bolts to 47 ft. lbs. Tighten the driveshaft bolts to 32 ft. lbs.

16. Check the adjustment of the shift linkage.

1985–90 Scirocco and Cabriolet

1. Disconnect the battery ground cable.

2. Support the left end of the engine at the lifting eye with the appropriate VW support tool. For 16V Scirocco, use support bar 10–222A with base 3180.

3. Remove the left transaxle mount bolts (between the transaxle and the firewall and ground strap.)

4. Detach the speedometer drive cable, backup light wire, and clutch cable. Plug the speedometer hole with a rubber cap.

5. Remove the engine-to-transaxle bolts. Remove the starter.

6. Turn the engine until the lug on the flywheel (to the left to the TDC mark) aligns with the flywheel timing pointer. The transaxle/engine must be in this position to be separated.

7. Disconnect the shift linkage.

8. Disconnect the front selector rod.

9. Remove the exhaust pipe bracket.

10. Remove the rear transaxle mount from the transaxle and body.

11. Unbolt the driveshafts from the transaxle and tie them up so they will be out of the way.

12. From underneath, remove the bolts for the large cover plate, but don't remove it. Unbolt the small cover plate on the firewall side of the engine. Remove the engine to transaxle nut immediately below the small plate.

13. Press the transaxle off the dowels and remove it from below the car.

To install:

14. Carefully, raise the transaxle into the vehicle and align as follows:

   a. Move the engine/transaxle from side-to-side until the rear mount is straight.

   b. Then, move the engine/transaxle assembly in a front-to-rear direction until the left and right mounts are centered in their brackets.

   c. Tighten the right, left and rear mount bolts to 25–30 ft. lbs.

   d. Position the front mount cup until the rubber core is centered in the cup.

   e. Torque the cup bolts to 38 ft. lbs.

15. Make sure that the exhaust system is aligned properly before completing the rest of the installation procedure. Re-align the exhaust system if necessary.

16. During the remainder of the installation, observe the following torque values:

- Large and small cover plate bolts: 78 inch lbs.
- Engine-to-transaxle bolts: 58 ft. lbs.
- Starter bolts: 33 ft. lbs.
- Driveshaft flange bolts: 33 ft. lbs.
- Rear mount bolts: 33 ft. lbs.

1985–90 Golf, GTI and Jetta

1. Disconnect the negative battery cable.

2. Disconnect the back-up light switch connector and the speedometer cable from the transaxle (plug the speedometer cable hole).

3. Connect the engine sling tool VW–10–222A and base 3180 to the engine and support slightly.

NOTE: *On 16 valve engines, the idle air stabilizer valve must be removed from the intake manifold before installing the engine support tools.*

4. Remove the upper transaxle-to-engine bolts.

5. At the transaxle housing, disconnect the clutch cable from the clutch release lever.

6. Remove the 3 mounting bolts from the right engine support.

7. At the gear selector lever shaft, disconnect the short rod and the connecting rod from the lever. Remove the long selector rod from the relay lever.

8. Remove the mounting bolt and the 2 upper bolts from the left transaxle housing-to-mount.

9. Remove the left wheel housing liner.

10. Detach the halfshaft from the transaxle and support on a wire.

11. Remove the large and the small cover plates from behind the right drive flange.

12. Remove the starter and the front mount assembly.

13. Remove the 3rd mounting bolt from the left transaxle mount.

14. Lower the transaxle slightly and remove the left transaxle mounting bolts.

15. Push the engine and transaxle assembly to the right as far as possible – at least 3mm.

16. Place a transaxle support jack under the transaxle, remove the lower transaxle-to-engine bolts and lower the transaxle from the vehicle.

17. To install, coat the input shaft lightly with Moly lube and observe the following torque values.

- Engine-to-transaxle bolts – 55 ft. lbs.
- Starter bolts – 44 ft. lbs.
- Halfshaft-to-flange – 33 ft. lbs.
- Transaxle-to-housing mount – 44 ft. lbs.

Corrado and Passat

1. Disconnect the negative battery cable.

2. Label and disconnect the electrical wires from the transaxle.

3. On Corrado, disconnect and plug the intercooler tubes.

4. Disconnect the gearshift cable from the transaxle gearshift lever. Disconnect the selector cable (with linkage lever) from the transaxle. Do not allow the cables to become twisted or kinked. Move them off to the side and out of the way.

5. Remove the cable support from the transaxle.

6. Unbolt the clutch slave cylinder and suspend it with wire. DO NOT disconnect the hydraulic lines.

7. Disconnect the speedometer cable from the transaxle.

8. Remove the upper engine/transaxle bolts.

9. If necessary, disconnect the air intake hose from the air flow sensor and move it off to the side and out of the way.

10. Remove the three right engine mount bolts.

11. Remove the hex head bolt from the left transaxle mount.

NOTE: *On vehicles equipped with ABS, the left transaxle bolt is hard to get at. On these vehicles, remove the cooling system overflow reservoir to gain access to this bolt.*

12. Remove the cooling fan, cover and mount.

13. Remove the front transaxle bracket nut.

14. Install VW support tool 10–222 with bases 10–222 A/1.

CAUTION: *These bases are formed to adapt to the angle of the body. If substitute bases are used, personal injury could occur!*

15. Tighten the support using the spindles.

16. Remove the starter and front transaxle bracket.

17. Unbolt the support bracket from the transaxle.

18. Remove the balance weight from the mount.

19. Remove the heat shield from the right inner CV-joint.

20. Unbolt the driveshafts from the transaxle flanges, swing them upward and tie them off.

21. Unbolt the transaxle bracket from the transaxle.

22. Using a large prybar, move the transaxle mount backward and remove the lower transaxle bracket mounting bolt.

23. Push the engine/transaxle mount to the right as far as it will go and lower the transaxle slightly by adjusting the left spindle.

24. Unbolt the gear gear carrier housing cover from the transaxle.

25. Support the transaxle with a jack and remove the lower engine/transaxle attaching bolt.

26. Pry the transaxle from the bushings and lower the unit from the vehicle.

To install:

NOTE: *Before installing the transaxle, press the clutch release lever toward the transaxle and hold it in place using a pin or M8 × 22mm bolt. The pin or bolt will be removed after the transaxle is in place.*

27. Raise the transaxle into the engine compartment and set it on the bushings.

28. Install the lower transaxle/engine attaching bolt. Torque the bolt to 59 ft. lbs.

29. Bolt the gear carrier housing cover to the transaxle.

30. Using the spindle, slightly raise the transaxle and push the transaxle/engine mount all the way to the left. Now, use the prybar to move the transaxle backward until you are able to insert the lower transaxle bracket mounting bolt. Torque the bolt to 44 ft. lbs.

31. Install the transaxle bracket and torque the bolts to 44 ft. lbs.

32. Connect the driveshafts and torque the flange bolts to 33 ft. lbs.

33. Install the right inner CV-joint heat shield.

34. Install the mount balance weight. Torque the bolts to 22 ft. lbs.

35. Install the support bracket. Torque the bolts to 44 ft. lbs.

36. Install the front transaxle bracket and starter. Torque the bracket and starter bolts to 44 ft. lbs.

37. Remove the support equipment.

38. Install the front transaxle bracket nut. Torque the nut to 44 ft. lbs.

39. Install the cooling fan, cover and mount.

40. Install the left transaxle mount hex bolt. Torque the bolt to 18 ft. lbs.

41. Install the three right engine mount bolts. Torque the bolts to 18 ft. lbs.

42. Connect the air intake hose to the air flow sensor.

43. Install the upper engine/transaxle bolts. Torque the bolts to 59 ft. lbs.

44. Connect the speedometer cable.

45. Attach the cable support to the transaxle. Torque the bolts to 18 ft. lbs.

46. Connect the transaxle cables.

47. On Corrado, connect the intercooler tubes.

48. Connect the wires to the transaxle.

49. Connect the negative battery cable.

50. Remove the pin from the clutch release lever and adjust the shift linkage.

Transaxle Overhaul

Cleanliness is an important factor in the overhaul of the manual transaxle. Before opening up this unit, the entire outside of the transaxle assembly should be cleaned, preferable with a high pressure washer such as a car wash spray unit. Dirt entering the transaxle internal parts will negate all the time and effort spent on the overhaul. During inspection and reassembly all parts should be thoroughly cleaned with solvent then dried with compressed air. Wiping cloths and rags should not be used to dry parts.

Wheel bearing grease, long used to hold thrust washers and lube parts, should not be used. Lube seals with clean transaxle oil and use ordinary, unmedicated petroleum jelly to hold the thrust washers and to ease the assembly of seals, since it will not leave a harmful residue as grease often will. Do not use solvent on neoprene seals, if they are to be reused, or thrust washers.

Before installing bolts into aluminum parts, always dip the threads into clean transaxle oil. Anti-sieze compound can also be used to prevent bolts from galling the aluminum and seizing. Always use a torque wrench to keep from stripping the threads. The internal snaprings should be compressed and the external rings should be expanded, if they are to be reused. This will help insure proper seating when installed.

Metric tools will be required to service this transaxle. Due to the large number of alloy parts used in this transaxle, torque specifications should be strictly observed. Before installing capscrews into aluminum parts, dip the bolts into clean transaxle oil as this will prevent the screws from galling the aluminum threads, thus causing damage.

Metric fastener dimensions are very close to the dimensions of the familiar inch system fasteners. For this reason replacement fasteners must have the same measurement and strength as the original fastener.

Do not attempt to interchange metric fasteners for inch system fasteners. Mismatched or incorrect fasteners can cause damage to the transaxle unit and possible personal injury. Care should be taken to reuse fasteners in their original locations.

Rabbit, Dasher and Fox

Certain variations are used in the application of this basic transaxle. The gear arrangement remains the same, the shifting mechanism differs in the shaping of various fingers and forks. The case is modified to adapt to the various vehicles in which it is used. Roller bearings are used in the majority of applications, while tapered bearings are used in the remainder. Needle cage bearings may be found as split, 1 piece or with a foldable cage. A pinion nut is used on varied transaxles, while a bolt and washer are used on others.

DISASSEMBLY

1. Mount the transaxle in a holding fixture.
2. Separate the shift housing from the transaxle.
3. Mount a dial gauge and zero the gauge with a 3mm preload.

NOTE: *Care must be taken when determining the thickness of the gasket and shim used between the shift housing and the gear carrier. The thickness of these two parts influence the position of the drive pinion. If the bearings for the mainshaft, pinion shaft are replaced, the measurements must be remade and new shim and gasket sizes selected.*

4. Measure the distance between the mainshaft bearing and the gear carrier. Record this reading. Make sure that the bearing is fully seated.
5. Measure the distance between the pinion bearing and the gear carrier. Record the reading. Make sure that the bearing is fully seated.
6. Measure the distance between the end face and the shim contact surface on the gear carrier. Record the reading.
7. Determine the shim thickness as follows; add the measurements from Step 4 and Step 6,

then subtract Step 5. This will give the shim thickness required.

8. The gasket thickness is determined by the mainshaft bearing projection obtained in Step 4.

NOTE: *When replacing the transaxle housing, gear carrier, 1st gear needle bearing or the pinion bearing, the exact location of the pinion must be determined before disassembly. Once the new parts have been installed, it will be necessary to set the pinion to its original position.*

9. Block the drive flange and remove the bolt.
10. Remove the final drive cover. Remove the differential assembly.

NOTE: *To perform the following operation, it is necessary to have special Volkswagen tools or equivalent.*

11. Assemble the universal bar tool. Zero the dial indicator with a 2mm preload.
12. Install the measuring plate tool on the pinion and install the measuring bar in the final drive housing.
13. Install the final drive cover and tighten the retaining nuts to 18 ft. lbs.
14. Move the second centering disc outward with the movable setting ring until the measuring bar can be turned by hand.
15. Turn the measuring bar until the measuring pin extension touches the plate on the pinion. Note the indicator needle at the point of maximum deflection. Record the reading.

NOTE: *After parts have been replaced, this setting must be reproduced as closely as possible.*

16. Separate the gear carrier from the final drive housing.
17. Drive the spring pin out of the 3rd/4th shift fork in the direction of the pinion.
18. Move the shift fork along the selector shaft and engage 3rd gear. Do not move the shaft.
19. Engage reverse gear. Place the gear carrier in the final drive housing. Loosen the pinion nut. Remove the gear carrier from the final drive housing. Remove the 3rd/4th shift fork.
20. Remove the mainshaft bearing using a suitable bearing puller. Remove the mainshaft.
21. Drive the reverse gear shaft out of the gear carrier.
22. Place the remaining gears in neutral and press the pinion shaft out of the gear carrier along with the 1st/2nd selector shaft and shift fork.
23. Remove the inner shift lever spring from the shift housing, remove the shift lever.
24. Press the transaxle rear mount off the shift housing.

25. Pry the inner shift lever oil seal out of the shift housing.

26. Drive the inner shift lever rear bushing out of the shift housing.

27. Press the inner shift lever from bushing out of the shift housing.

28. Pry the mainshaft oil seal out of the final drive housing from the final drive housing.

29. Drive the mainshaft sleeve out of the final drive housing from the gear carrier end.

30. Drive the mainshaft needle bearings out of the final drive housing from the front (flywheel side).

31. Remove the dowel pin from the pinion bearing and drive it out of the final drive housing.

32. Using a slide hammer, pull the clutch release shaft bushing out of the final drive housing.

33. Pull the starter bushing out of the final drive housing.

34. Drive the pinion bearing out of the gear carrier.

35. Remove the pin from the reverse gear selector shaft.

36. Drive the 1st/2nd and 3rd/4th interlock plungers through the gear carrier and remove through the access hole in the rear of the gear carrier.

37. Tap the remaining interlock plunger plug out.

38. Remove the circlip from the mainshaft which holds the 4th gear and the synchronizer ring. Remove the parts from the shaft.

39. Remove the circlip retaining the synchronizer hub, synchronizer ring and 3rd gear from the main shaft.

40. Press the synchronizer hub and 3rd gear off the mainshaft.

41. Press the pinion bearing inner race along with the 1st gear off the pinion shaft.

42. Press the synchronizer hub for 1st/2nd gear along with 2nd gear off the pinion shaft.

43. Remove the 3rd gear circlip from the pinion shaft.

44. Press the 3rd gear off the pinion shaft.

45. Press the 4th gear off the pinion shaft.

46. Remove the drive flange oil seal from the final drive housing by prying.

47. Drive the differential outer bearing race and shim out of the final drive cover.

48. Using a suitable puller, remove the differential bearing inner race/cage from the side opposite the ring gear.

49. Pull the bearing from the ring gear side of the differential assembly, along with the speedometer drive gear and bushing.

50. Remove the bolts holding the ring gear to the differential housing and drive the housing and gear apart.

51. Remove the circlip from the pinion gear shaft. Slide the shaft out of the differential housing.

52. Remove the pinion gears, side gears and the drive flange nuts.

ASSEMBLY

1. Insert the side gears and drive flange nuts. Bolt the drive flanges to the side gears.

2. Insert the pinion gears and move the drive flange until the pinion gears are aligned. Install the pinion shaft. Remove the drive flanges.

NOTE: *The drive pinion and the ring gears are matched units and can be replaced only as a matched set.*

3. Heat the ring gear to approximately 212°F (100°C) and center on the differential housing with a drift.

4. Install the bearing opposite to the ring gear by heating to 212°F (100°C) and pressing onto the differential housing.

5. Install the bearing on the ring gear side of the differential housing by heating to 212°F (100°C) and pressing onto the differential housing.

6. Insert 1.8mm shim onto differential housing and press drive gear bushing on.

7. Insert the shim into the final drive cover and drive the outer bearing race into place and insert the shim in the final drive housing.

8. Drive the right side drive flange oil seal into place in the final drive housing.

9. Press the 4th gear onto the pinion shaft while holding the bearing with the wide shoulder facing the pinion head.

10. Press the 3rd gear onto the pinion shaft.

11. Measure with a feeler gauge the space between the 3rd gear and the pinion shaft. Install a circlip of the correct size.

12. Position the three keys in the slots in the 1st/2nd gear synchronizer hub.

13. Place the synchronizer sleeve over the synchronizer hub and align marks.

14. Install the springs 120° offset with the angled ends engaged in the hollow of a key.

15. Position the shift fork slot and the groove in the synchronizer hub so that they face the 1st gear and press the synchronizer assembly onto the pinion shaft.

16. Press the synchronizer ring onto the 1st gear and measure the gap between the parts with a feeler gauge. New parts should be between 1.0–1.5mm and a used part should be no more than 0.6mm.

17. Install the 1st gear on the pinion shaft, slide on bearing and shim.

18. Press the inner race onto the pinion shaft.

19. Assemble the 3rd/4th gear synchronizer in the same way as the 1st/2nd synchronizer.

20. Press the synchronizer rings onto the 3rd and 4th gears. Check the gap between the synchronizer rings and the gears. New parts should measure 1.3–1.9mm and used parts should be no more than 0.6mm.

21. Install needle bearing on mainshaft.

22. Press the synchronizer hub along with the 3rd gear onto the mainshaft. The chamfer on the synchronizer hub inner splines faces 3rd gear.

23. Install the circlip on the mainshaft for the synchronizer assembly.

24. Install the needle bearing.

25. Install the spring pin in the mainshaft and align the pin with the slot in the 4th gear.

26. Install the 4th gear and shim, secure with the circlip.

NOTE: *Before measuring endplay, press the synchronizer and 3rd gear against the circlip located against the synchronizer hub.*

27. Measure the endplay between the shim and 4th gear. If the measurement is not between 0.10–0.40mm, remove the circlip and install a shim that will bring the measurement within limits.

28. Install the plunger and spring for the 1st/2nd shift selector shaft. Install the interlock plunger (between the 1st/2nd and the 3rd/4th shafts) from the top of the case.

29. Install the plunger and spring for the 3rd/4th selector shaft. Hold down the plunger and install the 3rd/4th shift selector shaft.

30. Install the pin for the reverse gear selector shaft.

31. Install the second interlock plunger from the top of the gear carrier.

32. Install the reverse gear selector shaft. Install the remaining spring and plunger. Install the reverse lever pin in selector shaft.

NOTE: *The 1st/2nd selector shaft is not installed until the gear train is in place.*

33. Install the plugs in the interlock plunger bores.

34. Install the reverse sliding gear. Insert the reverse lever with the shift segment.

35. Install the bolt and washer and press the reverse lever toward the center of the gear carrier.

36. Turn the bolt in until it touches the reverse lever. Press the lever against the bolt and make certain that the threads engage smoothly. Continue until the bolt is seated in the gear carrier. Tighten the bolt to 25 ft. lbs.

37. Check the operation of the reverse selector several times. Make sure that the lever moves easily in all positions. Remove the reverse sliding gear.

38. Press the pinion bearing into the gear carrier.

39. Install a new starter bushing into the final drive housing.

40. Install a new clutch release shaft bushing into the final drive housing.

41. Align the pinion bearing outer race with the hole in the final drive housing drive into place. The groove on the side must be toward the gear carrier. Install the dowel pin.

42. Install the mainshaft needle bearings into place in the final drive housing.

43. Install the mainshaft sleeve into position in the final drive housing.

44. Install the mainshaft oil seal into position.

45. Install the clutch bearing guide sleeve, the clutch release shaft and spring and the clutch release bearing.

46. Press the inner shift lever rear bushing into the shift lever housing until it is flush with shoulder.

47. Press the shift lever oil seal into the shift lever housing until it is flush with the housing.

48. Press the transaxle rear mount onto the shift housing.

49. Press the inner shift lever front bushing into the housing until it is flush.

50. Install the inner shift lever and install the spring.

51. Press the pinion shaft assembly into the ball bearing in the gear carrier.

52. Install the mainshaft bearing into the gear carrier assembly.

53. Position the 1st/2nd selector shaft and fork on the assembled pinion shaft assembly.

54. Press the pinion shaft assembly into the gear carrier assembly. Guide the shift selector shaft into the operating sleeve. Make sure that the selector shaft does not jam.

55. Place the pinion shaft in a vise and tighten the pinion nut to 14–21 ft. lbs. Install the gear carrier in the final drive housing and secure with 4 nuts.

56. Repeat the measurements from Steps 11–15 of disassembly. If the measurements are not the same as previously recorded, proceed as follows:

a. If the second measurement is smaller, a thinner shim must be installed (between the pinion shaft inner bearing race and needle bearing on the pinion shaft).

b. If the measurement is the same or very close to the original reading proceed to the next step.

c. If the measurement is larger, a thicker shim must be installed.

57. Remove the gear carrier from the final drive housing, install new shim if needed.

58. Place the mainshaft assembly in the gear carrier. Install the shim and circlip.

59. Install the 3rd/4th shift fork with the wider shoulder facing toward 4th gear. Secure the shift fork with a new spring pin.

60. Block the gear train and tighten the pinion nut to 72 ft. lbs.

61. Install the 1st/2nd gear selector dog.

62. Install the gear carrier assembly on the final drive housing. Install the dowel pins before tightening the nuts or bolts.

63. Install the differential assembly into the final drive housing.

64. Install the final drive cover.

65. Install the drive flanges and block with suitable drift.

66. Repeat the measurements from Steps 3–8 of disassembly. Select the proper shim and gasket to be installed between the gear carrier and shift housing.

67. Install the shift housing on the gear carrier assembly.

Except Rabbit, Dasher and Fox

DISASSEMBLY

1. Mount the transaxle assembly in a holding fixture.

2. Remove the end cover and gasket.

3. Remove the circlips from the clutch release shaft. Slide the shaft out of the gear carrier and remove the clutch lever and return spring.

4. Remove the clutch release bearing and clutch pushrod.

5. Mount a bar with a locknut and spacer across the final drive housing to support the mainshaft.

6. Remove the selector shaft cover. Remove the interlock plunger springs and the selector shaft.

7. Remove the circlip from the gear carrier side drive flange. Install the special tool with two bolts on the drive flange. Remove the drive flange.

8. Remove the plastic caps covering the clamping screws. Remove the clamping screw nuts.

9. Remove the reverse shaft retaining bolt.

10. Mount the special tool on the gear carrier assembly and lift the gear carrier off the final drive assembly while threading the special tool bolt in.

11. Drive the drive flange oil seal out of the gear carrier housing.

12. Pry the clutch operating shaft oil seal out of the carrier housing.

13. Pull the pinion shaft needle bearing out of the gear carrier.

14. Remove the shift fork assembly and the mainshaft from the final drive housing.

15. Remove the remaining drive flange as outlined in Step 7.

16. Remove the needle bearing stop and the 1st circlip from the pinion shaft. Lift 4th gear off the shaft.

17. Remove the 2nd circlip from the pinion shaft. Lift 3rd gear, 2nd gear, 2nd gear inner race and the needle bearing off the shaft.

18. Remove the reverse shaft and gear.

19. Using a gear puller, remove the synchronizer hub and 1st/2nd gear from the pinion shaft.

20. Remove the pinion bearing cover and outer bearing race. Remove the pinion shaft.

21. Remove the differential assembly.

22. Pry the mainshaft oil seal out of the final drive housing.

23. Drive the drive flange oil seal out of the final drive housing.

24. Pull the starter bushing out of the final drive housing.

25. Pull the pinion outer bearing race out of the final drive housing.

26. Drive the differential outer bearing race out of the final drive housing.

27. Pull the mainshaft needle bearing out of the final drive housing.

28. Remove the two circlips from the shift fork shaft and slide the components off the shaft.

29. Remove the 1st circlip from the mainshaft and discard. Press the bearing off the shaft.

30. Mount the separator assembly on 4th/5th gear and press the gear off the mainshaft. Remove the needle bearings.

31. Remove the 2nd circlip from the mainshaft and discard. Press 3rd gear and the synchronizer assembly off the shaft. Remove the needle bearings.

32. Slide a 10mm rod in the mainshaft and drive the clutch pushrod out.

33. Press the two tapered roller bearings off the pinion shaft.

34. Remove the circlips from the differential pinion shaft and drive out.

35. Remove the circlips from the drive flange shafts. Remove the side gears and thrust washers.

36. Press the tapered roller bearing off the housing side of the differential.

37. Remove the tapered roller bearing from the ring gear side of the differential.

38. Remove the ring gear.

ASSEMBLY

NOTE: *The ring gear and pinion shaft can be replaced only as a matched set.*

1. Heat the pinion shaft small tapered bearing to 212°F (100°C) and press it onto the shaft.

2. Heat the pinion shaft large tapered bearing to 212°F (100°C) and press onto the shaft.

3. Place a 0.75mm shim in the pinion bore in the final drive housing and press the small bearing outer position.

4. Install the pinion shaft and cover.

5. Assemble the pinion adjustment fixture tools. Place the end plate on the pinion shaft. Attach the dial indicator and zero it with a 1mm preload.

NOTE: *Do not turn the pinion shaft while measuring, because the bearings will settle and give an incorrect reading.*

6. Move the pinion shaft up and down and note the reading.

7. Specified bearing preload is obtained by adding the constant figure of 0.20mm to the measured reading and the shim thickness (0.75mm).

8. Remove the pinion shaft cover and the pinion shaft. Pull the pinion shaft cover and the pinion shaft. Pull the pinion shaft small bearing outer race of the final drive housing.

9. Install the correct shim and press the pinion shaft small bearing outer race into the final drive housing.

NOTE: *If new bearings have been installed on the pinion shaft, check the pinion shaft turning torque. Reading should be 4.4–13.1 inch lbs.*

10. Install the side gears and thrust washers in the differential housing.

11. Install the pinion gears and thrust washers. Drive the pinion shaft into the differential housing.

12. Install centering pins on the differential housing. Heat the ring gear to 212°F (100°C) and press it onto the differential housing.

13. Heat the housing side differential bearing to 212°F (100°C) and press the bearing into place.

14. Heat the ring gear side bearing to 212°F (100°C) and press the bearing into place.

NOTE: *If new bearings have been installed, the differential must be adjusted.*

15. Slide the drive flange shafts into the side gears. Determine the thickness of the circlip by pressing the drive flange shaft against the pinion gearshaft, while pressing the side gears against the housing. Insert the thickest possible circlip. The circlip should not be jammed sideways.

NOTE: *The differential inner and outer bearing races are matched to their bearings and cannot be interchanged.*

16. If new differential bearings have been installed, proceed as follows:

a. Install the race in the final drive housing with a 1mm shim.

b. Install the race in the gear carrier without a shim.

c. Place the differential assembly in the final drive housing. Install the gear carrier on the final drive housing, with the gasket.

d. Install the dial indicator fixture on the gear carrier tool and place the end plate on the drive flange. Install the dial indicator with a 1mm preload.

NOTE: *Do not turn the differential when making the measurements because the bearings will settle and give incorrect readings.*

e. Move the differential up and down and note the reading.

f. The correct bearing preload is determined by adding a constant figure or 0.40mm to the measured reading.

g. Remove the gear carrier from the final drive housing.

h. Pull the bearing race out of the gear carrier housing with a suitable extractor.

i. Install the shims in the gear carrier starting with the thickest. Install the bearing race.

17. With the differential in the final drive housing, install the pinion shaft and tighten the nuts on the cover plate to 14 ft. lbs.

NOTE: *Synchronizers can be replaced only as a matched unit.*

18. Position the keys in the slots in the synchronizer hub. Place the synchronizer sleeve over the hub and align the marks. Install the springs with a 120° offset with the angled ends engaged in the hollow of a key.

19. Press the synchronizer rings onto the 1st and 2nd gears. Check the gap between the ring and gear with a feeler gauge. The gap on new parts should be between 1.0–1.5mm and no less than 0.5mm on used parts.

20. Install the thrust washer and needle bearing for 1st gear on the pinion shaft. The recess in the thrust washers faces the roller bearing.

21. Align the grooves in the 1st gear synchronizer ring with the synchronizer shift keys. Position the shift fork slot in the operating sleeve toward 2nd gear. The groove on the synchronizer hub should face toward 1st gear.

22. Heat the 1st gear and synchronizer as an assembly to 250°F (121°C) and press onto the pinion shaft.

23. Drive the 2nd gear needle bearing race onto the pinion shaft.

24. Install the 2nd gear needle bearings and 2nd gear.

25. Install 3rd gear on the pinion shaft with the collar facing toward 2nd gear. Secure 3rd gear with the collar facing toward 2nd gear. Secure 3rd gear with the selective circlip which will give an axial play between 0–0.20mm. Measure the play with a feeler gauge between the circlip and 3rd gear.

26. Warm the reverse gear bushing and

press it on the reverse shaft until the top of the bushing is 41mm from the bottom of the shaft.

27. Install the reverse gear shaft retaining bolt in the shaft. Center the shaft and drive it in until the collar makes contact with the final drive housing. Remove the retaining bolt.

28. Assemble the 3rd/4th synchronizer.

29. Press the synchronizer rings onto 3rd and 4th gear.

30. Press the clutch pushrod bushing into the mainshaft until it is flush.

31. Install the 3rd gear needle bearings on the mainshaft.

32. Turn the synchronizer ring on 3rd gear until the grooves align with the shift keys in the synchronizer hub. The chamfer on the synchronizer hub inner splines must face toward 3rd gear.

33. Press the 3rd gear and synchronizer onto the mainshaft as a unit. Install the circlip.

NOTE: *If the mainshaft thrust washer is replaced, the mainshaft position must be re-adjusted.*

34. Install the 4th gear needle bearings on the mainshaft. Install 4th gear.

35. Press the mainshaft thrust washer on until it contacts 4th gear.

36. Drive the mainshaft oil seal into the final drive housing. Drive the mainshaft needle bearings into the final drive housing.

37. Make sure that the mainshaft support bar, locknut and spacer are in place. Insert the mainshaft. Install the shift fork assembly and secure with the circlips. Make sure that the gears are in Neutral.

38. Lift the shaft with the spindle until the play between 2nd gear on the pinion shaft and 3rd gear on the mainshaft can be checked. Measure the end-play with a feeler gauge. Measurement should be 1.0mm. Lock the spindle at the support bar and check the measurement to make sure it has not changed.

39. Install the measuring sleeve tool on the mainshaft. Place a new gasket on the final drive housing and install the gear carrier. Tighten the bolts to 14 ft. lbs.

40. Mount a dial indicator in a holding assembly and zero the indicator with a 3mm preload. Move the measuring sleeve up and down, record the indicator reading.

41. Remove the gear carrier from the final drive housing.

42. Install the shim (determined in Step 40) in the mainshaft bearing bore. Press the mainshaft bearing into the gear carrier and secure with the clamping screws and nuts. Tighten the nuts to 11 ft. lbs.

43. Install the drive flange oil seal into the final drive housing until it bottoms against the bearing race.

44. Install the drive flange on the final drive housing side, with the special tool (VW391), secure with a new circlip.

45. Install the starter bushing into the final drive housing.

46. Install the selector shaft oil seal into the gear carrier.

47. Install the clutch operating lever oil seal into the gear carrier.

48. Install the pinion shaft needle bearings into the gear carrier.

49. Install the drive flange oil seal into the gear carrier cover until it bottoms on the differential bearing race.

50. Position the gasket on the final drive housing. Install the gear carrier housing on the final drive housing. Make sure that the reverse gear shaft is aligned with the hole in the gear carrier, install the reverse shaft retaining screw.

51. Install the gear carrier-to-final drive housing bolts and tighten to 14 ft. lbs.

52. Install the mainshaft circlip through the clutch release bearing opening in the gear carrier.

53. Install the remaining driveshaft flange and circlip using special tools.

54. Remove the mainshaft support bar. Insert the clutch pushrod.

55. Insert the clutch release bearing assembly. Insert the clutch operating lever through the spring and clutch bearing lever. The bent end of the spring must contact the gear carrier. The center part of the spring is hooked over the end of the clutch bearing lever. Install the two circlips. Install the gasket and cover.

56. Insert the selector shaft and springs into the selector or opening in the gear carrier assembly. Lubricate the selector with a multipurpose grease before assembly. Install the selector shaft cover.

57. Install the interlock plunger assembly in the gear carrier assembly. Adjust the interlock plunger as follows:

a. Turn the slotted screw (interlock plunger) in until the nut starts to move out (bottoms).

b. Back the slotted screw out $1/4$ turn.

c. Install the plastic cap.

58. Install the plastic caps over the bearing clamping screws.

Axle Shaft (Halfshaft)
REMOVAL AND INSTALLATION
Dasher, Fox and Quantum

NOTE: *When removing the right axle shaft, you must detach the exhaust pipe from the manifold and the transaxle bracket. Be sure to buy a new exhaust flange gasket.*

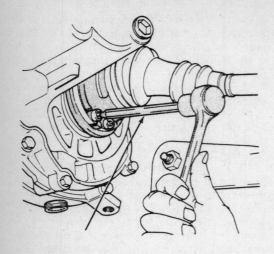

Remove the socket-head bolts retaining the axle shaft to the transaxle

1. With the car on the ground, remove the front axle nut.

NOTE: *Use a longer breaker bar with an extension (length of pipe).*

2. Raise and support the front of the vehicle.

3. Remove the socket head bolts retaining the axle shaft to the transaxle.

4. Pull the transaxle side of the driveshaft out and up and place it on the top of the transaxle.

5. Pull the axle shaft from the steering knuckle.

6. During installation, tighten the axle shaft flange bolts to 25–33 ft. lbs. The axle nut should be tightened to 145 ft. lbs. (M18 nut), or 170–175 ft. lbs. (M20 nut).

Except Dasher, Fox and Quantum

1. With the car on the ground, remove the front axle nut.

2. Raise and safely support the front of the vehicle.

3. Remove the socket head bolts retaining the halfshaft to the transaxle flange.

4. Remove the bolt holding the ball joint to the steering knuckle and separate the knuckle from the ball joint.

5. Removing the ball joint from the knuckle should give enough clearance to remove the axle shaft. It pulls right out of the steering hub. On Corrado and Passat, to remove the left side shaft, separate the left steering knuckle from the strut. To do this, remove the two knuckle bolts and swing the knuckle off to the side. Tie the knuckle off to a convenient suspension member.

6. During installation, tighten the axle

shaft flange bolts to 33 ft. lbs., the ball joint bolt to 21 ft. lbs. and the axle nut to 195 ft. lbs. on Golf, Jetta, GLI, GTI and Passat; 170–173 ft. lbs. on Rabbit, Scirocco, Cabriolet and Corrado. Be sure to check the alignment after work is completed.

NOTE: *The axle shafts on the Rabbit, Jetta and Scirocco differ in length from the left and right sides. The left side shaft is longer than the right side shaft. To insure that the shafts are in perfect balance with each other, the longer shaft is hollow, while the shorter shaft is solid, making both shafts weight exactly the same amount.*

AXLE SHAFT REPAIR

The constant velocity joints (CV-joints) of the axle shaft can be disassembled. However, Volkswagen states that the components making up the CV-joint are machined to a matched tolerance and that the entire CV-joint must be replaced as a set.

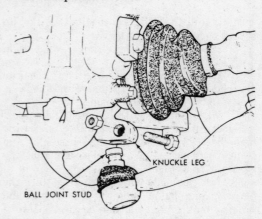

Remove the ball joint from the knuckle to remove the axle shaft for the Rabbit, Jetta and Scirocco

CLUTCH

CAUTION: *The clutch driven disc contains asbestos, which has been determined to be a cancer causing agent. Never clean clutch surfaces with compressed air! Avoid inhaling dust from any clutch surface! When cleaning clutch surfaces, use a commercially available brake cleaning fluid.*

Adjustments

NOTE: *1986–90 5-speed models are equipped with a self-adjusting clutch cable. The cable incorporates an adjustment mechanism on the transaxle side of the cable which automatically adjusts to compensate for normal clutch disc wear.*

Troubleshooting Basic Clutch Problems

Problem	Cause
Excessive clutch noise	Throw-out bearing noises are more audible at the lower end of pedal travel. The usual causes are: • Riding the clutch • Too little pedal free-play • Lack of bearing lubrication A bad clutch shaft pilot bearing will make a high pitched squeal, when the clutch is disengaged and the transmission is in gear or within the first 2″ of pedal travel. The bearing must be replaced. Noise from the clutch linkage is a clicking or snapping that can be heard or felt as the pedal is moved completely up or down. This usually requires lubrication. Transmitted engine noises are amplified by the clutch housing and heard in the passenger compartment. They are usually the result of insufficient pedal free-play and can be changed by manipulating the clutch pedal.
Clutch slips (the car does not move as it should when the clutch is engaged)	This is usually most noticeable when pulling away from a standing start. A severe test is to start the engine, apply the brakes, shift into high gear and SLOWLY release the clutch pedal. A healthy clutch will stall the engine. If it slips it may be due to: • A worn pressure plate or clutch plate • Oil soaked clutch plate • Insufficient pedal free-play
Clutch drags or fails to release	The clutch disc and some transmission gears spin briefly after clutch disengagement. Under normal conditions in average temperatures, 3 seconds is maximum spin-time. Failure to release properly can be caused by: • Too light transmission lubricant or low lubricant level • Improperly adjusted clutch linkage
Low clutch life	Low clutch life is usually a result of poor driving habits or heavy duty use. Riding the clutch, pulling heavy loads, holding the car on a grade with the clutch instead of the brakes and rapid clutch engagement all contribute to low clutch life.

PEDAL FREE-PLAY ADJUSTMENT

Clutch pedal free-play should be 15mm for all Dashers and 1975-79 Rabbits and Sciroccos. 1979 and later models should have 21.5–25.0mm free-play.

Clutch pedal free-play is the distance the pedal can be depressed before the linkage starts to act on the throwout bearing. Clutch free-play insures that the clutch plate is fully engaged and not slipping. Clutches with no or insufficient free-play often wear out quickly and give marginal power performance.

1. Adjust the clutch pedal free-play by loosening or tightening the two nuts (or locknut and threaded sleeve) on the cable near the oil filter on Fox, Dasher and Quantum: or on the Rabbit, Jetta, GTI, Scirocco and Cabriolet the left side (drivers) at the front of the transaxle.

NOTE: *Correct free-play cannot be measured correctly if floor covering interferes with clutch pedal travel. See following section for instructions on late model adjustment.*

2. Loosen the locknut and loosen or tighten the adjusting nut or sleeve until desired play is present. Depress the clutch pedal several times

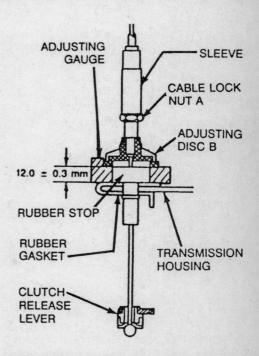

Clutch pedal freeplay checking and adjusting

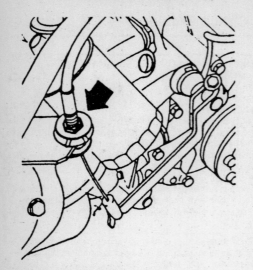

Clutch pedal freeplay adjuster

and recheck free-play. Readjust if necessary. Tighten locknut.

3. On late models, VW recommends that a special tool (US5043) be used to determine proper adjustment. The procedure for adjust-

ment follows: depress the clutch pedal several times. Loosen the locknut and insert the tool. Adjust the sleeve until zero clearance between sleeve and tool is reached. Tighten locknut. Remove tool and depress clutch pedal at least five times. Check free-play at clutch pedal.

CHECKING TOTAL CLUTCH PEDAL TRAVEL

Prior to free-play adjustment, check total pedal travel as follows:

1. Hook a tape measure to the top of the clutch pedal. Measure distance between the top of the pedal and the centerline of the steering wheel.

2. Depress the pedal and measure the total distance again. If the difference between the measurements exceeds 119mm, the floor covering may be interfering with pedal travel.

Clutch Cable
REMOVAL AND INSTALLATION
Except Self-Adjusting

1. Loosen the adjustment.
2. Disengage the cable from the clutch arm.

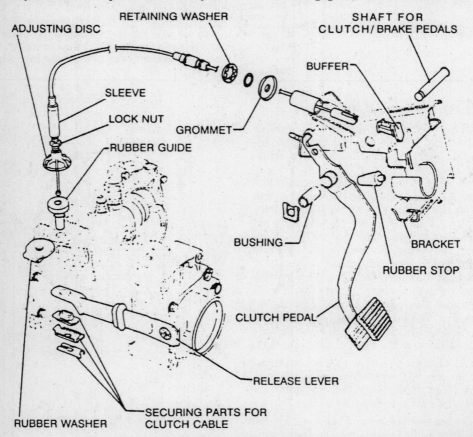

Self-adjusting clutch pedal and cable assembly

3. Unhook the cable from the pedal. Remove the threaded eye from the end of the cable. Remove the adjustment nut(s).

4. Remove the C-clip which holds the outer cable at the adjustment point. Remove all the washers and bushings, first noting their locations.

5. Pull the cable out of the firewall toward the engine compartment side.

6. Install and connect the new cable. Adjust the pedal free-play.

Self-Adjusting

1. Depress the pedal and release several times.

2. Compress the spring located under the boot at the top of the adjuster mechanism and remove the cable at the release lever.

3. Unhook the eye from the clutch pedal and remove the cable.

4. Install the new cable onto the pedal. Compress the spring and have a helper pull the cable down and install to the release lever.

5. If the adjuster spring is retained by a strap, remove the strap after cable installation.

6. Depress the clutch pedal several times to adjust the cable.

Driven Disc and Pressure Plate

REMOVAL AND INSTALLATION

CAUTION: *The clutch driven disc contains asbestos, which has been determined to be a cancer causing agent. Never clean clutch surfaces with compressed air! Avoid inhaling any dust from any clutch surface! When clean-* *ing clutch surfaces, use a commercially available brake cleaning fluid.*

Except Dasher, Fox and Quantum

NOTE: *You'll need special tool VW 547, VW 3190 or to center the clutch disc.*

These cars use a type of clutch more common to motorcycles than to cars. The pressure plate is bolted to the crankshaft and the flywheel bolted to the pressure plate; in other words, these two parts have switched places. The clutch release lever and bearing are in the left end of the transaxle. The clutch is actuated by a release rod which passes through a hollow transaxle shaft. The throwout bearing is in the transaxle and lubricated with transaxle oil.

1. Remove the transaxle.

2. Attach a toothed flywheel locking device and gradually loosen the flywheel to pressure plate bolts one or two turns at a time in a crisscross pattern to prevent distortion.

3. Remove the flywheel and the clutch disc.

NOTE: *If replacing the flywheel, the new one has only a TDC mark. Additional timing marks must be cut into the flywheel as shown.*

4. Use a small pry bar to remove the release plate retaining ring. Remove the release plate.

5. Lock the pressure plate in place and unbolt it from the crankshaft. Loosen the bolts one or two turns at a time in a crisscross pattern to prevent distortion.

6. On installation, use new bolts to attach the pressure plate to the crankshaft. Use a thread locking compound and torque the bolts in a diagonal pattern to 54 ft. lbs. on 1975-1984

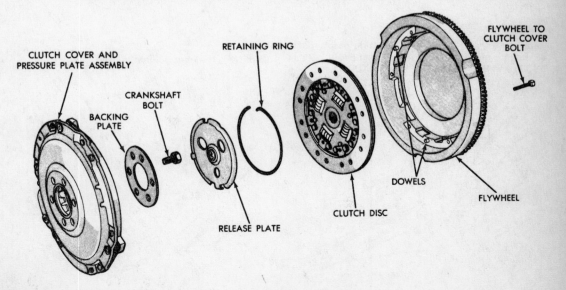

Rabbit, Jetta, and Scirocco clutch assembly

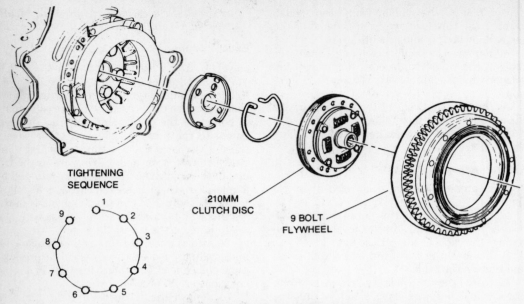

TIGHTENING
SEQUENCE

210MM
CLUTCH DISC

9 BOLT
FLYWHEEL

Late model 210mm clutch assembly, and flywheel tightening sequence

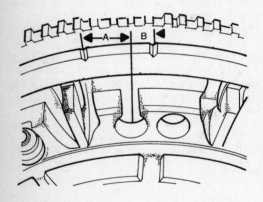

Rabbit, Jetta and Scirocco — a timing notch must be cut into new flywheels. A = 16mm ($^5/_8$ in.) ($7^1/_2°$ BTDC) and B = 2.5mm ($^3/_{32}$ in.) (3°ATDC)

Removing the clutch retaining ring

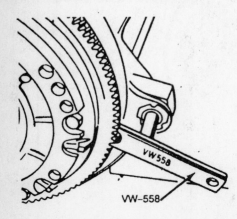

Locking the flywheel using holdng tool VW-558

VW–558

VW-558

VW–558

VW 558

Removing the clutch pressure plate using tool VW-558

models; 74 ft. lbs. on Corrado, Passat, Cabriolet, 1985–90 Sciricco, Golf, Jetta and GTI.

7. Lubricate the clutch disc splines, release plate contact surface, and pushrod socket with multipurpose grease. Install the release plate, retaining ring, and clutch disc.

8. Use special tool VW 547 or equivalent to center the clutch disc.

9. Install the flywheel, tightening the bolts one or two turns at a time in a crisscross pattern to prevent distortion. Torque the bolts to 14 ft. lbs.

10. Replace the transaxle. Adjust the clutch free-play.

Dasher, Fox and Quantum

1. Remove the transaxle.

2. Matchmark the flywheel and pressure plate if the pressure plate is being re-used.

3. Gradually loosen the pressure plate bolts one or two turns at a time in a criss-cross pattern to prevent distortion.

4. Remove the pressure plate and disc.

5. Check the clutch disc for uneven or excessive lining wear. The rivets in the plate should be tight and indented in the mating surface, not level with it.

6. Examine the pressure plate for cracking, scorching, or scoring. Replace any questionable components.

7. Install the clutch disc and pressure plate. Use a pilot shaft (available at most auto parts stores) or an old transaxle shaft to keep the disc centered.

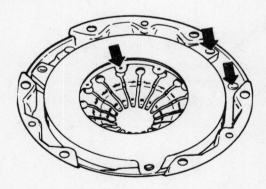

Check the Dasher pressure plate for surface wear. Make sure that the cover straps are not cracked or the rivets loose

NOTE: *The use of the proper pilot shaft is a necessity: if you can't obtain one, don't use dead reckoning to line up the clutch. You'll spend a long, sweaty time trying to force the transaxle spline into the misaligned clutch.*

8. Gradually tighten the pressure plate-to-flywheel bolts in a criss-cross pattern. Tighten the bolts to 18 ft. lbs.

9. Install the throwout bearing, if removed.

10. Apply a light film of grease to the input spline on the transaxle to aid in inserting it into the clutch. Don't go overboard with the amount of grease.

11. Install the transaxle.

Clutch Master Cylinder

The clutch master cylinder is located on the fire wall below the brake master cylinder. The clutch slave cylinder is located on top of the transaxle. The clutch master cylinder is supplied fluid from the brake fluid reservoir. Whenever any part of the system is removed or replaced the system must be bled to remove any air that may be in the lines.

REMOVAL AND INSTALLATION

NOTE: *On Corrado, remove the windshield washer reservoir before removing the clutch master cylinder.*

1. Remove and plug the pressure line from the rear of the clutch master cylinder.

2. Disconnect the fluid supply hose from the brake fluid reservoir.

3. Inside the vehicle, disconnect the push rod from the clutch pedal by removing the clip on the retaining pin.

4. Remove the two mounting bolts or nuts and pull the cylinder from the vehicle.

5. To install, insert the push rod through the firewall and install the cylinder mounting bolts. Torque the clutch master cylinder mounting bolts to 5–14 ft. lbs.

6. Install the supply line to the brake master cylinder and install the pressure line to the rear of the clutch master cylinder.

7. Fill the brake reservoir and bleed the clutch system.

Clutch Slave Cylinder

NOTE: *On Corrado and Passat, before removing the clutch slave cylinder, disconnect the linkage lever from the transaxle but leave the selector lever connected. DO NOT disconnect the selector lever.*

1. Raise and safely support the vehicle.

2. Disconnect and plug the pressure line to the slave cylinder.

3. Remove the slave cylinder by removing the spring pin and clip from the transaxle.

To install:

4. Align the slave cylinder on the transaxle housing and insert the spring pin and clip.

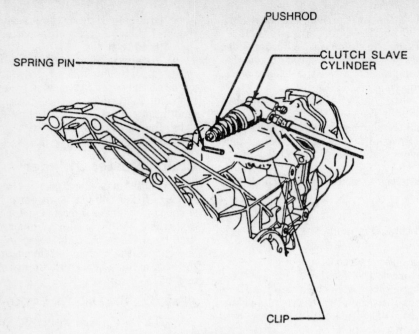

PUSHROD

CLUTCH SLAVE
CYLINDER

SPRING PIN

CLIP

Clutch slave cylinder

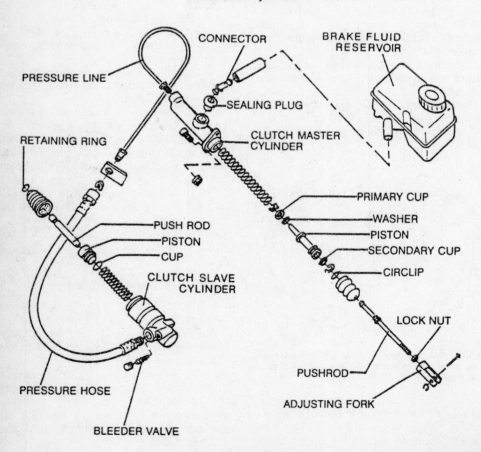

CONNECTOR

BRAKE FLUID
RESERVOIR

PRESSURE LINE

SEALING PLUG

CLUTCH MASTER
CYLINDER

RETAINING RING

PRIMARY CUP

WASHER

PISTON

PUSH ROD

SECONDARY CUP

PISTON

CIRCLIP

CUP

CLUTCH SLAVE
CYLINDER

LOCK NUT

PRESSURE HOSE

PUSHROD

BLEEDER VALVE

ADJUSTING FORK

Hydraulic clutch system components

5. Connect the pressure line and lower the vehicle.

6. Fill the brake reservoir and bleed the system.

BLEEDING THE HYDRAULIC CLUTCH

1. Clean all dirt and grease from the cap to make sure that no foreign substances enter the system.

2. Remove the cap and diaphragm and fill the reservoir to the top with the approved DOT 3 brake fluid. Fully loosen the bleed screw which is in the slave cylinder body next to the inlet connection.

3. At this point bubbles of air will appear at the bleed screw outlet. When the slave cylinder is full and a steady stream of fluid comes out of the slave cylinder bleeder, tighten the bleed screw.

4. Assemble the diaphragm and cap to the reservoir, fluid in the reservoir should be level with the step. Exert a light load of about 20 lbs. to the slave cylinder piston by pushing the release lever towards the cylinder and loosen the bleed screw. Maintain a constant light load, fluid and any air that is left will be expelled through the bleed port. Tighten the bleed screw when a steady flow of fluid and no air is being expelled.

5. Fill the reservoir fluid level back to normal capacity and if necessary repeat Step 4.

6. Exert a light load on the release lever, but do not open the bleeder screw as the piston in the slave cylinder will move slowly down the bore. Repeat this operation 2–3 times, the fluid movement will force any air left in the system into the reservoir. The hydraulic system should now be fully bled.

7. Check the the operation of the clutch hydraulic system and repeat this procedure if necessary. Check the push rod travel at the slave cylinder to insure the minimum travel 14.5mm.

AUTOMATIC TRANSAXLE

Normal maintenance such as fluid checking, adding and filter cleaning is discussed in Chapter 1.

Fluid Pan

REMOVAL AND INSTALLATION, STRAINER SERVICE

Passat

On Passat the ATF filter is mounted on top of the transaxle instead of on the bottom. Removal and installation of this filter is described in Chapter 1.

Dasher and Quantum

VW recommends that the automatic transaxle fluid be replace every 30,000 miles or 20,000 miles if used for trailer towing, mountain driving, or other severe service.

NOTE: *As of transaxle no. 13 03 8, an additional oil strainer is installed between the oil pump and the valve body inside the transaxle (see illustration). When installing it, be sure it fits into the locating lug of the transfer plate.*

1. Four (4) quarts of automatic transaxle fluid (Dexron®II) and a pan gasket are required.

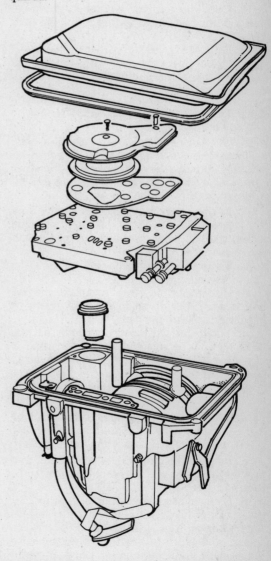

Beginning with transaxle 13 03 8, an additional strainer is used beneath the valve body. It cannot be installed on earlier models

2. Slide a drain pan under the transaxle. Jack up the front of the car and support it.

3. Remove the drain plug and allow all the fluid to drain.

NOTE: *Some models are not equipped with pan drain plugs. In this cases, empty the pan by loosening the pan bolts and allowing the fluid to drain out.*

4. Remove the pan retaining bolts and drop the pan.

5. Discard the old gasket and clean the pan with solvent.

6. Unscrew the strainer. If it is dirty, it should be replaced.

7. Install the strainer, but don't tighten the bolt too much specified torque is only 48 inch lbs.

8. Refill the transaxle with about 2.5L (2¾ qts.) of fluid. Check the level with the dipstick. Run the car for a few minutes and check again. Add fluid as necessary.

Golf, Rabbit, Scirocco, Cabriolet, GTI, GLI and Jetta

NOTE: *As of transaxle No. 09096 a new, cleanable oil filter is used which requires a deeper oil pan. Also beginning with transaxle number EQ–15 106, the drain plug was no longer installed in the oil pan.*

1. Remove the drain plug and let the fluid drain into a pan. If the pan has no drain plug, loosen the pan bolts until a corner of the pan can be lowered to drain the fluid.

2. Remove the pan bolts and take off the pan.

3. Discard the old gasket and clean the pan out. Be very careful not to get any threads or lint from rags into the pan.

4. The manufacturer recommends that the filter needn't be replaced unless the fluid is very dirty and burnt smelling. When replacing the strainer be careful, the specified torque for the strainer screws is 24 inch lbs.

NOTE: *Beginning with Transaxle number 13 03 8, there is an additional strainer under the valve body. When installing it, be sure it fits into the locating lug of the transfer plate.*

5. Replace the pan with a new gasket and tighten the bolts, in a criss-cross pattern, to 14 ft. lbs.

6. Using a long necked funnel, pour in 2.3L (2½ qts.) of Dexron®II automatic transaxle fluid through the dipstick tube. Start the engine and shift through all the transaxle ranges with the car stationary. Check the level on the dipstick with the lever in Neutral. It should be up to the lower end of the dipstick. Add fluid as necessary. Drive the car until it is warmed up and recheck the level.

Adjustments

LINKAGE ADJUSTMENT

Check the cable adjustments on all models as follows:

1. Run the engine at 1000–1200 rpm with the parking brake on and the wheels blocked.

2. Select the Reverse gear. A drop in engine speed should be noticed.

3. Select Park. Engine speed should increase. Pull the shift lever against the stop in the direction of Reverse. The engine speed should not drop (because reverse gear has not been engaged).

4. Move the shift lever to engage the Reverse. Engine speed should drop as the gear engages.

5. Move the shift lever into Neutral. An increase in engine speed should be noticed.

6. Shift into Drive. A noticeable drop in engine speed should result.

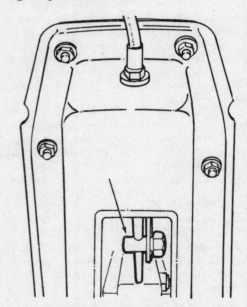

Dasher automatic transaxle linkage adjustment, before chassis number 3-5 2 044 957

7. Shift into 1. The lever must engage without having to overcome any resistance.

8. To adjust the cable, shift into Park. On Dashers, before chassis no. 3–5 2 044 957, remove the cover from the bottom of the shift lever case under the car and loosen the cable clamp. Using pliers, press the lever on the transaxle to the rear (against spring tension) until it hits the stop and tighten the clamp.

On Dashers from chassis no. 3–5 2 044 957 and later, and Quantum the shift cable clamp is loosened from inside the passengers compartment. Have an assistant under the car press the transaxle lever toward the Park position and tighten the clamp.

On all models except Dasher and Quantum shift into Park, loosen the cable clamp at the transaxle end of the cable, press the transaxle lever all the way to the left and tighten the cable clamp.

TRANSAXLE CABLE ADJUSTMENT

All Except 1985–90 Golf, Jetta and GTI

NOTE: *Early Dashers with the type 003 automatic transaxle (identified by the modulator hose attached to the driver's side front of the transaxle above the pan) have a kickdown switch rather than a throttle cable. See below for switch test.*

Make sure the throttle is closed, and the choke and fast idle cam are off (carbureted models).

1. Detach the cable end at the transaxle.
2. Press the lever at the transaxle into its closed throttle position.

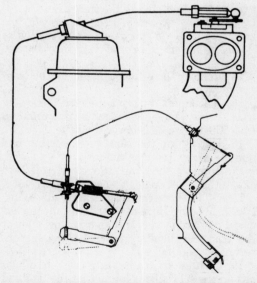

Rabbit, Jetta and Scirocco automatic transaxle cable arrangement on fuel injected engines

3. You should be able to attach the cable end onto the transaxle lever without moving the lever.
4. Adjust the cable length to the correct setting.

1985–90 Golf, Jetta and GTI

1. Warm up the engine and move the gearshift lever to Park.
2. Loosen the adjusting nuts and remove the accelerator cable.

3. Remove the nuts on the throttle cable support bracket.
4. Grasp the throttle cable by the sleeve and push it way from the lever until all play is removed from the cable. While doing this, make sure the throttle valve and the accelerator/transaxle linkage remain in the closed position.
5. When all slack is removed from the cable, hold it and tighten the adjusting nut until it contacts the support bracket. Tighten the locknut to 7 ft. lbs.
6. Install and connect the accelerator cable. **At this point an assistant will be needed to complete the adjustment procedure.**
7. Have an assistant press the gas all the way down until it hits the stop.
8. Move the transaxle operating lever against the kick-down stop and remove all the slack from the cable by turning the adjusting nut.
9. Let up on the gas pedal and push it all the way down again. Make sure the operating lever rests against the kick-down stop and tighten the locknut.

KICK-DOWN SWITCH CHECK

Dasher

NOTE: *Early Dashers with the type 003 automatic transaxle (identified by the modulator hose attached to the driver's side front of the transaxle above the pan) are the only VWs equipped with kickdown switches. All other models have throttle cable kickdowns (see above).*

1. Turn the ignition switch ON.
2. Floor the accelerator. You should hear a click from the solenoid on the transaxle.
3. Replace the solenoid if no sound is heard. The solenoid is housed in the valve body and is accessible only by removing this unit from the transaxle: a job you should depend on a qualified mechanic to perform.

1st AND 2nd GEAR (FRONT AND REAR) BAND ADJUSTMENTS

Dasher with Type 003 Transaxle Only

The type 003 transaxle is identified by the modulator hose attached to the driver's side front of the transaxle above the pan.

NOTE: *The transaxle must be horizontal when the band adjustments are performed.*

The adjustment screws are located at the top of the transaxle housing with the 1st gear band being closest to the front of the unit on the passenger's side of the car. The 2nd gear band adjustment screw is located toward the rear of the unit on the driver's side of the vehicle.

1. To adjust the 1st gear band, loosen the

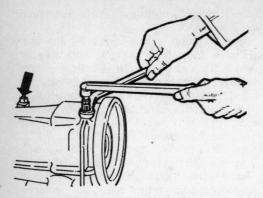

Dasher type 003 transaxle band adjustment — front band (first gear) being adjusted. The arrow locates second gear band adjustment screw

locknut and tighten the adjusting screw to 84 inch lbs.

2. Loosen the screw and retighten it to 42 inch lbs.

3. Turn the screw out $3^1/4$–$3^1/2$ turns and then tighten the locknut.

4. To adjust the 2nd gear band, repeat Steps 1 and 2 on the 2nd gear band adjusting screw, then turn the screw out exactly $2^1/2$ turns and tighten the locknut.

NEUTRAL START/BACKUP—LIGHT SWITCH

The combination neutral start and backup light switch is mounted inside the shifter housing. The starter should operate in Park or Neutral only. Adjust the switch by moving it on its mounts. The back—up lights should only come on when the shift selector is in the Reverse position.

Transaxle

REMOVAL AND INSTALLATION

Dasher and Quantum

The following procedures are for both types of Dasher automatic transaxles, the 003 and the 089. The model designation numbers are visible on the top of the automatic transaxle unit (as opposed to the differential unit) of the transaxle. Another way to tell the type 003 transaxle from the 089 is the type 003 has a vacuum modulator hose coming from the driver's side front of the transaxle above the pan. The type 089 does not. Don't confuse the ATF filler pipe with the above mentioned hose.

1. Disconnect the battery ground strap.

2. Raise the car and place the support stands so that you will have free access to the transaxle and axle shafts.

3. Disconnect the speedometer cable.

4. On the 089, remove the accelerator cable from the throttle valve housing.

5. Remove two of the upper engine/transaxle bolts. On the 089 transaxle, support the engine with either VW special tool 10–222 or an appropriate jack.

6. Disconnect the exhaust pipe.

7. Remove the torque converter cover plate. On the 003 transaxle, remove the vacuum modulator hose.

8. Remove the circlip holding the selector lever cable to the lever and remove the cable.

9. Remove the starter.

10. On the 003 disconnect the kickdown switch wires.

11. The torque converter is mounted to the flywheel by three bolts. The bolts are accessible through the starter hole. You'll have to turn the engine over by hand to remove all three.

12. Remove the axle shaft to transaxle socket head bolts.

13. Matchmark the position of the ball joint on the left control arm and remove the ball joint from the arm. Hold the wheel assembly out away from the arm to provide clearance between the axle shaft and the transaxle.

NOTE: *On Quantum Syncro models, the driveshaft to the rear axle assembly will also have to be removed in order to remove the transaxle.*

14. Remove the exhaust pipe from the transaxle bracket.

15. Disconnect the remaining transaxle controls. Those you cannot reach can be removed when the transaxle is lowered a little.

16. Unbolt the transaxle crossmember and remove it from the transaxle.

17. Support the transaxle on a jack and loosen the lower engine/transaxle bolts.

18. On the 089 transaxle, remove all engine/transaxle bolts. Have an assistant pull the left wheel out as far as it will go and slowly lower the transaxle, making sure the torque converter does not fall off.

19. On the 003 transaxle, loosen the union nut on the ATF filler pipe so that the pipe can be swivelled. Remove the engine/transaxle bolts and lower the unit. You may have to pull the left wheel out a little so that the axle shaft clears the transaxle case. Make sure the torque converter does not fall off.

20. During installation, observe the following:

a. The torque converter nipple must be about 21mm from the bellhousing face surface. If it sticks out further than this, the oil pump shaft has pulled out. To correct this realign the converter and shaft.

b. Tighten the engine/transaxle bolts to 40 ft. lbs. and the torque converter bolts to

20–23 ft. lbs. New torque converter bolts should be used. Torque the axleshaft bolts to 33 ft. lbs. and the ball joint-to-control arm bolts to 45 ft. lbs.

c. Check the shift linkage adjustment.

1975–84 Rabbit, Scirocco and Jetta

The engine and transaxle may be removed together as explained under "Engine, Removal and Installation" in Chapter 3, or the transaxle may be removed alone, as explained here.

1. Disconnect both battery cables.

2. Disconnect the speedometer cable at the transaxle.

3. Support the left end of the engine at the lifting eye. Attach a hoist to the transaxle.

4. Unbolt the rear transaxle carrier from the body then from the transaxle. Unbolt the left side carrier from the body.

5. Unbolt the driveshafts and wire them up.

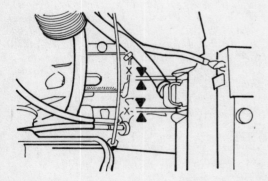

Align the engine/transaxle mount on Rabbit, Jetta and Scirocco. Dimension X must be equal

6. Remove the starter.

7. Remove the three converter to drive plate bolts.

8. Shift into Park and disconnect the floorshift linkage at the transaxle.

9. Remove the accelerator and carburetor cable bracket at the transaxle.

10. Unbolt the left side transaxle carrier from the transaxle.

11. Unbolt the front transaxle mount from the transaxle.

12. Unbolt the bottom of the engine from the transaxle. Lift the transaxle slightly, swing the left driveshaft up, remove the rest of the bolts, pull the transaxle off the mounting dowels, and lower the transaxle out of the car. Secure the converter so it doesn't fall out.

WARNING: *Don't tilt the torque converter!*

To install:

13. Push the transaxle onto the mounting dowels and install two bolts. Be sure the torque converter is fully seated on the clutch support. The distance **A** should be 30mm. Lift the unit until the left driveshaft can be installed and install the rest of the bolts. Torque them to 39 ft. lbs. Align the transaxle the left mount must be in the center of the body mount. Dimension **X** on both sides should be equal.

14. Tighten the front transaxle mount bolts to 39 ft. lbs. Install the left side transaxle carrier to the transaxle.

15. Connect the accelerator and carburetor cable bracket. Connect the floorshift linkage.

16. Tighten the torque converter to drive plate bolts to 22 ft. lbs. Torque the driveshaft bolts to 32 ft. lbs.

17. Connect the speedometer cable and battery cables.

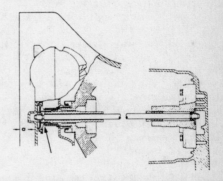

Rabbit, Dasher, Jetta, Scirocco — When attaching the transaxle to the engine, be sure the torque converter is seated on the one-way clutch support (arrow). When the converter is properly seated, A = 30mm (1³⁄₁₆ in.)

1985–90 Golf, GTI and Jetta

1. Disconnect the negative battery cable.

2. Remove the wheel ornaments and remove the axle nuts.

3. Raise and support the front end and remove the front wheels.

4. Disconnect the speedometer cable from the transaxle.

5. Install the engine support tool VW-10-222A or equivalent to the engine and lift it slightly.

6. Remove the left transaxle mount complete with the support.

7. Remove the upper engine-to-transaxle bolts.

8. Remove the upper through-bolts from the front engine-to-transaxle mount.

9. Remove the bolt that holds the coolant pipe to the front engine-to-transaxle mount.

10. Raise the vehicle.

11. Remove the lower bolts and remove the front engine-to-transaxle mount.

12. Remove the protective plate from the transaxle.

13. Disconnect the accelerator and selector cables from the transaxle levers and remove the support bracket with the cables attached.

14. Unbolt the axleshafts from the transaxle flanges.

15. Separate the ball joints and wheel bearing housing from each axle shaft and pull the shafts out of the transaxle.

16. Remove the right rear engine mount.

17. Remove the starter heat shield and brackets.

18. Remove the starter.

19. Remove the 3 torque converter bolts from the drive plate.

20. Remove the sub-frame mounting bolts and allow the sub-frame to hang freely.

21. Support the transaxle with a transaxle jack.

22. Remove the lower transaxle mounting bolt and carefully lower the transaxle out of the vehicle.

23. During installation use the following torque specifications:
- Transaxle-to-engine: 55 ft. lbs.
- Torque converter-to-drive plate: 26 ft. lbs.
- Halfshaft-to-flange: 33 ft. lbs.
- Upper rear mount bolts: 18 ft. lbs.
- Lower rear mount bolts: 59 ft. lbs.
- Upper front engine/transaxle mount bolts: 33 ft. lbs.
- Lower front engine/transaxle mount bolt (long): 52 ft. lbs.
- Lower front engine/transaxle mount bolt (short): 26 ft. lbs.

24. Adjust the accelerator cable and the shift selector lever.

1985–90 Scirocco and Cabriolet

1. Disconnect the negative battery cable.

2. Disconnect the speedometer cable from the transaxle and plug the hole.

3. Remove the upper engine-to-transaxle bolts.

4. Loosen the left transaxle mount fasteners.

5. Install engine support tool VW-10–222A or equivalent to the engine and lift it slightly.

6. Remove the rear transaxle mount (five bolts).

7. Disconnect the axleshafts and tie them up and out of the way.

8. Disconnect the starter harness which is located under heater control panel.

9. Remove the starter.

10. Remove the transaxle gravel guard and converter plate cover.

11. Remove the three torque converter bolts from the drive plate.

12. Place the shift selector lever in the Park position, remove the selector cable and bracket from the transaxle. Remove the accelerator cable and the accelerator pedal cable.

NOTE: *When removing the accelerator cable, DO NOT change the adjustment.*

13. Install transaxle support tool 4470 and connect the support to an engine hoist. Tension the hoist.

14. Remove the left engine-to-transaxle mount.

15. Remove the front mount.

16. Remove the lower transaxle bolt and nut.

17. Using the hoist, raise the transaxle slightly and carefully lower out of the vehicle.

NOTE: *When attaching the transaxle to the engine, the torque converter must be fully seated on the one way clutch support and should be able to be rotated by hand. When the torque converter is properly seated, distance from the face of the converter to the end of the transaxle housing should be 30mm.*

DO NOT allow the torque converter to slip during installation. If it slips, it could pull the shaft out of the oil pump and cause serious damage when the transaxle is bolted to the engine.

18. During installation, use the following torque specifications:
- Lower transaxle bolt (and nut): 58 ft. lbs.
- Engine-to-transaxle bolt mounts: 25 ft. lbs.
- Torque converter bolts: 22 ft. lbs.
- Starter bolts: 17 ft. lbs.
- Axle shaft bolts: 30 ft. lbs.
- Upper transaxle-to-engine bolts: 58 ft. lbs.
- Gravel guard bolts: 17 ft. lbs.

19. Align the engine to the transaxle as described in "Engine, Removal and Installation" in Chapter 3. Adjust the selector lever cable.

Passat

1. Disconnect the negative battery cable.

2. Disconnect the speedometer drive from the transaxle using VW special tool 3016 or its equivalent.

3. Remove the upper engine/transaxle bolts.

4. Install engine support bar 10–222 and support bases 10–22A/1 and raise the engine slightly using the support bar.

5. Remove the starter.

6. Shift the selector lever to the **P** position and disconnect the selector cable from the transaxle selector lever. Remove the cable retainer clip and route the cable off to the side and out of the way.

7. Remove the left mount.

8. Pinch and clamp the ATF cooler hoses and disconnect them from the ATF cooler.

9. Disconnect and label the wires and multi-plug connectors from the transaxle.

10. Remove the transaxle oil pan protective plate.

11. Remove the front mount.

12. Unbolt the driveshafts from the transaxle flanges, swing them upward and tie them off.

13. Remove the converter cover plate and unbolt the converter from the flywheel drive plate.

14. Lower the engine slightly using the support bar.

15. Support the transaxle with a transaxle jack.

16. Remove the lower engine/transaxle bolts.

17. Separate the transaxle from the engine and lower it from the vehicle. Wedge the torque converter to prevent it from falling out of the transaxle during removal.

To install:

NOTE: *Before installing the transaxle, make sure guide sleeves are in place and aligned properly.*

18. Raise the transaxle and mate it with the engine. Install the lower engine/transaxle bolts. Torque the 12mm bolts to 59 ft. lbs. and the 10mm bolts to 44 ft. lbs. During the step, make sure that the torque converter is wedged to prevent the unit from falling out of the transaxle. Once the transaxle is in place, remove the wedge.

19. Raise the engine slightly using the support bar.

20. Install the drive plate bolts and torque them to 44 ft. lbs. Install the converter cover and torque the cover bolts to 11 ft. lbs.

21. Connect the driveshafts to transaxle flanges. Torque the flange bolts to 33 ft. lbs.

22. Install the front mount. Torque the mount bracket bolts to 44 ft. lbs.

23. Install the transaxle oil pan protective plate.

24. Connect the wires and multi-plug connectors to the transaxle.

25. Connect the hoses to the ATF cooler.

26. Install the left mount. Torque the mount bracket/transaxle bolts to 44 ft. lbs. and the bracket/mount bolts to 18 ft. lbs.

27. Connect the transaxle selector cable and secure with the retainer clip.

28. Remove the engine support tools.

29. Install the starter.

30. Install the upper engine/transaxle bolts. Torque the 12mm bolts to 59 ft. lbs. and the 10mm bolts to 44 ft. lbs.

31. Connect the speedometer drive to the transaxle.

32. Connect the negative battery cable.

Axle Shaft (Halfshaft)
REMOVAL AND INSTALLATION
Dasher, Fox and Quantum

NOTE: *When removing the right axle shaft, you must detach the exhaust pipe from the manifold and the transaxle bracket. Be sure to buy a new exhaust flange gasket.*

1. With the car on the ground, remove the front axle nut.

NOTE: *Use a longer breaker bar with an extension (length of pipe).*

2. Raise and support the front of the vehicle.

3. Remove the socket head bolts retaining the axle shaft to the transaxle.

NOTE: *When removing the left side axle shaft, matchmark the ball joint (left side) mounting position in relation to the lower control arm. Remove the two ball joint retaining nuts and remove the ball joint from the control arm to create room to remove the axle shaft.*

4. Pull the transaxle side of the driveshaft out and up and place it on the top of the transaxle.

5. Pull the axle shaft from the steering knuckle.

6. During installation, tighten the axle shaft flange bolts to 25–33 ft. lbs. The axle nut should be tightened to 145 ft. lbs. (M18 nut), or 170–175 ft. lbs. (M20 nut).

NOTE: *Be aware that the axle shafts are two different lengths with the left side axle shaft being slightly longer than the right. They should not be interchanged.*

Except Dasher, Fox and Quantum

1. With the car on the ground, remove the front axle nut.

2. Raise and safely support the front of the vehicle.

3. Remove the socket head bolts retaining the halfshaft to the transaxle flange.

4. Remove the bolt holding the ball joint to the steering knuckle and separate the knuckle from the ball joint.

5. Removing the ball joint from the knuckle should give enough clearance to remove the axle shaft. It pulls right out of the steering hub. On Passat, to remove the left side shaft, separate the left steering knuckle from the strut. To do this, remove the two knuckle bolts and swing the knuckle off to the side.

6. During installation, tighten the axle shaft flange bolts to 33 ft. lbs., the ball joint bolt to 21 ft. lbs. and the axle nut to 195 ft. lbs. on Golf, Jetta, GLI, GTI and Passat; 170–173 ft. lb. on Rabbit, Scirocco and Cabriolet. Check the alignment after work is completed.

NOTE: *The axle shafts on the Rabbit, Jetta and Scirocco differ in length from the left and right sides. The left side shaft is longer than the right side shaft. To insure that the shafts are in perfect balance with each other, the longer shaft is hollow, while the shorter shaft is solid, making both shafts weight exactly the same amount.*

AXLE SHAFT REPAIR

The constant velocity joints (CV-joints) of the axle shaft can be disassembled. However, Volkswagen states that the components making up the CV-joint are machined to a matched tolerance and that the entire CV-joint must be replaced as a set.

NOTE: *Use a longer breaker bar with an extension (lenght of pipe).*

Suspension and Steering

FRONT SUSPENSION

Front Wheel Bearing Adjustments

There is no front wheel bearing adjustment. The bearing is pressed into the steering knuckle. The axle nut should be torqued to:
• Rabbits, Jettas and Sciroccos: 174 ft. lbs. (239 Nm)
• Dasher Fox and Quantum: 145 ft. lbs. (195 Nm) [M18 nut] or 175 ft. lbs. (237 Nm) [M20 nut]
• Passat and Corrado: 195 ft. lbs. (265 Nm)
Torque the nut with the wheels on the ground.

REMOVAL, PACKING AND INSTALLATION

Front Axle Only

1. In order to remove the wheel bearings, the steering knuckle must be removed.
2. Jack up the vehicle and remove the wheel and tire.
3. Straighten the lockplate at the wheel hub on the constant velocity joint side, loosen the wheel hub nut, and remove the nut with the lockplate.
4. Remove the tie rod end from the knuckle arm.
5. Remove the two cotter pins, castle nuts, spring washers, and the lower arm ball joint.
NOTE: *When the camber and caster adjusting cams are removed, remember the setting number for reassembly.*
6. After flattening the lockwasher, remove the nut and lockplate which joins the upper arm and the upper arm joint.
7. Remove the hub and knuckle assembly from the splined section of the axle shaft constant velocity joint side.

8. Separate the hub from the knuckle.
9. Remove the upper and lower ball joints and then remove the steering knuckle from the vehicle.
10. Straighten out the lockplate, loosen the bolt, and remove the bolt together with the spring washer and the lockplate.
11. Remove the inner oil seal from the bearing nut.
12. Remove the nut from the knuckle.
13. Remove the spacer.
14. Remove the outer oil seal from the knuckle.
15. Remove the bearing from the knuckle by pressing it out with a press. Remove the wheel bearing race using a puller with a clamping bracket.
16. Make sure that the bearings are installed in the same position as they were removed.
17. Before installing the bearing, clean and inspect it for damage. Repack the bearing with wheel bearing grease.
18. Press the outer and inner races, and the oil seal into the knuckle. Insert the outer oil seal into the knuckle. Insert the outer oil seal so that it protrudes from the knuckle end surface about 1mm. Coat the outer seal lip with grease when installing.
19. Insert the spacer making sure that the lip of the oil seal is not tucked up.
20. Tighten the bearing nut.
21. Align the lockplate groove with the nut groove and bend the lockplate and lock the nut.
22. Press the inner oil seal into the nut. Be careful not to damage the side lip of the oil seal. Coat the inner oil seal lip surface with grease when installing.
23. Assemble the steering knuckle to the vehicle in the reverse order of removal.

Strut

REMOVAL AND INSTALLATION

Dasher, Fox and Quantum

1. With the car on the ground, remove the front axle nut. Loosen the wheel bolts.

2. Raise and support the front of the car. Use support stands. Remove the wheels.

3. Remove the brake caliper from the strut and hang it with wire. Detach the brake line clips from the strut.

4. At the tie rod end, remove the cotter pin, back off the castellated nut, and pull the tie rod end from the strut with a puller.

5. Loosen the stabilizer bar bushings and detach the end from the strut being removed.

6. Remove the ball joint from the strut.

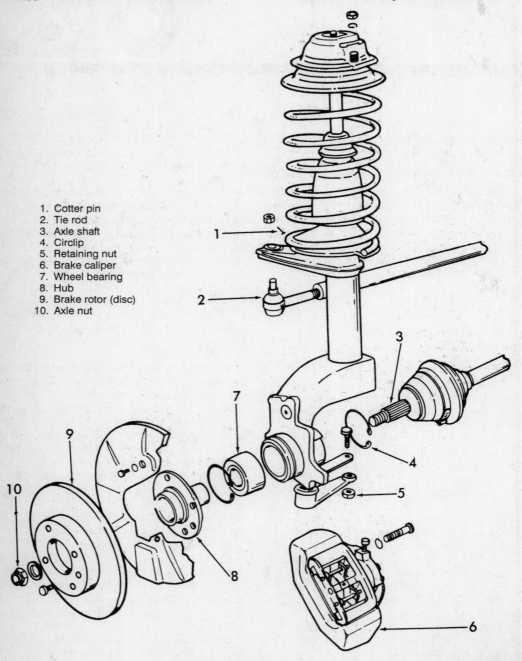

1. Cotter pin
2. Tie rod
3. Axle shaft
4. Circlip
5. Retaining nut
6. Brake caliper
7. Wheel bearing
8. Hub
9. Brake rotor (disc)
10. Axle nut

Dasher front suspension components

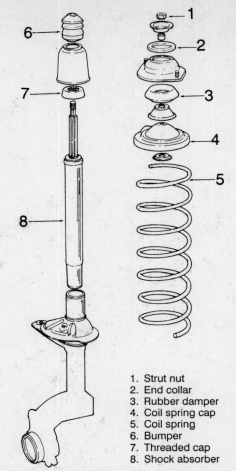

1. Strut nut
2. End collar
3. Rubber damper
4. Coil spring cap
5. Coil spring
6. Bumper
7. Threaded cap
8. Shock absorber

Dasher suspension strut, before chassis number 3-5 2 117 398

7. Pull the axle driveshaft from the strut.

8. Remove the upper strut-to-fender retaining nuts located under the engine hood.

9. Pull the strut assembly down and out of the car.

10. Installation is the reverse of removal. Observe the following torques:
• Axle nut: 145 ft. lbs. (195 Nm) [M18 nut] or 175 ft. lbs. (238 Nm) [M20 nut]
• Ball joint-to-strut nut: 25 ft. lbs. (34 Nm) [M8 nut] or 36 ft. lbs. (49 Nm) [M10 nut]
• Caliper-to-strut bolts: 44 ft. lbs. (60 Nm)
• Stabilizer-to-control arm bolts: 7 ft. lbs. (10 Nm).

Golf, Rabbit, Scirocco, Jetta and GTI

1. Jack up the front of the vehicle and support it on stands.
2. Remove the wheel.
3. Remove the brake hose from the strut clip.

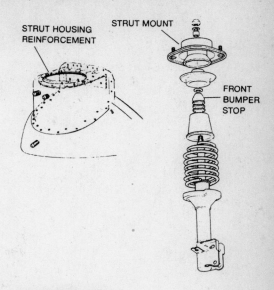

GTI strut installation

4. Mark the position of the camber adjustment bolts before removing them from the hub (wheel bearing housing).

5. Remove the upper mounting nuts and remove the strut from the vehicle.

6. Installation is the reverse of removal. Observe the following torques:
• Upper nuts: 14 ft. lbs. (19 Nm)
• Upper adjusting bolt-to-hub to 58 ft. lbs. (79 Nm)
• Lower adjusting bolt-to-hub to 43 ft. lbs. (58 Nm)

Use new washers on the lower bolts. If the shock absorber was replaced, camber will have to be adjusted. See procedures in this chapter.

Corrado and Passat

1. Raise the vehicle and support with jackstands under the lower control arms.
2. Mark the position of the lower strut bolts before removing. Remove the two bolts.
3. Remove the upper mounting nut and the strut from the vehicle.
4. Install the strut and torque the upper nut to 44 ft. lbs. (60 Nm). Install the lower knuckle-to-strut bolts and torque to 70 ft. lbs. (95 Nm).
5. Install the wheel, lower the vehicle and have the front end aligned by a qualified alignment technician.

STRUT OVERHAUL

NOTE: *You must obtain a spring compressor, either the Volkswagen type (VW 340/5 and VW 340) or its equivalent.*

1. Remove the strut from the vehicle. See above for procedures.

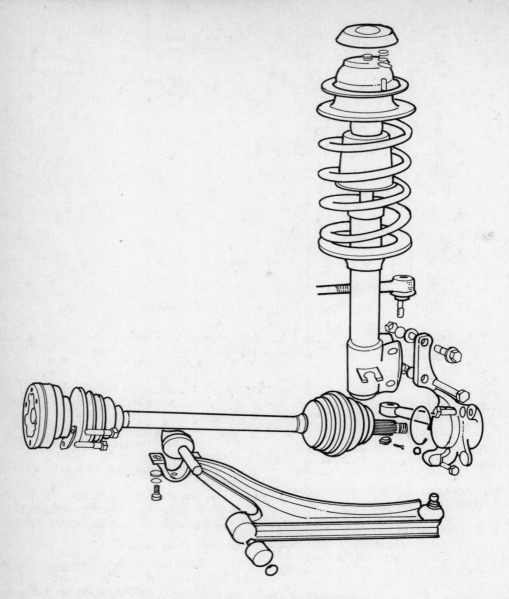

Rabbit, Jetta and Scirocco front suspension

2. Anchor the strut in a vise so it cannot move and attach the spring compressor. Be sure to follow the compressor instructions to the letter. The coil spring is under considerable pressure and has the potential to seriously harm you.

3. Compress the spring and loosen the center nut at the top of the strut assembly. To aid in removing the nut, fit an allen wrench in the top of the shock absorber rod and loosen the nut with a closed end wrench.

4. Remove the collar parts from the top of the spring and arrange the parts in the order of removal to aid you in reassembly.

5. Slowly release the pressure on the spring and remove the spring from the strut.

NOTE: *The springs are color coded. When replacing, make sure both replacement springs have the same color code.*

Dashers after chassis no. 3–5 2 117 398 and all Golfs, Rabbits, Jettas, GTIs and Sciroccos have nonremovable shock absorbers in the struts. If the shock absorbers on these models wear out, you must replace the entire strut assembly (except for the coil spring and its attaching parts).

To replace the removable shock absorber car-

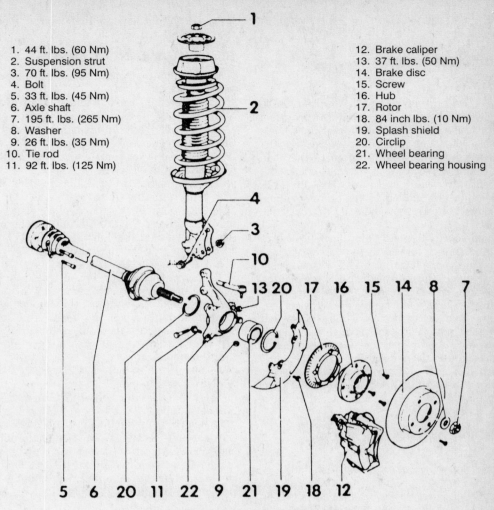

1. 44 ft. lbs. (60 Nm)
2. Suspension strut
3. 70 ft. lbs. (95 Nm)
4. Bolt
5. 33 ft. lbs. (45 Nm)
6. Axle shaft
7. 195 ft. lbs. (265 Nm)
8. Washer
9. 26 ft. lbs. (35 Nm)
10. Tie rod
11. 92 ft. lbs. (125 Nm)

12. Brake caliper
13. 37 ft. lbs. (50 Nm)
14. Brake disc
15. Screw
16. Hub
17. Rotor
18. 84 inch lbs. (10 Nm)
19. Splash shield
20. Circlip
21. Wheel bearing
22. Wheel bearing housing

Front suspension — Corrado and Passat

tridge in Dashers before chassis no. 3–5 2 117 398, and 1987–90 Foxes, proceed as follows:

6. Remove the rubber cap and collar on the shock tube and remove the round, threaded retaining cap. There is a special VW tool (40–201) for this job, but you should be able to loosen the cap with a pipe wrench. Be careful not to bend or dent the cap when removing.

7. Pull the shock absorber cartridge out of the strut. You may have to put the nut back on the shock absorber rod and use it as a stoppoint to tap the cartridge out of the strut. When installing, the threaded retaining cap should be tightened to 108 ft. lbs. (148 Nm).

8. Installation of the coil spring is the reverse of removal. Tighten the coil spring retaining nut to 44 ft. lbs. (60 Nm) on the Dasher, Fox and Quantum, 58 ft. lbs. (80 Nm) on the Rabbit, Golf, Jetta, GTI and Scirocco.

Make sure the coil spring fits into its grooves in the strut. If the strut has been replaced, the

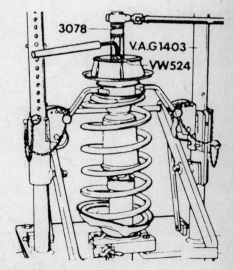

Compressing the strut spring

camber must be adjusted. See the section in this chapter.

Shock Absorbers

TESTING

The function of a shock absorber is to dampen harsh spring movement and provide a means of dissipating the motion of the wheels so that the roughness encountered by the wheels is not totally transmitted to the body and, therefore, to you and your passengers. As the wheel moves up and down, the shock absorber shortens and lengthens, thereby imposing a restraint on movement by its hydraulic action.

A simple way to see if your shock absorbers are functioning correctly is to push one corner of the car down a few times. This will compress the spring on that side of the car as well as the shock absorber. If the shock absorber is functioning properly, it will control the spring's tendency to remain in motion. Thus the car will level itself almost instantly when you release the downward pressure. If the car continues to bounce up and down several times, the shock absorber is worn out and should be replaced. Examine the strut body for heavy oil streaking, which would indicate shock leakage. Replace a leaky shock absorber.

REMOVAL AND INSTALLATION

Shock absorber removal and installation is contained in the strut overhaul section, above. Be aware, however, that on all models except Dashers up to chassis no. 3–5 2 117 398, and 1987–90 Foxes, replacing the shock absorber means replacing the strut itself (except for the coil spring and its attaching parts).

Coil Spring

REMOVAL AND INSTALLATION

Coil spring removal and installation procedures are contained in the strut overhaul section, above. The coil springs are color coded and must be matched with other springs of the same color code.

Ball Joints

INSPECTION

Visually check the ball joint rubber dust cap for cracks and rips. Make sure the ball joint is mounted securely on the lower control arm, and check the up and down play (as opposed to side to side movement) of the joint itself. If the

up and down play is more than 2.5mm, replace the ball joint.

REMOVAL AND INSTALLATION

1. Jack up the front of the vehicle and support it on jackstands.
2. Matchmark the ball joint-to-control arm position on the Dasher, Fox and Quantum.
3. Remove the retaining bolt and nut from the hub (wheel bearing housing).
4. Pry the lower control arm and ball joint down and out of the strut.
5. Remove the two ball joint-to-lower control arm retaining nuts and bolts on the Dasher, Fox or Quantum. Remove the three nuts and bolts on the Corrado and Passat. Drill out the rivets on the Rabbit, Jetta, GTI and Scirocco; enlarge the holes to 3mm.
6. Remove the ball joint assembly.
7. Install the Dasher, Fox or Quantum ball joint in the reverse order of removal. If no parts were installed other than the ball joint, align the match marks made in Step 2. No camber adjustment is necessary if this is done. Pull the ball joint into alignment with pliers. Observe the following torques:
   • Control arm-to-ball joint bolts: 47 ft. lbs. (65 Nm)
   • Strut-to-ball joint bolt: 25 ft. lbs. (34 Nm) [M8 bolt] or 36 ft. lbs. (48 Nm) [M10 bolt].
8. On the Golf, Rabbit, Jetta, GTI, Scirocco, Corrado and Passat bolt the new ball joint in place (bolts are provided with the replacement ball joint), and tighten them to 18 ft. lbs. (25 Nm). Tighten the retaining bolt holding the ball joint to the hub to 21 ft. lbs. (28 Nm).

Axle Shaft

REMOVAL AND INSTALLATION

Axle shaft removal and installation procedures are covered in Chapter 7.

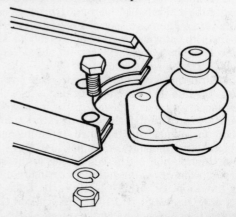

Rabbit, Jetta and Scirocco ball joint assembly

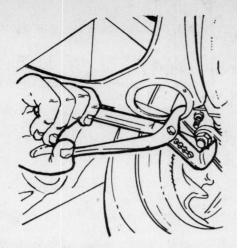

Aligning the ball joint on Dasher and Quantum

Lower Control Arm (Wishbone)

REMOVAL AND INSTALLATION

Volkswagen refers to the lower control arm as the wishbone.

NOTE: *When removing the left side (driver's side) control arm on the Rabbit, Jetta, GTI and Scirocco equipped with an automatic transmission, remove the front left engine mounting, remove the nut for the rear mounting, remove the engine mounting support and raises the engine to expose the front control arm bolt.*

1. Raise the vehicle and support it on jack stands. Remove the road wheel.
2. Remove the nut and bolt attaching the ball joint to the hub (wheel bearing housing) and pry the joint down and out of the hub.
3. Unfasten the stabilizer bar on the Dasher, Fox or Quantum.
4. Unbolt and remove the control arm-to-subframe (crossmember) mounting bolts on the Dasher or Quantum. On the Golf, Rabbit, Jetta, GTI and Scirocco remove the control arm mounting bolts from the frame.
5. Remove the control arm. See procedures above for ball joint removal and installation.
6. Installation is the reverse of removal. Observe the following torques:
• Dasher, Fox or Quantum control arm-to-subframe bolts: 50 ft. lbs. (37 Nm)
• Rabbit, Jetta, GTI and Scirocco control arm-to-frame front bolt: 43 ft. lbs. (57 Nm)
• Rabbit, Jetta, GTI and Scirocco control arm-to-frame rear bolts: 32 ft. lbs. (44 Nm)
• Rabbit, Jetta, GTI and Scirocco ball joint-to-hub bolt: 21 ft. lbs. (28 Nm)
• Dasher, Fox or Quantum ball joint-to-hub bolt: 25 ft. lbs. (34 Nm) [M8 nut] or 36 ft. lbs. (49 Nm) [M10 nut]

• Corrado and Passat arm-to-frame bolts: 96 ft. lbs. (130 Nm)

Front Wheel Bearings

The front wheel bearings are non-adjustable on all models and are sealed, so they should be maintenance free. Removing the front wheel bearings requires a stand press and a myriad of special Volkswagen tools, so the procedure is not given here.

Steering Knuckle

REMOVAL AND INSTALLATION

1. Raise the vehicle and support with jackstands.
2. Remove the front wheels.
NOTE: *The strut assembly does not have to be removed on all models except the Dasher. The Dasher's strut and knuckle is one assembly.*
3. Mark the knuckle-to-strut housing for installation alignment.
4. Remove the brake caliper and hang from a piece of wire to the frame. Do NOT allow the caliper to hang from the brake hose.
5. Remove the tie rod nut and cotter pin. Disconnect the tie rod using the proper separator.
6. Remove the axle nut and washer.
7. Disconnect the lower control arm from the knuckle.
8. Remove the two strut-to-knuckle bolts.
9. Slide the axle shaft out of the bearing and remove the knuckle.
10. Install the knuckle onto the vehicle and slide the axle shaft into the bearing.
11. Reconnect the lower ball joint, tie rod end, strut and caliper.
12. Torque the axle nut to 195 ft. lbs. (265 Nm).
13. Install the tire and lower the vehicle.

Front End Alignment

NOTE: *When checking wheel alignment, the car must be empty, tire pressure correct and on a level surface.*

CAMBER ADJUSTMENT

Camber angle is the number of degrees which the centerline of the wheel is inclined from the vertical. Camber reduces loading of the outer wheel bearing and improves tire contact while cornering.

Dasher, Fox and Quantum

Camber is adjusted by loosening the two ball joint-to-lower control arm bolts, and moving the ball joint in or out as necessary.

Golf, Rabbit, Scirocco, Jetta and GTI

Camber is adjusted by loosening the nuts of the two bolts holding the top of the wheel bearing housing (knuckle) to the bottom of the strut, and turning the top eccentric bolt. The range of adjustment is 2°.

Corrado and Passat

If the camber is out of adjustment, loosen the bolts securing the strut to the wheel bearing housing (knuckle) and move the top of the wheel in or out to obtain specifications. If the camber is out of specification range, replace the original top bolt with a special camber correction bolt Part No. N 101 740.01. The thinner diameter changes camber 1°.

CASTER

Caster angle is the number of degrees in which a line drawn through the steering knuckle pivots is inclined from the vertical, toward the front or rear of the car. Positive caster improves direction stability and decreases susceptibility to cross winds or road surface deviations. Other than the replacement of damaged suspension components, caster is not adjustable.

TOE-IN

Dasher and Quantum

Toe-in is checked with the wheels straight ahead. The left tie rod is adjustable. Loosen the nuts and clamps and adjust the length of the tie rod for correct toe-out. If the steering wheel is crooked, remove and align it.

Fox

NOTE: *Steering gear tool 3075 must be used to adjust toe on vehicles with top adjustable tie rods.*

1. Turn the steering gear to the center position.
2. Remove front bolt **A** from the steering gear cover.
3. Attach centering tool 3075 with bracket **B** over mounting nut on the left tie rod.
4. Remove the bolt from the spacer on the chain of the centering tool.
5. Put the spacer under the hole marked with an **L** and insert a bolt through this hole and the hole in the spacer, then tighten to the steering gear.
6. Measure and divide the total toe in half.
7. Loosen the clamps and outer lock nut on both sides.
8. Turn both tie rods until the specified setting for Toe is reached.

9. Tighten the clamps and lock nuts on the tie rods.
10. Check and reposition steering wheel in center position if necessary.
11. Remove the centering tool and tighten bolt **A** to 15 ft. lbs. (20 Nm).
12. If the steering wheel is crooked after the toe adjustment has been made, remove, straighten and reinstall the wheel.

Golf, Rabbit, Scirocco, Jetta, GTI, Corrado, Passat

Toe-in is checked with the wheels straight ahead. Only the right tie rod is adjustable, but replacement left tie rods are adjustable. Replacement left tie rods should be set to the same length as the original. Toe-in should be adjusted only with the right tie rod. If the steering wheel is crooked, remove and align it.

The top eccentric bolt provides camber adjustment on Rabbit, Scirocco and Jetta

REAR SUSPENSION

The Dasher rear suspension has a rear axle beam tube on each side. The trailing arms mount to the unit body in rubber bushings. A coil spring and shock absorber are located at each wheel. A Panhard rod locates the axle against side forces.

The Golf, Rabbit (except the Pick-up truck), Jetta, Scirocco, Corrado and Passat rear suspension includes a torsion beam which connects the two trailing arms. On these models, the coil spring and the shock absorber are combined into a strut. The Quantum rear axle assembly is similar to this type, but uses different axle bushings.

The Rabbit Pick-up truck has leaf springs mounted on a simple axle beam with conventional shock absorbers mounted at each side of the beam.

The Fox rear suspension has a rear axle beam tube on each side. The trailing arms mount to the unit body in rubber bushings. The coil spring and the shock absorber are combined into a strut.

Coil Spring

REMOVAL AND INSTALLATION

Dasher Only

NOTE: *This operation requires the use of either special tool VW 655/3 or a suitable spring compressor.*

1. Raise the car and support it on jack stands. Do not place the jack stands under the axle beam.
2. Remove the road wheel.
3. Attach special tool VW 655/3 between the axle beam and a prefabricated hook hung on the body frame above the beam. Use the special tool or spring compressor to compress the spring.
4. Unbolt the shock absorber from the axle beam. If you used a spring compressor, you should be able to remove the spring now. Do not allow the axle to hang by its body mounts. If you used special tool VW 655/3, lower the axle beam enough to remove the spring.
5. Installation is the reverse of removal.

NOTE: *It is not necessary to replace both springs if only one is damaged.*

Shock Absorber

REMOVAL AND INSTALLATION

Dasher Only

NOTE: *Only remove one shock absorber at a time. Do not allow the rear axle to hang by its body mounts only, as it may damage the brake lines.*

This operation requires the use of either special tool VW 655/3 or a suitable spring compressor and floor jack.

1. Raise the car and support it on jack stands. Do not place the jack stands under the axle beam.
2. Remove the wheel.
3. Attach special tool VW 655/3 between the axle beam and a prefabricated hook hung on the body frame above the beam. Jack the tool until you can see the shock absorber compressing. If you are using a spring compressor and a floor jack, compress the springs little and, placing the floor jack under the beam below the spring, jack it up until you see the shock absorber compress.
4. Unbolt and remove the shock absorber.
5. Installation is the reverse of removal. Tighten the shock absorber bolts to 43 ft. lbs. (58 Nm).

NOTE: *There are two types of shock absorbers for the Dasher and they have different*

mounts. *Make sure you get the correct type for your vehicle.*

Strut Assembly

REMOVAL AND INSTALLATION

Fox, Rabbit (Except Pick-Up), Scirocco, Jetta, Golf, GTI, Corrado and Passat

1. Raise the car on a lift or jack it up and support it on stands. Support the axle with a floor jack, but do not put any pressure on the springs.
2. Remove the rubber guard from inside the car.
3. Remove the nut, washer and mounting disc.
4. Unbolt the strut assembly from the rear axle and remove it.
5. Installation is the reverse of removal. Tighten the top mount bolt to 23 ft. lbs. (29 Nm) and the bottom bolt to 32 ft. lbs. (45 Nm).

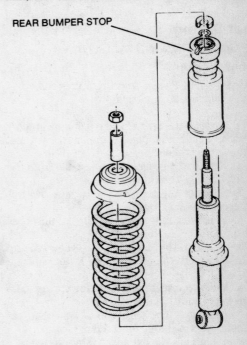

REAR BUMPER STOP

GTI rear strut installation

Quantum

1. Remove shock strut cover inside car.
2. Unscrew strut from body.
3. Slowly lift vehicle until wheels are slightly off ground.
4. Unscrew strut from axle.
5. Take strut out of lower mounting. Press wheel down slightly when removing strut.

CAUTION: *Do not remove both suspension struts at the same time as this will overload the axle beam bushings.*

6. Guide strut out carefully between wheel and wheel housing. Do not damage paint on spring and wheel housing.

7. Installation is the reverse of removal.

STRUT OVERHAUL (COIL SPRING AND SHOCK ABSORBER)

A spring compressor is necessary for this operation. Also, do not interchange a Rabbit, Jetta, or Scirocco coil spring, since they are different in size and/or hardness.

1. Clamp the strut in a vise.

2. Attach the spring compressor and compress the spring.

3. Remove the slotted nut at the top of the strut and remove the collar and the spring.

4. Installation is the reverse of removal. Tighten the slotted nut to 14 ft. lbs. (19 Nm).

Leaf Spring

REMOVAL AND INSTALLATION

Rabbit Pick-Up

CAUTION: *The springs are under considerable tension, so be careful!*

1. Jack up the rear of the truck and support it with jackstands placed under the frame. Remove the wheel.

2. Remove the parking brake cable from the spring and cut the tie-wrap.

3. Support the rear axle on a jack. Do not put pressure on the spring.

4. Remove the bottom shock absorber mount bolt.

5. Remove the U-bolts and their spring plates. Loosen the upper and lower shackle bolts.

6. When removing the left side spring, perform these additional steps:

   a. Remove the three bolts from the exhaust system flange on the flex pipe.

   b. Unhook the exhaust system hangers.

   c. Remove the exhaust system.

7. Remove the lower shackle bolt.

8. Remove the front spring bolt and remove the spring.

9. Installation is the reverse of removal. The weight of the truck must be on the rear wheels before the leaf spring and shock absorber attaching bolts are fully tightened. Tighten the rear shackle bolts to 45 ft. lbs. (61 Nm), and the front bolt to 68 ft. lbs. (90 Nm). Tighten the U-bolt nuts and the lower shock absorber bolt to 29 ft. lbs. (40 Nm).

Shock Absorber

REMOVAL AND INSTALLATION

Rabbit Pick-Up

1. Jack up the rear of the truck and support the axle on jack stands.

2. Unbolt and remove the shock absorber, taking care to notice the direction of mounting bolts for installation.

3. Installation is the reverse of removal. Tighten the mounting bolts to 29 ft. lbs. (40 Nm).

Stub Axle

REMOVAL AND INSTALLATION

All Models

1. Remove the grease cap.

2. Remove the cotter pin, nutlock, adjusting nut, spacer, wheel bearing and brake drum.

3. Detach the brake line and plug it.

4. Remove the brake backing plate complete with brake assembly.

5. Unbolt and remove the stub axle.

6. Installation is the reverse of removal. Always replace the spring washer with a new

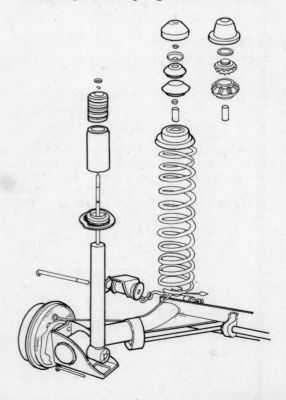

Rabbit, Jetta and Scirocco rear suspension, except Rabbit pickup. Note new parts used beginning in 1978

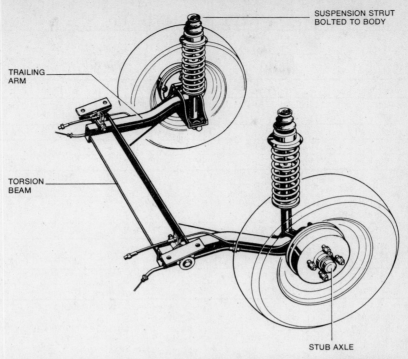

SUSPENSION STRUT
BOLTED TO BODY

TRAILING
ARM

TORSION
BEAM

STUB AXLE

Rabbit, Jetta and Scirocco rear suspension. Jetta models also have stabilizer bars

one and bleed the brakes. Pack the bearings and adjust the bearing end-play.

Axle Assembly

REMOVAL AND INSTALLATION

Except Rabbit Pick-up

1. Raise the vehicle and support with jackstands.
2. Remove the rear wheels. Remove the brake drums or the caliper and rotor depending on the vehicle.
3. Disconnect the brake hoses and parking brake cables. Plug the hydraulic hoses after disconnecting. Disconnect the ABS wheel sensors if so equipped.
4. Using a jack to support the axle.
5. Remove the strut-to-axle bolts and allow the axle to rest on the jack.
6. Remove the bolts to the sway bar and center mounting bracket.
7. Remove the bolts at the axle bushing and lower the axle using the jack.
8. Install the axle with the jack and install the axle bushing bolts.
9. Install the center support bracket, sway bar and strut bolts.
10. Connect the brake lines, cables and wires.
11. Install the brake drums or calipers.
12. Bleed the brake system, install the rear wheels and lower the vehicle.

Rear Wheel Bearings

ADJUSTMENT

Before attempting to adjust the wheel bearings, tighten the adjustment nut while turning the wheel to seat the bearings. Wheel bearing clearance is correctly adjusted when the thrust washer under the adjusting nut can be moved slightly with a suitable prybar. Do not twist or pry with the prybar. Install a new cotter pin.

REMOVAL AND INSTALLATION

1. Raise the vehicle and support with jackstands.
2. Remove the rear wheels.
3. Remove the grease cap, cotter pin, nut, washer and outer bearing.
4. Pull the brake drum or rotor from the axle using care not to damage the grease seal.
5. Remove the grease seal with a soft chisel and rubber hammer.
6. Remove the inner bearing.
7. Clean the grease cavity of all grease. Do NOT use liquid cleaner solution.
8. Remove the bearing outer races with a bearing race remover.
9. Install the bearing races using a race installer VW432.

NOTE: *Do not use old bearing with new races or vise versa. Only use bearings in a matched set.*

WHEEL ALIGNMENT

Year	Model	Caster ① Range (deg.)	Pref Setting (deg.)	Camber ② Range (deg.)	Pref Setting (deg.)	Toe-in ③ (in.)	Steering Axis Inclination ① (deg.)
All	Dasher	0 to 1°P	30' P	0 to 1°P	30' P	0.08	10½
1975–85	Rabbit, Fox Scirocco, Jetta	1°20' P to 2°20' P	1°50' P	10' N to 50' P	20' P	0.08	10½
1982–87	Quantum	0 to 1°P	30' P	1°10' N to 10' P	40' N	NA	NA
1985–90	Fox Sedan	1°40' P to 2°20' P	2°P	50' N to 10' N	30' N	0.08	NA
	Wagon	1°25' P to 2°25' P	1°55' P	50' N to 10' N	30' N	0.08	NA
1986–90	Golf, GTI, GLI, Jetta under 100 HP	1°P to 2°P	1°30' P	50' N to 10' N	30' N	0	NA
	Golf, GTI, GLI, Jetta from 102 HP	1°05' P to 2°05' P	1°50' P	1°05' N to 15' N	15' N	0	NA
	GTI 16V	1°05' P to 2°05' P	1°50' P	1°N to 20' N	50' N	0	NA
1986–90	Quantum	0 to 1°P	30' P	10' N to 1°10' P	40' P	0.20	NA
	Scirocco, Cabriolet	1°20' P to 2°20' P	1°40' P	10' N to 50' P	30' P	0.12	NA
1990	Passat	1°10' P to 2°10' P	1°50' P	1°40' N to 1°N	1°20' N	0	NA
	Corrado	1°05' P to 2°05' P	1°35' P	55' N to 15' N	35' N	0	NA

① Not adjustable.
② Rear wheel camber (not adjustable)
  Rabbit (to Ch. No. 176 3 241 690)—1°N ± 30'
  Rabbit (from Ch. No. 176 3 261 691)—1¼°N ± 30'
  Scirocco (all)—1°N ± 30'
  Dasher (all)—½°N ± 30'
  Quantum 1982—1°40' ± 20'
  Jetta—1¼°N ± 30'
  1986–90 Fox—2° ± –1
  1986–90 Quantum –1°20 to –2°
  1986–90 Scirocco –40 to 1°50'
        Cabriolet
  1990 Passat –1°40' ± 20'
      Corrado

③ Rear wheel toe-in (not adjustable)
  Rabbit—0° ± 15'
  Scirocco (to Ch. No. 536 2 031 722)—10°P ± 30'
  Scirocco (from Ch. No. 536 2 031 723)—20' P ± 30'
  Quantum +25 ± 15'
  Jetta—0° ± 15'
  1986–90 Fox 10° ± 36'
  1986–90 Quantum + 10 to + 40'
  1986–90 Scirocco –10 to + 50'
        Cabriolet
  1990 Passat +25 ± 15
      Corrado

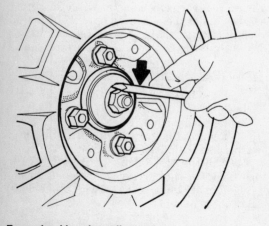

Rear wheel bearing adjustment

10. Pack the bearings with new high temperature grease.

11. Install the inner bearing and seal. Use a seal installer VW3074.

12. Install the rotor onto the axle. Be careful not to damage the grease seal.

13. Install the outer bearing, washer, nut and retainer.

14. Adjust the bearing as outlined in this section.

15. Install a new cotter pin and grease cap.

16. Install the rear wheels and lower the vehicle.

STEERING

The Dasher and Fox uses rack and pinion steering gear with center mounted tie rods. This allows very little toe-in change during suspension travel. A steering damper reduces road shock transmittal to the steering wheel. No maintenance is required.

The Golf, Rabbit, Jetta, GTI, Scirocco, Corrado and Passat are equipped with rack and pinion steering. The tie rods are end mounted. One tie rod is adjustable. No maintenance is required on the rack and pinion.

The Quantum, Corrado and Passat is equipped with standard power steering (rack and pinion). The only periodic maintenance required is a check of the power steering fluid reservoir, and a check when underneath the car (oil change time is convenient) for steering system leaks. Replace fluid reservoir filter when changing fluid or when replacing steering system components.

Steering Wheel

REMOVAL AND INSTALLATION

NOTE: *Beginning in August 1988 the steering wheels with modified inner splines were introduced into production on some models. The column remains unchanged except for the addition of a short splined adapter sleeve pressed onto the splines of the steering column. The short splined adapter was replaced by the longer sleeve starting in January 1989. The short splines P/N is 191 419 514 A and the long P/N is 191 419 514.*

1. Grasp the center cover pad and pull it from the wheel. (Cover varies depending on model).
2. Loosen and remove the steering shaft nut.
3. Matchmark the steering wheel position in relation to the steering shaft so that when you install it, the wheel is perfectly level when the road wheels are straight ahead.
4. Pull the steering wheel off the shaft. You may need a puller to perform this operation. Under no circumstances should you bang on the shaft to try to free the wheel, or you may damage the collapsible steering column.
5. Disconnect the horn wire.
6. Replace the wheel in the reverse order of removal. On the Rabbit, Jetta and Scirocco, install the steering wheel with the road wheels straight ahead and the canceling lug pointing to the left. On the Fox, Dasher and Quantum with the road wheels straight ahead, the canceling lug on the steering wheel must point to the right and the turn signal lever must be in the neutral position. Tighten the steering shaft nut to 36 ft. lbs. (48 Nm).

Turn Signal and Headlight Dimmer Switch

REMOVAL AND INSTALLATION

1. Disconnect the battery ground cable.
2. Remove the steering wheel.
3. Remove the switch retaining screws.
4. Pry the switch housing off the column.
5. Disconnect the electrical plugs at the back of the switch.
6. Remove the switch housing.
7. Replace in the reverse order of removal.

NOTE: *On the Rabbit, Jetta and Scirocco, tap spacer sleeve into column (carefully) until there is 2–4mm clearance between the wheel and the hub.*

Ignition Switch

REMOVAL AND INSTALLATION

The ignition switch is located at the bottom of the ignition key cylinder body. To remove the ignition switch, remove the steering lock body, see below for procedures. On all models except Dashers made before 1978, remove the switch by removing the screw at the bottom of the switch and pulling the switch out. On Dashers made before 1978, the screw is located in the side of the cylinder body. Installation is the reverse of removal.

Steering Lock

REMOVAL AND INSTALLATION

On some models, the hole in the lock body for removing the steering lock cylinder was not drilled by Volkswagen. To make the hole, use the following measurements in conjunction with the illustrations. Drill the hole where "a" and "b" intersect on the lock body. The hole should be drilled 3mm deep.

- 1974–77 Dasher
  a = 11.5mm
  b = 8.0mm
- 1975–76 Rabbit, Scirocco
  a = 11mm
  b = 11mm
- 1977–90 Rabbit, Jetta, Scirocco, 1978–87 Dasher, Quantum, Fox, Corrado, Passat
  a = 12mm
  b = 10mm

NOTE: *Measurements are given in metric form first because this unit of measurement will be easier to make.*

Remove the lock cylinder by pushing a small drill bit or piece of wire into the hole and pulling the cylinder out. It might be easier to insert the ignition key, turn it to the right a little and pull on it.

NOTE: *On 1976 Rabbits and Sciroccos, the lock cylinder can also be removed by removing the steering and windshield wiper components and removing the locking plate holding the cylinder with a pair of pliers. When installing the plate, peen it slightly to hold it in place.*

To remove the lock body, proceed as follows:

1. Remove the steering wheel and turn signal switch. See above for procedures. Remove the steering column shaft covers.
2. The lock is clamped to the steering column with special bolts whose heads shear off on installation. These must be drilled out in order to remove the switch.

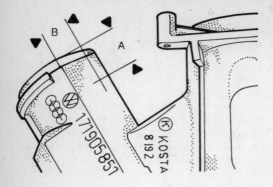

Lock cylinder removal for all Rabbit, Jetta and Scirocco and 1978–81 Dasher

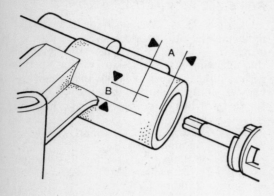

Lock cylinder removal for 1974–77 Dasher

3. On replacement, make sure that the lock tang is aligned with the slot in the steering column.

Steering Column

REMOVAL AND INSTALLATION

1. Disconnect the negative battery cable.

2. Working from the inside of the vehicle, remove the steering wheel as previously described.

3. Remove the turn signal/headlight and wiper/washer switches.

4. Remove the ignition switch and the ignition lock housing.

5. Remove the upper and lower column covers. Pry off the bearing support ring.

6. Remove the shear bolt cover and drill out the shear bolt(s). Then remove the steering shaft support bolts and lower the steering column.

7. Working from under the hood of the car, lower the dust boot and remove the bolt which secures the steering column to the universal joint shaft.

NOTE: *On the 1987 Fox the steering column is connected to a flange tube. Remove the retainer which holds the steering shaft to the flange tube and remove the column. During installation, hold the flange tube and the steering column together with water pump pliers and install the retainer.*

8. Working from inside the vehicle, remove the steering column.

9. Installation is the reverse of the removal procedures.

10. Torque the universal shaft bolt to 22 ft. lbs. (30 Nm).

11. Torque the steering shaft support bolt to 14 ft. lbs. (20 Nm).

12. Install new shear bolts and tighten until the heads shear off.

NOTE: *Do not push the steering column into the universal joint using more than 100–200 lbs. of force.*

13. Install the remaining components in the reverse of their removal.

14. Make sure that the road wheels are straight ahead when the steering wheel is installed.

15. Torque the steering wheel retaining bolt to 36 ft. lbs. (50 Nm).

Tie Rods

REMOVAL AND INSTALLATION

Dasher, Fox and Quantum

Because of the demand for optional wheel rims which require more clearance at the tie rod, several different length adjustable and non-adjustable tie rods are available. Which tie rod is right for your car depends on the transmission used (manual or automatic), and the year

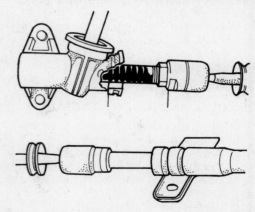

Rabbit, Jetta and Scirocco steering rack adjustment

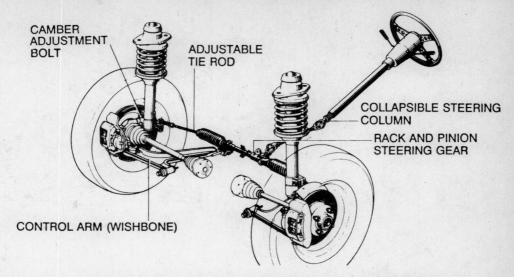

CAMBER ADJUSTMENT BOLT

ADJUSTABLE TIE ROD

COLLAPSIBLE STEERING COLUMN

RACK AND PINION STEERING GEAR

CONTROL ARM (WISHBONE)

Rabbit, Jetta and Scirocco steering and front suspension components

of production. Consult your dealer for this information.

1. Raise the car and remove the front wheels.

2. Disconnect the outer end of the steering tie rod from the steering knuckle by removing the cotter pin and nut and pressing out the tie rod end. A small puller or press is required to free the tie rod end.

3. Under the hood, pry off the lock plate and remove the mounting bolts from both tie rod inner ends. Pry the tie rod out of the mounting pivot and remove.

4. Installation is the reverse of removal. If you are replacing an adjustable tie rod, adjust the new tie rod to the same length. If replacing a new, non-adjustable shorter tie rod, the other side tie rod will have to be adjusted. Tighten the tie rod to steering knuckle nut to 22 ft. lbs. (29 Nm), and the inner pivot bolt to 40 ft. lbs. (54 Nm). Check the toe.

Golf, Rabbit, Jetta, GTI, Scirocco, Corrado and Passat

1. Center the steering wheel.

2. Remove the cotter pin and nut from the tie rod end.

3. Mark or measure the length of the tie rod for installation purposes.

4. Disconnect the tie rod from the steering rack after removing the rubber boot from the end of the rack. The left side tie rod end cannot be removed from the tie rod, therefore the entire tie rod must be replaced if the ball joint goes bad. Loosen the lock ring and unscrew the tie rod. See Steps 5 and 6 of the Rabbit and Scirocco Steering Gear Removal and Installation.

5. Adjust the appropriate tie rod to the specified length before installing.

• Rabbit, Scirocco, Fox, Golf, GTI, Jetta: 379mm Left side

• Corrado, Quantum: 379.5mm Left side

• Passat: 395mm Left side

6. Adjust the right tie rod for Toe. Tighten the tie rod end nuts to 21 ft. lbs. (28 Nm) and install new cotter pins.

Steering Gear

REMOVAL AND INSTALLATION

Dasher, Fox and Quantum

1. Pry off the lock plate and remove both tie rod mounting bolts from the steering rack, inside the engine compartment. Pry the tie rods out of the mounting pivot.

2. Remove the lower instrument panel trim.

3. Remove the shaft clamp bolt, pry off the clip, and drive the shaft toward the inside of the car with a brass drift.

4. Disconnect power steering hoses (if equipped). Remove the steering gear mounting bolts.

5. Turn the wheels all the way to the right and remove the steering gear through the opening in the right wheel housing.

6. For installation, temporarily install the tie rod mounting pivot to the rack with both mounting bolts. Remove one bolt, install the tie rod, and replace the bolt. Do the same on the other tie rod. Make sure to install a new lock plate. Torque the tie rod bolts to 39 ft. lbs. (54 Nm), the mounting pivot bolt to 15 ft. lbs. (19 Nm), and the steering gear to body mounting bolts to 15 ft. lbs. (19 Nm).

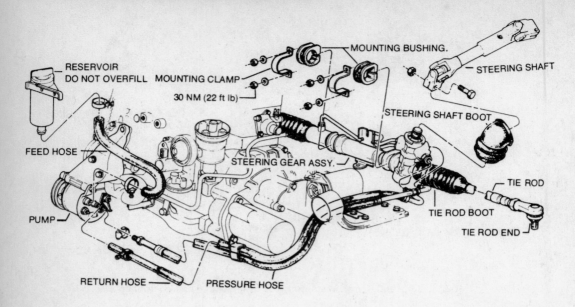

Typical rack and pinion power steering

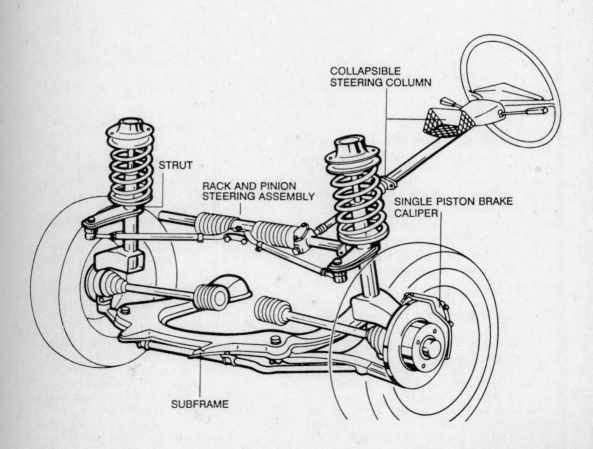

Dasher front suspension and steering components

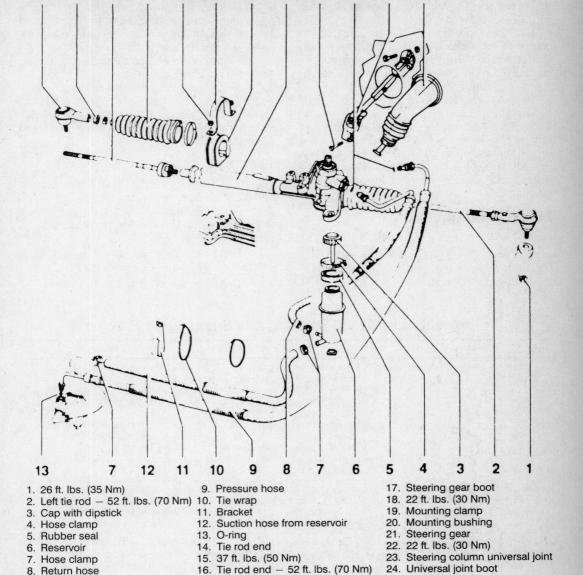

1. 26 ft. lbs. (35 Nm)
2. Left tie rod — 52 ft. lbs. (70 Nm)
3. Cap with dipstick
4. Hose clamp
5. Rubber seal
6. Reservoir
7. Hose clamp
8. Return hose
9. Pressure hose
10. Tie wrap
11. Bracket
12. Suction hose from reservoir
13. O-ring
14. Tie rod end
15. 37 ft. lbs. (50 Nm)
16. Tie rod end — 52 ft. lbs. (70 Nm)
17. Steering gear boot
18. 22 ft. lbs. (30 Nm)
19. Mounting clamp
20. Mounting bushing
21. Steering gear
22. 22 ft. lbs. (30 Nm)
23. Steering column universal joint
24. Universal joint boot

Power steering gear assembly

Golf, Rabbit, Scirocco, GTI and Jetta

1. Disconnect the steering shaft universal joint and wire up out of the way.

2. Disconnect the tie rods at the steering rack and wire up and out of the way. Disconnect power steering hoses (if equipped).

3. Remove the steering rack and drive.

4. Install the steering rack and drive and torque the attaching hardware to 14 ft. lbs. (20 Nm).

5. Set the steering rack with equal dis-

tances between the housing on the right side and left side.

6. Install the tie rods and screw both sides in until an equal distance is reached on both rods.

7. Install the steering shaft.

8. Check the front end alignment.

ADJUSTMENT

The steering gear on all models, except the Dasher before chassis no. 4 2 186 215, is adjustable. The adjustment is made at the junction where the steering wheel shaft meets the rack.

1. Loosen the locknut.

2. Hand tighten the adjusting screw in the center of the locknut until it just touches the thrust washer inside the gear housing. You can't see the thrust washer, but you should be able to tell by the feel of the screw.

3. Hold the screw in this position and tighten the locknut.

4. Road test the car. If the steering is stiff or does not center itself after a turn, the screw is probably too tight. If the steering still rattles, the adjustment is too loose, or other components of the steering system (tie rods, etc.) are wearing out.

Power Steering Pump

REMOVAL AND INSTALLATION

1. Place a catch pan under the power steering pump to catch the fluid.

2. Remove the suction hose and the pressure line from the pump, then drain the fluid into the catch pan (discard the fluid).

3. Loosen the tensioning bolt at the front of the tensioning bracket and remove the drive belt from the front of the drive pulley.

4. Remove the pumps mounting bolts and lift the pump from the vehicle.

5. To install, reverse the removal procedures. Torque the mounting bolts to 15 ft. lbs. (20 Nm). Tension the drive belt. Fill the reservoir with approved power steering fluid and bleed the system.

BLEEDING

1. Fill the reservoir to the MAX level mark with approved power steering fluid.

2. With the engine idling, turn the wheels from the right to the left side as far as possible, several times.

NOTE: *Continue bleeding the system until NO air bubbles are present in the fluid.*

3. Refill the reservoir to the MAX level.

Troubleshooting Basic Steering and Suspension Problems

Problem	Cause	Solution
Hard steering (steering wheel is hard to turn)	• Low or uneven tire pressure • Loose power steering pump drive belt • Low or incorrect power steering fluid • Incorrect front end alignment • Defective power steering pump • Bent or poorly lubricated front end parts	• Inflate tires to correct pressure • Adjust belt • Add fluid as necessary • Have front end alignment checked/adjusted • Check pump • Lubricate and/or replace defective parts
Loose steering (too much play in the steering wheel)	• Loose wheel bearings • Loose or worn steering linkage • Faulty shocks • Worn ball joints	• Adjust wheel bearings • Replace worn parts • Replace shocks • Replace ball joints
Car veers or wanders (car pulls to one side with hands off the steering wheel)	• Incorrect tire pressure • Improper front end alignment • Loose wheel bearings • Loose or bent front end components • Faulty shocks	• Inflate tires to correct pressure • Have front end alignment checked/adjusted • Adjust wheel bearings • Replace worn components • Replace shocks
Wheel oscillation or vibration transmitted through steering wheel	• Improper tire pressures • Tires out of balance • Loose wheel bearings • Improper front end alignment • Worn or bent front end components	• Inflate tires to correct pressure • Have tires balanced • Adjust wheel bearings • Have front end alignment checked/adjusted • Replace worn parts
Uneven tire wear	• Incorrect tire pressure • Front end out of alignment • Tires out of balance	• Inflate tires to correct pressure • Have front end alignment checked/adjusted • Have tires balanced

Troubleshooting the Steering Column

Problem	Cause	Solution
Will not lock	• Lockbolt spring broken or defective	• Replace lock bolt spring
High effort (required to turn ignition key and lock cylinder)	• Lock cylinder defective	• Replace lock cylinder
	• Ignition switch defective	• Replace ignition switch
	• Rack preload spring broken or deformed	• Replace preload spring
	• Burr on lock sector, lock rack, housing, support or remote rod coupling	• Remove burr
	• Bent sector shaft	• Replace shaft
	• Defective lock rack	• Replace lock rack
	• Remote rod bent, deformed	• Replace rod
	• Ignition switch mounting bracket bent	• Straighten or replace
	• Distorted coupling slot in lock rack (tilt column)	• Replace lock rack
Will stick in "start"	• Remote rod deformed	• Straighten or replace
	• Ignition switch mounting bracket bent	• Straighten or replace
Key cannot be removed in "off-lock"	• Ignition switch is not adjusted correctly	• Adjust switch
	• Defective lock cylinder	• Replace lock cylinder
Lock cylinder can be removed without depressing retainer	• Lock cylinder with defective retainer	• Replace lock cylinder
	• Burr over retainer slot in housing cover or on cylinder retainer	• Remove burr
High effort on lock cylinder between "off" and "off-lock"	• Distorted lock rack	• Replace lock rack
	• Burr on tang of shift gate (automatic column)	• Remove burr
	• Gearshift linkage not adjusted	• Adjust linkage
Noise in column	• One click when in "off-lock" position and the steering wheel is moved (all except automatic column)	• Normal—lock bolt is seating
	• Coupling bolts not tightened	• Tighten pinch bolts
	• Lack of grease on bearings or bearing surfaces	• Lubricate with chassis grease
	• Upper shaft bearing worn or broken	• Replace bearing assembly
	• Lower shaft bearing worn or broken	• Replace bearing. Check shaft and replace if scored.
	• Column not correctly aligned	• Align column
	• Coupling pulled apart	• Replace coupling
	• Broken coupling lower joint	• Repair or replace joint and align column
	• Steering shaft snap ring not seated	• Replace ring. Check for proper seating in groove.
	• Shroud loose on shift bowl. Housing loose on jacket—will be noticed with ignition in "off-lock" and when torque is applied to steering wheel.	• Position shroud over lugs on shift bowl. Tighten mounting screws.
High steering shaft effort	• Column misaligned	• Align column
	• Defective upper or lower bearing	• Replace as required
	• Tight steering shaft universal joint	• Repair or replace
	• Flash on I.D. of shift tube at plastic joint (tilt column only)	• Replace shift tube
	• Upper or lower bearing seized	• Replace bearings
Lash in mounted column assembly	• Column mounting bracket bolts loose	• Tighten bolts
	• Broken weld nuts on column jacket	• Replace column jacket
	• Column capsule bracket sheared	• Replace bracket assembly

Troubleshooting the Steering Column (cont.)

Problem	Cause	Solution
Lash in mounted column assembly (cont.)	• Column bracket to column jacket mounting bolts loose	• Tighten to specified torque
	• Loose lock shoes in housing (tilt column only)	• Replace shoes
	• Loose pivot pins (tilt column only)	• Replace pivot pins and support
	• Loose lock shoe pin (tilt column only)	• Replace pin and housing
	• Loose support screws (tilt column only)	• Tighten screws
Housing loose (tilt column only)	• Excessive clearance between holes in support or housing and pivot pin diameters	• Replace pivot pins and support
	• Housing support-screws loose	• Tighten screws
Steering wheel loose—every other tilt position (tilt column only)	• Loose fit between lock shoe and lock shoe pivot pin	• Replace lock shoes and pivot pin
Steering column not locking in any tilt position (tilt column only)	• Lock shoe seized on pivot pin	• Replace lock shoes and pin
	• Lock shoe grooves have burrs or are filled with foreign material	• Clean or replace lock shoes
	• Lock shoe springs weak or broken	• Replace springs
Noise when tilting column (tilt column only)	• Upper tilt bumpers worn	• Replace tilt bumper
	• Tilt spring rubbing in housing	• Lubricate with chassis grease
One click when in "off-lock" position and the steering wheel is moved	• Seating of lock bolt	• None. Click is normal characteristic sound produced by lock bolt as it seats.
High shift effort (automatic and tilt column only)	• Column not correctly aligned	• Align column
	• Lower bearing not aligned correctly	• Assemble correctly
	• Lack of grease on seal or lower bearing areas	• Lubricate with chassis grease
Improper transmission shifting— automatic and tilt column only	• Sheared shift tube joint	• Replace shift tube
	• Improper transmission gearshift linkage adjustment	• Adjust linkage
	• Loose lower shift lever	• Replace shift tube

Troubleshooting the Ignition Switch

Problem	Cause	Solution
Ignition switch electrically inoperative	• Loose or defective switch connector	• Tighten or replace connector
	• Feed wire open (fusible link)	• Repair or replace
	• Defective ignition switch	• Replace ignition switch
Engine will not crank	• Ignition switch not adjusted properly	• Adjust switch
Ignition switch wil not actuate mechanically	• Defective ignition switch	• Replace switch
	• Defective lock sector	• Replace lock sector
	• Defective remote rod	• Replace remote rod
Ignition switch cannot be adjusted correctly	• Remote rod deformed	• Repair, straighten or replace

Troubleshooting the Turn Signal Switch

Problem	Cause	Solution
Turn signal will not cancel	· Loose switch mounting screws · Switch or anchor bosses broken · Broken, missing or out of position detent, or cancelling spring	· Tighten screws · Replace switch · Reposition springs or replace switch as required
Turn signal difficult to operate	· Turn signal lever loose · Switch yoke broken or distorted · Loose or misplaced springs · Foreign parts and/or materials in switch · Switch mounted loosely	· Tighten mounting screws · Replace switch · Reposition springs or replace switch · Remove foreign parts and/or material · Tighten mounting screws
Turn signal will not indicate lane change	· Broken lane change pressure pad or spring hanger · Broken, missing or misplaced lane change spring · Jammed wires	· Replace switch · Replace or reposition as required · Loosen mounting screws, reposition wires and retighten screws
Turn signal will not stay in turn position	· Foreign material or loose parts impeding movement of switch yoke · Defective switch	· Remove material and/or parts · Replace switch
Hazard switch cannot be pulled out	· Foreign material between hazard support cancelling leg and yoke	· Remove foreign material. No foreign material impeding function of hazard switch—replace turn signal switch.
No turn signal lights	· Inoperative turn signal flasher · Defective or blown fuse · Loose chassis to column harness connector · Disconnect column to chassis connector. Connect new switch to chassis and operate switch by hand. If vehicle lights now operate normally, signal switch is inoperative · If vehicle lights do not operate, check chassis wiring for opens, grounds, etc.	· Replace turn signal flasher · Replace fuse · Connect securely · Replace signal switch · Repair chassis wiring as required
Instrument panel turn indicator lights on but not flashing	· Burned out or damaged front or rear turn signal bulb · If vehicle lights do not operate, check light sockets for high resistance connections, the chassis wiring for opens, grounds, etc. · Inoperative flasher · Loose chassis to column harness connection · Inoperative turn signal switch · To determine if turn signal switch is defective, substitute new switch into circuit and operate switch by hand. If the vehicle's lights operate normally, signal switch is inoperative.	· Replace bulb · Repair chassis wiring as required · Replace flasher · Connect securely · Replace turn signal switch · Replace turn signal switch
Stop light not on when turn indicated	· Loose column to chassis connection · Disconnect column to chassis connector. Connect new switch into system without removing old.	· Connect securely · Replace signal switch

Troubleshooting the Turn Signal Switch (cont.)

Problem	Cause	Solution
Stop light not on when turn indicated (cont.)	Operate switch by hand. If brake lights work with switch in the turn position, signal switch is defective.	
	• If brake lights do not work, check connector to stop light sockets for grounds, opens, etc.	• Repair connector to stop light circuits using service manual as guide
Turn indicator panel lights not flashing	• Burned out bulbs • High resistance to ground at bulb socket	• Replace bulbs • Replace socket
	• Opens, ground in wiring harness from front turn signal bulb socket to indicator lights	• Locate and repair as required
Turn signal lights flash very slowly	• High resistance ground at light sockets	• Repair high resistance grounds at light sockets
	• Incorrect capacity turn signal flasher or bulb	• Replace turn signal flasher or bulb
	• If flashing rate is still extremely slow, check chassis wiring harness from the connector to light sockets for high resistance	• Locate and repair as required
	• Loose chassis to column harness connection	• Connect securely
	• Disconnect column to chassis connector. Connect new switch into system without removing old. Operate switch by hand. If flashing occurs at normal rate, the signal switch is defective.	• Replace turn signal switch
Hazard signal lights will not flash— turn signal functions normally	• Blow fuse • Inoperative hazard warning flasher	• Replace fuse • Replace hazard warning flasher in fuse panel
	• Loose chassis-to-column harness connection	• Conect securely
	• Disconnect column to chassis connector. Connect new switch into system without removing old. Depress the hazard warning lights. If they now work normally, turn signal switch is defective.	• Replace turn signal switch
	• If lights do not flash, check wiring harness "K" lead for open between hazard flasher and connector. If open, fuse block is defective	• Repair or replace brown wire or connector as required

Troubleshooting the Manual Steering Gear

Problem	Cause	Solution
Hard or erratic steering	• Incorrect tire pressure	• Inflate tires to recommended pressures
	• Insufficient or incorrect lubrication	• Lubricate as required (refer to Maintenance Section)
	• Suspension, or steering linkage parts damaged or misaligned	• Repair or replace parts as necessary
	• Improper front wheel alignment	• Adjust incorrect wheel alignment angles
	• Incorrect steering gear adjustment	• Adjust steering gear
	• Sagging springs	• Replace springs
Play or looseness in steering	• Steering wheel loose	• Inspect shaft spines and repair as necessary. Tighten attaching nut and stake in place.
	• Steering linkage or attaching parts loose or worn	• Tighten, adjust, or replace faulty components
	• Pitman arm loose	• Inspect shaft splines and repair as necessary. Tighten attaching nut and stake in place
	• Steering gear attaching bolts loose	• Tighten bolts
	• Loose or worn wheel bearings	• Adjust or replace bearings
	• Steering gear adjustment incorrect or parts badly worn	• Adjust gear or replace defective parts
Wheel shimmy or tramp	• Improper tire pressure	• Inflate tires to recommended pressures
	• Wheels, tires, or brake rotors out-of-balance or out-of-round	• Inspect and replace or balance parts
	• Inoperative, worn, or loose shock absorbers or mounting parts	• Repair or replace shocks or mountings
	• Loose or worn steering or suspension parts	• Tighten or replace as necessary
	• Loose or worn wheel bearings	• Adjust or replace bearings
	• Incorrect steering gear adjustments	• Adjust steering gear
	• Incorrect front wheel alignment	• Correct front wheel alignment
Tire wear	• Improper tire pressure	• Inflate tires to recommended pressures
	• Failure to rotate tires	• Rotate tires
	• Brakes grabbing	• Adjust or repair brakes
	• Incorrect front wheel alignment	• Align incorrect angles
	• Broken or damaged steering and suspension parts	• Repair or replace defective parts
	• Wheel runout	• Replace faulty wheel
	• Excessive speed on turns	• Make driver aware of conditions
Vehicle leads to one side	• Improper tire pressures	• Inflate tires to recommended pressures
	• Front tires with uneven tread depth, wear pattern, or different cord design (i.e., one bias ply and one belted or radial tire on front wheels)	• Install tires of same cord construction and reasonably even tread depth, design, and wear pattern
	• Incorrect front wheel alignment	• Align incorrect angles
	• Brakes dragging	• Adjust or repair brakes
	• Pulling due to uneven tire construction	• Replace faulty tire

Troubleshooting the Power Steering Gear

Problem	Cause	Solution
Hissing noise in steering gear	• There is some noise in all power steering systems. One of the most common is a hissing sound most evident at standstill parking. There is no relationship between this noise and performance of the steering. Hiss may be expected when steering wheel is at end of travel or when slowly turning at standstill.	• Slight hiss is normal and in no way affects steering. Do not replace valve unless hiss is extremely objectionable. A replacement valve will also exhibit slight noise and is not always a cure. Investigate clearance around flexible coupling rivets. Be sure steering shaft and gear are aligned so flexible coupling rotates in a flat plane and is not distorted as shaft rotates. Any metal-to-metal contacts through flexible coupling will transmit valve hiss into passenger compartment through the steering column.
Rattle or chuckle noise in steering gear	• Gear loose on frame	• Check gear-to-frame mounting screws. Tighten screws to 88 N·m (65 foot pounds) torque.
	• Steering linkage looseness	• Check linkage pivot points for wear. Replace if necessary.
	• Pressure hose touching other parts of car	• Adjust hose position. Do not bend tubing by hand.
	• Loose pitman shaft over center adjustment	• Adjust to specifications
	NOTE: A slight rattle may occur on turns because of increased clearance off the "high point." This is normal and clearance must not be reduced below specified limits to eliminate this slight rattle.	
	• Loose pitman arm	• Tighten pitman arm nut to specifications
Squawk noise in steering gear when turning or recovering from a turn	• Damper O-ring on valve spool cut	• Replace damper O-ring
Poor return of steering wheel to center	• Tires not properly inflated	• Inflate to specified pressure
	• Lack of lubrication in linkage and ball joints	• Lube linkage and ball joints
	• Lower coupling flange rubbing against steering gear adjuster plug	• Loosen pinch bolt and assemble properly
	• Steering gear to column misalignment	• Align steering column
	• Improper front wheel alignment	• Check and adjust as necessary
	• Steering linkage binding	• Replace pivots
	• Ball joints binding	• Replace ball joints
	• Steering wheel rubbing against housing	• Align housing
	• Tight or frozen steering shaft bearings	• Replace bearings
	• Sticking or plugged valve spool	• Remove and clean or replace valve
	• Steering gear adjustments over specifications	• Check adjustment with gear out of car. Adjust as required.
	• Kink in return hose	• Replace hose
Car leads to one side or the other (keep in mind road condition and wind. Test car in both directions on flat road)	• Front end misaligned	• Adjust to specifications
	• Unbalanced steering gear valve	• Replace valve
	NOTE: If this is cause, steering effort will be very light in direction of lead and normal or heavier in opposite direction	

Troubleshooting the Power Steering Gear (cont.)

Problem	Cause	Solution
Momentary increase in effort when turning wheel fast to right or left	• Low oil level • Pump belt slipping • High internal leakage	• Add power steering fluid as required • Tighten or replace belt • Check pump pressure. (See pressure test)
Steering wheel surges or jerks when turning with engine running especially during parking	• Low oil level • Loose pump belt • Steering linkage hitting engine oil pan at full turn • Insufficient pump pressure • Pump flow control valve sticking	• Fill as required • Adjust tension to specification • Correct clearance • Check pump pressure. (See pressure test). Replace relief valve if defective. • Inspect for varnish or damage, replace if necessary
Excessive wheel kickback or loose steering	• Air in system • Steering gear loose on frame • Steering linkage joints worn enough to be loose • Worn poppet valve • Loose thrust bearing preload adjustment • Excessive overcenter lash	• Add oil to pump reservoir and bleed by operating steering. Check hose connectors for proper torque and adjust as required. • Tighten attaching screws to specified torque • Replace loose pivots • Replace poppet valve • Adjust to specification with gear out of vehicle • Adjust to specification with gear out of car
Hard steering or lack of assist	• Loose pump belt • Low oil level **NOTE:** Low oil level will also result in excessive pump noise • Steering gear to column misalignment • Lower coupling flange rubbing against steering gear adjuster plug • Tires not properly inflated	• Adjust belt tension to specification • Fill to proper level. If excessively low, check all lines and joints for evidence of external leakage. Tighten loose connectors. • Align steering column • Loosen pinch bolt and assemble properly • Inflate to recommended pressure
Foamy milky power steering fluid, low fluid level and possible low pressure	• Air in the fluid, and loss of fluid due to internal pump leakage causing overflow	• Check for leak and correct. Bleed system. Extremely cold temperatures will cause system aeriation should the oil level be low. If oil level is correct and pump still foams, remove pump from vehicle and separate reservoir from housing. Check welsh plug and housing for cracks. If plug is loose or housing is cracked, replace housing.
Low pressure due to steering pump	• Flow control valve stuck or inoperative • Pressure plate not flat against cam ring	• Remove burrs or dirt or replace. Flush system. • Correct
Low pressure due to steering gear	• Pressure loss in cylinder due to worn piston ring or badly worn housing bore • Leakage at valve rings, valve body-to-worm seal	• Remove gear from car for disassembly and inspection of ring and housing bore • Remove gear from car for disassembly and replace seals

Troubleshooting the Power Steering Pump

Problem	Cause	Solution
Chirp noise in steering pump	• Loose belt	• Adjust belt tension to specification
Belt squeal (particularly noticeable at full wheel travel and stand still parking)	• Loose belt	• Adjust belt tension to specification
Growl noise in steering pump	• Excessive back pressure in hoses or steering gear caused by restriction	• Locate restriction and correct. Replace part if necessary.
Growl noise in steering pump (particularly noticeable at stand still parking)	• Scored pressure plates, thrust plate or rotor • Extreme wear of cam ring	• Replace parts and flush system • Replace parts
Groan noise in steering pump	• Low oil level • Air in the oil. Poor pressure hose connection.	• Fill reservoir to proper level • Tighten connector to specified torque. Bleed system by operating steering from right to left—full turn.
Rattle noise in steering pump	• Vanes not installed properly • Vanes sticking in rotor slots	• Install properly • Free up by removing burrs, varnish, or dirt
Swish noise in steering pump	• Defective flow control valve	• Replace part
Whine noise in steering pump	• Pump shaft bearing scored	• Replace housing and shaft. Flush system.
Hard steering or lack of assist	• Loose pump belt • Low oil level in reservoir **NOTE:** Low oil level will also result in excessive pump noise • Steering gear to column misalignment • Lower coupling flange rubbing against steering gear adjuster plug • Tires not properly inflated	• Adjust belt tension to specification • Fill to proper level. If excessively low, check all lines and joints for evidence of external leakage. Tighten loose connectors. • Align steering column • Loosen pinch bolt and assemble properly • Inflate to recommended pressure
Foaming milky power steering fluid, low fluid level and possible low pressure	• Air in the fluid, and loss of fluid due to internal pump leakage causing overflow	• Check for leaks and correct. Bleed system. Extremely cold temperatures will cause system aeration should the oil level be low. If oil level is correct and pump still foams, remove pump from vehicle and separate reservoir from body. Check welsh plug and body for cracks. If plug is loose or body is cracked, replace body.
Low pump pressure	• Flow control valve stuck or inoperative • Pressure plate not flat against cam ring	• Remove burrs or dirt or replace. Flush system. • Correct
Momentary increase in effort when turning wheel fast to right or left	• Low oil level in pump • Pump belt slipping • High internal leakage	• Add power steering fluid as required • Tighten or replace belt • Check pump pressure. (See pressure test)
Steering wheel surges or jerks when turning with engine running especially during parking	• Low oil level • Loose pump belt • Steering linkage hitting engine oil pan at full turn • Insufficient pump pressure	• Fill as required • Adjust tension to specification • Correct clearance • Check pump pressure. (See pressure test). Replace flow control valve if defective.

Troubleshooting the Power Steering Pump (cont.)

Problem	Cause	Solution
Steering wheel surges or jerks when turning with engine running especially during parking (cont.)	• Sticking flow control valve	• Inspect for varnish or damage, replace if necessary
Excessive wheel kickback or loose steering	• Air in system	• Add oil to pump reservoir and bleed by operating steering. Check hose connectors for proper torque and adjust as required.
Low pump pressure	• Extreme wear of cam ring • Scored pressure plate, thrust plate, or rotor • Vanes not installed properly • Vanes sticking in rotor slots • Cracked or broken thrust or pressure plate	• Replace parts. Flush system. • Replace parts. Flush system. • Install properly • Freeup by removing burrs, varnish, or dirt • Replace part

Brakes

9

BRAKE SYSTEM

The base model 1975–78 Rabbit is equipped with front and rear drum brakes. The optional 1975–78 Rabbit, and most 1979–84 and later Rabbits, and all Quantums, Dashers, Jettas, Fox and Sciroccos are equipped with front disc brakes and rear drum brakes. The Golf, Scirocco 16V, GTI, Quantum, Passat and Corrato are equipped with front and rear disk brakes. The 1990 Passat and Corrado are equipped with Anti-lock brakes as an option.

The hydraulic system is a dual circuit type that has the advantage of retaining 50% braking effectiveness in the event of failure in one system. The circuits are arranged so that you always have one front and one rear brake for a more controlled emergency stop. The right front and left rear are in one circuit; the left front and right rear are in the second circuit.

There is also a brake failure switch and a proportioning valve. The brake failure unit is a hydraulic valve/electrical switch which warns of brake problems by the warning light on the instrument panel. A piston inside the switch is kept centered by one brake system pressure on one side and the other system pressure on the opposite side. Should a failure occur in one system, the piston would go to the failed side and complete an electrical circuit to the warning lamp. This switch also functions as a parking brake reminder light and will go out when the parking brake is released. The proportioning valve, actually two separate valves on manual transmission Dasher sedans, provides balances front-to-rear braking during hard stops.

Extreme brake line pressure will overcome the spring pressure on the piston within the valve causing it to proportionately restrict pressure to the rear brakes. In this manner, the rear brakes are kept from locking. The propor-

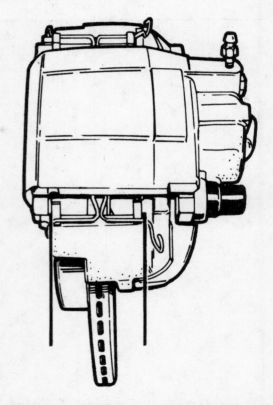

The GTI is equipped with a vented disc brake rotor. Brake pads, on the these models, should be replaced when a minimum thickness, including backing plate, reaches 9.5mm (³/₈ in.)

tioner doesn't operate under normal braking conditions.

Anti-lock brake system (ABS) is optional on the Passat, Corrado, Jetta Carat and Jetta GLI 16V. The Teves® ABS system is a three circuit brake system. This means that there is one brake control for each front wheel and one circuit for both rear wheels.

Adjustment

The front disc brakes require no adjustment, as disc brakes automatically adjust themselves to compensate for pad wear. The drum brakes on some models must be adjusted whenever free-play is $^1/_3$ or more of the total pedal travel. All 1979 and later Dashers and Quantums, and some 1979 and later Rabbits and Sciroccos are equipped with self-adjusting rear drum brakes. The only way to tell if the brakes are self-adjusting without removing the drum is the absence of the adjusting holes in the brake backing plate. All Golf, Fox, Rabbit Pick-up and Jetta models have self-adjusting rear brakes.

FRONT DRUM BRAKES

Rabbit Only

1. Raise and support the front of the car. Block the rear wheels.
2. Remove the rubber plugs covering the adjusters.
3. Insert a screwdriver through the hole and turn the adjuster clockwise until the brake locks.
4. Back off the adjuster until the wheel can be turned. The shoes should drag lightly.
5. Back off the adjuster two notches. The wheel should spin without brake drag. Replace the rubber plugs.

REAR DRUM BRAKES

All Models

NOTE: *On most models except manual transmission Dasher sedans, it is necessary to push the brake pressure regulator lever toward the rear axle to relieve the pressure in the right rear brake line.*

1. Raise the rear of the car and support on stands. Refer to Jacking in Chapter 1.
2. Block the front wheels and release the

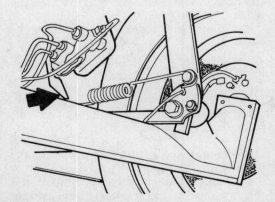

Relieving pressure at the brake pressure regulator valve — Dasher shown. Push the lever in the direction of the arrow

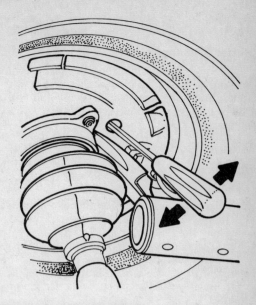

Typical drum brake assembly

parking brake. Step on the brake pedal hard to center the linings.
3. Remove the rubber plug from the rear of the backing plate on each wheel.
4. Insert a brake adjusting tool or wide-bladed screwdriver and turn the adjuster wheel clockwise until the brakes drag as you turn the wheel in the forward direction.
5. Turn the adjuster in the opposite direction until you just pass the point of drag.
6. Repeat on the other wheel.
7. Lower the car and road test. Readjust, if necessary.

Wheel Bearings

There is no front wheel bearing adjustment. The bearing is pressed into the steering knuckle. The axle nut should be torqued to 174 ft. lbs. on all Rabbit, Fox, Jetta and Scirocco and either 145 ft. lbs. (M18 nut) or 175 ft. lbs. (M20 nut) on the Dasher and Quantum. Tighten the nut with the wheels on the ground.

NOTE: *For rear wheel bearing adjustment, see Suspension and Steering, Chapter 8.*

Brake Light Switch

REMOVAL AND INSTALLATION

Pedal Mounted Switch

The brake switch is mounted on the brake pedal support bracket. Disconnect and remove the switch by pulling the switch from the adjusting clip. **To adjust:** depress the brake pedal and push in the switch as far as it will go. Pull the pedal back by hand as far as it will go. The switch is adjusted after no clicks are heard.

Master Cylinder Mounted

Disconnect the switch from the master cylinder and remove. Lubricate the switch with brake fluid and torque to 18 ft. lbs. (25 Nm). Connect the wire and bleed the system as outlined in this chapter.

Master Cylinder

REMOVAL AND INSTALLATION

Non-ABS

1. To prevent brake fluid from spilling out and damaging this paint, place a protective cover over the fender.
2. Disconnect and plug the brake lines.
3. Disconnect the electrical plug from the sending unit for the brake failure switch.
4. Remove the two master cylinder mounting nuts.

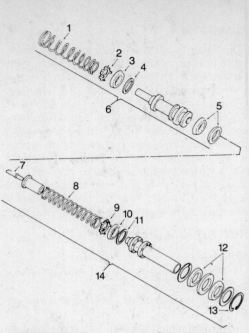

1. Conical spring
2. Spring seat
3. Primary cup
4. Washer
5. Secondary cups
6. Primary piston
7. Stroke limiting screw
8. Cylindrical spring
9. Spring seat
10. Primary cup
11. Washer
12. Secondary cups
13. Circlip
14. Secondary piston

Exploded view of the master cylinder, with power brakes

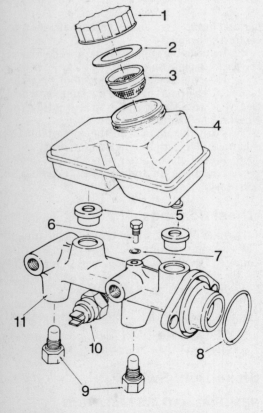

1. Reservoir cap
2. Washer
3. Filter screen
4. Reservoir
5. Master cylinder plugs
6. Stop screw
7. Stop screw seal
8. Master cylinder seal
9. Residual pressure valves
10. Warning light sender
11. Master cylinder housing

Typical master cylinder body and reservoir

5. Lift the master cylinder and reservoir out of the engine compartment being careful not to spill any fluid on the fender. Empty out and discard the brake fluid.

CAUTION: *Do not depress the brake pedal while the master cylinder is removed!*

6. Position the master cylinder and reservoir assembly onto the studs for the booster and install the washers and nuts. Tighten the nuts to no more than 10 ft. lbs.
7. Remove the plugs and connect the brake lines.
8. Bleed the entire brake system as explained further on in this chapter.

OVERHAUL

Purchase a genuine VW overhaul kit and sufficient brake fluid before starting this procedure.

1. Remove the master cylinder from the booster.
2. Firmly mount the master cylinder in a vise. Use clean rags to protect the cylinder from the vise jaws.
3. Grasp the plastic reservoir and pull it out of the rubber plugs. Remove the plugs.

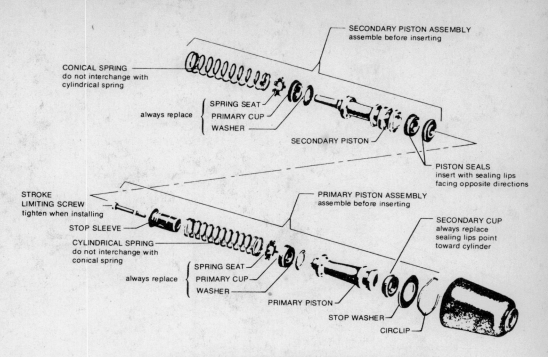

CONICAL SPRING
do not interchange with
cylindrical spring

SECONDARY PISTON ASSEMBLY
assemble before inserting

always replace { SPRING SEAT
PRIMARY CUP
WASHER

SECONDARY PISTON

PISTON SEALS
insert with sealing lips
facing opposite directions

STROKE
LIMITING SCREW
tighten when installing

PRIMARY PISTON ASSEMBLY
assemble before inserting

STOP SLEEVE

CYLINDRICAL SPRING
do not interchange with
conical spring

SECONDARY CUP
always replace
sealing lips point
toward cylinder

always replace { SPRING SEAT
PRIMARY CUP
WASHER

PRIMARY PISTON

STOP WASHER

CIRCLIP

Exploded view of the master cylinder, without power brakes

4. Remove the stop-screw from the center of the cylinder. Discard the stop screw seal, a new one is in the kit.

5. At the end of the master cylinder is a snapring (circlip); remove it, using snapring pliers.

6. Shake out the secondary piston assembly. If the primary piston remains lodged in the bore, it can be forced by applying compressed air to the open brake line fitting.

7. Disassemble the secondary piston. The secondary ring(s) will be replaced with those in the rebuilding kit. Save the washers and spacers.

8. Carefully clamp the secondary piston, slightly compress the spring and screw out the stroke limiting bolt.

9. Remove the secondary piston stop sleeve bolt, spring, spring seat, and support washer.

10. Replace all parts with those supplied in the overhaul kit.

11. Clean all metal parts in denatured alcohol and dry them with compressed air.

12. Check every part you are reusing. Pay close attention to the cylinder bores. If there is any scoring or rust, have the master cylinder honed or replace it.

13. Lightly coat the bores and cups with brake fluid. Assemble the cylinder components in the exact sequence shown in the illustration.

14. Install the primary piston assembly, notice that the primary spring is conically

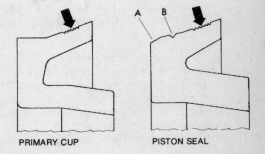

PRIMARY CUP   PISTON SEAL

The primary cup and piston seal have identifying marks

shaped. Be sure that you aren't using the secondary spring.

NOTE: *Models with either Teves or ATE master cylinders (the cylinder body should be marked with the brand name), the primary cup and the secondary cup(s) of the secondary (inner) piston have small grooves on their lips. Use the illustrations to tell the cups apart.*

15. Using a plastic rod or other nonmetallic tool, push the primary piston assembly into the housing until the stop bolt (with a new seal) can be screwed in and tightened.

16. Assemble the secondary piston. Fasten the spring, spring seat, primary cup, and stop sleeve to the piston with the stroke limiting bolt.

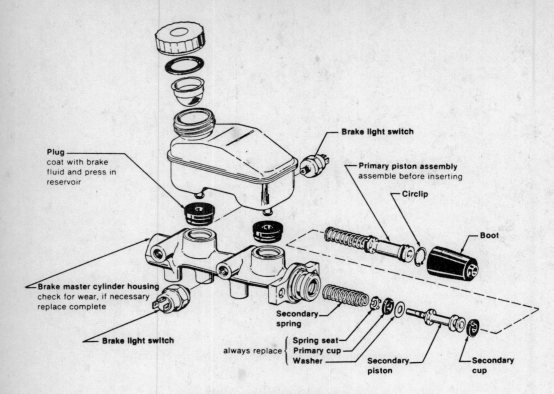

Plug
coat with brake
fluid and press in
reservoir

Brake light switch

Primary piston assembly
assemble before inserting

Circlip

Boot

Brake master cylinder housing
check for wear, if necessary
replace complete

Brake light switch

Secondary
spring

always replace { Spring seat
Primary cup
Washer

Secondary
piston

Secondary
cup

Exploded view of the Bendix master cylinder

17. Assemble the remaining master cylinder components in the reverse order of disassembly. Ensure that the snapring is fully seated and that the piston caps are properly positioned. Install the secondary piston with master cylinder opening face down.

18. Install and tighten the brake failure warning sending unit.

Bleeding

NOTE: *Use only new, unused and approved brake fluid (DOT3 or DOT4).*

Anytime a brake line has been disconnected the hydraulic system should be bled. The brakes should also be bled when the pedal travel becomes unusually long (soft pedal) or the car pulls to one side during braking. The proper bleeding sequence is: right rear wheel, left rear wheel, right front caliper, and left front caliper. You'll need a helper to pump the brake pedal while you open the bleeder valves.

NOTE: *If the system has been drained, first refill it with fresh brake fluid. Following the above sequence, open each bleeder valve by $1/2$–$3/4$ of a turn and pump the brake pedal until fluid runs out of the valve. Proceed with the bleeding as outlined below.*

1. Remove the bleeder valve dust cover and install a rubber bleeder hose.

2. Insert the other end of the hose into a container about $1/3$ full of brake fluid.

3. Have an assistant pump the brake pedal several times until the pedal pressure increases.

4. Hold the pedal under pressure and then start to open the bleeder valve about $1/2$–$3/4$ of a turn. At this point, have your assistant depress the pedal all the way and then quickly close the valve. The helper should allow the pedal to return slowly.

NOTE: *Keep a close check on the brake fluid in the reservoir and top it up as necessary throughout the bleeding process.*

5. Keep repeating this procedure until no more air bubbles can be seen coming from the hose in the brake fluid.

6. Remove the bleeder hose and install the dust cover.

7. Continue the bleeding at each wheel in sequence.

NOTE: *Don't splash any brake fluid on the paintwork. Brake fluid is very corrosive and will eat paint away. Any fluid accidentally spilled on the body should be immediately flushed off with water.*

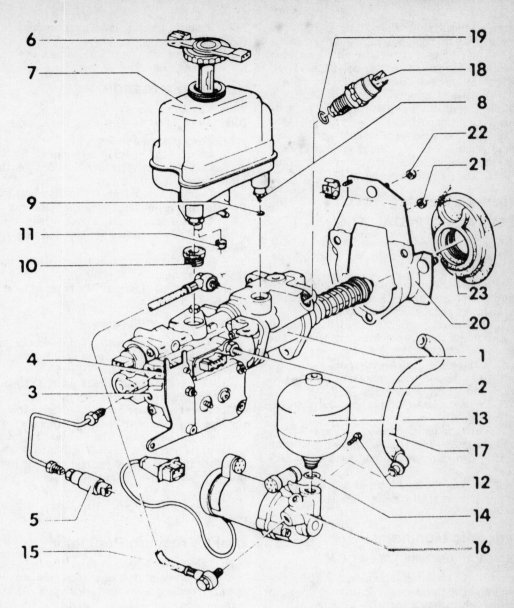

1. Hydraulic modulator
2. Brake line connection
3. Brake line connection
4. Brake line connection
5. Pressure regulator valve
6. Cap
7. Brake fluid reservoir
8. Sleeve
9. O-ring
10. Sealing plug
11. Reservoir mounting retainer
12. 86 inch lbs. (10 Nm)
13. Pressure regulator
14. O-ring
15. Brake line
16. Hydraulic pump
17. Connecting hose
18. Pressure warning switch
19. Seal
20. 18 ft. lbs. (25 Nm)
21. Hydraulic modulator
22. Gasket
23. Bracket
24. 18 ft. lbs. (25 Nm)
25. 18 ft. lbs. (25 Nm)
26. Gasket

ABS brake system

ABS Equipped Vehicles

PRECAUTIONS

1. Before working on the ABS system, switch the ignition switch OFF and disconnect the negative battery cable.

2. Reduce the high line pressure in the reservoir by pressing the brake pedal frequently (about 20 times) until a noticeable increase in pedal effort is felt.

3. Disconnect the ABS control unit connector located on the left side A-pillar before using any electric welding devices.

4. Remove the control unit if using a paint

drying system greater then 203°F (95°C). The unit may fail if exposed to high temperatures.

5. The ABS modulator assembly is capable of self-pressurizing up to 3045 psi (21,000 kpa). Serious injury may result if service is performed without properly depressurizing the system. Pump the brake at least 25–35 times with the ignition key OFF.

6. The following components can be replaced separately; hydraulic modulator, reservoir, pressure warning switch, pressure accumulator and pump subassembly.

Pressure Warning Switch

REMOVAL AND INSTALLATION

NOTE: *If the pressure warning switch is damaged, the pump relay must be replaced also.*

1. Switch the ignition switch to the OFF position and depressurize the system by pressing on the brake pedal at least 25–35 times.
2. Disconnect the negative (–) battery cable.
3. Remove the pressure warning switch connector.
4. Remove the switch with tool 3228.
5. Coat the seal with brake fluid, install the switch and torque to 18 ft. lbs. (25 Nm).
6. Connect the switch harness and negative battery cable.
7. Turn the ignition switch to the ON position. The pump must start running and shut off after a maximum running time of 60 seconds.
8. Depress the brake pedal 2–3 times and the pump must start running again.

Hydraulic Modulator

REMOVAL AND INSTALLATION

1. Switch the ignition switch to the OFF position and depressurize the system by pressing on the brake pedal at least 25–35 times.
2. Disconnect the negative (–) battery cable.
3. Disconnect all cable terminals from the ABS unit.
4. Drain the brake fluid from the reservoir with a suction bottle.
5. Remove the brake lines from the unit with flare nut wrenches only. Plug the open lines and bores.
6. Remove the left shelf under the instrument panel.
7. Remove the bolts from the pushrod clevis.
8. Remove the lock nuts on the ABS component and remove the unit.
9. Install the unit and torque the nuts to 18 ft. lbs. (25 Nm).

10. Install the brake lines and torque to 18 ft. lbs. (25 Nm).
11. Connect the electrical connectors and bleed as outlined in this section.

ABS SYSTEM BLEEDING

With Pressure Bleeder (US1116 or Equivalent)

1. Turn the ignition key OFF.
2. Depress the brake pedal about 20 times.
3. Connect the pressure bleeder to the brake reservoir and turn on.
4. Connect a hose from the bleeder bottle to the left front caliper and open the bleeder.
5. Depress the brake pedal slowly until brake fluid flows without bubbles and close the bleeder screw.
6. Bleed the right front, left rear and right rear in same manner.
7. Make sure the reservoir never runs out of fluid while bleeding.

Without Pressure Bleeder

NOTE: *Use a clear bottle and hose with the bottle about half full of new brake fluid.*

1. Turn the ignition key OFF.
2. Depress the brake pedal about 20 times.
3. Fill the reservoir to the upper edge.
4. Insert the hose of the bleeder bottle on the bleeder screw of either front caliper.
5. Open the bleeder and depress the brake pedal until brake fluid flows without bubbles. Bleed the other front caliper and then the right and left rear calipers. Refill the reservoir with new fluid.
6. Make sure the reservoir never runs out of fluid during the bleeding procedures.

Brake Pressure Regulator

NOTE: *The Dasher has two different kinds of brake pressure regulators: two pressure sensitive regulators mounted at the master cylinder and one load sensitive regulator mounted at the rear axle. Other models have only load sensitive regulators.*

The Brake Pressure Regulator insures that the front and rear brakes evenly distribute the stopping load in order of their efficiency. With only the driver in the car, most of the weight of the vehicle is hung over the front wheels (in the form of the engine and transaxle.) In this situation, the front disc brakes receive the lion's share of the stopping responsibility. As the rear compartment of the vehicle is loaded and the body sits lower on the rear springs, a lever on the brake pressure regulator attached to the rear axle by a spring is pulled, allowing the rear brakes to take on more of the stopping load.

The brake pressure regulator is located on

the left rear side of the car near the rear axle (except the Rabbit Pickup and Dasher). The Dasher and Fox regulator is on the right rear side near the axle. The Rabbit Pick-up is at the center rear of the vehicle in front of the rear axle. The pressure ratio of the regulator can be adjusted by your Volkswagen dealer with special pressure gauges and alignment tools.

NOTE: *Not all Rabbits and Sciroccos are equipped with brake proportioning valves.*

Brake Booster

REMOVAL AND INSTALLATION

1. Remove the master cylinder from in front of the booster.

2. In the driver's compartment, remove the clevis pin on the end of the booster pushrod by unclipping it and pulling it out of the clevis.

3. On the gasoline engine models, remove the vacuum line running from the booster to intake manifold. On diesel engines, the line connects to a special vacuum pump located where the distributor on a gasoline engine would be. Remove the line.

4. On the Rabbit, Jetta and Scirocco, unbolt the booster bracket where it connects to the firewall. On the Dasher, Fox and Quantum remove the two nuts from inside the driver's compartment, or the four nuts holding the booster to its bracket. Remove the booster.

5. The brake booster cannot be repaired and must be replaced if its diaphragm leaks or it fails to operate.

6. Installation is the reverse of removal.

NOTE: *On 1974–77 Dashers, the clevis and booster push have been shortened. When replacing the brake booster on these models, you'll have to enlarge the clevis pin hole in the brake pedal to 8mm. Also, the booster used in 1978–81 Dashers is 25mm wider (228mm) than the old model (203mm).*

7. Bleed the brakes after installing the master cylinder. See above for procedures.

8. After the system is installed, check to make sure that the rear brake lights work. If not, you have misaligned the light switch at the brake pedal.

Vacuum Pump

REMOVAL AND INSTALLATION

Diesel Engines with Power Brakes Only

One line of the vacuum pump runs to the power brake booster and the other line runs to the engine. Unclamp and remove both lines. Unbolt and remove the pump. The diaphragm inside the pump is replaceable. Remove the screws holding the vacuum hose inlet cover to the pump body and remove the cover. Unscrew the retaining nut and remove the diaphragm. Install the new diaphragm with the molded center toward the top. Don't overtighten the retaining nut.

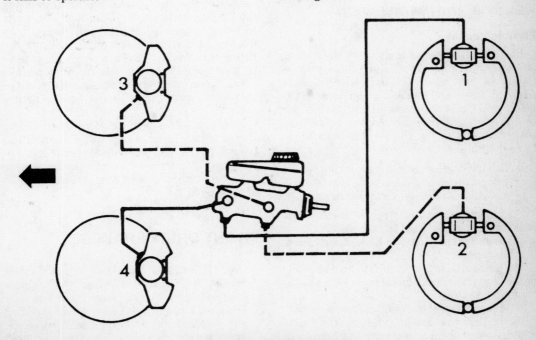

Proper brake bleeding sequence

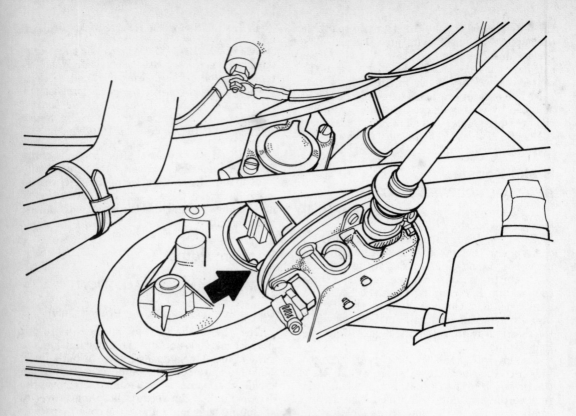

Diesel engine brake booster vacuum pump

Brake Lines

REMOVAL AND INSTALLATION

Flexible Hoses

Flexible rubber hoses are used at the moving suspension points. There is one for each axle. Solid rear axle assemblies only have one hose for both axles. The one end is mounted to the frame and the other is mounted to the caliper or the rear axle housing. As the suspension moves up and down, the flexible hose maintains hydraulic pressure to each wheel.

WARNING: *When removing any brake line or hose, always use a flare nut wrench to prevent damage to the soft metal fittings.*

1. Using a flare nut wrench, remove and plug the brake hose from the caliper.
2. Remove the frame-to-brake hose clamp, if so equipped.
3. Using a flare nut wrench to hold the steel brake line, remove the brake hose with a suitable flare nut wrench.
4. Plug the steel brake line after removal.
5. Install the brake hose in the same manner as removal and torque the fittings to 20 ft. lbs. (27 Nm).

Steel

Loosen the steel brake line fittings using flare nut wrenches only. If the steel line starts to twist, stop and lubricate with penetrating oil. Move the wrench back and forth until the fitting turn freely. A backup wrench may have to used when loosening steel-to-rubber brake hoses. When installing, apply a small amount of anti-seize compound onto the fitting threads only.

Steel brake lines can be repaired by installing a double flare after the damaged portion has been removed. The tools needed for this procedure may be purchased at a local hardware or auto parts store. Steel brake lines MUST be double flared.

FRONT DRUM BRAKES

CAUTION: *Some brake pads contain asbestos, which has been determined to be a cancer causing agent. Never clean the brake surfaces with compressed air! Avoid inhaling any dust from any brake surface! When cleaning brake surfaces, use a commercially available brake cleaning fluid.*

The early model Rabbit and Dasher vehicles are equipped with front drum brakes.

Brake Shoes

ADJUSTMENT

Refer to the procedure in the beginning of this chapter for front drum brake adjustment.

REMOVAL AND INSTALLATION

1. Raise the vehicle and support with jackstands.
2. Remove the front wheel and brake drum assembly. The adjuster may have to be loosened to remove the brake drum.
3. Use a pliers to unlock the lower return springs.
4. Pull the lower part of the shoes over the wheel hub and unhook the upper return springs.
5. Remove the adjuster and locating spring.
To install:
1. Hook the upper return spring into the brake shoes.
2. Slide the adjuster into the shoes.
3. Push the lower ends of the brake shoes over the wheel hub.
4. Hook the lower return springs into the brake shoes and install the retaining springs.
5. Hook the upper return springs into the bracket on the backing plate.
6. Install the brake adjuster and locating spring.
7. Install the brake drum and adjust the shoes as outlined in the beginning of this chapter.
8. Install the front wheels and lower the vehicle.
9. Check the brake fluid and pump the pedal and road test.

Wheel Cylinders

REMOVAL AND INSTALLATION

1. Raise the vehicle and support with jackstands.
2. Remove the front wheels and brake drums.
3. Remove the brake shoes and move out of the way to access the wheel cylinders.
4. Using a flare nut wrench, remove the brake hose from the wheel cylinder.
5. Remove the two retaining bolts and wheel cylinder.
6. Install the cylinder and torque the bolts to 15 ft. lbs. (20 Nm).
7. Install the brake hose and torque to 15 ft. lbs. (20 Nm).

8. Install the brake shoes, drum and bleed both wheel cylinders as outlined in this chapter.

FRONT DISC BRAKES

CAUTION: *Some brake pads contain asbestos, which has been determined to be a cancer causing agent. Never clean the brake surfaces with compressed air! Avoid inhaling any dust from any brake surface! When cleaning brake surfaces, use a commercially available brake cleaning fluid.*

There are four types of disc brake calipers used on these Volkswagens. Refer to the illustrations to identify the type used on your car.

NOTE: *The 1985 Golf and Jetta use the style MARK II front brake caliper. The wheel bearing housing is designed to form an integral part of the brake assembly. Thus making removal and replacement of the brake pads simpler. Removal and installation of the new Mark II style caliper and the brake pads are similar to the procedure for the Kelsey-Hayes floating type caliper.*

Brake Pads

REMOVAL AND INSTALLATION

Kelsey-Hayes Floating Caliper

This unit is a single piston, one piece caliper which floats on two guide pins screwed into the adapter (anchor plate). The adaptor, in turn, is held to the steering knuckle with two bolts. As the brake pads wear, the caliper floats along the adapter and guide pins during braking.

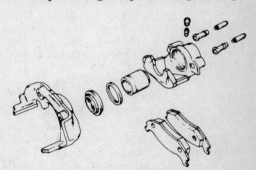

Kelsey-Hayes floating caliper

1. Raise the front of the vehicle and support it with jackstands. Remove the wheel.
2. Siphon some brake fluid from the master cylinder reservoir to prevent its overflowing when the piston is retracted into the cylinder bore.
3. Disconnect the brake pad warning indicator if so equipped.

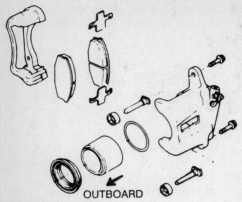

OUTBOARD

Girling floating caliper

4. Using a pair of needlenose pliers or the like, remove the anti-rattle springs.

5. Using an Allen wrench, back out the two guide pins that attach the caliper to the anchor plate.

NOTE: *When replacing pads only, it is not necessary to remove the guide pins completely from the rubber bushings, as they may be difficult to reinstall.*

6. Lift off the caliper and position it out of the way with some wire. You need not remove the brake lines.

CAUTION: *Never allow the caliper to hang by its brake lines.*

7. Slide the outer pad out of the anchor plate and then remove the inner pad. Check the rotor as detailed in the appropriate section. Check the caliper for fluid leaks or cracked boots. If any damage is found, the caliper will require overhauling or replacement.

8. Carefully clean the anchor plate with a wire brush or some other abrasive material. Install the new brake pads into position on the anchor plate. The inner pad usually has chamfered edges.

NOTE: *When replacing brake pads, always replace both pads on both sides of the vehicle. Mixed pads will cause uneven braking.*

9. Slowly and carefully push the piston into its bore until it's bottomed and then position the caliper onto the anchor plate. Install the guide pins and tighten them to 25–30 ft. lbs. (34–41 Nm).

NOTE: *The upper guide pin is usually longer than the lower one.*

CAUTION: *Use extreme care so as not to cross-thread the guide pins when tightening!*

10. Install the anti-rattle springs between the anchor plate and brake pads ears. The loops on the springs should be positioned inboard.

11. Fill the reservoir with brake fluid and pump the brake pedal several times to set the piston. It should not be necessary to bleed the system; however, if a firm pedal cannot be obtained, the system must be bled (see Bleeding the Brakes in this section).

12. Install the wheel and lower the vehicle.

Girling Floating Caliper

Although similar in many respects to a sliding caliper, this single piston unit floats on guide pins and bushings which are threaded into a mounting bracket. The mounting bracket is bolted to the steering knuckle.

Variations in pad retainers, shims, anti-rattle and retaining springs will be encountered but the service procedures are all basically the same. Note the position of all springs, clips or shims when removing the pads. Work on one side at a time and use the other for reference.

1. Raise and support the front of the vehicle on jackstands. Remove the wheel.

2. Siphon a sufficient quantity of brake fluid from the master cylinder reservoir to prevent the brake fluid from overflowing the master cylinder when removing or installing new pads. This is necessary as the piston must be forced into the cylinder bore to provide sufficient clearance to remove the pads.

3. Grasp the caliper from behind and pull it toward you. This will push the piston back into the cylinder bore.

4. Disconnect the brake pad lining wear indicator if so equipped. Remove any anti-rattle springs or clips if so equipped.

NOTE: *Depending on the model and year of the particular caliper, you may not have to remove it entirely to get at the brake pads. If the caliper is the swing type, remove the lower guide bolt, pivot the caliper on the upper bolt and swing it upward exposing the brake pads. If this method is employed, skip to Step 7.*

5. Remove the caliper guide pins.

6. Remove the caliper from the rotor by slowly sliding it out and away from the rotor. Position the caliper out of the way and support it with wire so that it doesn't hang by the brake line.

7. Slide the outboard pad out of the adapter.

8. Remove the inboard pad. Remove any shims or shields behind the pads and note their positions.

9. Install the anti-rattle hardware and then the pads in their proper positions!

10. Install any pad shims or heat shields.

11. Reposition the caliper and install the guide pins.

NOTE: *If the caliper is the "swing" type, you need only pivot it back into position and install the lower guide pin.*

12. Refill the master cylinder with fresh brake fluid.

13. Install the tire and wheel assembly and then pump the brake pedal several times to bring the pads into adjustment. Road test the vehicle.

NOTE: *If a firm pedal cannot be obtained, bleed the system as detailed in Bleeding the Brakes.*

Sliding Yoke Caliper

This unit is a single piston, two piece caliper. It has a fixed mounting frame which is bolted to the steering knuckle. The pads are retained in the fixed frame. A floating frame, or yoke, slides on the fixed frame. The cylinder attaches to this yoke, creating a caliper. Braking pressure forces the piston against the inner pad. The reaction causes the yoke to move in the opposite direction, applying pressure to the outer pad.

1. Raise the front of the vehicle and support it with jackstands. Remove the wheel.

2. Siphon a sufficient quantity of brake fluid from the master cylinder reservoir to prevent the brake fluid from overflowing the master cylinder when removing or installing new pads. This is necessary as the position must be forced into the cylinder bore to provide sufficient clearance to remove the pads.

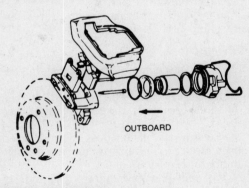

Sliding yoke caliper

3. Disconnect the wire connector leading to the brake pad wear indicator.

4. Remove the brake pad retaining clips on the inside of the caliper and then drive out the retaining pins. Don't lose the pad positioner (spreader) that is held down by the pins.

5. Pull out the inner brake pad.

6. The outer pads are secured by a notch at the top of the pad. Grasp the caliper assembly from the inside and pull it toward yourself. Remove the pad and detach the wear indicator.

7. Check the brake disc (rotor) as detailed in the appropriate section.

8. Inspect the caliper and piston assembly for breaks, cracks or other damage. Overhaul or replace the caliper as necessary.

9. Use a C-clamp and press the piston back into the cylinder bore.

10. Install the wear indicator on the outer pad and then install both pads.

11. Installation of the remaining components is the reverse order of removal.

12. Top off the master cylinder with fresh brake fluid.

13. Pump the brake pedal several times to bring the pads into adjustment. Road test the vehicle. If a firm pedal cannot be obtained, bleed the brakes as detailed in Bleeding the Brakes.

Girling Sliding Yoke Caliper

This unit is a double piston, one piece caliper. The cylinder body contains two pistons, back-to-back, in a through-bore. The cylinder body is bolted to the steering knuckle, with both pistons inboard of the rotor. A yoke, which slides on the cylinder body, is installed over the rotor and the caliper.

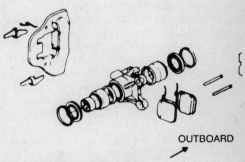

Girling sliding yoke caliper

When the brakes are applied, hydraulic pressure forces the pistons apart in the double ended bore. The piston closest to the rotor applies force directly to the inboard pad. The other piston applies force to the yoke, which transmits the force to the outer pad, creating a friction force on each side of the rotor.

One variation has a yoke that floats on guide pins screwed into the cylinder body.

Some designs incorporate parking brake mechanisms which are actuated by a lever and cam working between the piston and the yoke. The yokes do not have to be removed to replace the brake pads.

1. Raise and support the front of the vehicle on jackstands. Remove the wheel.

2. Siphon a sufficient quantity of brake fluid from the master cylinder reservoir to prevent the brake fluid from overflowing the

master cylinder when removing or installing new pads. This is necessary as the piston must be forced into the cylinder bore to provide sufficient clearance to remove the pads.

3. Disconnect the brake pad lining wear indicator if so equipped.

4. Remove the dust cover and/or anti-rattle (damper) clip if so equipped.

5. Lift off the wire clip(s) which hold the guide pins or retaining pin in place.

6. Remove the upper guide pin and the two hanger springs. Carefully tap out the lower guide pin.

CAUTION: *The lower guide pin usually contains an anti-rattle coil spring. Be careful not to lose this spring. If a retaining pin is used, pull the pin out and remove the two hanger springs.*

7. Slide the yoke outward and remove the outer brake pad and the anti-noise shim (if so equipped).

8. Slide the yoke inward and repeat Step 7.

9. Check the rotor as detailed in the appropriate section.

10. Inspect the caliper and piston assembly for breaks, cracks or other damage. Overhaul or replace the caliper as necessary.

11. Push the piston next to the rotor back into the cylinder bore until the end of the piston is flush with the boot retaining ring.

CAUTION: *If the piston is pushed further than this, the seal will be damaged and the caliper assembly will have to be overhauled.*

12. Retract the piston farthest from the rotor by pulling the yoke toward the outside of the vehicle.

13. Install the outboard pad. Anti-noise shims (if so equipped) must be located on the plate side of the pad with the triangular cutout pointing toward the top of the caliper.

14. Install the inboard pad with the shims (if so equipped) in the correct position.

15. Replace the lower guide pin and the anti-rattle coil spring.

16. Hook the hanger springs under the pin and over the brake pads.

17. Install the upper guide pin over the ends of the hanger springs.

NOTE: *If a single two sided retaining pin is used, install the pin and then install the hanger springs as in Steps 16–17.*

18. Insert the wire clip locks into the holes in the guide pins or retaining pin.

19. Refill the master cylinder with fresh brake fluid.

20. Install the tire and wheel assembly. Pump the brake pedal several times to bring the pads into adjustment. Road test the vehicle. If a firm pedal cannot be obtained, refer to "Bleeding the Brakes".

Corrado, Passat and Jetta 16V

CAUTION: *Some brake pads contain asbestos, which has been determined to be a cancer causing agent. Never clean the brake surfaces with compressed air! Avoid inhaling any dust from any brake surface! When cleaning brake surfaces, use a commercially available brake cleaning fluid.*

1. Remove about half of the fluid from the reservoir.

2. Remove the lower mounting bolt and hold the guide pin with an open end wrench.

3. Swing the caliper up and remove the brake pads.

4. Push the piston into the caliper housing with a large C-clamp.

5. Install the new brake pads and heat shield.

6. Swing the caliper down and torque the bolts to 26 ft. lbs. (35 Nm).

7. Refill the reservoir with new brake fluid. Pump the pedal about three times before moving the vehicle.

Brake Caliper
REMOVAL AND INSTALLATION

1. Remove the caliper from the mounting bracket.

2. Using a flare nut wrench, remove the brake line from the caliper.

3. Plug the open brake line to prevent excessive fluid lose.

OVERHAUL

1. Place the caliper in a vise or holding fixture.

2. Make sure the bleeder screw will loosen. If the screw breaks off, the caliper will have to replaced.

3. Remove the piston dust cover. Place a wooden block in the caliper to prevent damage or injury to the piston.

4. Use only enough compressed air to force the piston out of the bore.

5. Using a seal pick, remove the piston seal from the bore.

6. Clean all components with denatured alcohol and dry with compressed air.

7. Remove any rust or corrosion from the piston and bore with very fine emery paper and clean again. Excessive corrosion will cause the caliper to leak. Replace caliper if the corrosion can not be removed with fine emery paper.

8. Install the piston seal into the groove and make sure it is not twisted.

9. Lubricate the piston and bore with brake grease or brake fluid. Only use grease formulated for brake applications. Any thing else may cause damage to the rubber.

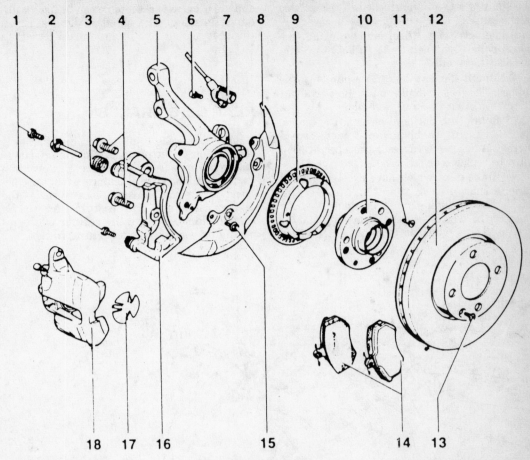

Front brake assembly — Corrado, Passat and Jetta 16V

1. 26 ft. lbs. (35 Nm)
2. Guide pin
3. Protective cap
4. 92 ft. lbs. (125 Nm)
5. Wheel bearing housing
6. 84 inch lbs. (10 Nm)
7. Wheel speed sensor
8. Splash shield
9. Rotor
10. Wheel hub
11. Screw
12. Brake disc
13. Countersunk screw
14. Brake pads
15. 84 inch lbs. (10 Nm)
16. Brake pad carrier
17. Heat shield
18. Brake caliper

10. Install the piston and insert the inner lip of the dust cover into the groove in the brake caliper. The outer lip must slip into the groove in the piston. Make sure the dust cover is secure before installing the caliper.

11. Install the caliper, pads and connect the brake hose.

12. Bleed the system as outlined in this chapter.

13. Test the brake performance before driving the vehicle at road speed.

Brake Rotor

REMOVAL AND INSTALLATION

1. Raise the vehicle and support with jackstands.

2. Remove the front wheel assemblies.

3. Remove the brake caliper as outlined in this chapter.

4. Remove the rotor retaining Phillips® screw and remove the rotor.

5. If the rotor sticks, tape on the hub area with a plastic hammer to break the rust loose.

6. Install the rotor and torque the retaining screw to 15 ft. lbs. (20 Nm). Do NOT overtighten. The screw may be difficult to remove in the future.

INSPECTION AND CHECKING

Brake discs may be checked for lateral runout while installed on the car. This check will require a dial indicator gauge and stand to mount it on the caliper. VW has a special tool for this purpose which mounts the dial indicator to the caliper, but it can also be mounted on the shaft of a C-clamp attached to the outside of the caliper.

1. Remove the wheel and reinstall the wheel bolts (tightened to 65 ft. lbs.) to retain the disc to the hub.

2. Mount the dial indicator securely to the caliper. The feeler should touch the disc about 13mm (1/2 in.) below the outer edge.

3. Rotate the disc and observe the gauge. Radial runout (wobble) must not exceed 0.1mm. A disc which exceeds this specification must be replaced or refinished.

4. Brake discs which have excessive radial runout, sharp ridges, or scoring can be refinished. First grinding must be done on both sides of the disc to prevent squeaking and vibrating. Discs which have only light grooves

and are otherwise acceptable can be used without refinishing. The standard disc is 12mm thick. It should not be ground to less than 10.5mm.

REAR DISC BRAKES

Rear disc brake removal and installation is very similar to the procedure for Kelsey-Hayes floating caliper front disc brakes removal and installation. The main difference is that the emergency brake mechanism is located inside the caliper assembly. **The piston has to be turned clockwise into the caliper while applying pressure with a turning tool.**

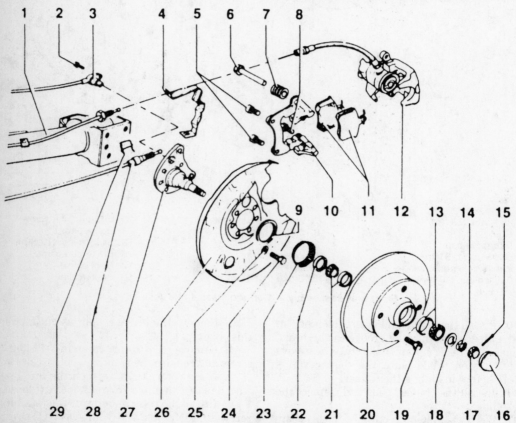

1. Axle beam
2. 84 inch lbs. (10 Nm)
3. Wheel speed sensor
4. Brake hose bracket
5. 48 ft. lbs. (65 Nm)
6. Guide pin
7. Protective cap
8. 26 ft. lbs. (35 Nm)
9. Cover ring
10. Brake pad carrier
11. Brake pads
12. Brake caliper
13. Outer wheel bearing
14. Nut
15. Cotter pin
16. Grease cap
17. Slotted cap
18. Thrust washer
19. 81 ft. lbs. (110 Nm)
20. Brake disc
21. Inner wheel bearing
22. Seal
23. Rotor
24. 44 ft. lbs. (60 Nm)
25. Dished washer
26. Splash shield
27. Stud axle
28. Parking brake cable
29. Spring clip

Rear disc brake assembly

Calipers

NOTE: *The caliper piston has to be turned clockwise into the bore with a turning tool. Damage to the caliper may occur if the piston is forced into the bore as the front calipers.*

REMOVAL AND INSTALLATION

1. Jack up the front of the car and support it on stands.

2. Remove the brake pads as outlined above if caliper mounted. If support mounted, the pads may be allowed to remain in place.

3. If you are removing the caliper for overhaul, disconnect and plug the brake line at the caliper. If not, do not remove the hose, hang it by a wire. Disconnect the emergency brake cable.

4. Remove the two caliper-to-strut retaining bolts and remove the caliper.

5. Installation is the reverse of removal. Tighten the two retaining bolts to 43 ft. lbs. for the Dasher, 36 ft. lbs. for other models.

6. Bleed the brakes.

OVERHAUL

NOTE: *Purchase an overhaul kit and sufficient brake fluid before starting.*

1. Remove the caliper as outlined above.

NOTE: *Remove and overhaul one caliper at a time. In this way you can use the other caliper as a reference.*

2. Mount the caliper in a soft jawed vise or place rags over the jaws to protect the caliper.

3. Depending on type, pry the fixed mounting frame off the floating frame.

4. Or, drive the caliper cylinder off the floating frame with a brass drift. Do not damage the piston(s).

5. On all models, remove the dust boot(s) and retaining ring(s) from the piston(s) either by hand or using a screwdriver. Some models do not have a retaining ring.

6. Remove the piston(s) from the cylinder. If the piston(s) is stubborn, remove the bleeder screw and use compressed air to force it out.

CAUTION: *Hold the piston(s) between blocks of wood when doing this, as they will fly out with considerable force.*

7. When the piston pops out of the caliper, remove the rubber seal with a wood or plastic pin to avoid damaging the seal groove.

8. Clean all metal parts in denatured alcohol. Never use a mineral based solvent such as gasoline, kerosene, acetone or the like; these solvents deteriorate rubber parts. Inspect the pistons and their bores. They must be free of scoring and pitting. Replace the cylinder if there is any damage.

9. Discard all rubber parts. The caliper rebuilding kit includes new boots and seals which should be used as the caliper is reassembled.

10. Lightly coat the cylinder bore, piston and seal with brake assembly paste or fresh brake fluid.

11. Install the piston into the cylinder. Fit the dust cover.

12. Installation is the reverse of removal. Be sure to install the guide or mounting springs in the correct position.

13. Install the pads and caliper and bleed the brakes.

REMOVAL AND INSTALLATION

1. Loosen the wheel bolts. Remove the hub cap.

2. Jack up the front of the car and place it on stands. Remove the wheel(s).

3. Remove the caliper as outlined above.

4. Remove the disc-to-hub retaining screw.

5. Grip the disc with both hands and give it a sharp pull to remove it. A stubborn disc should be removed with a puller. Never strike the disc with a hammer.

6. The disc is installed in the reverse order of removal. Don't forget to install the retaining screw. Install the caliper and bleed the brakes.

7. Install the wheel and lower the car. Tighten the wheel bolts diagonally to 65 ft. lbs. (88 Nm). This is doubly important because the bolts not only retain the wheels, but attach the disc to the hub.

REAR DRUM BRAKES

Brake Drums

REMOVAL AND INSTALLATION

1. On all but rear self adjusting brakes, jack up vehicle and remove the wheels. On self adjusting models, jack up vehicle, remove one lug bolt, position and using a screw driver through the lug hole push the adjusting wedge upward.

2. Remove and discard the cotter pin.

3. Remove the castellated nut, hex nut and washers.

4. Work the inner race of the wheel bearing out.

NOTE: *On models with self adjusting rear brakes, leave the road wheel attached to the brake drum when removing.*

5. Pull off the brake drum. Be careful not to lose the inner race of the outer bearing.

NOTE: *If the brake drum is stubborn, remove the rubber cover at the backing plate and back off the brake adjuster with an ad-*

justing tool or wide bladed screwdriver. If this doesn't work, use a puller. Never heat the drum or beat on it with a hammer.

6. Check the brake drum for any cracks, scores, grooves, or an out-of-round condition. Replace a drum which slows cracking. Smooth light scoring with fine emery cloth. If scoring is extensive have the drum turned. Never have a drum turned more than 0.8mm.

7. The stub axle bearings in the brake drum must be pressed out for replacement. Take the drum(s) to a competent machinist to have them removed. Always use new seals on reassembly.

8. After greasing the bearings and installing them in the drum with new seals, place the drum onto the sub axle.

9. Install the washer and the hex nut. Tighten the nut and then loosen it. Retighten the nut slightly so that the washer between the nut and the bearing can just be moved with a suitable prybar (refer to the illustration). Correct bearing play is 0.03–0.07mm.

Brake Shoes

REMOVAL AND INSTALLATION

Adjustable Rear Brake Shoes

NOTE: *Only do one side at a time. This way, you will always have one side intact as a reference.*

1. Remove the brake drum. See above for procedures.

2. On the Rabbit and the Scirocco, remove the horseshoe shaped spring with a pair of pliers. Be careful, the spring is under pressure.

3. Remove the lower springs. Remove the spring clips holding the shoes to backing plate.

4. Detach the parking brake cable by pressing back the spring with a pair of needle nose pliers and then disconnecting the cable at the lever.

5. On the Rabbit and Scirocco, remove the brake shoes with the adjusting mechanism. On the Dasher, raise up the brake shoes from the bottom and remove the adjusting mechanism. Lift up the brake shoes and remove the upper springs. Remove the brake shoes.

6. Clean and inspect all brake parts. Spray solvents are available for brake cleaning which do not affect linings. Do not spray rubber parts with solvent.

7. Check the wheel cylinders for boot condition and leaking.

8. Installation is the reverse of removal. When completed, install the drum and make an initial adjustment by turning the adapter wheel until a slight drag is felt between the shoes and drum, and back off about 1/4 turn. Complete adjustment as described earlier in this chapter.

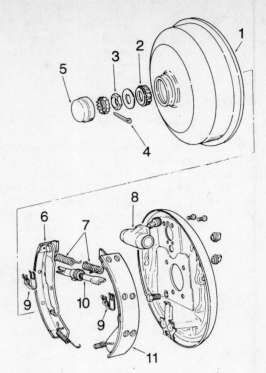

1. Brake drum	
2. Wheel bearing	7. Return spring
3. Retaining nut	8. Wheel cylinder
4. Cotter pin	9. Holddown spring
5. Grease cap	10. Adjuster
6. Brake shoe	11. Brake shoe

Dasher adjustable brake components

Self–Adjusting Rear Brake Shoes

NOTE: *Only do one side at a time. This way, you will always have one side intact as a reference.*

1. Remove the brake drum. See above for procedures.

2. Remove the spring retainers which hold the shoes to the brake backing plate by pressing in against the springs and turning the little cap until its slot lines up with the pin head.

3. Pull the bottom of the brake shoes free of their stop and allow them to come together close enough to remove the bottom spring.

4. Unhook the parking brake cable from its lever by pulling the spring on the cable back with a pair of needle nose pliers and then unhooking the cable.

5. Unhook the three springs at the top of the shoes (except the adjustment rod spring) and remove the shoes.

6. Place the adjustment rod in a vise and unhook the tension spring.

7. To install new brake shoes, with the adjustment rod in the vise, hook the tension

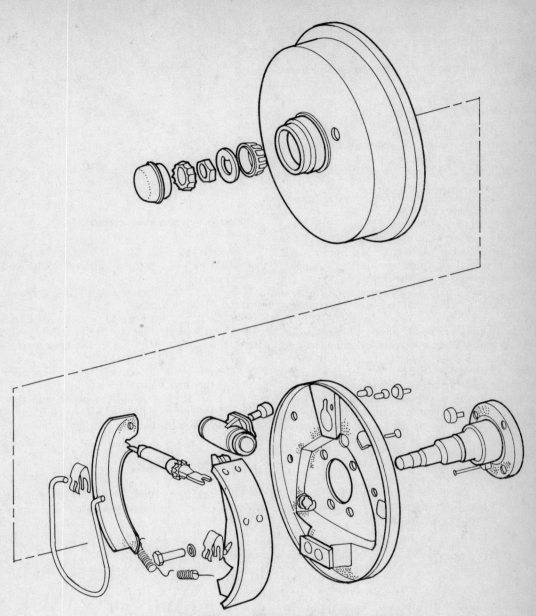

Rabbit and Scirocco adjustable rear drum brakes

spring on the rod and brake shoe. Insert the adjusting wedge with the lug on the wedge facing the backing plate.

8. Attach the other brake shoe with the lever to the adjusting rod.

9. Install the upper return spring.

10. Place parking brake lever into its cable.

11. Fit the shoes on the brake cylinder pistons. Hook the lower return spring into the brake shoe.

12. Remaining installation is the reverse of removal. See section in this chapter for wheel bearing adjustment.

Wheel Cylinders

REMOVAL AND INSTALLATION

1. Remove the brake shoes.

2. Loosen the brake line on the rear of the cylinder, but do not pull the line away from the cylinder or it may bend.

3. Remove the bolts and lockwashers that attach the wheel cylinder to the backing plate and remove the cylinder.

4. Position the new wheel cylinder on the backing plate and install the cylinder attaching bolts and lockwashers.

5. Attach the metal brake line or rubber hose by reversing the procedure given in step two or three.

6. Install the brakes and bleed the brake system.

OVERHAUL

1. Remove the brakes.

2. Place a bucket or some old newspapers under the brake backing plate to catch the brake fluid that will run out of the wheel cylinder.

3. Remove the boots from the ends of the wheel cylinders.

4. Push one piston toward the center of the cylinder to force the opposite piston and cup out the other end of the cylinder. Reach in the open end of the cylinder and push the spring, cup, and piston out of the cylinder.

5. Remove the bleeder screw from the rear of the cylinder, on the back of the backing plate.

6. Inspect the inside of the wheel cylinder. If it is scored in any way, the cylinder must be honed with a wheel cylinder hone or fine emery paper, and finished with crocus cloth if emery paper is used. If the inside of the cylinder is excessively worn, the cylinder will have to be replaced, as only 0.08mm of material can be removed from the cylinder walls. Whenever honing or cleaning wheel cylinders, keep a small amount of brake fluid in the cylinder to serve as a lubricant.

7. Clean any foreign matter from the pistons. The sides of the pistons must be smooth for the wheel cylinders to operate properly.

8. Clean the cylinder bore with alcohol and

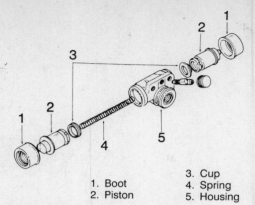

1. Boot
2. Piston
3. Cup
4. Spring
5. Housing

Exploded view of a wheel cylinder

a lint-free rag. Pull the rag through the bore several times to remove all foreign matter and dry the cylinder.

9. Install the bleeder screw and the return spring in the cylinder.

10. Coat new cylinder cups with new brake fluid and install them in the cylinder. Make sure that they are square in the bore or they will leak.

11. Install the pistons in the cylinder after coating them with new brake fluid.

12. Coat the insides of the boots with new brake fluid and install them on the cylinder. Install and bleed the brakes.

PARKING BRAKE

The parking brake activates the rear brake shoes through a cable attached to the lever between the seats.

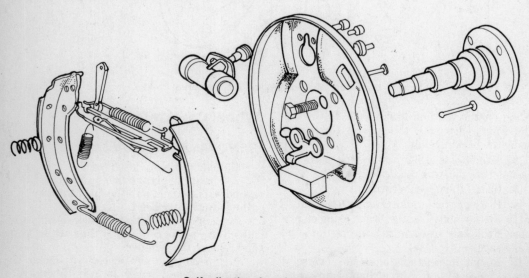

Self-adjusting drum brake assembly

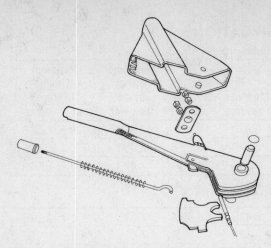

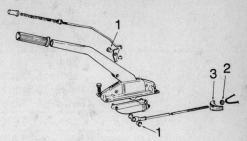

1. Retaining pin
2. Parking brake adjusting nut
3. Cable compensator

Dasher parking brake assembly

4. Release the parking brake lever and check that both wheels can be easily turned.

Rear Disc Brakes

Adjustment of the parking brake is only necessary when the parking brake cables, rear brake calipers, brake pads or discs have been replaced.

1. Put the parking brake lever in the down position.

2. Tighten the adjusting nuts until the levers at the calipers just move off their stops.

3. The maximum allowable distance from stop is 1.5mm.

4. Apply, release the parking brake and check that both rear wheels rotate freely.

Cable

REMOVAL AND INSTALLATION

Drum Brakes

CAUTION: *Some brake pads contain asbestos, which has been determined to be a cancer causing agent. Never clean the brake surfaces with compressed air! Avoid inhaling any dust from any brake surface! When cleaning brake surfaces, use a commercially available brake cleaning fluid.*

Rabbit, Jetta and Scirocco parking brake handle assembly

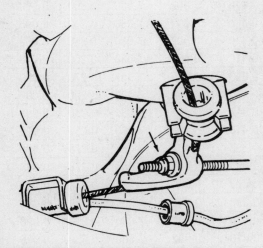

Dasher parking brake adjusting nut (arrow)

Cable

ADJUSTMENT

Rear Drum Brakes

Parking brake adjustment is made at the cable compensator, which is attached to the lever push rod underneath the car, or at the cable end nuts on top of the handbrake lever.

1. Block the front wheels. Raise the rear of the car.

2. Apply the parking brake so that the lever is on the second notch.

3. Tighten the compensator nut or adjusting nuts until both rear wheels can just be turned by hand. On the Rabbit, Jetta and Scirocco, and Dashers with self adjusting rear brakes, you shouldn't be able to turn them at all.

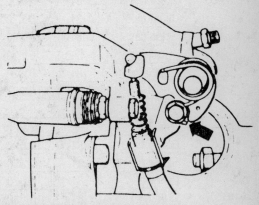

Rear disc parking brake adjustment

BRAKE SPECIFICATIONS

All measurements in inches unless noted.

Year	Model	Lug Nut Torque (ft. lbs.)	Master Cylinder Bore	Brake Disc		Maximum Brake Drum Diameter	Minimum Lining Thickness	
				Minimum Thickness	Maximum Runout		Front	Rear
1974–78	Dasher	65	0.820	0.410	0.004	7.870	0.078	0.098
	Rabbit, Scirocco	65	0.820	0.410	0.004	7.080	0.078	0.098
1979–81	Dasher	80	0.820	0.410	0.004	7.870	0.250	0.098
1979–85	Rabbit, Jetta Scirocco, Quantum	80	0.820	0.410	0.004	7.080	0.250 ①	0.098
1983	Jetta	80	0.820	0.410 ②	0.002	7.080	0.250	0.098
	Quantum	80	0.820	0.410 ②	0.002	7.080	0.250	0.098
	Rabbit	80	0.820	0.410 ②	0.002	7.080	0.250	0.098
	Scirocco	80	0.820	0.410 ②	0.002	7.080	0.250	0.098
1984	Jetta	80	0.820	0.410 ②	0.002	7.080	0.250	0.098
	Quantum	80	0.820	0.410 ②	0.002	7.080	0.250	0.098
	Rabbit	80	0.820	0.410 ②	0.002	7.080	0.250	0.098
	Scirocco	80	0.820	0.410 ②	0.002	7.080	0.250	0.098
1985	Jetta	80	0.820	0.393 ③④	0.002	7.087	0.276	0.098 ⑤
	Quantum	80	0.820	0.410 ②	0.002	7.080	0.250	0.098
	Rabbit	80	0.820	0.410 ②	0.002	7.080	0.250	0.098
	Scirocco	80	0.820	0.410 ②	0.002	7.080	0.250	0.098
	GTI	80	0.820	0.393 ③④	0.002	7.087	0.276	0.098 ⑤
	GLI	80	0.820	0.393 ③④	0.002	7.087	0.276	0.098 ⑤
	Golf	80	0.820	0.393 ③④	0.002	7.087	0.276	0.098 ⑤
1986	Jetta	80	0.820	0.393 ③④	0.002	7.087	0.276	0.098 ⑤
	Quantum	80	0.820	0.410 ②	0.002	7.080	0.250	0.098
	Scirocco	80	0.820	0.410 ②	0.002	7.080	0.250	0.098
	GTI	80	0.820	0.393 ③④	0.002	7.087	0.276	0.098 ⑤
	GLI	80	0.820	0.393 ③④	0.002	7.087	0.276	0.098 ⑤
	Golf	80	0.820	0.393 ③④	0.002	7.087	0.276	0.098 ⑤
1987	Jetta	81	0.820	0.393 ③④	0.002	7.087	0.276	0.098 ⑤
	Quantum	81	0.820	0.410 ②	0.002	7.080	0.250	0.098
	Scirocco	81	0.820	0.410 ②	0.002	7.080	0.250	0.098
	GTI	81	0.820	0.393 ③④	0.002	7.087	0.276	0.098 ⑤
	GLI	81	0.820	0.393 ③④	0.002	7.087	0.276	0.098 ⑤
	Golf	81	0.820	0.393 ③④	0.002	7.087	0.276	0.098 ⑤
	Fox/GL	81	0.820	0.393	0.002	7.087	0.276	0.098 ⑤
1988	Jetta	81	0.820	0.393 ③④	0.002	7.100	0.276	0.098 ⑤
	Quantum	81	0.820	0.410 ②	0.002	7.900	0.276	0.098 ⑤
	Scirocco	81	0.820	0.410 ②	0.002	—	0.276	0.098 ⑤
	Cabriolet	81	0.820	0.393 ③④	0.002	7.100	0.276	0.098 ⑤
	Golf	81	0.820	0.393 ③④	0.002	7.100	0.276	0.098 ⑤
	Fox/GL	81	0.820	0.393	0.002	7.100	0.276	0.098

BRAKE SPECIFICATIONS (cont.)

Year	Model	Lug Nut Torque (ft. lbs.)	Master Cylinder Bore	Brake Disc Minimum Thickness	Brake Disc Maximum Runout	Maximum Brake Drum Diameter	Minimum Lining Thickness Front	Minimum Lining Thickness Rear
1989–90	Jetta	81	0.820 ⑥	0.393 ③④	0.002	7.100	0.276	0.098 ⑤
	Quantum	81	0.820	0.410 ②	0.002	7.900	0.276	0.098 ⑤
	Scirocco	81	0.820	0.410 ②	0.002	—	0.276	0.098 ⑤
	Cabriolet	81	0.820	0.393 ③④	0.002	7.100	0.276	0.098 ⑤
	Golf	81	0.820	0.393 ③④	0.002	7.100	0.276	0.098 ⑤
	Fox/GL	81	0.820	0.393	0.002	7.100	0.276	0.098
	Passat	81 ⑦	0.870	0.708 ⑧	0.002	—	0.276	0.276
	Corrado	81 ⑦	0.870	0.708 ⑧	0.002	—	0.276	0.276

*NOTE: Minimum lining thickness is as recommended by manufacturer. Due to variations in state inspection regulations, the minimum thickness may be different than that recommended by the manufacturer.
① Rabbit front brake drums—9.05–9.06 in.
② Vented disc—0.728
③ Vented disc—0.708
④ Rear disc brake—0.315
⑤ Disc brake—0.276
⑥ ABS optional (anti-lock brakes)
⑦ With ABS—0.811
⑧ Rear disc—0.315

1. Raise the rear of the vehicle and support with jackstands.

2. Remove the rear wheels and brake drums as outlined in this chapter.

3. Remove the brake shoes and disconnect the cable from the secondary brake shoe.

4. Using a pliers or suitable tool, remove the cable retainer from the brake backing plate.

5. Disconnect the frame-to-cable retainers.

6. Remove the nut and washers from the cable adjuster in the middle of the vehicle.

7. Slide the cables out of the vehicle noting their location.

8. Route the cables into the vehicle in the same location as removal.

9. Connect the cable to the cable adjuster and install the nut and washers loosely.

10. Thread the cable into the backing plates and connect the end of the cable to the secondary brake shoe.

11. Install the frame-to-cable retainers.

12. Adjust the parking brake cables as outlined in this section.

Disc Brakes

CAUTION: *Some brake pads contain asbestos, which has been determined to be a cancer causing agent. Never clean the brake surfaces with compressed air! Avoid inhaling any dust from any brake surface! When cleaning brake surfaces, use a commercially available brake cleaning fluid.*

1. Raise the rear of the vehicle and support with jackstands.

2. Remove the rear wheels.

3. Using a pliers or suitable tool, remove the cable retainer from the brake cable retainer. Slide the cable end out of the actuator arm.

4. Disconnect the frame-to-cable retainers.

5. Remove the nut and washers from the cable adjuster in the middle of the vehicle.

6. Slide the cables out of the vehicle noting their location.

7. Route the cables into the vehicle in the same location as removal.

8. Connect the cable to the cable adjuster and install the nut and washers loosely.

9. Thread the cable into the cable retainers and connect the end of the cable to the actuator arm.

10. Install the frame-to-cable retainers.

11. Adjust the parking brake cables as outlined in this section.

Troubleshooting the Brake System

Problem	Cause	Solution
Low brake pedal (excessive pedal travel required for braking action.)	• Excessive clearance between rear linings and drums caused by inoperative automatic adjusters	• Make 10 to 15 alternate forward and reverse brake stops to adjust brakes. If brake pedal does not come up, repair or replace adjuster parts as necessary.
	• Worn rear brakelining	• Inspect and replace lining if worn beyond minimum thickness specification
	• Bent, distorted brakeshoes, front or rear	• Replace brakeshoes in axle sets
	• Air in hydraulic system	• Remove air from system. Refer to Brake Bleeding.
Low brake pedal (pedal may go to floor with steady pressure applied.)	• Fluid leak in hydraulic system	• Fill master cylinder to fill line; have helper apply brakes and check calipers, wheel cylinders, differential valve tubes, hoses and fittings for leaks. Repair or replace as necessary.
	• Air in hydraulic system	• Remove air from system. Refer to Brake Bleeding.
	• Incorrect or non-recommended brake fluid (fluid evaporates at below normal temp).	• Flush hydraulic system with clean brake fluid. Refill with correct-type fluid.
	• Master cylinder piston seals worn, or master cylinder bore is scored, worn or corroded	• Repair or replace master cylinder
Low brake pedal (pedal goes to floor on first application—o.k. on subsequent applications.)	• Disc brake pads sticking on abutment surfaces of anchor plate. Caused by a build-up of dirt, rust, or corrosion on abutment surfaces	• Clean abutment surfaces
Fading brake pedal (pedal height decreases with steady pressure applied.)	• Fluid leak in hydraulic system	• Fill master cylinder reservoirs to fill mark, have helper apply brakes, check calipers, wheel cylinders, differential valve, tubes, hoses, and fittings for fluid leaks. Repair or replace parts as necessary.
	• Master cylinder piston seals worn, or master cylinder bore is scored, worn or corroded	• Repair or replace master cylinder
Decreasing brake pedal travel (pedal travel required for braking action decreases and may be accompanied by a hard pedal.)	• Caliper or wheel cylinder pistons sticking or seized	• Repair or replace the calipers, or wheel cylinders
	• Master cylinder compensator ports blocked (preventing fluid return to reservoirs) or pistons sticking or seized in master cylinder bore	• Repair or replace the master cylinder
	• Power brake unit binding internally	• Test unit according to the following procedure: (a) Shift transmission into neutral and start engine (b) Increase engine speed to 1500 rpm, close throttle and fully depress brake pedal (c) Slow release brake pedal and stop engine (d) Have helper remove vacuum check valve and hose from power unit. Observe for backward movement of brake pedal. (e) If the pedal moves backward, the power unit has an internal bind—replace power unit

Troubleshooting the Brake System (cont.)

Problem	Cause	Solution
Spongy brake pedal (pedal has abnormally soft, springy, spongy feel when depressed.)	• Air in hydraulic system	• Remove air from system. Refer to Brake Bleeding.
	• Brakeshoes bent or distorted	• Replace brakeshoes
	• Brakelining not yet seated with drums and rotors	• Burnish brakes
	• Rear drum brakes not properly adjusted	• Adjust brakes
Hard brake pedal (excessive pedal pressure required to stop vehicle. May be accompanied by brake fade.)	• Loose or leaking power brake unit vacuum hose	• Tighten connections or replace leaking hose
	• Incorrect or poor quality brakelining	• Replace with lining in axle sets
	• Bent, broken, distorted brakeshoes	• Replace brakeshoes
	• Calipers binding or dragging on mounting pins. Rear brakeshoes dragging on support plate.	• Replace mounting pins and bushings. Clean rust or burrs from rear brake support plate ledges and lubricate ledges with molydisulfide grease. **NOTE:** If ledges are deeply grooved or scored, do not attempt to sand or grind them smooth—replace support plate.
	• Caliper, wheel cylinder, or master cylinder pistons sticking or seized	• Repair or replace parts as necessary
	• Power brake unit vacuum check valve malfunction	• Test valve according to the following procedure: (a) Start engine, increase engine speed to 1500 rpm, close throttle and immediately stop engine (b) Wait at least 90 seconds then depress brake pedal (c) If brakes are not vacuum assisted for 2 or more applications, check valve is faulty
	• Power brake unit has internal bind	• Test unit according to the following procedure: (a) With engine stopped, apply brakes several times to exhaust all vacuum in system (b) Shift transmission into neutral, depress brake pedal and start engine (c) If pedal height decreases with foot pressure and less pressure is required to hold pedal in applied position, power unit vacuum system is operating normally. Test power unit. If power unit exhibits a bind condition, replace the power unit.
	• Master cylinder compensator ports (at bottom of reservoirs) blocked by dirt, scale, rust, or have small burrs (blocked ports prevent fluid return to reservoirs).	• Repair or replace master cylinder **CAUTION:** Do not attempt to clean blocked ports with wire, pencils, or similar implements. Use compressed air only.
	• Brake hoses, tubes, fittings clogged or restricted	• Use compressed air to check or unclog parts. Replace any damaged parts.
	• Brake fluid contaminated with improper fluids (motor oil, transmission fluid, causing rubber components to swell and stick in bores	• Replace all rubber components, combination valve and hoses. Flush entire brake system with DOT 3 brake fluid or equivalent.
	• Low engine vacuum	• Adjust or repair engine

Troubleshooting the Brake System (cont.)

Problem	Cause	Solution
Grabbing brakes (severe reaction to brake pedal pressure.)	· Brakelining(s) contaminated by grease or brake fluid	· Determine and correct cause of contamination and replace brakeshoes in axle sets
	· Parking brake cables incorrectly adjusted or seized	· Adjust cables. Replace seized cables.
	· Incorrect brakelining or lining loose on brakeshoes	· Replace brakeshoes in axle sets
	· Caliper anchor plate bolts loose	· Tighten bolts
	· Rear brakeshoes binding on support plate ledges	· Clean and lubricate ledges. Replace support plate(s) if ledges are deeply grooved. Do not attempt to smooth ledges by grinding.
	· Incorrect or missing power brake reaction disc	· Install correct disc
	· Rear brake support plates loose	· Tighten mounting bolts
Dragging brakes (slow or incomplete release of brakes)	· Brake pedal binding at pivot	· Loosen and lubricate
	· Power brake unit has internal bind	· Inspect for internal bind. Replace unit if internal bind exists.
	· Parking brake cables incorrrectly adjusted or seized	· Adjust cables. Replace seized cables.
	· Rear brakeshoe return springs weak or broken	· Replace return springs. Replace brakeshoe if necessary in axle sets.
	· Automatic adjusters malfunctioning	· Repair or replace adjuster parts as required
	· Caliper, wheel cylinder or master cylinder pistons sticking or seized	· Repair or replace parts as necessary
	· Master cylinder compensating ports blocked (fluid does not return to reservoirs).	· Use compressed air to clear ports. Do not use wire, pencils, or similar objects to open blocked ports.
Vehicle moves to one side when brakes are applied	· Incorrect front tire pressure	· Inflate to recommended cold (reduced load) inflation pressure
	· Worn or damaged wheel bearings	· Replace worn or damaged bearings
	· Brakelining on one side contaminated	· Determine and correct cause of contamination and replace brakelining in axle sets
	· Brakeshoes on one side bent, distorted, or lining loose on shoe	· Replace brakeshoes in axle sets
	· Support plate bent or loose on one side	· Tighten or replace support plate
	· Brakelining not yet seated with drums or rotors	· Burnish brakelining
	· Caliper anchor plate loose on one side	· Tighten anchor plate bolts
	· Caliper piston sticking or seized	· Repair or replace caliper
	· Brakelinings water soaked	· Drive vehicle with brakes lightly applied to dry linings
	· Loose suspension component attaching or mounting bolts	· Tighten suspension bolts. Replace worn suspension components.
	· Brake combination valve failure	· Replace combination valve
Chatter or shudder when brakes are applied (pedal pulsation and roughness may also occur.)	· Brakeshoes distorted, bent, contaminated, or worn	· Replace brakeshoes in axle sets
	· Caliper anchor plate or support plate loose	· Tighten mounting bolts
	· Excessive thickness variation of rotor(s)	· Refinish or replace rotors in axle sets
Noisy brakes (squealing, clicking, scraping sound when brakes are applied.)	· Bent, broken, distorted brakeshoes	· Replace brakeshoes in axle sets
	· Excessive rust on outer edge of rotor braking surface	· Remove rust

Troubleshooting the Brake System (cont.)

Problem	Cause	Solution
Noisy brakes (squealing, clicking, scraping sound when brakes are applied.) (cont.)	• Brakelining worn out—shoes contacting drum of rotor	• Replace brakeshoes and lining in axle sets. Refinish or replace drums or rotors.
	• Broken or loose holdown or return springs	• Replace parts as necessary
	• Rough or dry drum brake support plate ledges	• Lubricate support plate ledges
	• Cracked, grooved, or scored rotor(s) or drum(s)	• Replace rotor(s) or drum(s). Replace brakeshoes and lining in axle sets if necessary.
	• Incorrect brakelining and/or shoes (front or rear).	• Install specified shoe and lining assemblies
Pulsating brake pedal	• Out of round drums or excessive lateral runout in disc brake rotor(s)	• Refinish or replace drums, re-index rotors or replace

Body

10

EXTERIOR

Doors

REMOVAL AND INSTALLATION

1. Open the door and support it securely. Remove the door check strap sleeve and remove the door check strap.

2. If equipped with electric accessories, disconnect the wiring harness before removing the door bolts.

3. Have an assistant hold the door, and remove the door hinge bolts.

4. Remove the door from the vehicle.

5. Position the door to the door hinges.

6. Make sure to install new door hinge bolts and tighten the bolts securely.

7. Install the check strap and sleeve, connect the electrical wiring harnesses and check the operation of the door.

ADJUSTMENT AND ALIGNMENT

When checking door alignment, look carefully at each seam between the door and body. The gap should be constant ad even all the way around the door. Pay particular attention to the door seams at the corners farthest from the hinges; this is the area where errors will be most evident. Additionally, the door should pull against the weatherstrip when latched to seal out wind and water. The contact should be even all the way around and the stripping should be about half compressed.

The position of the door can be adjusted in three dimensions: fore and aft, up and down, in and out. The primary adjusting points are the hinge-to-body bolts.

Apply tape to the fender and door edges to protect the paint. Two layers of common masking tape works well. Loosen the bolts just enough to allow the hinge to move. With the help of an assistant, position the door and re-tighten the bolts. Inspect the door seams carefully and repeat the adjustment until correctly aligned.

The in-out adjustment (how far the door sticks out from the body) is adjusted by loosening the hinge-to-door bolts. Again, move the door into place, then retighten the bolts. This dimension affects both the amount of crush on the weatherstrips and the amount of "bite" on the striker.

Further adjustment for closed position and smoothness of latching is made at the latch plate or striker. This piece is located at the rear edge of the door and is attached to the bodywork; it is the piece the latch engages when the door is closed.

Although the striker size and style may vary between models or from front to rear, the method of adjusting it is the same:

1. Loosen the large cross-point screw(s) holding the striker. Know in advance that these bolts will be very tight; an impact screwdriver is a handy tool to have for this job. Make sure you are using the proper size bit.

2. With the bolts just loose enough to allow the striker to move if necessary, hold the outer door handle in the released position and close the door. The striker will move into the correct location to match the door latch. Open the door and tighten the mounting bolts. The striker may be adjusted towards or away from the center of the car, thereby tightening or loosening the door fit. The striker can be moved up and down to compensate for door position, but if the door is correctly mounted at the hinges this should not be necessary.

NOTE: *Do not attempt to correct height variations (sag) by adjusting the striker.*

3. Additionally, many models use one or more spacers or shims behind the striker. These shims may be removed or added in combination to adjust the reach of the striker.

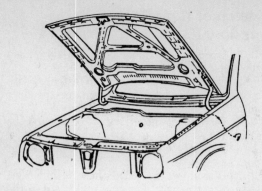

Hood removal

4. After the striker bolts have been tightened, open and close the door several times. Observe the motion of the door as it engages the striker; it should continue its straight-in motion and not deflect up or down as it hits the striker.

5. Check the feel of the latch during opening and closing. It must be smooth and linear, without any trace of grinding or binding during engagement and release.

It may be necessary to repeat the striker adjustment several times (and possibly re-adjust the hinges) before the correct door to body match is produced.

Door Locks

REMOVAL AND INSTALLATION

1. Lock the door lock with either the locking knob or the key.

2. Remove both of the door lock retaining

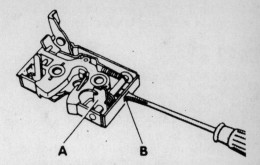

Door lock assembly—hold the lever A at 90 degrees through the opening B

screws, and pull the lock approximately 10–12mm ($^3/_8$–$^1/_2$ in.) away from the door.

3. Insert a screwdriver into the access hole at the bottom of the lock mechanism and hold the remote control lever in the pulled out position.

4. Detach the remote control lever from the pull rod.

5. Pull the locking lever, at the top of the mechanism, out of the sleeve.

6. Remove the lock from the door.

7. Close the rotary latch and lock it with the locking lever.

8. Insert a screw driver into the access hole at the bottom of the lock mechanism and hold the remote control lever in the pulled out position.

9. Insert the locking lever into the sleeve and attach the remote control lever to the pull rod.

10. Pull the screwdriver out of the access hole.

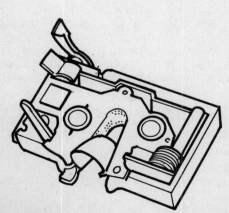

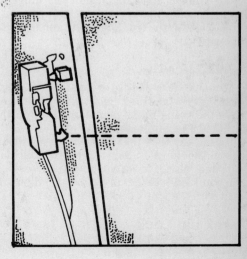

Door lock installation

11. Mount the door lock to the door, insert the retainer screws and tighten securely.

Hood

REMOVAL AND INSTALLATION

1. Raise the hood and support it securely. Cover the painted areas of the body to protect the finish from being damaged. Scribe the hood hinge-to-hood locations for installation.
2. While an assistant holds the hood, remove the hinge-to-hood retaining bolts.
3. Remove the hood from the vehicle.
4. With an assistant, install the hood to the original position and torque the bolts to 15 ft. lbs. (20 Nm).

ALIGNMENT

Loosen the hinge to hood attaching bolts and move the hood from side to side until there is an equal amount of clearance on both sides of the hood and fender. Tighten the hood attaching bolts.

Trunk Lid

REMOVAL AND INSTALLATION

1. Open and support the trunk lid securely.
2. Mark the position of the trunk lid hinge in relation to the trunk lid.
3. With an assistant, remove the two bolts attaching the hinge to the trunk lid.
4. Remove the trunk lid from the vehicle.
To Install:
1. Align the marks on the trunk lid with the hinges.
2. With an assistant, install the hinge-to-trunk lid bolts.
3. Tighten the trunk lid bolts and adjust if necessary.

ADJUSTMENT

To make the to-and-fro or side-to-side adjustment, loosen the trunk lid attaching bolts and move the trunk lid as necessary. Tighten the trunk lid attaching bolts.

To make the up-and-down adjustment, loosen the hinge-to-hinge support attaching bolts and raise or lower the hinge as necessary. The trunk lid is at the correct height when it is flush with the trunk deck.

Trunk Lid Lock

ADJUSTMENT

To adjust the trunk lid lock, loosen the striker attaching bolts, and move the striker as required, then tighten the attaching bolts.

Hatch or Rear Door

REMOVAL AND INSTALLATION

1. Open the rear door fully and disconnect the negative battery cable.
2. Carefully remove the trim fasteners with a flat screwdriver and and remove the door trim.
3. Disconnect the wiring couplings and the ground wire.
4. Pull out the wiring harness from the rear door.
5. Disconnect the washer hose at the nozzle located on the back door and pull it out of the rear door (if equipped).
6. Support the rear door with a suitable bar. Then remove the ball studs from both the upper and lower ends of the stay dampers. Remove the struts.
   CAUTION: *Never disassemble the support strut, as it is filled with high pressure gas. Do not apply oil or paint on the piston rod. Be careful not to damage the piston rod. Do not turn the piston rod and the cylinder when the piston rod is extended. When discarding the strut, drill a 2–3mm (0.08–0.12 in.) hole in the bottom of the damper or use a hack saw to release the gas. Make sure to protect yourself against any metal particles that may be thrown into the air by the compressed gas during drilling.*
7. Remove the rear door-to-hinge attaching bolts and remove the rear door.
8. Installation is the reverse of the removal procedure.

ALIGNMENT

1. To align the to-and-fro position of the door, loosen the hinge attaching bolts on both the back door and the body.
2. To adjust the door for the up and down position, loosen the hinge attaching bolts on the back door side, the door lock attaching bolts, and the door striker attaching bolts.
3. Adjust the rear for closing, by moving the door lock and striker.
4. Make all necessary adjustments by moving the rear door in the appropriate directions for the desired adjustments and tighten the attaching bolts.

Hatch and Rear Door Lock

REMOVAL AND INSTALLATION

1. Using a flat screwdriver, gently remove the trim fasteners and remove the door trim.
2. Disconnect the rod for the push button release.
3. Remove the push button securing clip and remove the push button.

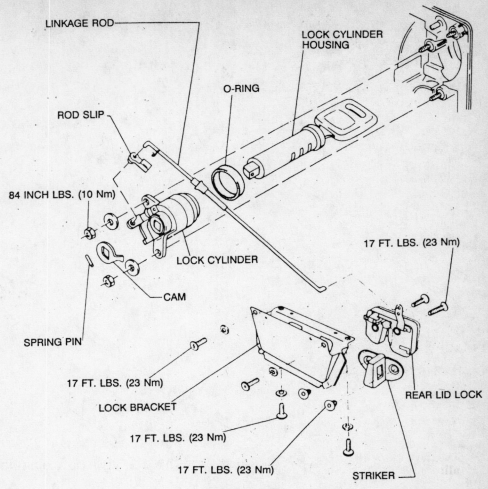

Rear hatch lock

4. Remove the door lock attaching bolts and remove the door lock.

5. Installation is the reverse of the removal procedure.

6. Adjust the door as described above.

Bumpers

REMOVAL AND INSTALLATION

Front

FOX

1. Disconnect the negative (–) battery cable.

2. Remove the air intake hose, bracket and air duct box cover.

3. From inside the engine compartment, remove the upper bumper bracket bolts.

4. Disconnect the turn signal wiring and remove the bumper.

5. Install the bumper, bolts and connect the wiring.

6. Install the air intake hose, bracket and air duct.

GOLF, GTI AND JETTA

1. Raise the vehicle and support with jack-stands.

2. Remove the bracket on both body long members and bolts from underneath the vehicle.

3. Remove the ventilation grille and bumper bracket bolts and remove the bumper from the vehicle.

4. Install the bumper and torque the bolts to 59 ft. lbs. (83 Nm).

QUANTUM AND SCIROCCO

1. Raise the vehicle and support with jack-stands.

2. Remove the right side bumper bracket mounting bolts, radiator cowling and A/C receiver/drier bracket.

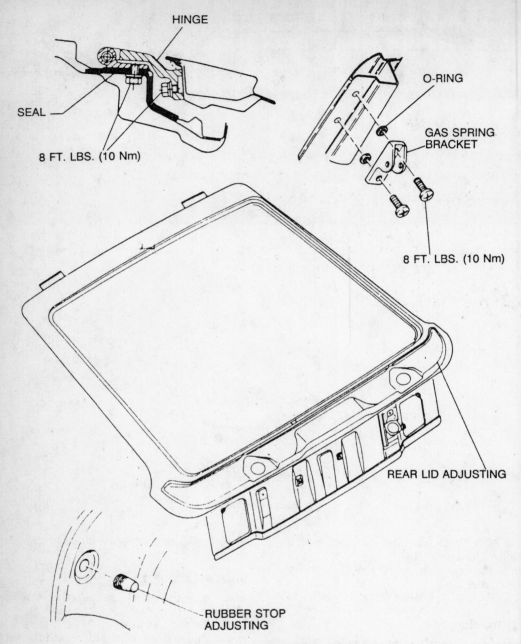

HINGE

SEAL

8 FT. LBS. (10 Nm)

O-RING

GAS SPRING BRACKET

8 FT. LBS. (10 Nm)

REAR LID ADJUSTING

RUBBER STOP ADJUSTING

Rear hatch — Corrado and Passat

3. Remove the left side bumper bracket and remove the bumper by sliding the bumper back off the guides.

4. Install the bumper and tight the bolts, receiver/drier bracket and lower the vehicle.

CORRADO AND PASSAT

1. Raise the vehicle and support with jackstands.

2. Remove the clips between the cover and front engine mount.

3. Remove the bolts from the engine mount and bracket.

4. Pull the bumper forward out of the plastic retainers with an assistant.

5. Pry the fasteners out of the plastic clips with a suitable prybar.

Rear

GOLF, GTI AND JETTA

1. Raise and support the vehicle with jackstands.

CHILTON'S
AUTO BODY
REPAIR TIPS

**Tools and Materials • Step-by-Step Illustrated Procedures
How To Repair Dents, Scratches and Rust Holes
Spray Painting and Refinishing Tips**

With a little practice, basic body repair procedures can be mastered by any do-it-yourself mechanic. The step-by-step repairs shown here can be applied to almost any type of auto body repair.

TOOLS & MATERIALS

You may already have basic tools, such as hammers and electric drills. Other tools unique to body repair — body hammers, grinding attachments, sanding blocks, dent puller, half-round plastic file and plastic spreaders — are relatively inexpensive and can be obtained wherever auto parts or auto body repair parts are sold. Portable air compressors and paint spray guns can be purchased or rented.

Auto Body Repair Kits

The best and most often used products are available to the do-it-yourselfer in kit form, from major manufacturers of auto body repair products. The same manufacturers also merchandise the individual products for use by pros.

Kits are available to make a wide variety of repairs, including holes, dents and scratches and fiberglass, and offer the advantage of buying the materials you'll need for the job. There is little waste or chance of materials going bad from not being used. Many kits may also contain basic body-working tools such as body files, sanding blocks and spreaders. Check the contents of the kit before buying your tools.

BODY REPAIR TIPS

Safety

Many of the products associated with auto body repair and refinishing contain toxic chemicals. Read all labels before opening containers and store them in a safe place and manner.

• Wear eye protection (safety goggles) when using power tools or when performing any operation that involves the removal of any type of material.

• Wear lung protection (disposable mask or respirator) when grinding, sanding or painting.

Sanding

1 Sand off paint before using a dent puller. When using a non-adhesive sanding disc, cover the back of the disc with an overlapping layer or two of masking tape and trim the edges. The disc will last considerably longer.

2 Use the circular motion of the sanding disc to grind *into* the edge of the repair. Grinding or sanding away from the jagged edge will only tear the sandpaper.

3 Use the palm of your hand flat on the panel to detect high and low spots. Do not use your fingertips. Slide your hand slowly back and forth.

WORKING WITH BODY FILLER

Mixing The Filler

Cleanliness and proper mixing and application are extremely important. Use a clean piece of plastic or glass or a disposable artist's palette to mix body filler.

1 Allow plenty of time and follow directions. No useful purpose will be served by adding more hardener to make it cure (set-up) faster. Less hardener means more curing time, but the mixture dries harder; more hardener means less curing time but a softer mixture.

2 Both the hardener and the filler should be thoroughly kneaded or stirred before mixing. Hardener should be a solid paste and dispense like thin toothpaste. Body filler should be smooth, and free of lumps or thick spots.

Getting the proper amount of hardener in the filler is the trickiest part of preparing the filler. Use the same amount of hardener in cold or warm weather. For contour filler (thick coats), a bead of hardener twice the diameter of the filler is about right. There's about a 15% margin on either side, but, if in doubt use less hardener.

3 Mix the body filler and hardener by wiping across the mixing surface, picking the mixture up and wiping it again. Colder weather requires longer mixing times. Do not mix in a circular motion; this will trap air bubbles which will become holes in the cured filler.

Applying The Filler

1 For best results, filler should not be applied over ¼" thick.

Apply the filler in several coats. Build it up to above the level of the repair surface so that it can be sanded or grated down.

The first coat of filler must be pressed on with a firm wiping motion.

Apply the filler in one direction only. Working the filler back and forth will either pull it off the metal or trap air bubbles.

REPAIRING DENTS

Before you start, take a few minutes to study the damaged area. Try to visualize the shape of the panel before it was damaged. If the damage is on the left fender, look at the right fender and use it as a guide. If there is access to the panel from behind, you can reshape it with a body hammer. If not, you'll have to use a dent puller. Go slowly and work the metal a little at a time. Get the panel as straight as possible before applying filler.

1 This dent is typical of one that can be pulled out or hammered out from behind. Remove the headlight cover, headlight assembly and turn signal housing.

2 Drill a series of holes 1/2 the size of the end of the dent puller along the stress line. Make some trial pulls and assess the results. If necessary, drill more holes and try again. Do not hurry.

3 If possible, use a body hammer and block to shape the metal back to its original contours. Get the metal back as close to its original shape as possible. Don't depend on body filler to fill dents.

4 Using an 80-grit grinding disc on an electric drill, grind the paint from the surrounding area down to bare metal. Use a new grinding pad to prevent heat buildup that will warp metal.

5 The area should look like this when you're finished grinding. Knock the drill holes in and tape over small openings to keep plastic filler out.

6 Mix the body filler (see Body Repair Tips). Spread the body filler evenly over the entire area (see Body Repair Tips). Be sure to cover the area completely.

7 Let the body filler dry until the surface can just be scratched with your fingernail. Knock the high spots from the body filler with a body file ("Cheese-grater"). Check frequently with the palm of your hand for high and low spots.

8 Check to be sure that trim pieces that will be installed later will fit exactly. Sand the area with 40-grit paper.

9 If you wind up with low spots, you may have to apply another layer of filler.

10 Knock the high spots off with 40-grit paper. When you are satisfied with the contours of the repair, apply a thin coat of filler to cover pin holes and scratches.

11 Block sand the area with 40-grit paper to a smooth finish. Pay particular attention to body lines and ridges that must be well-defined.

12 Sand the area with 400 paper and then finish with a scuff pad. The finished repair is ready for priming and painting (see Painting Tips).

Materials and photos courtesy of Ritt Jones Auto Body, Prospect Park, PA.

REPAIRING RUST HOLES

There are many ways to repair rust holes. The fiberglass cloth kit shown here is one of the most cost efficient for the owner because it provides a strong repair that resists cracking and moisture and is relatively easy to use. It can be used on large and small holes (with or without backing) and can be applied over contoured areas. Remember, however, that short of replacing an entire panel, no repair is a guarantee that the rust will not return.

1 Remove any trim that will be in the way. Clean away all loose debris. Cut away all the rusted metal. But be sure to leave enough metal to retain the contour or body shape.

2 Grind away all traces of rust with a 24-grit grinding disc. Be sure to grind back 3-4 inches from the edge of the hole down to bare metal and be sure all traces of paint, primer and rust are removed.

3 Block sand the area with 80 or 100 grit sandpaper to get a clear, shiny surface and feathered paint edge. Tap the edges of the hole inward with a ball peen hammer.

4 If you are going to use release film, cut a piece about 2-3″ larger than the area you have sanded. Place the film over the repair and mark the sanded area on the film. Avoid any unnecessary wrinkling of the film.

5 Cut 2 pieces of fiberglass matte to match the shape of the repair. One piece should be about 1″ smaller than the sanded area and the second piece should be 1″ smaller than the first. Mix enough filler and hardener to saturate the fiberglass material (see Body Repair Tips).

6 Lay the release sheet on a flat surface and spread an even layer of filler, large enough to cover the repair. Lay the smaller piece of fiberglass cloth in the center of the sheet and spread another layer of filler over the fiberglass cloth. Repeat the operation for the larger piece of cloth.

7 Place the repair material over the repair area, with the release film facing outward. Use a spreader and work from the center outward to smooth the material, following the body contours. Be sure to remove all air bubbles.

8 Wait until the repair has dried tack-free and peel off the release sheet. The ideal working temperature is 60°-90° F. Cooler or warmer temperatures or high humidity may require additional curing time. Wait longer, if in doubt.

9 Sand and feather-edge the entire area. The initial sanding can be done with a sanding disc on an electric drill if care is used. Finish the sanding with a block sander. Low spots can be filled with body filler; this may require several applications.

10 When the filler can just be scratched with a fingernail, knock the high spots down with a body file and smooth the entire area with 80-grit. Feather the filled areas into the surrounding areas.

11 When the area is sanded smooth, mix some topcoat and hardener and apply it directly with a spreader. This will give a smooth finish and prevent the glass matte from showing through the paint.

12 Block sand the topcoat smooth with finishing sandpaper (200 grit), and 400 grit. The repair is ready for masking, priming and painting (see Painting Tips).

Materials and photos courtesy Marson Corporation, Chelsea, Massachusetts

PAINTING TIPS

Preparation

1 SANDING — Use a 400 or 600 grit wet or dry sandpaper. Wet-sand the area with a ¼ sheet of sandpaper soaked in clean water. Keep the paper wet while sanding. Sand the area until the repaired area tapers into the original finish.

2 CLEANING — Wash the area to be painted thoroughly with water and a clean rag. Rinse it thoroughly and wipe the surface dry until you're sure it's completely free of dirt, dust, fingerprints, wax, detergent or other foreign matter.

3 MASKING — Protect any areas you don't want to overspray by covering them with masking tape and newspaper. Be careful not get fingerprints on the area to be painted.

4 PRIMING — All exposed metal should be primed before painting. Primer protects the metal and provides an excellent surface for paint adhesion. When the primer is dry, wet-sand the area again with 600 grit wet-sandpaper. Clean the area again after sanding.

Painting Techniques

P aint applied from either a spray gun or a spray can (for small areas) will provide good results. Experiment on an old piece of metal to get the right combination before you begin painting.

SPRAYING VISCOSITY (SPRAY GUN ONLY) — Paint should be thinned to spraying viscosity according to the directions on the can. Use only the recommended thinner or reducer and the same amount of reduction regardless of temperature.

AIR PRESSURE (SPRAY GUN ONLY) — This is extremely important. Be sure you are using the proper recommended pressure.

TEMPERATURE — The surface to be painted should be approximately the same temperature as the surrounding air. Applying warm paint to a cold surface, or vice versa, will completely upset the paint characteristics.

THICKNESS — Spray with smooth strokes. In general, the thicker the coat of paint, the longer the drying time. Apply several thin coats about 30 seconds apart. The paint should remain wet long enough to flow out and no longer; heavier coats will only produce sags or wrinkles. Spray a light (fog) coat, followed by heavier color coats.

DISTANCE — The ideal spraying distance is 8"-12" from the gun or can to the surface. Shorter distances will produce ripples, while greater distances will result in orange peel, dry film and poor color match and loss of material due to overspray.

OVERLAPPING — The gun or can should be kept at right angles to the surface at all times. Work to a wet edge at an even speed, using a 50% overlap and direct the center of the spray at the lower or nearest edge of the previous stroke.

RUBBING OUT (BLENDING) FRESH PAINT — Let the paint dry thoroughly. Runs or imperfections can be sanded out, primed and repainted.

Don't be in too big a hurry to remove the masking. This only produces paint ridges. When the finish has dried for at least a week, apply a small amount of fine grade rubbing compound with a clean, wet cloth. Use lots of water and blend the new paint with the surrounding area.

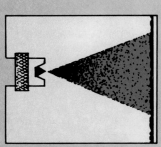

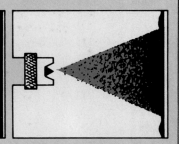

WRONG

Thin coat. Stroke too fast, not enough overlap, gun too far away.

CORRECT

Medium coat. Proper distance, good stroke, proper overlap.

WRONG

Heavy coat. Stroke too slow, too much overlap, gun too close.

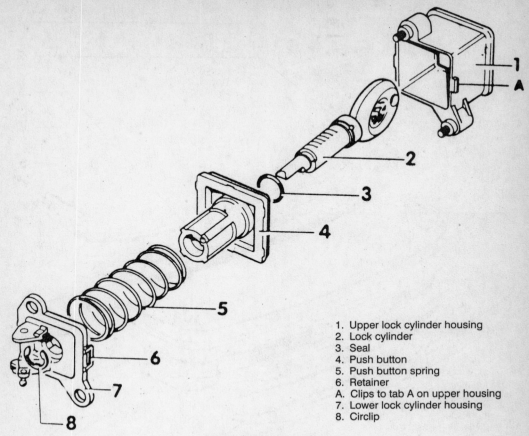

1. Upper lock cylinder housing
2. Lock cylinder
3. Seal
4. Push button
5. Push button spring
6. Retainer
A. Clips to tab A on upper housing
7. Lower lock cylinder housing
8. Circlip

Rear hatch lock — Passat

2. Remove the rear bumper bracket from both side of the floor panel located under the floor panel.

3. Remove the bolts from each side of the luggage compartment.

4. Slide the bumper assembly away from the body.

5. Install the bumper and torque the bolts to 29 ft. lbs. (40 Nm).

QUANTUM

1. Raise the vehicle and support with jackstands.

2. Remove both side bumper bracket mounting bolts and side the bumper off the guides.

3. Install the bumper and tighten the bolts.

CORRADO AND PASSAT

1. Raise the vehicle and support with jackstands.

2. Remove the bolts from the trunk floor area and pull the bumper rearward out of the plastic retainers with an assistant.

3. Install the bumper assembly and torque the bolts to 55 ft. lbs. (75 Nm).

Grille
REMOVAL AND INSTALLATION

Unclip the radiator grille at the lock carrier and remove upward. Check the rubber supports for damage.

To remove the Passat front panel; remove the top bolts and withdraw the panel at an angle and upwards from the lock carrier.

Outside Mirrors
REMOVAL AND INSTALLATION

Sail Mount

NOTE: *If equipped with electric mirrors, remove the door trim panel and disconnect the wiring harness before removing mirror assembly.*

1. Disconnect the negative (–) battery cable.

2. Remove the remote knob and unscrew the control lever.

3. Remove the trim cover, retaining screws and clamps.

4. Remove the mirror and outer shim.

5. Install the mirror and tighten the retaining screws.

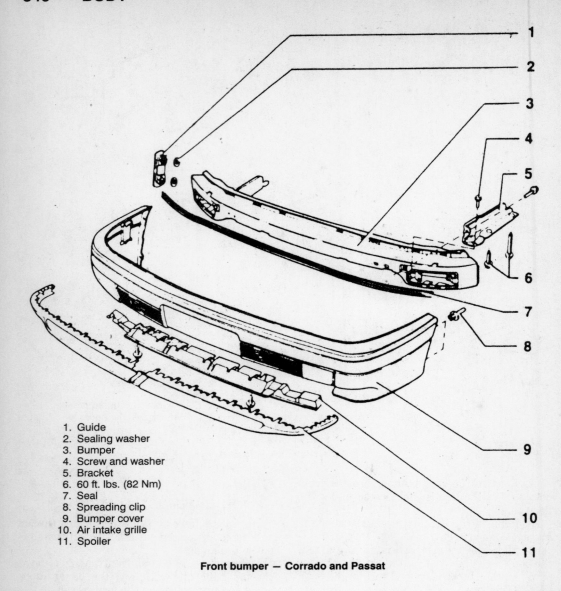

1. Guide
2. Sealing washer
3. Bumper
4. Screw and washer
5. Bracket
6. 60 ft. lbs. (82 Nm)
7. Seal
8. Spreading clip
9. Bumper cover
10. Air intake grille
11. Spoiler

Front bumper — Corrado and Passat

Door Mount

1. Remove the door trim panel as outlined in this chapter.

2. Remove the adjusting knob, bezel and locking nut.

3. Remove the mirror trim cover, retaining screws and mirror.

4. Install the mirror, screws, trim cover and remote wire.

5. Install the locking nut, bezel and adjusting knob.

6. Install the trim panel.

Antenna

REMOVAL AND INSTALLATION

1. Disconnect the negative (–) battery cable.

2. Remove the radio assembly and instrument cluster.

3. Remove and antenna cable from the foam tube and note the routing for installation.

4. Remove the rubber grommet and unclip the antenna cable from the water tray.

5. Remove the inner wheelhouse liner.

6. Remove the mast retainer nut from the top of the fender.

7. Pull the assembly downward into the inner wheelhouse and remove the lower mounting bracket.

8. Install the antenna and route the wire through the vehicle. Keep the cable away from the heater control cables.

9. Tighten the mast nut.

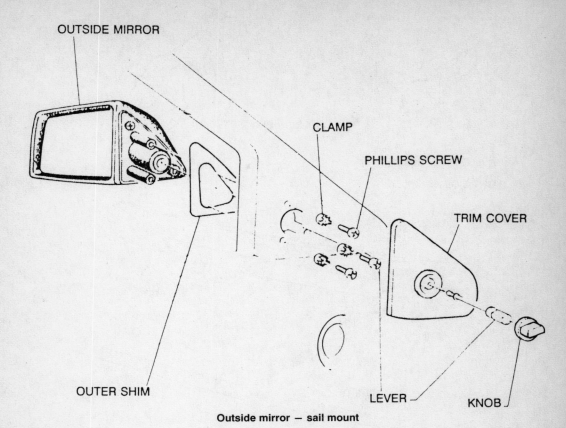

OUTSIDE MIRROR

CLAMP

PHILLIPS SCREW

TRIM COVER

OUTER SHIM

LEVER

KNOB

Outside mirror — sail mount

Windshield

NOTE: *Bonded windshields require special tools and procedures. For this reason we recommend that all removal, installation and repair work be referred to a qualified technician.*

REMOVAL AND INSTALLATION

Special tool set (431 898 099A) is required to perform this procedure. You will also need VW glass cutting tool 1351, double suction pad holders, for holding the glass, and a caulking gun for applying the bonding and sealing compound.

1. Remove the rear view mirror, sun visors, front pillar trim, and front header trim.
2. Remove the wiper arms and cowl grille.
3. Remove the front window molding.
4. Remove the glass by separating the glass from the sealant using a commercial power or manually operated remover tool, or use the following procedure.

   a. Use an awl to make a hole in the sealant.

   b. Pass a piece of piano wire, about 3mm ($^1/_8$ in.) in diameter, through the hole, and attach wood bars to both ends.

   c. Two people should hold the bars, one inside and one outside the vehicle, and then "saw" the sealant from around the glass, cutting along the border between the glass and the sealant.

   d. Then, with the help of an assistant, remove the glass from the vehicle. Make sure that no spacers or clips are lost during windshield removal.

To install:

1. Use a knife to smoothly trim the sealant on the body. Leave a layer about 1–2mm (0.04–0.08 in.) thick.

NOTE: *If there are small gaps or flakes in the sealant use new sealant to patch it.*

2. Carefully clean and remove any dirt or grease from a 50mm (1.97 in.) wide area around the circumference of the glass and the remaining bond of the body.

3. Bond a dam along the circumference of the glass 5mm (0.20 in.) from the edge.

NOTE: *Securely bond the dam and allow it to dry before proceeding to the next step.*

4. Apply primer with a brush to the circumference of the glass and the body, and allow it to naturally dry for 20 to 30 minutes.

CAUTION: *Be sure not to allow dirt, water, oil, etc. to come in contact with the coated surfaces and do not touch it with your hand!*

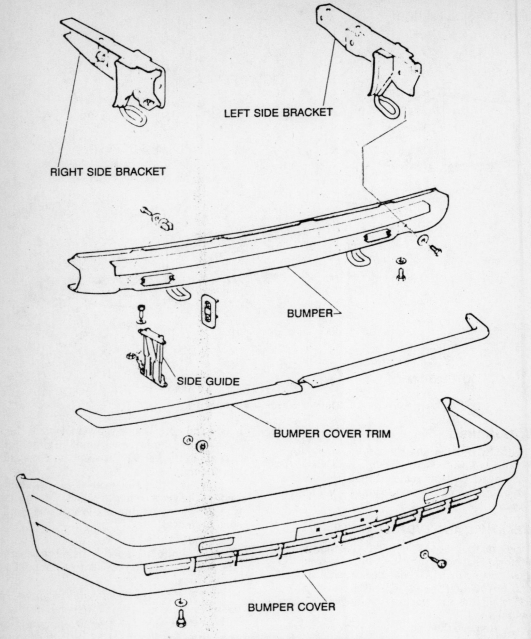

LEFT SIDE BRACKET

RIGHT SIDE BRACKET

BUMPER

SIDE GUIDE

BUMPER COVER TRIM

BUMPER COVER

Front bumper — Except Corrado and Passat

5. Install the spacers in the positions shown in the figure. Replace any clips with flaws.

6. When the primer has dried, apply an 11mm (0.43 in.) thick bead of repair seal, 7mm (0.28 in.) from the frame of the glass using a sealant gun. Cut the nozzle of the sealant gun to the angle shown in the figure. If necessary, smooth the repair seal to correct any irregularities.

7. Place the windshield into the frame.

Fully lower the side windows to prevent any pressure from being exerted on the windshield should the doors be closed suddenly. Keep the door glass open until the repair seal dries to some degree.

8. Remove any access, or add repair seal where necessary.

9. Check the windshield for water leaks. If a leak is found, wipe off the water and add repair seal.

10. After checking for water leakage, mount

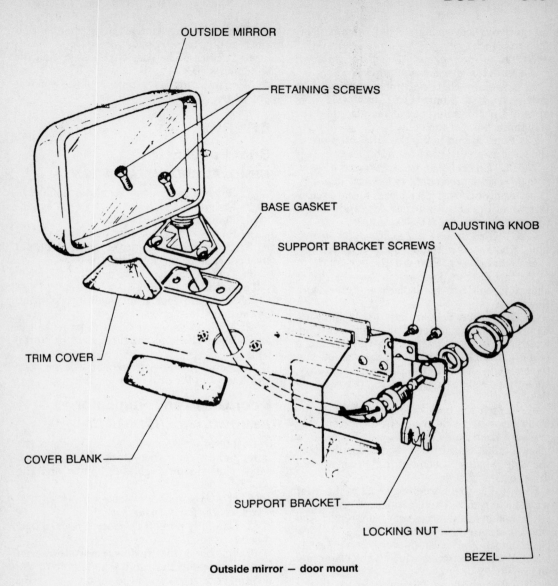

OUTSIDE MIRROR

RETAINING SCREWS

BASE GASKET

ADJUSTING KNOB

SUPPORT BRACKET SCREWS

TRIM COVER

COVER BLANK

SUPPORT BRACKET

LOCKING NUT

BEZEL

Outside mirror — door mount

the pillar garnish, cowl panel, cowl grill, wipers, etc.

11. Attach the front header trim, sun visor, interior mirror, etc.

Rear Window Glass
REMOVAL AND INSTALLATION

The procedure for removing and installing the rear window glass is the same as the front windshield removal and installation procedures.

Hatchback Window Glass
REMOVAL AND INSTALLATION

1. Remove the wiper arm, wiper motor, back door trim and defogger connector.

2. Remove the rear window molding.

3. Use an awl to make a hole in the sealant.

4. Pass a piece of piano wire, about 3mm ($^1/_8$ in.) in diameter, through the hole, and attach wood bars to both ends.

5. Two people should hold the bars, one inside and one outside the vehicle, and then "saw" the sealant from around the glass, cutting along the border between the glass and the sealant.

6. Then, with the help of an assistant, remove the glass from the vehicle. Make sure that no spacers or clips are lost during windshield removal.

To install:

1. Use a knife to smoothly trim the sealant

on the body. Leave a layer about 1–2mm (0.04–0.08 in.) thick.

NOTE: *If there are small gaps or flakes in the sealant use new sealant to patch it.*

2. Carefully clean and remove any dirt or grease from a 50mm (1.97 in.) wide area around the circumference of the glass and the remaining bond of the body.

3. Bond a dam along the circumference of the glass 8mm (0.31 in.) from the edge.

NOTE: *Securely bond the dam and allow it to dry before proceeding to the next step.*

4. Apply primer with a brush to the circumference of the glass and the body, and allow it to naturally dry for 20 to 30 minutes.

CAUTION: *Be sure not to allow dirt, water, oil, etc. to come in contact with the coated surfaces and do not touch it with your hand!*

5. Install the spacers in the positions shown in the figure. Replace any clips with flaws.

6. When the primer has dried, apply an 11mm (0.43 in.) thick bead of repair seal, 7mm (0.28 in.) from the frame of the glass using a sealant gun. Cut the nozzle of the sealant gun to the angle shown in the figure. If necessary, smooth the repair seal to correct any irregularities.

7. Attach the back door glass to the body. Fully lower the side windows to prevent any pressure from being exerted on the back door glass should the doors be closed suddenly. Keep the side windows open until the repair seal dries to some degree.

Refer to the seal hardening chart in the front windshield removal and installation section.

8. Remove any access, or add repair seal where necessary.

9. Check the back door glass for water leaks. If a leak is found, wipe off the water and add repair seal.

10. After checking for water leaks, install the molding.

11. Install the wiper arm, wiper motor door trim and defogger connector.

Side Quarter Glass

REMOVAL AND INSTALLATION

1. Pry the cover from the door handle using a flat screwdriver, remove the screws and detach the door handle.

2. Wind down the rear window and remove the window regulator handle.

3. Remove the door trim panel from the door and remove the bolts and oversize spring washers.

4. Remove the screw at the top of the door and the two bolts on the inside of the door, that secure the window guide channel.

5. Remove the window guide channel and the rear quarter window.

6. Lubricate the seal on the rear quarter window.

7. Installation is the reverse of the removal procedure.

INTERIOR

Door Panels

REMOVAL AND INSTALLATION

1. Remove the window regulator handle.
2. Remove the arm rest.
3. Remove the door lock knob.
4. Remove the inner door handle cover.
5. Using a flat screwdriver, gently separate the door trim panel clips from the door.
6. Remove the door trim panel.

To install:

1. Place the door trim panel into position on the door.
2. Apply pressure to the trim panel in the areas where the trim panel clips attach to the door.
3. Install the inner door handle cover, door lock knob and the arm rest.

Door Glass and Regulator

REMOVAL AND INSTALLATION

1. Lower the window glass and remove the inner handle cover, door lock knob (if necessary), the window regulator handle and the door trim panel.

NOTE: *On vehicles with power windows, disconnect the wiring coupling.*

2. Carefully peel off the door screen so that it can be reused.

3. On convertible models remove the seven screws attaching the window regulator to the door and one screw from the winder.

NOTE: *The window regulator may be riveted to the door on later model vehicles. Drill the rivets out to remove and use nuts, bolts and lock washers for installation.*

4. On all other models replace the window regulator handle and position the door glass so that the door glass installation bolts can be removed from the service hole.

5. Remove the door glass installation bolts.

6. On convertible models, remove the door glass and take out the window regulator through the large access hole.

7. On all other models, remove the door glass. Disconnect the retainer clips from the window winder, then remove the winder through the service access hole.

8. Installation is the reverse of the removal procedure.

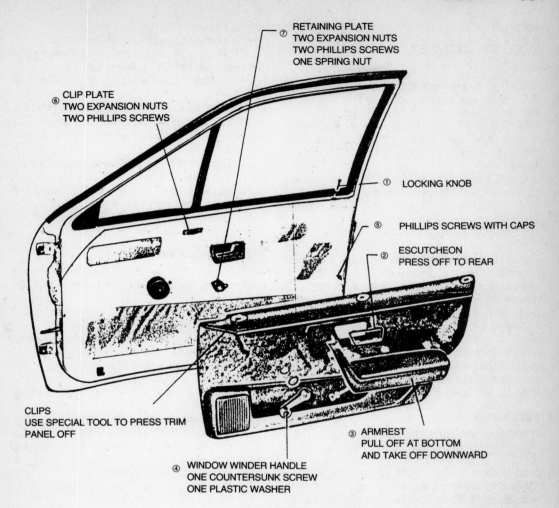

RETAINING PLATE
⑦ TWO EXPANSION NUTS
TWO PHILLIPS SCREWS
ONE SPRING NUT

CLIP PLATE
⑥ TWO EXPANSION NUTS
TWO PHILLIPS SCREWS

① LOCKING KNOB

⑤ PHILLIPS SCREWS WITH CAPS

ESCUTCHEON
② PRESS OFF TO REAR

CLIPS
USE SPECIAL TOOL TO PRESS TRIM
PANEL OFF

③ ARMREST
PULL OFF AT BOTTOM
AND TAKE OFF DOWNWARD

WINDOW WINDER HANDLE
④ ONE COUNTERSUNK SCREW
ONE PLASTIC WASHER

Exploded view of a door panel

Electric Window Motor

REMOVAL AND INSTALLATION

1. Lower the window glass and remove the inner handle cover, door lock knob (if necessary), the window regulator handle and the door trim panel.

2. Disconnect the wiring coupling. Carefully peel off the door screen so that it can be reused.

3. Pull the glass run channel out of the window guide. Remove the retaining screws that secure the front and rear window guides and remove the window guides. Then remove the front quarter window glass from the vehicle.

NOTE: *The window regulator may be riveted to the door on later model vehicles. Drill the rivets out to remove and use nuts, bolts and lock washers for installation.*

4. On the convertible models remove the six bolts attaching the window regulator to the door.

5. On all other models replace the window regulator handle and position the door glass so that the door glass installation bolts can be removed from the service hole.

6. Remove the door glass installation bolts.

7. On the convertible models, remove the door glass and take out the window regulator through the large access hole.

8. On all other models, remove the door glass. Remove the winder cable installation clips, and then remove the window winder through the service access hole.

9. Remove the window motor mounting bolts, then remove the motor from the regulator/winder cable.

10. Lubricate the front quarter window glass gasket.

11. Installation is the reverse of the removal

Seats

REMOVAL AND INSTALLATION

Front

1. Disconnect the negative (–) battery cable.
2. Slide the seat forward to the stop and remove the track cover beside the tunnel.
3. Remove the acorn nut, washer and bolt.
4. Release the retaining rod from the seat guide, push the seat to the rear and lift out of tracks.
5. Slide the seat assembly into the tracks and install the bolt, washer and nut.
6. Install the track cover and check operation.

Rear

1. Fox, Golf, Jetta, Quantum: lift the seat up and pull forward to remove.
2. Scirocco, Cabriolet, Passat, Corrado: remove the retaining bolts and detach the cover caps.
3. Release the seat backrest and fold forward.
4. Release the locking lug in the mounting and pull the backrest out of the mounting.
5. Install the seat and fold back.
6. Install and tighten the retaining bolts.

Headliner

REMOVAL AND INSTALLATION

Vehicles without a Sunroof

1. Remove the rear view mirror, sun visors, sunvisor holders and the assist grip.
2. Remove the lens of the interior light and remove the screws.
3. Disconnect the interior lamp harness coupler.
4. Remove the weatherstrip.
5. Remove the seaming welt.
6. Remove the front door trim by prying with a flat screwdriver.
7. Remove the center pillar trim.
8. Remove the weatherstrip, fasteners, and then remove the rear pillar trim.
9. Remove the fasteners from the roof lining.
10. Remove the floor lining rear end plate.
NOTE: *On the sedan, remove the plate while pushing the weatherstrip away from the end plate.*
11. Remove the rear of the roof lining by pulling it free from the corners.
12. Move the roof lining brace rearward and remove the front part of the roof lining.
13. Installation is done in the reverse of the removal procedure.

Vehicles with a Sunroof

1. Remove the overhead console, rear view mirror, sun visors, sunvisor holders and the assist grip.
2. Remove the lens of the interior light and remove the screws.
3. Disconnect the interior lamp harness coupler and remove the interior lamp.
4. Remove the seaming welt from the sunroof opening.
5. Remove the front of the door opening seaming welts.
6. Remove the front pillar trims.
7. Remove the roof lining front lace.
8. Remove the rear of the door opening seaming welts.
9. Remove the rear pillar trim.
10. Remove the roof lining rear lace.
11. Remove the side pillar trim.
12. Remove the attaching screws of the roof lining side lace and remove the side lace.
13. Remove the fasteners at the side of the roof lining and remove the roof lining.
14. Installation is the reverse of the removal procedure.

Mechanic's Data

11

TAX
1":254mm
10.16mm
Liter
Parts
Overhaul

General Conversion Table

Multiply By	To Convert	To	
		LENGTH	
2.54	Inches	Centimeters	.3937
25.4	Inches	Millimeters	.03937
30.48	Feet	Centimeters	.0328
.304	Feet	Meters	3.28
.914	Yards	Meters	1.094
1.609	Miles	Kilometers	.621
		VOLUME	
.473	Pints	Liters	2.11
.946	Quarts	Liters	1.06
3.785	Gallons	Liters	.264
.016	Cubic inches	Liters	61.02
16.39	Cubic inches	Cubic cms.	.061
28.3	Cubic feet	Liters	.0353
		MASS (Weight)	
28.35	Ounces	Grams	.035
.4536	Pounds	Kilograms	2.20
—	To obtain	From	Multiply by

Multiply By	To Convert	To	
		AREA	
.645	Square inches	Square cms.	.155
.836	Square yds.	Square meters	1.196
		FORCE	
4.448	Pounds	Newtons	.225
.138	Ft./lbs.	Kilogram/meters	7.23
1.36	Ft./lbs.	Newton-meters	.737
.112	In./lbs.	Newton-meters	8.844
		PRESSURE	
.068	Psi	Atmospheres	14.7
6.89	Psi	Kilopascals	.145
		OTHER	
1.104	Horsepower (DIN)	Horsepower (SAE)	.9861
.746	Horsepower (SAE)	Kilowatts (KW)	1.34
1.60	Mph	Km/h	.625
.425	Mpg	Km/1	2.35
—	To obtain	From	Multiply by

Tap Drill Sizes

National Coarse or U.S.S.

Screw & Tap Size	Threads Per Inch	Use Drill Number
No. 5	40	39
No. 6	32	36
No. 8	32	29
No. 10	24	25
No. 12	24	17
1/4	20	8
5/16	18	F
3/8	16	5/16
7/16	14	U
1/2	13	27/64
9/16	12	31/64
5/8	11	17/32
3/4	10	21/32
7/8	9	49/64

National Coarse or U.S.S.

Screw & Tap Size	Threads Per Inch	Use Drill Number
1	8	7/8
1 1/8	7	63/64
1 1/4	7	1 7/64
1 1/2	6	1 11/32

National Fine or S.A.E.

Screw & Tap Size	Threads Per Inch	Use Drill Number
No. 5	44	37
No. 6	40	33
No. 8	36	29
No. 10	32	21

National Fine or S.A.E.

Screw & Tap Size	Threads Per Inch	Use Drill Number
No. 12	28	15
1/4	28	3
6/16	24	1
3/8	24	Q
7/16	20	W
1/2	20	29/64
9/16	18	33/64
5/8	18	37/64
3/4	16	11/16
7/8	14	13/16
1 1/8	12	1 3/64
1 1/4	12	1 11/64
1 1/2	12	1 27/64

Drill Sizes In Decimal Equivalents

Inch	Dec-imal	Wire	mm
1/64	.0156		.39
	.0157		.4
	.0160	78	
	.0165		.42
	.0173		.44
	.0177		.45
	.0180	77	
	.0181		.46
	.0189		.48
	.0197		.5
	.0200	76	
	.0210	75	
	.0217		.55
	.0225	74	
	.0236		.6
	.0240	73	
	.0250	72	
	.0256		.65
	.0260	71	
	.0276		.7
	.0280	70	
	.0292	69	
	.0295		.75
	.0310	68	
1/32	.0312		.79
	.0315		.8
	.0320	67	
	.0330	66	
	.0335		.85
	.0350	65	
	.0354		.9
	.0360	64	
	.0370	63	
	.0374		.95
	.0380	62	
	.0390	61	
	.0394		1.0
	.0400	60	
	.0410	59	
	.0413		1.05
	.0420	58	
	.0430	57	
	.0433		1.1
	.0453		1.15
3/64	.0465	56	
	.0469		1.19
	.0472		1.2
	.0492		1.25
	.0512		1.3
	.0520	55	
	.0531		1.35
	.0550	54	
	.0551		1.4
	.0571		1.45
	.0591		1.5
	.0595	53	
	.0610		1.55
1/16	.0625		1.59
	.0630		1.6
	.0635	52	
	.0650		1.65
	.0669		1.7
	.0670	51	
	.0689		1.75
	.0700	50	
	.0709		1.8
	.0728		1.85

Inch	Dec-imal	Wire	mm
	.0730	49	
	.0748		1.9
	.0760	48	
	.0768		1.95
5/64	.0781		1.98
	.0785	47	
	.0787		2.0
	.0807		2.05
	.0810	46	
	.0820	45	
	.0827		2.1
	.0846		2.15
	.0860	44	
	.0866		2.2
	.0886		2.25
	.0890	43	
	.0906		2.3
	.0925		2.35
	.0935	42	
3/32	.0938		2.38
	.0945		2.4
	.0960	41	
	.0965		2.45
	.0980	40	
	.0981		2.5
	.0995	39	
	.1015	38	
	.1024		2.6
	.1040	37	
	.1063		2.7
	.1065	36	
	.1083		2.75
7/64	.1094		2.77
	.1100	35	
	.1102		2.8
	.1110	34	
	.1130	33	
	.1142		2.9
	.1160	32	
	.1181		3.0
	.1200	31	
	.1220		3.1
1/8	.1250		3.17
	.1260		3.2
	.1280		3.25
	.1285	30	
	.1299		3.3
	.1339		3.4
	.1360	29	
	.1378		3.5
	.1405	28	
9/64	.1406		3.57
	.1417		3.6
	.1440	27	
	.1457		3.7
	.1470	26	
	.1476		3.75
	.1495	25	
	.1496		3.8
	.1520	24	
	.1535		3.9
	.1540	23	
5/32	.1562		3.96
	.1570	22	
	.1575		4.0
	.1590	21	
	.1610	20	

Inch	Dec-imal	Wire & Letter	mm
	.1614		4.1
	.1654		4.2
	.1660	19	
	.1673		4.25
	.1693		4.3
	.1695	18	
11/64	.1719		4.36
	.1730	17	
	.1732		4.4
	.1770	16	
	.1772		4.5
	.1800	15	
	.1811		4.6
	.1820	14	
	.1850	13	
	.1850		4.7
	.1870		4.75
3/16	.1875		4.76
	.1890		4.8
	.1890	12	
	.1910	11	
	.1929		4.9
	.1935	10	
	.1960	9	
	.1969		5.0
	.1990	8	
	.2008		5.1
	.2010	7	
13/64	.2031		5.16
	.2040	6	
	.2047		5.2
	.2055	5	
	.2067		5.25
	.2087		5.3
	.2090	4	
	.2126		5.4
	.2130	3	
	.2165		5.5
7/32	2188		5.55
	.2205		5.6
	.2210	2	
	.2244		5.7
	.2264		5.75
	.2280	1	
	.2283		5.8
	.2323		5.9
	.2340	A	
15/64	.2344		5.95
	.2362		6.0
	.2380	B	
	.2402		6.1
	.2420	C	
	.2441		6.2
	.2460	D	
	.2461		6.25
	.2480		6.3
1/4	.2500	E	
	.2520		6.
	.2559		6.5
	.2570	F	
	.2598		6.6
	.2610	G	
	.2638		6.7
17/64	.2656		6.74
	.2657		6.75
	.2660	H	
	.2677		6.8

Inch	Dec-imal	Let-ter	mm
	.2717		6.9
	.2720	I	
	.2756		7.0
	.2770	J	
	.2795		7.1
	.2810	K	
9/32	.2812		7.14
	.2835		7.2
	.2854		7.25
	.2874		7.3
	.2900	L	
	.2913		7.4
	.2950	M	
	.2953		7.5
19/64	.2969		7.54
	.2992		7.6
	.3020	N	
	.3031		7.7
	.3051		7.75
	.3071		7.8
	.3110		7.9
5/16	.3125		7.93
	.3150		8.0
	.3160	O	
	.3189		8.1
	.3228		8.2
	.3230	P	
	.3248		8.25
	.3268		8.3
21/64	.3281		8.33
	.3307		8.4
	.3320	Q	
	.3346		8.5
	.3386		8.6
	.3390	R	
	.3425		8.7
11/32	.3438		8.73
	.3445		8.75
	.3465		8.8
	.3480	S	
	.3504		8.9
	.3543		9.0
	.3580	T	
	.3583		9.1
23/64	.3594		9.12
	.3622		9.2
	.3642		9.25
	.3661		9.3
	.3680	U	
	.3701		9.4
	.3740		9.5
3/8	.3750		9.52
	.3770	V	
	.3780		9.6
	.3819		9.7
	.3839		9.75
	.3858		9.8
	.3860	W	
	.3898		9.9
25/64	.3906		9.92
	.3937		10.0
	.3970	X	
	.4040	Y	
13/32	.4062		10.31
	.4130	Z	
	.4134		10.5
27/64	.4219		10.71

Inch	Dec-imal	mm
	.4331	11.0
7/16	.4375	11.11
	.4528	11.5
29/64	.4531	11.51
15/32	.4688	11.90
	.4724	12.0
31/64	.4844	12.30
	.4921	12.5
1/2	.5000	12.70
	.5118	13.0
33/64	.5156	13.09
17/32	.5312	13.49
	.5315	13.5
35/64	.5469	13.89
	.5512	14.0
9/16	.5625	14.28
	.5709	14.5
37/64	.5781	14.68
	.5906	15.0
19/32	.5938	15.08
39/64	.6094	15.47
	.6102	15.5
5/8	.6250	15.87
	.6299	16.0
41/64	.6406	16.27
	.6496	16.5
21/32	.6562	16.66
	.6693	17.0
43/64	.6719	17.06
11/16	.6875	17.46
	.6890	17.5
45/64	.7031	17.85
	.7087	18.0
23/32	.7188	18.25
	.7283	18.5
47/64	.7344	18.65
	.7480	19.0
3/4	.7500	19.05
49/64	.7656	19.44
	.7677	19.5
25/32	.7812	19.84
	.7874	20.0
51/64	.7969	20.24
	.8071	20.5
13/16	.8125	20.63
	.8268	21.0
53/64	.8281	21.03
27/32	.8438	21.43
	.8465	21.5
55/64	.8594	21.82
	.8661	22.0
7/8	.8750	22.22
	.8858	22.5
57/64	.8906	22.62
	.9055	23.0
29/32	.9062	23.01
	.9219	23.41
59/64	.9252	23.5
15/16	.9375	23.81
	.9449	24.0
61/64	.9531	24.2
	.9646	24.5
31/32	.9688	24.6
	.9843	25.0
63/64	.9844	25.0
1	1.0000	25.4

AIR/FUEL RATIO: The ratio of air to gasoline by weight in the fuel mixture drawn into the engine.

AIR INJECTION: One method of reducing harmful exhaust emissions by injecting air into each of the exhaust ports of an engine. The fresh air entering the hot exhaust manifold causes any remaining fuel to be burned before it can exit the tailpipe.

ALTERNATOR: A device used for converting mechanical energy into electrical energy.

AMMETER: An instrument, calibrated in amperes, used to measure the flow of an electrical current in a circuit. Ammeters are always connected in series with the circuit being tested.

AMPERE: The rate of flow of electrical current present when one volt of electrical pressure is applied against one ohm of electrical resistance.

ANALOG COMPUTER: Any microprocessor that uses similar (analogous) electrical signals to make its calculations.

ARMATURE: A laminated, soft iron core wrapped by a wire that converts electrical energy to mechanical energy as in a motor or relay. When rotated in a magnetic field, it changes mechanical energy into electrical energy as in a generator.

ATMOSPHERIC PRESSURE: The pressure on the Earth's surface caused by the weight of the air in the atmosphere. At sea level, this pressure is 14.7 psi at 32°F (101 kPa at 0°C).

ATOMIZATION: The breaking down of a liquid into a fine mist that can be suspended in air.

AXIAL PLAY: Movement parallel to a shaft or bearing bore.

BACKFIRE: The sudden combustion of gases in the intake or exhaust system that results in a loud explosion.

BACKLASH: The clearance or play between two parts, such as meshed gears.

BACKPRESSURE: Restrictions in the exhaust system that slow the exit of exhaust gases from the combustion chamber.

BAKELITE: A heat resistant, plastic insulator material commonly used in printed circuit boards and transistorized components.

BALL BEARING: A bearing made up of hardened inner and outer races between which hardened steel balls roll.

BALLAST RESISTOR: A resistor in the primary ignition circuit that lowers voltage after the engine is started to reduce wear on ignition components.

BEARING: A friction reducing, supportive device usually located between a stationary part and a moving part.

BIMETAL TEMPERATURE SENSOR: Any sensor or switch made of two dissimilar types of metal that bend when heated or cooled due to the different expansion rates of the alloys. These types of sensors usually function as an on/off switch.

BLOWBY: Combustion gases, composed of water vapor and unburned fuel, that leak past the piston rings into the crankcase during normal engine operation. These gases are removed by the PCV system to prevent the buildup of harmful acids in the crankcase.

BRAKE PAD: A brake shoe and lining assembly used with disc brakes.

BRAKE SHOE: The backing for the brake lining. The term is, however, usually applied to the assembly of the brake backing and lining.

BUSHING: A liner, usually removable, for a bearing; an anti-friction liner used in place of a bearing.

BYPASS: System used to bypass ballast resistor during engine cranking to increase voltage supplied to the coil.

CALIPER: A hydraulically activated device in a disc brake system, which is mounted straddling the brake rotor (disc). The caliper contains at least one piston and two brake pads. Hydraulic pressure on the piston(s) forces the pads against the rotor.

CAMSHAFT: A shaft in the engine on which are the lobes (cams) which operate the valves. The camshaft is driven by the crankshaft, via a belt, chain or gears, at one half the crankshaft speed.

CAPACITOR: A device which stores an electrical charge.

CARBON MONOXIDE (CO): A colorless, odorless gas given off as a normal byproduct of combustion. It is poisonous and extremely dangerous in confined areas, building up slowly to toxic levels without warning if adequate ventilation is not available.

CARBURETOR: A device, usually mounted on the intake manifold of an engine, which mixes the air and fuel in the proper proportion to allow even combustion.

CATALYTIC CONVERTER: A device installed in the exhaust system, like a muffler, that converts harmful byproducts of combustion into carbon dioxide and water vapor by means of a heat-producing chemical reaction.

CENTRIFUGAL ADVANCE: A mechanical method of advancing the spark timing by using flyweights in the distributor that react to centrifugal force generated by the distributor shaft rotation.

CHECK VALVE: Any one-way valve installed to permit the flow of air, fuel or vacuum in one direction only.

CHOKE: A device, usually a moveable valve, placed in the intake path of a carburetor to restrict the flow of air.

CIRCUIT: Any unbroken path through which an electrical current can flow. Also used to describe fuel flow in some instances.

CIRCUIT BREAKER: A switch which protects an electrical circuit from overload by opening the circuit when the current flow exceeds a predetermined level. Some circuit breakers must be reset manually, while most reset automatically

COIL (IGNITION): A transformer in the ignition circuit which steps up the voltage provided to the spark plugs.

COMBINATION MANIFOLD: An assembly which includes both the intake and exhaust manifolds in one casting.

COMBINATION VALVE: A device used in some fuel systems that routes fuel vapors to a charcoal storage canister instead of venting them into the atmosphere. The valve relieves fuel tank pressure and allows fresh air into the tank as the fuel level drops to prevent a vapor lock situation.

COMPRESSION RATIO: The comparison of the total volume of the cylinder and combustion chamber with the piston at BDC and the piston at TDC.

CONDENSER: 1. An electrical device which acts to store an electrical charge, preventing voltage surges.
2. A radiator-like device in the air conditioning system in which refrigerant gas condenses into a liquid, giving off heat.

CONDUCTOR: Any material through which an electrical current can be transmitted easily.

CONTINUITY: Continuous or complete circuit. Can be checked with an ohmmeter.

COUNTERSHAFT: An intermediate shaft which is rotated by a mainshaft and transmits, in turn, that rotation to a working part.

CRANKCASE: The lower part of an engine in which the crankshaft and related parts operate.

CRANKSHAFT: The main driving shaft of an engine which receives reciprocating motion from the pistons and converts it to rotary motion.

CYLINDER: In an engine, the round hole in the engine block in which the piston(s) ride.

CYLINDER BLOCK: The main structural member of an engine in which is found the cylinders, crankshaft and other principal parts.

CYLINDER HEAD: The detachable portion of the engine, fastened, usually, to the top of the cylinder block, containing all or most of the combustion chambers. On overhead valve engines, it contains the valves and their operating parts. On overhead cam engines, it contains the camshaft as well.

DEAD CENTER: The extreme top or bottom of the piston stroke.

DETONATION: An unwanted explosion of the air/fuel mixture in the combustion chamber caused by excess heat and compression, advanced timing, or an overly lean mixture. Also referred to as "ping".

DIAPHRAGM: A thin, flexible wall separating two cavities, such as in a vacuum advance unit.

DIESELING: A condition in which hot spots in the combustion chamber cause the engine to run on after the key is turned off.

DIFFERENTIAL: A geared assembly which allows the transmission of motion between drive axles, giving one axle the ability to turn faster than the other.

DIODE: An electrical device that will allow current to flow in one direction only.

DISC BRAKE: A hydraulic braking assembly consisting of a brake disc, or rotor, mounted on an axle, and a caliper assembly containing, usually two brake pads which are activated by hydraulic pressure. The pads are forced against the sides of the disc, creating friction which slows the vehicle.

DISTRIBUTOR: A mechanically driven device on an engine which is responsible for electrically firing the spark plug at a predetermined point of the piston stroke.

DOWEL PIN: A pin, inserted in mating holes in two different parts allowing those parts to maintain a fixed relationship.

DRUM BRAKE: A braking system which consists of two brake shoes and one or two wheel cylinders, mounted on a fixed backing plate, and a brake drum, mounted on an axle, which revolves around the assembly. Hydraulic action applied to the wheel cylinders forces the shoes outward against the drum, creating friction, slowing the vehicle.

DWELL: The rate, measured in degrees of shaft rotation, at which an electrical circuit cycles on and off.

ELECTRONIC CONTROL UNIT (ECU): Ignition module, module, amplifier or igniter. See Module for definition.

ELECTRONIC IGNITION: A system in which the timing and firing of the spark plugs is controlled by an electronic control unit, usually called a module. These systems have no points or condenser.

ENDPLAY: The measured amount of axial movement in a shaft.

ENGINE: A device that converts heat into mechanical energy.

EXHAUST MANIFOLD: A set of cast passages or pipes which conduct exhaust gases from the engine.

FEELER GAUGE: A blade, usually metal, of precisely predetermined thickness, used to measure the clearance between two parts. These blades usually are available in sets of assorted thicknesses.

F-HEAD: An engine configuration in which the intake valves are in the cylinder head, while the camshaft and exhaust valves are located in the cylinder block. The camshaft operates the intake valves via lifters and pushrods, while it operates the exhaust valves directly.

FIRING ORDER: The order in which combustion occurs in the cylinders of an engine. Also the order in which spark is distributed to the plugs by the distributor.

FLATHEAD: An engine configuration in which the camshaft and all the valves are located in the cylinder block.

FLOODING: The presence of too much fuel in the intake manifold and combustion chamber which prevents the air/fuel mixture from firing, thereby causing a no-start situation.

FLYWHEEL: A disc shaped part bolted to the rear end of the crankshaft. Around the outer perimeter is affixed the ring gear. The starter drive engages the ring gear, turning the flywheel, which rotates the crankshaft, imparting the initial starting motion to the engine.

FOOT POUND (ft.lb. or sometimes, ft. lbs.): The amount of energy or work needed to raise an item weighing one pound, a distance of one foot.

FUSE: A protective device in a circuit which prevents circuit overload by breaking the circuit when a specific amperage is present. The device is constructed around a strip or wire of a lower amperage rating than the circuit it is designed to protect. When an amperage higher than that stamped on the fuse is present in the circuit, the strip or wire melts, opening the circuit.

GEAR RATIO: The ratio between the number of teeth on meshing gears.

GENERATOR: A device which converts mechanical energy into electrical energy.

HEAT RANGE: The measure of a spark plug's ability to dissipate heat from its firing end. The higher the heat range, the hotter the plug fires.

HUB: The center part of a wheel or gear.

HYDROCARBON (HC): Any chemical compound made up of hydrogen and carbon. A major pollutant formed by the engine as a byproduct of combustion.

HYDROMETER: An instrument used to measure the specific gravity of a solution.

INCH POUND (in.lb. or sometimes, in. lbs.): One twelfth of a foot pound.

INDUCTION: A means of transferring electrical energy in the form of a magnetic field. Principle used in the ignition coil to increase voltage.

INJECTION PUMP: A device, usually mechanically operated, which meters and delivers fuel under pressure to the fuel injector.

INJECTOR: A device which receives metered fuel under relatively low pressure and is activated to inject the fuel into the engine under relatively high pressure at a predetermined time.

INPUT SHAFT: The shaft to which torque is applied, usually carrying the driving gear or gears.

INTAKE MANIFOLD: A casting of passages or pipes used to conduct air or a fuel/air mixture to the cylinders.

JOURNAL: The bearing surface within which a shaft operates.

KEY: A small block usually fitted in a notch between a shaft and a hub to prevent slippage of the two parts.

MANIFOLD: A casting of passages or set of pipes which connect the cylinders to an inlet or outlet source.

MANIFOLD VACUUM: Low pressure in an engine intake manifold formed just below the throttle plates. Manifold vacuum is highest at idle and drops under acceleration.

MASTER CYLINDER: The primary fluid pressurizing device in a hydraulic system. In automotive use, it is found in brake and hydraulic clutch systems and is pedal activated, either directly or, in a power brake system, through the power booster.

MODULE: Electronic control unit, amplifier or igniter of solid state or integrated design which controls the current flow in the ignition primary circuit based on input from the pick-up coil. When the module opens the primary circuit, the high secondary voltage is induced in the coil.

NEEDLE BEARING: A bearing which consists of a number (usually a large number) of long, thin rollers.

OHM:(Ω) The unit used to measure the resistance of conductor to electrical flow. One ohm is the amount of resistance that limits current flow to one ampere in a circuit with one volt of pressure.

OHMMETER: An instrument used for measuring the resistance, in ohms, in an electrical circuit.

OUTPUT SHAFT: The shaft which transmits torque from a device, such as a transmission.

OVERDRIVE: A gear assembly which produces more shaft revolutions than that transmitted to it.

OVERHEAD CAMSHAFT (OHC): An engine configuration in which the camshaft is mounted on top of the cylinder head and operates the valves either directly or by means of rocker arms.

OVERHEAD VALVE (OHV): An engine configuration in which all of the valves are located in the cylinder head and the camshaft is located in the cylinder block. The camshaft operates the valves via lifters and pushrods.

OXIDES OF NITROGEN (NOx): Chemical compounds of nitrogen produced as a byproduct of combustion. They combine with hydrocarbons to produce smog.

OXYGEN SENSOR: Used with the feedback system to sense the presence of oxygen in the exhaust gas and signal the computer which can reference the voltage signal to an air/fuel ratio.

PINION: The smaller of two meshing gears.

PISTON RING: An open ended ring which fits into a groove on the outer diameter of the piston. Its chief function is to form a seal between the piston and cylinder wall. Most automotive pistons have three rings: two for compression sealing; one for oil sealing.

PRELOAD: A predetermined load placed on a bearing during assembly or by adjustment.

PRIMARY CIRCUIT: Is the low voltage side of the ignition system which consists of the ignition switch, ballast resistor or resistance wire, bypass, coil, electronic control unit and pick-up coil as well as the connecting wires and harnesses.

PRESS FIT: The mating of two parts under pressure, due to the inner diameter of one being smaller than the outer diameter of the other, or vice versa; an interference fit.

RACE: The surface on the inner or outer ring of a bearing on which the balls, needles or rollers move.

REGULATOR: A device which maintains the amperage and/or voltage levels of a circuit at predetermined values.

RELAY: A switch which automatically opens and/or closes a circuit.

RESISTANCE: The opposition to the flow of current through a circuit or electrical device, and is measured in ohms. Resistance is equal to the voltage divided by the amperage.

RESISTOR: A device, usually made of wire, which offers a preset amount of resistance in an electrical circuit.

RING GEAR: The name given to a ring-shaped gear attached to a differential case,or affixed to a flywheel or as part a planetary gear set.

ROLLER BEARING: A bearing made up of hardened inner and outer races between which hardened steel rollers move.

ROTOR: 1. The disc-shaped part of a disc brake assembly, upon which the brake pads bear; also called, brake disc.
2. The device mounted atop the distributor shaft, which passes current to the distributor cap tower contacts.

SECONDARY CIRCUIT: The high voltage side of the ignition system, usually above 20,000 volts. The secondary includes the ignition coil, coil wire, distributor cap and rotor, spark plug wires and spark plugs.

SENDING UNIT: A mechanical, electrical, hydraulic or electromagnetic device which transmits information to a gauge.

SENSOR: Any device designed to measure engine operating conditions or ambient pressures and temperatures. Usually electronic in nature and designed to send a voltage signal to an on-board computer, some sensors may operate as a simple on/off switch or they may provide a variable voltage signal (like a potentiometer) as conditions or measured parameters change.

SHIM: Spacers of precise, predetermined thickness used between parts to establish a proper working relationship.

SLAVE CYLINDER: In automotive use, a device in the hydraulic clutch system which is activated by hydraulic force, disengaging the clutch.

SOLENOID: A coil used to produce a magnetic field, the effect of which is to produce work.

SPARK PLUG: A device screwed into the combustion chamber of a spark ignition engine. The basic construction is a conductive core inside of a ceramic insulator, mounted in an outer conductive base. An electrical charge from the spark plug wire travels along the conductive core and jumps a preset air gap to a grounding point or points at the end of the conductive base. The resultant spark ignites the fuel/air mixture in the combustion chamber.

SPLINES: Ridges machined or cast onto the outer diameter of a shaft or inner diameter of a bore to enable parts to mate without rotation.

TACHOMETER: A device used to measure the rotary speed of an engine, shaft, gear, etc., usually in rotations per minute.

THERMOSTAT: A valve, located in the cooling system of an engine, which is closed when cold and opens gradually in response to engine heating, controlling the temperature of the coolant and rate of coolant flow.

TOP DEAD CENTER (TDC): The point at which the piston reaches the top of its travel on the compression stroke.

TORQUE: The twisting force applied to an object.

TORQUE CONVERTER: A turbine used to transmit power from a driving member to a driven member via hydraulic action, providing changes in drive ratio and torque. In automotive use, it links the driveplate at the rear of the engine to the automatic transmission.

TRANSDUCER: A device used to change a force into an electrical signal.

TRANSISTOR: A semi-conductor component which can be actuated by a small voltage to perform an electrical switching function.

TUNE-UP: A regular maintenance function, usually associated with the replacement and adjustment of parts and components in the electrical and fuel systems of a vehicle for the purpose of attaining optimum performance.

TURBOCHARGER: An exhaust driven pump which compresses intake air and forces it into the combustion chambers at higher than atmospheric pressures. The increased air pressure allows more fuel to be burned and results in increased horsepower being produced.

VACUUM ADVANCE: A device which advances the ignition timing in response to increased engine vacuum.

VACUUM GAUGE: An instrument used to measure the presence of vacuum in a chamber.

VALVE: A device which control the pressure, direction of flow or rate of flow of a liquid or gas.

VALVE CLEARANCE: The measured gap between the end of the valve stem and the rocker arm, cam lobe or follower that activates the valve.

VISCOSITY: The rating of a liquid's internal resistance to flow.

VOLTMETER: An instrument used for measuring electrical force in units called volts. Voltmeters are always connected parallel with the circuit being tested.

WHEEL CYLINDER: Found in the automotive drum brake assembly, it is a device, actuated by hydraulic pressure, which, through internal pistons, pushes the brake shoes outward against the drums.

ABBREVIATIONS AND SYMBOLS

A: Ampere

AC: Alternating current

A/C: Air conditioning

A-h: Ampere hour

AT: Automatic transmission

ATDC: After top dead center

μA: Microampere

bbl: Barrel

BDC: Bottom dead center

bhp: Brake horsepower

BTDC: Before top dead center

BTU: British thermal unit

C: Celsius (Centigrade)

CCA: Cold cranking amps

cd: Candela

cm^2: Square centimeter

cm^3, cc: Cubic centimeter

CO: Carbon monoxide

CO_2: Carbon dioxide

cu.in., in^3: Cubic inch

CV: Constant velocity

Cyl.: Cylinder

DC: Direct current

ECM: Electronic control module

EFE: Early fuel evaporation

EFI: Electronic fuel injection

EGR: Exhaust gas recirculation

Exh.: Exhaust

F: Fahrenheit

F: Farad

pF: Picofarad

μF: Microfarad

FI: Fuel injection

ft.lb., ft. lb., ft. lbs.: foot pound(s)

gal: Gallon

g: Gram

HC: Hydrocarbon

HEI: High energy ignition

HO: High output

hp: Horsepower

Hyd.: Hydraulic

Hz: Hertz

ID: Inside diameter

in.lb.; in. lb.; in. lbs: inch pound(s)

Int.: Intake

K: Kelvin

kg: Kilogram

kHz: Kilohertz

km: Kilometer

km/h: Kilometers per hour

kΩ: Kilohm

kPa: Kilopascal

kV: Kilovolt

kW: Kilowatt

l: Liter

l/s: Liters per second

m: Meter

mA: Milliampere

mg: Milligram

mHz: Megahertz

mm: Millimeter

mm^2: Square millimeter

m^3: Cubic meter

$M\Omega$: Megohm

m/s: Meters per second

MT: Manual transmission

mV: Millivolt

μm: Micrometer

N: Newton

N-m: Newton meter

NOx: Nitrous oxide

OD: Outside diameter

OHC: Over head camshaft

OHV: Over head valve

Ω: Ohm

PCV: Positive crankcase ventilation

psi: Pounds per square inch

pts: Pints

qts: Quarts

rpm: Rotations per minute

rps: Rotations per second

R-12: A refrigerant gas (Freon)

SAE: Society of Automotive Engineers

SO_2: Sulfur dioxide

T: Ton

t: Megagram

TBI: Throttle Body Injection

TPS: Throttle Position Sensor

V: 1. Volt; 2. Venturi

μV: Microvolt

W: Watt

∞: Infinity

<: Less than

>: Greater than

CHILTON'S REPAIR MANUAL MODEL INDEX
Car and truck model names are listed in alphabetical and numerical order

Part No.	Model	Repair Manual Title
6980	Accord	Honda 1973-88
7747	Aerostar	Ford Aerostar 1986-90
7165	Alliance	Renault 1975-85
7199	AMX	AMC 1975-86
7163	Aries	Chrysler Front Wheel Drive 1981-88
7041	Arrow	Champ/Arrow/Sapporo 1978-83
7032	Arrow Pick-Ups	D-50/Arrow Pick-Up 1979-81
6637	Aspen	Aspen/Volare 1976-80
6935	Astre	GM Subcompact 1971-80
7750	Astro	Chevrolet Astro/GMC Safari 1985-90
6934	A100, 200, 300	Dodge/Plymouth Vans 1967-88
5807	Barracuda	Barracuda/Challenger 1965-72
6844	Bavaria	BMW 1970-88
5796	Beetle	Volkswagen 1949-71
6837	Beetle	Volkswagen 1970-81
7135	Bel Air	Chevrolet 1968-88
5821	Belvedere	Roadrunner/Satellite/Belvedere/GTX 1968-73
7849	Beretta	Chevrolet Corsica and Beretta 1988
7317	Berlinetta	Camaro 1982-88
7135	Biscayne	Chevrolet 1968-88
6931	Blazer	Blazer/Jimmy 1969-82
7383	Blazer	Chevy S-10 Blazer/GMC S-15 Jimmy 1982-87
7027	Bobcat	Pinto/Bobcat 1971-80
7308	Bonneville	Buick/Olds/Pontiac 1975-87
6982	BRAT	Subaru 1970-88
7042	Brava	Fiat 1969-81
7140	Bronco	Ford Bronco 1966-86
7829	Bronco	Ford Pick-Ups and Bronco 1987-88
7408	Bronco II	Ford Ranger/Bronco II 1983-88
7135	Brookwood	Chevrolet 1968-88
6326	Brougham 1975-75	Valiant/Duster 1968-76
6934	B100, 150, 200, 250, 300, 350	Dodge/Plymouth Vans 1967-88
7197	B210	Datsun 1200/210/Nissan Sentra 1973-88
7659	B1600, 1800, 2000, 2200, 2600	Mazda Trucks 1971-89
6840	Caballero	Chevrolet Mid-Size 1964-88
7657	Calais	Calais, Grand Am, Skylark, Somerset 1985-86
6735	Camaro	Camaro 1967-81
7317	Camaro	Camaro 1982-88
7740	Camry	Toyota Camry 1983-88
6695	Capri, Capri II	Capri 1970-77
6963	Capri	Mustang/Capri/Merkur 1979-88
7135	Caprice	Chevrolet 1968-88
7482	Caravan	Dodge Caravan/Plymouth Voyager 1984-89
7163	Caravelle	Chrysler Front Wheel Drive 1981-88
7036	Carina	Toyota Corolla/Carina/Tercel/Starlet 1970-87
7308	Catalina	Buick/Olds/Pontiac 1975-90
7059	Cavalier	Cavalier, Skyhawk, Cimarron, 2000 1982-88
7309	Celebrity	Celebrity, Century, Ciera, 6000 1982-88
7043	Celica	Toyota Celica/Supra 1971-87
8058	Celica	Toyota Celica/Supra 1986-90
7309	Century FWD	Celebrity, Century, Ciera, 6000 1982-88
7307	Century RWD	Century/Regal 1975-87
5807	Challenger 1965-72	Barracuda/Challenger 1965-72
7037	Challenger 1977-83	Colt/Challenger/Vista/Conquest 1971-88
7041	Champ	Champ/Arrow/Sapporo 1978-83
6486	Charger	Dodge Charger 1967-70
6845	Charger 2.2	Omni/Horizon/Rampage 1978-88

Part No.	Model	Repair Manual Title
6739	Cherokee 1974-83	Jeep Wagoneer, Commando, Cherokee, Truck 1957-86
7939	Cherokee 1984-89	Jeep Wagoneer, Comanche, Cherokee 1984-89
6840	Chevelle	Chevrolet Mid-Size 1964-88
6836	Chevette	Chevette/T-1000 1976-88
6841	Chevy II	Chevy II/Nova 1962-79
7309	Ciera	Celebrity, Century, Ciera, 6000 1982-88
7059	Cimarron	Cavalier, Skyhawk, Cimarron, 2000 1982-88
7049	Citation	GM X-Body 1980-85
6980	Civic	Honda 1973-88
6817	CJ-2A, 3A, 3B, 5, 6, 7	Jeep 1945-87
8034	CJ-5, 6, 7	Jeep 1971-90
6842	Colony Park	Ford/Mercury/Lincoln 1968-88
7037	Colt	Colt/Challenger/Vista/Conquest 1971-88
6634	Comet	Maverick/Comet 1971-77
7939	Comanche	Jeep Wagoneer, Comanche, Cherokee 1984-89
6739	Commando	Jeep Wagoneer, Commando, Cherokee, Truck 1957-86
6842	Commuter	Ford/Mercury/Lincoln 1968-88
7199	Concord	AMC 1975-86
7037	Conquest	Colt/Challenger/Vista/Conquest 1971-88
6696	Continental 1982-85	Ford/Mercury/Lincoln Mid-Size 1971-85
7814	Continental 1982-87	Thunderbird, Cougar, Continental 1980-87
7830	Continental 1988-89	Taurus/Sable/Continental 1986-89
7583	Cordia	Mitsubishi 1983-89
5795	Corolla 1968-70	Toyota 1966-70
7036	Corolla	Toyota Corolla/Carina/Tercel/Starlet 1970-87
5795	Corona	Toyota 1966-70
7004	Corona	Toyota Corona/Crown/Cressida/Mk.II/Van 1970-87
6962	Corrado	VW Front Wheel Drive 1974-90
7849	Corsica	Chevrolet Corsica and Beretta 1988
6576	Corvette	Corvette 1953-62
6843	Corvette	Corvette 1963-86
6542	Cougar	Mustang/Cougar 1965-73
6696	Cougar	Ford/Mercury/Lincoln Mid-Size 1971-85
7814	Cougar	Thunderbird, Cougar, Continental 1980-87
6842	Country Sedan	Ford/Mercury/Lincoln 1968-88
6842	Country Squire	Ford/Mercury/Lincoln 1968-88
6983	Courier	Ford Courier 1972-82
7004	Cressida	Toyota Corona/Crown/Cressida/Mk.II/Van 1970-87
5795	Crown	Toyota 1966-70
7004	Crown	Toyota Corona/Crown/Cressida/Mk.II/Van 1970-87
6842	Crown Victoria	Ford/Mercury/Lincoln 1968-88
6980	CRX	Honda 1973-88
6842	Custom	Ford/Mercury/Lincoln 1968-88
6326	Custom	Valiant/Duster 1968-76
6842	Custom 500	Ford/Mercury/Lincoln 1968-88
7950	Cutlass FWD	Lumina/Grand Prix/Cutlass/Regal 1988-90
6933	Cutlass RWD	Cutlass 1970-87
7309	Cutlass Ciera	Celebrity, Century, Ciera, 6000 1982-88
6936	C-10, 20, 30	Chevrolet/GMC Pick-Ups & Suburban 1970-87

Chilton's Repair Manuals are available at your local retailer or by mailing a check or money order for **$14.95** per book plus **$3.50** for 1st book and **$.50** for each additional book to cover postage and handling to:

**Chilton Book Company
Dept. DM
Radnor, PA 19089**

NOTE: When ordering be sure to include your name & address, book part No. & title.

CHILTON'S REPAIR MANUAL MODEL INDEX
Car and truck model names are listed in alphabetical and numerical order

Part No.	Model	Repair Manual Title
8055	C-15, 25, 35	Chevrolet/GMC Pick-Ups & Suburban 1988-90
6324	Dart	Dart/Demon 1968-76
6962	Dasher	VW Front Wheel Drive 1974-90
5790	Datsun Pickups	Datsun 1961-72
6816	Datsun Pickups	Datsun Pick-Ups and Pathfinder 1970-89
7163	Daytona	Chrysler Front Wheel Drive 1981-88
6486	Daytona Charger	Dodge Charger 1967-70
6324	Demon	Dart/Demon 1968-76
7462	deVille	Cadillac 1967-89
7587	deVille	GM C-Body 1985
6817	DJ-3B	Jeep 1945-87
7040	DL	Volvo 1970-88
6326	Duster	Valiant/Duster 1968-76
7032	D-50	D-50/Arrow Pick-Ups 1979-81
7459	D100, 150, 200, 250, 300, 350	Dodge/Plymouth Trucks 1967-88
7199	Eagle	AMC 1975-86
7163	E-Class	Chrysler Front Wheel Drive 1981-88
6840	El Camino	Chevrolet Mid-Size 1964-88
7462	Eldorado	Cadillac 1967-89
7308	Electra	Buick/Olds/Pontiac 1975-90
7587	Electra	GM C-Body 1985
6696	Elite	Ford/Mercury/Lincoln Mid-Size 1971-85
7165	Encore	Renault 1975-85
7055	Escort	Ford/Mercury Front Wheel Drive 1981-87
7059	Eurosport	Cavalier, Skyhawk, Cimarron, 2000 1982-88
7760	Excel	Hyundai 1986-90
7163	Executive Sedan	Chrysler Front Wheel Drive 1981-88
7055	EXP	Ford/Mercury Front Wheel Drive 1981-87
6849	E-100, 150, 200, 250, 300, 350	Ford Vans 1961-88
6320	Fairlane	Fairlane/Torino 1962-75
6965	Fairmont	Fairmont/Zephyr 1978-83
5796	Fastback	Volkswagen 1949-71
6837	Fastback	Volkswagen 1970-81
6739	FC-150, 170	Jeep Wagoneer, Commando, Cherokee, Truck 1957-86
6982	FF-1	Subaru 1970-88
7571	Fiero	Pontiac Fiero 1984-88
6846	Fiesta	Fiesta 1978-80
5996	Firebird	Firebird 1967-81
7345	Firebird	Firebird 1982-90
7059	Firenza	Cavalier, Skyhawk, Cimarron, 2000 1982-88
7462	Fleetwood	Cadillac 1967-89
7587	Fleetwood	GM C-Body 1985
7829	F-Super Duty	Ford Pick-Ups and Bronco 1987-88
7165	Fuego	Renault 1975-85
6552	Fury	Plymouth 1968-76
7196	F-10	Datsun/Nissan F-10, 310, Stanza, Pulsar 1976-88
6933	F-85	Cutlass 1970-87
6913	F-100, 150, 200, 250, 300, 350	Ford Pick-Ups 1965-86
7829	F-150, 250, 350	Ford Pick-Ups and Bronco 1987-88
7583	Galant	Mitsubishi 1983-89
6842	Galaxie	Ford/Mercury/Lincoln 1968-88
7040	GL	Volvo 1970-88
6739	Gladiator	Jeep Wagoneer, Commando, Cherokee, Truck 1962-86
6981	GLC	Mazda 1978-89
7040	GLE	Volvo 1970-88
7040	GLT	Volvo 1970-88
7593	Golf	VW Front Wheel Drive 1974-90
7165	Gordini	Renault 1975-85
6937	Granada	Granada/Monarch 1975-82
6552	Gran Coupe	Plymouth 1968-76
6552	Gran Fury	Plymouth 1968-76
6842	Gran Marquis	Ford/Mercury/Lincoln 1968-88
6552	Gran Sedan	Plymouth 1968-76
6696	Gran Torino 1972-76	Ford/Mercury/Lincoln Mid-Size 1971-85
7346	Grand Am	Pontiac Mid-Size 1974-83
7657	Grand Am	Calais, Grand Am, Skylark, Somerset 1985-86
7346	Grand LeMans	Pontiac Mid-Size 1974-83
7346	Grand Prix	Pontiac Mid-Size 1974-83
7950	Grand Prix FWD	Lumina/Grand Prix/Cutlass/Regal 1988-90
7308	Grand Safari	Buick/Olds/Pontiac 1975-87
7308	Grand Ville	Buick/Olds/Pontiac 1975-87
6739	Grand Wagoneer	Jeep Wagoneer, Commando, Cherokee, Truck 1957-86
7199	Gremlin	AMC 1975-86
6575	GT	Opel 1971-75
7593	GTI	VW Front Wheel Drive 1974-90
5905	GTO 1968-73	Tempest/GTO/LeMans 1968-73
7346	GTO 1974	Pontiac Mid-Size 1974-83
5821	GTX	Roadrunner/Satellite/Belvedere/GTX 1968-73
5910	GT6	Triumph 1969-73
6542	G.T.350, 500	Mustang/Cougar 1965-73
6930	G-10, 20, 30	Chevy/GMC Vans 1967-86
6930	G-1500, 2500, 3500	Chevy/GMC Vans 1967-86
8040	G-10, 20, 30	Chevy/GMC Vans 1987-90
8040	G-1500, 2500, 3500	Chevy/GMC Vans 1987-90
5795	Hi-Lux	Toyota 1966-70
6845	Horizon	Omni/Horizon/Rampage 1978-88
7199	Hornet	AMC 1975-86
7135	Impala	Chevrolet 1968-88
7317	IROC-Z	Camaro 1982-88
6739	Jeepster	Jeep Wagoneer, Commando, Cherokee, Truck 1957-86
7593	Jetta	VW Front Wheel Drive 1974-90
6931	Jimmy	Blazer/Jimmy 1969-82
7383	Jimmy	Chevy S-10 Blazer/GMC S-15 Jimmy 1982-87
6739	J-10, 20	Jeep Wagoneer, Commando, Cherokee, Truck 1957-86
6739	J-100, 200, 300	Jeep Wagoneer, Commando, Cherokee, Truck 1957-86
6575	Kadett	Opel 1971-75
7199	Kammback	AMC 1975-86
5796	Karmann Ghia	Volkswagen 1949-71
6837	Karmann Ghia	Volkswagen 1970-81
7135	Kingswood	Chevrolet 1968-88
6931	K-5	Blazer/Jimmy 1969-82
6936	K-10, 20, 30	Chevy/GMC Pick-Ups & Suburban 1970-87
6936	K-1500, 2500, 3500	Chevy/GMC Pick-Ups & Suburban 1970-87
8055	K-10, 20, 30	Chevy/GMC Pick-Ups & Suburban 1988-90
8055	K-1500, 2500, 3500	Chevy/GMC Pick-Ups & Suburban 1988-90
6840	Laguna	Chevrolet Mid-Size 1964-88
7041	Lancer	Champ/Arrow/Sapporo 1977-83
5795	Land Cruiser	Toyota 1966-70
7035	Land Cruiser	Toyota Trucks 1970-88
7163	Laser	Chrysler Front Wheel Drive 1981-88
7163	LeBaron	Chrysler Front Wheel Drive 1981-88
7165	LeCar	Renault 1975-85

Chilton's Repair Manuals are available at your local retailer or by mailing a check or money order for **$14.95** per book plus **$3.50** for 1st book and **$.50** for each additional book to cover postage and handling to:

Chilton Book Company
Dept. DM
Radnor, PA 19089

NOTE: When ordering be sure to include your name & address, book part No. & title.

CHILTON'S REPAIR MANUAL MODEL INDEX
Car and truck model names are listed in alphabetical and numerical order

Part No.	Model	Repair Manual Title
5905	LeMans	Tempest/GTO/LeMans 1968-73
7346	LeMans	Pontiac Mid-Size 1974-83
7308	LeSabre	Buick/Olds/Pontiac 1975-87
6842	Lincoln	Ford/Mercury/Lincoln 1968-88
7055	LN-7	Ford/Mercury Front Wheel Drive 1981-87
6842	LTD	Ford/Mercury/Lincoln 1968-88
6696	LTD II	Ford/Mercury/Lincoln Mid-Size 1971-85
7950	Lumina	Lumina/Grand Prix/Cutlass/Regal 1988-90
6815	LUV	Chevrolet LUV 1972-81
6575	Luxus	Opel 1971-75
7055	Lynx	Ford/Mercury Front Wheel Drive 1981-87
6844	L6	BMW 1970-88
6844	L7	BMW 1970-88
6542	Mach I	Mustang/Cougar 1965-73
6812	Mach I Ghia	Mustang II 1974-78
6840	Malibu	Chevrolet Mid-Size 1964-88
6575	Manta	Opel 1971-75
6696	Mark IV, V, VI, VII	Ford/Mercury/Lincoln Mid-Size 1971-85
7814	Mark VII	Thunderbird, Cougar, Continental 1980-87
6842	Marquis	Ford/Mercury/Lincoln 1968-88
6696	Marquis	Ford/Mercury/Lincoln Mid-Size 1971-85
7199	Matador	AMC 1975-86
6634	Maverick	Maverick/Comet 1970-77
6817	Maverick	Jeep 1945-87
7170	Maxima	Nissan 200SX, 240SX, 510, 610, 710, 810, Maxima 1973-88
6842	Mercury	Ford/Mercury/Lincoln 1968-88
6963	Merkur	Mustang/Capri/Merkur 1979-88
6780	MGB, MGB-GT, MGC-GT	MG 1961-81
6780	Midget	MG 1961-81
7583	Mighty Max	Mitsubishi 1983-89
7583	Mirage	Mitsubishi 1983-89
5795	Mk.II 1969-70	Toyota 1966-70
7004	Mk.II 1970-76	Toyota Corona/Crown/Cressida/Mk.II/Van 1970-87
6554	Monaco	Dodge 1968-77
6937	Monarch	Granada/Monarch 1975-82
6840	Monte Carlo	Chevrolet Mid-Size 1964-88
6696	Montego	Ford/Mercury/Lincoln Mid-Size 1971-85
6842	Monterey	Ford/Mercury/Lincoln 1968-88
7583	Montero	Mitsubishi 1983-89
6935	Monza 1975-80	GM Subcompact 1971-80
6981	MPV	Mazda 1978-89
6542	Mustang	Mustang/Cougar 1965-73
6963	Mustang	Mustang/Capri/Merkur 1979-88
6812	Mustang II	Mustang II 1974-78
6981	MX6	Mazda 1978-89
6844	M3, M6	BMW 1970-88
7163	New Yorker	Chrysler Front Wheel Drive 1981-88
6841	Nova	Chevy II/Nova 1962-79
7658	Nova	Chevrolet Nova/GEO Prizm 1985-89
7049	Omega	GM X-Body 1980-85
6845	Omni	Omni/Horizon/Rampage 1978-88
6575	Opel	Opel 1971-75
7199	Pacer	AMC 1975-86
7587	Park Avenue	GM C-Body 1985
6842	Park Lane	Ford/Mercury/Lincoln 1968-88
6962	Passat	VW Front Wheel Drive 1974-90
6816	Pathfinder	Datsun/Nissan Pick-Ups and Pathfinder 1970-89
5790	Patrol	Datsun 1961-72
6934	PB100, 150, 200, 250, 300, 350	Dodge/Plymouth Vans 1967-88
5982	Peugeot	Peugeot 1970-74
7049	Phoenix	GM X-Body 1980-85
7027	Pinto	Pinto/Bobcat 1971-80
6554	Polara	Dodge 1968-77
7583	Precis	Mitsubishi 1983-89
6980	Prelude	Honda 1973-88
7658	Prizm	Chevrolet Nova/GEO Prizm 1985-89
8012	Probe	Ford Probe 1989
7660	Pulsar	Datsun/Nissan F-10, 310, Stanza, Pulsar 1976-88
6529	PV-444	Volvo 1956-69
6529	PV-544	Volvo 1956-69
6529	P-1800	Volvo 1956-69
7593	Quantum	VW Front Wheel Drive 1974-87
7593	Rabbit	VW Front Wheel Drive 1974-87
7593	Rabbit Pickup	VW Front Wheel Drive 1974-87
6575	Rallye	Opel 1971-75
7459	Ramcharger	Dodge/Plymouth Trucks 1967-88
6845	Rampage	Omni/Horizon/Rampage 1978-88
6320	Ranchero	Fairlane/Torino 1962-70
6696	Ranchero	Ford/Mercury/Lincoln Mid-Size 1971-85
6842	Ranch Wagon	Ford/Mercury/Lincoln 1968-88
7338	Ranger Pickup	Ford Ranger/Bronco II 1983-88
7307	Regal RWD	Century/Regal 1975-87
7950	Regal FWD 1988-90	Lumina/Grand Prix/Cutlass/Regal 1988-90
7163	Reliant	Chrysler Front Wheel Drive 1981-88
5821	Roadrunner	Roadrunner/Satellite/Belvedere/GTX 1968-73
7659	Rotary Pick-Up	Mazda Trucks 1971-89
6981	RX-7	Mazda 1978-89
7165	R-12, 15, 17, 18, 18i	Renault 1975-85
7830	Sable	Taurus/Sable/Continental 1986-89
7750	Safari	Chevrolet Astro/GMC Safari 1985-90
7041	Sapporo	Champ/Arrow/Sapporo 1978-83
5821	Satellite	Roadrunner/Satellite/Belvedere/GTX 1968-73
6326	Scamp	Valiant/Duster 1968-76
6845	Scamp	Omni/Horizon/Rampage 1978-88
6962	Scirocco	VW Front Wheel Drive 1974-90
6936	Scottsdale	Chevrolet/GMC Pick-Ups & Suburban 1970-87
8055	Scottsdale	Chevrolet/GMC Pick-Ups & Suburban 1988-90
5912	Scout	International Scout 1967-73
8034	Scrambler	Jeep 1971-90
7197	Sentra	Datsun 1200, 210, Nissan Sentra 1973-88
7462	Seville	Cadillac 1967-89
7163	Shadow	Chrysler Front Wheel Drive 1981-88
6936	Siera	Chevrolet/GMC Pick-Ups & Suburban 1970-87
8055	Siera	Chevrolet/GMC Pick-Ups & Suburban 1988-90
7583	Sigma	Mitsubishi 1983-89
6326	Signet	Valiant/Duster 1968-76
6936	Silverado	Chevrolet/GMC Pick-Ups & Suburban 1970-87
8055	Silverado	Chevrolet/GMC Pick-Ups & Suburban 1988-90
6935	Skyhawk	GM Subcompact 1971-80
7059	Skyhawk	Cavalier, Skyhawk, Cimarron, 2000 1982-88
7049	Skylark	GM X-Body 1980-85

Chilton's Repair Manuals are available at your local retailer or by mailing a check or money order for **$14.95** per book plus **$3.50** for 1st book and **$.50** for each additional book to cover postage and handling to:

**Chilton Book Company
Dept. DM
Radnor, PA 19089**

NOTE: When ordering be sure to include your name & address, book part No. & title.

CHILTON'S REPAIR MANUAL MODEL INDEX
Car and truck model names are listed in alphabetical and numerical order

Part No.	Model	Repair Manual Title
7675	Skylark	Calais, Grand Am, Skylark, Somerset 1985-86
7657	Somerset	Calais, Grand Am, Skylark, Somerset 1985-86
7042	Spider 2000	Fiat 1969-81
7199	Spirit	AMC 1975-86
6552	Sport Fury	Plymouth 1968–76
7165	Sport Wagon	Renault 1975-85
5796	Squareback	Volkswagen 1949-71
6837	Squareback	Volkswagen 1970-81
7196	Stanza	Datsun/Nissan F-10, 310, Stanza, Pulsar 1976-88
6935	Starfire	GM Subcompact 1971-80
7583	Starion	Mitsubishi 1983-89
7036	Starlet	Toyota Corolla/Carina/Tercel/Starlet 1970-87
7059	STE	Cavalier, Skyhawk, Cimarron, 2000 1982-88
5795	Stout	Toyota 1966-70
7042	Strada	Fiat 1969-81
6552	Suburban	Plymouth 1968-76
6936	Suburban	Chevy/GMC Pick-Ups & Suburban 1970-87
8055	Suburban	Chevy/GMC Pick-Ups & Suburban 1988-90
6935	Sunbird	GM Subcompact 1971-80
7059	Sunbird	Cavalier, Skyhawk, Cimarron, 2000, 1982-88
7163	Sundance	Chrysler Front Wheel Drive 1981-88
7043	Supra	Toyota Celica/Supra 1971-87
8058	Supra	Toyota Celica/Supra 1986-90
6837	Super Beetle	Volkswagen 1970-81
7199	SX-4	AMC 1975-86
7383	S-10 Blazer	Chevy S-10 Blazer/GMC S-15 Jimmy 1982-87
7310	S-10 Pick-Up	Chevy S-10/GMC S-15 Pick-Ups 1982-87
7383	S-15 Jimmy	Chevy S-10 Blazer/GMC S-15 Jimmy 1982-87
7310	S-15 Pick-Up	Chevy S-10/GMC S-15 Pick-Ups 1982-87
7830	Taurus	Taurus/Sable/Continental 1986-89
6845	TC-3	Omni/Horizon/Rampage 1978-88
5905	Tempest	Tempest/GTO/LeMans 1968-73
7055	Tempo	Ford/Mercury Front Wheel Drive 1981-87
7036	Tercel	Toyota Corolla/Carina/Tercel/Starlet 1970-87
7081	Thing	Volkswagen 1970-81
6696	Thunderbird	Ford/Mercury/Lincoln Mid-Size 1971-85
7814	Thunderbird	Thunderbird, Cougar, Continental 1980-87
7055	Topaz	Ford/Mercury Front Wheel Drive 1981-87
6320	Torino	Fairlane/Torino 1962-75
6696	Torino	Ford/Mercury/Lincoln Mid-Size 1971-85
7163	Town & Country	Chrysler Front Wheel Drive 1981-88
6842	Town Car	Ford/Mercury/Lincoln 1968-88
7135	Townsman	Chevrolet 1968-88
5795	Toyota Pickups	Toyota 1966-70
7035	Toyota Pickups	Toyota Trucks 1970-88
7004	Toyota Van	Toyota Corona/Crown/Cressida/Mk.II/Van 1970-87
7459	Trail Duster	Dodge/Plymouth Trucks 1967-88
7046	Trans Am	Firebird 1967-81
7345	Trans Am	Firebird 1982-90
7583	Tredia	Mitsubishi 1983-89
7040	Turbo	Volvo 1970-88
5796	Type 1 Sedan 1949-71	Volkswagen 1949-71
6837	Type 1 Sedan 1970-80	Volkswagen 1970-81
5796	Type 1 Karmann Ghia 1960-71	Volkswagen 1949-71
6837	Type 1 Karmann Ghia 1970-74	Volkswagen 1970-81
5796	Type 1 Convertible 1964-71	Volkswagen 1949-71
6837	Type 1 Convertible 1970-80	Volkswagen 1970-81
5796	Type 1 Super Beetle 1971	Volkswagen 1949-71
6837	Type 1 Super Beetle 1971-75	Volkswagen 1970-81
5796	Type 2 Bus 1953-71	Volkswagen 1949-71
6837	Type 2 Bus 1970-80	Volkswagen 1970-81
5796	Type 2 Kombi 1954-71	Volkswagen 1949-71
6837	Type 2 Kombi 1970-73	Volkswagen 1970-81
6837	Type 2 Vanagon 1981	Volkswagen 1970-81
5796	Type 3 Fastback & Squareback 1961-71	Volkswagen 1949-71
7081	Type 3 Fastback & Squareback 1970-73	Volkswagen 1970-70
5796	Type 4 411 1971	Volkswagen 1949-71
6837	Type 4 411 1971-72	Volkswagen 1970-81
5796	Type 4 412 1971	Volkswagen 1949-71
6845	Turismo	Omni/Horizon/Rampage 1978-88
5905	T-37	Tempest/GTO/LeMans 1968-73
6836	T-1000	Chevette/T-1000 1976-88
6935	Vega	GM Subcompact 1971-80
7346	Ventura	Pontiac Mid-Size 1974-83
6696	Versailles	Ford/Mercury/Lincoln Mid-Size 1971-85
6552	VIP	Plymouth 1968-76
7037	Vista	Colt/Challenger/Vista/Conquest 1971-88
6933	Vista Cruiser	Cutlass 1970-87
6637	Volare	Aspen/Volare 1976-80
7482	Voyager	Dodge Caravan/Plymouth Voyager 1984-88
6326	V-100	Valiant/Duster 1968-76
6739	Wagoneer 1962-83	Jeep Wagoneer, Commando, Cherokee, Truck 1957-86
7939	Wagoneer 1984-89	Jeep Wagoneer, Comanche, Cherokee 1984-89
8034	Wrangler	Jeep 1971-90
7459	W100, 150, 200, 250, 300, 350	Dodge/Plymouth Trucks 1967-88
7459	WM300	Dodge/Plymouth Trucks 1967-88
6842	XL	Ford/Mercury/Lincoln 1968-88
6963	XR4Ti	Mustang/Capri/Merkur 1979-88
6696	XR-7	Ford/Mercury/Lincoln Mid-Size 1971-85
6982	XT Coupe	Subaru 1970-88
7042	X1/9	Fiat 1969-81
6965	Zephyr	Fairmont/Zephyr 1978-83
7059	Z-24	Cavalier, Skyhawk, Cimarron, 2000 1982-88
6735	Z-28	Camaro 1967-81
7318	Z-28	Camaro 1982-88
6845	024	Omni/Horizon/Rampage 1978-88
6844	3.0S, 3.0Si, 3.0CS	BMW 1970-88
6817	4-63	Jeep 1981-87

Chilton's Repair Manuals are available at your local retailer or by mailing a check or money order for **$14.95** per book plus **$3.50** for 1st book and **$.50** for each additional book to cover postage and handling to:

**Chilton Book Company
Dept. DM
Radnor, PA 19089**

NOTE: When ordering be sure to include your name & address, book part No. & title.